A-level General Principles of English Law Textbook

A-level
General Principles
of English Law
Textbook

P A Read
LLB, DPA, Barrister

Fifth Edition

HLT Publications

HLT PUBLICATIONS
200 Greyhound Road, London W14 9RY

First published 1989
Fifth edition 1995

© The HLT Group Ltd 1995

ISBN 0 7510 0298 4

British Library Cataloguing-in-Publication.

A CIP Catalogue record for this book is available from the British Library.

Printed and bound in Great Britain

Contents

Foreword by Brian Heap

A-level work, comprising two, three or even four subjects, is a challenging course of study. It follows a period of general education leading to the GCSE in which you have experienced a 'taster' course of up to ten subjects presented to you in a highly structured teaching system. Thereafter, it becomes necessary to make a choice of subject areas for a more concentrated period of study – two years – in which more time will be spent in 'private study' – literally, teaching yourself.

Inevitably, private study is a new experience for most students and the time normally allocated is rarely used to the best advantage. The assimilation of facts, whilst working on your own, can be difficult since it also necessitates identifying the important issues from a range of books and a wealth of information. The framework of your course is naturally vital, not simply in terms of passing your A-level exams but in achieving the right grades you need to enter the university or college degree course of your choice.

My A-level series aims to provide you with this essential framework. This book will give you the support you need to work through your syllabus and to reinforce the knowledge you will need to be sure of success at the end of your school or college career.

Brian Heap

Preface

The contents and sequence of every book are shaped to a large extent by the requirements of the audience to whom it is addressed. There are a number of textbooks on general principles of English law; one or two of those are specifically for 'A' Level students. But it should be remembered that there are many Examination Boards offering 'A' Level law and the syllabi vary quite markedly. This book is aimed specifically at those students studying law at 'A' and 'AS' Level examinations as set by the Associated Examining Board, and by the University of Oxford Delegacy of Local Examinations.

While it is hoped that it will prove equally useful for students studying for other examinations, the student must first verify the extent to which the syllabi of the various courses diverge or coincide. This text is set out in such a way so as to cover, in approximately the same order and with the same emphasis on subject matter, the syllabi of these two examining bodies. Since the last edition of this book, it has been revised to take into account the special needs of students sitting these examinations.

It is up to date as of January 1995 and takes into account all major new legislation and case-law.

Acknowledgement

The publishers and author would like to thank the Incorporated Council of Law Reporting for England and Wales for kind permission to reproduce extracts from the Weekly Law Reports.

Cover

The author and publishers would like to thank the General Council of the Bar, the Institute of Legal Executives and the Artwork Company Ltd for the loan of pictures and permission to reproduce them on the cover of this book. We would also like to thank George Southall of Peter Van Arden Productions for photographs of the wig and the entrance to the Law Society. Finally, we would like to thank Master McKenzie QC Registrar of Criminal Appeal for the loan of the wig and other objects which appear in that photograph.

Key

1 Wig.
2 The General Council of the Bar logo.
3 Lincoln's Inn.
4 The Royal Courts of Justice.
5 The Law Society.
6 The crest of the Institute of Legal Executives.
7 The Institute of Legal Executives.

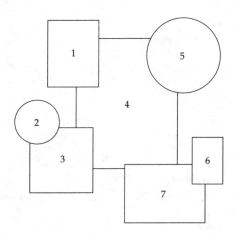

Table of cases

Introduction to Law | 1

Introduction to the study of law and the course

The question of what 'law' is has occupied the minds of legal theorists for centuries. Definitions and descriptions have gone in and out of fashion. The current view seems to be that, really, there is little point in defining law as a single concept anyway; since it can mean so many things according to context – political, social, economic, religious, and so on.

This book may be basically divided into four more or less equal sections. In the first part we shall be looking at various ideas of what law is, the functions of law in society and the creation and uses of law in Britain today.

Inevitably at different times, legal theorists, who are mainly experts in jurisprudence (or the science of law) have put forward a large number of theories as to the meaning of the term 'law' and its role in society. Reference to, at least, some of the main authorities is unavoidable, indeed wherever possible the student should read further than the bare minimum of authorities quoted here.

In the other parts of the book we shall look at some of the main areas of law – contract, tort, and criminal law.

While studying law a student acquires skills in the logical application of rules to factual situations, and should be able to predict the probable outcome should a dispute go to court, or some other dispute resolving institution.

No lawyer 'knows' all the law, no matter how able; and no student on any law course should have such an objective. Rather, a lawyer will know where the relevant law is to be found, and will be able to apply such knowledge in seeking out the particular rules applying to a given situation and applying those rules by analogy to the particular facts of his client's situation. Lawyers will be able to advise their clients as to the chance of success if the problem is taken before a court. Lawyers may also have certain practical skills such as drawing up a formal contract, or writing a will, or representation of a client in court.

Not all lawyers will possess all these skills – to a large extent it is a question of specialisations.

Some terms discussed

Most legal terminology is (hopefully) defined as the text proceeds. Remember in any case that there are such things as legal dictionaries! However, while it is not the purpose of this introduction to provide a glossary of terms, it may be useful to look briefly at one or two preliminary concepts.

Civil law

It used to be said with absolute certainty that civil law was the area of law that governed the relationship between individuals as individuals and it was the concern of the state merely to provide facilities and guidelines through which this branch of law would operate. For example, matter such as the rules in company law regulating the relationship of the members of the company to the company itself or the formation, performance and discharge of contractual agreements at law. Where an individual felt that the other individual had not performed his part under the law then it was for that individual to pursue his remedy at law. It was not a matter in which the state was involved. If the aggrieved person did not seek a remedy then that was an entirely private matter which was no one else's business.

This picture is no longer completely accurate. It is now recognised that there is a need for the whole of society to be involved in what was previously regarded as an entirely private matter. The legislation on consumer protection and the rules on wrongful trading, among many others, provide examples where the State is involving itself on behalf of the whole of society in areas that were previously in the private domain.

Criminal law

The question 'what is crime' is rather a vexing one. There exist a plethora of definitions and explanations that go far beyond the scope of this course. Indeed many of the complex jurisprudential theories are more concerned with *why* a crime is committed – material which more properly belongs in a course on criminology. However, there are one or two ideas which are worth looking at briefly:

Crimes as moral wrongs
Lord Denning inclines towards the view that crimes involve moral wrongs. If this were so it would be difficult to accept why adultery, for example, is not a crime. Having said that, it should be observed that there is no widely shared morality in a pluralistic society such as Britain. A conception of morality, if not shared, would be difficult to enforce and would not find acceptance. The criminal law would not then reflect morality but a particular group's conception of morality.

Crimes as legislative enactments
If a crime is what the legislature has declared to be illegal conduct then such a definition would not distinguish it from certain torts, such as under the Defective Premises Act 1972 or in situations where liability will be imposed where a duty is broken, for example s47(2) Health and Safety at Work Act 1974.

Such a definition would not encompass those crimes declared by the courts. An example, although the most extreme, would be *Shaw v DPP* [1962] AC 220 where the courts exercised a residual power they claimed to possess as guardians of public morals to impose retrospective criminal responsibility in an area where the legislature had not acted and in which there had been no direct precedent.

In some instances the legislature has declared that what was previously a crime will no longer amount to criminal conduct. Prior to the Suicide Act 1961 attempted suicide was an offence. That Act removed the application of the criminal law to this conduct – although it retained liability for aiding and abetting suicide: *Attorney-General* v *Able* (1984) 78 Cr App R 197.

Criminal law and civil law compared

Whilst we deal in some detail in areas of criminal law in part two there are some areas of apparent distinction between crime and civil wrongs which it would be instructive briefly to examine.

a Crimes are said to be wrongs committed against society as a whole and prosecuted in the name of society by a public body. Torts are said to be private wrongs and involve the regulation of relationships between private individuals.

b There are procedural differences. Certainly the organisation of the court structure is geared to separating criminal from civil matters although even in this area the separation is not complete. Some criminal courts have some civil jurisdiction, eg magistrates' courts.

   A civil case is of course brought by a private individual whereas a criminal prosecution is generally brought by a public body. There are opportunities for private prosecutions although these are rare. Indeed in some instances the consent of the Attorney-General or the DPP is required before any prosecution can be instituted. This is because some cases are said to involve important constitutional matters. An example would be the crime of inciting racial hatred. It is said that the consent of the Attorney-General is required before a prosecution can be brought because this offence has serious implications for the freedom of speech. The Attorney-General has the power to stay any criminal prosecution (nolle prosequi), however, he would not normally interfere in any private civil suit.

   The victim in a criminal prosecution may forgive the accused; however that would not affect the criminal proceedings which are brought, not on behalf of the victim, but in the name of society as a whole. On the other hand, where a victim in a civil matter decides to discontinue the court action, that is the end of the matter and it will then be dropped from the court's agenda. There are many reasons why such a case may be 'dropped' not least that it has been settled 'out of court'. There is no such facility with regard to criminal prosecutions.

c The consent of the victim will often negate or at least mitigate the civil liability of a defendant; however, in many crimes, though not all, the consent of the victim is irrelevant, eg murder. This is because the criminal law generally adopts a paternalistic approach to individual members of society. There are some crimes where lack of any consent given by the victim is an element in the definition of the offence and in those instances evidence as to consent would be material. An example would be rape.

d A further distinction lies with regard to the available remedies. It is said that a civil suit will lead to the compensation of the victim and a criminal prosecution to the punishment of the offender. This is, however, a simplistic view. Exemplary damages are awarded in tort (*Rookes* v *Barnard* [1964] AC 1129) and these are designed to punish a wrongdoer who may have profited from his civil wrong. In a criminal prosecution (s35 of the Powers of the Criminal Courts

Act 1973) the court may order that compensation be paid by any person convicted of certain offences to a victim. This can be imposed in addition to any other sentence available to the court. Thus there is also an overlap with regard to remedies.

The common law

Common law is a term used in different ways. The type of law in this country has been described as the common law. By which term is meant that the judges have a major role in the development of the law through their decisions, which by operation of rules such as *stare decisis* bind future judges deciding cases of the same legal matter on the same material facts. The actual term common law came into existence to describe the application of law common to all, that followed the system of assizes developed by the Norman conquerors of England by which judges were sent around the country to apply the law of the conquerors to all. The term is of historical interest only today and has, as indicated, taken on the meaning first mentioned.

Overlap of terms

It should be noted that some legal terminology overlaps considerably and more attention will be paid to this later in the book.

For the moment it is enough to note that many legal authorities use the terms common law and civil law almost interchangeably – meaning unwritten law, judge made law: that is, as opposed to law created by statute.

Notice also that some criminal law is also common law: not all criminal law has been absorbed into legislation.

It is also common to split law into private and public law. Civil law is sometimes called private law for obvious reasons, being concerned with private individuals, their rights and duties. Public law, while potentially much wider than criminal law, does not stop there, but also includes constitutional, administrative and other 'public' areas like welfare law.

The principal sources of law

The principal sources of law in this common law system are discussed in considerable depth in this text and represent an important part of this course. Briefly these sources are in order of legal priority: Regulations of the European Community (EC); Directives and Decisions of the EC; statute law, being Acts of Parliament and delegated legislation; case law, with greater priority being given to the higher courts. Thereafter reference can be made to academic texts, extrinsic aids and custom (although for the purposes of this course these latter ones are not significant). However it should be noted that this order of importance is not necessarily reflected in practical terms. Case law probably provides a source for most of our law, with statute a close second. The fact that EC law has legal priority does not mean it has first place as a source of new law.

Contract

The rules of contract are discussed in detail later. For present purposes a contract may be defined as an agreement between two or more persons of capacity to effect a lawful purpose with the intention that their agreement create legal relations governing the agreement between them.

The need for such a body of rules is clear where persons can define their rights and duties by agreement.

Tort

Tort is the area of law that concerns the liability of one individual for his breach of a duty to another individual outside the relationship of contract and which is not considered criminal. It is an area of private law which has developed very considerably over the last fifty years. It is governed primarily by the fault principle but there have been important proposals recently to change this. At present where loss is caused to an individual by another individual who owed that individual a duty to take reasonable care in all the circumstances then, subject to policy considerations, damages may be available to the aggrieved individual.

Obviously this chapter is intended only to give a working definition of these terms and, as the course develops, there will be a need to return to this chapter and to expand thereon.

Right from the start, however, it is clearly of importance to be careful with terminology. A great deal of help can be gleaned from the context in which the particular word or phrase appears.

The idea of law (1)   2

Law as a marker of boundaries of 'acceptable conduct'

a When one speaks of the part that law plays in ordering society, the distinction between what is 'right' and what is 'wrong' in that society's standards must be determined.

Remember that what the law says is right will be legal; what is wrong, illegal. Legality is not necessarily, however, the same thing as morality.

The law at any given moment is not an exact mirror of the ethical standards that exist in society at any particular time. Indeed there is always a wide divergence of opinion as to what constitutes morality.

Consider the following list:

Prostitution	Feminism
Suicide	Drug taking
Smoking	Apartheid
Euthanasia	Abortion
Telling lies	Terrorism
Chauvinism	Homosexuality
Drinking	Mugging
Snobbery	Adultery
Racism	Exceeding the speed limit

b Some people might not only consider every item on this list immoral but they might produce an even longer list. Others might consider only one or two things on the list to be immoral; equally, there is a wide divergence as to what acts ought, or ought not, to be considered illegal.

Only when ideas of morality and principles of law touch and follow the same course does the result seem logical. All wrongs fall into two categories: wrongs according to moral principles and wrongs according to law.

c *Sir John Salmond* spoke of the two types of wrong, moral and legal, as being like intersecting circles. Both follow the same basic pattern, but they intersect only at those points of agreement that have been pre-determined, either by the intentional rejection of moral principles on the ground of social convenience, or alternatively by the imperfect historical development of the legal system.

Natural wrongs and legal wrongs, natural justice and legal justice, rights and duties all follow the same basic principles, and because of this it must be recognised that some divergence is inevitable. The inherent dualism of law and morals in the social system means that circumstances change situations. Lying is a good example. The telling of a lie would be regarded in most circumstances as an immoral act only. But if the lie is told in court, the crime of perjury is committed and it becomes a legal wrong.

d Morals are one of the ways in which a society influences the way in which its members think. The views put forward by its political and religious leaders will have an impact on individual members of the society. If all the members uphold the legal, moral and traditional social rules of a society, that society is likely to be a stable one, but this sort of static situation may also perpetuate injustice by being inflexible towards change.

e   A society may also be hypocritical. It will deplore the actions of another country on the grounds of violation of human rights but at the same time it will continue to trade with that country out of self-interest. What is worse, the condemning State itself may be violating human rights in other more subtle ways.

f   The early positivist theorists sought to draw a distinction between law as it 'is' and law as it 'ought' to be. They concluded that it was not accurate to derive an 'ought' statement from any number of 'is' statements. There is, therefore, according to the positivists, no necessary correlation between law and morality and to the extent that there is such a correlation that is a matter of coincidence and not design. On the other hand the natural law theorists insisted that a law which was not a just law could not properly be regarded as law.

g   When people talk about 'human rights' they are incorporating the 'ought' into their thinking. Some constitutions are written and contain a Bill of Rights under which the individual's liberty is assured. In Britain we have no written Bill of Rights. We are, however, a party to the European Convention on Human Rights and have been found by that Court to have been 'inhumane' in our treatment of prisoners in the prisons of Northern Ireland. There are also the Universal Declaration of Human Rights and organisations such as Amnesty International, trying to see that states uphold its declarations. Different states have different ideas of morality just as individuals do.

h   Many people, including judges, still adhere to the Natural Law theory though in a modern form. Crime is still equated with sin. The fear is that if these ultimate public standards are flaunted then society will disintegrate.

i   The Natural Law theory is, however, fast disintegrating itself. Its philosophers differ as to the content of their code and it cannot be tested scientifically or empirically, nor do societies agree as to what is moral, and morals change.

j   There is no consensus on what is moral on many issues. It might be argued that criminal offences against the person and property are generally thought of as immoral. But on the whole offences against the person and property affect everyone and society cannot function unless such behaviour is outlawed. These were the earliest types of recognised criminal offences and still account for a large part of the work of the Criminal Courts.

k   But if these offences against person and property are taken away there is still a large area of morality where the law intervenes in spite of the fact that there is no general consensus as to whether that particular act constitutes immorality or not. Also attitudes change and when they change there is a move towards accepting the new morality or relinquishing the old. If the morality is embodied in a legal rule there will be a call for law reform. What changes attitudes? The social, economic and political climate will make up one factor but the other more subtle persuader will be the strongest of the interest groups involved in the struggle. In our society, which is based on the idea of sole ownership of property, rather than sharing, it is obvious that interest groups who are large property owners will have a great deal of influence particularly where legal rules are concerned. The majority of our law is concerned with the protection of property.

The nature of the debate regarding enforcement of morality by the law

It is important to set out the area in which the debate surrounding the problem of the use of law to enforce a particular conception of morality is conducted. One of the leading philosophers of the twentieth century, *Professor Isaiah Berlin*, has identified two types of freedom. He calls these 'negative liberty' by which he means the absence of constraint on human desires being itself an intrinsic value; and 'positive liberty' referring to the truly free man as the ideal, and justifies coercion in order to attain the truly free state. For example, compulsory attendance at school in order to become 'educated'. The coercion is justified in terms of the attainment of positive liberty. One of the major moral objections involved is with the necessary restriction on negative liberty that would be involved through the enforcement of morals by means of the criminal law.

By examining the moral grounds for enforcement of morality we can conclude that anything outside these would be subject to moral objection. There are various views on this topic, each directed from a particular political perspective relating to the relationship between the individual and the state and the extent to which, if at all, the state has a role in limiting negative liberty in the area of morality/immorality.

The liberal view

In 1957 *Wolfenden* wrote that there remains an area of private morality and immorality that is not the law's business. His report was heavily influenced by the writings of *John Stuart Mill* whose *Essay on Liberty* (1859) asserts the primacy of individual liberty. *Mill* admits that tyranny can exist in a democracy although not through law, rather through the morality of the ruling class. Liberation for *Mill* therefore means that the law should be used not to uphold a particular morality but rather to prevent harm to citizens. *Mill* has been criticised by *Dias* in *Jurisprudence* who points out that *Mill* therefore relies on a premise that it is immoral for law to uphold morality.

In his essay *Mill* outlined his 'harm principle' as the sole valid end for interfering in negative liability. He put it thus: 'The only purpose for which power can be rightfully exercised over any member of a civilised community, against his will, is to prevent harm to others. His own good, either physical or moral, is not sufficient warrant.'

A problem that arises here is as to the definition of 'harm'. For *Mill* the harm must be direct and physical. This would probably now include direct psychological harm, such as nervous shock but it would exclude indirect harm such as distress at what others are doing in private. This would be an area of private morality and immorality which is not the law's business.

By enforcement of morality is meant that society is using law to uphold certain moral standards. On this matter The Wolfenden Committee *Report on Homosexual Offences and Prostitution* (1957) was quite clear. Unless society is prepared to equate crime with sin, as stated, 'there must remain a realm of private morality and immorality which is not the law's business'. Reviewing the topics within his terms of reference *Wolfenden* recommended that prostitution should not be punishable, but the activities that surround it ought to be illegal, for example soliciting, pimping, running a brothel and so on, the reason being that these may cause direct harm to those not seeking the services of a prostitute. With regard to homosexual acts between adult consenting males in private this should no longer be an offence. This, it is said, causes no harm to non-participants.

The strict enforcement view

Stephen J, a famous criminal law judge of the last century, attacked *Mill* in *Liberty, Equality, Fraternity* (1873). The essence of *Stephen's* criticism, is that there is no clear distinction between acts that harmed others and acts that harmed oneself. He would advocate that the 'grosser forms of vice' should be punished per se. That was a legitimate function of legislation. This leads to the rule of the majority at the expense of the rights of the minority and this is further problematical to the extent that there is a danger that they might not be right. The major problem with such a view is in asserting that the majority are always right. This is not so. Did the world only become spherical when the majority of people ceased to believe it to be flat?

The moderate view

The major attack on *Wolfenden's* statement has come from *Lord Devlin* whose lecture entitled *The Enforcement of Morals* (1959) initially was supportive of *Wolfenden's* finding but then, upon reflection, according to its author, thought that the application by *Wolfenden* of *Mill's* harm principle is too restrictive. *Devlin* insisted that he still preferred individual liberty but at a lower level than *Mill*. Society has the right to punish any act which in the opinion of the right minded man is grossly offensive and immoral. *Devlin's* test is, then, that society should tolerate what the reasonable man would tolerate, and where conduct is so immoral that the reasonable man would feel disgust, society should ban that activity.

Devlin's second prong of attack against *Wolfenden* and the harm principle asserts that indecent and similar terms can only be understood if measured against society's morality.

A recognised morality is essential to societal existence. Therefore the enforcement of Christian morals is an act of societal self defence. The problem here is, how do we identify the content of this shared morality? *Devlin* contends that even if the act is done 'in private' it still weakens the fabric of the society. Private vice for *Devlin* makes the individual a less useful member of society. We could then query whether this would cover smoking. Does *Devlin* mean to suggest that a smoker is a less useful member of society because he will more likely require medical treatment and will not work as efficiently? Could he not also argue that the person will die earlier and will not require a pension and therefore be a relief to the society?

Devlin is not referring to every immoral act. It should be noted that the immoral act must still be sufficiently grave as to cause disgust in the reasonable man. Still law should enforce morality only to the extent strictly required by the exigencies of the situation in order to protect and preserve society.

It is not here being said that the majority in the House of Lords in the celebrated Ladies Directory Case (*Shaw* v *DPP* (1962)) followed *Devlin's* notion, but Viscount Simmonds did have this to say ' ... There is in the Courts as custodes morum of the people a residual power, where no statute had yet intervened to supersede the common law, to superintend those offences which were prejudicial to the public welfare ... '. That residual power to enforce the supreme and fundamental purpose of the law is 'to conserve not only the safety and order, but also the moral welfare of the State ... '. There is much which is similar to *Devlin's* views here.

Dworkin, in *Taking Rights Seriously*, ascribes to *Devlin* two arguments used to support the interference of the law in an area of 'private morality'. First, that society has a right to protect its own existence. Second, that the majority has a right to follow its own moral convictions in defending its social environment from change it opposes. *Dworkin* recognises that whilst the first is readily identifiable from *Devlin's* lecture, the second is derived from his various essays, where it is presented in a somewhat disjointed form.

Devlin's argument goes like this: There are moral principles that people adhere to but do not require adherence from others (religion) and there are also certain principles that are placed beyond toleration. In order to preserve its own existence society has the right to insist on conformity to the latter principles. If society has that right then it also has the right to use the institutions of the state to enforce that right. With regard to immorality, however, enforcement should not in every case be resorted to. *Devlin* put it thus, '(there) ... must be toleration of the maximum individual freedom that is consistent with the integrity of society ... '. *Devlin's* justification entitles society to preserve itself without vouching for the morality that holds it together.

Devlin's theory rests on society having formed certain moral institutions which form part of its own particular fabric, for example marriage. As an institution this is common to many societies although the method and precise rules that govern it may vary, for instance the number of brides permitted. In so far as these are part of the fabric of any given society then that society is entitled to protect and preserve them and in so doing protect and preserve itself. Thus *Devlin* compares contravention of this morality to treason.

Devlin cannot be regarded as a 'moral campaigner' of the 'Mary Whitehouse type' and this is clear from his outlining of the limits within which the law may act as follows:

1 There should be the maximum freedom consistent with the integrity of society.

2 The limit of tolerance is reached when the ordinary man would feel indignation and disgust.

3 Law makers should be slow to change.

4 Privacy should be respected as far as possible.

5 Laws should be concerned with the minimum not the maximum standards.

Reference has been made to *Devlin*'s reasonable man test. The reasonable man, like the jury, reaches his opinion after full, informed and educated discussion of all relevant points of view. Even so we may find opinion divided, in which case, *Devlin* requires that the majority view shall prevail. This test has been criticised on the grounds that it is too vague to apply in practice, as is the criterion of disgust. It does not define the limits of legal interference. Also there are difficulties in establishing the criteria for describing 'the reasonable man'.

Dworkin believes that there is an intellectual sleight of hand in *Devlin*'s argument with regard to public outrage being presented as the threshold that places the practice in a category which the law is no longer forbidden to regulate. Thus homosexuality would be outlawed without any proof that it represented a threat to the fabric of society. There is implicit in *Devlin*'s second argument as identified by *Dworkin* a need for the law to balance between freedom and the threat to the institutions of society. With regard to a matter like homosexuality, how is this balance to be struck? It is a matter of opinion. According to *Devlin* the legislature must respond to the consensus because a democracy is based upon a democratic consensus and the community must protect itself according to its own perception of the threats.

Dworkin seeks to examine *Devlin*'s arguments on their own terms and concludes that they are not valid because *Devlin* has misunderstood what it is to disapprove on moral principle. However popular *Devlin*'s thesis that the criminal law should be drawn from public morality, *Dworkin* believes it to be fundamentally wrong.

Devlin requires only good faith in the reasonable man arriving at his disgust. The essence of *Dworkin*'s critique of *Devlin* on this point is that *Devlin* uses the term 'moral position' in the anthropological sense, which is not necessarily the same as a moral position in the legal context.

Dworkin acknowledges another point of practical politics in a democracy whereby a legislator cannot afford to ignore the public reaction but insists that confusion is avoided between the facts of political life and the principles of political morality.

Paternalism

Professor HLA Hart in *Law Liberty and Morality* criticised *Devlin* on two points – namely that there is no widely shared morality and that there can be no freedom if we can do only that which others approve of. We will deal with the former.

According to *Hart* there is no widely shared morality. There is morality but it amounts only to his 'minimum content of natural law' which is by definition universal. *Hart* has said that 'some shared morality is essential to the existence of any society'. This cannot be proved by evidence, hence it is a statement which he regards as self evident. Society is pluralistic. There is a mixture of tolerated moralities rather than one shared morality. He allows that the majority may be wrong, for example Hindu prohibition on killing cows. The Saudi imprisonment of Europeans who have consumed alcohol would be supported by *Devlin*'s argument for the cohesion of their society. *Hart* argues that a change in morality has not the same effect as if treason were successful and therefore the analogy that *Devlin* draws between them does not lie. Morality is not a seamless web. We do not have to accept an all or nothing situation.

This can be illustrated in the case of *R v Lemon; R v Gay News* (1979) on blasphemous libel concerning the publication of a poem and cartoon about the Crucifixion with homosexual undertones – why does the law only protect the deity of the Christians? The Law Commission Report on *Offences Against Religion and Public Worship* (1985) (no. 145) received many objections to extending the offence to other religions but nonetheless concluded 'in the circumstances now prevailing in this country, the limitation of the offence to the protection of Christianity and, it would seem, the tenets of the Church of England, cannot be justified.' The majority recommended the complete abolition of the common law offence. That recommendation has not yet been adopted. With the publication of Salman Rushdie's book, *The Satanic Verses*, the need for reform has been given fresh impetus.

In addressing the issue of when the law ought to enforce a particular morality *Hart* favours paternalism. According to this thesis society may prevent people from harming themselves. Consent is rejected not because the act is wrong but because it is harmful. *Hart* also distinguishes between offence through public spectacle and offence through knowledge. He would act only against the former since the latter would involve the punishing of people for the doing of actions that we do not want them to do.

Hart in some respect goes further than *Mill*. He acknowledges the difficulty in defining 'harm' to others and proceeds that the law may be used in a paternalistic way to prevent people from harming themselves. *Dias* criticises *Hart*'s paternalism on the grounds that *Hart* relies on paternalism to justify the prohibition on homosexual intercourse among the young for fear of 'corruption'. *Dias* rightly points out that 'corruption' implies the taking of a moral position prior to paternalism. He suspects that *Hart* uses paternalism in this way to justify the outlawing of that which society holds offensive. *Hart* accepts the distinction drawn by the Wolfenden Committee between public and private spheres of morality. *Dias* criticises this proposition. He maintains that the same acts are differentiated depending on whether there is an immoral purpose. The example he uses is the accosting and solicitation of money by a woman. The immoral purpose would be for prostitution. A perfectly moral purpose would be for a student charity.

Hart explains the prohibition on bigamy as analogous to public nuisance – it is an affront to the marriage ceremony and throws the legal obligations of the parties into confusion. He appears here to support *Devlin*'s contention that bigamy is immoral because monogamy is an accepted moral institution in this society. In effect *Hart* maintains that *Devlin* has not proved that every act of immorality threatens the survival of the society. *Devlin* responded to this criticism in his 1965 edition in which he says that he was looking at immorality's potential to threaten the existence of society. *Devlin* uses an analogy with drunkenness. He maintains that if a large proportion of the population became drunk every night that would threaten the existence of the society yet he insists that society cannot take account of the numbers when legislating against an action. Would it be illegal if only some people became drunk? How many? This surely reduces the argument to absurdity.

Devlin argues that if the law is entitled to show a paternalistic interest in the matters that *Hart* outlines then why ought it not also to show a paternalistic interest in the morals of the community? The paternalism of *Hart* also assumes that the majority or the powerful can and do decide for all others what is in their best interests. Perhaps people do not want to be 'looked after' any more? Perhaps they wish to take full responsibility for their own actions including responsibility for the consequences of those actions. If a person wishes to drive a motor cycle without a crash helmet it is only his head that will be injured. Why should society be interested in imposing a law on him that requires his wearing of a helmet? *Dias* strongly supports *Devlin*. He also believes that there reaches a point when fragmentation of values destroys cohesion and coexistence in a society. Those who advocate moral pluralism assume that with tolerance there will still be a bond that holds the society together. *Dias* doubts that it is possible to preserve that underlying unity in a society if the law is confined to interference only when there is harm to others.

In support of moderation

It is common ground that the law should uphold moral positions because these are central to our way of life. The disagreement seems to be on what criteria should the law act. There is much agreement. No one advocates not protecting minors or others suffering from incapacity; no one doubts that the law has a role to protect life, limb and property. The area of difficulty is over moral principles that do not cover these matters.

Dias believes that permissive societies are always in danger of becoming weak societies unless a stand is taken at some point to uphold a broad basis of cohesive values. He insists that since the state is very much concerned with the behaviour of its citizens, it may rightly continue to concern itself with moral attitudes while renouncing interest in beliefs. Further, he continues that another justification for restraint is that social existence depends upon coordination which in turn requires restraint in individual action. It follows that to relax legal restraints at a time when there is less and less assurance of self discipline is the path to social destruction.

Dias is of the opinion that the civil law is inappropriate as to a remedy but that there are also disadvantages with the use of the criminal law. Although geared to advance the interests of the society (state) the remedy at criminal law involves punishment. In the case of immorality there has however usually been no victim. Further, it is accepted that punishment is not a cure. The emphasis on cure does however presuppose that immorality is a disease. *Dias* wants a system that upholds and reinforces societal morals yet does not criminalise the persons involved.

Dias proposes a complex calculus in place of the other formulae. He lists the following as relevant:

1 The danger of the activity to others.

2 The danger to the actor himself.

3 Economy of forces needed for detection and pursuit.

4 Equality of treatment.

5 The nature of the sanction.

6 Possible hardship caused by the sanction.

7 Possible side effects.

Empirical difficulties

The prior position that one would adopt with regard to the relationship of the state to the individual will determine the view one would take on the question of the empirical difficulties involved in the enforcement of morality through the criminal law. The moral question is hence seen as prior to this. The empirical difficulties are rather obvious. The state would have to sanction burdensome interference in negative liberty and in privacy. There would be all the problems of detection and the unpleasant aspects of surveillance, blackmail and hypocrisy would be raised.

Conclusion

We can therefore conclude that the question of the legal enforcement of morality is a complex political, moral and legal question on which opinion is sharply divided. The view expressed in the Wolfenden Committee is but one approach – one that is closely based on *Mill*'s philosophy of liberty of the individual. If one is of a view that the state has a paternalistic task to perform then one would be prepared to have the state intrude into private lives to the extent required to prevent the individual from harming himself. The so called 'caring society' is also the interfering society. The line between caring (in a paternalistic way as a father cares for his child) and interference is one that perplexes both parents and the society as a whole. It is not at all clear where in practice that line ought to be drawn. From a different perspective one may argue that it is the role of the state to protect values and moral institutions. If this is the case, in a pluralistic society such as Britain an assumption would have to be made as to which set of values is the correct one. This would entail obvious difficulties and would certainly alienate substantial minority views if the majority position was adopted. A further perspective would allow for complete invasion of private lives and would justify the same by reference to absolute truths – namely the contention that certain conduct is vice and ought to be punished per se whether committed in public or private. Whilst there is a point to be made here it would have to be stated that certain conduct is not immoral if done in private; whereas the same conduct would be considered immoral if done in public just for the reason of offence to sensibility.

With the discussion that has taken place so far, it should be possible, at least in part, to provide an answer to the question, 'Does the law define the boundaries of acceptable conduct?'

The answer must be a qualified 'yes'. There are certain legal rules which have as their purpose the definition of what behaviour is socially acceptable. At the same time, however, it must be recognised that there are many other non-legal rules within society that also help in defining what is acceptable.

As was noted earlier, many legal rules are normative – that is they provide a standard of how people ought to act. The clearest example, of course, is the criminal law, which in general can be reformulated in the phrase, 'you shall not'. Therefore, you shall not commit murder, rape, theft, burglary, is the typical substance of the criminal law. Such laws clearly have as their purpose the definition of what is socially unacceptable behaviour. On the other hand, however, as *Hart* pointed out, not all such rules of law can be formulated in this way, in that some rules are 'enabling rules' – that is they provide a means by which individuals within society can create certain relationships. Hence, the law of contract is not normative, in the sense that it states how a person ought to act; rather, it is an enabling rule in that it provides the means by which individuals can enter into legally binding agreements, which will be enforced by the law. Similarly with the law of trusts and company law, the former states how an individual is able to create a trust, the latter a company. Therefore, it is not true to say that all rules of law have as their purpose the definition of what is socially acceptable behaviour.

The idea of law (2) | 3

Law and justice

All agree that the aim of the law should be to achieve justice. Yet, no-one can agree as to what justice is. The first thing to note is that justice has two meanings – a wide sense and a narrow sense.

Wide sense

The word justice is frequently used as the equivalent to morality. It was in this sense that *Aquinas* used the word when he said 'An unjust law is no law'. Justice, in its wide sense, therefore, is the same as morality.

Narrow sense (formal justice)

a Justice, as used in its narrow sense, refers to a specific branch of morality, and not to all of morality. Justice and morality are not, therefore, co-extensive. This can be illustrated by the way in which language is used: an unjust man is automatically immoral, but an immoral man is not automatically unjust.

b On this view, 'justice is that specific part of morality which requires the treatment of like cases alike'. Therefore, injustice is that specific breach of morality which consists of failing to treat like cases alike. It was Aristotle who first argued that justice is that specific moral principle which requires the treatment of like cases alike. Formal justice, he said, consists of two elements: distributive justice and corrective justice:

   i Distributive justice is that area which is concerned with the determination of what is a fair division of the benefits and burdens within society. Preference is, therefore, towards the legislature and the constitution, for it is these organs that determine the division of goods within society. Therefore, it is for the legislature to ensure that all like cases are treated alike, so that all get the benefits (the right to vote) and burdens (the obligation to pay tax).

   ii Corrective justice operates when the fair balance determined by distributive justice is upset. For example, if X stops Y from voting in breach of the rules of distributive justice, then corrective justice is required in the form of an order requiring X to pay compensation to Y. Corrective justice is, therefore, the main concern of the courts.

c Justice, therefore, as viewed by *Aristotle*, is a narrow, formal requirement. It says nothing as to the content of the laws; it merely requires that these laws should be applied equally to all people. Therefore, to *Aristotle* an immoral law would still be a just law (in the sense of satisfying the requirements of justice) if it were applied equally to all people.

d It is quite clear that justice is an entirely subjective notion, and that one person's appreciation of what is just will differ from that of another. Yet having said that, it must be recognised that most people still regard justice (whatever that might mean) as being the ultimate aim of a legal system.

Are judges concerned with justice?

The traditional view of the function of the judge is that the judge is only required to apply the law. He should not try to modify or adapt the law according to what is his concept of justice, in that this would involve him in the constitutionally unacceptable role of creating new law.

This attitude is typified in the following quotation by Megarry V-C in *Tito* v *Waddell* [1977] Ch 106:

> 'However, the question for me is not whether the Banabans ought to succeed as a matter of fairness or ethics or morality. I have no jurisdiction to make an award to the plaintiffs just because I reach the conclusion (if I do) that they have had a raw deal. This is a Court of Law and Equity (using equity in its technical sense) administering justice according to the law and equity, and my duty is to examine the plaintiffs' claim on that footing.'

Essentially, therefore, Megarry is saying that to the judge, considerations of substantive fairness are irrelevant, and that the only function of the judge is to apply the law.

In comparison, some other judges, notably Lord Denning have always shown an acute concern for what is just, and he has always stated that the function of the law is to do justice as between the parties. There is no doubt that many of his legal decisions have involved modification to the law so as to achieve justice in the particular case. The difficulty of this approach is twofold:

a that it involves the judge in the constitutionally unacceptable function of creating new law;

b the decision will only reflect the judge's own particular concept of justice. Since this is inevitably subjective, many others may disagree with the decision.

Some conceptions of justice

Many people have put forward ideas of justice in social arrangements, and it will not be possible to consider them all; it is worth at the outset sowing a seed of scepticism and doubt. Can any of the theories discussed below in reality be termed anything other than subjective? Aren't all the arguments aimed at showing 'what justice is', really only showing good arguments for a particular arrangement, and not conclusive?

A first differentiation can be made between 'collectivist' and 'individualistic' positions. Collectivists, (notably in the present day Communists/Marxists,) view arrangements from the point of view of society as a whole or of institutions having a reality greater than the individuals who make them up (cf *Savigny's* 'Volksgeist';

Hegel's state), whereas individualists view them from the standpoint of the individual. (Marxists do of course consider that in a communist state the individual will fully realise his freedom.) The theories mentioned and discussed below are individualist. There are various ways of categorising theories. Perhaps the three most influential and important have been social contract theories, natural rights theories and utilitarian theories. In fact the first two go together very often, as we shall see; we differentiate them now because the modern theorists *Rawls* and *Nozick* do not combine them, but use a social contract and a natural rights model respectively.

Social contract theories

These base the justice of society's organisation on the fact that the individuals in the society have – or would have, or may be presumed to have – entered into a contract agreeing that society should be so patterned.

Natural rights theories

These emphasise the importance of society being formed in such a way as to protect and not infringe upon 'natural rights', rights which people have either from God or from their nature.

The major exponents of social contract theory in its first heyday in the seventeenth century also placed great emphasis on natural rights: because of their different stresses it seems right to consider *Hobbes's* as a social contract view, and *Locke's* a natural rights one, but both included the idea of a state of nature including natural rights, and a contract leading to civil society.

Hobbes: men had their natural rights in a state of nature. Since men had a tendency to compete and infringe on the rights of others (and, in the famous words, the state of nature would therefore be 'nasty, brutish and short') they would find this state of nature unsatisfactory, and would therefore wish to join a society where the urge to competition was controlled and restrained by a political sovereign. This sovereign could become so by force or by contract. People in the state of nature would be prepared to covenant or contract to transfer their natural right to protect themselves and all their powers to a sovereign. They were then subject to an all powerful illimited sovereign (cf *Austin*): subject to political obligation because of a contract they had made or would be prepared to make.

Locke: In state of nature, man had rights including that of appropriation of land. The two limits to this (to prevent waste, and to leave enough and as good for others) can be shown to be removed by the advent of money, leaving an *unconditional* right of appropriation, along with a right to protection of life, liberty and estate. Man could live in the state of nature, but some will try to gain property by trespass rather than just acquisition. To protect their property, men will enter into a covenant agreeing to a civil society. This society is there to ensure natural rights, and the state is still subject to them; if the state passed laws infringing these rights, rebellion would be justified.

A third theorist tying together social contract and natural rights was *Rousseau*, whose work was seized as a philosophical justification for the French Revolution. By the 'social contract', a man transferred his rights not to an actual sovereign but to society which was the 'general will': to obey this was to obey oneself. The state should grant the citizen his freedom, and if it did not, it could be overthrown or revoked by the 'general will'.

At first, difficulty might be seen in relating these theories to our theme of justice, since *Hobbes*, for example, concentrates on political obligations to the state, not the obligations of the state to conform to standards of justice. Clearly the 'natural rights' stress of *Locke* does suggest a standard of justice (a society will be just if it respects the natural rights of its citizens) a view shared by *Rousseau* and *Nozick*. However, although *Hobbes* does not allow the social contract to be used in the direction of obligations of the state, it seems that individuals who were contracting in such a way would lay down conditions to control the state, and determine how it would operate. So the social contract model suggests a standard of justice as well (a society will be just if it follows the conditions which contracting members of society would impose and accept.) This sort of approach can also be seen in the work of *Rawls*.

Utilitarian theories

Perhaps the most common political viewpoint of the nineteenth and twentieth centuries, utility, was pioneered by *Jeremy Bentham*. He thought that society's decisions should be taken on the basis of creating by those decisions the 'greatest happiness of the greatest number', or more specifically by maximising utility. This can be done in one or two ways; either maximising the average of the utilities of everyone in the society, or by maximising the total utility of the society as a whole.

It will be convenient to mention the major criticisms of 'utility' here: the modern theories, particularly *Rawls*, can be seen as attacks on utilitarianism and attempts to remove it from its pre-eminent position. The criticism mostly made of *total utility* is that it ignores the lot of the average person: if by increasing the total population by a large number the total utility can be slightly increased, society should follow a programme of encouraging production of children, even though on average everyone's lot will be less happy. For this reason *average utility* is preferable, but this too is unacceptable. For a start, how does one measure utility or happiness or welfare: is it psychological, is it based on want satisfaction or what? How does an unemotional man's quiet happiness measure against the super-sensitive person's ecstasy?

Assuming a measure can be found, we still must face the fact that utility is not a theory which should be acceptable. Three points can be made:

a Some preferences or wants must be disregarded for reasons of consistency: for example, preferences for anti-utilitarian arrangements (for example a ban on alcohol for religious reasons); or more fundamentally, desires for a state run following the rules of a religion, even if that did not match happiness or want maximisation.

b Utility would offend our intuitions of justice, because it would countenance unacceptable inequality. We should test all possible conceptions of justice against our own convictions of what is right in particular situations; when we apply utility to one or two factual situations, we can see that it goes counter to these convictions. To take a simple case, of a slave-owning society: should we keep slavery? Assume that we are measuring utility in terms of satisfaction of wants or preferences. If 20 per cent of the population are slaves, they would have to feel four times as strongly about becoming free as the 80 per cent slave owners feel about life without slaves. It is not implausible to assume that slavery will be kept. Thus, utility will frequently accept situations where the majority benefit from the poverty or oppression of a minority.

c A more complex example can lead us to a further point. Should discrimination against blacks be illegal? A decision on this question, on any utility scale, will take into account the views (wants, happiness, preferences) of those who see blacks as unequal, and therefore less deserving of respect: the very decision will therefore be based on an unequal view of blacks. And yet, utilitarians would claim to be egalitarian in that each person is counted as the same weight. The discrimination decision clearly does not give them that weight.

Dworkin argues that this latter point extends to all 'external preferences' for his attempted rescue of the utilitarian position. Other types of rescue attempt can be made: one perhaps stronger than the others. This is to mix utility with another factor, *a* minimum standard: once the minimum standard is reached for all, decisions are taken on the basis of utility. This attempt fails: it answers the major thrust of the second criticism (against allowing poverty), but does not meet the third criticism (against external preferences).

Social contract, natural rights and utilitarian theories are only three of the types of individualistic theories of justice. Others include perfectionism which organises things to promote a particular good or value, and intuitionism which denies that any acceptable complete criteria of justice can be worked out, and therefore results in each decision being made by the intuition of the decision taker. The former is only acceptable if we accept the idea in question; the second only if no complete criterion proves satisfactory.

The theories mentioned above can be divided in another way, ie in relation to traditional labels put on political views – libertarian, egalitarian, liberal, etc.

Since different meanings are attributed to these labels at different times, it is not possible to be certain of the correct use: the following 'definitions' are thus rather subjective.

'Libertarian' would seem to mean basing views on the importance of individual freedoms from interference, whereas 'liberal' relates to views which emphasise the importance of allowing the individual to pursue any course he chooses.

These two are not by any means the same; by these definitions, a liberal theory could advocate redistribution of wealth to allow the freedom to a greater number of people, which redistribution would not be acceptable to a libertarian as it encroaches on the freedoms, or liberty, or rights, of the people from whom the wealth is taken.

'Egalitarian' is capable of at least two definitions. By one of these, an egalitarian would advocate that everything in society should be distributed equally; by the other, that in the decisions a society has to make, everyone should have an equal weight, an equal vote and value.

The second meaning of egalitarian is called by *Dworkin* 'equal concern and respect' and he sees it as being the basis of *Rawls's* and indeed of any liberal theory: society allows the individual freedom to follow his chosen course because his course is as important and valid as anyone else's; in making decisions about allocation and resources, etc, his feelings and wishes and the course he chooses are given weight equal to everyone else's.

Of the theories above, natural rights theories are libertarian, concentrating on the freedoms the individual has by right; social contract theories might be libertarian (as with *Locke*), liberal-egalitarian (as with *Rawls*), or none of these (as with *Hobbes*, a theory of political obligation not justice); and utilitarianism purports to be egalitarian, but has problems with external preferences and prejudices, as considered above.

The most complete argument for a theory of justice is possibly that provided by *Rawls*, who argues for his two principles of justice in *A Theory of Justice*. His theory is of *justice as fairness*, accepting those principles that would result from an 'original position'. In this 'original position', the parties set out, subject to conditions considered reasonable and fair, to agree the principles by which their society should be organised. It is thus a social contract position, although the contract is a hypothetical one.

Robert Nozick's Anarchy, State and Utopia is a fascinating book, containing a new natural rights theory as well as criticisms of utilitarianism and *Rawls*, a plea for vegetarianism, and much more. It is recommended as a stimulating 'read' on justice and some related topics.

In brief, *Nozick's* theory is as follows. Man has certain natural rights, including the right to acquire property. These rights must not be violated by anyone, without the consent of the right-holder: they act as moral 'side-constraints' on action. To be justified, a state must be such that it would arise from a no-state position (the state of nature) without infringing the rights of anyone who did not consent; only a minimal state offering protection against violence, theft and breach of agreement would emerge in this way. Any further state is not justified; particularly, a state redistributing wealth is not justified, and taxation to bring this about is the equivalent of forced labour. The only legitimate way of coming to hold property is by just acquisition, just transfer, or rectification of a past injustice.

Nozick's theory is interesting and a strong challenge to *Rawls*, but must ultimately be rejected as being unrealistic, particularly his views on taxes and the welfare state.

Law and freedom

Both England and America are sometimes referred to as 'the land of the free'. How is that freedom ensured? In America, freedom is ensured by the American Constitution. The phraseology of the constitution is clear and unambiguous:

> 'Congress shall make no law respecting an establishment or religion or prohibiting the free express thereof, or abridging the freedom of speech, or of the press, or the right of the people peaceably to assemble and petition the Government for a redress of grievance.'

If any legislation is passed by Congress or the individual states which contravenes these provisions, then the Supreme Court of the United States may intervene and declare the law null and void. Freedom, therefore, to the extent provided by the Constitution, is ensured in that nobody has the jurisdiction to pass legislation taking away those freedoms.

No such structure exists in the UK. Freedom is provided in the UK by what may be called 'The Golden Principle' of the English Constitution – namely that everything is lawful, unless it is specifically decreed by Parliament to be unlawful. For example, nothing in English law guarantees freedom of speech, but due to the Golden Principle (that everything is lawful except if it is decreed to be unlawful) we have freedom of speech except in so far as the law specifically limits that freedom.

As a consequence of the above, an analysis of the freedoms enjoyed in the UK and America must follow very different lines. The analysis in America will be on the basis of an examination of the positive freedoms ensured by the Constitution. In England, however, one would start by examining all the laws which deny freedom of action, and one would then know that because of the 'Golden Principle', freedom exists in all other areas.

There is no such thing as absolute freedom: one man's freedom is another's duty, the duty to respect the freedom. Without such respect, the freedom is meaningless. Each right carries with it duties.

Restriction of freedom for one actually extends freedom for another; there must be some restriction on freedoms to allow everyone to exercise theirs, otherwise only the most powerful could do so.

The law must strike a balance between conflicting freedoms; where the balance is struck is not a legal matter but a political one.

For example under s17 of the Public Order Act 1986, which defines the offence of incitement to racial hatred, a prosecution can only be brought with the consent of the Attorney-General: this signifies that it is recognised that this particular provision involves a political decision as complying with it could severely curtail freedom of speech. This puts the Attorney-General in a difficult position, as he has to strike the balance between freedom of speech on the one hand and freedom for other people to go about their daily lives without racial harassment on the other.

Some freedoms are meaningless without certain rights to go with them. The USSR claims that freedom of speech is no use unless you first have the right to accommodation, right to education etc, so these must come before you can be given any such freedom. In this country we have freedom of labour – you are free to choose your profession, where you practise it and when – but no right to work; in the USSR the situation is reversed – you have the right to work, but not the freedom to choose what you do, where or when. Freedoms can therefore conflict with rights.

The famous Justice of the United States Supreme Court, *Oliver Wendell Holmes*, once said that as soon as you interfere with a right it is no longer a right but a privilege enjoyed at another's sufferance.

The problem is that some may seek to exercise their rights in order to deny others theirs. In the USA, there are no restrictions on personal freedom (following *Wendell Holmes*); you may be a racist, etc if you wish. In the UK, however, the opposing view is held, that it is necessary to restrict some people's rights in order that others may exercise theirs.

The European Convention, article 17, says that no-one may use his rights to deny rights to another – this was invoked in 1957 against the German Communist Party, who were denied their rights of association on the grounds that if they were allowed then they would seek to use them to deny others their own rights of association etc.

Article 15 of the Convention states that the rights and freedoms protected in the Convention may be abandoned or at least diminished in time of war or other emergency which threatens the life of the nation (such a clause is essential in an international treaty). The Convention seeks to balance this by showing that there are certain rights and freedoms which may never be derogated from: the right to life, freedom from torture and freedom from retroactive criminal legislation. This has been used on several occasions: against Greece, during the rule of the military junta which took power in 1967 – the European Court of Human Rights said that there was no sufficient emergency and therefore the ruling junta could not derogate from the Convention; against the UK because of the treatment in Northern Ireland of suspected IRA prisoners; against Cyprus and Turkey during the troubles there in 1974/75.

The problem in the UK is that our constitution is not written down. We do not therefore have any safeguard against what Lord Hailsham called 'the instrument of tyranny', ie the House of Commons. There is no court which can challenge an Act of Parliament, unlike in the USA, where Congress can pass a bill and the Supreme Court can void it for being inconsistent with the constitution. Everything is alright so long as Parliament is concerned about liberties and freedoms, but should a time come when it is not there would be no safety valve. Also no Parliament can bind its successors, so that what one Parliament does the next can undo.

If Parliament passed a bill of rights setting out freedoms, the next Parliament could change it completely.

At present there is an arrangement for cases to be appealed to the European Court of Human Rights, but under Article 5 of the European Convention on Human Rights this is subject to review by the government at five-year intervals (ie they could withdraw their agreement); internationally, however, this right is inalienable (ie one country can take another to it and the court's decision will be binding on that other). In fact the UK government allows 800 cases a year to go to the Court of Human Rights, which is far more than any other country. France, for instance, will not allow its citizens to appeal to it. The UK loses many of these cases; in theory it has a contractual duty to the other states to change its legislation in respect of lost cases (thus detracting from the sovereignty of Parliament). But in fact such changes in the legislation do not always materialise (see para (e) below).

It may be questioned whether Britain needs any formal rights guarantee. However, Lord Scarman, an ardent supporter of the concept of a bill of rights, in an article in *The Independent* newspaper, cited the fact that every year about 800 provisional UK files are opened under the Convention, and that no other signatory state sends so many claims. He also pointed out that between 1953 and 1984, of the 57 cases where the Court actually decided that there had been a violation of rights, 18, nearly one-third, were cases originating in the United Kingdom.

It is said by some that our freedoms are sufficiently guaranteed by the Strasbourg process (ie referral to the European Commission of Human Rights). However, it can be argued that this is not so. Although the British Government is under an obligation to amend any law which violates the freedoms guaranteed by the European Convention, certain cases have shown that this is not so. For example, in *Young, James and Webster* v *United Kingdom* (1981) E Ct HR, it was held that the 'closed shop' was a restriction on freedom, yet Britain has done nothing to correct this. Nevertheless, the recent reforms in the Dockworkers' terms of employment and the proposed reforms of the legal profession, are an indication of this Government's determination to stamp out the 'closed shop'. Even if the Government decides to act, the measures which it takes are often unsatisfactory. For example, Harriet Harman, a solicitor who had been found to be in 'contempt of court' by allowing a journalist to see documents which had been read out in open Court, took her case to the European Commission, arguing that the English law of contempt was a violation of her right to freedom of speech under Article 10 of the European Convention. The Government in 1986 finally reached an agreement with Ms Harman, agreeing to amend the law of contempt and to pay all her costs.

On the other hand, *Lord McCluskey* in the Reith Lectures does not think that freedoms in Britain are threatened. He said:

'The position today is that the law professes the principle of equality; and, although at a social and private level, discrimination and prejudice still exist, the law itself does not in principle deny equality to minority groups in the claiming of their fundamental human rights and immunities. Of course, most of us would acknowledge or even protest about particular instances which illustrate that to be a female or a homosexual or a member of some ethnic or religious minority carries with it certain economic, cultural or other disadvantages, including legal ones, but my point is that the fundamental human rights made available in other Common Law democracies, by the entrenchment of specific and general rights, are not withheld by law in the United Kingdom. Nor is there any political party likely to win power that seeks to deny such rights to such groups. I do not argue that our treatment of minorities is exemplary; merely that our record will stand comparison with that of the USA, where the constitution has always professed freedom and equality.

The conclusion that I would suggest on this point is that, in our society, the absence from our recent history of institutionalised discrimination having its formal origins in the law, and the absence of any recent history of an unholy alliance between the lawmakers and oppressors, make it unnecessary to enact a Bill of Rights to betoken a national repentance for the sins of our forefathers: or to protect us against non-existent threats. The threat of a flood is too remote to warrant the building of a legal dam. The mechanisms of our existing legal and political structures can handle all the foreseeable rainfall.'

He follows on to say that even a Bill of Rights cannot succeed in 'preserving the fundamental rights of the citizens in those countries more effectively than does the ordinary law as applied in the United Kingdom', and concludes that the issue is whether the disadvantages of such a measure outweigh the advantages.

One is drawn to the view expressed by the American Judge, *Learned Hand* and quoted by *Lord McCluskey*:

'I often wonder whether we do not rest our hopes too much upon constitutions, upon laws and upon courts. These are false hopes; believe me, these are false hopes. Liberty lies in the hearts of men and women; when it dies there is no constitution, no law, no court can save it; no constitution, no law, no court can even do much to help it. While it lies there it needs no constitution, no law, no court to save it.'

Since there is clearly a potential conflict between competing rights and freedoms, it is important that a balance should be struck. This raises the important question of how the balance is decided.

Returning to the Golden Principle, since all things are legal (and thus there is freedom of action) except where a particular course of conduct is declared to be illegal, then those establishments that can declare something to be illegal are the establishments which determine the balance between the conflicting freedoms.

Two institutions have this power to declare an act illegal:

a *The Courts*

The Courts can limit freedom (by making an act illegal) in one of two ways:

i   By creating new offences – *Shaw* v *DPP* (1962) (but it should be noticed that this was disapproved in *Knuller* v *DPP* (1972)). Even so, the Courts effectively created a new offence in *R* v *Lemon; R* v *Gay News* (1979). Their power here, however, is clearly limited.

ii Through the interpretation of statutes and existing case law – since the Courts are entrusted with deciding the correct interpretation of the law, they clearly have the power to limit freedom by interpreting statutes and cases in a wide way, so as to increase the scope of what is illegal. If one examines labour law, for example, one cannot doubt the ability of the Courts to restrict the freedom of unions to strike. Similarly, the way in which the Courts interpret the case law on individual freedom (such as the extent of police powers of stop and search) can affect the extent of the freedoms involved.

b *Parliament*
Since Parliament is sovereign, and can thus pass any law, on any matter, Parliament is clearly central in deciding what freedoms we enjoy.

Finally, however, it should be noticed that in practice the scope of our freedom is largely determined by how effectively the law is enforced. For example, one has no practical freedom (despite the wording of the law) if the police (or any other body) continually break the law. One has no individual freedom if the police continually break the law relating to search and seizure or if they continually hold suspects for longer than is allowed.

Therefore, whether the law is obeyed, and enforced when broken, also helps determine the balance between competing freedoms. It is probably in this area that there is most dissatisfaction – for instance see the complaints of black youths in Brixton who say that they have little personal freedom because of continuing police harassment.

The above explains why the question of freedom within society is such a vexed problem; namely because freedoms conflict, and so one man's freedom may be another's loss of freedom. Freedom is only relative, and so a careful balance must be struck. It is because of the nature of freedom that the following seemingly contradictory statements do make sense: 'By limiting freedom, we increase it' and 'The law creates freedom by restricting it'.

Is there a loss of freedom?

It is in the light of the above considerations that the question of whether we are losing our freedoms must be answered. Many point to the increasing degree to which Government and legislation interfere in individuals' lives, and suggest that this is conclusive proof that we are losing our freedoms. For example, legislation in criminal law such as the prohibition on drinking and driving, and the obligation to wear a crash helmet on a motorbike, or seat belts in a car or, in another area the proliferation of planning restrictions, are cited as instances of this loss of freedom.

Yet does the above really mean that we are losing our freedom? It should be remembered that each of these provisions, while restricting one person's freedom, increases the freedom of others. The prohibition on drinking and driving increases the freedom of other drivers to use the roads in safety. Seat belt and crash helmet legislation reduces the cost of road accidents, and thus increases the freedom of all others who have to pay for this cost through increased taxes. Planning restrictions give freedom not to be adversely affected by our neighbours' activities.

Therefore, because of the potential conflicting freedoms, whenever one is asked whether a particular piece of legislation reduces freedom, one must always ask the question: 'Is there a possible increase in somebody else's freedom, which offsets the loss of freedom caused by the law's limitation of this sort of action?'

People will always disagree over the answer to this question, but it must be realised that the question of whether we are losing our freedoms cannot be answered simply by listing new legislation which limits previously free acts. One must always consider whether the legislation has not produced a greater freedom in some other area.

Can we list freedoms?

There has always been controversy as to how widely 'freedom' should be defined, and as such, what should be viewed as a 'freedom' ensured by the law. The following includes all 'freedoms' that would be included in the widest possible definition of freedom. It remains for the student to decide himself whether all of the following are correctly viewed as freedoms.

Lloyd lists the following as freedoms guaranteed by the law:

a Equality and democracy;

b Freedom of contract;

c The right of property;

d The right of association;

e Freedom of labour;

f Freedom from want;

g Freedom of speech and the press;

h Freedom of religion;

i Personal freedom.

A more conservative definition might include only the freedoms of association, labour, speech, religion and personal freedom.

These freedoms will now be examined:

Equality and democracy

Equality consists not in falsely pretending that all people are the same, but requires that before the law all people should be treated equally and that all matters of colour, race, creed or sex should be ignored.

The notion of democracy being expressed as a freedom may at first sight seem strange. Democracy, however, is essentially the freedom of self-determination. If one compares the principles of a dictatorial regime to those of a democracy, it will be seen that democracy is itself a form of freedom.

Freedom of contract

Freedom of contract may be viewed as an extension of the democratic principle of self-determination – namely that it is for the individual to decide for himself the nature of the contract he would make; in this matter he should have entire freedom. Freedom of contract, however, no longer exists to the same extent as earlier this century, as evidenced by the provisions of the Unfair Contract Terms Act 1977, and the Sale of Goods Act 1979, and other legislation.

The right of property

Property as used here is not limited to land, but includes anything that is capable of being taken into ownership. The right of property, therefore, essentially means the right to own whatever is capable of being owned.

The right of association

This is the question of the right of various types of groups, whether social, political or economic, or of any other kind, to organise themselves and to conduct their affairs. It also includes the right to hold public meetings – a freedom which may clash with the right that society has to preserve public order.

Freedom of labour

This includes the freedom to work for whomever one wishes; it also includes the right to strike and picket. The extent of this freedom has frequently been controversial. But it should be realised that the dispute has only ever been about the extent to which civil immunity against actions in tort should be granted for those on strike. From the time union activity became legal in this country it has never been suggested insofar as the majority of workers are concerned that the right to strike should be removed by making strikes illegal.

Freedom from want

The need to protect everyone, not merely from grinding poverty but also in a reasonable standard of enjoyment, has gradually established itself as one of the supreme values of the modern state. The aim to ensure freedom from poverty and sickness is reflected in the system of social services, the National Health Service and the comprehensive cover against the risks of unemployment.

Freedom of speech and the press

Freedom of speech is, of course, necessary if the democratic system is to operate fully. Similarly, the right of association would be an empty right were it not for the complementary right of freedom of speech. The limits on the right of free speech are: the Law of Defamation; the Obscene Publications Act 1959; the Public Order Act 1986; and the Race Relations Act 1976.

Freedom of religion

This is nowadays taken for granted, yet historically it is one of the most hard fought for freedoms. Every person has the right to choose and follow his own religion, and will not be persecuted on account of his chosen religion.

Personal freedom

Perhaps the most vitally important (but least considered) aspect of personal freedom is, that everyone should be free to come and go as he pleases, to take up or reject any employment that he may wish and to reside wherever he may desire, and generally speaking to lead the sort of life which, subject to compliance with the law of the land, may seem good to him.

Conclusion

Whether one accepts that there is any necessary correlation between law and justice or whether or not it is the proper function of law to advance and protect individual freedom will depend primarily on one's own political perspective. It is not the function of this text nor indeed of this course to mould those views. What is required is a recognition of the political nature of the matter and the formulation of reasoned arguments around the political topic.

Functions of law in society | 4

Introduction

In this chapter we will discuss the function of law from two angles: its function in practice and the theoretical question of whether there are some areas which are 'none of the law's business'. Finally there will be a short section on the origin of law, asking whether it is possible to see the development of our law by looking at various primitive societies.

Recognition of relationships

The law must recognise and define legal relationships between persons before it can implement legal rules. It does this by legally defining certain concepts.

We will see that the concepts of freedom and justice have great significance within the English legal system. There are other concepts which are embodied in the laws themselves, eg the property concept of ownership. This type of concept explains the legal relationship between individuals and concrete situations. Such concepts are basic or fundamental to the working of the system. Three other such concepts in this category are 'rights', 'duties' and 'persons'.

It is not easy to define a moral, human or civil right. Certainly some of these rights are not the subject of law until incorporated in it by statute or case law, and some such 'rights' never are incorporated. Legal rights are those which are the subject of the law and have been legally formulated and enforced by the state. Legal rights are legally protected.

If Y has a legal right to be paid a debt owed to Z then he has a legally protected right to sue Z in a court of law.

Many jurists have attempted to define a right. The two main classifications of legal rights are:

a   deriving from subject-matter on the right of the human will; and

b   basing the conception of the right upon the protection of an interest.

The English jurist *Salmond* felt that a right was similar to an interest.

Oliver Wendell Holmes defined a right as 'nothing but a permission to exercise certain natural powers and upon certain conditions to obtain protection, restitution, or compensation, by the aid of "public force" '.

Holland defined a right as 'Capacity residing in one man of controlling, with the assent and assistance of the State, the actions of others'.

Buckland saw a right as 'An interest of expectation guaranteed by law'. And *Allen* saw a right as 'The legally guaranteed power to realise an interest'.

Austin defined right and duty as correlatives. Put simply, the idea is that where X has a right Y will have a corresponding duty. He said 'Duty is an act or forbearance, compelled by the State, in respect of a right vested in another, and the breach of which is a wrong'.

The modern American jurist *Hohfeld* amplified *Austin*'s simple dichotomy of right-duty. *Hohfeld* says that the simple dichotomy of right-duty (a correlative relationship of two sides (as a coin) or persons) inseparably linked together is inadequate. *Hohfeld* says that each concept of right or duty is a bundle of ideas. Clarity consists of separating them. *Hohfeld*, therefore, elaborated on the simple correlation of rights and duties. He analysed legal relationships as involving the working of four concepts – rights, privileges, powers and immunities. This scheme of jural relations is discussed in more depth in chapter 6.

In spite of *Hohfeld*'s very well thought out scheme, there is still no answer to the question whether there is a complete definition of legal rights and legal duties. One of the difficulties is that certain duties have no corresponding rights, eg criminal law duties.

Professor Hart says that such an answer is not possible and it is necessary instead to look at specific legal contexts before an understanding of the legal right and legal duty can be reached. *Hart* does not use a synonym for the word 'right' but presents a formula which gives us a situation where we would find a right. The difficulty of the formula is that it presupposes a crystal clear legal rule. In factual situations this is not the case. The judge often has to decide whether the particular legal rule applies to a given situation. Statute made law and the common law do not always have clearly defined boundaries of operation.

The case of *Donoghue* v *Stevenson* [1932] AC 562 involved a new situation to come before the courts and there was no crystal clear legal rule for the judges to point to. D drank ginger beer, manufactured by S, from an opaque bottle which contained the decomposed remains of a snail. D became ill as a result. The drink had been sold by a retailer to a friend of D. In this situation the Court held that the manufacturers ought to have foreseen the probability that a consumer would drink the ginger beer, consequently a duty of care was owed to her to ensure that the bottle did not contain any objectionable matter. This duty had been broken and the manufacturer was liable in negligence.

The Court did not magic this 'new' rule out of the air; they drew on a previous legal rule and modified it to apply to this new situation. English legal rules are dynamic. They expand or restrict themselves according to the needs of the given case. Perhaps that is why they are so difficult to define.

This flexibility of legal rules responds to the changing nature of society as well as to given cases. The claim in *Donoghue* v *Stevenson* had not been brought before. It was a result of the changing social situation in which consumers are far apart from the multi-national manufacturers who make their products. This claim of right was recognised by the Court; it could have been recognised by Parliament instead.

In *Hedley Byrne & Co Ltd v Heller & Partners Ltd* [1964] AC 465 B, advertising agents, were instructed by E Ltd, one of their clients, to make advertising contracts which would involve B in personal liability to the advertisers. They made inquiries with H, merchant bankers, concerning the credit worthiness of E Ltd and were told 'in confidence and without responsibility on our part' that E Ltd were good for

£100,000. Relying on that statement, B placed further orders on behalf of E Ltd, but losses of £17,000 were incurred when E Ltd went into liquidation. It was held that H was not liable for the losses sustained by reason of their express disclaimer of liability. Their Lordships went on to explain, obiter, that a negligent though honest misrepresentation, whether written or spoken, could give rise to an action in tort for negligence in certain situations, thereby creating a new form of right.

Here again, the Court recognised the claim of right but because of the defendant's disclaimer, the plaintiff's right to a legal remedy was not recognised in this particular case.

Solution of disputes without using the courts

A second function of the law is between persons. It would be most unusual for a family argument, or an argument at work, however bitter it may be, to arrive on the doorsteps of the Court. In developed societies conflict is usually channelled into non-legal institutions such as the family or professional associations. This code of ethics or familial obligations can be seen as custom operating outside the legal system. However, some custom will be incorporated into the legal system and then used to solve disputes which non-legal custom cannot solve. It has been shown that the majority of interest groups, including businessmen, have no wish to 'go to law'. Law is expensive and litigation can often be tedious and prolonged; therefore, the well developed society will have mechanisms for solving disputes which do not involve legal rules or legal institutions.

Businessmen often provide in their contracts for private arbitration, should anything go wrong.

Modern society has seen the growth of new and powerful interest groups but some have not yet established the necessary mechanisms for avoiding the Court system. An example of such an interest group is the trades union movement. Their power lies in their ability to withdraw a whole labour force. This sort of action could affect the economic and political status quo of the country and so by the 1960s, Governments began to make efforts to regulate the behaviour of the trade unions.

There was the ill-fated Conservative Industrial Relations Act 1971 which established the National Industrial Relations Court and laid down formal legal procedures which the trade unions had to follow in order to pursue their activities. The Trade Union and Labour Relations Act 1974 passed by the Labour Government repealed the Industrial Relations Act and set up the Advisory Conciliation and Arbitration Service which was independent of Government machinery.

Other new situations have seen the need for other new types of dispute solving agencies. The Sex Discrimination Act 1975 made it illegal to discriminate against a person on the grounds of that person's sex. The Act is enforced and supervised by the Equal Opportunities Commission. The Race Relations Act 1976, passed to eliminate discrimination on the grounds of race, is supervised by the Commission for Racial Equality. If problems arise as to immigration policies and practices then enquiries and appeals can be made to the United Kingdom Immigration Advisory Service.

Since the emergence of the Welfare State there has been an enormous amount of legislation relating to the rights of individual citizens as members of interest groups to certain State benefits. If all this work was handled by the Courts the system would disintegrate under the heavy work load. The answer has been to provide a system of administrative tribunals.

In general, the High Court exercises a supervisory control over these tribunals by means of prerogative orders, but sometimes a declaration or injunction may be granted. There are also certain statutory rights of appeal. The supervisory jurisdiction of the High Court by means of prerogative orders may not be used unless:

a the body has legal authority;

b the body has power to determine questions affecting the rights of subjects; and

c the body has a duty to act judicially.

The claimant may appeal where he alleges a breach of the rules of natural justice or where the tribunal has acted ultra vires in exceeding its statutory authority.

This diversity of tribunals working in specialised areas led to the growth of different procedures in different tribunals. This did not lead to 'formal' justice and as a result of the Franks Committee Report in 1957 on Administrative Tribunals the Tribunals and Inquiries Act was passed. The Franks Committee stressed three important characteristics of tribunals. They must be open, fair and impartial. The Act implemented these concepts and the Council on Tribunals reviews the constitution and working of tribunals.

At present legal aid is only available in certain tribunals. The Royal Commission on Legal Services published a report in 1979 that recommended legal aid should be made available in a wide range of circumstances so that persons appearing can be legally represented. There are two possible disadvantages to this. Procedure in the tribunals, which is at present informal, might be less so, and the standard of performance by legal representatives might leave much to be desired as few of them are trained in welfare law. The Citizens' Advice Bureaux usually pass on tribunal cases to the Free Representation Unit (FRU) which supplies the client with a representative who will prepare the case for him and present it at the hearing. The FRU representatives are trained and do not require payment for their work. They are usually law students or pupil barristers.

Most disputes are settled outside the Courts system but because the Higher Courts are dealing with the most important economic, social and political matters of our times, what is said in those Courts has tremendous significance for our daily lives. The Courts' pronouncements therefore have a disproportionate importance in view of the numbers of cases they actually deal with compared to other dispute-solving mechanisms.

Maintenance of social order

There is disagreement as to whether our legal system represents social consensus or social conflict. The view a person has of law will be influenced by his political and social background. Law will be seen by some as the State's mechanism for regulating social activities and interests and controlling society for its own ends. By others the law may be seen as the mother of freedom and justice protecting the weak and harnessing the powers of the strong.

If the law is neutral then it will protect everyone's social values and will show social consensus. If the law is not neutral then it will treat only some values and interests as worth protecting.

Talcott Parsons, the American writer, took the view that the factors pointed towards social consensus. His critics have argued that there are other elements which point towards a social conflict situation.

We have seen that society does not share the same values and there are, therefore, conflicts between individuals and groups which the law has to resolve. Many people may disagree with a legal rule, eg the prohibition of cannabis, and this may mean that the 'social consensus' view of society is too simplistic. It cannot be said that the law treats all persons the same because it treats those groups of people with a different value-system from the one it implements, as being less equal than those who agree with the value-system.

The unitary consensus model does not adopt this viewpoint. Instead it says that law is enacted for the common good by a Parliament which represents all of us, and interpreted by the Courts who treat all equally. Only individuals will set themselves up in conflict against it.

The pluralist consensus model allows for the fact that there are different interest groups all jostling with one another to secure their aims but that because the bargaining powers of each are on the whole equal they balance each other out and help to increase rather than decrease stability in society. In this model the state and law are onlookers and do not interfere except by providing the machinery for solving disputes in the form of policy-making by the executive, political debate by the legislature and principle stating by the judiciary. This view relies on the assumption that all interest groups possess equal power – an assumption which is self-evidently not true.

Should this lead us to accept the unitary consensus model? There is a 'middle of the road model' (the liberal democratic view) of a society in which the legitimate process of law and Government is used to resolve conflicts between interest groups.

These models are very different from that developed by the German philosopher *Karl Marx*. He drew a model of capitalist society which took a more cynical view of the 'agreed' values in the consensus model (eg equality, freedom and the legitimate process of law and Government). He saw these as the ideological constructs of capitalism used to gain acceptance of and continuance of the capitalist system.

Marx did not formulate a systematic theory of law. Instead he and his fellow writers (including *Engels*) attempted to treat law as one facet of a wide variety of social phenomena all of which are alike ultimately determined by the play of economic forces. It could, therefore, be described as a sociological approach to law because it concerns the part which law has played and is playing in society. The approach looks at the content of law, the nature of which is regarded as being but a reflex of an economic substratum. It can also be described as an historical approach in so far as the approach sought to unfold a pattern of evolution.

The rise of the economic approach was due to a mixture of factors. Contemporary science had made massive advances which had challenged existing standards. The outlook of positivism had made people look critically at the accepted social structure. Materialist ideals had replaced religious ones. The object of the movement was to improve the lot of the poor and the working classes.

The approach looked at the economic system within the State. It had developed from the feudal system to the capitalist system and according to *Marx* the next natural historical development would be to the communist system.

The main defects of the capitalist system arose from the nature of the system itself:

a The system was based on the class struggle. There was the ruling class in the form of the bourgeoisie, and they employed labour and attempted to get the most out of their employees by exploitation. They were in conflict with the proletariat (the working classes) who were the employees trying to get as much money for as little work as possible.

b Capitalism produces a boom-slump economic cycle, the slump bringing again the hardships of unemployment.

These factors are coupled with a tendency for industry to concentrate, resulting in multi-national industries producing monopolies and higher prices. All this was seen by *Marx* as the result of the profit motive, the evil of over-production and the centralisation of decision making.

The proletariat realise their lot is worsening and when the situation becomes desperate there is a revolt by the proletariat. The proletariat would take over the means of production: 'the expropriators are expropriated'. The aim was to reach a full communist State: 'from each according to his ability to each according to his needs'.

The original Marxist interpretation challenged the indispensability of law and foreshadowed its eventual disappearance. At the communist stage (the classless society) inequalities would vanish and with them the State and law would disappear as well.

'Law' in Marxist theory lumps together laws and their administration. He sees law as a tool used by the economic rulers to keep the masses in subjection. The bourgeois picture of society is an ideology distorted to suit the situation of those who present it, ie the ruling class, in whose interest it is to give the false picture and quieten the working classes and further their own ends.

There is no real social consensus, the ruling classes have domination of the ideology, attitudes and opinions of the masses. The ruling classes also have control of the institutions which repress by force any sign of revolt by the masses. Law and State together form an apparatus of compulsion wielded by the minority to oppress and exploit the masses. This is why, according to *Marx*, the masses accept the fact of domination by the ruling classes both in a political and economic sense. According to *Marx*'s approach social consensus is a myth and hides the means by which the power groups perpetuate their hold on the 'national' and 'public' interest, and 'law and order'.

Origins of law

Introduction

Law in primitive society has long been of interest to jurists, in that it was hoped that by studying the origins of law, more would be understood about its nature. The writings of various jurists will be examined, and in conclusion the question will be considered as to whether an understanding of primitive law is useful to an understanding of modern law. The work of five jurists will be considered – *Savigny, Maine, Durkheim, Malinowski* and *Gluckman*.

Savigny

Savigny rejected the thinking of both Natural Law and Positivism, and was perhaps the greatest writer of the German Historical School of Thought. He rejected the views that law had some divine origin and authority (Natural Law) or that law was a deliberately created product (the Positivists). For him, law was a slow organic distillation of the spirit of a particular people – 'The Volksgeist' (The Spirit of the People). Law, therefore, was the product of a long and continuing historical process, reflecting the people's own inherent views of what is right. Law, therefore, was the reflection of the people's popular consciousness, and hence should be in accord with the 'spirit of the people'.

Much of what *Savigny* says seems obscure to contemporary thought, and there is no doubt that his theory can be criticised:

a The people of a nation do not always display the 'collective consciousness' required if *Savigny*'s theory is to be considered correct.

b His theory does not adequately account for the fact that law is made by a 'creative minority' or a 'power elite'.

c It does not explain the wholesale introduction of foreign legal systems into domestic laws – such as the introduction of Roman Law into German Law in the sixteenth century.

However, his writing does reveal an important truth – namely that law is not just an abstract set of rules imposed on society, but is an integral part of that society, deeply rooted in the social and economic climate in which it functions, and embodying traditional values which are meaningful within a particular society.

It is, of course, for this reason that *Savigny* is relevant to a consideration of the importance of primitive law; for he shows that the origin of modern law lies in that of primitive law, which is in turn the embodiment of the attitudes of a people.

Maine

The importance of *Maine* is the approach which he adopted. Much of what he said, however, has been subsequently proved to be wrong (for instance, he was opposed tooth and nail to the doctrine that all men are created equal, the falsity of which he said was demonstrated by every piece of historical evidence!).

Maine was the first to adopt a scientific, empirical approach to Primitive Law. In comparison to the speculating and philosophising of such people as *Savigny*, *Maine* actually studied primitive societies, such as Greece, Rome and India. He concluded that all laws had as their origin religious ritual and observance. As such, he believed that in most primitive societies, it was impossible to distinguish law and religion.

He suggested that law developed in the following three stages:

a *Themistes (individual decisions by a leader)*
At the earliest stages law did not exist as established rules. In the event of a dispute, the conflict would be brought before a particular person (the King or the Leader) who would give his decision.

b *Custom*
By collecting the individual decisions (Themistes), customs developed which could be used to decide disputes, in that these were generalised statements of how the Leader would decide such individual disputes were he called upon to do so. Groups emerged, who had the task of applying the law (mainly priests).

c *Institution of the Codes*
This stage marks the development to a modern legal system. The law is specifically recorded and means are provided to reform the law.

Durkheim

Durkheim's main purpose in considering primitive societies was to find an answer to the question 'What provides social cohesion within a society?' His views of primitive society are most interesting. *Durkheim* compared primitive and advanced societies.

Durkheim argued that in primitive society the whole group exists and acts towards one commonly accepted collective goal. It is this unity of purpose which provides the cohesion within the society. *Durkheim* termed this 'mechanical solidarity'.

The function of the law in such primitive societies was simply to punish deviancy from the collective purpose, thereby ensuring the maintenance of the social cohesion.

Therefore, he saw primitive society as being based on commonly accepted goals, and that the function of the law was to punish deviancy from that aim.

In an advanced society, however, there is no unity of purpose. This arises from occupational specialisation. Since all have different functions, then they also have different aims. But, since all have specialised, no-one is self-sufficient – all are mutually dependent, and it is this inter-dependence which provides social cohesion within society. Further, the function of the law is no longer to punish deviancy (it could not be, since there is no longer a collective goal). Rather, its purpose is to resolve disputes between the individuals inter se.

Malinowski and Gluckman

In the twentieth century *Malinowski* conducted field research among tribal people and gained a better understanding of the working of customary rules in an undeveloped society. It is now accepted that tribal people do possess a system of law in a genuine state.

More recent studies have shown that all societies to a greater or lesser extent have legal rules enforced by legally controlled sanctions. One particular study by *Gluckman* led him to conclude that the judicial process of tribal peoples corresponds with more than it differs from the judicial process in Western society. Laws in primitive societies are flexible and new ones can be created and old ones reinterpreted.

Much of the common law was undoubtedly customary and showed this same flexibility. No clear demarcation exists between custom and anthropology since custom is an essential part of the wider category, and is also the foundation of law in its evolutionary aspect. There are three stages of custom. First, as in primitive society. Second, as emerging law. Third, as in advanced society including both general and English local custom.

Primitive society evolves as follows: First societies have customs but no law. Then societies have institutions which create law. Then societies are fully law-based. Custom gradually becomes law as it crystallises out and the need for the community to enforce it becomes a common interest.

Conclusion

Two important points have been made.

a All writers recognise that even in primitive societies some form of authority for the resolution of disputes is required. Whether this authority is classified as 'law' or an embryonic legal system is largely irrelevant. The point has been made that the need for law does not arise simply because of the complexity of modern day society. Whatever type of society one considers, no matter how primitive, the need for law or its equivalent is felt. When one considers that the function of law is to guide human behaviour, and to resolve disputes, this is hardly a surprising conclusion.

b The law is at least to some extent organic in origin; that is it has developed from the beginnings of the society itself. Law and the legal system is not, therefore, something which should be simply imposed upon a society.

Finally, it should be noted that there is no reason why the meaning of 'Primitive Society' should be defined in the narrow way in which it has been in the above discussion. Children, gangs or any other social grouping are as much a primitive society as the types of society mentioned above. Likewise, it would be possible to analyse the social rules which exist in these groupings.

Social aspects of English law | 5

Legal regulation of relationships

As has been discussed earlier, the law is used in the regulation of relationships between persons. Later in the book, we shall examine in depth the ways in which law is used to regulate contractual relationships where the parties combine to effect a mutual purpose: in criminal law where law is used to protect persons and property in order that they may live without undue fear of their life limb and property being violated; in tort law, designed effectively to protect the same interests as the criminal law save that in tort the interests are viewed not as those of the state or society as a whole but as an individual interest and where culpability is less morally reprehensible. These are not the only areas where law regulates relationships. For example, in the next chapter we shall briefly examine the concept of corporate personality where the law employs a fiction (of the separate legal personality of a company) to organise the relationships between the company and its members as well as outsiders. There are other such forms of law regulating relationships, which have no place in this book.

An entire series of volumes could be written on this topic. In this chapter we shall merely examine a theoretical setting for this regulation and look in particular at *Hohfeld*'s scheme of jural relations which seeks to explain the relationship between rights and duties with particular regard to their use by law in the regulation of relationships.

Analytical and normative jurisprudence

In chapter 8 we shall examine the normative jurisprudence of rights which is essentially an area of law which looks at the rights that people have or ought to have. It was said that normative jurisprudence was about the moral foundation of rights. In this section we will look at the analytical jurisprudence of rights. Analytical jurisprudence concerns itself with analysis of concepts. Although we did not address the subject at the time as such the imperative theorists (dealt with in the earlier chapters) can be regarded as engaging in analytical jurisprudence in their search for a definition of 'law'. So far as this chapter is concerned we shall be examining the nature of rights from an analytical point of inquiry. In a later chapter we shall look at another concept, namely legal personality, from the point of view of analytical jurisprudence. It is neither entirely possible nor it is submitted would it be desirable to separate analytical and normative jurisprudence. The reason being that many would say normative jurisprudence gives meaning to the exercise of analytical jurisprudence. Before examining what a right is, it is desirable to ascertain what rights ought to be and who ought to have them and when – that is to say under what circumstances it would be 'legitimate' to restrict or otherwise limit the enjoyment of those 'rights'.

Hohfeld's scheme of jural relations

Within the area of the analytical jurisprudence of rights the starting point for any study must be the work of *Wesley N Hohfeld. Hohfeld's* writing on the subject of rights was undertaken at the early years of the twentieth century and it could indeed be said with some justification that he has made a considerable, though hardly acknowledged contribution, to our understanding of law. In his work, *Fundamental Legal Conceptions as Applied in Judicial Reasoning, Hohfeld* stated that the aim of his theory was to clarify different kinds of legal relations and the different uses to which certain words that are employed in legal reasoning are made. He sought to expose the ambiguities and to eliminate the confusion that surrounds these words. He was concerned to give meaning to the phrase 'X has a right to R' and to explain the set of jural relations that such a statement gives rise to. That objective can be achieved by the concept of right (which he also referred to as a claim); of privilege (liberty); of power and of immunity. These he saw as the lowest common denominators in which legal problems about rights could be stated. That proposition is one that is not without criticism. Indeed the contention of his critics is that whilst his scheme works for some propositions in which the phrase 'X has a right to R' could be fitted; it does not always work because his scheme could not take account of paternalistic criminal law. It is proposed to deal with this criticism in more depth below.

For *Hohfeld* these words (claim; privilege; power and immunity) are to be explained in terms of correlatives and opposites, as each of these concepts has both a jural opposite and a jural correlative. These contain eight fundamental conceptions and all legal problems could be stated in their terms. They thus represented a sort of lowest common denominator in terms of which legal problems could be stated. The eight fundamental concepts might therefore be listed as follows:

a *Jural opposites – right/no right; privilege/duty; power/disability; immunity/liability.*

b *Jural correlatives – right/duty; privilege/no right; power/liability; immunity/disability.*

These terms can be defined as follows:

a By a right (claim) he meant that everyone is under a duty to allow X to do R and that X would have a claim against anyone from everyone to enforce that right.

b By a privilege/liberty he meant that X is free to do or refrain from doing that which is the subject of R. Y has no claim against X if X either exercises or refrains from exercising that liberty.

c By a power he meant that X is free to do an act whether or not he has a claim or a privilege and that this act would have the effect of altering the legal rights and duties of others.

d   By an immunity he meant that X is not subject to anyone's power to change his legal position.

e   By a duty he meant that Y must respect X's right.

f   By no claim he meant that where X has a liberty Y has no claim that X should not exercise that liberty.

g   By disability he meant that the party has an inability to change another person's legal position.

It is important to emphasise that *Hohfeld* was examining legal rights and that the meanings attributed to his terms are technical and do not necessarily accord with their common usage.

The aim of *Hohfeld* was to provide a model for the correct solution of legal problems and to make that solution easier and more certain. He would advocate that the judge and the legal theorist employ the above scheme in order to ensure greater understanding of these legal concepts. He wrote of the need to use the term 'right' in a very strict sense and not indiscriminately to cover a privilege, power and immunity. Nonetheless, it would not be necessary to *Hohfeld* that the legal practitioner actually employ the terms claim, power, etc so long as he thinks in terms of *Hohfeld*'s scheme. It is thus possible to think *Hohfeld* without talking *Hohfeld*. This in my view adequately deals with the criticism of *Hohfeld* that he has adopted an unusual terminology which it would be naive to expect the legal profession to adopt overnight. Indeed *Hohfeld*'s scheme was developed seventy years ago and still nothing much has happened by way of the legal profession adopting his terminology in the effort to clarify legal problems. Nonetheless, his contribution has been quite substantial although underrated to date. His scheme provides an excellent starting point for any theoretical discussion of rights.

Evaluation of Hohfeld's scheme

Whilst *Hohfeld*'s scheme of jural relations is useful not only for illustrating the different forms which the word 'right' can take it also illustrates the interrelationships between these words. It is thus useful for distinguishing between claims, liberties, powers and immunities but it is argued that it would also be both necessary and desirable to retain a general concept of 'right' to denote institutions such as ownership or possession. As *Cook*, who was the editor of *Hohfeld*'s work and generally sympathetic to his task observes, *Hohfeld* mistakenly considers all rights as sets of any number of his four elementary rights, namely: claim, privilege, power and immunity. Not all rights are neat sets of the four basic concepts. Their possession entails the possession of other rights or of powers and duties. For example, the concept of ownership includes rights of possession, transfer, sale, hire, use and enjoyment. Thus ownership creates a set of claims and powers. The concept of ownership can be seen as a package of rights.

There are important criticisms of *Hohfeld*'s scheme. In that he purports to analyse fundamental legal concepts he does so without taking account of any concept of law as a whole. He fails to provide an explanation of the process by which those conceptions are given their legal character. He further assumes that there is only one concept of duty. It is said that this is because his examples are drawn from civil and private law only.

In criminal law his scheme hardly works. This, it is submitted, is because of the nature of the duty under criminal law. The duty is not owed to the prosecution but to the society as a whole. That duty does not give rise to a right in anyone. *Hohfeld*'s scheme is designed to cover one to one relations and not the relations between an individual and the society. Furthermore, it is suggested that with respect to paternalistic criminal law such as the laws that govern the wearing of seat belts in cars and the law of murder which forbids the defence of consent of the victim, the nature of the duty is one that the individual owes both to the society and to himself. As such when an individual has both a claim and a duty with regard to the same thing the scheme would be without application.

In spite of these criticisms viewed in a chronological frame his contribution has been substantial. There have however since his work been further developments and elucidations such as the works of *Hart* and *MacCormick* on rights.

The nature of rights: choice protection or interest protection?

In this context the debate between *Hart* and *MacCormick* over the role and nature of legal rights is particularly informative. The essence of the debate should be viewed within its political perspective.

Hart's Will Theory

Hart views rights as legally protected choices. He emphasises the power or option of one person to waive someone else's duty. Thus having a right is to do with the legal or moral recognition of some individual's choice as being pre-eminent over the will of others as to a given subject matter in a given relationship. This is applicable in the civil law area in matters such as contract. The essence of the holding of a right is that the holder has the choice whether to waive the duty owed to him. The connection with *Hohfeld*'s scheme of jural relations is apparent in that such a view assumes a correlativity of rights and duties.

MacCormick's Interest Theory

MacCormick criticises *Hart*'s theory on the grounds that there are some rights which do not seem to involve the exercise of a choice at all. He argues that particularly in the area of paternalistic criminal law, the law limits the power of waiver without destroying a substantive right. An example would be in respect of assault or of murder. The law will not admit the consent of the victim in defence to a prosecution. *MacCormick* argues that if one cannot consent to assault it follows that one is not exercising a choice on the right to freedom of the person. *MacCormick* maintains that the nature of rights can be viewed as protecting the interests of the right holder.

Looking at the difficult example of the 'rights' of a child *MacCormick* draws a distinction between the substantive right and the right to enforce the substantive right. He shows that the child possesses the substantive right to have its interest protected but lacks the right to enforce that right – the right to enforce is exercisable by the child's guardian on behalf of the child. Further the child cannot in fact nor in morals nor in law relieve his or her parents of their duty towards it (though some of the recent Scandinavian cases of children 'divorcing' their parents would seem to cast some doubt on this statement!) *MacCormick* then prefers the view of rights as protecting certain interests in the sense that either moral or legal normative constraints are imposed on the acts and activities of other people with respect to the objects of one's interest. *Hart* admits that if rights are all about choice then a young child would not possess any rights in that sense. As to the question of the protection of the child *Hart* maintains that rights are not the only moral basis for protection and that other factors such as humanity, love and compassion also provide the basis for protection. If that is so then there would be no need for a formal assignment of rights to the child on its attaining the age of choice – perhaps the traditional 'key of the door' or other ceremonies of attaining adulthood also imply an assignment of rights from the parent to the child. Until that assignment of rights the parent would act as the child could have acted had it possessed the power to choose. A problem with the idea that rights are founded on love, etc is that emotions are impossible to enforce.

Legal personality | 6

Introduction

Why are certain entities treated in law as 'persons' and some (trade unions, partnerships, unincorporated associations) generally not?

The issue of personality may be examined under three main heads.

Firstly, what different types of personality are known to English law?

Secondly, how useful is the concept of personality? This may be illustrated with particular reference to corporations; for example, what does it imply legally to say that a company is a 'person'?

Thirdly, what theories are used to explain the concept of legal personality and what are the main criticisms of these theories?

Different types of legal personality

There are three types of personality recognised in English law; in relation to any question, you should ask yourself if it is about one or all three. From the beginning it should be recognised that there is a difference between legal personality and legal capacity. The law may recognise the personality of say a child, or a corporate body, but place limits on the capacity of that individual or body.

Human beings

No distinction is drawn in law between legal and natural persons. But it should be noted that the notion of a human being is more flexible than might be thought. We shall examine two aspects of this concept:

a *A foetus*. What is the legal status of an unborn child ? The example of the legal personality of a foetus has raised interesting and emotive questions recently. In the case of *C v S* (1987) the question arose for consideration. Briefly, in that case a man who claimed to be the father of a foetus attempted to prevent the mother of the foetus from proceeding with an abortion after their relationship broke down. His grounds were to invoke the criminal law against the destruction of a child 'capable of being born alive' (s1 Infant Life Preservation Act 1929). The rather controversial interpretation given to that phrase by the House of Lords need not detain this text. What is of importance is the observation that it took the father (or any other interested person) to bring the action and not the foetus, yet if the foetus had been a legal person it could have brought the action itself. Practical problems of instructing solicitors, etc, from the womb can in this legal system be overcome – there are procedures to enable the (physically as well as legally) incompetent to be party to actions. The implication though is wide. The foetus would have a separate legal personality to the mother carrying it. The mother would merely be a walking incubator for another legal person. The mother would owe that person a duty of care that would give rise to that 'person' having a cause of action where for example through smoking cigarettes the mother caused the foetus damage. If the foetus is a legal person then it would be party to an action to prevent an abortion, etc. The question as to whether or not a foetus possesses legal personality has not been fully resolved. However since the courts have, on a number of occasions, decided that an action may be brought for injuries/deformities sustained while in the womb, the concept of foetal personality, if not yet fully established, would appear to be gaining recognition. Recently in *R* v *Tait* [1990] 1 QB 291 the question arose as to whether a threat to kill an unborn baby could be a threat to kill contrary to the Offences Against the Person Act 1981. The decision of the Court of Appeal indicated that the current judicial attitude is that the foetus is *not* a person and has no identity separate from the mother.

b *A dead person*. Legal personality extends to those humans who are alive and of an existence independent of their mother. What is the position with regard to the dead? They have legal interests such as that their wishes as expressed in their will are carried out, for example. The law has studiously avoided any definition of death – see *R* v *Malcherek; R* v *Steel* (1981) – probably for the very sound reason that advances in medical science and technology would outstrip the capacity of the law to keep pace and we would arrive at a situation, as we have for example in criminal law, where the definition of insanity has become fossilised in 1843 (*M'Naghten's Case*) in spite of very considerable advances since then. So quite what constitutes legal death is not that clear. The dead may have certain rights, to have their property disposed of according to their legal wishes, but that is as far as it goes.

Corporations sole

A corporation sole is a person with a perpetual existence, ie an office, the personification of an official capacity. Examples are various clergy, and the Crown (the Queen has a different personality for each country where she is the monarch). The main rationale behind the corporation sole is that the continuity of jural relations, such as the holding of property, is made possible. This need hardly detain us further.

Corporations aggregate

These are companies or other corporations created by charter, statute or under the Companies Acts. They are treated as persons in law unless the contrary is stated (statutes use 'individuals' if they mean humans and unincorporated associations but not corporations). Some unincorporated associations are given some of the attributes of corporations but they are still not 'persons'. Partnerships, for example, can issue writs in their own name and can make contracts – but the individual partners remain fully liable as individuals.

Is legal personality a useful concept?

The flexibility of treatment given to the notion of a human being is useful and corporations sole have their limited effectiveness allowing in the continuation of property ownership and contractual relations. This question as to the usefulness of the concept of legal personality is, though, most relevantly considered with regard to the corporations aggregate.

The uses of corporations aggregate

These have been stated as:

a *Convenience*
   The convenience offered by conferring powers and liabilities on a unit rather than on each individual shareholder involved (imagine suing British Telecom if it were otherwise!).

b *Limited liability*
   Shareholders do not attract liability except to the extent of their respective shareholdings, and directors and employees are only liable for their personal negligence; this is subject to the frequent requirement of personal guarantees, from participants in small companies.

c *Perpetuity of succession*
   This applies on death, retirement, sale of shares.

d *Ability to sue*
   Can sue or be sued, can own property.

e *Separate ownership*
   Ownership and control can be separated, allowing investors to risk their money but under the control of expert management. In many public quoted companies, ownership and control is totally divorced in this way.

f *Other advantages*
   Generally, an individual trader can escape personal liability (subject to personal guarantees) and it is easier for a company to raise capital than for a sole trader. Note though that the courts do sometimes lift the corporate veil (there is a list of instances of this in *Dias*). Note also that some of the advantages can be achieved without a separate personality being used. For example, writs can be served on partnerships, and property is often held by some only of the partners. This allows ownership to be passed more easily. Also, a big partnership will often split its management from the bulk of the owning partners. Think also of the special treatment of trades unions and employers' associations in English law.

Problems with corporations aggregate

Corporations aggregate also raise the following problems:

a *Groups*
English law has difficulties in dealing with the idea of a group of companies: for most purposes they are treated as separate units rather than as a collective entity, which is most unrealistic. Some inroads have however been made into this problem; group companies now submit consolidated accounts and are taxed as a unit, for example.

b *Inflexibility*
Even small companies have to fulfil statutory requirements suitable for much larger outfits. The present government is committed to relaxing some of these requirements and it is already the case that small companies have to submit less complete accounts, for instance.

c *Unfairness*
Small creditors never have security and so can lose heavily in an insolvency. There are some restrictions in the Insolvency Act 1986 on directors involved in setting up a similarly named company to escape liability in such cases (only time will tell on their effectiveness) and there are various possibilities of penalties or civil remedies (including disqualifications) against directors involved in an insolvency see the Companies Directors Disqualification Act 1986. But these generally will not benefit small unsecured creditors, who can't afford to rely on them. It is a myth that a customer or supplier is safer dealing with a limited company than an individual trader or partnership – often the reverse is the case.

d *Inconsistency*
It is not at all clear why some legal rules and regulations apply to all companies but not to other (often larger) organisations which organise themselves as partnerships. Often the choice of business medium is based on taxation considerations rather than on which medium is more suitable in terms of its inherent characteristics.

The theories: what theories are used to explain legal personality?

There are four main theories for us to consider, albeit in each case rather briefly. We will try to analyse for each theory which elements of the law it can, and cannot, account for. None of the theories performs spectacularly well!

Fiction theory

First, we will look at the 'fiction theory', supported by *Savigny* and in England by *Coke, Blackstone* and especially *Salmond*. Juristic or artificial persons are only treated as if they are persons, under this view. They are fictitious, not known as persons apart from the law. The law gives them proprietary rights, grants them legal powers and so on, but they have no personality and no will (except to the extent a will is implied by the law). This is an obviously flexible viewpoint, since it can account for any apparent inconsistency in legal treatment by simply saying that they are only treated as persons 'to that extent'. The doctrine of *ultra vires,* under which a company cannot do anything not authorised by its memorandum of association might be thought to support the fiction theory, on the basis that the law only gives personality to the limit of the memorandum and so might the doctrine that a company is separate from its members, epitomised in the leading case of *Salomon* v *Salomon* (1897). This case shows the law treats the company as a separate unit, even though in fact it is not, especially in the one-man company cases like *Salomon.*

Further support for this theory could be claimed from the criminal law, which originally accepted that a company could not commit a criminal offence which depends on mental intention. The fiction view explains this on the basis of the 'will' of the 'person' only being that given by law, and therefore presumably being limited to lawful intention. Recent developments show a more pragmatic and sensible approach to the question of corporate liability, with companies being subject to more criminal liability (and also subject to liability for the torts of their servants). Also, the cases where the law allows the corporate veil to be turned aside can be explained as limitations on the grant of the fictitious personality.

Acceptable explanations, then, are provided by the fiction theory for many aspects of company law (although many of them can be explained acceptably by other theories, see below).

Hohfeld's theory

This theory is not mirrored in English writing on the subject. Since only human beings have juristic relations, one must, according to *Hohfeld,* explain companies in a complex way by looking at the capacities, rights, powers and liabilities of the individuals involved. This view is clearly related to the *Hohfeld*'s analysis of rights; however, it fails to give us an explanation of why the notion of a company is used, the notion of a separate personality.

Realist

This view sees an 'artificial person' as a real personality, having a real mind, will and power of action. It is associated with *Gierke, Dicey, Pollock* and *Maitland.*

If independent power of action was the only requirement of our definition of a 'person' and 'personality', perhaps an artificial person would qualify (but has a company really got a power of action independent of its members and officials?); surely though there is something more. To say a corporation is a real person implies an individuality, and that implies some consciousness, experience, inner unity. Some groups may seem to have such a unity and consciousness – but do all legal personalities fit? Surely a corporation sole (consisting of successive holders of one office) hasn't a 'consciousness', nor has a multi-national company, nor even a small company? Perhaps a university might be thought to fit?

In any case, even if the legal personalities could be counted as real persons, a further problem arises. If a two-man company is a person in reality, why not a two-man partnership? If a one-man company, why not a one-man business? If a university, why not a private law college – one that is unincorporated? The 'realist theory' fails to explain why the legal definition of personality does not match the extended realist definition.

Returning to some of the aspects of English law already considered, Realist theory can account for the ultra vires doctrine (the real personality constituted by the company as set up by its documents), though it would seem a weakness to have to refer to legal documents to establish the limits of reality, but can't successfully accommodate the tearing aside of the corporate veil. If the company is a real entity distinct from its members, surely it should always be viewed as such and not sometimes viewed as a collection of its members?

Finally, realism can account for those instances where criminal law applies to a company: but can it account for those when it doesn't (if a board meeting orders an execution, the company isn't guilty of murder: why not)? The reason why it would not in the likelihood of a board resolution so ordering be guilty of murder is that it is incapable of forming the necessary *mens rea* for murder. Obviously, considerations as to suitable penalty will also be relevant (it is impractical to imprison a company!) The recent prosecution of company officials, (as well as the Captain and some crew) following the Zeebrugge Ferry disaster shows that the law is changing in this respect. But equally the rapid collapse of the prosecution demonstrates the problems of establishing corporate liability for such crimes as manslaughter.

Purpose

The final view is the purpose theory developed by *Brinz* and in England by *Barker*. On this view, only human beings are persons, but the law protects certain purposes other than human beings. The creation of artificial persons just gives effect to a purpose (for example, a charitable corporation is created to give effect to various devices by which the law aids the charitable cause). So company property is held not by a person, but for a purpose.

This view has a fundamental flaw. It does not answer the question. It is obviously true that companies and other artificial legal persons are given their status for a purpose (or various purposes). The question remains – why call them 'persons'? What aspect of these entities makes them so akin to real people that the law uses the same name and to a great extent applies the same rules?

A purpose view can explain the ultra vires doctrine (a company is limited to its express purposes, as mentioned in the memorandum), and even the tearing aside of the veil (the countering weight of other legal purposes), cannot explain the concept of an artificial person.

It will be seen at this point that none of the various explanations given of the nature of corporate personality is really satisfactory.

Law: a balancing of conflicting interests 7

Introduction

In this chapter we shall examine both the theoretical setting for the topic of the use of law as a balancer of conflicting interests and then consider some examples of how the law may be used in this manner. The topic does however depend on an assessment of the role of society and the nature of its organisation. On this matter there are sharply divided views. Whilst it would be necessary eventually to formulate a view on this at this stage the alternatives between a conflict model or a consensus model will be discussed. It will become apparent that if the idea of law as a balancer of conflicting interests is to work then the society will need to reflect the essence of a consensus model.

Conflict or consensus model?

The whole thesis that the law can or does act as a balancer of conflicting interests depends on the view that one takes of the nature of society – namely whether society is essentially a reflection of the consensus or of the conflict model. It is proposed briefly to examine these two polar views on the nature of society.

A consensus model is one which sees society as having shared values and traditions, and law serves the interests which are to the ultimate benefit thereof. Law therefore, may be seen as a value consensus, representing the shared values of the society, and adjusting conflicts and reconciling interests to match with the consensus. Such a model may be seen, explicitly or implicitly, in the works of *Pound* and *Durkheim*.

It is also the basis of the framework provided by *Parsons*, who views the legal system as having a function of integration, of preventing, via the set of rules, the disintegration of social interaction, into conflict. He splits the legal from the political system: in the former, the courts hold centre stage with their work of interpretation; in the latter, the legislature formulates policy.

Pound put it thus: 'The success of any particular society will depend on the degree to which it is socially integrated and so accepts as common ground its basic postulates'. Such a view claims that law adjusts and reconciles conflicting interests according to the requirements of social order.

The problem with this view of society is that in effect it is a representation of a static and homogeneous society where such a society does not exist.

A conflict model, on the other hand, suggests that society involves not a value consensus but a value conflict; that law, rather than reconciling conflict interests in a compromise, instead imposes one interest at the expense of the other. Such a model is expounded by *Quinney*, and of course, the Marxists.

Which is a correct reading of the English legal system? Is the conflict model a simple one, with one ruling class (of which judges are a part: see *JAG Griffith, The Politics of the Judiciary*) or competing interest groups with varying amounts of power? Both views can claim support from particular pieces of evidence; either showing a social consensus (major crimes, civil liberties protection?) or rules that are the product of conflict (rules of property and contract).

The philosophy of Ihering

The main question posed by the theorists is – what is the function or purpose of law? Many theorists – *Pound, Bentham* and *Summers* among them – have given their versions of law's purpose. For *Bentham*, for instance, the purpose of the institution (as with that of other institutions) was utility maximisation. The other major concern follows from that basic enquiry: having decided on the law's purpose or function, how does it achieve that? If law is a method of social control, for example, in what ways does it control? This leads to a concentration on the actual working of institutions. Many theorists look at this from a conceptual point of view; on a rather less grand (but more practical?) level, socio-legal researchers address themselves to it in a factual way.

One of the first theorists to discuss these questions was *Ihering*.

Writing in the nineteenth century, he developed a thesis that saw laws as instruments of society, arising from the need to further and protect the interests of society. Society needed to balance interests, since the interests of individuals would necessarily conflict with the interests of society as a whole: these interests had to be balanced and individuals reconciled to a society. Individuals' interests had to be altered to conform with society's, and this was done by rewards, coercion, duty and love. Law was state-organised coercion for this purpose.

It is possible to note three things about these views:

a There is little indication of how the balancing is done, what weight should be attached to what interests, and when an individual's interest 'trumps' (in *Dworkinian* terminology) that of the state; except that:

b *Ihering* was a utilitarian, like *Bentham*, and it seems clear that social aims are more important than those of individuals.

c His theory clearly places law as one method of carrying out a particular function of society.

Introduction to Roscoe Pound's theory

The extensive writings of *Roscoe Pound* spread as they are over a long period of time represent the culmination of the legal philosophy of the past. *Pound* was an academic lawyer and an advocate for socio-legal studies. His concern was to examine 'law in action' as opposed to the dry topic of 'law in books'. Again it should be emphasised that his primary concern was with law reform and his theory ought to be read with this in mind. He was developing a technology to redraft the law to take account of social reality. He saw 'Law as a social phenomenon' which translated into policy action meant that in the making, interpretation and application of laws due account should be taken of law as a social fact.

The fact that he was by training a botanist may, it has been suggested, explain his tendency for engaging in classifications. It seems difficult to imagine a situation where a candidate will be examined on his/her ability to recite the various classifications that *Pound* developed. It is not expected that you would learn these by rote. What is required is an overview of his aims and of his general categorisations.

Nonetheless for the sake of a complete record the following represent the task of the purposes of the legal order:

a   factual study of the social effects of legal administration;

b   social investigations as preliminary to legislation;

c   constant study of making laws more effective;

d   study – both psychological and philosophical of judicial method;

e   sociological study of legal history;

f   allowance for the possibility of a just and reasonable solution of individual cases;

g   a Ministry of Justice to undertake law reform;

h   the achievement of the purposes of the various laws.

In order to achieve these purposes of the legal order it would first be necessary to achieve the recognition of certain interests which operate on different levels. These levels are the:

a   individual;

b   public;

c   social.

Secondly, it would be necessary to arrive at a definition of the limits within which such interests will be legally recognised and given effect to. And thirdly, the securing of those interests within the limits as defined.

Again we stay with these lists in order to identify what would according to *Pound* be required in order to achieve this. He listed the following as necessary:

a   preparation of an inventory of classified interests;

b   selection of interests which should be legally recognised;

c   demarcation of limits of securing the interests so selected;

d   consideration of the means whereby laws might secure the interests when these have been acknowledged and delimited;

e   evolution of the principles of valuation of the interests.

As stated above in doing this rather protracted task *Pound* sought to harmonise 'law in books' with 'law in action'. It is not at all clear that he has succeeded in this aim or indeed that anyone could have succeeded. However in order to give due regard to his attempt we shall examine his efforts in this further. In particular we shall examine his concept of social engineering and the balancing of conflicting interests and the use of his jural postulates in the achievement of the balancing act.

Social engineering

Following very much on the consensus model of society and in explaining the process of the balancing of conflicting interests *Pound* has used an analogy with engineering. He sees the task as one to build as efficient a structure of society as possible, which requires the satisfaction of the maximum of wants with the minimum of friction and waste. Thus by identifying and protecting certain interests the law ensures social cohesion.

The idea of the balancing of conflicting interests was derived from *Ihering* and can be stated as the giving effect to as much as possible of conflicting claims 'which men assert de facto about which the law must do something if organised societies are to endure.'

Balancing of conflicting interests

It would be appropriate to examine further the notion of the balancing of conflicting interests. In doing so *Pound* looks at actual assertion of claims in a particular society as manifested in legal proceedings and this of course includes rejected as well as accepted claims.

Again there is more classification involved. However with this matter it is worth learning the three different levels on which *Pound* identified interests operating. These are:

a   *Individual interests.* These are claims as seen from the standpoint of individual life. The following are examples:

   i   Personality – eg interest in person, honour, privacy;

   ii   Domestic relations – as distinct from social interest in institutions such as family – eg parent;

   iii Interest of substance – eg property, freedom of association.

b   *Public interests.* These are claims asserted by individuals but viewed from the standpoint of political life. These are less important but would include:

i   Interests of the State as a juristic person – looking at the personality of the State (*note:* this is not relevant in Britain); and

ii Interests of the State as guardian of social interests.

c   *Social interests.* These are the most general and according to *Pound* the preferred level on which to balance conflicting interests. They are claims as viewed of in terms of social life or generalised as claims of the social group. This includes the social interest in:

i   general security – ie to be secure against threats to existence from disorder and matters such as health;

ii security of social institutions – which acknowledges the existence of tension and the need to protect religious institutions;

iii general morals – ie such matters as prostitution and gambling which are said to be offensive to moral sentiments;

iv conservation of social resources – this is comparable to *Rawls'* 'just savings principle' and is in conflict with the individual interest in one's own property;

v   general progress – which would cover free speech and free trade (but nonetheless ignores the tendency for resale price fixing); and

vi individual life – according to which one should be able to live life according to standards of society.

These are just examples. The important point according to *Pound* is that these must be balanced on the same level otherwise the decision is already made in that if this were not done the preference for type of interests would dictate the outcome of the supposedly scientific exercise in balancing out these interests. It is noteworthy that *Ihering* did not insist on this when he spoke of balancing conflicting interests. *Pound's* insistence on balancing conflicting interests on the same level is not matched by any explanation of just *how* conflicting interests are to be identified and compared. *Lloyd* summed it up thus, ' ... Unlike *Ihering*, who assumed that social and individual interests should always be directly compared, *Pound* insisted that a fair balancing of interests could only be achieved by examining a conflict on the same plane or level.'

Jural postulates

In circumstances where an accommodation of interests is not possible there would according to *Pound* be no objective way of resolving disputes. To meet this defect *Pound* developed the notion of jural postulates as the means of testing new interests. These jural postulates are the presuppositions of legal reasoning which embody the fundamental purposes of the legal system. They are in effect the basic assumptions upon which society is based. One cannot help but conclude that *Pound* was using a new term to describe something that was already well recognised. He has not discovered the wheel he has merely called it something else.

Pound's methodology was that of incremental legal reasoning. This method of legal reasoning which is well known to common law lawyers would allow new claims only if claims of that sort are already recognised. The speech of Lord Buckmaster in *Donoghue* v *Stevenson* (1932) would represent one of the most famous to adopt incremental legal reasoning. In essence Lord Buckmaster was saying that unless Mrs Donoghue could show that in a previous case a claim such as that she was bringing to the court was admitted then whatever the particular merits of her case her claim would have to be rejected.

Balancing interests: practical applications

Property is considered to be one of the most important interests in our society, because our economic structure depends on ownership. That structure must be protected and that protection is given in the interest of national security or public interest. There are other interests; personal, social and economic. Legal rules embody the rights which protect these interests. Sometimes the interests conflict as we have seen in cases such as *Donoghue* v *Stevenson*.

If the law acts as a balancer of interests it does this to protect interest groups from 'injury' by one another and to preserve the security of the State. In such cases the judges must rate one interest as more important.

The balance between interest groups is also achieved by the Bill stage of the making of legal rules by Parliament. There will be many compromises and amendments before the Bill becomes an Act of Parliament. The advantage of having several political parties in Parliament is that no single party can say 'it is good for us, it must be good for them'.

There are, however, powerful interest groups and classes within our society. These groups influence the view of Ministers, Civil Servants and the judiciary so that the proposition that legislation is the mirror of public opinion may be a false one.

Many politicians are wealthy and influential men. They may possess large shareholdings in companies and have directorships or other connections. It would be strange if they did not listen to the voice of the Confederation of British Industry which represents management and business ownership, and is frequently heard opposing the policies of the trades unions who represent the worker's interest.

In contrast we have seen that Parliament passes laws which are sometimes advantageous to the weaker interest groups and disadvantageous to the powerful groups. There is, for example, the consumer law legislation and legislation designed to protect the worker in the fields of employment, including health and safety at work. There are many more examples of this type of protective legislation. In his book *Introduction to Law*, Harris argues that such Acts are not rigorously enforced and, in fact, aid the stronger group while appearing to aid the weaker one. For instance, because of the protection for consumers and employees, industry and commerce are able to enjoy a better image with the public and so further their own aims.

Another fault described by *Harris* is that often the agencies dealing with the complaints are composed of members of the industry itself, eg the Press Council, the Law Society, the Advertising Standards Authority.

Other reasons for protective legislation have been put forward. One view is that in order to maintain a stable society in the twentieth century the Government must legislate to see that the status quo between powerful groups and weaker ones is maintained, or it will face the modern weapon of terrorism.

There are also times when there is a consensus of opinion as to the passing of certain legislation; for instance, pensions for the old and disabled. That is not to say there are not economically powerful groups who seek to have some of that money diverted to industry and away from public services.

In the courts judges must balance priorities. Thus, for example:

a Nuisance cases show quite clearly how the judges make value judgments in order to find the more important interest which it will protect.

b In family law it must balance the interests of a man and a woman with regard to their children and their property.

c In employment law the balance of interests is between the employer's right to pursue his business and the employee's right to work.

d In the law of defamation the Court must weigh freedom against the right to protect one's reputation.

Finally, freedom is always balanced against 'national' security and normally loses.

Legal protection of rights and freedoms | 8

Introduction

In this chapter we shall consider the theoretical justification for rights and their relationship to law. We will also consider the impact of the European Convention on Human Rights and Fundamental Freedoms 1950 on the human rights situation in this country and the areas where permissible derogations, restrictions and limitations may be placed on respect for the human rights and fundamental freedoms protected by that instrument. We have already discussed much of the content of the Convention in chapter 3 and students are therefore referred back to that chapter as being relevant to this chapter.

What rights ought people to have?

It is proposed to discuss this topic from three different perspectives. It is recognised that there are other perspectives not discussed here. There is no reason why the student conversant with these ought to be deterred from discussing them fully if the opportunity arose under examination conditions. The three perspectives discussed are the left, liberal and libertarian. The question is discussed primarily from the left/liberal/libertarian perspective; because it is here that the subject is most problematical.

The perspective from the left

A discussion of the views of the left on rights could occupy a doctorate thesis. In this short space it is proposed merely to summarise the main elements of the classical Marxist and the new left perspective. The student will recognise that there are other 'left' perspectives which are not considered herein.

a *Marxist perspective*
  From a Marxist perspective individual rights are incompatible with socialism in that social change is not effected by moralising about rights. *Marx* spoke of the distinction between the rights of the citizen being those political rights exercised in common with others and which therefore involve participation in the community and the rights of man which he thought were private rights exercised in isolation from others and therefore allowed for withdrawal from the community.

b *The new left*
  The new left also reject rights as such as these as being not required in a classless society. *Campbell* in *The Left and Rights* identifies the reasons for such rejection as legalism, coerciveness, individualism and moralism. By legalism is meant that rights subject human behaviour to the governance of rules; by coerciveness that rights protect the interests of capital; by individualism that rights protect the self interested scattered individuals and by moralism the point is made that

they are essentially utopian and therefore irrelevant to reality. Yet even under socialism there is a requirement for rules to facilitate social interactions and that in so doing certain rights will be enunciated. Under socialism then the right to work is more important than the freedom of labour. So that everyone has the right to do some work because it is only through work that the individual can fully realise his potential as a person. This means that it will be the socialist state that will determine what work people will do. Under the freedom of labour which is the prevalent philosophy under liberal capitalism the individual chooses his profession and whether to work it all. Under socialism and the right to work in some instances it will not be possible to satisfy everyone's preference for the type of work they wish to engage in. Hence the prior decision about political preferences will determine much of the discussion on the protection of 'rights' and the circumstances under which they can be justifiably overridden.

A liberal conception of rights

The views of *Ronald Dworkin* are particularly illuminating in this regard. These have been mentioned in previous chapters. However by way of relevant summary it is important to bear in mind the following: *Dworkin* refers to the political neutrality of the state in that the state will treat everyone with equal concern and respect. He speaks of auction equality on the desert island where decisions are taken on the basis of a majoritarian democratic process on the basis of utility but subject to the proviso that the basic rights of the minority not being infringed. Every majority decision infringes the rights of the minority. However the rights that *Dworkin* is referring to are those which a liberal holds as fundamental human rights. Thus in order to avoid the excesses of utilitarianism *Dworkin* speaks of 'protected interests'. Although there is no list of these provided it is submitted that those rights that are non derogable in the European Convention on Human Rights and Fundamental Freedoms (1950) probably express the more important of these and would therefore include the right to life, to freedom from torture or other inhumane or degrading punishment and the right not to be subject to retrospective criminal legislation. These protected interests of *Dworkin* possibly go even further than this list.

The libertarian perspective

The libertarian view is discussed in chapter 3. There, considerable emphasis was placed on the importance of natural rights.

With regard to the libertarian view, the main difficulty is that those theorists taking this view fail to recognise welfare rights. It is thus unlikely that the libertarian viewpoint would gain any foothold of support in any of the political groups proposing an agenda of change in Britain today. By welfare rights is meant what an individual can expect from the state if he should find himself in need of assistance. The preference of the libertarian viewpoint is for philanthropy rather than rights in the welfare field. Their reasoning for this position is discussed in detail in the previous chapter and it is not proposed to repeat that discussion herein – suffice to conclude that it is by reference to their opposition to patterned conceptions of justice that interfere with just historical entitlements arising out of the natural and inviolable right to the product of one's labour and property freely transferred in open market transactions.

The European Convention on Human Rights and Fundamental Freedoms and limitations on rights

Given that, one is generally in support of the existence of people's rights the question arises as to whether there exist any circumstances where it would be desirable to limit those rights on the protection of which importance is placed. Having addressed the main different perspectives from which the normative question of what rights ought to be, it may be more helpful to approach the question of limitations from a substantive law viewpoint. However this cannot be divorced from the theoretical background which is discussed above.

In order then to answer the question a distinction would have to be made on the type of rights that one is prepared to override. Not all rights are overridable with legitimate justification. I have in mind the ones mentioned above as non derogable. However the European Convention provides that in certain circumstances other rights and freedoms may be justifiably overridden. It lists two other categories of rights. Firstly, those that are subject to limitation or restriction and secondly, those that are derogable in times of war or other public emergency threatening the life of the nation. However such derogation is legitimate to the extent strictly required by the exigencies of the situation. The jurisprudence of the Council of Europe allows a certain margin of appreciation to the state concerned in the determination of how far this goes see the *Greek Junta Cases* (1969) ECHR Yearbook Vol 12 and *Ireland v United Kingdom* [1978] 2 EHRR 25 concerning conditions at prison camps in Northern Ireland. *Dworkin* would view the restrictions on rights in line with the derogation clause of Article 15 of the European Convention as a restriction on policy grounds whereas with regard to other restrictions such as that contained in Article 17 as one on grounds of principle.

Article 17 provides that the rights contained in the Convention cannot be pleaded in order to defeat the exercise or enjoyment of rights by others. There are ample case authorities illustrating the legitimacy of the denial of rights to those who seek to deny the rights of others. The *Federal German Communist Party Case* (1957) illustrated the denial of the freedom of association to an organisation which it was thought sought to deny the right of others. In those circumstances one would support the jurisprudence of the organs of the Council of Europe in their justifiable overriding of the rights of some.

Thus *Dworkin's* rights thesis sees rights as of overriding importance placing individual rights over considerations of general welfare and that these rights ought not be interfered with unless one is faced with the type of situation covered by either Article 15 or 17 of the European Convention. The problem is that such a view is not devoid of political considerations whatever *Dworkin* may say about the political neutrality of the state in this matter.

Any discussion on rights is inevitably going to make political assumptions. It is on these political assumptions that most criticism is made. What is clear from *Dworkin* and to a certain extent a view now hijacked by the new left is that rights are anterior to law. When rights can justifiably be overridden depends then firstly, on political assumptions about the nature of rights, secondly, on the type of rights whether substantive or procedural and thirdly, on the circumstances one is minded to allow for such restriction.

We turn now to freedoms (and limitations on those freedoms) in Britain today. It will be recalled from Chapter 3 that because the British constitution is unwritten the so-called 'Golden Principle' applies. That is to say, Parliament or the courts may impose restrictions on certain activities, for reasons of public policy. Whatever activities remain un-proscribed can be called freedoms.

In the following paragraphs we deal with the major freedoms.

Substantial protection: freedom of association

In general, there are no limitations imposed by the law upon the freedom of individuals to associate together. However this is subject to certain qualifications.

The Public Order Act 1936, s2, prohibits quasi-military organisations. Under this section it is an offence to control, manage, organise or train an association of persons for the purpose of usurping the functions of the police or the armed forces or for the use or display of physical force in promoting any political object. In 1963 the leaders of Spearhead, a neo-Nazi organisation, were convicted under s2.

The Prevention of Terrorism (Temporary Provisions) Act 1984 contains in Part I of the Act a series of offences which may be committed by persons supporting proscribed organisations. Several organisations are proscribed under the Act, including the Irish Republican Army (IRA) and the Irish National Liberation Army. By s1 of the Act, it is an offence to belong or profess to belong to such an organisation, to solicit or invite financial or other support for it, to make or receive contributions to its resources, or to arrange, assist in the arrangement or address its meetings.

Members of the armed forces, the police and senior civil servants may be prevented by their conditions of service from engaging in political activities and may not therefore join political associations.

Freedom of assembly

The basic rule is that anyone is free to assemble provided that no law is breached. The law in this area consists in essence, of the restrictions that Parliament and the courts have felt necessary over the years to impose on the freedom to assemble in public, in the interests of maintaining order. The law thus reflects the slow process of historical development.

The right to hold meetings

Meetings on private and public property

There is no legal right to hold a meeting on private premises without the consent of the owner or occupier. Unless permission has been granted, a person holding such a meeting becomes a trespasser and the owner or occupier of the premises may use reasonable force in evicting the trespasser.

Meetings in public places are subject to a number of limitations. Places such as Hyde Park Corner or Trafalgar Square which are traditionally used for public meetings are Crown property and there is no right to hold meetings in them. For any meeting to take place the permission of the Secretary of State for the Environment is needed, and he can if he wishes impose restrictions on any meeting for which permission has been granted.

Many local authority premises are also subject to regulations governing meetings. If there are by-laws which require permission to be obtained before a meeting may take place on local authority property, then any meeting held without permission will be a criminal offence. Local authorities have a wide discretion to stop meetings being held in their parks or buildings but their decisions are open to judicial review. A decision to refuse permission to any meeting, or any meeting by a particular organisation, may be unreasonable under the principles laid down in *Associated Provincial Picture Houses* v *Wednesbury Corporation* [1948] 1 KB 223.

There is, however, a statutory right under the Representation of the People Act 1983 for candidates in General or local elections to have access to local authority premises for the purpose of holding election meetings. It has been argued that this statutory right ought to be extended to all meetings following recent decisions by some local authorities to refuse the National Front permission to hold meetings on their premises.

Imposing conditions on public assemblies

The Public Order Act 1986, s14 contains a new power for a senior police officer to impose conditions in relation to public assemblies. If the senior police officer, having regard to the time or place at which and the circumstances in which any public assembly is being held or is intended to be held, reasonably believes that (a) it may result in serious public disorder, serious damage to property or serious disruption to the life of the community, or (b) the purpose of the persons organising it is the intimidation of others with a view to compelling them not to do an act they have a right to do, or to do an act they have a right not to do, he may give directions imposing on the persons organising or taking part in the assembly such conditions as to the place at which the assembly may be (or continue to be) held, its maximum duration, or the maximum number of persons who may constitute it, as appears to him necessary to prevent such disorder, damage, disruption or intimidation.

Section 16 defines 'public assembly' as an assembly of 20 or more persons in a public place which is wholly or partly open to the air.

Meetings on the highway

At common law, the highway is land dedicated to the public use for the primary purpose of the passing and repassing of pedestrians and traffic. If either exceed this function then they will be using the highway unreasonably and will be subject to a number of sanctions.

The owners of the highway can sue anyone in trespass if that person uses the highway for an improper purpose. The surface of the highway is usually vested in the local authority, but adjacent landowners have an interest in the subsoil and can also sue in trespass and nuisance. In *Hickman* v *Maisey* [1900] 1 QB 752 a racehorse trainer successfully sued in trespass a person who stood on the highway to time the trainer's racehorses. Similarly, in *Harrison* v *Duke of Rutland* [1893] 1 QB 142 a person who objected to the Duke shooting grouse walked up and down the highway crossing the grouse moor opening and closing his umbrella so as to frighten the birds. He was held to be an unreasonable user of the highway and therefore a trespasser who could not complain when the Duke's gamekeeper used reasonable force to eject him from the moor.

Under the Highways Act 1980 s137(1), it is a criminal offence wilfully to obstruct the free passage along a highway. If the highway is obstructed then a constable can arrest those causing the obstruction. Obstruction, in this context, is a very flexible term. In *Gill* v *Carson* (1917) it was held that there was no necessity to show that anyone was actually obstructed. In *Homer* v *Cadman* (1866) 55 LJMC 110 it was held that it is no defence to show that there was a way around the obstruction. Therefore, if you erect a street stall on a wide pavement, leaving plenty of room for people to pass, this will still constitute an obstruction. In *Arrowsmith* v *Jenkins* [1963] 2 QB 561, Arrowsmith was arrested for obstructing the highway under s121 of the Highways Act 1959. She argued that the prosecution had to show that she had an intention to obstruct the highway. Lord Parkes rejected this argument and refused to introduce mens rea into the Act, stating that 'if a person does an act according to their free will which results in an obstruction, it will be sufficient for the offence of obstruction'.

Processions

Processions along the highway, being mobile, will generally be lawful at common law since the highway is being used for passage. However, if the procession goes beyond what is a reasonable use of the highway, then it may constitute a public nuisance. This offence is rare but it was used in the case of *R* v *Clarke (No 2)* [1964] 2 QB 315. Clarke was charged with inviting others to obstruct the highway around Whitehall. The police had blocked the path of the demonstration and Clarke was said to have told the crowd to go around the blockade. It was argued that this amounted to an incitement to commit a public nuisance. The accused was convicted and given a sentence of 18 months' imprisonment. The conviction was quashed on appeal. The court held that the question that must be asked is whether there had been an unreasonable use of the highway. It was held to be irrelevant that some obstruction had occurred if the use of the highway was reasonable.

The Public Order Act 1986, ss11, 12 and 13

Under the Public Order Act 1986 advance notice of public processions must be given in certain circumstances. Section 11 provides that proposals to hold a public procession must be notified to the police if it is a procession intended to demonstrate support for or opposition to the views or actions of any person or body of persons; or publicise a cause or campaign; or mark or commemorate an event. Written notice must be given to the police not less than six clear days before the date of the procession, or as soon as is practicable. The organisers commit an offence if they fail to satisfy these requirements or, if in general, the conduct of the procession differs from that indicated in the notice.

The Public Order Act 1986, ss12 and 13, replaces the provisions first enacted in s3 of the Public Order Act 1936. The 1936 Act was enacted following the disorder caused by the Fascist marches in the East End of London. Powers to control the route of processions had long existed, in the Metropolitan Police Act 1839 and the Town Police Clauses Act 1847, but s3 of the 1936 Act introduced for the first time the power to ban processions. These provisions are now contained in ss12 and 13 of the 1986 Act. They are directed to preventing serious public disorder rather than dealing with it when it has occurred. The framework of control has two stages, in order to ensure that banning orders are used only as a measure of last resort.

Section 12 provides that:

'If the senior police officer, having regard to the time or place at which and the circumstances in which any public procession is being held or is intended to be held and to its route or proposed route, reasonably believes that –

a) it may result in serious public disorder, serious damage to property or serious disruption to the life of the community, or
b) the purpose of the persons organising it is the intimidation of others with a view to compelling them not to do an act they have a right to do, or to do an act they have a right not to do,

he may give directions imposing on the persons organising or taking part in the procession such conditions as appear to him necessary to prevent such disorder, damage, disruption or intimidation, including conditions as to the route of the procession or prohibiting it from entering any public place specified in the directions.'

If, however, it is considered that these powers will not be sufficient to prevent serious disorder, then the second stage of the process is used.

Section 13 provides that:

'If at any time the chief officer of police reasonably believes that, because of particular circumstances existing in any district or part of a district, the powers under section 12 will not be sufficient to prevent the holding of public processions in that district or part from resulting in serious public disorder, he shall apply to the council of the district for an order prohibiting subject to the consent of the Home Secretary (s13(2)) for such period not exceeding 3 months as may be specified in the application the holding of all public processions (or of any class of public procession so specified) in the district or part concerned.'

In the City of London or the metropolitan police district, the Commissioner of Police for the City of London or the Commissioner of Police of the Metropolis may make such orders with the consent of the Home Secretary (s13(3), (4)).

The only way to appeal against such a ban is to show that it was unreasonable.

Metropolitan Police Act 1839, s52

Under s52 of the Metropolitan Police Act 1839 the Commissioner of Police of the Metropolis may make regulations for preventing obstruction of the streets within the vicinity of Parliament. Any contravention of those regulations is a criminal offence. Although this is a wide power there are some limits to it. In *Papworth v Coventry* [1967] 1 WLR 633, the accused was convicted of ignoring a s52 order that the streets around Parliament should be kept clear. He appealed on the grounds that the seven protesters could not have caused an obstruction. The appeal was upheld.

The police also have the power to stop potential disorderly processions by bringing the possible demonstrators before the magistrates before the demonstration. They may then be bound over to keep the peace. Should they refuse to be bound over then they can be imprisoned for up to six months.

Responsibility for causing disorder

The general principle is that a lawful act does not become unlawful just because others act unlawfully.

In *Beatty v Gillbanks* (1882) 9 QBD 308 the Salvation Army regularly held processions through the town of Weston-super-Mare. These processions were regularly confronted by a group called the Skeleton Army. The confrontations frequently resulted in violence and general disorder. The local magistrates purported to ban marches by the Salvation Army. The Salvation Army ignored the ban and violence occurred. Members of the Salvation Army were convicted of unlawful assembly by the magistrates, but this was reversed on appeal. The Divisional Court held that as the disorder had been caused by the Skeleton Army, and the Salvation Army did not incite the counter- demonstration, the disorder was not a natural consequence of the procession.

Per Field J: 'The present decision of the justices ... amounts to this, that a man may be punished for acting lawfully if he knows that his so doing may induce another man to act unlawfully – a proposition without any authority to support it.'

However the general principle laid down in *Beatty v Gillbanks* is today subject to certain qualifications.

a The Public Order Act 1986, s13 refers to processions which may result in serious public disorder. Therefore innocent marches may be stopped if their march is likely to be the occasion for serious disorder caused by others.

b If the police reasonably apprehend an imminent breach of the peace they may take any action which is necessary to control or prevent it, including arresting those who are responsible. The police may also limit numbers in any particular place in order to prevent breaches of the peace.

In *O'Kelly* v *Harvey* (1883) 15 Cox CC 435, a magistrate was held to be justified in dispersing a lawful meeting on the basis that he had reasonable grounds for supposing that those opposed to the meeting would use violence and that there was no other way in which the peace could be preserved.

In *Moss and Others* v *McLachlan* (1984) 149 JP 167, the police were held to be entitled to stop and turn back pickets otherwise lawfully on the highway during the miners' dispute.

c The principle in *Wise* v *Dunning* [1902] 1 KB 617 that if the speakers or demonstrators use insulting language which is likely to cause a breach of the peace then they can be successfully prosecuted for 'disturbing the peace'. This case is in keeping with the general principle in *Beatty* v *Gillbanks*. In that case the disorder was not the natural or probable consequence of the procession, but in *Wise* v *Dunning*, it was.

Public order offences and police powers

Common law police powers: breach of the peace

The concept of a breach of the peace derives from the early days of the common law. Breach of the peace is not in England and Wales a substantive offence, but it forms the basis of important police powers. If the police reasonably apprehend an imminent breach of the peace they may take any action which is necessary to control or prevent it, including arresting those who are responsible. The police may also limit numbers in any particular place in order to prevent breaches of the peace. The common law power to disperse an unlawful assembly derives from the general power of the police to control breaches of the peace. The police may also bring anyone who threatens the peace before the courts to enter into a recognisance and find sureties to keep the peace or to be of good behaviour, or in default to be imprisoned for up to six months. This preventive power to bind someone over to be of good behaviour is traced back to the Justices of the Peace Act 1361, and is still frequently used in public order cases.

Statutory public order offences

Statutes in the field of public order law have generally been enacted in response to a particular mischief.

The Unlawful Drilling Act 1819 prohibits assemblies for the purpose of training or drilling in the use of arms or practising military exercises without lawful authority.

The Public Meeting Act 1908 makes it an offence to endeavour to break up a public meeting by acting in a disorderly manner for the purpose of preventing the transaction of the business for which the meeting was called together.

The Representation of the People Act 1983, s97 makes it an offence to cause a disturbance at an election meeting.

The Public Order Act 1936

Section 1 places a general prohibition on the wearing of political uniforms in any public place or at any public meeting except for uniforms worn on ceremonial, anniversary or other special occasions where public disorder is not likely to be provoked. (The Prevention of Terrorism (Temporary Provisions) Act 1984 contains a similar prohibition in respect of proscribed organisations.)

Section 2 creates an offence of controlling, managing, organising or training an association of persons for the purpose of usurping the functions of the police or the armed forces or for the use or display of physical force in promoting any political object.

Section 6 makes it an offence to act in a disorderly manner for the purpose of disrupting a public meeting.

The Police Act 1964

Section 51(1) makes it an offence to assault a police officer in the execution of his duty.

Section 51(3) makes it an offence to wilfully obstruct the police in the execution of their duty.

In *Duncan* v *Jones* [1936] 1 KB 218, Duncan intended to hold a meeting outside a government training centre. At a previous meeting there had been a disturbance. As she was about to start speaking a police officer asked her to move about 150 yards down the road. She refused to move and was arrested and charged with obstructing a police officer in the execution of his duty. She was convicted and appealed. The Divisional Court upheld the conviction. They found that Duncan must have realised that a probable consequence of holding the meeting was a disturbance, and that the police officer had reasonable grounds for believing that a breach of the peace might ensue and therefore was under a duty to stop the meeting taking place.

However it can be argued that *Duncan* v *Jones* was wrongly decided. Mrs Duncan committed no offence other than the obstruction. She did not incite anyone to commit a breach of the peace, nor was she causing an obstruction. It would seem that in such a case the court should have followed *Beatty* v *Gillbanks* and adhered to the principle that a lawful act does not become unlawful merely because other people act unlawfully.

The Criminal Law Act 1977, s6 makes it an offence to use or threaten to use violence for the purpose of securing entry to any premises, where there is someone opposed to such entry. (For example demonstrators trying to occupy diplomatic premises.)

The Public Order Act 1986

The Public Order Act 1986 was passed on 7 November 1986. Some provisions came into force on 1 January 1987. Most of the rest of the Act came into force on 1 April

1987. The Act introduced several new offences and abolished or repealed several common law and statutory offences. The ancient common law offences of riot, rout, unlawful assembly and affray have been abolished. Three offences were created as replacements: riot, violent disorder and affray.

Section 1 redefines the offence of riot. Where 12 or more persons who are present together use or threaten unlawful violence and the conduct of them (taken together) is such as would cause a person of reasonable firmness present at the scene to fear for his personal safety, each of the persons using unlawful violence for the common purpose is guilty of riot. A person guilty of riot is liable on conviction on indictment to imprisonment for a term not exceeding ten years or a fine or both.

Section 2 creates a new offence of violent disorder. Where three or more persons who are present together use or threaten unlawful violence and the conduct of them (taken together) is such as would cause a person of reasonable firmness present at the scene to fear for his personal safety, each of the persons using or threatening unlawful violence is guilty of violent disorder. A person guilty of violent disorder is liable on conviction on indictment to imprisonment for a term not exceeding five years or a fine or both, or on summary conviction to imprisonment for a term not exceeding six months or a fine or both.

Section 3 redefines the offence of affray. A person is guilty of affray if he uses or threatens unlawful violence towards another and his conduct is such as would cause a person of reasonable firmness present at the scene to fear for his personal safety. A person guilty of affray is liable on conviction on indictment to imprisonment for a term not exceeding three years or a fine or both, or on summary conviction to imprisonment for a term not exceeding six months or a fine or both. The case of *R* v *Dixon* [1993] Crim LR 579 illustrates s3(3) as to the meaning of 'affray'. The appellant had been involved in a domestic argument with his common law wife. The police were called and the appellant made off, accompanied by his dog. When eventually cornered by the police, the appellant ordered the dog, which was in an agitated state, to attack the officers. Two officers suffered bites in an attack by the dog. The dog returned to the appellant who then ordered it to kill the officers. At this point the officers retreated awaiting reinforcements. The appellant was convicted of affray, and appealed on the grounds that his words alone could not constitute the affray; that there was insufficient evidence to show that the dog had been responding to his commands; and that the trial judge may have given the jury the impression that passivity on the part of the appellant might be sufficient actus reus for the offence.

The court held that the appeal would be dismissed. The offence could not comprise the use of words alone, but in the present case the prosecution had relied upon the actions of the appellant in deliberately setting the dog on the officers and the words he had uttered at the time. It was not a requirement that the prosecution prove that the dog had responded to the commands uttered by the appellant. The trial judge might have achieved greater clarity had he indicated that the actus reus of the offence comprised the words spoken to the dog, coupled with the dog being in a highly agitated state.

Section 4 largely replaces s5 of the Public Order Act 1936 with the new offence of causing fear or provocation of violence. A person is guilty of an offence if he (a) uses towards another person threatening, abusive or insulting words or behaviour, or (b) distributes or displays to another person any writing, sign or other visible representation which is threatening, abusive or insulting with intent to cause that person to believe that immediate unlawful violence will be used against him or another by any person, or to provoke the immediate use of unlawful violence by that person or another, or whereby that person is likely to believe that such violence will be used or it is likely that such violence will be provoked. As to the definition of 'threatening behaviour' see: *R v Afzal* [1993] Crim LR 791 and *Kwasi Poku v DPP* [1993] Crim LR 705. Both cases concerned the question of whether self-defence is to be considered reasonable conduct, or will amount to threatening or abusive behaviour.

Section 5 introduces the controversial offence of causing harassment, alarm or distress. A person is guilty of an offence if he (a) uses threatening, abusive or insulting words or behaviour, or disorderly behaviour, or (b) displays any writing, sign or other visible representation which is threatening, abusive or insulting, within the hearing or sight of a person likely to be caused harassment, alarm or distress thereby. A constable may arrest a person without warrant if he engages in offensive conduct which the constable warns him to stop, and he engages in further offensive conduct immediately or shortly after the warning. The maximum penalty on summary conviction is a fine.

Section 5 provides for three specific defences. First, that the defendant had no reason to believe that there was anyone within hearing or sight of his conduct who was likely to be harassed, alarmed or distressed; second, that he was inside a dwelling and had no reason to believe that the conduct would have been seen or heard by anyone outside; third, that his conduct was reasonable. These are all objective tests.

Sections 17–23 of the 1986 Act deal with racial hatred and replace s5A of the 1936 Act. The Act creates six offences all of which require the consent of the Attorney General to institute proceedings. All of these offences concern conduct which is threatening, abusive or insulting and which is intended or which is likely, having regard to all the circumstances, to stir up racial hatred. They are: using such words or behaviour or displaying such materials (s18); distributing or directing such materials (s19); presenting or directing a public play which involves such words or behaviour (s20); distributing, showing or playing a recording of such visual images or sounds (s21); certain participation in a broadcast or cable programme service which includes such images or sounds (s22); possessing such material or recordings with a view to its being displayed, published, distributed, broadcast or included in a cable broadcast service (s23).

Section 30 empowers a court by or before which a person is convicted of an offence connected with football to make an exclusion order prohibiting him from entering premises to attend a prescribed football match or matches.

Section 38 creates various offences connected with contamination of or interference with goods.

Section 39 deals with mass trespass and gives the most senior police officer present power to direct trespassers to leave land. The officer may arrest anyone who, knowing that such a direction has been given, fails to leave as soon as is reasonably practicable or, having left, re-enters within three months of the direction.

Police powers of entry to private meetings

In the case of *Thomas* v *Sawkins* [1935] 2 KB 249 it appears that the police have a power to enter a public meeting even though it is held on private premises and permission has been withheld, if they reasonably apprehend a breach of the peace. The facts of the case were as follows:

A meeting was held against the Incitement to Disaffection Bill. Two police officers entered the meeting and the organiser asked them to leave. One police officer grabbed him and then 30 other officers entered the meeting. Thomas prosecuted the police officer for battery. The magistrate held that the police had a right to enter the meeting and, therefore, there was no battery.

It appears that the Divisional Court decided that if the police apprehended both the possibility of seditious speeches and a breach of the peace, then they have a power of entry. What is unclear is whether a mere apprehension of a breach of the peace gives them this power. It has been argued that the decision has given the police 'a right to attend private meetings in private premises where they believe that the appropriate offences are likely to be committed if they are not there'.

This is an enormous extension of police powers and does not have any precedent. Perhaps the balance between public order and free speech has been weighed too heavily in favour of public order in this case.

The Criminal Justice and Public Order Act 1994

Sections 61–71 of this Act are now operative. This part of the Act creates new offences, in particular aggravated trespass. It also strengthens the Public Order Act 1986, by introducing new powers for the police to ban meetings from being held on private land without the consent of the owner.

Pickets and picketing

Picketing by strikers usually involves a few of them standing at the works gate and informing their fellow workers that a strike is taking place. Mass picketing is simply picketing in large numbers. There are three ways in which pickets can become involved with the law. Firstly, if the picketing is unlawful then the employer can use the civil law to obtain an injunction ordering the pickets to stop. Secondly, the pickets may be prosecuted for breaches of the criminal law. Finally, anyone can obtain an injunction to stop pickets who are 'unreasonable users' of the highway: *Hubbard* v *Pitt* [1976] 1 QB 142.

The civil law

Generally there is no 'right' to picket because it will not be a reasonable use of the highway unless for passing and repassing. However, under s15 of the Trade Union and Labour Relations Act 1974, picketing is lawful if it is in 'contemplation or furtherance of a trade dispute' and at or near the strikers' own workplace 'for the purpose only of peacefully obtaining or communicating information or peacefully persuading any person to work or to abstain from working'. It follows from this that picketing someone else's place of work is illegal and the employer can obtain an injunction to stop it. (This is so-called secondary picketing.)

For the picketing to be legal it must fall within each of the following categories:

a The people picketing must be employees, their trade union officials or those sacked during the dispute.

b The only places that can be picketed are the entrances to the premises, or if there is more than one place of work or it is impracticable to picket the workplace (for example seamen), then they can picket 'those offices of their employer from which they receive their instructions or pay packets, or depot or garage from which their vehicles operate'.

c The picketing is only lawful if it is peaceful. The Code of Practice states: 'The main cause of violence and disorder on the picket line is excessive numbers … Accordingly, pickets and their organisers should ensure that in general the numbers of pickets do not exceed six at any entrance to a workplace … ' The Code is not law. It is, therefore, not legally binding but the courts must take it into account when considering whether to grant an injunction.

d Unless the picketing is in 'furtherance of a trade dispute' it is unlawful. In *Hubbard v Pitt* [1976] 1 QB 142, it was held that consumers picketing an estate agent could be stopped by an injunction.

Conclusion

Whilst it is not envisaged that a detailed knowledge of the rules relating to the various freedoms discussed herein will be examinable it is thought desirable that an appreciation of the substantive rules be gained in order to appreciate the role that the law, particularly the criminal law, can have in the protection rather than the suppression of freedoms. An unrestricted freedom may well curtail others' freedoms. X's freedom to kill violates Y's right to life. There is little doubt that the criminal law ought to be used to protect Y's right to life as a priority over X's freedoms in this regard. The same principle will apply in other areas also. Through the maintenance of order the law enables persons to live together as a society. In a state of total anarchy no such freedoms would be available for only the strong would prosper as the law would be the law of the jungle. That is not to say that the law must be totally inflexible. We have seen that as the nature of the society changes there is a need for the law to reflect these changes. This may require the development of further protective machinery. An example would be that after the Second World War society changed to the extent that women were participating in all aspects of life on an equal footing with men there was a clear need for the law to encourage this development and to provide remedies where sex discrimination emerged – see Equal Pay Act 1970 and the Sex Discrimination Act 1975. It is interesting to note that the impetus for these laws came from the EC.

Note: Now that we are moving away from matters jurisprudential the student may find it useful to note the reading list on p577.

Law and adaptation to social change | 9

Introduction

In this chapter we shall consider a variety of matters connected to the way in which law adapts, if at all, to social change. We shall consider the nature of the English court structure as an understanding of the structure is deemed essential in an elucidation of the ways in which the courts can function in a changing society. However in order not to overburden an already detailed chapter very little descriptive material will be included on the court structure, but further details may be found in chapters 16–18. Proposals for the reform of the court structure are also considered. We shall further look at the way in which the jurisdiction of equity has historically been utilised to avoid some of the perceived inadequacies of the common law. An examination of the process of statute creation would be necessary in an assessment of the utility of statute as a mechanism for change. A note on the mechanisms of law reform will conclude this chapter.

} equity

Jurisdiction

A criterion affecting the position of a court in the hierarchy concerns the question whether the court is one where the original trial takes place (the court of first instance) or whether it exists to hear appeals from lower Courts. Magistrates' Courts and County Courts are both courts of first instance; the Court of Appeal and the House of Lords are both appellate Courts only. The courts which lie in between these levels of the structure may, depending on the case before them, be either of first instance or appellate jurisdiction.

The three divisions of the High Court, Chancery, Queen's Bench and Family, are civil courts (except for the criminal appellate jurisdiction of the Queen's Bench Division) which deal, in the main, with first instance trials. But each of the three divisions may also in some circumstances be appellate courts hearing appeals on matters heard at first instance in the Magistrates' Court or County Court. See the diagrams on the following pages which indicate the relative positions of the courts and channels of appeal in the main courts of law in this country.

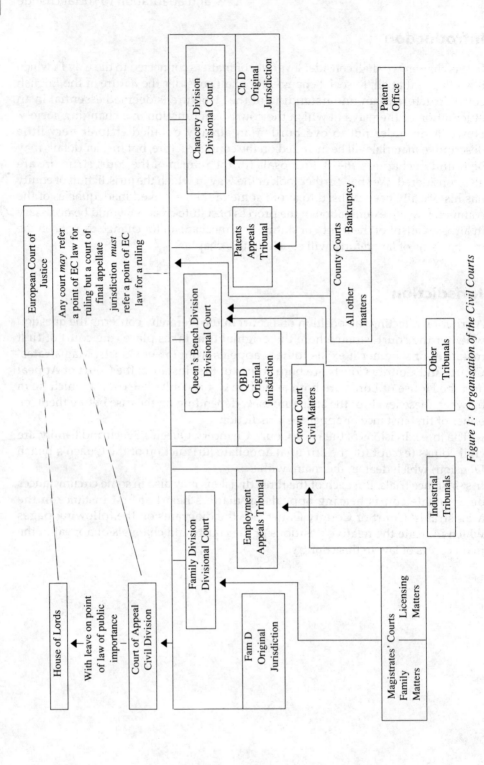

Figure 1: Organisation of the Civil Courts

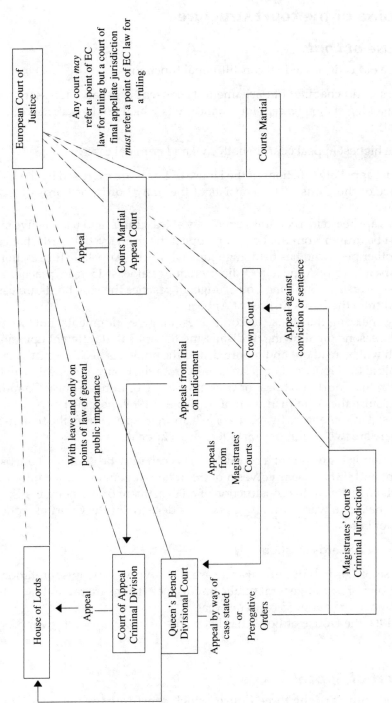

Figure 2: Organisation of the Criminal Courts

An outline of the court structure

The House of Lords

The House of Lords has a dual constitutional function:

a As the second chamber of Parliament its consent is usually necessary for the passing of legislation (except for Finance Acts which can be passed without its consent).

b It is the highest appeal court in both civil and criminal cases.

The judicial appellate functions of the House of Lords are exercised by the Judicial Committee of the House. This consists of the 'Law Lords' or Lords of Appeal in Ordinary.

Appeals are heard in a committee room by at least three, and usually five judges who must be drawn from the Lords of Appeal in Ordinary, the Lord Chancellor, and any other peer who has held 'high judicial office' (Appellate Jurisdiction Act 1876). To be a Lord of Appeal in Ordinary requires at least 15 years practice at the Bar, or two years as a Supreme Court judge. In practice the Law Lords are usually appointed from the Lords Justices of Appeal.

Strictly speaking the House of Lords does not give 'judgments' but 'opinions' stating its reasons for allowing or dismissing the appeal. If different opinions are held, each will be read out and reported, and the appeal is decided on a vote.

Appeals to the House of Lords are usually from the Court of Appeal, with leave either from the Court of Appeal or from the House of Lords Appeal Committee. However, since the Administration of Justice Act 1969 the Court of Appeal may be by-passed in some cases by means of a 'leap-frog' appeal from the first instance court. There are two conditions for a 'leap-frog' appeal:

a The trial judge must grant a certificate. This can only be done if all the parties consent and if the case involves a point of law of general public importance and which relates to the construction of an enactment or is a point in respect of which the judge was bound by a previous decision of the Court of Appeal or House of Lords.

b The House of Lords must grant leave.

The House of Lords will only hear a case if it involves the interpretation of a difficult point of law of general public importance. There are rather few of these, usually numbering about 85 cases per year.

Since 1966 the House of Lords has been able to depart from its own previous judgments.

The Court of Appeal

This is the highest of the three Courts which constitute the Supreme Court of Judicature, the others being the High Court and the Crown Court.

The Court of Appeal is theoretically composed of ex officio judges who are the Lord Chancellor, the Lord Chief Justice, the Master of the Rolls, the President of the Family Division, Lords of Appeal in Ordinary and former Lord Chancellors, and of the Lords Justices of Appeal. In practice only the Master of the Rolls and the Lord Chief Justice of the ex officio judges sit in the civil and criminal divisions respectively. Puisne judges (that is those judges of the High Court who do not have specific titles) may also sit with Lords Justices, and frequently do so in the criminal division. The normal number is three, but when a difficult and important point of law is in issue, the Court may consist of five. Interlocutory appeals may be heard by two judges and in the criminal division a single judge hears applications for leave to appeal.

Since the Criminal Appeal Act 1966 the Court of Appeal has consisted of two divisions. The civil division has the jurisdiction exercised by the old Court of Appeal which is exclusively civil and almost entirely appellate. Appeal is by rehearing but normally the only evidence given is the written transcript of evidence given at the trial.

The criminal division replaces the old Court of Criminal Appeal which was set up in 1907. Its jurisdiction is exclusively criminal and appellate, hearing appeals from the Crown Court and considering points of law referred by the Attorney General when the Crown Court trial ended in an acquittal.

Sir John Donaldson, a former Master of the Rolls, described the function of the Court of Appeal as:

> '... to develop and define the law where it has not previously been considered or where the law is in doubt ... It would also overrule an error of law made by a lower court.'

There is always a large backlog in the waiting list of cases before the Civil Division of the Court of Appeal. This has important ramifications since justice delayed is justice denied. The court authorities are certainly aware of this. There is currently being undertaken a review on the reorganisation of the Civil Division; however at the time of writing such proposals have not reached an advanced stage.

At the Court of Appeal the original parties are seldom present. No fresh evidence is usually entered into while the judges have before them a transcript of the proceedings in the lower courts. The hearing in the Court of Appeal concentrates on the legal argument and has been described as a forum for the sober discussion of difficult points of law.

Abolition of the House of Lords?

As can be seen from the above, both the Court of Appeal and the House of Lords are purely appellate courts, in that they never sit as courts of first instance, and only hear appeals from other courts' decisions. Further, since one can appeal from the Court of Appeal to the House of Lords, this means that the litigant, should he so wish, can have the decision of two purely appellate courts. As *A P Herbert* pointed out, this is somewhat strange. He gave a medical analogy, arguing that if a patient has had his appendix removed by a distinguished surgeon he would not expect to be referred to a body of three other surgeons who might recommend that the appendix be replaced. Still less would he expect to be referred to a further body of surgeons who may recommend that the original operation was the right one. Such an experience is commonplace in the law in that the Court of Appeal can overturn the decision of the first instance judge and then be overturned itself by the House of Lords. The analogy between law and medicine drawn by *A P Herbert* is of course unfair in that law never purported to be an exact science. Yet the question still remains, why do we have two purely appellate Courts especially since, as has been seen, the personnel of the two courts overlaps considerably.

The first point to be made is that the Court of Appeal could not be abolished, leaving the House of Lords as a single appeal body. The House of Lords quite simply could not cope with the amount of work. In 1980 the House of Lords heard a total of 85 cases, while the Court of Appeal Civil Division in 1980 heard 872 cases, and the Criminal Division heard some 2,419. The Court of Appeal is thus an essential Court; but can the same be said for the House of Lords? Is the House of Lords required as a second appeal court?

Arguments in favour of retaining the House of Lords

The House of Lords is a better tribunal, and its decisions are more fully argued

Such a view is so subjective that it is difficult to evaluate. *Jackson's* (*The Machinery of Justice*) argument seems strong, namely that since the strength of the two Courts depends upon the persons who are sitting in them, since these people change, so too will the relative strengths of the two Courts. It is thus difficult either to support or reject the view that the House of Lords gives better decisions.

The rigidity of the Court of Appeal requires the retention of a second Appeal Court

The argument in favour of the House of Lords is that the fact that the Court of Appeal binds itself means that from time to time there must be poor decisions which have come to be regarded as wrong or seriously inconvenient. This problem can be overcome by retaining a superior court, the House of Lords, to review the work of the Court of Appeal. The alternative solution, however, would be to give the court the right to depart from its own previous decision where justice demands it. The Court of Appeal would thus have the powers which the House of Lords gave itself in 1966, and thus it is said the House of Lords could be abolished. Such a solution, however, is not without its difficulties. Since the Court of Appeal in fact consists of several different courts (this is required by the sheer volume of work), one would always face the danger that different Courts in the same Court of Appeal Division would be applying different views of the law. At least this danger is minimised by having the House of Lords which can supervise all that the Court of Appeal does.

The House of Lords has a general supervisory function over the whole of the law, and guides its future development

Blom-Cooper in *A Study of the House of Lords in Its Judicial Capacity*, an extensive study of the role of the House of Lords, essentially argues the above. He argues that the House of Lords should be retained, not because of the desirability of giving the litigant a second bite at the cherry (indeed he recognises *A P Herbert*'s criticism) but because the House of Lords 'still has a general supervisory role over the judicial process, which is analogous to its medieval position as a council to the royal "fountain of justice". In effect it is the alter ego of a sovereign legislature which does not merely hand down statute law but also exercises a considerable measure of control over the manner in which the judges interpret and apply the law.'

Essentially therefore, *Blom-Cooper* argues in favour of the retention of the House of Lords in that the House of Lords is able to oversee the whole legal system, and ensure that the system does administer justice. This view has of course become increasingly tenable after the House of Lords 1966 Practice Direction. The House of Lords, he suggests, can and should adopt a more creative role, and should be willing to reform the law from the top.

Arguments in favour of abolishing the House of Lords

There is no good reason for retaining it

Those who argue in favour of abolishing the House of Lords argue that the fact that there is nothing to be said in favour of retaining it is a strong reason for abolishing it.

The use of the House of Lords as an appellate court is potentially unfair

This argument is that it is unfair that a litigant should lose the case when the majority of judges have held in his favour. For example, if the trial judge finds in favour of X, Y may appeal to the Court of Appeal. If all the judges there uphold the decision in favour of X, Y may still appeal to the House of Lords.

If three Law Lords hold in Y's favour in the House of Lords, he will of course win the case and be entitled to all his costs even though six judges in all have found in favour of X and only three in favour of Y, counting both appeals.

Appeal to the House of Lords adds further expense and delay before a final decision can be given

Blom-Cooper in his extensive study in 1972 does not suggest that the House of Lords is inefficient or particularly expensive, but there is no doubt that the appeal to the House of Lords does add to the cost and the time of the case. In 1972 appeal to the

House of Lords on average took an additional 11 months, and of course added substantially to the costs since QCs will usually be instructed.

The main merit of a House of Lords' decision is finality and this could be achieved without recourse to the House of Lords
Jackson asks the question: why do people appeal to the House of Lords? He examined the 15 appeals made to the House of Lords in 1973 and noted that eight involved government departments or National authorities, five were disputes between commercial concerns, and the other two were miscellaneous. He comments:

> 'It is noticeable that half of the appeals concerned government departments or the like. Why? These bodies are engaged in work on lines that they conceive as being authorised or required by legislation: if judicial decisions "obstruct" them, then their reaction is that the obstruction must be removed. The simplest step is to see what the final Court will say, for a successful outcome may remove the "obstruction" whilst if this fails, the matter can be put right by legislation if the relevant minister will take the appropriate action. The point is that the appeal must be final before legislation is contemplated, and there is no magic in finality coming from a second appeal Court rather than a single appeal Court. It is probable that the five appeals by commercial concerns (or their insurers) were also in pursuit of finality.'

The theme is simple therefore: the only merit of the House of Lord's decision is its finality – and that could be equally well given by a single Court of Appeal sitting as a final appeal court.

Reform of the County Court

The County Courts were first established in 1846 to deal speedily and cheaply with relatively minor civil litigation. The aim was to make the Courts accessible to the average man in the street, and ensure that the costs of litigation would remain within his means. As such the Courts were intended to be quicker and cheaper and the procedure such that the average man unaided could pursue his own claim. Indeed The County Court Practice Book begins with the words:

> 'The County Courts are adapted to the needs of the great masses of the population by the maximum of ... simplicity of procedure, suitors being able in fact to obtain relief and defend themselves without legal assistance.'

In fact the present system does not operate in such a way at all:

The procedure is not so simple
The County Court Practice (1986) contains some 319 pages of county court rules and 204 pages of court forms. Whereas the procedure to a lawyer may seem simple, to the average man in the street the procedure remains complex and intimidating.

Filing a claim is difficult

Even the initial stage of filing a claim will prove too complex for most unrepresented litigants. Further, the County Court staff are not allowed to help draft it (though sometimes they do help).

Few lay persons understand the rules of evidence

The County Court is still a full court and so is bound (except in small claims arbitration) by the rules of evidence. They are complex and do not always accord with what common sense would suggest. Since few lay persons understand the rules of evidence, it is not uncommon to see a litigant producing 'evidence' on a vital point, only to be told by the judge that he cannot receive it. Little wonder that ordinary people who have been through the courts frequently complain that 'the judge would not listen to me'.

The procedure at the hearing is such that the litigant is frequently unable to 'tell his story'

Procedure at the hearing is quite beyond the capability of most people. 'Instead of each side telling its story, the case is presented to the judge by means of a gladiatorial combat between the parties.' Yet very few people are able to examine and cross-examine effectively the first time they try it. Consequently, many litigants, even if they do have a strong case, will lose if they are unrepresented, simply because they are unable to present their side of the story adequately.

The cost of litigation is prohibitive

It has been pointed out by many commentators that the cost of taking a case to the County Court is beyond the reach of many potential litigants. The difficulties of procedure, filing a claim and the rules of evidence mean that most people would require legal advice before going to court. Necessarily such advice is expensive and if representation in court is also required the costs can be huge.

Taking all of the above together, it is quite clear that the quote given from *The Court Practice* is over-optimistic to the point of being wildly inaccurate. The Consumer Council paper on the County Courts (1970) entitled *Justice Out of Reach* is a far more accurate description of the present County Court system. That report is most interesting in that it suggests the development of an alternative procedure, so that the Courts could indeed be used by the ordinary person. The following recommendations were made.

It should be a genuine people's court

Only people should be allowed to use the court. Hence companies and partnerships would not be allowed to start proceedings in the court. This was justified on the basis of the American experience in that unless companies were prohibited from appearing in the courts, before long the court procedure adapted to that which was more suitable for company litigation, to the detriment of the ordinary person.

No legal representation

It was argued that to allow lawyers to appear would increase the procedural complexity of the hearing and would destroy the informality of the Court. Further, if legal representations were allowed, those who could not afford lawyers would be discouraged from appearing before the Court for fear that the other person would have the 'unfair' advantage of legal representation. If this happened then the whole aim behind the new system – namely to make the courts open to the normal person – would have been destroyed.

The procedure – the court should help the parties

The basic principle of the court procedure would be that the Court should help the parties. Hence the litigant would not have to draft his own claim. He would explain it in his own words to a court officer, who would then draft the appropriate document. The Registrar would hold the hearing in his own office – not in a court room – and provision should be made to hear the case outside of the parties' working hours if this would be more convenient to them. The Registrar would then conduct the hearing in the way a reasonable man would do, letting the parties tell their stories and asking questions where more information is required. The hearing would not be governed by the rules of evidence, or any rules of procedure: the Registrar's function would simply be to find out the story of what happened as best as he could, and then apply his judgment to it.

The fundamental aim of the Registrar should be to act as arbitrator with the aim of helping the parties reach an amicable settlement. If this fails, then the Registrar should have the power to give his decision on the matter, which would bind the parties.

Costs

Since no legal representation would be allowed the costs would be kept as low as possible. Further, however, it was suggested that as a basic principle, both parties should be required to bear their own costs, although the 'winning' party would be able to recover his 'filing fee'.

Quite clearly, if such a scheme could be established in practice, it would have many advantages over the present County Court system. Since the Court would be there to help the litigant, and since there would be none of the pomp and formality usually associated with courts, the whole process of litigating would be far less intimidating. Further, the cost of taking an action to the court would be minimal, so that it would at last be possible to say that the courts of England are open to all people whatever their financial means. Such a development would represent the biggest step yet towards making the law accessible to the average man in the street.

Magistrates' Courts

A more detailed description of the structure and work of the Magistrates' Courts is discussed in chapter 16.

The system of justice in Britain rests heavily on the role of the lay magistrates (Justices of the Peace). As stated earlier, every criminal case begins one way or another in the Magistrates' Court – either the case is heard summarily by the court, or if the offence is indictable, committal proceedings will begin. Magistrates are thus the people who make all important decisions regarding bail of the accused.

The importance of the Magistrates' Court was strikingly put by *Esther Moir* in 1969 when she wrote that one in forty persons in England appears before justices every year and of all cases heard in the different courts 97.5 per cent were dealt with by lay magistrates.

Given this fact, that one in every forty persons in this country will appear before a magistrate within the year, it is sensible to view the Magistrates' Court as one of the courts that rank highest in importance, rather than viewing it as the court at the bottom of the hierarchy of importance as it is usually viewed.

The volume of work which confronts the Magistrates' Court necessitates that the procedure in court should be fast. This is indeed the great strength of the Magistrates' Court, but it is also its greatest weakness. They are very quick, but bearing in mind the need for justice to be seen to be done, there is something almost indecent in the speed with which the cases are disposed of: even an occasional plea of 'not guilty' acts only as a temporary brake on the rapidly moving procession of defendants through the court. Further, the courts do not state the reasoning underlying their decisions, and this only adds to the rough and ready appearance of the justice which they administer.

Few would suggest that magistrates are consciously biased in favour of one party or the other, but it is frequently suggested that the magistrates are far too willing to accept police evidence; consequently Magistrates' Courts have often gained the reputation of being 'Police Courts'.

Thus, the Magistrates' Court is, out of necessity, a Court which must deal with cases quickly. Injustice will also inevitably result, and this must be accepted in that we cannot afford a more sophisticated machine to process the vast amount of petty crime. Some try to suggest that this is unimportant in that the punishments which the Magistrates' Court gives are only relatively small (six months imprisonment and/or £5,000 fine). Yet as *Drewry* argues 'smallness of sentence is a relative concept'. Even a relatively small fine can have a crippling effect on a person living on a financial knife edge. Further, a small penalty can have heavy side effects – for instance, a third endorsement for a relatively minor motoring offence automatically means the loss of one's driving licence, and this can have drastic consequences for those whose livelihood is dependent upon driving.

Thus, in a sense, the Magistrates' Court can be viewed as one of the most important courts in the court structure. However, it must be admitted that the court does administer a rather 'rough and ready' notion of justice, and that injustice is bound to occur.

Civil Justice Review and the Courts and Legal Services Act

In the light of the problems highlighted in recent years – increasing cost and length of litigation, and the consequent backlog of cases – on 11 March 1987 the Lord Chancellor's Department published its *Civil Justice Review*. The aims were to speed up the machinery of justice by modernising antiquated court procedures, and to reduce cost of litigation. The main proposals are set out below:

Amalgamation of the High Court and County Court

As an alternative, to retain formal separation but for the two courts to be much more closely integrated than at present. Civil procedure to be streamlined with more emphasis placed on pre-trial procedures which, it is hoped, would encourage more out of court settlements and hence reduce the number of cases going to trial. Penalties to be imposed for introducing into court a large number of irrelevant documents.

Court powers to strike out delayed cases

More emphasis to be placed on arbitration

The Department repeated its earlier recommendation that the financial limits in the Small Claims procedure should be raised to £1,000. It is also proposed 'in-court arbitration' for claims between £1,000 and £5,000, thus bringing the advantages of the inquisitorial method to claims at present heard by the adversarial process in the County Court.

Extend Civil Court sittings by one hour per day

Abolish the High Court long vacation in the summer with the aim of increasing the number of sitting days for a High Court judge to match that of a Circuit Judge. In addition, it was suggested that a number of High Court judges be located permanently in the regions (at the moment, all are based in London, of which about one-third travel the circuits).

Lord McCluskey in the *Reith Lectures* 1986 entered on a wide review of the present system of justice in England with particular reference to the need for improvement, and the role of the judges in that improvement. His views on Civil Justice reflect those of the Lord Chancellor's Department. The relevant parts of his lecture are set out below:

'No one can be satisfied with the administration of justice as it is in 1986. The delays, costs and complexities are notorious. No doubt they have been worse at other times and are worse in other countries, but that is no comfort to the potential litigant. And the problems do not yield readily to administrative solutions, such as providing more judges or building more courts or spending more on legal aid, however necessary or desirable such measures appear to be …

'What, I believe, is needed is to engage the judge's experience of making such judgments at a much earlier stage in litigation, particularly civil litigation, so that he plays a substantial part in defining and articulating the issues which are justiciable and which have to be resolved. Our present procedures allow too much time for each party to set out his stall before the judge is brought in to judge the competition … We cannot rest content with a system in which the ordinary litigant finds himself joining a queue which shuffles fitfully towards an uncertain destination.'

The Courts and Legal Services Act 1990 has in fact incorporated most of these proposals. The major change has been to transfer many cases from the High Court to the County Court, vastly increasing the latter courts' workload. For further details see chapters 16–18.

Custom

In a wide sense of the word, 'custom' is of great historical significance in that before the developing common law extinguished the local variations of law, all English law was 'custom' in the sense that, with the exception of limited royal intervention, law varied from area to area, shire to shire, town to town.

These local customary laws were not written down and were administered by the local courts. However, with the rapid development of the royal courts and royal justice which provided a law 'common' to the entire realm (it was of even application and did not vary with the locality), the local customary law went into a decline and disappeared. However, though not much is known about communal, customary justice, it is clear that parts of it did exert an influence on the developing common law.

In the modern law, custom has a very limited role to play, and a narrower meaning, namely a particular rule which has existed since 'time immemorial' and must have obtained legal status within a particular location. Custom should be distinguished from mere trade *usage* which is simply a factual question of usual practice within a given trade and which is not subject to the stringent tests for establishing custom providing the usage is legal and reasonable. One use for trade usage is to imply terms and contracts.

Basic definition

In the *Tanistry Case* (1608) Dav Ir 28 custom was defined as 'such usage as has obtained the force of law' and is binding as regards the particular places, persons and things with which it is concerned.

The main characteristics of custom are:

a It must have existed in fact, or by presumption, since *time immemorial* that is since 1189 (see below).

b The custom must be *local*, that is: confined to a particular locality. A custom cannot exist in one place which purports to confer a right to something in a different locality: *Re Ecclesfield Inhabitants* (1818) 1 B & Ald 348. Contrast this with the common law which is not (within England and Wales) confined to any particular locality.

c Custom is an *exception* to the normal operation of the common law – though many customs have been abolished by legislation (see Law of Property Act 1925).

Essential elements of custom

Time immemorial

The custom must be shown to have existed since 1189, the time fixed by the Statute of Westminster 1, 1275 as 'time immemorial' (that is, the first year of the reign of Richard I): see *Angus* v *Dalton* (1877) 3 QBD 85 at pp 103–4. In some cases, it is sufficient to raise a *presumption* of antiquity, eg by showing that a continuous customary user has existed for as long as living memory can go: *Angus* v *Dalton*, above. Of course, such a presumption is open to rebuttal, such as by evidence indicating that the custom began after 1189. For example, to say that a customary use of land has existed since time immemorial, would speedily be disproved if it could be established that the land in question was under water until say, the seventeenth century, or whatever.

Must be reasonable

This requirement means that if the alleged custom is without a legal reason, it will not be upheld. 'Unreasonableness' in this context can mean that the custom arose from accident or by the permission of another, eg a royal grant and not from a right arising in ancient times – *Alfred F Beckett* v *Lyons* [1967] 2 WLR 421 CA. The reasonableness of a custom is to be adjudged at the time it began, and a custom is not unreasonable merely because it is not consistent with the common law: *Tanistry Case*, above.

Further, if the custom is repugnant to the principles of the common law it will not be upheld, eg it entails placing a disproportionate burden on some for the benefit of others: *Wolstanton Ltd* v *Newcastle under Lyme Corporation* [1940] 3 All ER 101 HL.

Must be certain

The custom alleged must be clear and certain not only in respect of the nature of the right claimed but as to the custom itself. A custom must be certain:

a as to its general nature;

b as to the persons alleged to be affected;

c as to the locality in which it is alleged to be effective, eg a town, manor, parish or county.

Must be obligatory

Unless the custom carries with it obligatory force it will not be upheld since, in that case it does not have the characteristic of a rule of law.

Must not have been interrupted

To be valid a custom must have existed without interruption since time immemorial. A mere lack of use for a period does not necessarily mean that the custom has been extinguished, though it makes it more difficult to establish.

Creation and enjoyment

Provided that the requirements stated above have been fulfilled, it is unnecessary to prove how the custom originated. However, the right claimed by virtue of custom must be enjoyed as of *right* (by virtue of the custom) and without violence, secrecy or the permission of another (nec vi nec clam nec precario): *Beckett* v *Lyons*, above.

As noted above, non-user will not of itself extinguish the custom though it may raise an inference that no such custom existed particularly if non-user was not accidental or due to natural causes.

Equity

The common law of England and Wales evolved from spontaneously observed rules and practices which were shaped and formalised by decisions made by judges declaring and pronouncing the law in relation to the particular facts before them. It was so-called to distinguish it from local laws as well as from any law that was particular or special, for example, Roman law or law merchant.

From the fifth to the eleventh century the principles applied in local courts reflected broadly the customs of local communities. After the Norman Conquest in 1066, (a watershed in English legal history) the King's judges – itinerant justices, moulded the customs into a general body of principles to be uniformly applied on their travels around the country and later in the Royal Courts – Common Pleas, King's Bench and Exchequer. From the twelfth to the thirteenth century, the writ system developed – actions in the common law courts were initiated by writs obtained from the Chancery. During this period many writs were issued, in various forms and gradually a register of writs appeared. By harsh legislation – the Provisions of Oxford 1258 – the Chancellor's office was temporarily restricted from creating new writs. The severity of the Provisions of Oxford was alleviated to some extent by the passing of the Statute of Westminster 1285. This provided that new writs could be issued, but only if they were similar in nature (in consimili casu) to writs already existing. The effect of this statute was that though the development of the common law did continue, very slowly, it was not until the introduction of the *action on the case* in the 1370s that some flexibility was restored to the common law system, but what had not been envisaged was the growth of the jurisdiction of the Chancellor himself.

The medieval common law was defective in that it did not cover the whole field of obligations; it had no means to extract the truth from litigants (since oral evidence was not received until the 16th century); its judgments were not capable of being adapted to special circumstances. Dissatisfied litigants petitioned the Sovereign or his Council, and later, the Chancellor who was 'keeper of the King's conscience'. Initially the Chancellor made recommendations to the council but eventually (in the fifteenth century) petitions were delivered to the Chancellor himself.

The Chancellor's jurisdiction proved more popular because:

a   the Court of Chancery could enforce rights not recognised at common law (trusts and married women's property);

b   in contract, it could provide an alternative and more efficient remedy to that of the common law;

c   the court could compel the disclosure of documents;

d   it could protect third party rights.

In these ways, the Court of Chancery afforded an improved means of obtaining justice. A number of equitable maxims developed, one being 'Equity follows the law' and by the seventeenth century, equity was locked in a fierce battle with the common law – the latter threatened by the new usurper. *The Earl of Oxford's Case* 1615 (see below) brought the crisis to a head when it was resolved that in the event of a conflict equity should prevail.

Thereafter equity developed rules and procedures and by the eighteenth century was itself a settled doctrine.

Reforms were made in 1873 and 1875 by the Judicature Acts which established the Supreme Court and provided that both common law and equity could be applied by it – s25 Judicature Act 1873.

Equity developed as a gloss on the common law. 'Equity' is not peculiar to the English legal system and is recognised also by continental systems but in the common sense of 'natural justice' or 'fairness'. This is not the correct meaning in English law, although such notions certainly played a part in its growth. *Maitland* defined 'Equity' as:

'that body of rules which, were it not for the operation of the Judicature Acts, would be administered by those Courts which would be known as the Courts of Equity.'

In other words, modern Equity in English law can only be understood by reference to its origins and historical development.

The practice grew up for litigants dissatisfied with 'justice' as administered by the common law courts to petition the King to exercise his prerogative in their favour. These petitions were at first dealt with by the King himself, in Council, but later the task was delegated to the Lord Chancellor (who was the King's principal Minister and controlled the issue of writs out of Chancery, was custodian of the Great Seal and judge in Council and Exchequer Chamber). The first recorded instance of a Chancellor issuing a decree in his own name and not in that of the King was in 1474 – this marked the beginning of the independence of the Court of Chancery from the King in Council.

The early Chancellors were members of the clergy (and to this day Equity is concerned to a large extent with morals and 'justice'). After the fall of Cardinal Wolsey in 1529, they were appointed from the ranks of common lawyers. This was significant for the subsequent development of Equity as the common lawyers brought with them the system of precedent and applied this to the rules of Equity so that it became a coherent body of rules.

The Chancellor's Court was the Court of Chancery. Here appeals were heard from litigants who felt they had been denied a remedy to which they were entitled at common law. It also developed an original jurisdiction through the recognition and enforcement of a set of principles now identifiable as the rules of Equity.

Proceedings in the Court of Chancery were not commenced by writ; therefore, formal procedure did not determine the success or failure of a case as it did at common law. Proceedings were begun instead by petition, which could be in any form, and evidence was brought in the form of a sworn affidavit.

At first, the Lord Chancellor was the only judge. Later, as pressure of work increased, he was assisted by Chancery Masters, the head of whom was the Master of the Rolls. In 1813 Lord Chancellor Eldon appointed the first Vice-Chancellor.

By 1851 there had developed in addition the Court of Appeal in Chancery to hear appeals from Vice-Chancellors and the Master of the Rolls. This Court was abolished by the Judicature Acts 1873–75 and its jurisdiction transferred to the Court of Appeal.

Another, albeit shortlived, Court of Equity should be mentioned. This was the Court of Requests, which existed during the fifteenth century to provide relief to poor litigants in minor cases where they had been denied a remedy at common law. This Court was declared illegal in 1598 as it had 'not any power by Commission, by Statute or by common law', and it was not revived after the Restoration; it was generally felt that its links with the Council were too close.

The major development of Equity occurred between 1529 and 1827. But its rules continue to develop to meet the needs of modern times, as demonstrated in cases of land law concerning interests in property in equity during the latter half of this century, and in the principle of 'equitable estoppel' enunciated by Lord Denning in *Central London Property Trust Ltd* v *High Trees House Ltd* [1947] KB 130. (See the later chapters on contract.)

Principal rights protected by equity

Trusts

A 'trust' arises where A transfers property to B with the express intention that B is to hold that property not for his own benefit but for the benefit of C. B is a 'trustee' of the property so transferred and C is a 'beneficiary' or 'cestui que trust'.

The common law would look no further than the form of transfer, ie it would recognise B as the legal owner of the property transferred and would not go behind B's legal title to recognise the interest of C. Thus under the common law in such circumstances B, if he was unscrupulous, could keep the property for his own use, contrary to his moral obligation to C.

Equity, however, recognised and enforced the rights of the beneficiary – not only as against the trustee but also against any transferee of the legal interest who knew of the interest of the beneficiary.

Thus the beneficiary had an equitable interest in the property which the Courts of Equity would protect.

Mortgages

The classical form of common law mortgage was a conveyance of land to the mortgagee (lender), subject to an agreement to re-convey to the mortgagor (borrower) on repayment of the loan, and interest, by a specified date. At common law the right to 'redeem' was lost if the mortgagor did not repay the loan in time.

Injustice could be caused by persons advancing money to a mortgagor in this way, and then absenting themselves until after the date for repayment had passed, thus retaining the land mortgaged plus any proportion of the money which had actually been handed over by the mortgagor.

Equity provided a means of preventing such abuse through the 'equity of redemption' which gave the mortgagor the right to redeem after the set date provided certain formalities are complied with, eg payment of interest. The equity of redemption was recognised as an equitable interest in land which, like the beneficiary's interest under a trust, was capable of binding transferees of the mortgaged property as well as the original mortgagee. The only way in which the equity redemption could be overcome was for the mortgagee to apply to the Court of Chancery for an order for foreclosure of the mortgage.

Principal remedies of equity

a *Injunction*. This is an order of the Court compelling or restraining the performance of some act, for protection of both equitable and common law rights.

b *Specific performance*. This is an order compelling a party to an agreement (eg contract or trust) to carry out his promise or be guilty of a contempt of Court.

c *Rectification*. An order altering the words of a written document which has failed truly to express the intentions of the parties to it.

d *Rescission*. The restoration of parties to a contract to their pre-contract status quo.

All equitable remedies are discretionary as opposed to those of the common law courts which are available 'as of right'. In deciding whether to exercise its discretion to make an order providing an equitable remedy, the Court of Chancery developed many principles or 'maxims'.

Contemporary application of equitable maxims

Equity has developed a series of maxims to aid its decisions in the achievement of fairness. Whilst these maxims have now become well embedded in our system it may be useful to list the main ones for use as examples.

He who seeks equity must do equity

A person who seeks equitable relief must be prepared to act fairly towards his opponent as a condition of obtaining relief.

In the case of *Chappell* v *Times Newspapers Ltd* [1975] 1 WLR 482 workers who had been threatened with dismissal if they refused to withdraw their strike action applied for an injunction preventing the threat from being carried out.

It was held that the workers had not come to equity willing to do equity as they were not prepared to give an undertaking that they would fulfil their contracts (ie not take strike action) if the injunction were granted. Therefore, the injunction was refused.

He who comes to equity must come with clean hands

Not only must the plaintiff 'do equity' by making present concessions for the defendant, but his conscience must be clear as to his past conduct.

In the case of *D & C Builders* v *Rees* [1966] 2 QB 617 the defendant claimed the benefit of the principle of equitable estoppel. She had tried to take advantage of the plaintiffs' financial difficulties in persuading them to agree to accept a lower sum in satisfaction of a debt she owed them.

It was held that the defendant had not come to equity with clean hands, having tried to exert undue or improper influence; and, therefore, the doctrine of equitable estoppel could not apply to her.

Delay defeats equities

Unreasonable delay will prevent a plaintiff from claiming an equitable remedy. The reasonableness of the delay is a question of fact in all the circumstances.

In the case of *Leaf* v *International Galleries* [1950] 2 KB 86 L brought an action claiming rescission for misrepresentation and/or mistake arising out of a contract of sale of a painting five years previously.

It was held that the five-year delay prevented the plaintiff from obtaining rescission.

This rule is sometimes referred to as the 'doctrine of laches'.

Equality is equity

For example, since specific performance of a contract cannot be ordered against an infant, it cannot be invoked by him.

Equity looks to the intention, not the form

This is demonstrated in relation to mortgages and trusts.

Equity acts in personam

Originally equitable decrees were enforced against the person of the defendant (ie by imprisonment) and not against any property involved in the dispute. Alternatively, the defendant's property could be confiscated until he obeyed the decree. Today more convenient methods are available. For example, the court can order a person to execute a document, and, if he does not do so, the court will appoint someone to execute it on his behalf.

Relationship between equity and common law

Common law and equity developed to some extent in conflict with one another until 1875, when the Judicature Acts finally resolved the conflicts. The difficulties arose out of the fact that the Courts of Equity would provide a remedy where the common law courts would not, and this had the effect of omitting the common law courts' jurisdiction. The conflict came to a head in 1615 with *The Earl of Oxford's Case* (1615) 1 Rep Ch 1, where Merton College, Oxford, had been granted a lease of Covent Garden for 72 years at £9 per year. Fifty years later the College sold the lease to the Earl of Oxford at a rent of £15 per year. Later the College retook possession of part of it, on the basis that an Elizabethan statute prevented the sale of ecclesiastical and College lands so that the conveyance to the Earl was void. The Earl brought an action to eject the College from the land, and the common law found in favour of the College, saying that they were bound by the statute. The Earl filed a bill in equity for relief – Lord Ellesmere LC granted it, saying that the College had acted against all good conscience.

Lord Ellesmere declared that the Court of Chancery had the power to set aside common law judgments, 'not for any error or defect in the judgment but for the hard conscience of the party'.

The question was referred to King James I, who consulted Sir Francis Bacon, and decided in favour of the supremacy of the Court of Chancery.

Gradually the Courts of Equity became undisputed Courts of Law (ie as opposed to conscience) and a clear body of rules emerged which were applied there.

The Judicature Acts 1873–75 finally fused the two systems of law, common law and equity, and provided that both (or all) were available in all law courts.

Thus, today both common law and equity are English law, both rely on the doctrine of precedent, both are applied in all law courts, and both have been partly embodied in statutes.

Where a principle of equity conflicts with one of common law, equity prevails, under the Judicature Acts.

Legislation as a principal source of law

Introduction

The modern importance attached to legislation and the overriding effect of Parliament's will manifested through statute has not always existed, though statutes (in one form or another) have existed for many centuries. Traditionally, though incorrectly, the first is the Statute of Merton (1236). This is not entirely correct; there were earlier equivalents but ancient statutes did not follow the modern form nor did they always enjoy the respect and obedience given to modern legislation by the judiciary. Indeed, an official edition of statutes did not appear until 1822.

Parliament initially played a minor role in law-making though it gradually developed functions of ratification of royal decrees and initiator of royal legislation (by presenting grievances to the Crown). The Tudor period, with its great outburst of legislative activity, saw the origins of modern parliamentary procedure – though the influence of the Crown was still great.

In the modern law, statute law fulfils a number of important functions, since it not only expresses the will of the democratically elected Parliament (insofar as their will is clearly expressed in statute – see *Black-Clawson* v *Papierwerke* [1975] AC 591) but carries out social, legal and administrative reforms. With the generally conservative approach of the judiciary and the constraints of the doctrine of precedent, major legal reform is left to Parliament: see, for example, *Lim Poh Choo* v *Camden and Islington Area Health Authority* [1980] AC 174 HL where the House declined to initiate major reforms of the law governing damages for personal injury:

' ... so radical a reform can be made neither by judge nor by modification of rules of court. It raises issues of social, economic and financial policy not amenable to judicial reform, which will almost certainly prove to be controversial and can only be resolved by the legislature after full consideration of factors which cannot be brought into clear focus, or be weighed and assessed, in the course of the forensic process ... it is this limitation, inherent in the forensic process, which sets bounds to the scope of judicial law reform ...' (Lord Scarman).

The 'limitation' referred to is that the court is always confined to the issues raised and argued by the litigants and is very rarely in a position (if at all) to consider the full implications of a major change in the law. Parliament is, however, in such a position and is further able to make use of reports of the *Law Commission* (a permanent body set up to consider issues of law reform) or a *Royal Commission* specially set up to consider a particular area of the law.

Modern legislation

Since 1973 there have been two major sources of legislation binding within the English legal system: the traditional Parliamentary legislation was joined by that of the European Communities on the coming into force of the European Communities Act 1972. European law is dealt with in chapter 12.

The modern authority of statute law is clear and is quite able to alter and abolish sections of the common law: subject to the restraints of the democratic system, laws may also be enacted contrary to morality or religion. Further, international law is only made part of English law by statutory incorporation, see Lord Atkin in *Attorney-General for Canada* v *Attorney-General for Ontario* [1937] AC 326, at pp347–8.

With the exception of private member's bills most legislation is initiated by the Crown. The initial impetus may be that of the government seeking to implement its own party policy, or from the Law Commission (or Royal Commission – see above) pointing out defects in the existing law and making recommendations for reform. Government bills are usually dealt with by the government ministry or department most concerned and their proposals form the basis of instructions sent to *Parliamentary Counsel* who draft the bills. The drafting of a bill involves consultation between counsel (who is a qualified barrister) and the relevant ministry (or even the Cabinet if it is sufficiently important).

Prior to its introduction into Parliament, the final draft of the relevant bill is approved by the department whose concern it is. It is also attended by counsel who drafted it, and who will draft any subsequent amendments made during its passage. The basic stages in the passage of a bill are:

a Introduction of the bill.

b First reading. (No debate.)

c Second reading. (Principle of the bill debated on the floor of the House.)

d Committee stage. (Clause-by-clause scrutiny in standing committee.)

e Report stage. (Amendments considered on floor.)

f Third reading. (Final version debated on floor of the House.)

g House of Lords. (Stages similar to those in Commons are heard in the House of Lords. If the Lords make any amendments the bill may have to be referred back to the Commons.)

h Royal Assent.

Since 1962 (Acts of Parliament Numbering and Citation Act 1962) the date of an Act is the calendar year rather than the regnal year and in practice one short title is used, eg 'Criminal Justice Act 1948' instead of 11 and 12 Geo 6 c.58.

If older statutes are consulted, it may be found that they are referred to solely by the regnal year of the monarch in whose reign it was enacted, eg 18 Ed. I (statute of the eighteenth year of Edward I's reign – *Quia Emptores*, 1290).

Form and functions of modern legislation

Form

In brief, there are a number of forms of legislation. The most important form is, of course, an *Act of Parliament* which is enacted in accordance with the unlimited legislative power of Parliament subject to compliance with European Law (though English theory holds that should Parliament wish it, this could be overridden: see *Macarthys* v *Smith* [1981] 1 All ER 111). It is now well established that no court may impugn an Act or go behind it in order to see if there were irregularities of procedure: *British Railways Board* v *Pickin* [1974] AC 765.

The most commonly used version of an Act is the Queen's Printer's Copy (published by HMSO), though various editions appear in both commentaries and as appendices to practitioner's works. *Current Law Statutes* publishes each statute with a detailed commentary on the various provisions outlining any relevant case law. Statutes with detailed commentary are also privately published in *Halsbury's Statutes*, now in the course of its fourth edition. Statutes in this series and in the official publication, *Statutes in Force*, are arranged by subject rather than chronologically.

Functions

a *Reform and revision of law*

This function of legislation that is, reform of 'lawyers' law' is not a function in which Parliament generally takes an active part, except where it has other implications. The initiative for legal reform usually comes from the Law Commission or specially appointed Royal Commissions (usually on ministerial recommendation). The first permanent body set up to which matters of private law could be referred was the Law Revision Committee (set up between the Wars), followed by the Law Reform Committee. In 1965, the Law Commission, consisting of five full-time members, was set up to consider major legal reform and also to recommend such reform. A separate Criminal Law Revision Committee deals with reform of the Criminal law.

Reform initiated by such bodies includes the Theft Act 1968, the Courts Act 1971 and the Foreign Limitation Periods Act 1984.

b *Social legislation*

This form of legislation deals with wider and often more fundamental issues than simple revision of the substantive law. It often involves a wholesale abolition of existing principles and the creation of a new system or structure of rules, eg major reforms of taxation – such as the creation of capital transfer tax in the Finance Act 1975 (consolidated in the Capital Transfer Tax Act 1984). Whilst some minor revisions of the law (and some major, such as the new approach to tax planning – *Furniss* v *Dawson* [1984] 2 WLR 226 HL) are carried out by the courts, particularly the House of Lords, social reform is almost wholly outside the scope of the activities of the judiciary. Indeed, it is not in a position to take such steps (see Lord Scarman's dictum above) and the judges are not democratically acceptable as instigators of social reform – even if their generally and necessarily conservative stance permitted them so to be.

Social reforms, such as the creation of new rules governing landlord and tenant (eg Landlord and Tenant Act 1954, Rent Act 1977) are often matters of great political (and moral, eg reform of sexual offences) controversy. Indeed the judiciary may often find such reforms difficult to operate, because of the new ideas they contain and the new concepts they employ. For example, the Leasehold Reform Act 1967 which permits tenants, in certain circumstances, to 'enfranchise' their leases, ie force their landlords to sell them the freehold, has given rise to not only controversy but legal difficulties of implementation (largely in the County Court which has exclusive first instance jurisdiction in this area).

c *Consolidation*

It often happens that when Parliament enacts a statute on a particular topic (eg the parts of the Finance Act 1975 dealing with Capital Transfer Tax), the new law requires amendment which is dealt with by subsequent statutes – and additions and deletions are made as the effects and problems of the new law become apparent with time. A consolidating statute is one which brings together all the statutory provisions on a given topic and, together with any consequential amendments, puts them into one statute, such as the Inheritance Tax Act 1984 amending and consolidating the capital transfer tax provisions.

d *Codification*

In areas of the law which are well developed and the principles of which are well worked-out in a body of case law and statute, statutes are sometimes enacted which bring together all the rules (both common law and statutory) and present them in a single statutory code. From thenceforth, the new statute is the starting-point in that area of the law and case law will, in time, build up around the codified provisions. See, for example, the Criminal Law Act 1977 (conspiracy), the Criminal Attempts Acts 1981 and the Police and Criminal Evidence Act 1984.

Areas of law which are still developing (eg the tort of negligence) are obviously unfit for such treatment since it remains to be seen how new developments work in practice.

The operation of statutes

Geographical operation

There is a presumption that an Act of Parliament is operative throughout the United Kingdom but nowhere else unless a contrary intention appears in the Act, though often law reform statutes extend only to England and Wales since Scotland and Northern Ireland have separate systems of law.

Temporal operation

A statute comes into force on the day it receives the Royal Assent unless some other date is specified in the Act itself. Very commonly now Acts provide that they are to come into force on 'a day to be appointed' usually by a Minister or by Order in Council (ie by Statutory Instrument).

Often sections of an Act are brought into operation at different times, eg Civil Jurisdiction and Judgments Act 1982, parts of which have only at the beginning of 1987 been brought into operation. While administratively convenient this practice makes it difficult for lawyers and others to determine the law exactly.

There is a presumption against retrospective operation except for certain financial and revenue statutes: *R v Fisher* [1969] 1 All ER 100 and *Wilson v Dagnall* [1972] 1 QB 509.

Obsolescence

A statute never becomes ineffective due to the passage of time and, if it is desired that it should no longer be in force, it must be repealed, unless it was stated to be for a fixed period, or for a particular purpose, long since gone. Repeal must be by statute, and can be either express or implied, implied repeal of an earlier statute being the result of an enactment of a later inconsistent statute. Since 1965 the Law Commission has been systematically reviewing the statute book and repealing obsolete statutes in regular Statute Law Repeal Acts. As a result, generally only effective legislation remains in force.

Criticisms of existing legislative methods

In 1975, the Report of the Renton committee, *The Preparation of Legislation*, set out the major problems with existing legislation.

Statutory language is often too complex and obscure and the meaning and effect of the language is uncertain.

The desire for certainty often leads to over-elaboration since it tries to cover every contingency to deal with possible future circumstances.

The structure of Acts is often neither logical nor helpful. *Renton* suggested that the main purpose of a bill should be made clear very early on so that both Parliament and the courts would be able to understand more readily the purpose of the intended legislation and be able to interpret it once enacted. Intention is very rarely expressly set out.

Renton suggested:

a the use of more trained draftsmen;

b the use of statements of principle, with detailed guidance in schedules;

c complexity of language should be avoided;

d the use of more statements of the purpose of enactments;

e supervision of statute law by the Statute Law Committee with regular reports.

Amendment is not always simple, and Acts and further Acts are enacted to amend existing legislation. Accordingly, it is not always easy to ascertain the current law in a given area since there are a number of different statutory provisions governing that area.

Further criticisms (many similar to *Renton's*) were made by *Sir William Dale* in *Legislative Drafting – A New Approach* (1977). He contrasted the complexity and detail of English statutory drafting with the more succinct continental approach which deals in much broader terms of principle and intention – leaving details of application to the courts. *Dale* also pointed out that there was no adequate body to review draft legislation. Amongst his suggestions were:

a reduce complexity by being more general and concise, worrying less about detail. A statute should deal with principle first, then set out the detail;

b an advisory body should be set up to consider draft bills;

c more advice from experts on the given topic should be taken, rather than simply that of drafting experts;

d a Parliamentary Committee should be set up to examine legislation before it reaches Parliament.

Renton disagreed with certain of *Dale's* proposals, (b) on the basis that such matters were best left to the relevant government departments and (d) on the footing that it would place an additional strain on Parliamentary resources. Very little has been done to implement any of these proposals. Indeed, the government specifically rejected (e) (*Renton*) – giving no reasons.

Mechanisms of law reform

The process

The problem of keeping the law abreast of changing times and values faces every legal system. *Norman Marsh* (*Law Reform in the United Kingdom*) 1971 proposed five considerations which suggest that English law cannot rely on judge-made law as the main instrument of law reforms.

a Judge-made reforms are dependent *only* on the issue coming before the courts, and more particularly on the issue reaching where the judge is prepared to overrule or distinguish any difficult or awkward precedent.

b Complex cases make not so much, bad law, but *more* law. The judge merely prepares the way for further litigation.

c The 'reforming' decision may be extremely unjust to the losing party. The danger of injustice was emphasised by the House of Lords in a 1966 Practice Statement.

d The fifth consideration involves recognising the importance of 'stare decisis' – the doctrine of precedent.

e The Court generally relies on arguments presented by counsel for the parties. It does not have the opportunity to consult with interested bodies as to what type of reform is most needed or most beneficial.

> 'The courts are not helped as they could and ought to be in the adaptation of law to justice. The reason ... is because there is no one whose business it is to give warning that help is needed ... Some agency must be found to mediate between the legislature and the courts.' *Benjamin Cardozo*, Judge, New York 1921.

Reforming bodies

The responsibility for the law in general and its administration is divided between the Home Secretary and the Lord Chancellor. It is a somewhat complex division: the Home Secretary is concerned with the criminal law, preventing offences, catching offenders, part of the process of trying them and virtually all treatment of offenders. The Lord Chancellor is concerned with the composition of all courts, parts of civil procedure and everything which relates to procedural criminal law. Other departments have responsibility for certain parts of the law. (For example, the Department of the Environment is responsible for housing, planning, transport and local government.) There is too much work involved for the staff of the Lord Chancellor and Home Secretary to undertake. When one considers the steady increase of legislation from Victorian times to the present day; it is obvious that the present system is slowly failing. Although ad hoc committees have been created from time to time to carry out the investigations necessary for the formulation of new legislation, this can only be a stop-gap measure.

Parliamentary law making (1) | 10

Introduction

In chapter 9 we considered the process of legislation and some of the mechanisms for law reform. We shall develop those themes in this chapter paying particular attention to the pressures that lead to legislative activity and the agencies for law reform in this country.

Pressures producing legislation

Legislation, which must be regarded now as the principal source of law, is effected by or with the authority of Parliament. In this section we shall examine the pressures that tend to produce particular types and pieces of legislation. We shall consider the factors as follows:

Political parties

It is hardly surprising that political parties can be regarded as the prime moving force in producing legislation. The manifestos of political parties outline their proposals for legislative programmes at every general election. In theory they seek a mandate on the basis of these manifestos although the reality is quite different as they are in no way bound by such a 'mandate' and the manifestos are drafted in suitably wide language as to be almost incapable of precise definition.

In this country, with but a few major national parties, it can be stated that every party is in effect a coalition of various views and that the policy making processes in each of these parties can be seen as the pressures for priority of one view over another. Some parties are more vocal in their internecine squabbles than others but in all the process is more or less the same. Each section of the political party represents particular views and interests. It would be pointless to list these as they may be prone to change through time. (Perhaps the most controversial are the privatisation of services such as electricity and water.) This is seen as an article of faith by certain powerful sections of the ruling party. This is an example of legislation for reasons of ideology. There are also examples of legislation which fit a certain ideology but which are seen as a reaction to certain events rather than as part of a larger plan. An example of this may be the Public Order Act 1986 which can be seen as a response to the massive violence that ensued during the Coal Miner's strike of 1984.

The amount of legislation which results from such party political pressure is surprisingly small – perhaps no more than ten per cent of the total volume. The largest volume is routine, eg Finance Act, on the raising of taxes and other fiscal matters.

Pressure groups

Some legislation may be heavily influenced by pressure groups. Whereas political parties can be seen as wide coalitions, pressure groups are narrower having merely a single or a few items on their agenda. Some pressure groups are highly effective, others less so. They will lobby members of parliament with a view to getting their items on the legislative agenda – they compete with each other for parliamentary time and attention. Perhaps the most powerful are those that represent the interests of the legal profession as they can almost certainly secure legislation to give effect to their wishes – probably due to the large proportion of lawyers in parliament. *Dugdale et al* in their book on *A Level Law* cite as an example The Law Society having secured greater disciplinary powers to itself over the solicitors' profession. Although they have failed to prevent many of the Lord Chancellor's proposals for reform of the legal profession, which will be dealt with later.

Other pressure groups may adopt so called 'moral campaigns' such as the National Viewers and Listeners organisation inspired by Mrs Whitehouse – who must rank as one of the most effective lobbyists of recent times. Their agenda includes the eradication of any pornography including violence and abusive language from the broadcasting media. Again there is little attempt to prove the connection between so called pornography and violence in the real world, but the issue has been made so emotive that in order to counter argue their case opponents are almost forced to support pornography.

In a democracy the role of such pressure groups freely allowed to campaign cannot be overstated.

It would really be the function of a course on government and politics to take this matter much further. The organisation/functions/effectiveness of pressure groups is not primarily a legal concern.

The Civil Service

Although hardly recognised as a pressure group, and perhaps that is its strength, the civil service is nonetheless assigned the task of implementing legislation. More than that the ministers of the government rely very heavily on their senior civil servants for information and advice on the options open to the government on any given matter. Although highly professional, and as neutral (in the party political sense) as it may be possible to be, the civil service does engage in a policy role in the legislative process. In explaining the options, emphasis can be given to that favoured by the institution itself – it would be a well informed and courageous minister who would consistently act in direct contravention of the advice of his senior civil service staff. Perhaps because of the continuity of their service – not being political appointees changing with any change in the governing party – the civil servants can formulate and pursue their own goals. To suggest that a body as large and as powerful as the Civil Service has no such goals is considered naive.

Agencies for law reform and reforming bodies

It has already been noted in the previous chapter that *Marsh* has suggested a number of reasons why law reform cannot be left as the sole responsibility of judges and the court system.

It was also noted that pressure of work means that the Lord Chancellor's department alone cannot cope with the necessary background work to formulate proposals for new bills to put before Parliament. In the next two sections we shall look at the role of certain types of committee in the field of law reform.

Standing committees

In 1959 the Home Secretary set up the Criminal Law Revision Committee to examine such aspects of criminal law as the Home Secretary may from time to time refer to it. The first important reference was the law of larceny and similar offences which resulted in the Theft Act 1968. The Lord Chancellor has the Statute Law Commission, the Law Reform Commission and the Commission on Private International Law. The Law Reform commission was set up in 1953 and has to consider what changes are necessary in legal doctrines which are referred to it having special regard to judicial decisions. It produces a report most years and has been responsible for much important legislation including the Occupiers Liability Act 1957, the Misrepresentation Act 1967 and the Civil Evidence Act 1968.

Ad hoc committees

Over the last 100 years many changes in law have been based on the reports of Royal Commissions or official committees. They are made up of a wide cross section of people who are often experts or are concerned in the matters in question. These committees are impartial and non-political. However, the members are not sitting full time and so they are slow and not suitable for matters requiring long term continuing examination. The committee makes recommendations which must be considered by the Minister concerned and if he is satisfied proposals are put before Parliament.

In 1963 Lord Gardiner proposed the setting up of a permanent law reforming body. In 1965 the Law Commission was set up under the Law Commissioners Act 1965. Two full time committees were set up one for England and one for Scotland. Section 3(1) provides that:

'It shall be the duty of each of the commissions to take and keep under review all the law with which they are respectively concerned with a view to its systematic development and reform, including in particular the codification of such law, the elimination of anomalies, the repeal of obsolete and unnecessary enactments, the reduction of the number of separate enactments and generally the simplification and modernisation of the law.'

There is a duty to promote but not a mandate to perform. Five commissioners are appointed by the Lord Chancellor from those appearing 'to be suitably qualified by the holding of judicial office or by experience as a barrister or a solicitor or as a teacher of law in a University.'

The Commission produces a working paper outlining aspects of special concern, courses open and its own provisional conclusions. These are then made available to organisations and individuals and comment is invited. Several reports are produced each year. The Animals Act 1971 and the Powers of Attorney Act 1971 are amongst the legislation to have resulted from this body (NB one important report not legislated is the Interpretation of Statutes). A programme for reform is also published approximately every three years. 'Justice', the British section of the International Commission of Jurists (a self appointed body), issues reports regularly on areas needing reform.

A ministry of justice in Britain?

Outside the United Kingdom this is very common.

In Britain, there is no such ministry. If there were its functions might be shared between the following:

a   Lord Chancellor to be responsible for the courts.

b   Home Secretary to be responsible for police and prisons.

c   Attorney-General to be responsible for giving the Government legal advice.

d   Director of Public Prosecutions to be responsible for criminal prosecutions.

e   Representatives of the two branches of the legal profession which would make their own arrangements for the education and training and discipline of lawyers.

The creation of a Law Commission has weakened the argument that a Ministry of Justice is needed to facilitate law reform. However, an uncomfortable division of function remains. Opponents of the idea claim that the danger to the legal system would be that it would rest under the control of a Minister in the House of Commons.

Proposals for such a Ministry date back to 1918. Yet 'successive holders of office have testified that it is beyond the strength of any one man to perform the work that ought to be done.' (Jackson).

It has always been difficult to get government attention on law reform, yet it was suggested several decades ago that perhaps the Home Secretary could be Minister in charge, by transferring certain Home Office work to other departments leaving the Minister with his present duties namely: legal administration.

If so, ought such a minister to sit in the House of Commons? There is always the fear that 'justice' would come under his control.

Parliamentary law making (2) | 11

Introduction

In chapter 9 we considered the process of statute creation. That section should be referred to in this chapter as it is also relevant. The doctrine of parliamentary sovereignty means that the Queen in Parliament can make or unmake any law. The courts cannot question the validity of this primary legislation, either on its merits, or on the grounds of procedural impropriety, even when the allegation is one of fraud: *British Railways Board* v *Pickin* [1974] AC 765.

Despite the ever increasing volume of primary legislation, the complexities of governing modern society necessitates the delegation of legislative functions to inferior bodies, such as ministers and local authorities. Clearly Parliament simply does not have the time or resources to enact in the form of primary legislation, which can be fully debated and scrutinised by both Houses, every single piece of legislation that is needed. The result is subordinate (or delegated) legislation, that is legislation produced by an inferior body which nevertheless has the force of law.

The reasons for subordinate legislation

Pressure upon parliamentary time

The formal procedure for enacting legislation can be both slow and cumbersome. If Parliament itself attempted to enact all the legislation necessary to govern the United Kingdom, the legislative machinery would break down. By delegating the formulation of detailed rules and regulations to subordinate authorities, Parliament can concentrate its attention on discussing the essential principles of legislation. Delegated legislation saves parliamentary time.

The need to deal with future contingencies

When a new piece of legislation is being enacted, Parliament cannot foresee all the possible contingencies that may affect the operation of that particular statute in the future. By delegating power to the relevant minister to introduce new measures to deal with unforeseen situations that may arise, Parliament avoids the need for amending legislation to be enacted and thus enhances both the speed and flexibility of the legislative process.

Technical content

Few Members of Parliament have the expert knowledge necessary effectively to scrutinise highly technical legislation. It may be more effective to leave such legislation to be made by the appropriate minister in consultation with his expert advisers and other interested parties. This procedure also avoids Acts of Parliament becoming a mass of highly complex and unintelligible detail.

Emergency

In times of war or other emergency the Government may need to act quickly and in excess of its normal powers. For example, an Act of Parliament could not be passed in a short enough time to provide the response needed to control an outbreak of foot and mouth disease among cattle. In cases involving matters of great national importance Parliament should clearly have the opportunity to consider what action is to be taken. It is argued, however, that it is vital for Parliament to arm the Executive in advance to meet emergencies that might arise. Thus, following the unilateral declaration of independence by the Government of Southern Rhodesia in 1965, Parliament, by the Southern Rhodesia Act 1965, granted wide legislative powers enabling the Queen in Council to take whatever steps were necessary in order to bring about the resumption of lawful government in the colony.

Classification of subordinate legislation

Subordinate legislation may be classified:

a   according to purpose; or

b   according to procedure.

Classification according to purpose

Regulations for the purpose of bringing a statute into operation
Some statutory instruments are designed to bring into force the whole or part of an Act of Parliament which for some reason it is not desired to put into effect immediately upon Royal Assent. There may be more than one of these Commencement Orders per Act (the Town and Country Planning Act 1971 had 75 such Orders) and there is in general no requirement as to the time after Royal Assent in which such an Order must be brought in (for example the Easter Act 1928 has not yet had a Commencement Order made).

Regulations for the purpose of amending statutory provisions
For example the European Communities Act 1972, s2(2) delegates power to give effect to Community obligations. Orders in Council and ministerial regulations made under these delegated powers have the effect of Acts of Parliament and may be made even where they conflict with Acts of Parliament.

Regulations which add to, explain, or give effect to general statutory provisions or which define terms referred to in the parent Act

Regulations for the purpose of clothing a Statute

The general principles of a piece of legislation may be expounded in the 'framework' statute, but it is left to the subordinate authority to clothe that statute, by means of delegated legislation, with the detail necessary to give it effect. 'Framework' acts have become increasingly common, because of pressures on Parliamentary time.

Classification according to procedure ie the way of implementing the law making power

The main kinds of delegated legislation are:

Orders in Council

These are the oldest and most 'dignified' form of delegated legislation, and are made by the Queen 'by and with the advice of Her Majesty's Privy Council'. Only those Orders in Council made under Statutory authority may be classified as delegated legislation, and they must be distinguished from those Orders in Council made under the Royal Prerogative.

Ministerial regulations

Ministers of the Crown may be empowered to make regulations and issue directions, rules and orders relating to matters within their departmental jurisdiction. The Rules Committee of the Supreme Court also has power, under the Supreme Court Act 1981, to make Rules of the Supreme Court. These have the same status as ministerial regulations.

Local authority and other by-laws

These comprise rules made by local authorities and other statutory undertakers, for example the British Railways Board, for the regulation, administration or management of the district or service administered by the authority or undertaking concerned.

Miscellaneous categories

These include local authority orders (for example compulsory purchase orders), and measures taken by the General Synod of the Church of England.

Creation of subordinate legislation

Originally the only provisions regulating the methods by which a law making power could be exercised by the minister or other body to whom the power had been entrusted by Parliament were those contained in the parent statute. The Rules Publication Act 1893 made provision for certain kinds of subordinate legislation to be numbered, printed and sold by the Queen's printer. Before that date, although it was not uncommon for enabling statutes to make provision for notification and sometimes publication in the London Gazette, no general requirements as to notification existed. The Act provided that notice of the proposal to make any subordinate legislation to which it applied should be given at least forty days in advance in the London Gazette. During those forty days any public body was to have the opportunity of obtaining a copy of the proposed subordinate legislation and of making representations or suggestions on it.

The Act went some way toward curing the confusion and resentment caused by the lack of information about new subordinate legislation, but it failed to go far enough. It applied only to 'statutory rules' as defined in s4 and that definition was a narrow one. As a result a great deal of subordinate legislation still came into effect without prior notification and publication.

The Statutory Instruments Act 1946, which came into operation generally on 1 January 1948 applies to a wider range of instruments, but by no means to all subordinate legislation. It repealed the Rules Publication Act 1893; defined the new expression 'statutory instrument' (s1) and made new provision as to the printing and publication of statutory instruments (s2). A number of provisions were introduced relating to Parliamentary control over the making of statutory instruments (ss4, 5 and 6).

Statutory instruments

The term 'statutory instrument' is a comprehensive expression which describes all those categories of subordinate legislation subject to the Statutory Instruments Act 1946.

Section 1(1) of the 1946 Act provides:

'Where by this Act or any Act passed after the commencement of this Act power to make, confirm or approve orders, rules, regulations or other subordinate legislation is conferred on His Majesty in Council or on any Minister of the Crown then, if the power is expressed –

a) in the case of a power conferred on His Majesty, to be exercisable by Order in Council;
b) in the case of a power conferred on a Minister of the Crown, to be exercisable by statutory instrument,

any document by which that power is exercised shall be known as a "statutory instrument" and the provisions of this Act shall apply thereto accordingly.'

The effect of this is that if the delegated power conferred in the parent statute does not come within the categories described in s1(1) it is not a statutory instrument for the purposes of the Act and the provisions of the Act as to laying before Parliament and publication do not apply. Even where the 1946 Act does apply, the precise laying procedure to be followed will still be determined by the parent statute. Therefore, after the 1946 Act there are two different methods of creating subordinate legislation, within the 1946 Act and outside it. If the 1946 Act applies, its provisions as to laying before Parliament and publicity must be followed unless other provision is made in the parent statute. Where the 1946 Act does not apply, the regulations and procedures for making the subordinate legislation will be found in the parent statute.

Control of subordinate legislation

There are four main ways in which control may be exercised over subordinate legislation:

a pre-drafting consultation;

b parliamentary proceedings;

c judicial review;

d publicity.

Pre-drafting consultation

As the creation of subordinate legislation is a legislative function, the authority for which has been delegated by Parliament, the rules of natural justice do not apply, and failure to consult parties likely to be affected does not amount to a breach of natural justice: *Bates v Lord Hailsham* [1972] 1 WLR 1373. However, see *R v Secretary of State for Health, ex parte United States Tobacco International Inc* [1991] 3 WLR 529 and note the desirability of 'fairness and candour' (see 'Judicial review' following). It is the general practice that before regulations are made by a Department, prior consultation takes place with advisory bodies and other groups with an interest in the proposed legislation. Very often the parent Statute makes such consultation obligatory. Often the body to be consulted will be specifically named in the Statute. For example ss10 and 11 of the Tribunal and Inquiries Act 1971 provides that the power to make procedural rules for any of the tribunals listed in Schedule 1 to the Act may not be exercised by a Minister except after consultation with the Council on Tribunals. In some statutes the requirement to consult may be stated more generally, requiring: 'such consultation as the minister thinks appropriate with such organisations as appear to him to represent the interest concerned'. In addition there are many examples of ministers voluntarily consulting with outside interests before exercising the power to make subordinate legislation.

While there is no statutory definition of 'consultation', where consultation is required by statute, any consultation which takes place must be genuine. If the consultation is not adequate then any subordinate legislation subsequently made will be invalid on the grounds of procedural ultra vires. See *Agricultural, Horticultural and Forestry Training Board v Aylesbury Mushrooms Ltd* [1972] 1 WLR 190. However, if the bodies specified in the statute are consulted, they cannot challenge the validity of any instrument made on the grounds that their views were not accepted or adopted by the minister.

Parliamentary proceedings

Two of the reasons for delegating legislative powers are the need to relieve the pressure on parliamentary time and the fact that often the nature of the subject matter of the legislation is highly technical. If Parliament therefore had to examine each instrument in detail, it would defeat the main objects of delegating the legislative power in the first place. However, some parliamentary control is exercised; the actual procedure depending upon the terms of the parent statute.

The parent statute may or may not require the instrument to be laid before Parliament. Some statutory instruments are not subject to any parliamentary procedure. They therefore simply become law on the date stated in them. Such instruments are, in general, not contentious nor often particularly important. But, even if there is no requirement as to laying, a Member of Parliament may still raise the matter in debate or put down a question about it to the responsible minister.

Usually, however, the parent statute provides that an instrument shall be laid, or laid in draft, before Parliament, subject to the negative resolution procedure. Under this procedure the instrument is laid before Parliament and will become law on the date specified in it. However the instrument will be nullified if either House (the Commons only, in the case of instruments dealing with financial matters) passes a motion calling for its annulment within a certain time (usually 40 days during periods when Parliament is sitting). Such a motion, known as a prayer, usually takes the following form: 'That a humble address be presented to Her Majesty praying that the (name of instrument) be annulled.'

Any Member may put down a motion to annul a statutory instrument subject to the negative resolution procedure. Such motions are now generally put down as Early Days Motions, that is, motions for which no time has been fixed, and in the vast majority of cases, for which no time is likely to be available. An annulment motion put down by a backbencher is not certain to be dealt with. However, a motion put down by the Official Opposition will usually be accommodated, though there is no absolute certainty of this. Broadly speaking, if an instrument does arouse comment or interest then it is fairly likely that it will be discussed in some form.

The provisions of the Parliament Acts 1911–1949 do not apply to subordinate legislation. Instruments (with the exception of those dealing with financial matters) may therefore be vetoed by the House of Lords. For example, in 1968 the House of Lords rejected an order imposing sanctions against the Rhodesian Government made under the Southern Rhodesia Act 1965.

In the case of some instruments the parent Acts require them to be laid, or laid in draft, before Parliament, subject to an affirmative resolution of one or both Houses. Unless a Motion approving the instrument is passed within the period specified in the parent Act (commonly 28 or 40 days) the instrument ceases to have effect or, if laid in draft, cannot be made. The affirmative resolution procedure is used only for the most important instruments, for example those of special constitutional importance. As a vote has to be taken on the motion to affirm the instrument, time must be made available by the Government for debate and any opposition to the Instrument may then be raised. It is very rare however for the Government not to obtain a majority when a vote is taken on an Instrument in the Commons.

Statutory instruments cannot, except in extremely rare instances where the parent Act provides otherwise, be amended or adapted by either House. The House simply expresses its wish for them to be annulled or passed into law, as the case may be.

By s4 of the Statutory Instruments Act 1946 where an instrument must be laid before Parliament after being made, it must generally be laid before it comes into operation. Where however it is essential for the instrument to become operative at once, the reason must be notified to the Lord Chancellor and the Speaker forthwith.

Note that certain parent statutes require an instrument to be laid before Parliament 'for information only'. The only value this has would appear to be that, if at all unusual or apparently ultra vires, it will presumably arouse interest, and be the subject of questioning by MPs.

Standing Committees on statutory instruments

The House of Commons has in recent years found difficulty in making time available for the debate of statutory instruments. These debates, normally on motions to approve or annul instruments, may take place on the floor of the House (they are commonly but not exclusively taken late at night), or in one of the Standing Committees on Statutory Instruments. They were first set up in the 1973–74 session in order to relieve pressure of time in the House itself, and are quite distinct from the Joint Select Committees on Statutory Instruments. Standing Committees on Statutory Instruments are commonly composed of 17 members, though any member may attend and speak (but not vote). Only ministers may make a motion to commit an instrument to a Standing Committee, and the instrument will be referred to such a Committee only if fewer than 20 members object to such a course when the referral motion is made in the Chamber.

Joint Committee on Statutory Instruments

To assist the parliamentary examination of statutory instruments there is a Joint Committee of both Houses on Statutory Instruments. The Committee consists of seven members appointed from each House, of whom two are a quorum. The members from the Commons sit separately to scrutinise those instruments which are laid only in the Commons. They have the services of Counsel to Mr Speaker and the Lord Chairman of Committees available to them in their deliberations. They may, like other select committees, take oral or written evidence from the responsible Government department on instruments they are considering.

The terms of reference of the committee are to consider all statutory instruments of a general nature and all other instruments which, under the parent statute were laid or laid in draft before Parliament, with a view to deciding whether the special attention of the Houses should be drawn to an instrument on any of the following grounds:

a that it imposes a charge on the public revenues or contains provisions requiring payments to be made to the Exchequer or any Government department or to any local or public authority in consideration of any licence or consent, or of any services to be rendered, or prescribes the amount of any such charge or payments;

b that it is made in pursuance of an enactment containing specific provisions excluding it from challenge in the courts, either at all times or after the expiration of a specified period;

c that it purports to have retrospective effect where the parent Statute confers no express authority so to provide;

d that there appears to have been unjustifiable delay in the publication or in the laying of it before Parliament;

e that there appears to have been unjustifiable delay in sending a notification under the proviso to s4(1) of the Statutory Instruments Act 1946, where an instrument has come into operation before it has been laid before Parliament;

f that there appears to be a doubt whether it is intra vires or that it appears to make some unusual or unexpected use of the powers under which it was made;

g that for any special reason its form or purport calls for elucidation;

h that its drafting appears to be defective.

The committee may also report on an instrument on any ground 'which does not impinge on its merits or on the policy behind it; and to report their decisions with the reason thereof in any particular case.'

The committee may not consider the merits of any instrument and an opportunity must be provided for the department concerned to put its case before an adverse report on any instrument is made. While the report of the committee itself has no effect upon a particular instrument, it does draw the attention of members to the instrument and they may then pray for its annulment or oppose the affirmative resolution.

Other opportunities for scrutiny

Parliament may also exercise some control over the creation of subordinate legislation when the parent statute is being debated by the House of Commons, or the House of Lords. Members can consider:

a whether a minister needs to be given powers to issue subordinate legislation. If he does:

b the form that the subordinate legislation will take, ie whether by statutory instrument or circular;

c if by statutory instrument they can demand that one of the laying procedures be followed;

d generally whether a minister is being given any wide or unusual powers.

Other measures

No formal parliamentary procedure exists for the scrutiny of other forms of subordinate legislation, such as circulars, guidelines and codes of conduct, etc. However the traditional methods of control, such as questions to ministers, etc, may be utilised to draw attention to apparent irregularities or excesses.

Judicial review

Unlike primary legislation, subordinate legislation may be reviewed by the courts and where necessary may be declared invalid. Note, for example, the recent case of *R v Secretary of State for Health, ex parte United States Tobacco International Inc* [1991] 3 WLR 529 in which the validity of subordinate legislation was the subject of judicial review. It was held that the Minister had acted unfairly in not consulting fully with the manufacturers of oral snuff, that the statutory consultation period was inadequate, and that the firm should have been given full opportunity to know and respond to the evidence on which the government had relied. 'Fairness demanded (the firm) be treated with candour.' An order of certiorari was granted and the regulations were quashed. This seems to be only a whisker away from taking into account that the rules of natural justice, although it has always been stated (see above) that the rules of natural justice need not be taken into account in enacting subordinate legislation. In the absence of any express exclusion in the parent statute, the doctrine of ultra vires will operate so as to contain the making of subordinate legislation within its legal bounds. However it should be remembered that judicial review as a means of controlling undesirable delegated legislation is, to say the least, haphazard. The 'review' in question is not on any regular or wholesale basis, but depends entirely on an individual challenging one particular statutory instrument (or a part thereof). It would not be at all unlikely for a court to decide that, for example, a by-law is unreasonable and ultra vires years after its enactment. It has not suddenly become so, it is simply that for the first time an individual has chosen to challenge the by-law in question. It would be equally possible of course for no such challenge to occur and for the by-law (ultra vires or not) to affect the lives of other individuals who are not so questioning (or, more likely, lack the financial resources) and therefore do not challenge the operation of the by-law in question. This hit-and-miss system of challenge hardly merits the use of the word 'review'. However, it is true that once challenged in courts a statutory instrument may be thoroughly reviewed by the courts and all aspects of it examined with a view to testing its legality.

Procedural ultra vires

One ground upon which an individual may seek to challenge the validity of subordinate legislation is that the procedure laid down in the parent statute and/or the Statutory Instruments Act 1946 for making, laying and publishing the measure in question, has not been complied with.

In this respect the courts classify these procedural requirements as either mandatory or directory. Non-compliance with a mandatory requirement will render the Instrument invalid. If however the requirement is merely directory, failure to comply with it will not usually affect the validity of the Instrument.

Difficulty may arise however in ascertaining which procedural requirements are likely to be construed by the courts as mandatory and which as directory.

In *Agricultural, Horticultural and Forestry Training Board* v *Aylesbury Mushrooms Ltd* [1972] 1 WLR 190, failure to comply with a statutory requirement as to consultation resulted in the order being declared invalid.

But, in *Bailey* v *Williamson* (1873) LR 8 QB 118 a conviction under the Rules made pursuant to the Parks Regulation Act 1872 was upheld, even though at the time, the Rules had not been laid before Parliament because of the Summer recess. The court found that the Rules did not depend upon the laying procedures for their validity, and that consequently such procedural requirements were merely directory.

Judicial review of circulars, etc

As will have been noted above the validity of statutory instruments can be challenged in the courts. Is the same true of material such as circulars, codes of practice and ministerial guidelines? The problem is that if, as is often suggested, such material has no legal status, it need not be challenged to assess its validity since, in theory, it can be ignored anyway. There have been a number of cases which attempt to deal with the problem, probably the most recent is *R* v *Secretary of State for Social Services, ex parte Stitt* (1990) The Times 23 February. It is clear that the courts consider ministerial directives much closer to the narrow concept of delegated legislation and they are more likely to scrutinise such directives more closely than say, routine circulars. This is especially true where the parent Act makes no further provision for any requirement for Parliamentary approval of such directives. On the topic of routine circulars, leaflets etc, it is useful to look at at *R* v *Secretary of State for the Environment, ex parte Greenwich LBC* (1989) The Times 17 May.

Substantive ultra vires

Challenge for substantive ultra vires is usually based on the ground that the measure in question goes beyond what was envisaged by Parliament in the parent Statute or, contrary to the intention of Parliament, purports to be of retrospective effect or sub-delegate the legislative power conferred.

The case of *Commissioners of Customs and Excise* v *Cure and Deeley Ltd* [1962] 1 QB 340 is relevant here. The Finance (No 2) Act 1940 empowered the Commissioners to make regulations providing 'for any matter for which provision appears to them necessary for the purpose of giving effect to the Act'. The Commissioners, purporting to act under this provision, had made a regulation under which they could determine the amount of tax due from the tax payer in the event of a tax return being submitted late. The High Court invalidated the regulations, inter alia, on the grounds that the Commissioners were only empowered to collect the amount of tax due at law, not the amount they thought fit. They had, therefore, purported to give themselves power by way of subordinate legislation going far beyond what was envisaged by Parliament when it passed the parent statute.

Partial invalidity

In some circumstances the courts may be prepared to uphold part of a statutory instrument, or to limit the scope of its application so as to render it intra vires.

In *DPP* v *Hutchinson; R* v *Secretary of State for Defence, ex parte Parker; R* v *Same ex parte Hayman* [1989] 3 WLR 281 the court was faced with delegated legislation (a by-law) which covered more than was permitted by the empowering Act. Schiemann J noted that the court could adopt a number of possible approaches:

a   never to enforce any part of the subordinate legislation;

b   only to enforce those parts of the subordinate legislation permitted by the empowering Act, but to do so consistently;

c   to enforce such parts of the subordinate legislation permitted by the empowering Act as seem appropriate according to the court's discretion.

In certain circumstances the court would reduce the ambit of the decision so as to preserve those parts of it which were intra vires – this would only be done where the court was sure that the altered decision represented that which the decision maker would have made had he appreciated the limitation on his powers. (On the facts this meant that the defendants could be lawfully convicted of an offence against a by-law which was wider than permitted by the enabling statute because, had the by-law been drawn only as widely as the enabling Act authorised, the persons charged would still have been properly convicted.)

After noting that similar issues had been considered in the cases of *Dunkley* v *Evans* [1981] 1 WLR 1522 and *Thames Water Authority* v *Elmbridge Borough Council* [1983] 1 QB 570 he said that: 'It is clear that the approach I have adopted is stricter as against the by-law maker than that warranted by these two cases. If I have erred, I have erred in favour of those challenging the by-law.'

It may therefore be that the courts are moving towards a more stringent application of the ultra vires doctrine as applied to delegated legislation generally. Note, however, that the court felt that it had the jurisdiction to effectively 're-write' those parts of the by-law which were not ultra vires so as to preserve them. This is an approach which courts have not, before, taken and in this respect represents a departure from established practice.

Publicity

Ignorance of the law is no excuse. However, given the great volume of subordinate legislation, that doctrine can operate so as to cause severe hardship, especially as an instrument may have legal effect before it is published. Generally, however, departments try to ensure that instruments do not come into operation for twenty one days after being laid before Parliament. A uniform procedure for numbering, printing, publishing and citing statutory instruments has also been laid down by the Statutory Instruments Act 1946, s2. However certain instruments, such as local Acts, temporary instruments, or those where publication before coming into operation would be contrary to the public interest, may be exempt in whole or part from the publication requirements of the 1946 Act.

Section 3(2) of the Statutory Instruments Act 1946 provides a defence of non-publication:

> 'In any proceedings against any person for an offence consisting of a contravention of any such statutory instrument, it shall be a defence to prove that the instrument had not been issued by His Majesty's Stationery Office at the date of the alleged contravention unless it is proved that at the date reasonable steps had been taken for the purpose of bringing the purport of the instrument to the notice of the public, or to persons likely to be affected by it, or of the person charged.'

By-laws

By-laws comprise rules made by local authorities and other statutory undertakers, for example British Railways Board, for the regulation, administration or management of the area or service administered by the authority or undertaking concerned. Many by-laws will give rise to criminal liability if violated.

The making of by-laws by local authorities is governed by the Local Government Act 1972. This provides that by-laws must be:

a made under the common seal of the local authority;

b advertised in the local press at least one month before confirmation;

c confirmed by the appropriate Minister;

d available for local inspection.

The making of by-laws by other bodies is usually governed by similar provisions laid down in the parent statute.

By-laws are subject to review by the courts in the same way and for the same reasons as other categories of subordinate legislation. However, in addition to these general grounds of review by-laws will also be void if they are:

Uncertain or vague as to their object or terms

In *Nash* v *Finlay* (1901) 85 LT 682 the court declared void for uncertainty by-laws prohibiting 'wilfully annoying passengers in the street'.

Unreasonable

In *Kruse* v *Johnson* [1898] 2 QB 91 the Divisional Court declined to declare a by-law to be invalid on the ground of unreasonableness, but accepted that such a challenge was possible. The Lord Chief Justice suggested that a by-law could be invalidated if it was found to be partial and unequal in operation as between different classes; manifestly unjust; disclosed bad faith; or involved an oppressive and gratuitous interference with the rights of individuals.

Contrary to statute

Unlike statutory instruments by-laws can never include a power to amend statutes.

Criticisms of subordinate legislation

The main criticisms of subordinate legislation are as follows:

Matters of general principle

It is the function of Parliament to determine legislative policy. The power to make regulations on matters of general principle should not therefore be delegated by Parliament unless the boundaries of the delegate's discretion are clearly defined in the parent Statute. There is the fear that the delegation to legislate on matters of principle, as opposed to procedural and administrative detail, could lead to a failure of Parliamentary supervision over matters affecting the rights of individuals.

Exclusion of the jurisdiction of the courts

The courts may review subordinate legislation and declare it ultra vires and void on the grounds of procedure or substance. However, the conferring of discretionary legislative powers upon a minister in such broad terms as to effectively oust or frustrate review by the court may lead to abuse of power by those exercising the delegated function.

Retrospective operation

Parliament, being supreme, may enact legislation which has retrospective effect. However, such legislation is repugnant to the doctrine of the rule of law and its introduction by the Executive through means of delegated legislation can never be justified.

Authority to make regulations amending acts of Parliament

Clauses which empower the minister to alter the provisions of the enabling Act itself, 'so far as may appear to him to be necessary for the purpose of bringing this Act into operation' have been widely criticised and are rarely found today. It has been recommended that such 'Henry VIII' clauses, which confer such a wide legislative discretion on the Minister, should never be used except for the purpose of bringing an Act into operation and should be subject to strict time limitations (usually one year from the passing of the Act).

Some power to amend statutory provisions is conferred under the European Communities Act 1972. Sections 2(2) and 2(4) of the Act enable the Executive to give effect to Community law even where this conflicts with Act of Parliament. It provides that:

> 'Her Majesty may by Order in Council, and any designated Minister or department may, by regulation, make provision:
>
> i) for the purpose of implementing any Community obligations; or
>
> ii) for the purpose of dealing with matters arising out of or related to such obligations.'

The power to tax or levy charges

Generally no imposition or changes of taxation may be effected except by Act of Parliament. Historically taxation has always been considered too important to be delegated by Parliament. However, nowadays Parliament has, subject to certain controls, delegated certain taxing powers to the Government. These include powers to vary the rates of indirect taxation and customs duties.

Sub-delegation

Only Parliament has the power to delegate its legislative functions. The recipient of the delegated powers should be clearly identified in the parent statute and no sub-delegation of those powers should be made to unauthorised or unnamed persons. The phrase 'delegatus non potest delegare' – delegates cannot delegate, should be borne in mind.

European Community law | 12

The structure of the European Community

Basic points

The European Community is at present composed of fifteen Western European States, namely, France; Belgium; Netherlands; Italy; Germany; Luxembourg; Denmark; Ireland; United Kingdom; Greece; Spain; Portugal; Austria; Finland and Sweden. Together they form the world's largest trading unit and the major importer of goods from the Third World. The European Communities or the EC as they are now widely known are in reality a club of democratic states. This is evidenced by the refusal to admit Spain and Portugal while these countries were under military rule or dictatorship. The application of Turkey to join the EC has been put on the back burner until the other countries are satisfied that Turkey really has returned to a democratic political system. So we can say that a precondition of membership is a liberal democratic political structure. The EC acts as a large customs area but the major political premise of the EC is political unity in Western Europe. This high goal had humble origins.

The first treaty (1951) was largely the work of *Monet* and *Schumann* whose basic purpose was to prevent another war, and to provide a solid front against Eastern Europe, the latter combined into an economic alliance called 'COMINFORM' (set up in 1947).

A laissez-faire (freedom of competition) economic system has been adopted. In order to facilitate a reasonably free market, it is proposed that the method of setting up trading companies should be the same in each member state. This and other matters in establishing a common market point to the need to harmonise laws. A clear example of this is the need to have a joint agreement to restrict imports, so as to allow the development of industries within the communities.

Foundation

The communities came into existence at different times:

On 18 April 1951, the Treaty of Paris established the European Coal and Steel Community.

On 21 March 1957, the Treaty of Rome established the European Economic Community.

On 25 March 1957, the European Atomic Energy Authority was established under a Treaty of Rome.

The original structure of the communities provided for separate administration for each organisation. It was later agreed that to serve all three communities there should be a single Court and a single Assembly, and since, that there should be a single Council and a single Commission. These now unified institutions will have the separate functions assigned by the Treaties.

United Kingdom entry was given statutory force by the passing of the European Communities Act 1972.

Limitations on national sovereignty

The object of the EC is set out in Article 2 of the Treaty of Rome (which set up the EC):

'... to promote ... a harmonious development of economic activities, a continuous and balanced expansion, an increase in stability, an accelerated raising of the standard of living and closer relations between the States belonging to it ...'

The EC is not a federal state, since unlike a federal government, the real political power lies in the constituent member states – through their representatives on the Council of Ministers. The Community is, in fact, a *supra-national* body: a body exercising a jurisdiction over and above that of the member states, directing certain activities by law common to all members (though existing in limited areas only, namely coal and steel industry, atomic energy, economic and agricultural matters) – though there are various theories as to how this fits into constitutional and international law.

According to Community law:

'the Community constitutes a new legal order of international law for the benefit of which the states have limited their sovereign rights, albeit within limited fields ... independently of the legislation of Member States, Community law therefore not only imposes obligations on individuals but is also intended to confer upon them rights which become part of their legal heritage.' ECJ in the *Van Gend en Loos* case [1963] ECR 1.

European law was incorporated into English law by the European Communities Act 1972. In particular, s2(1) provides:

'All such rights, powers, liabilities, obligations and restrictions from time to time created or arising by or under the Treaties, and all such remedies and procedures from time to time provided for by or under the Treaties, as in accordance with the Treaties are without further enactment to be given legal effect or used in the United Kingdom shall be recognised and available in Law, and be enforced, allowed and followed accordingly; and the expression "enforceable Community right" and similar expressions shall be read as referring to one to which this subsection applies.'

Section 2(4) subjects 'any enactment passed or to be passed' by Parliament to s2(1), that is to European law, and requires English statute law to be construed accordingly.

In creating the EC the Member States have to a certain extent limited their national sovereignty by conferring limited although very real and expanding powers to the institutions of the EC. Most of these institutions are the creation of the various founding treaties of which today the most important is undoubtedly the Treaty of Rome 1957. However not all of the work of the EC is done through these institutions. Much of the high profile work of the EC is done at the biannual summits of the Heads of Governments of the twelve and obviously these summits require considerable preparation behind the scenes by government officials. By virtue of the European Communities (Amendment) Act 1986, which came into force on 1 January 1987, the Single European Act was given statutory force and certain far reaching changes were made to the original treaty provisions. In particular, The European Council is now formally recognised as part of the European Communities' institutional framework and by Art. 2 must meet, at least twice a year. Although, unanimity was previously required, this has been replaced by qualified majority voting in an increased number of areas concerning the internal market. A state may now find itself under an obligation to comply with rules or a policy to which it was opposed. Failure to comply would amount to a breach of the provisions of the Treaty. While it is clear that this is largely a political question it has major legal ramifications.

The Treaty on European Union (the Maastricht Treaty) was signed by the United Kingdom government on 7 February 1992.

The European Communities (Amendment) Act 1993 s1(1) gives effect to the Maastricht Treaty, with the exception of the Protocol on Social Policy, by providing that references in the European Communities Act 1972 to 'Community Treaties' now include the Treaty on European Union. Section 1(2) provides that, for the purposes of s6 of the European Parliamentary Elections Act 1978 (which provides that no treaty which provides for any increase in the powers of the European Parliament shall be ratified by the United Kingdom unless it has been approved by an Act of Parliament), the Maastricht Treaty (meaning 'the Treaty ... signed at Maastricht ...') has received such parliamentary approval. The purpose of this provision is that, once enacted, the United Kingdom government becomes entitled to exercise its prerogative power in order to ratify the Maastricht Treaty without contravening s6 of the European Parliamentary Elections Act 1978, as the treaty referred to in s1(2) is the Maastricht Treaty in its entirety, and not just those parts of the Treaty referred to in s1(1). Section 2 of the 1993 Act provides that no notification shall be given to the Council of the European Communities that the United Kingdom intends to move to the third stage of economic and monetary union unless a number of preconditions have been satisfied. These include (inter alia) the requirements that a draft of that notification should have been approved by Act of Parliament, and that the government has reported to Parliament on its proposals for the co-ordination of economic policies. Section 7 provides that the Act can come into force only after each House of Parliament has come to a resolution on a motion tabled by a minister of the Crown considering the question of adopting the Protocol on Social Policy.

The resolution required by s7 was considered by the House of Commons on 22 July. Before the vote could take place, however, the House had to consider an Opposition amendment which called for the adoption of the Protocol on Social Policy before ratification of the Maastricht Treaty. The vote on the opposition motion produced an apparent dead heat, the Speaker exercising her casting vote in the government's favour. In the subsequent vote on the substantive motion, put forward by the government for the purposes of satisfying the requirements of s7 of the 1993 Act, a number of rebel Conservative MPs voted with the opposition and the motion was defeated by 324 votes to 316. The following day the Prime Minister tabled a motion stating that 'This House has confidence in the policy of Her Majesty's Government on the adoption of the Protocol on Social Policy'. The motion was carried. The Act received royal assent on 20 July 1993, and came into force on 23 July 1993. The Maastricht Treaty was ratified on 2 August 1993.

A question may remain as to whether or not the motion passed on 23 July, which was in effect a confidence motion, was the type of motion envisaged by Parliament in enacting s7 of the 1993 Act. The judiciary may be precluded from commenting on the propriety or otherwise of parliamentary proceedings, but it would be open to them to consider the wording of s7 with a view to evaluating what type of resolution it required.

Institutions of the EC

It is proposed to examine briefly the role of the various institutions of the EC.

The European Parliament

This is not a Parliament in the normal sense, having no legislative powers.

The European Parliament, formerly referred to as the Assembly, is composed of 626 Euro-MPs directly elected since 1979 by the citizens of the various member states in elections of universal adult suffrage. A second election was held in 1984, a third in 1989 and a fourth in June 1994. With the expansion of the EC to include fifteen members seats are now allocated more or less in proportion to their respective population as follows:

Germany	99
France, Italy and the United Kingdom	87
Spain	64
Netherlands	31
Greece, Portugal and Belgium	25
Sweden	22
Austria	21
Denmark and Finland	16
Ireland	15
Luxembourg	6

Direct elections have caused some constitutional crises; however it was agreed that states would hold direct elections only after it was established that the direct elections would not affect the powers of the respective institutions. Indeed the Parliament (the name can be deceptive) was intended to be a constitutional body rather than a legislative body. Now that the members of Parliament are directly elected, the other organs tend to pay more attention to their views as they can claim to represent the electorate on the various proposals. Ever since the *Isoglucose Case* (1982) the Council of Ministers are obliged to consult the European Parliament and to obtain their opinion before acting legislatively. Furthermore, this position has been strengthened by the Single European Act 1986. By Art 238 association agreements now require the assent of the European Parliament. The Parliament has very considerable influence and since 1983 has started to propose on its own initiative various ideas that have subsequently been taken up by the Commission. The Parliament, it has been said, also has considerably more power over spending than does the British House of Commons in that it has the power to freeze community spending. However, it has no real power over the raising of finances which remain a matter outside its ambit. This budgetary power has been and is being used by the Parliament as a political weapon to gain more power.

Other aspects of the European Parliament's powers include the right to sack the entire Commission – it has no power to sack an individual Commissioner – although it would have to be said that this is a power used more in the implied threat than is, in the real world, viable.

The Parliament also has the right to take the other institutions of the EC to the European Court of Justice where alleged infringements of the Treaty are involved. It did this in 1983 when it took the Council of Ministers before the European Court for failure to create a common transport policy as provided for in the Treaty.

Quite apart from these formal powers and hardly any less important is the power of the Parliament to raise public consciousness on any given topic and hence to pressurise governments and the Commission to act. This facility was referred to by the then leader of the British Labour Party faction, Barbara Castle, as 'raising Hell'. It should not be underestimated.

Since the third direct elections in 1989, it has been noticeable that the democratic imperative is working on the side of the Parliament. It has used Article 235 of the Treaty of Rome 1957, which provides that a matter not in the Treaty but which would benefit the EC can be adopted if there is unanimous support for it, to imply that what is not expressly forbidden by the Treaty is permitted. The wide range of activities of the various committees of the Parliament certainly attest to this.

The Council of Ministers

The Council of Ministers (Council) is an entirely intergovernmental institution composed of government ministers or their representatives from all the member states. It is said to be 'the effective centre of power' in the EC since this is where all the real decisions are taken. As indicated it is the view of this writer that its role has been somewhat superseded by the Summit of Heads of Government.

The Council is composed of twelve members, one from each of the Member States, who is chosen according to the subject matter being dealt with at that meeting. For example, on a matter relating to coal production the representatives would be Ministers of Energy in the national governments. The Council has the power to legislate – rather than the Parliament. It would act on the recommendation of the Commission and can amend any proposal of the Commission by a unanimous decision.

Voting in the Council is carried out in one of three ways:

a unanimous – all member states must agree;

b absolute majority – each member state has one vote and the proposal that receives a majority of the members (presently seven) would be adopted;

c qualified majority – this is where the states receive weighted votes as follows:

United Kingdom, Italy, France and Germany	10 votes each
Spain	8 votes
Belgium, Greece, Netherlands and Portugal	5 votes each
Austria and Sweden	4 votes each
Denmark, Ireland and Finland	3 votes each
Luxembourg	2 votes

A qualified majority would be achieved with 62 out of the total of 87 votes. However, in response to the accepted need to protect vital national interests the so called 'Luxembourg Compromise' of 1966 was worked out to provide that majority voting would not be imposed where important issues are at stake, rather the member states would work towards a political compromise. It is unlikely now that any state would risk a veto on the grounds that it would then lose an issue that was important to it. Hence we can observe that Council meetings are in effect horse trading exercises of 'give and take'. This was evidenced when in 1982 a proposal concerning farm prices was voted through in spite of a veto from the United Kingdom.

In effect, most of the work of the Council is now done by diplomats in the Committee of Permanent Representatives (COREPER) and in various other committees of the Council. The work load is too vast for national government ministers to devote the time and energy to matters of fine detail.

The Commission

The Commission is the executive branch of the EC. There are at present seventeen Commissioners, two each chosen from France, West Germany, Italy, the United Kingdom and Spain and one each from the other member states. They are collectively, though not individually, responsible to the Parliament. The Commission is responsible for initiating most of the proposals that emanate from the EC. They perform the task of guardian of the Treaties and bring any suspected breach before the European Court. They also have the job of investigating alleged breaches and of issuing a ruling and notifying the respective parties of the appropriate remedial action to be taken.

The Commission derives its powers from the Treaty of Rome and from subsequently derived Community Law. By the latter is meant those Council decisions that give the Commission extra powers and responsibilities.

The functions of the Commissions are:

a to act as the executive branch of the EC;

b to implement EC legislation;

c to initiate a Community Policy;

d to advocate the Community interest in the Council of Ministers.

The European Court of Justice

The role of supervising the uniform application of EC law within the Community falls to the European Court of Justice which sits in Luxembourg. It is important not to confuse this Court with the European Court of Human Rights which sits in Strasbourg and is the Court established under the Council of Europe's Convention on Human Rights and Fundamental Freedoms 1950. The European Court of Justice (ECJ) deals with matters of EC law. The European Court of Human Rights deals with, as its name suggests, alleged violations of the human rights protected in the Convention.

The European Court of Justice performs a special role both within the EC and within the national jurisdictions of the Member States.

Under Article 177 of the Treaty of Rome the ECJ may give preliminary rulings on questions of EC law which are referred to it by a national court involving:

a the interpretation of the treaties;

b the validity and interpretation of legal acts of the institutions of the EC;

c interpretation of the status of bodies established under the treaties, eg The Euro-Investment Bank.

It is important to note that there is no right of appeal to the ECJ, indeed there is no appeal. A national court or tribunal may request a court ruling in any of the above matters where that ruling would assist them in reaching their decision, for example where a matter of EC law covers part of the facts raised in the case before the national court. Hence any national court however low in the hierarchy may ask for a ruling directly from the ECJ.

However, where there is no further appeal from the decision of the national court then that court must refer the matter to the ECJ. Thus all courts of final appellate jurisdiction would be bound by this requirement, although it is difficult to envisage a situation where the matter was not realised to involve a matter of EC law before it reached the court of final appellate jurisdiction. In this way it is clear that any matter involving a question of EC law will eventually reach the ECJ for a preliminary ruling.

During the reference to the ECJ the case before the national court is adjourned. In all cases an area of discretion remains with the national judge. He must rule that the case requires the ECJ to give a preliminary ruling before it can be decided.

An exception would be where the legal rule is clear and there is no difficulty in interpretation. Such a situation is governed by Acte Clair.

An interesting aspect of the ECJ preliminary rulings is that they bind not only the court that requested the ruling but also all courts in the EC. In this way it is quite possible for a Magistrates' Court in England to request a preliminary ruling from the ECJ that will then bind the House of Lords and all the courts of all the other member-nations.

The purpose behind this mechanism is clear. It is to provide a uniform application of EC law throughout the whole Community.

It should be noted that the ECJ will not decide matters of national law nor will they decide the case or dispute. Hence, we say that there is no appeal to the ECJ. The ECJ will decide only on the matter of EC law. The application of any decision will be left to the relevant court of the country in question.

Under the European Communities Act 1972 British courts are to give judicial notice to the Treaties. Since the ECJ rules on the Treaties it is the task of the national court to apply the preliminary ruling from the ECJ to the facts of the case before it in arriving at a decision. The preliminary ruling may of course cover only a part of the dispute; however it may also be central to the whole case.

In contrast with foreign domestic judgments, decisions of the ECJ cannot be questioned in an English court.

In addition to its jurisdiction to give preliminary rulings the ECJ also has other heads of jurisdiction. These are:

a   decide matters of compensation for non contractual damage caused by the institutions of the EC;

b   act as a staff tribunal;

c   facilitate arbitration procedures between member states and private individuals on commercial matters.

The ECJ has no machinery for enforcement of its decisions and rulings. Enforcement is left to the national court system. The relationship between EC law and National law is both a legal and a political question. For further details see Chapter 17.

Community legislation

The Community has powers, which are conferred by specific Treaty provisions, to legislate on various topics. Over the present lifetime of the Community, a great deal of legislation has been enacted covering important areas, eg of agriculture, trade, sex discrimination, company law, competition law. Moreover, these matters impinge directly on individuals in many cases and are of great importance to the existence of the Member States since they regulate and attempt to 'harmonise' the laws of those states (within limited areas). Article 189 of the EC Treaty outlines the forms of Community legislation:

'In order to carry out their task the Council and the Commission shall, in accordance with the provisions of this Treaty, make regulations, issue directives, take decisions, make recommendations or deliver opinions.

A *regulation* shall have general application, it shall be binding in its entirety and directly applicable in all Member States.

A *directive* shall be binding, as to the result to be achieved, upon each Member State to which it is addressed, but shall leave to the national authorities the choice of form and methods.

A *decision* shall be binding in its entirety upon those to whom it is addressed.

Recommendations and *opinions* shall have no binding force.'

Regulations are of general effect, affecting wide categories of persons – and are the nearest Community measure to an English Act of Parliament. They are 'directly applicable', ie as soon as they are enacted they take effect immediately as part of the national laws of the Member States.

Directives merely set out an objective to be achieved by the Member States. They do not take effect immediately as part of national law (as do regulations) but need to be implemented by national legislation. However, in order to further the aims of Community law, the ECJ has held that if the relevant Member States do not implement a directive within the time limit set down then it will intervene to make the directive directly applicable: *Van Duyn* v *Home Office* [1974] ECR 1337; *Pubblico Ministero* v *Ratti* [1980] 1 CMLR 96.

Decisions are addressed to particular bodies, companies or individuals and only bind those to whom they are addressed: they are like executive acts which are designed to deal with particular cases.

The policy-oriented attitude taken towards European legislation by the ECJ is quite unlike the generally conservative stance of the English courts when interpreting English case law and statute. Indeed, in a series of important cases, the ECJ took it upon itself to adjudicate on the interaction of Community law and national law: see *Van Gend en Loos* (above); *Costa* v *ENEL* [1964] ECR 585; *Simmenthal* v *Italian Minister of Finance* [1976] ECR 1871, and others. The policy of the ECJ has always been that of the supremacy of Community law over national law – though the English courts, with the traditional theory of the sovereignty of Parliament, do not accept that Parliament is always subject to European law and can never change its mind: see *Macarthys* v *Smith* [1981] 1 All ER 111.

effect of E.C legislation on English law.

Judicial law making (1) | 13

Introduction

The question addressed in this chapter is whether or not judges have discretion, and how they exercise it if they do. It is designed to set in a theoretical context the substantive subjects covered in the following chapters. In this short chapter we shall examine the jurisprudential approach to the role of the judge in making (or not making) law. We shall be concerned with the theory of *Dworkin* and the criticisms thereof. On the issue of whether judges have discretion it may be stated that even *Dworkin* admits a weak discretion, ie that officials make decisions which demand judgment and are not mechanical, and that sometimes these decisions are final and not reviewable by a higher authority. However, he denies that there is ever, for a judge, strong discretion, ie freedom to take decisions not covered by the available institutional material. The legal system, he claims, provides an authoritative answer to every case.

I think that the essence of this chapter has been expressed by *Lord Reid* in an extra-judicial capacity in an article he wrote entitled *The Judge as Law Maker* (1972) wherein he stated, '... There was a time when it was almost indecent to suggest that judges make law – they only declare it. Those with a taste for fairy tales seem to have thought that in some Alladin's cave there is hidden the Common Law in all its splendour and that on a judge's appointment there descends on him knowledge of the magic words 'Open Sesame'. Bad decisions are given when the judge has muddled the pass word and the wrong door opens. But we do not believe in fairy tales any more ... so we must accept the fact that for better or for worse judges do make law, and tackle the question how do they approach their task and how should they approach it ... '

Dworkin: rules, principles and policies

Taking Rights Seriously

Dworkin's Taking Rights Seriously has presented a serious challenge to our accepted viewpoints on many questions in the varied fields of moral and political philosophy, and jurisprudence. In jurisprudence, the major contribution is a consideration of how judges decide cases. In summary, his view is as follows. He rejects the notion, which he attributes to positivists, that law consists of rules, and that when rules run out in a particular case, the judge has discretion. Rather, a judge is bound by principles. These principles are developed from the previous institutional material (via the institutional thesis), and the ones based on principles rights (not policies – goals) can be used by the judges. These principles provide answers to all legal cases; the reasons never run out. Therefore, a judge has no discretion in a hard case (in the strong sense of discretion); he must follow the principles which emerge from the institutional and rights theses.

It would now be appropriate to explain *Dworkin's* argument in more detail. Remember that he claims both that this is how judges do behave (descriptive) and how they should behave (prescriptive). We shall have to decide if either or both of these claims stand up to scrutiny.

Not just rules: principles

Dworkin attributes three ideas to positivism, and aims to dispel each of them.

a Laws are rules, identified by a test of pedigree (like the rule of recognition) and not content.

b Outside rules; judges are not bound: they have discretion.

c There is only a legal obligation if there is a legal rule.

The reason the positivists are wrong, says *Dworkin*, is that they do not include the notion of legal principles. Even if a case is not covered by a strict rule (which may be provided by a section in a statute, or a particular case precedent) there are principles in the legal system which will dictate the result. In earlier writings, *Dworkin* seemed to suggest that these principles could even override rules. He discussed *Riggs* v *Palmer* 115 NY 506 (1899) a US case where the rules of succession were not followed because that would have resulted in the murderer of the deceased taking the estate, contrary to the equitable principle that no one can benefit from his own wrong. He now seems to have withdrawn from this position, and says that principles only operate outside the rules regulated area (the core area, in easy cases). We look, then, at the penumbra: at the 'grey' cases, not clearly covered by established rules.

We discuss the derivation of these principles, from the rights and institutional theses, below. *Dworkin* distinguishes two characteristics of principles showing that they differ from rules. First, counter-instances do not disprove a principle (although they do disprove a rule), and second, principles have weight. They do not operate in an all-or-nothing fashion, but can be balanced against each other.

Most positivists could accept that outside the area of rule regulation there are legal principles at work. They would, however, not accept that these principles bind judges. Let us assume, for the moment, that they do so – that the rights and institutional theses are correct, and there are principles covering all cases and dictating a particular decision. Couldn't a positivist still claim that his rule of recognition (R of R) could capture them all?

No, says *Dworkin*. The various possibilities he discusses would involve either a surrender (to the idea of non-discretion), or would not be able to capture the full weight of the principles. As we shall see, the institutional thesis provides a theory of content as well as pedigree, and so accepting in the R of R the principles given by the institutional theses would be a climb down by positivists, who see the R of R as a test of pedigree-validity-system membership, not content.

The main argument used by *Dworkin* is one that it is hard to accept. Positivists' objections to his principles, he claims, are based on *Hart*'s thesis that for a right or duty to exist there must be a uniform social practice of recognising it. *Dworkin*'s principles are uncertain, so cannot be the subject of such a practice, and therefore the principles cannot give rise to rights or duties.

Dworkin argues that *Hart* is wrong, confusing the social acceptance which often backs up the normative content of a rule with the normative content itself.

Dworkin may have simply misunderstood: *Hart* makes no such claims. True, *Hart* does discuss rules in the context of social rules, but this is not because they are the only type of rule (it is because he wants to contrast them with the similar notion of a general habit of obedience). Indeed, legal rules in a developed system do not depend on social recognition, but on validity. Further, *Hart* discusses the notion that such legal rules do have penumbral areas of doubt; and this is true of the detailed parts of the R of R: the acceptance of the R of R is a question of acceptance by the judges, but they can clearly accept the notion of Parliamentary supremacy without deciding on its details (eg the effect of the EC Treaty).

Which principles? The institutional thesis
The principles used to decide hard cases form part of the theory developed by a judge to explain the institutional material to date. *Dworkin* illustrates this with his explanation of how Hercules, an omnicompetent judge, would take on board the institutional structure and political philosophy of the constitution, the statutes and common law decisions, and form a total theory giving principles explaining it all. The process will differ from area to area; of particular interest is the common law area, where some decisions will be limited to their enactment force, and some given a wider, gravitational effect.

The judge's own philosophy will have a pervasive influence. Background morality enters the picture, because the judge needs both to decide which bits of material to reject (as mistakes), and which of the possible alternative 'fits' to choose. (Obviously some rejected material will remain the source of legal rules, which cannot be ousted: a House of Lords decision rejected as a mistake remains as an embedded mistake. It does not, however, form part of a principle.)

Is the institutional thesis true? Should it be? Judges do look at previous institutional material in making decisions, but they do not form anything like the complete theory of institutional material suggested by *Dworkin*. Whether or not *Dworkin*'s thesis should be followed by judges can more properly be left to the discussion of the rights thesis.

Which principles? The rights thesis
The law and institutional thesis will include two types of principles: what *Dworkin* calls 'principles' and 'policies'. Judges in complex cases should only apply principles, and not policies. Decisions generated by policy, eg to create jobs, are not decisions which create any requirement of consistency, whereas those based on principle do require consistency, and give one of the parties to a later dispute a right to have a similar decision made in his favour.

The problem with the principles-policy distinction is that it does not remain constant. Originally, *Dworkin* made the distinction on the basis of individuation of beneficiaries. If the basis of the argument was that it helped an individual or supported his rights, it was a principle; if its basis was not an individual but community welfare, it was a policy. Such policy decisions did not, as I have said, create any pull of consistency: once decision makers consider a policy has been satisfied, it can be dropped in favour of different policies.

However, *Dworkin* later admits that any argument of policy can be substituted by an argument of principle: a policy looked at another way is a principle. Allowing substitutability, and admitting that both principles and policies can be supported by arguments involving the consequences of the action (such arguments not being limited simply to policy claims), weakens the distinction.

Is there descriptive or prescriptive truth in the rights thesis? We have seen that *Dworkin's* problems with the principles-policy distinction has led to a watered-down version; but surely once we allow that consequential arguments can be used (of the form 'if we make X decision, this will happen') for principles, and not solely non-consequential ones ('I have a right to this decision, irrespective of the consequences'), the distinction is practically useless?

Let us assume, however, that there is a distinction which is a reality. *Dworkin* suggests that the argument ranged against judges making law, do not hit home against principles. These arguments are from democracy (judges are not elected, and it is undemocratic to allow them to make law) and retrospectivity (that if judges do make law and apply it to a particular case at bar, that law is retrospectively applied). They do not apply to principles as strongly because one party has a right to a particular decision dictated by principles from the institutional thesis.

It would appear that *Dworkin* has attempted to fit the descriptive into the prescriptive and in so doing has distorted both. If his thesis is only descriptive then, it is submitted, it is inaccurate. The most that can be said if it is intended to be merely prescriptive is that it is open to objection from a subjective perspective.

No discretion: always a right answer?

Dworkin not only says that there are principles which bind judges apart from rules; he also suggests that these principles, these reasons for decisions, never run out. Legal argument, he thinks, only takes one of two forms – either the law requires X, or it does not. There is no middle ground, where it is uncertain whether or not the law requires X. To back this up, he points to legal language: lawyers never claim uncertainty, but rather always say to a judge 'this is the case'.

Surely this is not the case. Lawyers do not think of the law as a seamless web, giving answers to every possible problem. Rather they see definite rules in many areas, and outside these rules they admit to an area of doubt. Legal principles and analogies from other institutional material do play a role, but not a conclusive one: often, judges follow their own notions of what is required by policy in a given situation.

The reason why lawyers speak in such definite terms is obvious: they are attempting to persuade the judge to say that 'the law is X'. In private, they would agree that the notion of an omnipresent common law which exists even before decisions are made is a fiction. They will be quite prepared to tell clients that the law is uncertain and advise as to the probabilities of one or other decision in a case. Textbook writers frequently admit uncertainties, gaps in the law which remain to be filled by judicial action.

Dworkin's Law's Empire

Dworkin's book, *Law's Empire*, develops his earlier theories on the nature of law and of the judicial process outlined in his *Taking Rights Seriously*. His book is an important and refreshing study on the judicial process. It is not though without its flaws nor its critics.

In essence *Dworkin* sees *Law's Empire* as the interpretative approach which he maintains is the technique adopted by the judges in their deciding of cases and interpretation of statutes. In so doing the judge will decide the case in the light of principles of political fairness; substantive justice and procedural due process. In deciding what principle of law best fits the case the judge looks at existing decisions. *Dworkin* uses the analogy with a chain written novel to emphasise that there is always a right answer to every legal question and that is found in principles which according to him are existing statements about rights. That is, he uses the example of a series of authors, each writing a chapter based on what has gone before – each author obliged to use and build on work already done. The judge will not refer to policy in the sense of statements about goals to be achieved by the legal system as this is the proper preserve of the legislature. *Dworkin* is concerned to protect the judiciary from the type of criticism that was levelled against them in, for example, the cheap London Transport fares case in which transport was subsidised from rates (local government taxation on property: see *London Borough of Bromley* v *Greater London Council* [1983] 1 AC 768 wherein the Court of Appeal held that it was illegal to subsidise fares from rates. The popular press pilloried the judges asking who elected them. This respect for the democratic process and the requirement for a democratic mandate in order to enter policy decisions is an important element of *Dworkin's* premises. His other contention in this regard is that any policy decision on the part of the judge would since it was not drawn from already existing statements about rights be retrospective law making on his part and therefore unfair to the disputants.

From this *Dworkin* speaks of law being a seamless web. There is always a right answer to every legal question – law never runs out – the only difficulty being in finding the right answer. There never comes a point in the adjudicative process when reasons run out. We do not hear our judges say '… there is no law on this point so we shall have to make some up … '. What *Dworkin* seems to confuse is the point that the judges do not frame their decisions in such terms does not mean that they are not actually acting in such a way. Take the celebrated 'Ladies Directory' case (*Shaw* v *DPP* [1962] AC 220) in which it was not at all apparent that there existed any law on the matter yet the courts created a jurisdiction that they were custodes morum of the nation and went on to declare that the events surrounding the publication of the directory amounted to a conspiracy to corrupt public morals. The speech of Lord Reid, dissenting, in that case is most illuminating in this regard yet a decade later when he was invited to overrule that decision in *Knuller Ltd* v *DPP* [1972] 3 WLR 143 he said that he would follow an 'already established decision '!

Dworkin argues that the judge examines the choices presented from the story of law contained in the previous decisions and in the statutes and then considers his own conception of justice as to which to apply. He then considers the community's view of justice. To the extent that these correlate there is no problem. If the community view of justice differs from his own the judge will then consider whether it would be fair to impose his views over those of the community. That idea of fairness is at the heart of *Dworkin*'s conception of justice and as such might be expected of an adherent to the democratic liberal tradition. It is not though the only conception of justice. A socialist might argue that fairness in the sense of treating everyone with equal concern and respect subject only to the 'trump card' rights of the minority would not take adequate account of social and economic inequalities.

In a revealing passage towards the conclusion of the book *Dworkin* writes that '... Law's attitude is constructive: it aims, in the interpretative spirit, to lay principle over practice to show the best route to a better future, keeping the right faith with the past ...' This perhaps opens him up to the accusation that he is a dreamer. He contends that 'every hard decision is a vote for one of law's dreams ' and that these dreams are fed into the system by philosophers. In an attack on *Dworkin*'s thesis written before *Law's Empire*, *Hart* thought that the difficulty with *Dworkin*'s thesis was that it forced the lawyer to choose between the nightmare of there being no established principles and the noble dream of there always being a right answer to every legal question. *Hart* argued that a sensible lawyer would settle for a good night's sleep somewhere between the two positions acknowledging that there will be a few cases where reasons will run out and that in those circumstances a wide discretion should be available to the judge to decide in essence on policy grounds how to decide the case (see '*American Jurisprudence through English Eyes: The Nightmare or the Nobel Dream*'). One criticism of his analysis is that he insists that his thesis is descriptive of what the judiciary actually do rather than prescriptive as to what they ought to do yet in so doing *Dworkin* has sought to merge the descriptive element with the prescriptive to the extent that he has sacrificed reality to a noble dream.

However, dreams have their place. They are better than nightmares. This dream looks at what the law can achieve. It sees a purpose to law rather than a mere instrument for social control. The dream is most refreshing.

Evaluation of Dworkin's thesis

Dworkin does not quite manage to escape the arguments about democratic mandate and retrospectivity in fact. First, the democratic argument. In a hard case, ex hypothesi, the judge applies a new standard, makes a legal decision. Any attempt to hide the anti-democratic nature of this process by talking of applying principles inherent in the material of the system, is misleading. Anyway, *Dworkin*'s judges discover these principles through a process which involves a heavy use of their own political views. Is this democratic?

Second, the retrospectivity argument. The complaint is that the parties do not know what law will be applied to their case. Is this overcome by suggesting that the decision is gleaned from present institutional material? When this process is controversial, judges may come to different results and so the parties cannot discover in advance what the results will be?

Dworkin's attempt to show that here is no judicial discretion ultimately fails, however captivating his power of argument was en route. Judges do not engage in the complex process of forming an institutional thesis, nor do they limit themselves solely to arguments based on principles not policies. Many counter examples forced *Dworkin* to weaken, fatally, the principles v policy distinction. Nor is there always one right answer to a case. Many questions of law which arise in cases are not capable of being settled solely by principles justifying the present law.

Judicial discretion

If the pun may be excused perhaps there is no right answer to the question whether judges have or exercise discretion. We shall herein examine some of the main arguments raised in this debate.

Once we decide that judges do have discretion in hard cases (and even in some 'easy' cases, when they use their powers to overrule or distinguish earlier cases), how should they exercise that discretion? What factors should they take into account?

The main debate centering on that question is to what extent it is acceptable for judges to use arguments of policy, of utility, of value judgments. On the one hand, some people argue that they should be limited to extending by analogy the present institutional material. (*Dworkin*, who sees this as a legal and not just a political/moral duty, is an extreme example of this.) Others say that judges must, and should, be concerned with questions other than institutional logic and purity, and should have an eye for whether or not a particular decision would be right/have good consequences.

There are various strands of thought on the side of analogy-logic. In statutory interpretation, judges must try to give effect to the wishes of Parliament, and must often try to limit themselves to the words/will of Parliament. We discuss this under statutory interpretation in chapter 15. Considerations of historical development, logical consistency, the requirements of certainty, and the argument that questions of right/wrong and political values are for elected representatives all suggest that maybe judges should not use policy considerations.

There are, however, strong counter-arguments. In hard cases, judges inevitably make law, and this must be accepted. Why force them to make it in an artificial manner, possibly leading to absurd results because they are not allowed to consider the sort of things a legislator would always consider? And why should consistency and certainty stand in the way of progress and fairness?

It seems that the approach might be allowed to differ from area to area. For example, in constitutional matters regarding Bills of Rights, fundamental questions of fairness might be considered as more important than consistency; on the other hand, in company law and insurance, certainty to enable affairs to be arranged in advance might dictate logical extensions of rules even with absurd results.

Judicial law making (2) | 14

Introduction

The judge has two tasks. He must resolve the dispute before him and he must reach his decision by reference to some impartial rule of law. One of the most obvious aspects of formal justice is that all cases should be treated alike; one of the commonest and most noteworthy features of many human institutions (clubs, societies, companies, etc, as well as States) is the tendency to repeat earlier practice and follow earlier patterns. For these, and other, reasons, most legal systems have developed a system of precedent, including the use of past decisions as a guide to present decision. A moment's thought by any student of English law should bring scores of decisions based on precedents to mind.

As we shall see, though, the English system – the common law system – in fact uses precedent in a slightly different way from the civil law systems of most European countries. In England, precedents of an appropriate authority not only guide decisions in later cases, but bind the judges in those later cases: within the given hierarchical structure, a judge in an inferior court must obey the decision of a higher court on the same point. This is the doctrine of stare decisis.

Any system using precedents will require a method of keeping them in an acceptable and accessible form; this need for law reports is obviously greater where precedents are law (since they bind later decisions, they are actual law, and not just guides to what the law is). In the stare decisis based system there will also need to be a defined hierarchy, and an established way of working out what part of an earlier case is binding: we call this the ratio decidendi (reason for deciding.)

Traditionally it is said that judges do not make law, but only declare what the law is, by considering and applying rules laid down in previous cases, which themselves were based on the rules of earlier cases and so on. However this 'declaratory' theory of law is simplistic in that:

a It overlooks the fact that the judges must of necessity extend and modify existing rules in that the established rules must be applied to new cases, to new situations. In the words of *Lord Radcliffe*:

> 'Judicial law is always a reinterpretation of principles in the light of new combinations of facts ... true, judges do not reverse principles, once well established, but they do modify them, extend them, restrict them or even deny their applicability to the combination in hand.' (*Not in Feather Beds* (1968)).

b It overlooks the creative function of the more 'dynamic' lawmakers amongst the judiciary (more apparent at certain periods of history than others) who develop existing rules into a new form which it is possible to categorise as 'new law'. For example, the 'distillation' of the principle in *Hughes v Metropolitan Railway Co* (1877) 2 App Cas 439 by Denning J in *Central London Property Trust Ltd v High Trees House Ltd* [1947] KB 130 to 'create' a new form of equitable forbearance (promissory estoppel). The classic statement of the heart of the modern tort of negligence, the duty of care, by Lord Atkin in *Donoghue v Stevenson* [1932] AC 562 was a departure from precedent and a generalisation of more limited rules.

Despite these criticisms, it remains true that the process of applying and developing the law is largely a conservative one and radical change is left to Parliament.

Precedent, in the sense of treating like cases alike and following established rules of law and practice, has been present in the English legal system for many centuries as is clear from the continued interest in law reporting from the thirteenth century onwards. However, the medieval view of decided cases was not that of the twentieth century, which sees the decision in the case itself as binding. The medieval attitude was that decisions were examples of the application of rules of law, several examples demonstrating an established custom which would be very persuasive in a medieval court.

The modern doctrine only emerged in the nineteenth century with the establishing of an official system of reliable law reporting which, of course, is indispensable to the operation of the doctrine. Generally, any report of a case made by a barrister will be regarded as reliable as this is usually a precondition to the citation of a report in court. Although there is no rule that an unreported decision may not be put before the court in a subsequent case, almost invariably precedents will be contained in law reports. Indeed, in the case of *Roberts Petroleum Ltd* v *Bernard Kenny Ltd* [1983] AC 192, Lord Diplock opined that the House of Lords should not allow the citing before it of transcripts of unreported judgments of the Court of Appeal unless they contained a statement of some principle of law the substance of which could not be found in any law report.

Given the importance law reports have, it is not surprising that in 1865 the first moves began to take law reporting out of private hands. In 1870 the Incorporated Council of Law Reporting for England and Wales was founded, a semi-official body, not funded by the state. (In fact its legal status has been defined as that of a non-profit-making charity.)

While not an official body as such, its regulation is in the joint hands of the Inns of Court and the Law Society. All reporters are barristers, who must vouch for the accuracy of the reports. However, there are criticisms, the main one being the informality of the system. No case is *obliged* to be reported and some undoubtedly do get missed. At the same time some get duplicated and appear in several different reports. With the advent of computerisation a number of data bases are now available (LEXIS, EUROLEX and so on).

This is one of the reasons why unreported cases, along with foreign case law, have suddenly become more accessible, and it is partly this which has led to decisions such as that in *Roberts Petroleum* (supra).

There are still one or two private law reports published, probably the best known being the All England Reports.

In addition to the generally conservative views of judges, the doctrine is upheld for a number of reasons:

a It is based on a principle of *fairness*, that is treating 'like cases alike'. This is also convenient in that it is obviously wasteful of effort to reconsider every like case and consider what the applicable principles should be. Precedent allows a judge to have a ready-made solution to hand, with the possibility of distinguishing previous decisions if they are significantly different. Most cases do not involve disputes as to the principles to be applied at all, since these are usually clear, but disputes as to the facts and the application of the rules to those facts.

b *Certainty*: in theory, with the large number of points of law which have already been decided, it should be a relatively simple matter to discover the relevant principles applying in the particular case. Of course, the many variations in facts and circumstances mean that in some cases, the relevant principles are unclear (or their application is uncertain). However, the great majority of cases do not involve disputes as to the law, only as to the facts and the application of those rules.

c *Flexibility*: the fact that the decisions are decisions of judges and not statutory provisions, means that they can be subsequently overruled or distinguished (see below) where they are incorrect, cease to be applicable or are simply not applicable to the instant case.

d *Predictability*: related to the certainty argument. With the large number of reported decisions it should, in theory at least, be relatively easy to predict on the basis of those decisions the relevant rules applicable and the result of the present case. This enables legal advisers to give to their clients more precise and accurate advice as to what are their chances of success in bringing or defending a particular claim. Consequently, the settlement of claims and disputes, saving time and money for all concerned, becomes more likely.

A fairly typical example of the judicial attitude is shown by Russell LJ's speech in *Gallie* v *Lee* [1969] 2 Ch 17 CA:

'I am a firm believer in a system by which citizens and their advisers can have as much certainty as possible in the ordering of their affairs ... an abandonment of the principle that this court follows its own decisions on the law would I think lead to greater uncertainty and tend to produce more litigation ...'

See also Cumming-Bruce LJ in *Davis* v *Johnson* [1979] AC 264 at 311:

'It seems to me that in any system of law the undoubted public advantages of certainty in civil proceedings must be purchased at the price of the risk of injustice in difficult individual situations. I would think that the present practice holds the balance just about right.'

Continental legal systems, and Community law, do not have this doctrine. Judges look at previous decisions for guidance only, and decide cases on broad principles. Nevertheless even though precedents are not binding, continental Courts tend to follow them as this does give certainty.

It is not the whole decision which is binding, but only the rule of law contained in the decision. This binding element is termed the 'ratio decidendi' (the reason for the decision), and a lawyer must be able to analyse in order to discover the ratio.

The ingredients of a decision

Every decision contains three basic ingredients:

a findings of material facts, direct and inferred. An inferred finding is one which the judge or jury draws from the direct facts, eg from a finding of the direct facts that a car was driven at a particular speed in particular road conditions, the fact of negligent conduct may be inferred;

b statements of principles of law relevant to the legal problems disclosed by the facts; and

c judgment based on applying the law to the facts.

The parties are concerned with the outcome of the case, in other words, with the conclusion the court reaches when it applies the law to the facts. Lawyers, though, are interested in the statements of legal principle made by the judge. It is these statements of principle which form the ratio decidendi of the case. Therefore, it is these statements of legal principle which will be looked at in future cases where the same point of law falls to be decided.

The ratio decidendi must always be distinguished from obiter dicta. Obiter dicta are statements made 'by the way', which do not form part of the reasons behind the decision. Obiter dicta may be of two kinds:

a Statements based on facts which either were not proved to have existed, or if they did exist, were not proved to be relevant. For example, see the case of *Central London Property Trust Ltd* v *High Trees House Ltd* [1947] KB 130 dealt with in Chapter 12. In this case Denning J expressed his view that the landlords would not have been able to claim rent for the war years, even though they had not asked for that back-rent.

b Statements based on the facts proved, but on which the court did not rely when reaching its decision. For example, see *Hedley Byrne & Co Ltd* v *Heller & Partners Ltd* [1964] AC 465 dealt with in chapter 16. In that case the House of Lords made certain general observations about the duty of care which the bank owed to its customers when giving advice, and it was said that the bank had been negligent, but because of the disclaimer clause these statements were irrelevant and the bank was not liable.

While obiter dicta are not of binding authority there is no doubt that the dicta of superior courts and eminent judges have a strong persuasive authority. Thus the principles laid down as obiter dicta in both the above examples have now been accepted by all the superior courts as established rules of equity and law respectively.

Some precedents are not binding on later courts. There are three possible reasons for a precedent not to be binding:

Persuasive authorities

These may be obiter dicta statements of any court, ratio decidendi of an inferior court, or ratio decidendi of Scottish, Commonwealth, or foreign courts, and statements of the Judicial Committee of the Privy Council. This latest authority is the equivalent appellate court to the House of Lords in respect of appeals from Commonwealth courts, and consequently its statements have very strong persuasive authority and may be followed in preference to earlier English authorities, even of the Court of Appeal.

Precedents which have been overruled, either by statute or a superior court

In general, judges are reluctant to overrule precedents as to do so reduces the certainty of the law, and also the authority of a case tends to increase with the passage of time. Judicial overruling operates retrospectively, because the theory is that the earlier decision is deemed to have been based on a misunderstanding of the law, so that the overruling is simply a correct re-statement of the law (this is the 'declaratory theory' of the common law). Statutory overruling only operates retrospectively if the statute expressly states that this is to happen. (*Note*: do not confuse 'overruled' with 'reversed'. The latter expression refers to the reversing of a case on appeal which alters the outcome (ie the actual decision binding the parties), whereas overruling affects the ratio decidendi of the case.) Sometimes cases are distinguished, rather than overruled. This means that the Court finds that the material facts are different so that the previous precedent does not have to be followed. The process of distinguishing is a major factor in keeping the doctrine of precedent flexible. As the ratio is based on the facts of the case, a judge in a later case may find a significant distinction in the facts of the case to allow him not to follow the earlier case. Clearly the facts in any two cases are never absolutely identical, so an unpopular decision may be avoided by careful distinguishing.

Per incuriam statements

'Per incuriam' means in error through lack of notice of the law. This means that the Court in reaching its decision failed to consider some relevant statute or precedent. This is rarely used. (Note: sometimes a case is 'disapproved'. This means that a judge in a later case, without overruling an earlier case, gives his opinion that it was wrongly decided.)

In *Secretary of State for Trade and Industry* v *Desai* (1991) The Times 5 December, Scott LJ said that to come within the category of per incuriam it must be shown not only that the decision involved some slip or error, but also that if the decision were left to stand it would be likely to result in some inconvenience in the administration of justice or significant injustice to citizens.

The principle of res judicata must be mentioned. That principle states that once the courts have given their final decision in a case, that case cannot be reopened. This does not mean that there can never be an appeal, but once all appeals have been heard the courts will not reopen the case, even if a later decision overrules the principle of law which was applied. For example in the case of *Re Waring (No 2)* [1948] Ch 221 W left annuities to H and L 'free of income tax'. In 1942 an appeal was made by H and it was held that income tax must be deducted. In 1946 a similar case between different parties was heard by the House of Lords and they overruled the Court of Appeal case of 1942. In 1948 H and L both applied to the Court to determine whether their annuities should be paid in full in view of the 1946 House of Lords' decision.

It was held that the original decision had to be applied between the parties, even though it no longer represented the law. Therefore, the annuity had to be paid to H with tax deducted, but L was not a party to the original case, so his annuity should be paid without deduction.

The relationship of the doctrine of precedent with the hierarchy of the courts

Introduction

The doctrine of precedent depends for its operation on the fact that each court stands in a definite position in relation to every other court (see diagrams in chapter 9, above). Broadly speaking, decisions of higher courts are binding on lower courts.

The European Court and precedent

The European Court of Justice's decisions bind all British courts, in matters concerning the interpretation of the Treaties, the validity and interpretation of acts of the Community institutions and the interpretation of statutes of bodies established by the Treaties or by the institutions of the Community. Its decisions are not binding on the ECJ itself in future cases, however.

The House of Lords and precedent

The decisions of the House of Lords bind all other courts, civil and criminal. Until 1966 the House of Lords was bound by its own previous decisions. In 1966 a Practice Direction by Lord Gardiner LC altered this:

'Their Lordships regard the use of precedent as an indispensable foundation on which to decide what is the law and its application to individual cases. It provides at least some degree of certainty upon which individuals can rely in the conduct of their affairs, as well as a basis for orderly development of legal rules.

Their Lordships nevertheless recognise that too rigid adherence to precedent may lead to injustice in a particular case and also unduly restrict the proper development of the law. They propose, therefore, to modify their present practice and while treating former decisions of this House as normally binding, to depart from a previous decision when it appears just to do so.

In this connection they will keep in mind the danger of disturbing retrospectively the basis on which contracts, settlements of property and fiscal arrangements have been entered into, and also the special need for certainty as to the criminal law.

This announcement is not intended to affect the use of precedent elsewhere than in this House.'

The interesting aspect of this statement is the emphasis that is placed on certainty. The House of Lords has, in fact, rarely used this power to divert from its previous decisions, emphasising the importance placed by the House of Lords on certainty in the law. It should be noted, therefore, that the fact that the House of Lords now views a previous decision as being either wrong or unjust is not of itself sufficient reason for departing from that decision. The Practice Direction impliedly recognises that a previous unjust decision might still be followed, if the effect of departing from that decision would be to produce uncertainty.

The Court of Appeal Civil Division

The Court of Appeal is clearly bound by House of Lords decisions. Further, the House of Lords has made it clear that the Court of Appeal is bound by its own decisions, except in the limited circumstances stated in *Young* v *Bristol Aeroplane Co* [1944] KB 718, namely:

a   where there are two previously conflicting Court of Appeal decisions;

b   where a previous Court of Appeal decision conflicts with a later House of Lords decision;

c   where a previous Court of Appeal decision was 'per incuriam'.

Lord Denning, however, led a campaign to have the rule in *Young* v *Bristol Aeroplane Co* relaxed. Essentially, he tried to argue that a rule to the same effect as the 1966 Practice Direction should apply to the Court of Appeal – namely, that the Court of Appeal would generally be bound by its own previous decisions, but that where it appeared right to do so, the Court of Appeal could depart from its previous decisions. Lord Denning argued this point in two cases: *Miliangos* v *George Frank (Textiles)* [1975] 3 WLR 758 and *Davis* v *Johnson* [1979] AC 264. In both cases, however, Lord Denning was firmly rebuked by the House of Lords, who re-asserted that the Court of Appeal is always bound by its previous decisions, except in the limited circumstances specified in *Young* v *Bristol Aeroplane Co*.

The House of Lords argued that if a previous Court of Appeal decision is wrong, then the correct way to remedy this is for an appeal to be taken to the House of Lords, and then the House of Lords will consider and, if necessary, overrule the Court of Appeal decision. For the following reasons, however, Lord Denning regarded this as an inadequate solution. The following are the points Lord Denning made in *Davis* v *Johnson*:

a An appeal may never be made to the House of Lords. If no appeal is made, then the incorrect Court of Appeal decision may stand as the law for years.

b No appeal may be made either because the litigant does not have the financial resources to pay for an appeal to the House of Lords, or because the case is settled. Many large companies, such as insurance companies, once they obtain a favourable decision in the Court of Appeal will buy the litigant off, by paying him ample compensation. The company then gains the advantage of a wrong decision in the Court of Appeal until an appeal is eventually taken to the House of Lords. Lord Denning suspects this happened in relation to the much criticised decision in *Oliver* v *Ashman* [1961] 3 WLR 669 which, although wrong, was very much to the advantage of the insurance companies. It was some 20 years before an appeal on this point was finally taken to the House of Lords who then overruled the decision in *Oliver* v *Ashman*.

c Even if an appeal is made to the House of Lords, the appeal may take some 12 months, and during this time the law remains in a state of acute uncertainty.

As yet, however, the House of Lords has not accepted Lord Denning's views and the position as stated in *Young* v *Bristol Aeroplane Co* remains. The House of Lords still insists that to allow the Court of Appeal to overrule its own decisions would introduce too great a degree of uncertainty into the law.

However, in *Rickards* v *Rickards* (1989) The Times 3 July, the Court of Appeal modified their approach for cases where review by the House of Lords was not possible. It was decided that in exceptional cases, concerning jurisdiction, the court was justified in not following their earlier decision where it had been wrongly decided. The then Master of the Rolls, Lord Donaldson of Lymington, set out the following considerations:

a The preferred course must always be to follow the previous decision but to give leave so that the House of Lords might remedy the error.

b Certainty in relation to the substantive law was usually to be preferred to correctness, since it enabled the public to order their affairs with confidence. Erroneous decisions as to procedural rules affected only the parties engaged in relevant litigation. Since that was a much less extensive group a departure from established practice was to that extent less undesirable.

c An erroneous decision involving the jurisdiction of the court was particularly objectionable, either because it would involve an abuse of power, if the true view was that the court had no jurisdiction, or a breach of the courts statutory duty, if in truth the court was wrongly declining jurisdiction. Such a decision of which the present case was an example, was thus in a special category.

The Court of Appeal Criminal Division

The same rules apply to the Criminal Division, except that the Court need not follow its own previous decisions where this would cause injustice to the appellant. The reason for this is that where human freedom is at stake the need for justice exceeds the desire for certainty. The leading authority on this point is *R v Gould* [1968] 2 QB 65.

The High Court

The High Court Divisional Courts are subject to the same rules as the Court of Appeal, so far as their own previous decisions are concerned.

The High Court (judges at First Instance) are not bound by decisions of other High Court judges, but these will be of persuasive authority.

Inferior courts

Magistrates' Courts, County Courts, and other inferior tribunals are not bound by their own previous decisions since they are less authoritative and are rarely reported.

Within the hierarchy

In *Derby & Co* v *Weldon* [1989] 1 WLR 1244 the question arose as to how far a Court of Appeal decision would bind a judge at first instance if the decision of the Court of Appeal was subject to an appeal to the House of Lords which had not yet been heard. It was stated that a judge in such a situation had the right to take into account the possibility of the Court of Appeal decision being reversed.

Avoiding awkward precedents

Introduction

The above analysis of the rules of precedent suggests that the doctrine of stare decisis is rigid and inflexible. It suggests that only the House of Lords has any creative function (in that only this House can overrule its own decisions) and that all other courts must slavishly follow previous decisions whether they be right or not. If this were how the doctrine were applied in practice, it would indeed be open to the criticism that its inflexibility leads to injustice.

In practice, however, the courts have found methods by which they can avoid awkward precedents. An awkward precedent is a previous court decision which the lower court is bound to follow, and yet it does not want to follow in that it feels that decision is wrong. The very notion of an 'awkward precedent' is an interesting idea. Traditionally judges were not meant to form their own opinions of what is right and wrong. Their function was simply to apply the relevant precedents to the facts of the present case, and thus reach their decision. If this is the judge's approach, then there can be no such thing as an 'awkward precedent'. The notion of an 'awkward precedent' only makes sense if in fact the courts approach the deciding of cases in a different way. If a judge decides what is a fair and just solution to the case, without reference to the relevant precedents, then one can understand what an 'awkward precedent' is. An awkward precedent would be a decision of a previous court which binds him, and prevents him from reaching the decision which he regards as the correct one. The notion, therefore, of an awkward precedent only makes sense if one presumes that judges are not just concerned with applying the law, but are also concerned with whether the decision they reach is a fair and just one.

There are thought to be at least seven ways in which an awkward precedent can be avoided.

a By saying that the same point is not raised in the later case. By doing this, the judge is, in fact, simply saying that the former 'awkward precedent' is not a relevant precedent for the case he now has to decide.

b By distinguishing the awkward precedent. This is, in fact, slightly different from the above method and consists in the judge saying that the ratio of the former case is different in some material respect from the case which is now to be decided.

c By arguing that the 'awkward precedent' has no ratio decidendi. This can arise in various situations: for example where each judge in the former case has given a different reason for the decision. Alternatively, if two judges in the House of Lords have taken one view, two judges express another view, and the fifth agrees with none of the others, the latter court can say that the previous decision has no clear ratio decidendi.

d By giving the awkward precedent a very narrow ratio decidendi. The ratio decidendi – the binding part of the precedent – consists of only that part of the decision which is necessary for the decisions reached. If a court does not like an 'awkward precedent', it can sometimes give the case a very narrow ratio, and thus say that it does not cover the present case. For instance, if a court did not like the decision made in *Hedley Byrne & Co Ltd* v *Heller & Partners Ltd* [1964] AC 465 the court could have said that since the only part of the judgment necessary for the decision in the case was the finding that the exclusion clause was valid, the latter court could say that this is the ratio of the case. The latter court could thus avoid being bound by the more generalised statements as to the liability for negligent mis-statements, in that this would not be part of the ratio.

e By confining the case to its facts. If a later court found the decision in *Donoghue* v *Stevenson* [1932] AC 562 in the sense explained earlier, the Court could have limited the case to its facts. This would consist of saying that the case is only relevant authority in relation to the liability of a manufacturer of ginger beer for foreign bodies in the beverage. *Donoghue* v *Stevenson* would, therefore, not be a binding authority except in relation to that type of case.

f By claiming that the 'awkward precedent' is inconsistent with a subsequent decision of a higher court. This is to argue that the decision has been impliedly overruled.

g By claiming the previous decision is per incuriam. This has been explained earlier.

Therefore, the judge does have many devices by which he can avoid an awkward precedent if he so chooses. That this is the case is undoubtedly a good thing in that it prevents the law becoming too inflexible, and allows the judge to avoid making unjust decisions. On the other hand, since a judge will in general be bound to follow the previous decisions of the court, a fair degree of certainty in the law is ensured.

The following quotation from Lord Denning may be used in conclusion in relation to the correct use of precedent by the courts:

'Let it not be thought from this discourse that I am against the doctrine of precedent. I am not. It is the foundation of our system of case law. This has evolved by broadening down from precedent to precedent. By standing by previous decisions, we have kept the common law on a good course. All that I am against is its too rigid application – a rigidity which insists that a bad precedent must necessarily be followed. I would treat it as you would a path through the woods. You must follow it certainly so as to reach your end. But you must not let the path become too overgrown. You must cut out the dead wood and trim off the branches, else you will find yourself lost in thickets and brambles. My plea is simply to keep the path to justice clear of obstructions which would impede it.'

An alternative: prospective overruling

The main argument for stare decisis is certainty. Certainty is a value in a legal system because it allows people to arrange their affairs in accordance with the law, both not breaking it (crime) and taking advantage of its facilities (contract, wills, etc). If judges departed from their decisions at will, these arrangements would be upset; further, the individual case would be in effect a retrospective law, changing the law as it was and applying the new law to the present case.

An American Judge, Cardozo J, stated that in order to avoid this problem the court might adopt prospective overruling. This is a method of treating the present case on the old law, but announcing the new law for future cases. This only, of course, avoids the retrospective argument; could it be so arranged (eg by applying the new law to future arrangements only?) to avoid affecting settled arrangements? Also, wouldn't it be extremely unfair to the losing litigant, who would have persuaded the judge(s) to accept his legal argument but still have lost the case?

The question that is really being asked is whether certainty and development of the law go together?

Judicial law making (3) | 15

An introduction to statutory construction

As our law becomes increasingly statutory, with upwards of sixty new public Acts of Parliament each year (as well as innumerable statutory instruments (SIs)), the interpretation of those statutes becomes increasingly the judge's central role. There will always be a need for such interpretation and construction. Words are ambiguous, phrases and paragraphs are more so; and no legislator can cover every possible future case clearly. *Professor Hart* has spoken of the core of settled meanings of words and the penumbral area of doubt. It is in these penumbral areas of doubt that the litigation is brought before the courts. Since under our Constitution matters of law are decided by the judges, the task of working out the meaning of the unclear statutory provision, and seeing if it applies to the (frequently unforeseen) case before them, falls to the judges. The problem was clearly identified by Lord Macdermott when he stated that the difficulty lies with finding unambiguous words with which to convey the intention of the legislature.

Various sorts of problems can arise. A distinction is often attempted between interpretation (deciding the meaning of the words) and construction (seeing if the words apply to a particular case): the definitions in brackets are only one variant. This distinction is perhaps too simplistic, bear in mind that apart from those cases where the meaning is obvious and straightforward (enabling both the judge and the layman organising his affairs to see what the statute means immediately), there are cases where a particular word or phrase is ambiguous, cases where it is unclear whether a particular fact-situation was meant to be included, cases where the particular punishment intended is not clear, cases where the legislature appears to have left out an obvious case, and cases where the result on the straightforward meaning of the words is absurd.

Note the frequent use of the words 'meant' and 'meaning'. Judges often say that they seek 'the intention of Parliament': the 'great debate' between the literal meaning and the mischief-purpose approach is said to hinge on whether Parliament's intention is to be gleaned merely from its exact words ('he meant what he said') or also from a consideration of why the statute was passed (its purpose) and what Parliament would have done if it had had the particular case in mind. Any search for 'intention', purpose, etc, is to an extent a fiction. A body like Parliament is made up of many people, who may not vote at all on a measure, or may vote for the measure for tactical reasons without considering its consequences, or may vote for it for tactical reasons apart from the actual content. Often votes are on general principles, and yet the matters that come before the courts will be detailed and perhaps highly technical.

To that extent, then, one cannot say that Parliament 'intended'. However, the judges are looking at Parliament's words and must (under the parliamentary supremacy doctrine) follow and attempt to apply those words. While guidance may not be available on a particular matter, it is clearly the case that, on general principles at least, it does not seem so absurd to search for a parliamentary 'intention'. Surely the Sex Discrimination Act was *intended* to remedy some aspects of discrimination against women, the Unfair Contract Terms Act was *intended* to control exemption clauses and the Supplementary Benefits Acts are *intended* to set up a scheme providing those with no income with a state safety-net? And more specific provisions can be seen to be *intended* – a provision repealing an earlier provision or overturning an earlier case; a provision following a Law Commission recommendation where no-one in Parliament argued with the Commission's reasons. Whether it be intention of the draftsman, or intention of the proposer, or intention of the majority, there is some sense in the concept 'Parliament's intention'.

Having said that, it should be emphasised that most often in difficult cases Parliament's intention is not clear. On a disputed provision, did Parliament intend to protect from that specific type of exemption clause? It is precisely because the words do not make clear what the intention is that the problem arises in that case, and in general – if the words are not clear, how are the courts to decide what 'Parliament's intention' was? To put it another way, what do the words as enacted by Parliament legally mean?

Canons and presumptions

Apart from the major rules considered herein, in cases where statutory words are obscure or unclear judges may use one or other of the following canons of construction and presumptions.

Canons

The statute must be read as a whole
The words of the particular sub-section in question must not be read in isolation, but must be read with the other sections (particularly any interpretation section) and with the Schedules. As we shall see below, this canon is now subsumed by *Professor Cross*'s reformulation of the major rules, where he emphasises that the context of the words is in account.

Eiusdem generis
If a general word follows two or more specific words, the general word must be restricted in meaning to a meaning of the same kind (eiusdem generis). For example, *Powell* v *Kempton Park Racecourse Co* [1899] AC 143 turned on whether in relation to places of betting the words 'house, office, room or other place' included the racecourse itself: no, said the House of Lords, since the general words 'other place' were restricted to a meaning of the same kind as the specific words, ie an indoor place of betting.

Narrow construction of penal provisions
The individual gets the benefit of any doubt if a criminal or tax liability is imposed by statute, in particular against the imposition of liability without fault.

1978 Interpretation Act

This Act gives presumptive interpretations to common words and phrases in statutes: so 'men' includes 'women' (and vice versa), singular includes the plural, distances are to be measured in a straight line on the horizontal plain, time refers to Greenwich Mean Time and so on: all subject to contrary intention (which must sometimes be expressly stated, but most often must just 'appear').

Presumptions

Against alteration of the law

This presumption does not work against a change in the general (common) law which appears clearly from the literal meaning of the words; but if there is a doubt, Parliament will be presumed to have left the law unaltered.

Against imposition of without-fault liability

To create a strict liability offence, Parliament must use clear words.

Against ousting the jurisdiction of the courts

The courts are very protective of their own jurisdiction; although Parliament may alter the courts' jurisdiction even fundamentally, it must do so clearly. In administrative law, for example, in several cases the courts have evaded statutory attempts to forestall judicial review (*Anisminic* v *Foreign Compensation Commission* [1969] 2 AC 47, *Padfield* v *Minister of Agriculture* [1968] AC 997 and *Pyx Granite Ltd* v *MHLG* [1960] AC 260.)

Against the Crown being bound by a statute

The Crown must be expressly named, or it is not bound by a statute.

    Lord Advocate v *Dumbarton District Council; Lord Advocate* v *Strathclyde Regional Council* [1989] 3 WLR 1346: there was a rule of construction that the Crown was not bound by statute save where expressly named, or by necessary implication.

Against depriving a person of a vested right

The above are just examples. It may be quite possible to find canons and presumptions to support quite conflicting contentions.

The three rules of statutory construction

It is often said that there are three rules of statutory interpretation, these being the mischief, literal, and golden rules. As we shall see they are to an extent contradictory; all can claim judicial support.

Mischief rule

This rule was prevalent in the sixteenth century. The courts have regard to the purpose of the Act, and interpret it in such a way that the purpose is fulfilled or enhanced. The classic statement of the rule is contained in *Heydon's Case* (1584) 3 Co Rep 74 where the Barons laid down four things to be considered when interpreting statutes: the common law before the Act, the mischief that the law did not provide for, the remedy appointed for that mischief, and the true reason of the remedy. Of course, not all statutes are altering the common law today, and the exact formulation therefore needs changing. The approach – while not now as prevalent as it was – still commands judicial support, and has authorities following it in many areas.

A recent example can be taken form the law against racial discrimination. Although there is a requirement in the mischief rule that the express words of the statute must reasonably bear the purposive meaning given to them, in *Mandla* v *Dowell Lee* [1983] 2 AC 548 the House of Lords interpreted the Race Relations Act where it is stated that it is an offence to discriminate in certain matters against a person 'on grounds of his race, colour, ethnic or national origin' in quite a different manner. The facts of the case were that a young Sikh male wanted to join a public (fee paying) school. He was granted admission but was required to conform to uniform regulations and remove his turban and cut his hair. For reasons of faith he was unwilling to do this. There were other Sikhs in the school who had conformed to the uniform requirement and there was no suggestion that Dowell Lee (the headmaster) had any inclination to discriminate against Sikhs. The Court of Appeal carefully considered the history of the Sikh people and concluded that they were a group identifiable only by their common religion and that as the statute makes no mention of religion then the actions of the school were reasonable and not illegally discriminatory. The House of Lords, relying on a New Zealand case concerning the position of the Jews (*King Ansell* v *The Police* [1979] 2 NZLR 531), held that the purpose of the section was to cover situations such as the present and that by a stretch the Sikhs could be regarded as a group identifiable by a common ethnic origin. The reason for so holding was to extend the protection afforded by the Act to Sikh people.

Had the court been minded to find otherwise then it might have followed the case of *Ealing London Borough Council* v *Race Relations Board* [1972] AC 342 which held to the literal approach (see below) in holding that discrimination against a Polish citizen in the granting of public housing was lawful because it was not on grounds of his national origin but on grounds of his citizenship or nationality. Perhaps this comparison between these two cases reinforces the view that in their choice of which rule of statutory construction to apply the judges in effect determine the outcome of the case.

Literal rule

Various factors, including the declining influence of the judges on legislation and the development of Parliamentary supremacy, led to a retreat from the mischief rule approach to the literal approach. Here, the intention of Parliament is considered as contained in the words passed: the literal meaning of those words must be taken, even if the result appears to be one which Parliament did not intend. Lord Esher in *R v City of London Court Judge* [1892] 1 QB 273 stated that '... the court has nothing to do with the question whether the legislature has committed an absurdity ...'. This follows on the constitutional provision that it is the role of the legislature to make law and the role of the judiciary to interpret the law the legislature so makes.

Many cases support this 'rule' of applying the clear and unambiguous words of Parliament. For example, in *Inland Revenue v Hinchy* [1960] AC 748 the House of Lords was construing a provision which visited upon people incorrectly completing tax returns a penalty of 'treble the tax that ought to be charged under this Act'. Presumably Parliament intended the punishment to be three times the excess owed: but those words meant three times the whole tax bill for the year, which cost poor Mr Hinchy £418 instead of £42!

Note at this stage two things. First, often words are not clear and unambiguous; two equally 'usual' meanings of a word might exist, or the application of words to particular cases might be in doubt, and so on. Second, it is not unknown for different judges to consider the 'literal meaning' of the words and end up with different results (eg *Liversidge v Anderson* [1942] AC 206).

Golden rule

Judges have often mitigated the strict literal approach by calling into play the 'golden rule', that is that if the usual interpretation results in consequences so absurd that Parliament could not possibly have intended them, any secondary meaning may be taken. In the case of *R v Allen* (1872) 11 NSWSCR 73 which concerned the definition given to the offence of bigamy in the Offences Against the Person Act 1861 as '... whoever being married, marries another ...' where it was observed that such a definition if applied literally would lead to the absurd conclusion that the offence could never be committed. A person cannot legally marry if they are already married. There the court held that, as Parliament could not have intended to legislate nonsense, the words should be changed to read 'whoever being married goes through a marriage ceremony with the intention to marry etc ...'. Then the offence has meaning which would probably be consistent with the intention of the legislature.

Obviously, the three rules above cannot really be taken as strict 'rules': they tend to contradict each other (for example, taking the literal meaning often obscures the purpose of the statute). At most they are possible approaches, with the judges choosing the most appropriate in the circumstances, generally plumping for the literal rule and taking the obvious plain meaning unless some good reason to the contrary appears.

Even this does not seem to be a good explanation of what happens if we accept that the judges generally follow the approach of looking at the literal meaning.

What of those cases where two meanings are equally 'usual' and neither of the other two approaches is relevant or helpful? What of technical words?

A rather more successful attempt at formulating the courts' approach has been made by *Professor Cross* in *Statutory Interpretation*. He suggests that the literal and mischief rules have been mixed, and the vital element of context added: the judges look to see what the ordinary (or, if appropriate, technical) meaning of the words used is in the general context (including the objects) of the statute. It is that ordinary meaning that may be displaced by a secondary meaning if the result would otherwise be absurd: and furthermore, in cases where what seem like simple mistakes make a statute unintelligible, absurd or totally unworkable, a judge may add or delete words, to change nonsense into sense (*Cross* cites *Adler* v *George* [1964] 2 QB 7 and Lord Denning in *Eddis* v *Chief Constable* [1969] 2 Ch 345).

The whole problem tends to originate from the old-fashioned idea that a statute is intended to cover every conceivable contingency. The modern idea of 'framework' acts which lay down general rules of guidance, and which, of necessity, will require some considerable degree of interpretation is compounded by poor drafting and imprecise use of words.

This is clearly stated by *Lord MacDermott* thus:

'... the difficulty of finding unequivocal language by which to convey the will of parliament ... [lies at the heart of the problem of statutory construction] ...'.

Hypothetical examples

Much of what judges do is obvious, even when they construe difficult or ambiguous sentences or phrases: although we must consider the pros and cons of judges following a 'purposive' as against the traditional 'literal' approach, we must also emphasise that in fact it is in comparatively few cases that a straightforward 'literal v purposive' clash occurs.

The following fact situations might help to make the point.

a   A particular word or phrase has a straightforward obvious 'usual' meaning, for example 'driving a motor-car at over 70 mph is an offence'. A driver knows that once the speedometer tops 70 he is committing an offence, the judge when he is deciding applies the obvious meaning of motor-car, driving and 70 mph and convicts.

   This is straightforward literal approach: in relation to this case, the words have only one meaning.

b   A particular word or phrase has several meanings: eg the verb 'wants' ('wishes' or 'lacks'?) the noun 'will' ('volition' or the document by which a deceased person leaves his property?).

   The context of the phrase in the statute usually makes it clear which sense is meant: eg a reference to providing what a lunatic 'wants' will refer to what he lacks; a reference to 'the will of the testator' in a statute on probate will generally mean the document (but could in context mean the volition, as 'the will of the testator was overborne by force').

The judge applies that obvious meaning. Not quite the literal approach, since there were two 'usual' meanings (and in the case of 'wants', the one chosen was, if anything, the less obvious or usual of the two). But can this really be called a purposive approach? We are looking at the in-context meaning, and purpose is relevant only as part of the context.

c As situation (a), except that this meaning either produces an absurd result, eg (ignoring the Interpretation Act) 'it is an offence to steal horses', and the defendant steals just one (so not guilty under literal meaning) or produces a result clearly against the intention of the Act, eg if the Race Relations Act defined 'racial group' in a technical way which excluded negroes. As to the absurd result, holding that the statute meant something else, this clearly involves the judge in rectification, which *Cross* allows as his third rule; not the golden rule, as there is only one meaning the words can bear (and therefore no secondary one to fall back on).

As to the result clearly against the intention of the Act, any suggestion that the judge acts in accordance with that intention and not the words of the Act does lead to a purpose v intention conflict. Note, however, that in general the courts have not invoked the mischief rule in this sort of case: an attempt by Lord Denning to fill in the gap left in a statute in the case of *Seaford Court Estates* v *Asher* [1949] 2 KB 481 was slapped down by the House of Lords, Viscount Simmonds rejecting this 'naked usurpation' of the legislative role (*Magor & St Mellons RDC* v *Newport Corporation* [1951] 2 All ER 839). If the result is not absurd, the courts will follow the wording of a statute if it only allows of one construction, even if that construction does not follow the general purpose of the statute.

d As situation (b), except that one meaning is clearly the more usual, but that result leads to either absurd consequences or is totally against the intention of the statute. An example of absurd consequences could be the facts of the tax case *Inland Revenue* v *Hinchy* [1960] AC 748: an example of being against the intention of the statute can be seen from the USA controversy of whether reverse or positive discrimination is against the constitutional provision; forbidding laws which deny 'equal protection of the laws'. Does that mean any discrimination is unlawful or could 'equal protection' be taken to include the effect of reverse discrimination in redressing the balance and hence making more equal?

If the judge takes a secondary meaning to avoid absurdity, that is the golden rule in operation; if he takes it to accord with the intention of the statute; that could be taken as using the context of the statute, if not he is using purpose to displace the literal rule.

e As situation (b), except the context does not assist, the purpose of the statute does not assist, and the consequences would not be (more) absurd either way.

The judge uses his discretion – but none of our stated approaches/rules and is left to shape his own approach.

Literal words v purpose

In (c) and (d) above, then, there are possibilities for a clash between words and purpose: should the judge follow the obvious or only meaning of a phrase or sentence if that goes against the purpose of the statute?

It may help at this stage to summarise the various pros and cons.

Briefly, the arguments for the Literal approach:

a certainty;

b avoids judicial legislation;

c deference shown to Parliament;

d often difficult to know 'purpose'; even if overall purpose, did Parliament intend this provision to follow the purpose or to be the limit of its extension?;

e encourages more careful drafting.

And for the purposive approach:

a often not possible to work out which is literal meaning;

b not really deference to Parliament, refusing to fulfil its purpose;

c judicial legislation is common, eg in common law.

Aids to construction

Where a statute's construction is ambiguous or uncertain, various aids may be used by the judge to help him come to his decision.

The rest of the statute

A statute must be read as a whole, as we have said above; the judge must therefore decide in the light of the rest of the enactment (including the long title). In cases of uncertainty, those parts of the statute which are not part of it (preamble, marginal notes, punctuation) may be called in aid.

Other statute in pari materia

If construction is uncertain, a statute of the same subject may be called in aid, if it is unambiguous.

International treaties

If an Act is stated to be intended to give effect to an international treaty, uncertainties may be decided by reference to the treaty.

Reports of committees

When a committee is responsible for a bill its report is admissible as evidence of the state of the law prior to the Act, and therefore the mischief to be remedied (eg Law Reform Committee, Law Commission).

The recent decision of the House of Lords in *Pepper* v *Hart* (1993) that to aid interpretation a judge may take into account reports of *Hansard* on debates, questions and other matters pertaining to ambiguous legislation will go considerably to clarify statutory interpretation. Note, however, that this will only be permitted where to interpret an ambiguous statute literally would lead to absurdity.

Are these exclusions justified? The exclusion of these matters, particularly of debates in Parliament, follows from the use of the literal approach: we are looking for Parliament's intentions as expressed in the words of the statute, the argument runs, and if the words do not express the intention, extrinsic evidence cannot be used to supply that intention. Further, using evidence from debates might lead to much longer submissions and much work for the lawyers (and expense for the litigants) wading through Hansard to find supporting passages, and unscrupulous MPs could say things in debate with a view to possible citation in favour of one side in a later case.

A joint report of the English and Scottish Law Commissions has suggested various reforms in this area. Of interest here is that they agree with the present position on legislative debates, but recommend that relevant reports on which the legislation is based should be admissible. They even tentatively suggest the use of material prepared to go with the statute to explain it; in terms of a possible future code they recommend that an explanatory statement and illustrative commentary on it could be authoritative. Also they urge the courts to accept constructions promoting the general underlying legislative purpose.

A later committee, the Renton Committee on the Preparation of Legislation 1975, follows this last recommendation, and the one proposing reference to any mentioned international treaty or agreement; but they demur from the recommendation about relevant committee reports.

Effect on drafting

Past and present practice of the courts on statutory interpretation clearly affect how draftsmen work on future legislation. An example from the nineteenth century Wills Act, cited by *Cross (Statutory Interpretation*, p12) shows how ridiculous were the lengths to which draftsmen then were driven to avoid the rigours of the full-blown literal approach. The courts are not quite as exacting any more, and do take at least the context into account with the words, but the enduring pre-eminence of the literal approach and the eagle-eyes of eager lawyers intent on taking every possible point for their clients do still affect the form and structure of present legislation.

Procedure

Generally, the procedure for drafting is a careful one, especially if the statute is 'lawyer's law', rather than dictated by party policy. For example, the Law Commission will issue a working paper, followed by a report with draft Bill, or the government will issue draft proposals (in Green or White Paper form) for consultation. As much time as possible is given to allow lawyers and others to look for, inter alia, drafting mistakes.

Detail

Often statutes go into great detail, to avoid unwanted interpretation: eg Employment Act 1980, sections defining the outlawed secondary action and secondary picketing. However, it should be noted that, as a general trend, there is a current 'fashion' for the framework or skeleton act.

Examples

Many statutes give examples of the instances intended to be covered as the factors to be taken into account: eg 1973 Matrimonial Causes Act, ss23–25, detailing the factors to be taken into account by a judge in deciding the financial provision on divorce as examples (because 'all the circumstances' are in account).

Discretion

When judges are intended to have discretion on a particular matter to decide in accordance with the statute's purposes, this is sometimes expressly stated in terms. Section 23 Matrimonial Causes Act is again a good example; the judge must do 'what is just and equitable in all the circumstances' in an attempt to put the parties in the position they would have been in if the marriage had not broken down.

Interpretation

Many statutes contain their own interpretation sections.

Dispute solving (1) | 16

Introduction

It cannot be in the interests of any society that seeks to achieve or maintain some form of consensus to have disputes between its subjects going unresolved for any considerable length of time. In this and the following chapters we shall consider mechanisms for the resolution of disputes by third parties. Where disputes are resolved by the parties themselves to the dispute then that is a matter of negotiation and agreement. Although the vast majority of disputes in our society are resolved in this manner it does not involve the work of the legal profession and as such is not deemed important for this course. We shall concern ourselves so far as the syllabus requires with mechanisms for the resolution of disputes that involve the participation of persons other than those directly concerned in the dispute. These are referred to as third party mechanisms. In this chapter we shall look at the court structure.

Courts may be classified in a number of different ways according to context.

Superior and inferior courts

Superior courts: with unlimited jurisdiction – including the House of Lords, the Privy Council, the Supreme Court and the Crown Court.

Inferior courts: with jurisdiction limited either by value or geographically or both, eg County Courts, Magistrates' Courts.

Courts of record and courts not of record

This is a historical division, based upon whether the court kept official records of its proceedings or not. This no longer applies, the essential difference now is that only courts of record have power to punish for contempt of court. (See Contempt of Court Act 1981.)

Civil and criminal

English law and procedure are divided into two categories, civil and criminal, and a case will fall within one classification or the other. This is not a clear distinction, however, since with one or two exceptions many courts deal with both.

Courts of common law and equity

Until the Judicature Act of 1873 the common law was administered solely by the courts of common law and the rules of Equity by the Court of Chancery, the two being quite separate – having different procedures, being based on different principles, and offering different remedies. However, ss24–25 of the 1873 Act 'fused' the administration of law and equity, the jurisdiction of both the superior common law courts and the Court of Chancery was transferred to the High Court and judges are now required to apply both sets of rules, where relevant. Thus the modern Chancery Division of the High Court, though it is assigned some specialist matters once dealt with exclusively by the old Court of Chancery, no longer is the sole administrator of Equity.

Courts of first instance and appellate courts

A court of first instance is one when cases are heard for the first time. The jurisdiction of such courts is 'original'. In the case of most courts, decisions they make may be challenged by an aggrieved party and the matter will come before an appeal court. Many courts have both original and appellate jurisdiction. The whole appellate system will be looked at in detail in the next chapter.

The civil courts

Inferior courts

The County Courts

These were established by the County Courts Act 1846 and have only civil jurisdiction. Their jurisdiction is limited geographically, that is actions must be brought in the court either where the defendant resides or carries on business or alternatively where the cause of action arose. They are also limited as to the cases they can hear by financial criteria (though see the note at the end of this section as to dual jurisdictions).

The Courts and Legal Services Act 1990 s1 gave the Lord Chancellor power to make orders dealing with allocation of cases and jurisdiction of the High Court and county courts respectively.

In pursuance of s1 the Lord Chancellor made the High Court and County Courts Jurisdiction Order 1991, which came into effect on 1 July 1991.

The main provisions are as follows:

Article 2

a A county court has jurisdiction under inter alia ss15 (contract and tort), 21 (recovery of land), 25 (inheritance and family law) of the County Courts Act 1984, 'whatever the amount involved …'.

b A county court has jurisdiction concerning local land charges and rent charges if the sum concerned does not exceed £5,000.

c A county court has jurisdiction under the Law of Property Act 1925 and Land Charges Act 1972, where the value of the land does not exceed £30,000.

d A county court has jurisdiction under the Solicitors Act 1974 where the claim relates partly or wholly to contentious business done in a county court and the amount claimed does not exceed £5,000.

Article 3
The High Court may hear an application for an injunction made in the course of or in anticipation of proceedings in a county court.

Article 4
Subject to articles 5 and 6, proceedings in which both courts have jurisdiction may be commenced in either court.

Article 5
Proceedings involving claims for personal injuries (including death, disease and nervous injuries) in which a county court has jurisdiction must be commenced in a county court if the amount claimed is below £50,000.

Article 6
Any claim which is less than £25,000 must be commenced in the county court unless:

a the county court considers the matter should be transferred and the High Court agrees to take the action; or

b the case was commenced in the High Court and the High Court is of the opinion it ought to try the action.
   (This article lists the criteria by which county courts and the High Court should assess which of them should have jurisdiction.)

Article 8
A judgment or order of the county court for payment of money to be enforced wholly or partly by execution against goods must be enforced in the High Court only when the sum sought is in excess of £5,000 (provided it is not a judgment arising out of the Consumer Credit Act 1974) and must be enforced in a county court only if the sum is less than £2,000. Between £2,000 and £5,000 it may be enforced in either court.

Article 9
Article 9 is concerned with the criteria for defining the value of an action.
Although they deal with relatively minor claims County Courts are important as they offer a comprehensive, speedy and cheap procedure. They tend to be less formal; solicitors as well as barristers have a right of audience. They deal with probably 75 per cent of civil litigation.
   There are about 400 County Courts in England and Wales. Some of these, however, are specially designated Divorce County Courts which deal primarily with undefended divorces and related matters and this jurisdiction is not limited geographically.
   The County Courts are grouped, for administrative convenience, into the same circuit system as Crown Courts. They are staffed by Circuit judges, most courts

having at least one judge permanently attached to that Court. Judges sit alone, save that on very rare occasions they may be assisted by a jury of eight people.

The administrative business is the concern of the County Court Registrar who will be a solicitor of at least seven years standing. The Registrar also deals with procedural matters and tries minor cases, for example those which are both undefended and concern amounts of less than £500.

Appeals are possible from the Registrar, as with any court hearing (see next chapter).

The County Courts Act 1984, a consolidating Act, now governs the operation of these courts.

Magistrates' Courts

The jurisdiction of the Magistrates' Courts is largely criminal and for that reason these courts will be dealt with primarily under the heading of 'Criminal Courts' (see below).

The Magistrates' Courts have, additionally, a very varied civil jurisdiction. This includes:

a   affiliation orders;

b   matrimonial – eg, protection against violence, maintenance orders;

c   children – custody, adoption and guardianship;

d   orders (eg, under Children Act 1989) committing children into local authority care;

e   enforcement of debt orders for eg, gas, electricity, water rates, poll tax, income tax and national insurance contributions;

f   granting and renewing licences especially those for a) sale of alcohol, b) betting and gaming premises.

When dealing with the first four items above, the Justices of the Peace (JPs) are specially trained, and at least one of the justices must be a woman. In these cases the bench is sometimes known as a 'domestic court'. The usual rules as to publicity are considerably restricted. Note that in 1985 the Law Society called for an end to the Magistrates' Courts' family jurisdiction and the establishment of a wholly separate system of 'family courts' to deal with this type of case.

Note that the civil work of the Magistrates' Courts is, to a large extent, governed by statute. See the later notes on the criminal aspects of the JPs' jurisdiction, and in particular take note that it would seem inevitable that sooner or later the whole system must be overhauled and reformed, or it will break down from sheer pressure of work.

The High Court

Supreme Court of Judicature

The Judicature Acts 1873–75 reorganised the system of civil courts by abolishing the various separate courts which had previously existed and replacing them with the Supreme Court (comprising the Court of Appeal and the High Court).

The Supreme Court Act 1981 now governs its day to day running.

The Court of Appeal will be dealt with in Chapter 17, which is concerned with appeals.

The High Court

Before the Courts Act 1971, the High Court sat solely in the Law Courts in the Strand, although High Court judges also tried some civil cases on assize.

The High Court has both civil and criminal jurisdiction, original and appellate functions. This chapter is concerned only with the Courts' original functions.

Procedure in the High Court (and Court of Appeal) is governed by the Rules of the Supreme Court ('The White Book'). Although all three divisions have equal competence, in practice they have separate jurisdiction, laid down partly by the Rules and partly by statute. There are no financial or geographical limitations to the High Court system (within England and Wales).

The Queen's Bench Division

The head of this Division of the High Court is the Lord Chief Justice. It has the largest number of puisne judges (approximately 50) and the widest jurisdiction of any of the three Divisions. Any action not specifically assigned to the other two Divisions will be heard here. Its original civil jurisdiction includes actions for tort, breach of contract and recovery of land.

Two specialised courts sit within the Queen's Bench Division: the Admiralty Court and the Commercial Court. Both courts have judges assigned to them on a permanent basis who 'specialise' in the relevant areas of law. They also have rather different procedural rules in order to deal more efficiently with the type of case assigned to them.

a   *The Admiralty Court* deals with such matters as claims for injury or loss through shipping accidents, marine insurance and salvage. It is common to find experienced laymen (known as assessors) sitting with a judge in the Admiralty Court.

b   *The Commercial Court* provides not only normal open-court hearings, but an arbitration service for businessmen and others. It is mainly concerned with insurance, banking, negotiable instruments (or other areas of law particularly concerned with the commercial world).

The Queen's Bench Division also exercises the supervisory powers of the old Court of King's Bench by means of the prerogative orders which the Divisional Court is empowered to grant (RSC O.53).

This function, that of judicial review, is of great importance; it has already, for example, been mentioned in the context of scrutiny of delegated legislation. Though the concern of the Divisional Court it is not, strictly speaking, an appellate function. The court does not take over the decision-making function itself; it merely checks the manner in which the decision is reached.

There are three prerogative orders and one prerogative writ:

a mandamus   –   used to compel the execution of a legal duty;

b prohibition   –   an order to prevent a particular form of activity;

c certiorari   –   an order that a decision taken without jurisdiction or contrary to the rules of natural justice should be corrected;

d habeas corpus –   the prerogative writ, probably better known than the prerogative orders.

The Chancery Division

This Division inherited the work formerly carried out by the old Court of Chancery; other functions have been assigned to it from time to time by statute.

The titular head of this Division is the Lord Chancellor, who in practice never sits, so the effective head is the Vice-Chancellor, who is also an ex-officio judge of the Court of Appeal. There are 12 puisne judges.

Most Chancery actions are heard in London, but they can also be tried at certain centres in the regions (eg the North of England, Birmingham).

This Division tries most matters concerned with land, and is given jurisdiction over contentious probate, bankruptcy, revenue matters, trusts, mortgages, company matters and winding up, landlord and tenant and so on.

Some matters are dealt with by specialist courts formed within the Division. For example, there are the Companies Court, the Patents Court and the Court of Protection (which deals with the affairs of mental patients under the Mental Health Act 1983).

The Family Division

This Division was created by the Administration of Justice Act 1970. There are 16 puisne judges and the senior judge is known as the President.

Its jurisdiction at first instance includes all defended matrimonial actions (undefended divorces being the province of the County Court), proceedings concerned with the validity of a marriage, proceedings for a declaration of presumption of death, wardship, adoption, guardianship, domestic violence and *some* matrimonial property matters.

Note:

By the High Court and the County Court's Jurisdiction Order (SI 1991/724 (L5)), which came into operation on 1 July 1991, the High Court and County Court have concurrent jurisdiction.

Generally, at the option of the plaintiff, it is now possible to use the County Court, or the High Court for contract or tort actions even when they exceed the usual County Court limit of £5,000. Inheritance claims under the Inheritance (Provision for Family and Dependants) Act 1975, even though the net estate exceeds £30,000, and landlord and tenant claims, even though the rateable value of the property exceeds £5,000, may also be brought in the County Court.

Personal injuries actions *must* be brought in the County Courts, unless the plaintiff realistically expects to recover more than £50,000.

Family proceedings and admiralty jurisdiction remain unaltered.

The criminal courts

The Crown Court

The Crown Court was created by the Courts Act 1971 which implemented the recommendations of the Beeching Commission. It is part of the Supreme Court and replaces all previous courts listed below.

History

Before 1972 the courts where trials on indictment took place were the 61 Assize Courts and the 173 Quarter Sessions together with the Central Criminal Court, commonly known as 'the Old Bailey', and the Crown Courts of Liverpool and Manchester. Both Assizes and Quarter Sessions had a local jurisdiction, so that in general they could only try crimes committed within their locality and also the methods of court administration varied from area to area.

The Assize system was founded by Henry II in the twelfth century. The most serious offences were tried at assize by a judge sitting, not by virtue of his normal office, but under Royal commissions of *oyer and terminer* and *gaol delivery* and included at each Assize two or more High Court judges who tried the most serious cases and also heard civil cases. The Assizes were grouped into circuits and the judges and the Assize court staff moved round this circuit on a fixed timetable. This caused a great deal of inconvenience and inefficiency.

Less serious offences were tried on indictment by the Quarter Sessions. These were held at least four times a year and were composed of the justices of the peace for the locality presided over by a legally qualified chairman. Many of the towns had a borough quarter session presided over by a Recorder, a qualified lawyer, who sat alone.

Jurisdiction today

Three main types of judge preside over the Crown Court, depending on the seriousness of the case: High Court judges, Circuit judges and a special type of part-time judge known as a Recorder (see the later chapter on Legal Personnel for further details).

The Crown Court works on a three-tier system. First-tier courts take the most important cases and, as might be expected, third-tier courts the least serious.

There are 26 first-tier centres which take some civil as well as criminal cases, 17 second-tier courts which take only criminal cases and 52 third-tier courts taking the least serious work.

As to what constitutes 'serious' cases, the system is such that all indictable offences (over which the Crown Court has exclusive jurisdiction) are divided into four categories.

According to the class of offence, different judges will preside.

a *Class 1* includes offences (very few nowadays!) where the death penalty survives, murder, genocide, offences under the Official Secrets Acts, incitement or conspiracy. These, the most serious offences (or attempts at any of them) are always heard by a High Court judge.

b *Class 2* includes manslaughter, infanticide, rape, unlawful abortion, child destruction, incest, unlawful intercourse with an under-age girl, sedition, mutiny, piracy, offences under the Geneva Convention 1957 and incitement, conspiracy or attempts at any of these. Any offence in Class 2 will be tried by a High Court judge unless he specifically releases it for trial by a Circuit judge.

c *Class 3* is a residual category, and any offence not specifically listed in Class 1 or 2, but triable on indictment only, will be a Class 3 offence. Any of the three types of judge can try them.

d *Class 4* offences are mainly causing death by reckless driving and burglary, and are often cases which could have been tried by the Magistrates' Court had the accused not opted for trial by jury (see below). Any of the three types of judge may hear such cases.

Obviously the severity of the case decides which tier of court the trial goes to.

For administrative convenience the tiers are divided into six circuits in England and Wales. The circuits are: Northern (based in Manchester), North Eastern (Leeds), Midland (Birmingham), Wales and Chester (Cardiff), Western (Bristol), and South Eastern (London). Each circuit has at least two presiding judges and a circuit administrator, whose function is managerial rather than judicial.

The Magistrates' Courts

The Magistrates' Courts have been operating, more or less in the same form, for over 600 years.

Magistrates' Courts are composed of Justices of the Peace (JPs) who are laymen not lawyers. In big cities a stipendiary (or professional salaried) magistrate may be appointed, who will be a solicitor or barrister of at least seven years' standing. Stipendiary magistrates are appointed on the Lord Chancellor's recommendation, but are payable by the local authority concerned. There are perhaps 60 or so stipendiary magistrates as against several thousand ordinary lay JPs.

For trying an information summarily there must be at least two and not more than seven magistrates (or one stipendiary magistrate). In theory a lay magistrate may sit alone, but nowadays his powers are so limited that this rarely occurs. In practice the bench normally consists of three lay justices so that in the event of disagreement a majority verdict may be given.

Magistrates' Courts have a wide and varied jurisdiction, only part of it being criminal, but their jurisdiction is not only confined to minor matters, but limited geographically, being normally restricted to offences arising in the locality.

There are three main criminal aspects:

a   petty crime;

b   preliminary/committal proceedings;

c   juvenile hearings.

Petty crime

Certain offences can *only* be tried summarily, ie in a Magistrates' Court, without a jury. Such petty crime work accounts for perhaps 95 per cent or more of all the criminal trials in this country. The sort of offences are obviously minor – drunkenness, driving offences, breaches of the peace.

An increasing number of cases, especially motoring cases, are heard in the absence of the offender.

Preliminary/committal proceedings

Certain offences can either be tried summarily or on indictment in the Crown Court. They tend to be crimes of a fairly serious nature, for example theft or violent crimes. In such cases the accused has a right to choose; he may, if he wishes, elect to go to the Crown Court. An offender is entitled to trial by jury in all cases except those which may only be tried summarily according to the Criminal Law Act 1977. If he opts for trial in the Magistrates' Court, the accused must be warned that, should he be found guilty, if the JPs do not have adequate sentencing power in view of his previous record, he may have to be sent to the Crown Court for sentencing anyway.

Certain cases cannot be tried summarily and *must* go on indictment to the Crown Court for trial by jury. Before a case can be tried it must have been sent there by a Magistrates' Court by means of committal proceedings. This is purely a preliminary inquiry to see whether there is a case to be sent to the Crown Court. The court does not try to pre-judge the issue or reach any decision, but simply tries to assess whether on the basis of an outline of prosecution evidence there is a prima facie case to answer.

Note: A consultation paper published on 27 July 1989 by the Lord Chancellor's Department described committal proceedings as 'cumbersome and in need of reform'. It was proposed that a new procedure be instigated whereby cases go straight to the Crown Court. The defence could, however, give notice that they wished to apply to the magistrates to have the charges dropped on the grounds that the evidence discloses no prima facie case. This would remove an automatic right to committal proceedings but would speed up criminal proceedings as a whole.

Juvenile hearings

There are special Magistrates' Courts known as Youth Courts which deal with people under the age of 17 who commit offences. A Youth Court is composed of at least three lay justices (of whom at least one must be male and one female), drawn from a panel of specially-trained JPs. The Youth Court must not sit in any place where an adult court has been sitting in the last hour and the proceedings are not public. Beside a limited jurisdiction to 'punish' the young offender the court may also make a care order (putting the child in the care of the local authority) or a supervision order (probation officer), or may order the parents to exercise proper care and control of the child.

The supervision of the court and its functions is in the hands of the Clerk to the Justices, who will normally be a barrister or solicitor of at least five years' standing. While he may not influence the magistrates' decision he must be available to advise them on points of law. Given the fact that (apart from stipendiary magistrates) the JPs are laymen with minimal legal training the role of the Clerk is an important one.

The findings of the *Le Vay* Inquiry appointed by the Home Office in 1989 were not encouraging. They felt that the present system of Magistrates' Courts were out of date and fragmented with a totally haphazard system.

If the recommendations made by *Le Vay* are implemented the whole system would be reorganised. In particular local authority ties would be cut and the Home Office would run the Magistrates' Courts from a central director-general's office.

(For further details of magistrates and their clerks see chapter 19.)

Courts not within the main system

Coroners' Courts

The office of coroner has existed since at least the twelfth century.

The coroner was originally the King's official responsible for ensuring that the King got the revenue due to him, including treasure trove and possible fines arising from unexplained deaths.

The coroner's jurisdiction is now statutory. He must be a barrister, solicitor or registered medical practitioner of at least five years' standing. His main jurisdiction is inquests into the death of persons who appear to have died a violent or unnatural death or when the death occurred in prison or mental homes. He also has jurisdiction over treasure trove, gold, silver or money, when the owner cannot be traced. If declared to be treasure trove, it becomes the property of the Crown, though the finder is often rewarded.

The purpose of an inquest is to establish the cause of death of the deceased. The coroner is not concerned with any question of civil or criminal liability for the death.

The coroner may summon a jury of between seven and eleven members to hold an inquest. The procedure is inquisitorial, which means that the coroner conducts the proceedings and questions the witnesses. Formerly, if the jury returned a verdict of murder, manslaughter or infanticide the coroner could commit the person named for trial. This power was abolished by s56(1) Criminal Law Act 1977. The practice is that whenever a person has been charged with the crime to adjourn the inquest until after the trial. There is no appeal but the Coroner's Court is subject to control by the High Court by means of prerogative orders.

Military Courts

While members of the armed forces are subject in the main to ordinary law, and the jurisdiction of the ordinary courts, there are additionally special military courts or Courts Martial. These are largely concerned with the enforcement of special disciplinary rules which apply only to servicemen and women.

Since 1951 there is a right of appeal to the Court Martial Appeals Court, which has a similar jurisdiction and status to the Criminal Division of the Court of Appeal.

Ecclesiastical Courts

These courts 'lost out' to the main system of courts and most of their jurisdiction in divorce and probate is now within the ambit of the County Courts, and the High Court.

Since the last century their function is confined to the hearing of disputes between clergy or otherwise affecting churches and consecrated land. In each diocese there is a Consistory Court with, ultimately a right of appeal to the Judicial Committee of the Privy Council.

Dispute solving (2): 17
appellate jurisdiction

The House of Lords

Originally Parliament was a court which exercised certain judicial functions but by Tudor times this jurisdiction came to be exercised exclusively by the House of Lords. Until the Appellate Jurisdiction Act 1876 which created Lords of Appeal in Ordinary, appointed from eminent judges and lawyers, to hear appeals, any peer (including laymen) could hear appeals and vote on the decision, and often the only lawyer present was the Lord Chancellor. One result of this was that House of Lords decisions before 1876 carried very little legal authority, except in cases where the judges were invited to advise the House of the law.

Perhaps 10 per cent of all cases in the lower appellate courts are taken further to the House of Lords. Apart from 'leap-frogging cases' (see below) further appeal lies only with leave either of the Court of Appeal or the Appeals Committee of the House of Lords (usually composed of three law lords). Such leave will be granted only in cases of general public importance. *Blom-Cooper and Drewry* ('*Final Appeal*' pp125, 134) point out that the House is also generally influenced by the prospects of success in an appeal and the level of disagreement the case may have engendered in the lower courts.

Appeals are heard by at least three, and usually five judges who must be drawn from the Lords of Appeal in Ordinary, the Lord Chancellor and any other peer who has held 'high judicial office' which is defined by the 1876 Act. In practice only the Lords of Appeal ('law lords') normally sit, although some Lord Chancellors have also sat in recent times, eg Lord Hailsham in *Hyam* v *DPP* [1975] AC 55. The law lords are usually appointed from Lord Justices of Appeal, although there are usually two who were Scottish High Court judges because the House of Lords is also the final appeal court for Scotland. They number between seven and eleven.

Appeals are heard generally in a committee room and their lordships do not wear robes. Strictly the lords do not give 'judgments' but instead give 'opinions' stating the reasons for their vote whether to allow or dismiss the appeal. If the House is equally divided the appeal is dismissed, and while normally this situation does not arise because an uneven number sits, it can occur – such as when a law lord dies before giving judgment and the House is otherwise equally divided: see *Kennedy* v *Spratt* [1972] AC 83 (Lord Upjohn died). The House is usually very reluctant to interfere with a trial judge's exercise of discretion, save in those cases where the judge is demonstrably wrong either in the light of further evidence, change of circumstances, or in point of law. Such an exercise of discretion will not be interfered with 'merely on the ground that the members of the appellate court would have exercised the discretion differently …' – Lord Diplock in *Hadmor Productions* v *Hamilton* [1982] 1 All ER 1042 at p1046 HL.

The House of Lords has very little original jurisdiction. The trial of one of its members 'by his peers' was abolished in 1948 and impeachment (prosecution of political offenders) is obsolete. The only remaining matters of original jurisdiction are breaches of privilege and disputed claims to peerages.

The jurisdiction of the House is almost entirely appellate, hearing appeals from:

a   the Court of Appeal (with the leave of either the Court of Appeal or the Appeals Committee of the Lords);

b   the High Court ('leap frog' procedure, with leave of the House of Lords, on a point of law of general public importance;

c   the Inner House of the Court of Session (Scotland);

d   the Court of Appeal (Northern Ireland).

The general Criminal appellate jurisdiction of the House was only created in 1907 by the Court of Criminal Appeal Act.

Note that the House of Lords is not part of the Supreme Court, even though it is the highest appellate court. This is due to the fact that when the Supreme Court was formed it was intended to abolish the Lords. This was only reversed by the 1876 Act.

One important question which should be considered is whether the luxury (if such it is) of a second appeal court is justifiable. The extra delays and costs of an appeal to the House of Lords can be great, and are often (as a matter of financial practicality) available only to such as the Inland Revenue, government departments, and large corporations. It can also seem very odd to a litigant to lose a case in the House of Lords by a bare majority of 3:2 when he had won at first instance and unanimously in the Court of Appeal; ie only three judges out of nine against him.

The question appears to be not one of the undoubted efficiency or speed of the conduct of an appeal: *Blom Cooper and Drewry* in their study of the Lords, *Final Appeal* (1972), suggest rather that it is simply a matter of 'social utility'. What is the function of the House of Lords? Certainly, as the second appeal court, the House of Lords is well-placed to supervise and direct major developments in the law, as well as correcting faulty decisions of the Court of Appeal. However, the House of Lords does not follow an actively law-making function and is frequently very concerned not to upset the status quo: this is particularly clear from their reluctance to depart from their own previous decisions. Yet, even if one sees the House of Lords as a body which *should* be more active in developing the law, what the House is able to do is largely a matter of chance, depending on which cases happen to be brought within their jurisdiction. Opinions vary greatly as to whether the House should be more active: a particular decision may cause dissatisfaction to some by not going far enough, by being too cautious, whereas to the more conservative it may seem to go too far, encroaching on the legislative function. These questions should be considered together with the issues raised in earlier chapters as to the function of the judiciary and the doctrine of precedent.

One important factor in favour of the current system is that whereas the Court of Appeal is bound by its own previous decisions the House is not. In this position there is a need for a final court to review these decisions – see Lord Diplock in *Davis v Johnson* [1979] AC 264 at p326:

'In an appellate court of last resort a balance must be struck between the need on the one side for the legal certainty resulting from the binding effect of previous decisions and on the other side the avoidance of undue restriction on the proper development of the law. In the case of an intermediate appellate court, however, the second desideratum can be taken care of by appeal to a superior appellate court if reasonable means of access to it are available ...'

However, it is not impossible that the House of Lords could be abolished and the Court of Appeal reconstituted so that, in certain cases, its own previous decisions could be reviewed. However, difficulties arise with the growing size of the Court of Appeal and the huge volume of work with which it must deal – with a possibly consequent lack of time to consider matters to the same extent as the House of Lords.

Civil appeals

Civil Appeals: introduction

Prior to the Judicature Acts of 1873–5 there was no general right of appeal – nor, indeed, was there any regular court of appeal. The main method of challenging a decision was by writ of error, heard by one of the courts of Exchequer chamber which lay merely for errors on the face of the court record. The Court of Appeal (civil appeals only) was created by the 1873 Act and a regular system of statutory appeals established. This was modelled partly on the Court of Appeal in Chancery which had been introduced in 1851 to deal with the particular problems facing the Court of Chancery in that period.

In the modern system, rights of appeal are statutory only and derive from the Judicature Acts – with more recent alterations and additions.

Court of Appeal (Civil Division)

This is the highest of the three courts which form the Supreme Court of Judicature, the other two being the High Court and the Crown Court.

The Court of Appeal has a number of ex officio judges including the Lord Chancellor, the Lord Chief Justice, the Master of the Rolls, the President of the Family Division, the Lords of Appeal in Ordinary and former Lord Chancellors. For all practical purposes, however, the Civil Division is composed of the Master of the Rolls and 26 Lords Justices of Appeal, though if needed High Court judges may also sit with Lords Justices of Appeal. In practice they rarely do so in the Civil Division, though it is common enough in the Criminal Division.

The normal number of judges is three, but when a difficult and important point of law occurs the court may consist of five. Interlocutory appeals may now be heard by a single judge sitting in chambers (in private). Further, appeals from County Courts are now usually heard by two judges, though three should sit if a difficult point arises. Recently, the procedure of the Court of Appeal (Civil

Division) underwent a number of changes, designed to speed up procedure and clear a backlog of cases, under the direction of Sir John Donaldson, the former Master of the Rolls. The administrative work of the divisions is supervised by two Registrars – the Registrar of Civil Appeals having been appointed first in 1982 as part of the remodelling of Civil Division procedure: see *Practice Note* [1982] 3 All ER 376.

Appeal is by rehearing using the original judge's notes and the written transcript of the trial. Arguments are heard from Counsel, witnesses are never normally heard a second time. Evidence which was available at the time of the original hearing but not used is never normally admitted, but in certain prescribed cases if fresh evidence is discovered a completely new hearing may be ordered.

Appeals to the Court of Appeal (Civil Division)

The rules governing appeals to the Court of Appeal were substantially amended in 1982, largely in order to speed up procedure and make it more efficient, and to clear up the large backlog of cases. For an explanation of the main points of these reforms, see *Practice Note* [1982] 3 All ER 376. The former Master of the Rolls, at p376, said:

'For a long time the delay in hearing civil appeals has been causing considerable anxiety. In February 1978 ... a committee was appointed under the chairmanship of Lord Scarman ... after a detailed study of the procedures of the court, it made a number of recommendations. The two most important were the creation of the office of registrar and a change in the law to enable a single judge of the Court of Appeal to deal with procedural matters.'

The recommendations of the Scarman Committee were implemented by the Supreme Court Act 1981 which, inter alia, made substantial changes to RSC O. 59 (Appeals to the Court of Appeal). The most significant change was the creation of the office of Registrar of Civil Appeals. See below.

Registrar's jurisdiction

The Registrar's function is to deal expeditiously with all incidental applications which are necessary pending an appeal (in chambers). Though the Scarman Committee did not recommend a change in the practice of presenting appeals orally (which 'lies at the heart of the English tradition' – [1982] 3 All ER 376 at 381), it did consider that the expensive preparations for the hearing of an appeal could be rationalised and directed in order to save time and cost. A substantial discretion is in the Registrar to give such directions as to 'matters incidental to the conduct of the appeal, as appear best adapted to secure the just, expeditious and economic disposal of the appeal'. (O.59 r 9(3), as amended).

Applications for such directions are made to the Registrar in chambers, and an appeal lies from his decision to a single Lord Justice of Appeal and thence to the Court of Appeal, with leave.

Applications to the Court of Appeal

Incidental applications may also be made to a *single judge* of the Court of Appeal in chambers (such were formerly made to two judges), or referred to him by the Registrar. Unlike the Registrar, a single judge has a jurisdiction to grant, vary or discharge injunctions or stays. A single judge may also grant leave to appeal. Appropriate applications may be made directly to the Court of Appeal or referred to it by a single Lord Justice.

Whereas appeals up to 1982 from both High Court and County Court were heard by three judges (or by a 'full' court of five or more in particularly important cases), the Supreme Court Act 1981 s54(4) now permits certain appeals (on the recommendations of the Scarman Committee) to be heard by two judges. These two-man courts may be used, inter alia, in the following cases:

a   Appeals from the County Courts;

b   Appeals from a single Lord Justice;

c   Interlocutory appeals from the High Court (including O. 14 appeals). In the event of deadlock arising in the form of the two Lords Justices disagreeing, the entire case must be re-argued before a reconvened Court of Appeal of three: s54(5) of the 1981 Act. If there is such disagreement there cannot be an appeal to the House of Lords without a reconvened hearing.

Procedure

The appellant prepares a *notice of appeal* (a type of notice of motion) setting out the grounds of appeal and specifying the order for which he applies. The Notice of Appeal must be served on all parties to the action within four weeks of the judgment in the court below (this time can be extended with the leave of the Registrar or Court of Appeal) and within seven days of service the appellant must set down the appeal for hearing. Appeals take on average from about three months to a year to come on for hearing.

A respondent to an appeal may contend that the order of the court below (or part of it) should be varied or affirmed on other grounds, or may cross-appeal that the decision was wrong. Otherwise, of course, a respondent (being the 'winner' in the court below) cannot appeal. His contentions are set out in a *respondent's notice*.

Once all the formalities have been completed, the Registrar gives all necessary directions (see above) – which are without a hearing unless either he or the party requires one (by summons).

In general, appeals are *by way of rehearing* though the Court of Appeal is not restricted to points raised in the lower court and can reconsider the case in the light of developments since the earlier hearing, eg new facts which have come to light (see below). However, the court does not hear all the evidence again but merely reads transcripts of the evidence given in the court below. However, a new practice has been encouraged in the production of *skeleton arguments* that is:

'a very abbreviated note of the argument ... (which) in no way usurp any part of the function of oral argument in court. They are an aide-memoire for convenience of reference before and during the hearing ...' (Sir John Donaldson MR, *Practice Note* [1983] 2 All ER 34)

Where evidence which was not given in the court below is sought to be admitted, the court will do so if it occurred since trial and may do so if otherwise providing; it could not have been discovered with reasonable diligence before trial; it is of importance to the case and is apparently credible.

Powers of the Court of Appeal

The Court of Appeal has full power to make any order which could have been made in the court below. However, the Court of Appeal is usually reluctant to upset the trial judge's finding of facts because he saw and heard the witnesses and was in a better position to assess their credibility. Further, the Court of Appeal is usually reluctant to interfere with a judge's exercise of his discretion where he has used it correctly, and with an award of damages unless it is out of proportion with awards in similar cases.

A successful appellant is normally awarded the costs of both the appeal and the original trial.

In appropriate cases the Court of Appeal may order a new trial. The grounds on which this may be done include a misdirection of the judge to the jury (in those few civil cases where it is still used), improper rejection of evidence, misconduct at the trial, judgment obtained by fraud.

Divisional Court of the High Court

In addition to its original jurisdiction, the High Court also exercises appellate jurisdiction for this purpose two or three judges sit together and constitute a Divisional Court.

Divisional Courts of the Queen's Bench Division may exercise both criminal (see below) and civil jurisdiction.

Civil appeals are heard from the decisions of certain tribunals (see next chapter).

The Divisional Court of the Chancery Division hears appeals from the County Courts on bankruptcy and other related matters. In the Family Division the Divisional Court hears Magistrates' Courts' appeals on domestic matters. The Divisional Court in the Queen's Bench Division, as well as its (largely criminal) appellate jurisdiction, hears applications for prerogative orders (see chapter 16 (above)). As has been noted earlier, this is not strictly an appellate function.

Criminal appeals

Before 1907 there was no *formal* system of appeals in criminal cases, only an informal arrangement where a trial judge might be prevailed upon to, effectively, consult with his brother judges. Following a miscarriage of justice which came to light in 1907, the Court of Criminal Appeal was established. In 1966 the Criminal Appeal Act further reformed the system. The present criminal appellate system is as follows:

The House of Lords

Though it has an appellate function in criminal cases (see above) this is not invoked as often as for civil cases. Probably the main reason is that few cases qualify on the criteria listed below as being one of sufficient general public interest to be heard by the Lords.

Either the prosecution or the defence may appeal from the Court of Appeal to the House of Lords if the following requirements are satisfied:

a the Court of Appeal certifies that a point of law of general public importance is involved in the decisions; and

b either the Court of Appeal or the House of Lords gives leave on the ground that the point in issue is one which ought to be considered by the House of Lords.

The House of Lords has the same powers as the Court of Appeal (see below) including those under 'the Proviso'.

Court of Appeal (Criminal Division)

The position is governed by the Criminal Appeal Act 1968 which sets out all rights of appeal available, following a trial on indictment. Appeal is to the Court of Appeal.

Appeal against conviction

There may be an appeal against conviction:

a on any ground which involves a question of law alone; and

b on any ground which involves a question of fact alone or of mixed law and fact, or any other ground which appears to the court to be a sufficient ground of appeal, with the leave of the Court of Appeal.

Leave may be granted by a single judge of the Court of Appeal.

Even if the defendant pleaded guilty, there may be an appeal against conviction, if the court is satisfied that the conviction is unsafe or unsatisfactory: *R v Lee* [1984] 1 WLR 578.

The Court of Appeal may allow an appeal against conviction if it considers:

a In all the circumstances of the case the conviction is unsafe or unsatisfactory.

b The judgment of the court should be set aside on the ground of a wrong decision of any question of law. This includes any misdirection by the judge to the jury in his summing-up.

c There was a material irregularity in the course of the trial.

It is to be noted particularly that it is always open to the Court of Appeal to rely on what is known as the 'Proviso'. The proviso states that even though the Court of Appeal opines that the appeal might be decided in favour of the appellant, it may dismiss the appeal if it considers that no miscarriage of justice has actually occurred: See s2(1) of the Criminal Appeal Act 1968.

It appears that the proviso will be applied if 'a reasonable jury, after a proper summing-up', could not have failed to convict the defendant.

The Court of Appeal has an additional power. Where:

a the jury could have found the defendant guilty of some other offence, and

b the jury must have been satisfied of the facts proving him guilty of that other offence,

it may substitute a conviction of that other offence and sentence the defendant accordingly: s3(1) of the Criminal Appeal Act 1968.

The Criminal Justice Act 1972 enabled the prosecution to appeal on a point of law to the Court of Appeal after an acquittal in the Crown Court. This did not mean that the jury's verdict of not guilty was overturned but it allowed for a misdirection on the law to be cleared up.

By s43 of the Criminal Justice Act 1988 the Court of Appeal may order a retrial where a conviction has been quashed.

Appeal against sentence
The defendant may appeal against the sentence passed by the Crown Court, but only with the leave of the Court of Appeal – s9 CAA 1968. There is no appeal against a sentence fixed by law.

The Court of Appeal will not interfere with the discretion of the judge below and will only interfere if the sentence is wrong in principle. It has power to reduce the sentence or substitute one form of detention for another.

On the recommendation of the Attorney-General the prosecution may appeal against an unduly lenient sentence to the Court of Appeal.

Section 36 Criminal Justice Act 1988

'(1) If it appears to the Attorney-General that the sentencing of a person in a proceeding in the Crown Court has been unduly lenient he may, with leave of the Court of Appeal, refer the case to them for them to review the sentencing of that person; and on such a reference the Court of Appeal may –

i) quash any sentence passed on him in the proceeding; and

ii) in place of it pass such sentence as they think appropriate for the case and as the court below had power to pass when dealing with him.'

This measure was introduced following an outcry in the media at the sentences imposed in certain cases.

Divisional Court of the Queen's Bench Division

Appeal here is made by way of 'case stated'.

By s111(1) of the Magistrates' Courts Act 1980, any person who was a party to proceedings before or aggrieved by the decision of the magistrates, may appeal against the proceeding on the ground that it is wrong in law or in excess of jurisdiction by applying to the magistrates, court to state a case for the opinion of a Divisional Court of the Queen's Bench Division.

Application must be in writing, made within 21 days after the date of the decision of the magistrates and indicating the point of law on which the opinion of the High Court is sought.

The 'case' to be stated by the magistrates must include the facts found by them and their decision. In settling a statement of the case the parties should also be consulted.

At the hearing before the High Court the parties will (usually) be represented by counsel and the court will determine the questions of law raised. The magistrates themselves are not usually represented, although they may file an affidavit dealing with any matters they consider to be of importance and relevance.

The High Court may:

a reverse, affirm or amend the magistrates' decision;

b remit the matter to the magistrates with its opinion;

c make such other order as it sees fit.

Note: Either party (but not a person aggrieved) to a decision of the Crown Court, other than one relating solely to trial on indictment, may apply for a case to be stated on the ground that the decision is wrong in law or in excess of jurisdiction.

The Crown Court

A defendant may appeal from the magistrates' court to the Crown Court.

a on conviction and sentence if he pleaded not guilty;

b on sentence only if he pleaded guilty.

There is no right of appeal against a committal to the Crown Court for sentencing. The procedure for appeal is as follows:

a Defendant gives notice of appeal within 21 days after the day on which the decision of the magistrates was given, to the magistrates' clerk and to the prosecution.

b By s48 of the Supreme Court Act 1981 the hearing before the Crown Court is a complete rehearing of the case. Therefore, the prosecution must prove its case afresh by calling its witnesses. New evidence may be tendered without leave of the court.

c On appeals against conviction, the crown court may confirm, reverse or vary the decision of the magistrates' court. This includes the power to increase the sentence to whatever the magistrates had the jurisdiction to impose.

On appeals against sentence, the crown court may impose any sentence which the magistrates' court could have passed.

d By s48(2) of the Supreme Court Act 1981 the Crown Court may 'make such other order in the matter as the court thinks just, and by such order exercise any power which the said authority might have exercised.'

Courts not within the main appellate system

Judicial Committee of the Privy Council

The Privy Council is the last remnant of the great council of the monarch (the curia regis). The curia regis was the source of most modern governmental and administrative institutions (eg Parliament, the courts, the Revenue) which gradually separated from it and became established in their own right. However, the Privy Council retains a small judicial jurisdiction which is exercised, on behalf of the Monarch, by the Judicial Committee (usually staffed by the Law Lords). Indeed the composition of the Judicial Committee corresponds to large degree with the membership of the House of Lords when sitting as a court of appeal, save insofar as certain judges from commonwealth countries may be empowered to sit in certain cases.

Although its judgments are not binding on English courts, they are strongly persuasive.

The jurisdiction of the Committee is as follows.

a Hearing appeals from outside the United Kingdom. The Privy Council hears appeals from the Channel Islands, the Isle of Man, British Colonies and protectorates and from the highest courts in those Commonwealth countries which have not abolished the right to appeal to the Privy Council.

b Admiralty jurisdiction. This is now limited only to appeals from the Admiralty court when sitting as a prize court (ie a court which determines issues concerning the ownership of ships and cargo captured by enemy warships).

c Appeals from ecclesiastical courts.

d Appeals from medical tribunals. A recent case on the general applicability of a Privy Council decision is *Peatfield* v *General Medical Council* [1987] 1 WLR 243 where Lord Keith of Kinkel, Lord Brandon of Oakbrook and Lord Mackay of Clashfern 'humbly advised' Her Majesty that various charges relating to the treatment of different patients were not bad for duplicity.

It may also advise on matters of law relating to the Commonwealth and Colonies. Membership includes all persons who have held high judicial office in the

Commonwealth but in practice the Court is usually composed of Law Lords, the usual number being five. When the Privy Council sits to hear ecclesiastical appeals, one archbishop (or the Bishop of London) and four other bishops sit as assessors, to advise. Only one majority opinion is given by the Committee, though dissenting opinions are recorded. The Committee does not give judgment, but simply advises the Sovereign who implements that advice by convention by Order in Council. The Committee may also be required by the Sovereign to advise on particular legal matters.

Employment Appeals Tribunal

Although this is called a tribunal it is in effect a court, a superior court of record, staffed by puisne judges and judges of the Court of Appeal one of whose number is appointed president (nominated by the Lord Chancellor), a judge from the Scottish Court of Session and lay members who are persons with special experience of industrial relations either as employers or trade unionists. The Tribunal was set up under the Employment Protection Act 1975 largely replacing the National Industrial Relations Court set up under the Industrial Relations Act 1971 passed by the Conservative government and repealed when the Labour party returned to power in 1974. Its jurisdiction is limited to hearing appeals, mainly on points of law from industrial tribunals. Hearings are informal, and the court sits with a judge and either two or four lay members.

The European Court of Justice

On 1 January 1973 by virtue of the European Communities Act 1972, the UK became a member of the European Communities – of which, at present, there are 12 member states. In fact, there are *three* distinct communities: the European Coal and Steel Community (ECSC), the European Economic Community (EEC) and the European Atomic Energy Community (EURATOM). However, the Communities are generally known by the name of the most publicised of the three, the EEC – 'the Common Market'. Each community was set up by a separate treaty, the Common Market by the Treaty of Rome (EEC Treaty).

The EEC Treaty gives the European Court of Justice (ECJ) jurisdiction to hear various matters concerning European law, including the power to review the legality of Community legislation (Articles 173–175 of the EEC Treaty). However, such actions take place entirely in the ECJ and are of no direct concern to the English courts. Article 177, on the other hand, is of direct interest here since it empowers the ECJ to hear references on questions of European law sent to it by the courts of the various member states, including England. The reference is *not* an appeal, and it is inaccurate to describe the ECJ as being situated within the structure of the appellate courts – especially since it may hear references addressed to it from any body exercising a judicial function (not just the House of Lords).

Article 177 gives the ECJ jurisdiction to hear references concerning:

a interpretation of the Treaty (the EEC Treaty);

b interpretation and validity of Acts of the Community Institutions (viz Community legislation);

c interpretation of the statutes of bodies established by the Council.

Any court or tribunal of a member state may make a reference – though if it is a court or tribunal from which there is no 'judicial remedy' (viz no appeal or judicial review) then it *must* make a reference on a point of European law if it is 'necessary' to reach a decision.

Where the English court has a discretion whether or not to make a reference, then it must consider the matters set out by Lord Denning MR in *HP Bulmer Ltd* v *J Bollinger SA* [1974] 3 WLR 202 CA, reaffirmed by Bingham J in *Customs & Excise Commissioners* v *APS Samex* [1983] 1 All ER 1042:

a only questions of Community law as opposed to domestic law may be referred;

b an English court will not refer a question unless the answer is 'necessary' to decide the particular case;

c if 'substantially the same question' has been answered in a previous case by the ECJ, the national court may follow that decision and not refer the matter;

d if a point is reasonably clear there is no need to refer it; and

e all the other surrounding circumstances must be taken into account eg the length of time, expense, the importance of not overloading the ECJ, the difficulty and importance of the point and the fact that the ECJ is the most appropriate court to consider European matters.

It may be questioned whether all of these items should legitimately be considered by an English court, eg the workload of the ECJ, given that it is the task of the ECJ to interpret Community law and such matters are better left for it to decide. However, Bingham J in the *APS Samex* case above did stress that it should be borne in mind that the ECJ is the appropriate court for deciding questions of Community law.

When a reference is made the court will stay the English proceedings (ie temporarily suspend) until it receives an answer to the point referred – which it must follow.

The court consists of eleven judges assisted by five Advocates General. Usually only seven judges and one Advocate General will sit to hear a case, though three smaller 'chambers' of three judges and one advocate general also sit. The business of the court is directed by the President of the Court, one of the judges elected by his fellows, and each Chamber has its own presiding judge. The judges and Advocates General are appointed from 'amongst persons of indisputable independence who fulfil the conditions required for the holding of the highest judicial office in their respective countries or who are jurists of recognised competence.' (Article 167(1) EEC).

Though the Advocates General have the same status as the judges they do not take part in the formal decisions of the ECJ. Their task is to make 'in open court, reasoned submissions on cases brought before the Court of Justice, in order to assist the Court ...' (Article 166 EEC). The Advocates General will give an independent opinion on the case which will be considered with great care by the judges, though they do not need to follow it. While the judges tend to be motivated by the needs of Community policy (much more blatantly than an English judge would be by policy considerations), it is the task of the Advocates General to give an impartial view of the case.

Only one judgment (always reserved) is given by the court, which is printed with the submissions of the Advocate General. Most of the representations to the court are in writing and oral procedure is used merely to expand existing submissions.

Where the court requires evidence to be given, this is done at an earlier stage in the preparatory inquiry – though, of course, this is not necessary on an Article 177 reference which is solely on a point of law.

The European Court of Justice has no enforcement machinery of its own to ensure that its rulings are complied with. Enforcement is left to the national courts and to their system of enforcement. We can conclude therefore that the relationship between the national courts of England and the European Court of Justice is both a legal and a political one.

Special orders and appeals

Applications to set aside orders by the courts which made them

Now that we have considered appeals proper, there should be noted the instances in which a court may set aside an order or judgment which it has made itself.
These include:

a   Orders which have been made in the absence of one party, particularly in cases of default judgment (see RSC O.13 and O.19) and ex parte orders, where one party has had no opportunity to be heard.

b   Consent orders are generally unappealable, and an application to set aside is the best method to challenge such an order. However, if the consent order indicates a genuine agreement between the parties then the court will only interfere with it on the same basis as it would interfere with any other contract. Where the consent order is not based upon a true agreement but merely on the basis that the parties do not object, then the court is free to vary the order – *Siebe Gorman* v *Pneupac Ltd* [1982] 1 WLR 185.

c   In the County Court, where no errors are alleged on the part of the trial court, application may be made to order a rehearing in order to correct technical or procedural slips. If errors are alleged, the correct procedure is an application to the Court of Appeal.

Under s17 Supreme Court Act 1981, provision is made for rehearing by the High Court.

Appeals from the orders of courts of first instance

Orders of masters or registrars

In certain types of case more suited to arbitration the case may be referred to a master or registrar. These are often non-judicial appointees or else have both a legal and other (eg accountancy, surveying) qualification. There is a general right of appeal to the High Court (masters) and to the County Court (registrars). In the High Court appeals are by way of rehearings, in the County Court appeals are actual appeals. The judge in either court is not bound by any earlier exercise of discretion (*Evans* v *Bartlam* [1937] AC 473), and there is no appeal from the actual arbitrational decision. The only remedy for a successful appellant will be an order to have an award set aside – the whole process will effectively have to be started all over again.

Orders of a High Court judge

Generally appeal lies to the Court of Appeal, though leave is necessary in the following cases:

a *Interlocutory orders* except (inter alia) those which affect the liberty of the subject, those granting/refusing injunctions or refusing unconditional leave to defend.

b *Final orders* where the order was a consent order or concerned costs only. Otherwise no leave for appeals from final orders needed.

The distinction between 'final' and 'interlocutory' orders is an elusive one: the best definition available is one which defines 'final orders' as those which finally dispose of the matter in dispute. See *Salter Rex* v *Ghosh* [1971] 2 QB 597 CA. No appeal will lie from a judge's refusal to grant leave.

Appeals may be made directly to the House of Lords (Administration of Justice Act 1969, ss12 and 13) providing all the parties consent, the House grants leave, and the trial certifies a point of law of general importance, for example:

a Statutory construction.

b Where the point has already been considered inconclusively by the House of Lords or Court of Appeal.

This is so-called 'leapfrog' appeal. There is no appeal from refusal to grant a certificate.

Orders of a County Court judge

With the following exceptions, the matters referred to in (b) above apply also to appeals from the County Court to the Court of Appeal:

a There are no 'leapfrog' appeals

b Leave is required for final orders if the claim was for less than half the relevant County Court limit, or if the order was one made by the judge on appeal from the registrar.

Dispute solving (3) | 18

Tribunals: introduction

Just as many people consider that the House of Lords and Court of Appeal are more worthy of consideration than the Magistrates' Court and County Court (the inaccuracy of which it is hoped has been shown earlier), so too many people dismiss the system of tribunals as being an unimportant part of the English legal system. In this chapter we shall consider the other third party mechanisms for dispute resolution apart from the courts and will pay particular attention to the body of tribunals and the availability of arbitration for certain types of dispute.

Reasons for having tribunals

The tribunal system is a massive structure which runs alongside the normal court system. One is as important as the other.

Reference must be made to a distinction first utilised by *Abel-Smith and Stevens* (*In Search of Justice*). They distinguished between two types of pressure leading to the creation of tribunals:

a pressure to take certain decisions out of the hands of Government, and give them to tribunals as independent centres of power, thus able to counter-balance Governmental power;

b pressure to provide more satisfactory adjudicatory bodies than the ordinary courts.

Policy orientated and court substitute tribunals

The pressures mentioned led to the development of two types of tribunal. Each will now be considered in turn.

The policy-orientated tribunal

During the twentieth century, as the economic and social structure in this country has become more complex, many new areas of dispute between individuals, groups and state agencies have arisen. The development of the welfare state has brought with it new rights and duties not formerly recognised by the law. The new welfare system is based upon a particular policy and conception of society. It is given effect by being written into the laws of the country, but it is the policy behind the written wording of the law that is important. Given this, it was quickly realised that the courts would be an inappropriate forum for determining disputes in this area. The courts would inevitably look at the strict wording of the statute, and consequently might arrive at decisions entirely contrary to the main policy of the legislation. What was required then, was an adjudicating body which would not only look at the wording of the legislation, but would also examine the spirit and policy of the legislation, so as to ensure that their decision would give effect to that policy

Therefore, the reason for creating these 'Policy Orientated Tribunals' was a recognition that a 'policy orientated' attitude would be required to ensure that the new welfare system would work effectively. It was correctly realised that no ordinary court would be willing to decide cases on the basis of policy since the court would be staffed by lawyers, they would almost inevitably fall back on the 'black letter law' of the legislation.

Two points of interest should be noted:

a   The above argument recognises that tribunals are involved with policy decision. From this, however, it should not be concluded that the distinction between tribunals and courts is that the former deal with matters of policy while the latter decide questions of law. This is inaccurate since both decide questions of law and policy.

b   The above explains why there is in general only a limited right of appeal to the courts from tribunals' decisions (see below). The purpose behind entrusting the initial decision to the tribunal was the belief that only a tribunal could make the necessary 'policy orientated decision'. It would entirely destroy this benefit if a wide right of appeal to the courts was then allowed since the courts, ignoring the policy considerations, might allow the appeal because as a matter of 'black letter law' the tribunal decision was not correct. Allowing a wide right of appeal to the courts might then destroy the advantages of the tribunals, 'policy orientated approach'. For this reason, the right of appeal is usually limited.

The court substitute tribunal

As mentioned earlier, the 'court substitute' tribunal fulfils essentially the same function as the court: it makes the same type of decision. Yet, for two reasons, it was realised that the courts could not have coped with the work that is presently entrusted to the tribunals.

Firstly, the courts would have collapsed under the sheer volume of the work. With the increasing growth of the welfare state more and more hitherto unregulated areas became subject to legal control: social security, unemployment benefits, industrial injury compensation, unfair dismissal, compulsory purchase and landlord and tenant problems. These pieces of legislation were themselves potential sources of dispute and so a forum to resolve these disputes would be required. The courts simply could not have dealt with the number of disputes likely to arise, and so the new tribunal system was created.

Secondly, it was realised that the courts were an inappropriate organ to deal with these disputes.

Again, therefore, one returns to the same theme that was examined when considering the need for a Small Claims Court. There it was argued that a Small Claims Court was required because the County Court was failing to meet the need – for what is required is a quick, cheap and informal means of resolving the dispute. Similarly here: tribunals were found to be the more appropriate organ in that they were able to provide what the courts failed to provide – namely a quick, cheap and informal means of resolving the dispute.

It can be seen that tribunals meet all these criteria.

Tribunals are cheap
Civil courts, with the exception of the Magistrates' Court, in certain cases charge fees: tribunals do not. Thus Rent Tribunals and the National Insurance Tribunal emphasise lack of expense. People appearing before these tribunals can be represented by persons other than lawyers, and this also helps reduce expenses. Further, a person who loses an action in a tribunal does not have to pay the costs of the other side: whatever the result, each party pays its own costs.

Tribunals are quick
Tribunal cases come on quickly and are usually dealt with within the day. Many tribunals even fix the time and the day on which the case will be heard. So those concerned need only attend for a minimum length of time, and are not kept waiting.

Tribunals may meet in private
It is a basic principle of English law that courts should be open to the public, so that they may attend at any time. This, however, does not always suit the parties who may prefer to have the matter heard in private. Tribunals have this additional flexibility that they may meet in private should the nature of the case justify this – such as appeals concerning supplementary benefit where a person's financial needs and personal circumstances must be made known.

Tribunals are informal
Tribunals are as informal as is consistent with an orderly conduct of their affairs. An attempt is usually made to create an atmosphere in which people who appear in court will not feel ill at ease or nervous. The approach, however, is still basically adversarial not inquisitorial. It is still, therefore, up to the litigant to present his own case. The strict rules of evidence, however, do not apply.

The above then explains at least in part, why the tribunal system has developed. Below, under the heading 'Tribunals: conclusions', a summary is given of the advantages/disadvantages of the tribunal system.

All tribunals use, to a greater or lesser extent, systems of arbitration, and the relevant sections should be studied in detail.

Meanwhile the following points should be noted.

Composition of tribunals

Tribunals do not comprise highly paid judges who are able to call on experts as witnesses. Rather, the tribunal normally consists of a chairperson (who will be legally trained) and two other non-legally qualified people, who have some particular expertise in the particular field over which the tribunal has jurisdiction. For example, the Industrial Tribunal will consist of a lawyer as the chairman, and one representative from the Trade Unions and one person to represent the views of the employers. The experts, therefore, sit on the decision making Board, and are not simply called to give expert evidence as would be the case in an ordinary court.

Types of tribunal

Tribunals dealing with employment (industrial tribunals)

These overlap with social security tribunals (see below).

Their main work is concerned with disputed claims for (inter alia) redundancy pay, industrial injury benefits and complaints of unfair dismissal and discrimination. They sit locally and have a panel comprised of a legally qualified chairman with two other members, chosen to represent employers/employees respectively. An appeal lies to the Employment Appeal Tribunal (see chapter 17).

Tribunals dealing with social security

The Social Security Acts provide for benefits to be paid, subject to certain conditions, in the event of sickness, death, unemployment, maternity, or various other situations causing financial hardship.

It is not surprising that these tribunals are some of the busiest and most important of all local tribunals, since disputes often arise as to whether a claimant is entitled to a particular benefit and, if so, as to the amount due.

There are, for example, more than 200 local social security appeal tribunals in England and Wales.

Each tribunal will have a panel of two lay members, headed by a legally qualified chairman. Above these are the Social Security Commissioners, to whom there is a right of appeal on a point of law, and since many of these appeals are concerned with medical facts, there are other tribunals, such as national health service tribunals, mental health review tribunals etc.

Tribunals dealing with use of land

There are a whole series of tribunals whose function might loosely be classified as to do with land. The Rent Assessment Committees, enabled under the Rent Act 1977 to pronounce on rents, security of tenure and allied matters, while not strictly a true 'administrative' tribunal, is a good example of such special tribunals. In the field of town and country planning and compulsory purchase there are, surprisingly, few special tribunals as such. However, if an aggrieved person wishes to appeal against an unfavourable decision on planning matters, or against a compulsory purchase order, he can appeal to the relevant Minister who will appoint an inspector to hold a public local enquiry – a procedure similar in all respects to a tribunal hearing.

Another tribunal concerned with land use is the Lands Tribunal, but it must be borne in mind that this has a status roughly equivalent to the High Court and the sort of cases it hears are of comparable importance.

Tribunals dealing with transportation

Of these probably the most important is the Transport Tribunal which (inter alia) deals with appeals over road haulage licences. The panel normally comprises five – a legally qualified President and four lay members; selected to include two with experience in the transport business, one with financial or economic business experience and one with commercial expertise.

Tribunals dealing with revenue

These are, in the main, tribunals that hear appeals against taxation and VAT assessments. Recently formed are the Valuation and Community Charge Tribunals (reconstituted from the old local valuation courts) which will be concerned with appeals against the community charge or poll or council tax.

Domestic tribunals

These tribunals are rather different from all the previous ones. Their use may be limited, for example those governing the internal workings of organisations such as trade unions. In this case the limits of the tribunal's jurisdiction is based on the rules of the organisation concerned. Their basis rests in contract law: if one joins such an organisation one is contractually bound to accept the decisions of the tribunal should disputes arise.

There are also similar domestic tribunals, whose creation is based on statute rather than contract (Professional Conduct Committee of the General Medical Council, established under the Medical Act 1983 or the Solicitors' Disciplinary Tribunal, formed under the Solicitors Act 1974).

This type of tribunal has formal mechanisms for appeal to the court system, which tribunals based on contractual law do not. However, *all* types of tribunal are subject to indirect supervision by the Divisional Court of the Queen's Bench Division (see earlier chapters on judicial review and the following section entitled 'Appeals from tribunals').

Control of tribunals

The tribunals described above are all creations of statute and have developed in a piecemeal fashion. In 1955 a committee was set up under the chairmanship of Sir Oliver Franks to consider administrative tribunals and inquiries. The committee reported in 1957 and its recommendations were substantially implemented by the Tribunals and Inquiries Act 1958 (now the Tribunals and Inquiries Act 1992). The 1992 Act provides that in the case of certain specified tribunals the chairman is to be selected from a panel appointed by the Lord Chancellor. In addition, there is a Council on Tribunals which has the task of keeping under review the constitution and working of tribunals and of making reports from time to time. The members of the Council are appointed by the Lord Chancellor and the Secretary of State, and the members are disqualified from membership of the House of Commons.

Appeals from tribunals

In most cases there is no appeal from a tribunal's decision to a court of law. However, some supervisory jurisdiction over tribunals may be invoked by way of judicial review in the High Court where the tribunal has acted ultra vires (beyond its powers) or had breached natural justice (ie has broken one of two rules: 'audi alteram partem' – each party should be given an opportunity to argue his case, or 'nemo judex in sua causa' – the tribunal must not be biased or partial in any way as regards the case before it).

The usual way in which this jurisdiction may be invoked is by the use of the prerogative orders of mandamus (ordering the tribunal to do something to fulfil its statutory obligations) prohibition (preventing the tribunal from doing something which is beyond its powers) and certiorari (striking out the record of the tribunal's decision on the grounds that it was ultra vires or in breach of natural justice). Alternatively, an aggrieved claimant may bring an action against the officers of the tribunal, claiming an injunction or declaratory relief. Such cases are heard in the Divisional Court of the Queen's Bench Division of the High Court.

In addition to these common law remedies, the Tribunals and Inquiries Act 1992 provides for any party to appeal or to require a tribunal to state a case on a point of law from certain administrative tribunals to the High Court. These appeals are also heard by the Divisional Court of the Queen's Bench Division. Other statutes provide rights of appeal to various branches of the Supreme Court, or may create a separate Appeal Tribunal, such as the Employment Appeal Tribunal which hears appeals on points of law from industrial tribunals and from which a further appeal lies to the Court of Appeal and ultimately to the House of Lords.

Tribunals: conclusions

Therefore, to conclude, what are the main strengths and weaknesses of the tribunal system?

Strengths

a They operate more quickly than the courts.

b They are much cheaper than the courts.

c They operate in a specialised field, and hence can build up an expertise in that area which no court could hope to achieve.

d They are more flexible than courts and do not work through precedent (though, of course, the tribunal will try to be consistent).

e They operate less formally than courts.

Weaknesses

a Tribunals have a tendency to behave too much like courts.

b There may be an appearance of injustice in that although the tribunal is said to be 'independent' it may be chaired by a person with an interest – for example, the clerks to Supplementary Benefit Appeal Tribunals are civil servants.

c There are too many kinds of tribunals with overlapping jurisdictions (such as those dealing with rent and rating).

d Even though procedure is relatively informal, lay persons, particularly those from humble backgrounds who constitute the majority of those applying for social security (etc) are likely to be very much out of their depth (and many potential applicants never go near tribunals because they do not know their rights). Legal aid and representation may be the answer here.

Inquiries

Before moving on to look at arbitration in more detail, brief note should be made of the role of Inquiries.

These hearings are different from courts and tribunals in that they tend to be set up on an ad hoc basis for one particular function, rather than to perform a series of continuing functions.

There are a number of different types of inquiries, in particular:

a Tribunals of Inquiry, set up as and when needed by Parliament to discover factual information about a particular event. Often, but not always, the event in question may be a disaster (Aberfan 1966, Bradford City fire 1986) though other matters might be the subject of such an inquiry (Profumo Scandal 1963, Guildford Four 1989).

b Inquiries into objections, for example public local inquiries into matters concerning compulsory purchase or planning law (see also 18.5(c)).

c Inquiries into company activities under the Companies Acts.

It should be noted from this that terminology is not an infallible guide. Certain 'one-off' inquiries are called tribunals, but this fact does not denote any degree of permanency. Inquiries as with tribunals are, under the Tribunals and Inquiries Act 1958 subject to review by the courts and the rules of natural justice must be observed.

Arbitration as an alternative to the courts

Any civil dispute brought before the courts will be heard by a judge who is an intelligent person trained to deal with far ranging and diverse fields. It is obvious, therefore, that at many stages throughout a court hearing the judge needs to be informed by expert witnesses and professionals from other fields since his general expertise is not adequate to deal with more complex and specific problems which arise. Undoubtedly, the effect on the hearing is to prolong it until the judge has assimilated the necessary facts; and this in turn causes expenses and costs to rise and also to crease a backlog of cases which is at present a very real characteristic of our courts.

The arbitration procedure is designed to try to minimise the use of a person as judge when he has not got the necessary knowledge or experience in a particular field; and maximise the use of the expert and the professional by placing them not in the witness box to inform another person acting as judge but instead, as it were, in the judge's seat by making them arbitrators in a new procedural format. Thereby, the process of dispute settlement becomes quicker comparatively, and, therefore, cheaper without as much delay for a case to be heard and settled. Keeping in mind that the court should theoretically have more time to devote to more straightforward cases, in turn the long delays should theoretically be shortened.

Invariably the areas in which experts are used are where the judge is unable to understand technical commercial matters, although with the advent of the commercial court which is manned by experienced commercial judges this has been minimised. But if the dispute contains a question of quality production, for example, and a thorough knowledge of a particular machine or product is required, then the most sensible approach is to obtain the services of someone who is acquainted with them; it has been glaringly obvious sometimes how difficult judges find dealing with such cases. Furthermore, since the judge would otherwise have it all explained to him by an expert witness time is wasted and, therefore, costs will invariably be greater. These increased practical problems have contributed greatly to arbitration being established.

This comparatively new system seems to be tailor-made to suit the commercial man for despite the fact that disputes range from a few pounds to many millions they are dealt with in a more expedient efficient manner so that the parties can have the disputes settled whenever and wherever they choose.

Speed is a high prerogative and in the quest for it, the rules of evidence and procedure can be relaxed despite the important consequences that the inbuilt safeguards they provide are partially forsaken. But businesses have different priorities, they want problems dealt with quickly, not having to wait up to 18 months or two years sometimes to have their dispute legally resolved. They may not want to jeopardise future negotiations with a party in dispute and often the courts' combative approach can do much to affect this. They, therefore, choose arbitration which may also mean that if the dispute is resolved speedily their assets can be redeployed instead of having to wait for statutory interest on the debt only.

Choosing an arbitrator

The arbitrator must be a person agreed upon by all the parties to the arbitration; obviously they will all protect their own interests and ensure:

a   he is not connected to any of the parties;

b   he has the necessary relevant expertise in the particular field;

c   that he has experience with the specific area of dispute.

Often you may have a lawyer deciding an arbitration especially if it is a technical arbitration (see below), where the interpretation of a trade clause is called for. It is also usual for the president of a professional association to be asked to be an arbitrator since obviously he will have good experience and be most suitable when a dispute arises in his area of expertise.

It is usual to consult a body known as the Institute of Arbitration when trying to find a suitable arbitrator. This body has lists of suitable applicants which it will give in order to find the necessary expert. However, it does not have a monopoly over arbitration in deciding which arbitrator should sit where. Obviously there are diverse areas of dispute but the Institute does have schemes for large organisations which are in need of quick dispute settlement, for example the Post Office, Rentokil, BP, Shell Mex, Mail Order Trades, The Grain and Feed Association.

Another body which brings together the Institute of Arbitrators, the London Chamber of Commerce and the City Corporation exists in relation to arbitration. This is known as the London Court of Arbitration. In fact, this was formed since London is probably one of the most important arbitration centres in the world where international trade is involved.

The arbitrator's duties

Once appointed, the arbitrator must accept the appointment. He thereupon becomes duty bound to come to a decision not as a judge, but as an arbitrator acting in a judicial manner.

The eventual decision which the arbitrator reaches is known as the 'award'. It is as binding on the parties as a judgment of the High Court.

It is to be remembered that arbitration is an alternative to the court and to the judge. Whereas a judge can find himself totally immersed and at a great disadvantage when dealing with complex commercial issues, the arbitrator who has been selected for his expertise is the most competent person. Lord Denning has said about arbitrators interpreting trade clauses:

> 'On such a clause, the arbitrator is just as likely to be right as the judge; probably more likely.'

and Lord Goddard talking about the arbitrator:

> '… in one sense he is the antithesis of a court. A person goes to arbitration because he does not want to go to court. Therefore, he sets up his own private judge to decide the case but the arbitrator is not deciding it as a judge, he is deciding it as an arbitrator and procedure rights and all matters relating to procedure are to be found in the Arbitration Act(s).'

The types of arbitration

Quality arbitration

It is this type of arbitration which is of most use in relieving the court and the judge of the problem he faces when a dispute is brought before him involving the quality of goods or services supplied. An expert acquainted with them does not necessarily need high legal expertise since often there is no question of law or interpretation but mere questions of production, standards of merchantability to be assessed in relation to a particular trade. The expert has this knowledge, he need not hear the evidence of others in order to arrive at a decision; he has the necessary qualification to do so; this will have been ensured by the parties in the first place when choosing him as their arbitrator.

Technical arbitration

An arbitration of this type necessitates the interpretation of a trade clause or of law; therefore, often the most suitable candidate to act as arbitrator is a lawyer of eminent counsel; a QC. It is in this type of arbitration that the decision of the arbitrator was most often criticised by judges on appeal, since it is in their field expertise; but rights of appeal have now been limited since the whole point of going to arbitration would otherwise be undermined if close judicial scrutiny were allowed.

Mixed arbitration

When a dispute is one concerning both a question of quality and also the interpretation of a clause or point of law, then it is described as a mixed arbitration. Obviously in this type of arbitration the choice of arbitrator is extremely important since he must possess quite wide-ranging skills and expertise and possibly legal training as well.

The law concerning arbitration

Parties agree contractually to go to arbitration by including in a contract an arbitration clause alongside the other possible clauses as to times of delivery, payment and price. The usual type of clause used is:

'any future and contingent dispute arising out of the contract will be settled by arbitration'.

So both parties must agree to its inclusion, and once it has been agreed then it becomes a condition of the contract and as such is binding.

If the parties later, in the event of dispute, attempt instead to have it resolved by the courts, the court will refuse to hear it and the parties will be forced to have it heard by an arbitrator.

Since the ability to go to arbitration is contractual then the normal rules as to capacity to enter into contracts apply (insanity, drunkenness, being of legal age). Similarly, if there is some question as to whether the contract itself which includes the arbitration clause, is valid, then this issue must be decided in order to see if the arbitration clause binds the parties, otherwise the clause would not be upheld.

Once that is validated, then the clause must be interpreted to ensure that it covers what is intended; for example, in *Heyman* v *Darwins* [1942] AC 356, the phrase:

'all disputes arising out of the contract'

was held to be wide enough to include repudiation or frustration.

The agreement to go to arbitration must be in writing if it is to be governed by the Arbitration Act 1950; it must clearly express the positive assertion to settle the dispute by arbitration; clarity is essential, ambiguity will defeat this objective. Otherwise if the agreement is oral only, it will be governed by the common law and many disadvantages will then exist. So if arbitration is the dispute-settlement method preferred, it is in the parties' best interests to bring it under the Arbitration Acts 1950 and 1979 and put their wishes in a written contract.

Similarly, if the main agreement is void through illegality for instance, then so too will the arbitration clause be void. Where several documents exist, then all must be read together to see if an Arbitration Clause is contained which will effect the overall agreement.

If one party attempts to go to court instead of arbitration then the other party can under s4 of the Arbitration Act apply to the court to stay proceedings (ie stop them from being heard); the basis for this is obviously to enforce a contractual term. The court will grant the application if:

a the person making it is a party to the arbitration agreement;

b he shows he is willing to assist in the proper conduct of the arbitration and files an affidavit stating this to be so;

c the court is satisfied that there is no sufficient reason why the matter should not be referred in accordance with the arbitration agreement;

d The contractual clause referring to arbitration covers the same matter which is asked to be resolved by the court.

But these powers are discretionary and the court can if it wishes take into account other factors particular to the case.

After an arbitrator has checked that he is qualified to be such under the particular arbitration agreement, it is usual for him to give details of the procedure. It will be followed in settling the dispute, or he may simply follow court patterns. Arbitrators will, therefore, convene a meeting to discuss matters and to settle on a final date.

Power of the arbitrator

The arbitrator must conduct the proceedings with fairness. Although not bound by strict rules of evidence or precedent he is obviously bound by the principles of natural justice, which are basic safeguards protecting important rights, and as such, can never be excluded. The rules of evidence, although formulated and developed to ensure impartiality, fairness, etc can, however, be excluded when both parties expressly agree.

The arbitrator must have effective powers in relation to calling necessary evidence, therefore he can compel witnesses to attend otherwise his task would be almost impossible; he can use under s12 of the Arbitration Act the power of the High Court to issue a subpoena to compel the attendance of any witnesses to the arbitration. Special provision also exists to ensure that any evidence which is given is made on oath and furthermore the laws of perjury also extend to arbitration in s1 of the Perjury Act 1911.

Once a decision is reached, technically known as the 'award', provision is made for its specific enforcement by making it a judgment of the High Court and, if not complied with, it will be enforced as one (using contempt for example).

The arbitrator also has discretionary powers in relation to costs; and as in the courts these can be used as a further way of compensating a party, for it is to be kept in mind that although arbitration tends to be cheaper than the courts, this is only comparatively speaking; it can sometimes be a very costly business itself.

Arbitration and the courts

If the purpose of arbitration is to conduct with greater speed and efficiency the settlement of a dispute, usually of a commercial nature, using people with expert knowledge and experience in a particular field, then the system will be totally undermined if, whenever the losing party chooses, he can simply appeal to the courts against the award; then the whole point of having a suitable alternative is defeated.

At the same time it must be remembered that to oust the jurisdiction of the courts totally is not a desirable objective either, and so if the system is to function effectively a balance must be achieved.

Before the Arbitration Act 1979 it was possible for the courts to exercise their supervisory powers to set aside an award on the grounds of error on the face of the award. If we keep in mind the fact that the expert as an arbitrator does not necessarily arrive at his conclusions in the same way as a legally trained person might, then criticism of his methods was quite easy and very commonplace. The effect was obviously that the losing party would not consider the award as final; he would not settle his liabilities immediately since he could delay the operation of the award to enforce payment, for example by appealing to the court. Again, this undermines the basic idea behind arbitration which is to conduct with speed and efficiency the settlement of a dispute so that assets in commerce in particular could be redeployed as quickly as possible.

The Act tries to ensure that parties who agree to arbitration cannot appeal to the High Court as easily as before by employing it as a tactical delay mechanism. The arbitrator can now even penalise defaulting parties by using the powers of a judge if parties fail to comply with his directions to file documents or defences for instance.

Furthermore, the Act now limits rights of appeal to instances where there has been a breach of natural justice (eg audi alterem partem or nemo judex in causa sua) or if all the parties give leave to do so or if the court itself gives leave.

Arbitrators can now give reasons for their award since the fear of judicial scrutiny has been removed to a great extent; the award cannot now be nullified on the reasoning alone as was the pre-Act position.

Lord Denning said in *Pioneer Shipping* v *BTP Tioxide* [1980] 3 WLR 326:

'... the purpose of the Arbitration Act 1979 was to do away with the drawbacks of the special case procedure: especially because it was used to delay payment ...'.

The desired effect was, therefore, achieved by the passing of the new Act since London regained its importance as an arbitration centre and respect for the system was re-established in the commercial world.

Summary

Advantages

a Arbitration costs less than a court hearing comparatively.

b The procedure is much quicker.

c Parties have a choice where the arbitration is to take place and when.

d The ability of the parties to choose who the arbitrator is to be promotes trust and confidence.

e Parties are protected since the proceedings are private unlike a court hearing, so that contractual terms or information about individual business are not made known.

f Arbitration is conducted in an atmosphere of compromise in comparison to the often combative approach characteristic of the courts with public cross-examination of witnesses.

g Future negotiations may still be possible if a dispute is resolved without hostility and this is a very important factor in a comparatively small commercial sector or trade.

h The number of International Trade cases which arbitration procedures in London attract brings a considerable number of benefits to the country, not the least of which is money.

i Since sums involved in arbitration are often great a protracted court hearing of the same matter can often create a situation of debt (eg if goods have not yet been paid for); therefore, the speed of the arbitration process often outweighs any possible disadvantages.

j Arbitration acts as a court substitute, therefore the courts are themselves relieved of much work and so the queues created should be shortened in relation to other civil matters.

Disadvantages

a The protection and safeguards which have been developed over the years are often substituted by the need for speed; this is especially so when the parties agree not to have the application of evidentiary rules of those of precedent.

b The arbitrator does not come to his decision in the same legal manner as a judge; this may seem inconsistent since it is a dispute settlement system which is an extension of the court structure and anomalies could, therefore, be created.

c Arbitration can still be costly and protracted.

d The question does arise as to whether or not the commercial court and arbitration are performing the same function.

e It may not be in the public interest that facts which ought to be disclosed are kept secret through arbitration procedures.

f Parties are not always aware of the consequences of agreeing to arbitration.

g Legal aid is not available.

Arbitration within the court system

New arbitration scheme for small claims in County Courts

Prompted by the pamphlet *Justice out of Reach* in 1973, the Lord Chancellor introduced the above scheme. For a claim up to £500, the claim is automatically referred to arbitration. If either party objects, then it is for the County Court Registrar to decide whether the matter should remain referred to arbitration; it is important to note that such an order would normally be given.

The hearing is conducted privately by the Registrar. The strict rules of evidence do not apply, and it is for the Registrar to adopt whatever procedure he may see fit to ensure a fair hearing. Consequently, studies have shown that the procedure adopted varies greatly from one court to the next – some Registrars adopt the inquisitorial approach, asking questions where necessary, whereas others still use the normal adversarial methods.

No costs are generally allowed in the Small Claims Courts, but contrary to the advice of the Consumer Council legal representation as well as lay representation is allowed. In about half the cases, neither side is represented and in about ten per cent of cases both sides are represented. It is noticeable that the average length of arbitrations is little different from that of an ordinary court case (about 12 weeks). It is interesting that the voluntary schemes (where no legal representation is allowed) are much faster, and one wonders whether allowing legal representation had slowed down the operation of the County Court Small Claims Arbitration.

Yet it must be stated that Small Claims Arbitration has not been entirely successful in bringing the courts within the reach of the ordinary person. Why more individuals have not come forward to pursue small claims is not clear but the fact that they have not is irrefutable. Further, of the small number of arbitrations brought, over a half were brought by firms and companies (usually collecting debts).

Voluntary arbitration scheme for small claims

Stimulated by the Consumer Council's pamphlet, a voluntary arbitration scheme was started in Manchester in 1971. For a fee of £2.50 a person with an unresolved consumer complaint for under £150, could ask for arbitration by someone on the panel. Since the arbitration is voluntary, both parties, however, must agree to appear before the arbitrator. In this sense, therefore, it cannot be viewed as an exact alternative to the County Court. Similar schemes have been started in other parts of the country, and the Manchester scheme has now raised its upper limit to £500.

The procedure is basically informal, and both parties submit their stories in writing. These statements are then sent to an appropriate expert – a solicitor, architect or car engineer – who may then give his decision. If he requires more information he may require the parties to appear before him. Legal representation is not allowed, but friends are allowed to help the claimant put his case. Hearings rarely last more than half an hour.

An assessment of the scheme

Since the parties only pay a nominal sum towards the cost of the arbitration (£2.50), the scheme clearly requires outside funding. This is the case, even though the arbitrators give their services free.

The problem of getting both parties to agree to arbitration has not been as great as expected. Whereas initially there was no such consent in 48 per cent of cases, this figure is now down to 20 per cent. If the scheme continues to operate effectively, thereby encouraging confidence in potential future parties to arbitration, there is good reason to suppose this figure will continue to fall.

From the point of view of the parties, the advantages are that the system is very quick and cheap. There is no lengthy pre-trial review, and the matter is usually settled at the first hearing. Most cases, therefore, from start to finish only take a few weeks.

The scheme, however, is limited in its scope – therefore, this system of arbitration is being mainly used by individuals for whom it was not chiefly designed.

Legal personnel | 19

Introduction

Unlike the position in most systems of law, the legal profession in England and Wales is not a single profession, exercising various functions, but is traditionally divided into two branches: barristers and solicitors. This division is a historical one and represents the latest stage in a development stretching back into the twelfth and thirteenth centuries, when as a result of the growing complexities of the developing royal justice men began to employ agents and experienced representatives to plead their cases for them before the King's justices. By the thirteenth century, these representatives became a profession, supervised by the judges. Even now it is still possible to appear in person in court without legal representation but such a course is fraught with difficulties and traps for the unwary.

By the fifteenth century, four or more groups of lawyers had become established: the *serjeants-at-law* (the senior advocate practitioners with sole rights of audience in the Court of Common Pleas); *barristers* (originally student advocates, but became the junior branch of the profession), who were the 'court room' lawyers; and *attorneys* and *solicitors*, who were the 'office room' lawyers (attorneys practising in the common law courts; solicitors in the Court of Chancery), the legal businessmen. Further, there were the lawyers of the Ecclesiastical and Admiralty courts, the *proctors*. The old divisions have largely been whittled down (eg in 1875 attorneys, solicitors and proctors were amalgamated) so that now only two branches remain, each with their own traditions, organisations, rules and functions.

Indeed, a question which deserves some consideration is whether the historical division of the legal profession can still be justified, or whether the two should be 'fused' to form a unified profession as in most legal systems. For a fuller discussion of this and other questions relating to reform of the legal profession, see below.

Solicitors

Solicitors greatly outnumber barristers, there being about 60,000 practising solicitors and 6,000 practising barristers (of which circa 4,000 practise in London).

A solicitor is more of a business man than a barrister, having an office to run and, substantial correspondence. He deals with the preparatory stages of litigation (interviewing witnesses and issuing writs, etc), and unlike barristers, deals with his clients directly. However, the bulk of a solicitor's work is non-litigious and includes conveyancing for reward, drafting wills, the supervision of settlements, administration of estates, matrimonial problems and matters arising from employment, immigration and company law. The majority of solicitors will handle a cross-section of work but there is a trend towards specialisation, especially in London. Solicitors may form partnerships but not companies. In recent years there has been a tendency for solicitors to form very large partnerships – sometimes with as many as 100 partners. A number of solicitors go into public employment (eg Local Government) or into Industry as legal advisors.

Solicitors are also officers of the Supreme Court and were originally regulated and controlled by the judges, though by the Solicitors Act 1974 this function is now exercised partly by the Law Society and partly by the Courts.

The Law Society is the controlling body and was constituted by Royal Charter in 1845 and re-named the Law Society in 1903. It has always been a voluntary organisation and about 85 per cent of solicitors are members. Under the Solicitors Act 1974, with the concurrence of the Master of the Rolls and the Lord Chief Justice it makes training regulations relating to examinations and articles. It maintains the Roll of solicitors, has a teaching college and provides club facilities for its members in Chancery Lane and produces a Gazette. It is responsible for the administration of the Legal Aid Scheme in civil proceedings.

The Law Society has the power to make rules regulating professional practice, conduct and discipline. The most important areas of control are:

a The keeping of accounts, handling clients' money, auditing accounts and sending accountants' reports to the Law Society.

b Where a solicitor can no longer be relied upon to continue handling his clients' affairs (eg bankruptcy, death of a sole practitioner, dishonesty) the Law Society may intervene.

c Solicitors must be insured against any claims arising from their work. (The Law Society has a master insurance policy.)

d Solicitors must make annual contributions to a compensation fund maintained by the Law Society which is used to alleviate the hardship of clients who have suffered loss through the dishonesty of solicitors.

Solicitors are subject to the law and also to sanctions for unprofessional conduct. They are Officers of the Court and are therefore subject to the direct discipline of judges (s50 Solicitors Act 1974). For example, a solicitor may be made personally liable for costs where he has been negligent. However, the main sanctions are imposed by the Solicitors Disciplinary Tribunal (formerly Solicitors Disciplinary Committee) a statutory body, set up by the Solicitors Act 1974. The Master of the Rolls appoints members consisting of solicitors of not less than ten years' standing and also lay members. Usually three members, including one lay member, sit and witnesses may be subpoenaed. It is independent of the Law Society and its proceedings are absolutely privileged. Its jurisdiction is threefold:

a To hear applications by a solicitor to have his own name removed from the Roll (eg to qualify for call to the Bar).

b To hear complaints by another party against a solicitor for breach of conduct. (This is the major part of its work.)

c To hear applications by the Law Society under s43 Solicitors' Act 1974 to restrain solicitors from employing clerks with previous criminal records or who have been involved in misconduct.

The Tribunal may make such order as it thinks fit. It may remove the solicitor's name from the Roll, suspend him from practice, order a fine and make an order for costs against him. It must strike off a solicitor who has assisted an unqualified person to act as a solicitor and it must either strike off or suspend a solicitor who has employed a person who has been struck off. Appeal lies to the Queen's Bench Divisional Court and with leave to the Court of Appeal.

An annual report is made to the Lord Chancellor by the Tribunal and this must be published.

In 1971 the *Ormrod Committee* reported on legal education in England and Wales and noted the greater role now played in legal education by universities – though it considered that the principal responsibility for training practitioners rested with the governing bodies of the two branches of the profession. It recommended a greater integration of academic and vocational stages in legal education – though their recommendations were not fully realised by either the Senate or Law Society.

The Law Society has, however, recently suggested that it intends its Solicitors' Finals course to follow a more 'practical' route, though as yet no firm dates for implementation exist.

From 1980 a prospective solicitor must have:

a A law degree: or

b A non-law degree; with the CPE (Common Professional Examination) which lasts one year; and

c Part II exams (professional exams – one year); and

d Two years of practical training as an articled clerk with a firm of solicitors; and

e Satisfy the Law Society as to his good character and suitability to practice as a solicitor.

If all these matters are completed and/or obtained satisfactorily, an entrant's name will then be entered on the Rolls and he will be 'admitted'. A practising certificate is a prerequisite to practising as a solicitor.

Solicitors may act as advocates in the Magistrates' Courts, County Courts and before certain Tribunals. As a general rule they cannot appear in the Crown Court but by virtue of a practice direction issued in [1972] 1 All ER 608 under the power conferred on the Lord Chancellor by s12 Courts Act 1971 they can now appear in proceedings on appeal from the Magistrates Court or in criminal cases where the case is referred to the Crown Court for sentence where either the solicitor or a member of his firm represented the client at the original hearing. However, the whole issue of right of audience is currently changing with the introduction of ss27–28, 31–33 of the Courts and Legal Services Act 1990. Additionally, the Lord Chancellor's Advisory Committee on Legal Education and Conduct made, in 1992, a number of recommendations as to rights of audience in the higher courts for solicitors in private practice and with additional experience and qualifications. In late 1993 the right of audience thus defined was confirmed by the Lord Chancellor, at least in principle. It has yet to be seen whether this right of audience will, in fact, be much utilised.

They have the same rights of audience as barristers in the European Court except for references under article 177. Solicitors of at least ten years standing may be appointed Recorders; after five years a Recorder may be appointed a Circuit Judge (ss16, 21 Courts Act 1971). A solicitor may also be appointed a Stipendiary Magistrate or a Master of the Supreme Court (other than Queen's Bench Division).

The Courts and Legal Services Act 1990 provides that solicitors will be eligible for appointment as QCs (see below) and High Court judges.

A solicitor can be sued in contract or tort by third parties. In the former his liability is usually governed by the law of agency. He can therefore be indemnified by his client for acts done within the scope of his authority. Where he acts without his clients' authority he can be sued for breach of warranty of authority: *Yonge* v *Toynbee* [1910] 1 KB 215. A solicitor's liability in tort is governed by the usual principles applicable under the law of torts. Under the rapidly developing tort of negligence, particularly in respect of negligence causing *economic loss* (purely financial loss), a solicitor may be liable to beneficiaries for loss caused by faulty drafting of a client's will – even though the beneficiary is not in a contractual relationship with that solicitor, *Ross* v *Caunters* [1979] 3 WLR 605.

As far as a solicitor's relationship with his client is concerned, a solicitor owes both contractual and tortious duties of care, arising from his *retainer* by his client – which also (depending upon its scope) gives him his authority to act for that client. There is limited immunity from a suit for damages for breach of that duty of care, but only so far as the solicitor is carrying out litigation work which would have been carried on by a barrister had one been engaged: *Saif Ali* v *Sydney Mitchell* [1978] 3 WLR 849 HL.

A solicitor also owes a fiduciary duty, derived from the equitable notion of fraud, to his client which requires him to act in good faith in all his dealings with and on behalf of his client. For example, in the giving of gifts by a client to his solicitor there is a presumption of undue influence namely that by reason of the solicitor's position as regards his client and his great influence over him, a solicitor must show in such circumstances (in order to rebut such a presumption) that such a gift was not made by reason of such influence, that the solicitor was not taking advantage of his client's weaker position: see *Allcard* v *Skinner* (1887) 36 Ch D 145 CA and also *Lloyds Bank* v *Bundy* [1974] 3 WLR 501 CA (bank manager – but the same principles apply).

The confidential relationship of solicitor and client which arises out of the solicitor's fiduciary duty has other important consequences, notably the fact that all communications between them are 'privileged' and cannot be required to be disclosed in evidence without the client's consent: *Wheeler* v *Le Marchant* (1881) 17

Ch D 675. The reason for this privilege is to allow the client to be free to obtain legal advice without fear of disclosure.

Much of the work done in a solicitor's office is carried out by legal executives who have their own professional association, the Institute of Legal Executives, and examination system.

The Office of Fair Trading has recommended that solicitors should be allowed to go into partnership with estate agents, valuers and surveyors. Joint practices are also suggested between solicitors and accountants, engineers, architects, patent agents, actuaries and medical practitioners. At present solicitors are prevented from joint practices by the Solicitors' Practice Rules 1936–1972 and the Solicitors Act 1974. The Monopolies Commission considered in 1970 that restrictions on freedom would lead to higher prices, but Benson opposed this and claimed that mixed practices were not in the public interest. Although the White Paper, discussed later, proposes that such partnerships be allowed.

The proportion of women solicitors is rapidly increasing. In 1984/85 14.3 per cent of practising solicitors were women and on 31 July 1990 it was 23.2 per cent; of the solicitors admitted in 1992–3, more than half were women. A 1991 Law Society survey revealed that nearly 50 per cent of assistant solicitors in private practice firms were women, but of partners women were only 10 per cent.

Barristers

The basic work of a barrister (or 'counsel' as he is also known) is advocacy and litigation, though there is a certain amount of paperwork to do in even the most litigous practices – typically settling pleadings and giving written opinions on difficult legal points and advising eg as to the strength of a client's case. More specialist practices (particularly 'Chancery' work, property, tax, company, landlord and tenant, wills, conveyancing, etc) tend to involve more paperwork, some practitioners devoting nearly all their time to advising and drafting and spending very little time in court. Barristers are not all of a type: some, as noted, specialise in certain cases (including also – tax, commercial, shipping, building contracts), some have 'general' practices doing a mixture of common law work, crime and matrimonial.

The Bar Council has recently made several changes in its code of conduct, which became effective from 31 March 1990. These changes are noted where relevant below.

Barristers cannot form a partnership, they are self-employed but they work together in a set of Chambers (on average 14 members in London and 11 in the provinces). The head of chambers is usually a QC. The chambers share secretarial facilities and a clerk. The clerk is not a legally qualified person but a business manager. He negotiates the fees with solicitors and distributes work amongst the barristers. He is usually paid 8–12 per cent commission on the total fees. Solicitors can only approach a barrister through his clerk.

However, as from 31 March 1990 barristers need no longer practise from established chambers, which have had the effect of regulating entries to the profession. They will now be able to practise on their own, without a clerk, working from home or other office. The concept of working from the Bar library has however been quietly dropped after a brief period of experimentation. (This new system is similar to that advocated by the General Council of the Bar in their publication 'Quality of Justice – The Bar's Response', and already in existence in Northern Ireland, Scotland and the Republic of Ireland.) The general rule that barristers cannot deal with clients directly (except when advising eg friends on a personal basis) has been relaxed to allow accountants and other professionals to instruct barristers directly.

Other changes effective from 31 March 1990 include: the abolition of the rule forbidding barristers to visit solicitors' offices and requiring all consultations between barristers and solicitors to be held in barristers' chambers; barristers are to be allowed to advertise their services in newspapers, though they will still not be able to see clients – save accountants and other professionals – without a reference from a solicitor.

Queen's Counsel (QCs) or 'silks' (because of their silk gowns) are the senior practitioners of the Bar. After about 10 years practice as a *junior* (all barristers who are not silks are known as 'juniors') a barrister may apply to the Lord Chancellor to 'take silk' (be appointed a QC) and on doing so changes his practice considerably: the heavy load of a junior in drafting pleadings and paperwork is lost and greater fees may be charged. There is also an increase in status, and judges will (naturally enough) tend to respect the arguments of silks to a greater extent than juniors. Indeed, almost all puisne judges are appointed from the ranks of the silks.

The rule that a QC could not appear in court without a junior was abolished in 1977, though it is still the usual practice – the junior bearing the greater part of the preliminary work (particularly the paperwork). In consequence of this, the client whose case is difficult enough to merit engaging a QC to argue it in court will have to pay both the QC's fees and those of his junior.

A barrister can only practise if he has been 'called to the Bar' of one of the four Inns of Court (Inner, Middle, Grays and Lincolns). These are very old institutions dating back to the 14th century. Their jurisdiction is derived from the judges and is not statutory, unlike that of the Law Society. The Inns are governed by the *Benchers* – judges and senior members of the Bar who have absolute control over admission of students and call of barristers. (Their appointment is by other Benchers, there being no outside control.) Appeal from their decision lies to the Lord Chancellor and judges of the High Court sitting as 'visitors'.

In order to be called to the Bar and to practise in England and Wales, a prospective applicant must have fulfilled certain requirements (altered partly to implement some of the recommendations of the *Ormrod Committee*).

a Have a law degree with at least upper second class honours; or

b Have a law degree with at least lower second class honours and complete a one year conversion course;

c If the degree is not law, then a degree (same standard) and the year's Diploma (in the 'core subjects' needed to practice);

d Join one of the Inns of Court;

e Eat the requisite number of dinners during the Inns' dining terms by 'keeping terms' (eight terms of three dinners each or four terms 'double dining' – six dinners per term). This is a relic of the days when the Inns were the centre of the social and educational life of the Bar and is still recommended to promote good relations with senior practitioners – though these rarely dine in great numbers now;

f For those intending to practice: attend the year's vocational course at the Council of Legal Education and to pass the course in 'practical exercises' (advocacy and pleading exercises);

g For those not intending to practice: pass the Bar Examination ('Bar Finals').

If the entrant wishes to practise he must then complete twelve months' *pupillage* with a senior member of the Bar during which he will have the opportunity to learn from his 'pupil-master' by watching him in practice, both with clients in conference and in court, and in learning how to plead and draft opinions. Unlike articled clerks, pupils are not paid and must support themselves. The Bar have, however, recently decided to implement a system whereby all pupils will be paid a minimum of £6,000 during their year of pupillage. Once pupillage has been completed, the pupil must find a 'tenancy': that is a space in chambers. Though there was a period in the 1970s when such tenancies were relatively easy to obtain, because of the increase then of the Bar's work, at the moment there are many more pupils than can be accommodated in chambers. The new provision allowing barristers to practise outside the traditional chambers system should help alleviate this problem.

The Senate of the Inns of Court and the Bar

The governing body of the Bar is the Senate of the Inns of Court and the Bar, established in 1974. The Inns have undertaken to abide by the general policy as laid down by the Senate. It regulates admissions, calls to the Bar, legal education and organises the finances of the Bar. It is also the disciplinary body, although the penalties are imposed by the Inn of which the individual Barrister is a member. It has up to ninety members including the Attorney-General, Solicitor-General, Chairman of the Council of Legal Education, twenty-four bench representatives, twelve hall representatives, thirty-nine Bar representatives (six must be non-practising members) and twelve additional members.

The Bar Council

The Bar Council was established in 1894. Prior to the setting up of the senate in 1974 it was the main organising body of the Bar. Most of its powers have now been transferred to the Senate. Its main functions now are to maintain the standards, honour and independence of the Bar, to promote, preserve and improve services and functions of the Bar and to represent and act for the Bar generally.

Unlike the solicitors' profession, the Bar is not regulated by Statute and its conduct is not prescribed by Parliament. However, the Conduct of the Bar is regulated by a strict 'Code of Conduct' drawn up and enforced by the Senate. One of the most important rules of conduct (sometimes referred to as rules of professional etiquette) is the *cab-rank* principle, that is to say

> 'A practising barrister is bound to accept any brief to appear before a Court in the field in which he professes to practice ... Special circumstances such as a conflict of interest or the possession of relevant and confidential information may justify his refusal to accept a particular brief ...' (Code of Conduct, para 21).

For the first time the latest version of the code mentions specifically that barristers are duty bound to take legal aid cases as well as those privately paid. Barristers will be forbidden to discriminate (in clients, or professional association) on grounds of race, ethnic origin, religion, sex or political persuasion.

Thus access may generally be had by any person to the barrister of his choice. *Benson* noted the importance of this principle, that it ensured that counsel would take a case 'without regard to his personal views whether about the client, the nature of the case or, in the case of crime, the offence charged'. (para 3.20). The Senate has called the rule 'a pillar of British liberty'.

A Barrister may be fined or imprisoned for contempt of court as any other individual but he is not an officer of the court (cf solicitors). He must be 'robed' in court (except in Magistrates' court). He owes a duty not only to his client but also to the court, and as an officer of justice must draw to the court's attention all relevant authorities even if harmful to his case. He must not conceal the facts or set up a defence where his client had made a confession of guilt to him. It is the duty of prosecuting counsel to assist in the court and not press for conviction.

The relationship between counsel and his client is not contractual. The fee is considered an honorary payment and a Barrister cannot sue for it though, as a matter of etiquette, the Council of the Law Society has stated that solicitors are liable to see that barristers are paid. Barristers cannot be sued for professional negligence, at least insofar as litigation in court and connected pre-trial work is concerned, on grounds of public policy for a barrister must be 'free to do his duty fearlessly and independently': *Rondel* v *Worsley* [1969] 1 AC 191.

This is partly in order to permit counsel to maintain his professional independence, but partly because he is not an entirely free agent since he owes a duty to the court (see above) and has an obligation to act under the 'cab-rank' rule. In *Saif Ali* v *Sydney Mitchell* [1978] 3 WLR 849 the House of Lords further considered the professional immunity of counsel and considered that it only applied to work outside court which was 'so intimately connected' with the conduct of the cause in court that 'it could fairly be said' to be a preliminary decision affecting the way the cause was conducted when it came to trial.

Note that the Code of Conduct now needs to be read in conjunction with the Courts and Legal Services Act 1990.

Proposals for reform of the legal profession

The legal profession, especially the Bar, has been greatly criticised over the years and there have been several proposals for reform. Most recently, the *Marre* committee reported in 1988 and in January 1989 the Lord Chancellor's Department issued three Green Papers. The Green Papers resulted in a hostile response from both the Judiciary and the Bar. The response from the Law Society was less hostile, but nevertheless critical. After a consultation period, the Government issued a White Paper with their final proposals. The Courts and Legal Services Act 1990 followed the White Paper closely. The main points will be dealt with below. It may, however, be appropriate at this point to raise the matter of fusion of the legal profession as perhaps the most far reaching proposal for reform – one which neither *Marre*, the earlier *Benson* Royal Commission, nor the Government have advocated.

Fusion

The arguments around the question of fusion have centered on the proposition that it would/ would not be better from the point of view of the litigant. Even distinguished members of the profession do not agree that the profession is as responsive to the needs of litigants as it could be. There is always room for further improvement. However it ought to be pointed out that not all change is necessarily for the better. Change itself is no good thing unless it brings with it some improvement. The legal profession is organised in a way that dates back several hundred years and is deeply rooted in tradition. It is perhaps worth noting that it has served the interests of litigants for all that time. That is not however the same as saying that the profession (or perhaps we ought to say professions) have fulfilled this task in the best way possible.

Samuel Beckett once said that 'lawyers are the cream of society – rich and thick'. He was referring to the rather poor image that lawyers have and one of the reasons for this poor image (although by no means the only reason) is what is perceived as their restrictive trade practices in respect of the divided profession between barristers and solicitors. The major proposal for reform of the legal professions is that they should be fused together to form one profession and in such a way that the interests of the litigants will be best served. In this chapter I shall consider the practical implications of fusion yet before doing so, it would be appropriate to examine the nature of the divided profession and the supposed problems that division carries with it.

It is said by litigants that the divided profession leads to duplication of work and also increases costs. This arises, it is said, because of the rule that only barristers may appear in the higher courts in that they have a monopoly of audience rights. A private individual may not approach a barrister directly and must always go through an instructing solicitor who then has to approach a barrister through that barrister's clerk of chambers. To the general public this seems like an extreme form of restrictive practice. Such a perception is not, however, altogether accurate.

It is said that the fused profession would overcome the extra cost element in hiring two lawyers – the solicitor and the barrister – but the experience of jurisdictions where there is a fused profession does not bear this assessment out. In Belgium, which recently fused its profession, there has been no noticeable reduction in the costs to the litigant of taking a case before a court. The work still has to be done by someone. The client will still have to pay for both the preparation and the presentation of the case in court (this obviously applies whether it is a private client or the legal aid fund). The only conceivable duplication that would be saved by fusion of the profession would be in the preparation of the brief by the instructing solicitor to the barrister. There would be no need to prepare a brief if the same lawyer who prepared the case, spoke to the client and gathered the evidence would also be the lawyer that presented the case in court.

In some jurisdictions with a fused profession, a single lawyer will prepare and present a case from start to finish. Obviously this would be so in a single lawyer practice. However, this is rare. The experience of the United States indicates that in a fused profession the lawyers tend to divide themselves between office practice lawyers and trial lawyers with each specialising in his own particular field. In the USA two lawyers also handle a single case. This would not necessarily cause a crisis of confidence on the part of the client who has built up a relationship with one lawyer only to find another lawyer handling the advocacy work before the courts. A good advocate will often quickly gain the confidence of the litigant by mastering the material before him/her. Indeed a litigant may feel more comfortable having two opinions on his case and having two lawyers working for him at no real additional cost. There is however a psychological/impressionistic reason surrounding the question of client confidence, the validity of which would vary from litigant to litigant.

Indeed on the point of cost, there is an argument that the present divided system is cheaper for many litigants (although not all). It is often less costly to retain a relatively junior barrister to attend court than for a solicitor with higher overheads (fixed costs) to spend a long time in court awaiting his case to be heard. Such considerations, it would have to be observed, would apply only to cases in the lower courts.

The fact that barristers are divorced from the preparation of a case before it comes to court enables the barrister to have a detached outlook. Not only will this have an advantage for the litigant in that his case will be presented objectively and dispassionately but also there will be a relationship of trust between the Bar and the Bench (judges). This trust will exist because the judge will know that the barrister's first duty as an officer of justice is to the court and then and only then to the litigant. For example, where the defendant has told the barrister that he is guilty and there is no technicality by which he may have misunderstood and that he was not guilty then, regardless of whether the barrister is of the opinion that he could 'get the defendant off' he is obliged to enter a plea of guilty. In the long term such a relationship is felt to be to the advantage of the litigant, yet it would not be possible in the event that the profession were fused.

A further advantage to the litigant of the divided profession is what is known as 'the taxi rank rule' according to which a litigant through his solicitor is able to retain the services of a specialist barrister for his particular case. If the profession were fused then not every law firm would have the relevant specialist for every dispute that was referred to them. In effect fusion would lead to whole chambers of barristers being swallowed up by the large City firms and leaving none of the rich pickings for other solicitor firms. Inevitably the litigant will suffer as he either has to pay the high prices of the City firms or do without the relevant specialists. This would also have an adverse affect on the solicitors practices that did not merge with the large firms. In a fused profession only the larger firms would have the necessary resources to retain specialists. Thus we can see that the taxi rank rule leads to a certain efficiency in the market place for legal services.

If there were fusion of the legal profession then it is clear that certain fundamental changes would be necessary. Such fusion would require that in the first instance solicitors be granted rights of audience in all courts and on the other side of the same coin that barristers be entitled to take instructions from the lay client directly. Inevitably this would result in barristers and solicitors entering into partnerships and the restriction against this would have to be removed. These are the immediate changes that one envisages would be necessary. No less necessary in the longer term would be a change in the professional stage of legal education. Currently there is a uniform system of core subjects covered at the academic stage of training and (at least in theoretical terms) the student does not need to choose which branch of the profession (s)he would want to enter until completion of this academic stage. Then an almost irrevocable choice has to be made. This choice would be eliminated as the students under a fused profession would all receive a common stage of professional training. Over the longer term a further consequence would be that all lawyers would become eligible for appointment to the Bench. At the moment only barristers are eligible for appointment to the High Court (and obviously beyond).

It would be appropriate in assessing whether one is in favour of fusion to ask the question as to who would benefit from fusion. There are not many lawyers who want to see fusion although some of the structural changes are being advocated (largely from a self interest point of view) eg some solicitors advocate that all solicitors should be given rights of audience in all courts. The past president of the Law Society Sir David Napley is a leading proponent of this cause.

The Marre Committee's recommendations

In their report entitled *A Time for Change* the *Marre* committee noted the massive growth in the provision of legal services and in the size of the professions. It also noted that if the profession does not adapt from within, unwelcome change 'will be forced upon them'. *Marre* recommended that the supervisory role of the Law Society and the General Council of the Bar should be retained but that only those rules which are essential for the maintenance of professional standards should remain.

In chapter 6 of their report they conclude that because lawyers have overriding duties to the rule of law, to their clients and to the court, commercial considerations cannot be paramount when considering the future supply of legal services.

The committee made several recommendations about the image of the profession and the availability of legal services (see below) but these can only be regarded as marginal in the light of their comment that there is 'a need for realism in determining the resources available to meet both needs and demands for legal services'.

The committee did not recommend fusion of the profession but did suggest that solicitors should have rights of audience in all cases in the Crown Courts subject to meeting certain standards (in advocacy) and, to compensate the Bar, that it be approachable directly by professional clients without the intermediary of the solicitor. Recommendations to explore the feasibility of changes in the law to enable a contractual relationship to be enforceable between the barrister and those instructing him/her (in order to recover fees at law) and a proposal that solicitors be considered eligible for appointment as High Court judges, were also mentioned.

Generally, the committee took quite a conservative view. On multi disciplinary practices it suggested awaiting the findings of the Law Society's examination of the issues but did suggest that moves towards more efficient practices were to be welcomed.

The White Paper and the Courts and Legal Services Act 1990

In July 1989, after much debate and controversy, the Lord High Chancellor isued a White Paper entitled 'Legal Services: A Framework for the Future'. This paper outlined the Government's proposals for the reform of the legal profession: the Courts and Legal Services Act, which closely followed the White Paper, received the Royal Assent on 1 November 1990. It has been steadily implemented since then. Its main provisions are:

Rights of audience
Barristers who are qualified in terms of the Bar's rules on education and training retain their full rights of audience in all courts and tribunals.

Solicitors retain their present rights of audience but, in addition, may seek certification from the Law Society to appear in the higher courts. They may be certified for each court or tribunal individually or obtain full rights. These rights will, however, only be granted where the Law Society is satisfied the solicitor has qualified in terms of regulations.

Rules issued by both the Bar and the Law Society governing rights of audience will be subject to the concurrence of the Lord Chancellor and of the Lord Chief Justice, the Master of the Rolls, The President of the Family Division and the Vice-Chancellor. They will act having regard to the Lord Chancellor's Advisory Committee on Legal Education and Conduct.

It shall be an offence to impersonate any qualified Advocate.

In future, all those advocates who hold rights of audience in the High Court or the Crown Court will be eligible for appointment as Queens Counsel as will other lawyers on an honorary basis. This will ultimately lead to solicitors being appointed to the senior ranks of the Judiciary.

Law Reporting will be open to those practitioners with rights of audience in the Supreme Court.

Litigation

Rights to litigate, which had previously only been held by solicitors will be open to all members of recognised professional bodies where they demonstrate the ability to set and maintain the appropriate standards of competence and conduct. It is probable that The Bar will pursue such rights for its members.

Conveyancing

Although there have been inroads into this traditional solicitors' preserve, the Act allows any body the right to provide conveyancing services provided they satisfy certain requirements. These are:

a suitability to provide conveyancing services;

b protection of clients' money from improper use;

c compliance with any applicable rules and regulations;

d ability to meet claims arising out of conveyancing services;

e investigation of complaints;

f suitable compensation arrangements;

g membership of the Conveyancing Ombudsman Scheme;

h adequate arrangements for protecting clients should an authorised practitioner cease to provide conveyancing services.

This has thus opened up conveyancing to banks, building societies and others who meet the specified requirements. Authorised practitioners will include solicitors, barristers and notaries where they are suitably qualified. The code of conduct will, with exceptions, prevent services being offered to both the buyer and seller of the same property. In the interest of fair competition services will not be offered at less than their true cost. That is, they cannot be cross-subsidised by more profitable aspects of the business. The provision of these services may not be offered on condition the client undertakes other services. Conveyancing will be regulated through an Authorised Conveyancing Practitioners Board and an Ombudsman scheme for complaints.

Probate

Previously, only solicitors, barristers and notaries were allowed by law to prepare the papers on which the grant of probate or letters of administration depend. Again the Government wished to open up this field to other suitably qualified bodies of practitioners, (for example, licensed conveyancers, authorised conveyancing practitioners, accountants, and legal executives) and the Act made similar provisions as for conveyancing.

The Advisory Committee

The Lord Chancellor's Advisory Committee on Legal Education and Conduct, to be known as the Advisory Committee, has been set up to 'advise upon the arrangements for legal education and training; the need for schemes recognising areas of specialisation, and how specialists should be trained; and on codes of conduct'; page 25 'Legal Services: A Framework for the Future'.

The Committee consists of 15 members. There is a chairman who must be either a Lord of Appeal in Ordinary or a Judge of the Supreme Court. There are to be two practising barristers, two practising solicitors, two academic lawyers and eight people drawn from outside the profession. The purpose behind this arrangement is to represent the user of legal services rather than the legal professions themselves. Every member is appointed by the Lord Chancellor after wide consultation.

Under certain circumstances, the Lord Chancellor, the professions and the Judiciary are 'to have regard' to advice from the Committee. This does not mean they have to follow that advice, but rather they must give reasons for not so doing.

Other provisions

Barristers are given the right to sue for their fees in the event of non-payment. This will be achieved by allowing barristers to enter into contracts for their services.

The barriers preventing multi-disciplinary partnerships have been largely removed and multi-national partnerships are now allowed. Multi-disciplinary partnerships could include eg accountants, surveyors.

A form of contingency fee is allowed similar to that already in operation in Scotland. The provision for 'no win, no fee' arrangements is designed mainly to help middle-income litigants who do not qualify for legal aid.

A Legal Services Ombudsman has been created to investigate how the professional bodies oversee complaints against lawyers and will be empowered to recommend that compensation be payable where appropriate. This is an important measure which should provide a more 'independent' check on the profession, while all lawyers will benefit from immunity against negligence claims for 'court work'.

Other matters covered in the White Paper which were incorporated into the Act, include provision of a scheme of properly accredited areas of specialisation, and giving the Bar the choice whether to allow direct access to their services by other professionals or members of the public.

The judiciary

The modern notion of the independence of the judiciary was not necessarily a medieval one: initially, the judges were appointed from the clerks by the King. The political crises of the fourteenth century indicate that the judges were a regular part of the political life of England. The growing professionalism of the lawyers led in the fourteenth and fifteenth century to a more 'objective loyalty' (*Baker*) to the Crown and to the common law, which derived its authority from the King.

A major upheaval occurred in 1616 when Coke CJ refused to accept James I's contention that the judges should be willing to stay a case on the request of the Crown: as a result Coke was dismissed. The political allegiances and biases of the sixteenth and seventeenth century judges depended much on the manner of their appointment and whether they were susceptible to political pressure: whether a judge was appointed whilst he was of good behaviour ('quam diu se bene gesserit') or at the pleasure of the monarch.

The growing practice in Tudor times was that of appointment during good behaviour but the Stuart monarchs were more inclined to control the judiciary especially late in the reign of Charles II and during the reign of James II (who dismissed twelve judges in four years). Following the 'Glorious Revolution' of 1689 and the deposition of James II the principle that judges shall hold office 'quam diu se bene gesserit' was established by statute.

Independence of the judiciary was further aided by the establishment of the principle that judges should continue automatically in office on the death of a monarch in 1760. Once this was done political influence over judges was mainly exercised by appointment; politics in particular played an important part in the appointment of judges, especially of chief justiceships. The appointment of Lord Ellenborough in 1806 was the last occasion on which a chief justice was also a member of the cabinet: since that date the judiciary have largely endeavoured to remain apart from politics.

Apart from the judges of the superior courts, the judiciary is still subject to removal by the Lord Chancellor (a political appointee) – but that power has generally been exercised with great care.

The main judicial appointments

The Lord Chancellor
The Lord Chancellor holds an office which is partly political, partly judicial.

Also a Minister of State and a member of the Cabinet, he presides over meetings of the House of Lords, but may take part in debates as a Government spokesman.

As head of the judicial system he has a number of ex officio jurisdictions, but obviously in practical terms pressure of work prevents his actively presiding over all the courts he heads. He presides over the House of Lords when sitting as a law court, also over the Judicial Committee of the Privy Council.

The Lord Chief Justice

The Lord Chief Justice holds the senior true (non-political) judicial office in this country. He presides over the Queen's Bench Division and the Criminal Division of the Court of Appeal.

Master of the Rolls

The Master of the Rolls presides over the Civil Division of the Court of Appeal and may sit in the Criminal Division.

Attorney General, Solicitor General, Director of Public Prosecutions

Strictly speaking these are *Law Officers* not judiciary. All three are political appointments.

Supreme Court Judges

High Court judges are appointed by the Crown (see below) on the advice of the Lord Chancellor. They must be barristers of at least ten years' standing. Upon appointment they receive a knighthood and a fixed salary. They are referred to as Mr Justice Smith or in writing as Smith J.

In order to sit as judges of the Court of Appeal or as a Lord of Appeal in Ordinary in the House of Lords, advice is sought from the Prime Minister, though the actual appointment is by the Lord Chancellor (see below).

Circuit judges

There are at present more than 400 circuit judges who serve mainly in the Crown Courts and County Courts. They must be barristers of at least ten years' standing. They are addressed as Judge Smith.

Recorders

There are something like 700 Recorders at present who are, effectively, part-time judges. They are appointed from solicitors or barristers of at least ten years' experience. The ranks of the Recorders are a fertile training ground for full-time Circuit judges; several solicitors have in fact entered the judiciary by this route.

Most Recorders are appointed from among practising barristers/solicitors who would not wish to give up a lucrative professional practice to become a permanent full-time judge. (For further details see the next section on 'appointment'.)

Appointment of judges today

Unlike some countries, England does not have a career structured judiciary, that is certain lawyers chosen at the beginning of their career to be judges and who work their way up the profession. All English judges, from the ranks of Appeal in ordinary to stipendiary magistrates are chosen from the ranks of practising lawyers, mainly from barristers. At High Court levels, becoming a judge is by 'invitation only'.

The Lord Chancellor is the only judge appointed on a 'political' basis. He is appointed by the Queen on the advice of the Prime Minister, he is a member of the Government, and when there is a change of Government there is a change of Lord Chancellor.

The Lord Chief Justice, the Master of the Rolls, the President of the Family Division, the Vice-Chancellor, the Lords of Appeal in Ordinary and the Lords Justices of Appeal are appointed by the Queen on the advice of the Prime Minister. Puisne judges of the High Court, Circuit judges and Recorders are appointed by the Queen on the advice of the Lord Chancellor. Justices of the Peace are appointed directly by the Lord Chancellor.

Until recently the only judicial office open to a solicitor was that of Recorder, but since 1971 a Recorder of five years' standing (altered to three years by the Administration of Justice Act 1977) may be appointed a Circuit Judge, and there are now some Circuit judges who were solicitors. Some solicitors, of course, reached high judicial office after they had switched to the Bar. A notable example was Lord Widgery CJ, who became Lord Chief Justice after a long career as a solicitor and lecturer. As mentioned above the *Marre* committee recommended that solicitors be considered eligible for appointment as High Court judges and the White Paper *Legal Services: A Framework for the Future* proposed that solicitors would be eligible for all appointments. The Courts and Legal Services Act now makes solicitors eligible for appointment as High Court judges.

The actual process of selecting a judge is 'shrouded in secrecy' (*M Berlins*). Undoubtedly, as the Bar grows in size and its composition alters socially, the Lord Chancellor, unlike his historical predecessors will not know every potential candidate. Information about 'good' senior barristers is stored in the so-called 'yellow sheets' and accumulated for future reference. Lord Elwyn-Jones Lord Chancellor 1974–79 says that the Lord Chancellor will have regard to a candidate's background and experience.

Reputation is all-important and clearly can be made or broken in court. One can guess that a barrister who has impressed a judge with his performance will not be forgotten lightly.

Professor JAG Griffith in his book *The Politics of the Judiciary* highlights several interesting features about judicial appointment:

a 'The most remarkable fact ... is that it is wholly in the hands of politicians'. Therefore, to what extent is any appointment 'political'? *Griffith* takes the view that the position is likely to vary with different Prime Ministers and differing sets of circumstances.

b From the data collated it seems to be unusual for the Prime Minister or Lord Chancellor to consult with other Ministers unless such a Minister is a distinguished member of the Bar.

c There is no evidence in recent times that Prime Ministers have asserted their influence or exercised their power of appointment. *Griffith* says 'the likelihood is that a modern Prime Minister would depart (from the decision of the Lord Chancellor) only in the most exceptional case'.

The Lord Chancellor when making appointments has a relatively small group to select from. In reality the grouping may consist of experienced barristers within the age range of forty and sixty years. The total number of 'real' or genuine possibles – the short list – could be as small as six.

Removal and retirement

Judges of the High Court and above, with the exception of the Lord Chancellor, hold office during good behaviour subject to a power of removal by Her Majesty on an address presented by both Houses of Parliament. This provision derives from the Act of Settlement 1701, and is now contained in The Supreme Court Act 1981.

Circuit Judges and Recorders, may be removed from office by the Lord Chancellor on the grounds of incapacity or misbehaviour.

Judges appointed after 1959 must now retire at 75, though the Lord Chancellor has indicated that he intends shortly to lower the retiring age to 70.

Immunity and independence

Immunity is an extension of the principle of an independent judiciary. A judge may not be sued in a civil action for anything done or said while acting in his judicial capacity. An authority for this is *Sirros v Moore* [1974] 3 WLR 459.

The immunity varies with the status of the judge:

a *Judge of Superior Court*: no action lies against him for anything he says or does in exercise of his judicial office even if he is malicious or acts in bad faith.

b *Judge of Inferior Court*: the same immunity as above but only when acting within his jurisdiction.

The independence of the judiciary is a key feature and one which runs parallel with immunity. The independence of the judiciary means that the judges are not controlled by the legislature or the executive. They do not take part in politics and cannot become MPs at the same time (although some were MPs before being appointed as judges). In the House of Lords the Law Lords do not, by convention, take part in political controversy or take part in party politics, although they do take part in debates on topics connected with the law. The Lord Chancellor, again by convention, keeps his political activities completely separate from his judicial responsibilities.

Security of tenure and adequate remuneration prevent influence and control being exerted.

English judges are said not to be promotion-minded in that the pay differential between High Court judges and members of the Court of Appeal or the House of Lords is not great. The nature of the work may, however, be more interesting the higher one reaches. It appears that the English judiciary do not seek elevation self-consciously and thus they remain free of the possible taint that their judgments are trimming and time-serving in order to please their political masters who hold the reins of patronage.

Judicial independence means that judges are not dependent on governments as is the case in several other legal systems. In addition to their immunity, they are not dismissible by any government, nor is their promotion a 'political' issue.

Social position and age

Professor Griffith has analysed the social class origins of judges from the period 1820 to 1968. He concluded that over this period the dominance of upper and middle classes is 'overwhelming'.

This is not at all surprising. The Bar was a profession historically for the educated and wealthy and as such would have seen its members educated at private, and public schools, Oxford or Cambridge and perhaps military service or a brief 'flirtation' with politics.

The public may have an image of the judge either through books or popularised television dramas or an actual court appearance. Two views may prevail:

a the embodiment of wisdom and impartiality;

b elderly, remote, nineteenth century figures.

Lord Edmund-Davies, a former Law Lord has said;

'Judges are human beings, have families of their own, families have troubles ... they are not set apart, they have to lead pretty normal lives off the bench.'

The role of the judge

The role of the judge can be stated as:

a supervisory – conduct of the trial;

b sole arbiter of any legal issue;

c in civil cases the judge alone decides fact and law – (except possibly libel cases) AJA 1933 s6;

d in civil cases the judge decides quantum of damages;

e to interpret, clarify and give effect to the law;

f in criminal cases, the role of summing up to a jury;

g in criminal cases, passing sentence.

The traditional view about the function of the judge is to decide and arbitrate disputes in accordance with the law. In addition, there is an implied assumption that judges are 'neutral'. The judiciary comprises one of the principal organs of state and a prime function is to maintain law and order, alongside the executive and Parliament.

Lord Devlin: in *The Dockers Case* [1973] AC 15; [1972] ICR 308:

'In theory the judiciary is the neutral force between government and the governed. The judge interprets and applies the law without favour to either ... it is not the judge's personal order; it is substantially the product of the law and only marginally of the judicial'.

Most of the work of a judge involves arbitration upon disputes, and to do this he must apply the existing rules of law to the facts of the case before him. In order to determine these rules of law he must interpret statutes and apply the doctrine of precedent. Whilst in theory the judges cannot create new rules of law, in practice this must inevitably happen. In the case of *Jones* v *Secretary of State for Social Services* [1972] 2 WLR 210 Lord Simon said, 'In this country it was long considered that judges were not makers of law but merely its discoverers and expounders. The theory was that every case was governed by a relevant rule of law, existing somewhere and discoverable somehow, provided sufficient learning and intellectual rigour were brought to bear. But once such a rule had been discovered, frequently the pretence was tacitly dropped that the rule was pre-existing; for example, cases like *Merryweather* v *Nixan* (1799) 8 TR 186 or *Priestley* v *Fowler* (1837) 150 ER 1030, were (rightly) regarded as new departures in the law. Nevertheless, the theory, however unreal, had its value – in limiting the sphere of law-making by the judiciary (inevitably at some disadvantage in assessing the potential repercussions of any decision, and increasingly so in a complex modern industrial society), and thus also in emphasising the central feature of our constitution, the sovereignty of parliament. But the true, even if limited nature of judicial law making has been widely acknowledged in recent years.'

However, when the function of a judge in a court of first instance was considered by the Chancery Division in *Derby & Co* v *Weldon* [1989] 1 WLR 1244, Vinelott J said:

'The function of a judge at first instance is to find the relevant facts and, with the assistance of counsel, ascertain the law as set out in any relevant statutory provisions and in any principles to be derived from the House of Lords and Court of Appeal and to draw the appropriate conclusions.

It is not open to the judge in performing this primary function to consider, far less express, an opinion as to the correctness of a decision in the Court of Appeal or the House of Lords, save in those rare cases when he is faced with conflicting decisions of the Court of Appeal and must choose which one to follow. There are, nonetheless, occasions when a judge is entitled as it were to stand outside and comment on ... the law. He may feel, for example, that a statute or a decision of the Court of Appeal ought to be reconsidered in the light of changed social and economic circumstances. That right should be sparingly exercised ...'

New rules, particularly of equity, have been evolved in recent years and an outstanding example is the principle of equitable estoppel enunciated by Denning J (as he then was) in *Central London Property Trust Ltd* v *High Trees House Ltd* [1947] KB 130.

Some judges consider change to be the province of Parliament for judges are faced with the immediate facts before them and cannot foresee the far reaching consequences of creating new law (see Lord Simon's speech, *Miliangos* v *George Frank (Textiles)* [1975] 3 WLR 758).

Extensions of the criminal law by judges are less favourably regarded by the higher courts and Parliament, but nevertheless the law of conspiracy was extended by the House of Lords in *Shaw* v *DPP* [1962] AC 220 to include 'conspiracy to corrupt public morals' and this decision has been tacitly accepted by parliament in the Criminal Law Act 1977.

In addition to this main judicial function judges exercise certain administrative functions. This is particularly true of justices of the peace who deal with many types of licensing, and another example is the Court of Protection. A High Court is often chosen as the chairman of a Royal Commission or a Tribunal of inquiry.

A case for an elected judiciary?

David Pannick has argued that it is unsatisfactory to have judicial appointments left in the hands of the Lord Chancellor rather than an 'elected' judiciary, and proposed that there could be a system introduced here analogous to certain states in America. In California for example, (and other states) judges are appointed by the governor for a period of one year after which time they must seek re-election before the electorate.

The New Law Journal (23 August 1979) took up these points and argued against *Pannick's* suggestion that the ballot paper should contain the simple question: 'should Mr Justice X be elected to the office of judge for a term of 12 years?'

There are some objections to this:

a Constitutional grounds. The 'democratic election' of the judiciary has been avoided out of regard for their independence and immunity from political pressure. Immunity means here, immunity from bribery. An argument against this could be that our MPs are elected.

b The public is not competent to select its judiciary. Obviously the counter argument is that they select their MPs.

c If the system were to be adopted, who would act as governor?

The suggestion by *David Pannick* is an interesting one. The separation of powers as enshrined in the Act of Settlement 1701 would be of little effect.

One should consider the following quotation:

In 1897, the Prime Minister (Lord Salisbury) wrote to the Lord Chancellor (Lord Halsbury), 'The judicial salad requires both legal oil and political vinegar'.
David Pannick concludes:

> 'An elected judiciary ... would introduce the political vinegar. It would ensure that those who make laws for us while deciding hard cases, would have their philosophies subjected to the test of public opinion.'

Magistrates

There are two types of magistrate – lay and stipendiary – and each shall be dealt with separately.

Lay justices

Until 1906 there was a property qualification for county justices, but there has never been a formal property qualification for borough justices. Justices are appointed by the Lord Chancellor from people who have been put forward by local party political organisations, others by leading members of the community or by voluntary organisations, and those put forward are in general people of standing, generally with a record of good service to the community. The Lord Chancellor is assisted by local advisory committees (about 100) and he attempts to maintain as far as possible a balance between the sexes, political parties, social classes and races.

The greatest difficulty in attempting to obtain justices representative of the community as a whole is that their services are unpaid, they are given their expenses only, so that many suitable people cannot afford to be appointed.

There are few formal qualifications. On appointment a magistrate must be over 21 and below 60 (50 in the case of a juvenile bench) and must normally reside within fifteen miles of the area of his court. There are no formal 'character' qualifications, although undischarged bankrupts are disqualified. The process of selection ensures that persons of good character will be appointed.

Justices retire at 70, and may be removed from office by the Lord Chancellor. By convention, he exercises this power in a judicial manner and justices may only be removed for good cause, and this includes infirmity or refusal to sit regularly.

Justices of the Peace are appointed in the name of the Crown under the hand of the Lord Chancellor, or, in Lancashire, the Chancellor of the Duchy of Lancashire. Local advisory committees assist the Lord Chancellor in assessing potential candidates and make formal recommendations. Ultimately, responsibility lies with the Lord Chancellor for appointment.

There are over 24,000 lay magistrates in England and Wales and at first sight some idea of their importance can be seen from the fact that most (90 per cent) of criminal cases start and finish in the Magistrates' Court. There is a heavy reliance on lay participation (as with juries) and the reasons are largely historical.

A frequent criticism is that lay justices do not need to be legally qualified. Newly appointed justices attend 'basic training'; they attend courses designed for them to 'get to know' procedure and familiarise themselves with basic elements of the law. Another criticism is that they are too ready to accept police evidence and to place undue reliance on the clerk of the court. To counter this, they play an important role in the administration of justice, and to replace them with qualified staff would be extremely costly. It has been said of the system that 'it enables the citizen to see that the law is his law, administered by men and women like himself' – Sir Thomas Skyrme, 1979, formerly Chief Official in the Lord Chancellor's department responsible for advisory committees.

It is interesting to look at the words 'like himself' a little closer:

a   84 per cent (approximately) of magistrates belong to the professional or middle classes;

b   16 per cent of magistrates from skilled or semi-skilled or working class;

c   category (b) above may not apply for fear of losing their jobs or pension prospects;

d   married women often look after young children or families – the ratio of men to women is about 3 to 2 (10,000 women approximately);

e   there is a low proportion of magistrates from the ethnic communities – in the 1970s about 100 black or Asian JPs – 1980s about 200;

f   average age is between 40–50 years, although some are in their twenties and thirties.

Stipendiary magistrates

The system of stipendiary (full time salaried) magistrates was first set up at the end of the eighteenth century to deal with the defects of the administration of justice in London. Most large conurbations now have stipendiary magistrates as well as lay magistrates, and this is necessary because of the vast quantity of work that has to be dealt with by the City Magistrates' Court.

A stipendiary magistrate is a professional lawyer (a barrister or a solicitor of seven years standing) who receives a 'stipend' (salary), and works full time. The total number of stipendiaries who can be appointed at any one time is limited and there are at present about 70 (therefore the reliance of the system on lay justices can be seen in relation to this figure). They are appointed by the Crown on the recommendation of the Lord Chancellor. Their salary is determined by the Home Secretary.

Stipendiary magistrates may be appointed to circuit judgeships and this is another route whereby a solicitor can become a judge.

There has never been any serious call to replace lay justices with stipendiaries but 'it is widely accepted' (*M Berlins*) that the 'justice' they dispense is of a different quality. Mostly such comments come from lawyers or defendants themselves who quickly 'get to know' the system if they are regular visitors.

One factor which is often mentioned by lawyers is that the stipendiary will dispense justice more quickly and fairly without undue time wasting or reliance on his clerk. London Magistrates' Courts are borrowing stipendiary magistrates from a pool to try to clear up the backlog of cases. There are two ideas behind this: firstly, to help to relieve the over-worked justices; secondly, to help the clerks to clear up the administrative backlog. It is thought that one stipendiary is able to do the work of two courts of lay justices and this therefore frees the clerk to cope with paperwork.

The justices' clerk

Lay justices can only sit if they have a legally qualified clerk, who therefore plays an important part in the administration of justice in Magistrates' Courts. The clerk must advise the justices as to the law and practice, but he must not interfere with their decision and the decision is liable to be quashed by an order of certiorari if this is seen to happen. The clerk, who must be a barrister or a solicitor, is a salaried official. He is a key figure in the Magistrates Courts, especially where they are staffed by lay justices. It is important that the magistrates themselves must make the decisions yet lay justices who are unqualified after all often need to call on the help of the clerk who brings points to their attention: The Justices of the Peace Act 1968.

Legal services | 20

Legal aid and advice

A national scheme for the provision of legal aid, that is funding for legal advice and proceedings was founded in 1949. It was governed by the Legal Aid Acts of 1974 and 1984 and administered by the Law Society together with the Bar Council. The Scheme is now administered by the Legal Aid Board which was set up by s3 of the Legal Aid Act 1988. The Act came into force on 1 April 1989 and has repealed the earlier Acts. There are few substantial changes in the administration of the system although moves are underfoot to do so. Money provided by the scheme comes from the Legal Aid Fund, which is state financed.

The Legal Aid Scheme has three aspects, each considered below, in relation to which the rules and procedure are very different. These three aspects are:

a   legal advice and assistance;

b   civil legal aid;

c   criminal legal aid.

Legal advice and assistance

The £5 fixed fee interview
Initially, it is to be noted that if someone is not sure whether he qualifies for legal aid or not, he may always ask a solicitor for a 'fixed fee interview' which costs £5.00. This will provide up to half an hour's advice and most solicitors who do legal aid work will provide this service.

The Green Form scheme
This scheme was first introduced by the Legal Advice and Assistance Act 1972, and is now contained in Part III (ie, ss8–18) of the Legal Aid Act 1988.

Services provided under the scheme include written or oral advice from a solicitor (or counsel) on any question of English law and on any steps which it may be appropriate for the applicant to take. This, therefore, will include the giving of general advice, writing letters, negotiating and preparing a written case if the applicant has to go before a tribunal.

Note: In 1990 the Lord Chancellor exercised his power under the Act to remove conveyancing and wills from the Green Form Scheme.

However, it is true to say that generally this scheme makes available advice only: if further representation is needed in either civil or criminal proceedings, that must be sought from the legal aid scheme proper (see below).

The name 'green form scheme' comes from the method of applying: Application is made at a solicitor's office by filling in a green form. This contains questions concerning the applicant's income and capital as legal advice and assistance is available only to applicants whose resources are within the limits specified in regulations pursuant to s9 of the Legal Aid Act 1988. It is for the solicitor himself to calculate whether the applicant qualifies: this is a necessary part of this aspect of the legal aid scheme as it ensures that the green form scheme of legal advice is given quickly and that administration costs are kept low.

The solicitor must assess two things:

a   is the applicant eligible for legal advice under the green form scheme;

b   if so, what, if any, contribution must he make.

Limitation

The scope of the scheme is limited by the Legal Aid Act 1988 in that advice and assistance may only be given immediately by a solicitor to the extent that he considers that giving it will take no more than two hours (or three hours in cases leading to the preparation of an undefended divorce or judicial separation petition). If the advice or assistance will take longer, the solicitor must obtain approval from the legal aid office before giving it.

The aim of the scheme, therefore, to give immediate initial advice is limited to a relatively small amount of advice and assistance.

Delay is involved in obtaining any greater amount of advice or assistance.

Although the Green Form Scheme is still operating it is the intention of the board to introduce a system of 'franchising' out legal aid work. They propose to contract with providers of legal services who meet certain criteria. For example, the Citizen's Advice Bureaux could be awarded such a contract.

Legal aid in civil proceedings

In a civil case, legal aid may be obtained to pay for all work leading up to and including the court proceedings and representation by a solicitor and if necessary, a barrister. The position is governed by Part IV of the Legal Aid Act 1988. Legal aid is available for proceedings in the following courts:

House of Lords
Court of Appeal
High Court
County Court
Magistrates' Court (certain proceedings)
Employment Appeal Tribunal (but *not* the Industrial Tribunal)
Restrictive Practices Court
Lands Tribunal

With very rare exceptions, legal aid is not available for:

Undefended matrimonial proceedings
Judicial and administrative tribunals
Arbitrations.

Eligibility for legal aid

The first condition of eligibility is that the applicant is within the financial requirements.

In order to qualify the applicant must meet the financial eligibility criteria as regards disposable income and capital. These figures change from time to time. In certain circumstances where the lower limits are exceeded but not the upper limits a contribution may be payable by the applicant. If the assisted person is liable to pay a contribution, this is payable directly to the Legal Aid Fund and not to the solicitor.

The second condition for eligibility is the 'merits of the case' test. This depends on whether the applicant who has satisfied the financial requirements has reasonable grounds for taking or defending an action in court and that it is reasonable to grant Legal Aid in the circumstances of the case.

Legal aid in criminal proceedings

The provision of legal aid for those charged with a criminal offence is governed by Part V of the Legal Aid Act 1988.

Application

Application for legal aid by a defendant in criminal proceedings is made to the magistrates in the Magistrates' Court which is dealing initially with the defendant's case. The magistrates make an immediate decision: delay in the provision of legal representation in criminal proceedings is undesirable and so the six week period of consideration in civil legal aid applications is avoided.

It is the clerk to the justices who in fact decides whether or not to grant legal aid or not. The decision is made on the basis of a 'statement of means' supplied by the defendant. An assessment of the defendant's precise resources may be ordered to take place subsequently in order to fix a contribution, if any. He may be ordered to pay such contribution as appears reasonable in the light of his commitments and resources.

If the clerk refuses legal aid appeal is as follows:

a   for summary offences – to the magistrates themselves;

b   for indictable or 'either way' offences – to the Legal Aid Board.

'Interests of justice'

Apart from financial considerations, it is laid down by s21(2) of the Legal Aid Act 1988 that legal aid must be granted where it is desirable in the interests of justice.

The criteria to be followed by the court are the criteria set out in s22 of the Legal Aid Act 1988 which are as follows:

a   the offence is such that if proved it is likely that the court would impose a sentence which would deprive the accused of his liberty or lead to loss of his livelihood or serious damage to his reputation;

b   the determination of the case may involve consideration of a substantial question of law;

c the accused may be unable to understand the proceedings or to state his own case because of his inadequate knowledge of English, mental illness or other mental or physical disability;

d the nature of the defence is such as to involve the tracing and interviewing of witnesses or cross-examination of a witness for the prosecution;

e it is in the interests of someone other than the accused that the accused be represented.

The *Marre Committee* noted that the reliance by the junior bar on the Criminal legal aid scheme was not desirable and that the rates for work in criminal legal aid should be increased. They went further in their recommendations on many practical matters connected with the legal aid and advice schemes including suggesting their extension to tribunals, retention for welfare matters of the availability of the green form scheme, and the availability of legal aid for petitioners of the European Court of Justice (in Luxembourg) and to the Court of Human Rights (in Strasbourg).

The unmet need for legal services

The *Marre Committee* noted that the biggest area of unmet need is in the provision of social welfare law and that the creation of new categories of legal rights without providing the funds to enforce those rights has led to a very high level of unmet need. This may be somewhat surprising in the light of the availability of legal aid and advice. However, a major criticism of the Legal Aid Scheme is that it provides no help for those of modest means and savings who nevertheless do not fall within its (relatively) low financial limits. Examples are obvious of people who may have disposable capital (within the definition of the Legal Aid Scheme) of several thousand pounds but who realistically are unable to undertake the risk of incurring the costs of High Court litigation. Unscrupulous insurance and other companies are able to make use of this, prolonging litigation and running up the costs in the hope that the plaintiff will give up. Also, people falling into this category will be at a great disadvantage if involved in litigation against a legally aided person: they are unlikely to recover their costs even if they win which surely must be an enormous disincentive.

However, there is no sign at present that the scope of the Legal Aid Scheme is to be extended. On the contrary, Lord MacKay (the Lord Chancellor) has recently (11 January 1995) spoken of the need to reform the legal aid system still further. A working paper has been circulated for comments and consultation. Whilst recognising the most basic defect of the present system to be that not enough money is available, the system has nevertheless to be controlled and managed in such a way as to control spiralling costs. One suggestion made by the Lord Chancellor was a 'fund-holding' (cf National Health Service) operation.

As we have seen although the Legal Aid Scheme is a scheme by which the state pays for a citizen to be provided with legal advice and representation by lawyers in private practice forming part of the 'mainstream' of the legal profession, it does not prove useful to everyone. In particular there are two circumstances when it may not come into play: first, a person may wish to obtain some advice without the trouble of formally approaching a solicitor and following the necessary procedure to be granted legal aid (albeit that it is a simple matter to obtain initial advice under the 'green-form scheme'). Secondly, a number of people may not be aware of what may be obtained on legal aid and in any event may be too intimidated by what they see as 'establishment figures' to enter a solicitors' office at all.

To help overcome unmet legal need stemming from these and similar causes, several sources of free legal advice have grown up. Although, in general, they can be of limited assistance, the following institutions have the useful function of putting those in need of help 'on the right track', that is, providing initial basic advice and, if appropriate, informing them of the Legal Aid Scheme and sending them to a solicitor willing to undertake such work.

The following are the sources of free legal advice:

Law centres

The establishment of 'local legal centres' was suggested in 1968 by the Society of Labour Lawyers in *Justice for All*. They were considered a good idea for the following reasons:

a They could provide a legal service outside office hours: it may not be practical for a working person to lose wages in order to pay a visit to a solicitor.

b They could provide a service of educating ordinary people in the rights and duties under the law: it is impractical for a private solicitor to do so to any great extent as he must charge for his time which, therefore, is better spent acting for a client and not educating him.

c They could acquire specialised knowledge of these areas of law of especial relevance to the poorer sections of the community such as landlord and tenant law and social security and employment law: many private practitioners will by necessity know more about company and tax law and conveyancing as these areas are of greater relevance to the majority of their clients.

In 1984 there were 45 law centres – most in poorer urban areas. Today, the law centres' main problems are concerned with attaining funds to provide their free services. Funds come from a variety of sources including government, local authorities and charities.

One effect of lack of funds is that although the centres are staffed by at least one or more qualified salaried solicitors full-time, such solicitors tend to be young with little experience and tend to return to private practice after two or three years. Assistance is given voluntarily part-time by qualified lawyers, for example for one afternoon or evening per week.

The future of law centres is uncertain: some face closure because of lack of funds and, it is argued, that none can function properly on a 'hand to mouth basis'. Increased and consistent government funding might ensure the future of this source of free legal advice which clearly goes some way to meet the unmet legal need.

Legal advice centres

These only provide legal advice and cannot undertake litigation. Because they are staffed by volunteers they cost very much less to run than the law centres. The majority of these centres are staffed by lawyers on a rota basis but there is no uniform pattern. Most university law faculties now run advice centres where second and third year students get practical experience of legal problems. When a client needs to start proceedings he is referred to a local solicitor.

Citizens' advice bureaux

These are charitable organisations, staffed by volunteers, who give advice on a wide variety of matters, including a simple legal problem. When a client requires more legal assistance he is referred to one of the solicitors on a list maintained by the bureau.

Duty solicitor schemes

These are organised locally on the initiative of the local law society. The first scheme was introduced in 1972 and there are now over 30 in existence. Volunteer solicitors who appear regularly in the Magistrates' Courts attend according to a rota and see all defendants in custody who are not legally represented and are making their first appearance. The duty solicitor will inform the defendant of his right to instruct any other solicitor, advise him and where necessary represent him in court in an application for bail. The scheme has recently been extended.

McKenzie man

'Any person whether he be a professional man or not may attend as a friend of either party, may take notes, may quietly make suggestions and give advice' (per Lord Tenterden in *Collier* v *Hicks* (1831) 2 B & Ad 663). This statement was approved by the Court of Appeal in *McKenzie* v *McKenzie* [1970] 3 WLR 472 where a party representing himself was assisted by an Australian barrister who was working for the solicitors who formerly represented him.

In *R* v *Leicester City Justices, ex parte Barrow* [1991] 3 WLR 368 the Court of Appeal decided that, in civil proceedings to which the public had a right of access, a litigant in person should have all reasonable facilities for exercising his right to be heard in his own defence, including quiet and unobtrusive advice from another member of the public accompanying him as an assistant or adviser.

Alternative dispute resolution

A Bar Council committee, chaired by Beldam LJ, has proposed pilot schemes in county courts and the High Court to evaluate ADR's potential in different kinds of proceedings. The legal rights of the parties would be unaffected by any mediation process and mediators would help the parties to find solutions rather than attempt to suggest or impose them. Mediators would be lawyers with at least seven years' experience and they would be given training in mediation techniques.

Some firms of solicitors already offer clients the benefits of mediation and they say that 82 per cent of cases referred to this service have been settled.

The Adam Smith Institute has recommended that legal aid be made available, in appropriate cases, to enable people to take advantage of ADR.

Legal expenses insurance

A person may take out insurance cover against sickness or accidental damage to property: it is suggested that the principle should be extended and people should insure against the heavy costs involved in litigation. On the continent this is becoming the norm, especially in West Germany where there is no legal aid system.

The introduction of such insurance schemes was recommended by the Royal Commission in 1976 and today they are available with certain insurance companies. The idea is good in principle and is used by companies and businesses: they can afford the premiums and are likely to make use of the services at some time.

However, as *M Berlins* has said, 'civil justice will continue to be the prerogative of the rich and the badly off'. In other words, it is only those in the middle-income who can neither afford litigation nor qualify for legal aid. Is legal expenses insurance of assistance to them? The answer to this question clearly depends on weighing the two factors of (i) the level of premiums and (ii) the likelihood that they will incur legal expenses. Clearly, the situation will vary from person to person. It is clear, however, that while companies, etc, are the main users of legal expenses insurance, premiums will stay high.

Criminal trials and the jury system

21

Introduction

Once the decision to prosecute has been made, the Prosecution must prepare for the trial of the Defendant at which it will be decided whether the Defendant is guilty or not guilty of the offence with which he is charged. In the English legal system there are two forms of trial. These have already been briefly discussed in the context of the courts system (see chapter 16).

First, there is 'Trial on Indictment' which takes place in the Crown Court before a judge and jury. This method of trial is used when more serious offences are charged.

Secondly, there is 'Summary Trial' which takes place in the Magistrates' Court and is used for less serious offences. The Magistrates will hear a case alone, without a jury, and decide both questions of law and fact (including the question of guilt) themselves.

Classification of offences

In order to determine which mode of trial is suitable all criminal offences may be classified in three groups.

Indictable offences

An indictable offence is an offence for which an adult (aged 17 or over) must or may be tried on indictment.

All common law offences are indictable. These include murder, manslaughter, rape and riot. Statutory offences are indictable if the statute which creates them indicates as such, for example, by imposing a penalty to follow conviction on indictment.

Summary offences

Summary offences must be tried by summary trial and are all statutory offences. Examples include driving without due care and attention under the Road Traffic Act 1972 and taking a pedal cycle without lawful authority under the Theft Act 1968.

The statute which creates the offence will show that the offence is summary by specifying a penalty which may be imposed upon summary conviction without specifying a further penalty to be imposed upon conviction on indictment.

Offences triable either way

As has already been stated, although a summary offence *must* be tried summarily, an indictable offence must or *may* be triable on indictment. This shows that some offences may be tried either summarily or on indictment; these are said to be 'triable either way'.

An offence is triable either way if either:

a   it is to be found in Schedule 1 to the Magistrates' Courts Act 1980. These include most offences under the Theft Act 1968, bigamy and indecent assault; or

b   it can be seen to be triable either way from the statute which creates it, such as reckless driving under the Road Traffic Act 1972.

Offences triable either way tend to be the sort of offences which are capable of varying in seriousness, depending upon the circumstances of the particular case. Whereas murder is always a serious crime no matter what the circumstances, theft, for example, may be serious or may be trivial depending, inter alia, upon the value of the goods stolen.

It should be noted that there are a few offences which are either triable either way or triable summarily depending upon the value of the property involved. An example of such an offence is s1 of the Criminal Damage Act 1971 which is triable summarily if the value of the property damaged is less than £2,000.

Determining the mode of trial

If an offence is an indictable offence which *must* be tried on indictment, or an offence which *must* be tried summarily, there is no difficulty because there is no choice of trial. If, however, the offence is triable either way the case will come initially before the Magistrates' Court. The procedure for making a decision is laid down by ss18–21 and s23 of the Magistrates' Court Act 1980. The decision may be made by a single lay justice, though it is more usual for there to be a panel of three.

The procedure is as follows:

a   The charge is read to the defendant.

b   The Prosecution and the Defence may each make submissions as to which method of trial is more suitable. Relevant factors for this purpose are the circumstances and nature of the case. For example, with theft, the value of the stolen goods and whether there was any violence involved.

c   The magistrate (or magistrates) decides which mode of trial is more suitable.

   In deciding he will consider the submissions of the Prosecution and the Defence and will also take into account in particular the Magistrates' Courts' power of sentence and whether it is adequate to punish the offence before him if the Defendant is found guilty.

d   If the magistrate(s) decides that trial on indictment is the suitable mode of trial, that is a final decision. The Defendant is informed of the decision by the Clerk to the Justices and Committal proceedings will follow (see below). The Defendant, in other words, does not have a *right* to summary trial.

e If the magistrate(s) decides that summary trial is more suitable, again the Defendant is informed of this. However, the Defendant has a *right* to trial on indictment and so he is then 'put to his election' and given the opportunity of exercising that right. In other words, the Defendant is asked whether he consents to summary trial or whether he wishes to be tried on indictment. Before making his choice, the Defendant is warned that if he is found guilty on summary trial and the magistrates consider they have insufficient powers to punish him (for example, in the light of his previous convictions of which they were not aware before conviction), they may send him to the Crown Court to be sentenced.

If the Defendant elects summary trial, the next stage will be the trial itself. If the Defendant elects trial on indictment, committal proceedings will follow (see below).

If the above procedure for determining the mode of trial is not followed precisely, and the magistrates proceed to try the Defendant summarily and convict him, that conviction is liable to be quashed: *R v Horseferry Road Justices, ex parte Constable* [1981] Crim LR 504.

Committal proceedings

If it has been decided that trial is to be an indictment in the Crown Court, committal proceedings must be held in the magistrates' court. When the magistrates sit for this purpose they are known as 'examining justices'.

The examining justices are *not* concerned with the question of whether or not the Defendant is guilty or whether or not the jury at the Crown Court will find him guilty. The question the examining justices must ask themselves is; 'does the evidence placed before them at the committal proceedings show a "prima facie" case that the Defendant has committed an indictable offence?'

If their answer is no, the Defendant must be discharged. If their answer is yes, the Defendant must be committed (sent) to the Crown Court for trial on indictment.

Committal proceedings will take one of two forms, the procedure for each being slightly different.

First, under s6(1) of the Magistrates' Courts Act 1980, there may be committal proceedings with consideration of the evidence.

The procedure for this is as follows:

a The prosecution outlines its case and the evidence it will call.

b The prosecution calls its evidence. If it is written it is read to the Court. If it is oral the witnesses are called to give their evidence and may be cross-examined by the Defence.

(*Note*: written evidence may be put in evidence only if s102 of the Magistrates' Courts Act 1980 is satisfied. This requires a written statement, inter alia, to be signed by its maker, with a declaration that it is true and that there be no objections by any party to its production in evidence.)

c The Defence may submit that there is 'no case to answer', that is that the Prosecution evidence has not raised a prima facie case.

d The examining Justices must decide whether there is a case to answer, that is, a prima facie case.

> 'A submission that there is no case to answer may be properly made and upheld: (a) when there has been no evidence to prove an essential element in the alleged offence; (b) when the evidence adduced by the prosecution has been so discredited as a result of cross-examination or is so manifestly unreliable that no reasonable tribunal could safely convict on it.' Lord Parker CJ: *Practice Note* [1962] 1 All ER 448

If the examining justices decide that there is a case to answer, they state in open court that they are committing the Defendant to Crown Court and they state on which charge or charges he is being committed. If the examining justices decide that there is no case to answer, the Defendant is discharged. A discharge, however, is not an acquittal and the prosecution is free to charge the Defendant afresh for the same offence at a later date, for example, if it obtains stronger evidence: *R v Manchester City Stipendiary Magistrate, ex parte Snelson* [1977] 1 WLR 911.

Secondly, under s6(2) of the Magistrates' Courts Act 1980, there may be committal proceedings without consideration of the evidence.

Under s6(2) there may be committal without consideration of the evidence where:

a *all* the evidence before the court consists of written statements tendered in evidence under s102 of the MCA 1980; and

b the Defendant has a solicitor acting for him; and

c there is no submission from the Defence that there is no case to answer.

Compliance with these requirements ensures that a 'short-form' committal will, in practice, be used only in circumstances in which if there had been committal with consideration of the evidence, the examining justices would have found there to be a case to answer.

The advantages of committal without consideration of the evidence are obvious, saving time and expenses for all concerned. It is not surprising, therefore, that most committals take this form. This is especially true given that a large majority of submissions of no case to answer at committals with consideration of the evidence, fail; this latter fact is understandable as the prosecution are unlikely to press ahead with a charge against a Defendant if it is clear or even possible that its evidence will not satisfy even the low burden of 'prima facie case'.

In a committal for trial on written statements (s6(2) of the Magistrates' Courts Act 1980) the Home Office has issued a circular encouraging solicitors not to attend court where a committal is made in this form. This, of course, produces a saving to the legal aid fund. It remains desirable for the solicitor to attend if the prosecution intends to apply for the withdrawal of bail or the imposition of fresh conditions. The defence should be informed in these circumstances.

Once a Defendant has been committed for trial a number of final points must be considered by the examining justices.

Witness orders

Witness orders must be made in relation to all the witnesses at the committal proceedings whether they gave oral evidence or written evidence under s102 of the Magistrates' Courts Act 1980. Witness orders may be full or conditional: the full order requires the witness to attend and give evidence at the trial at the Crown Court whereas the conditional order requires attendance only if subsequently a notice is sent to him to that effect. The latter order is used generally only when the witness' evidence is not in dispute.

Alibi warning

There is no obligation upon the Defendant to reveal his defence before trial. There is one exception to this and that is when the Defendant will seek to rely on an alibi; that is he will say that he was at a place other than the scene of the crime at the time of the crime. Without pre-warning, the prosecution would be denied the opportunity to investigate the truthfulness of the alibi.

If appropriate, at the end of the committal proceedings the Defendant must be warned of the effect of s11 of the Criminal Justice Act 1967 which provides that a Defendant may not adduce evidence of an alibi at his trial on indictment as of right, but only with the leave of the judge, unless he has given notice of particulars of his alibi either in court after the committal proceedings or in writing to the prosecution within seven days from the end of the committal proceedings.

Bail

The examining justices must decide whether the Defendant is to be committed on bail or in custody. The basis on which this decision is made as set out in chapter 8 of this text. It should be noted that the waiting period between committal proceedings and trial on indictment is likely to be many months and so this question is an important one to be answered only upon full consideration of all relevant factors.

Legal aid

The examining justices may well be asked to grant legal aid to the Defendant to cover the costs of the Defence at trial. They are unlikely to refuse, and where legal aid has already been granted thus far it is generally continued automatically.

Reform

On 27 July 1989 the Lord Chancellor's Department and the Home Office issued a joint consultation paper on the reform of committal proceedings. The Home Secretary, the Rt Hon Douglas Hurd CBE, MP, has said the existing procedure is 'cumbersome and in need of reform'. The document proposes a new procedure whereby the case would go straight to the Crown Court. The defence could, however, give notice that they wished to apply to the magistrates to have the charges dropped on the grounds that the evidence discloses no prima facie case. The evidence would be given in the form of written statements. This would effectively speed up the process and save in costs.

Summary trial

Summary trial will follow automatically if the Defendant is charged with a summary offence and may be chosen as the mode of trial for an offence triable either way.

Summary trial takes place in a Magistrates' Court before either three (exceptionally two) lay Magistrates or one Stipendiary Magistrate. The Magistrates sit as both judge and jury, that is they decide questions of fact and law (the latter with guidance from their legally-qualified clerk). Approximately 95 per cent of all criminal trials take place in the Magistrates' Courts.

The procedure of a summary trial is governed by the Magistrates' Courts Act 1980.

Magistrates Courts have geographical limits to their jurisdiction – and have jurisdiction to try any summary offence committed within the county. The purpose of this is to provide a Bench with 'local knowledge' eg of a stretch of road. However, Magistrates' Courts have jurisdiction to try offences either way no matter where allegedly committed.

In addition the Courts have jurisdiction to try a summary offence committed outside the county in the following situations:

a   A Magistrates' Court which tries a person for an offence (summary or triable either way) has jurisdiction to try him in addition for any other summary offence wherever committed: s2(6) MCA 1980.

b   If one Defendant is being prosecuted in a Magistrates' Court in xshire and it is necessary or expedient, with a view to the better administration of justice, that he be tried jointly with or in the same place as another person, xshire magistrate may issue a summons to bring that other person before xshire Magistrates' Court.

Attendance and representation

Attendance of the prosecution

If the prosecution fails to attend at a summary trial the Magistrates have a discretion: they may either

a   dismiss the information; or

b   adjourn the case: s15 MCA 1980.

If the case is part-heard and the prosecution fails to attend, the Magistrates have the further alternative of:

c   proceeding in the absence of the prosecution.

Attendance of the Defendant

The Defendant need not be present at his summary trial.

By s12 MCA 1980 the Defendant is entitled to plead guilty by post for any summary offence for which the maximum penalty does not exceed three months imprisonment. In suitable cases, a notice explaining this option is served on the Defendant with the summons. If he wishes to take advantage of this option the Defendant must write to inform the clerk to the magistrates. In his letter the Defendant may set out any mitigating factors he wishes the Magistrates to take into account when sentencing him. The clerk will inform the Prosecution of the Defendant's decision so the Prosecution need not attend either. On the day set for hearing, the clerk puts to the Magistrates, proof that the summons was served, the prosecution's brief statement of the facts of the offence and the Defendant's guilty plea with any mitigating circumstances.

The Magistrates should then proceed to sentence. However, they may not sentence the Defendant to imprisonment in his absence s11(3) MCA 1980. If this is contemplated, the matter should be adjourned and a warrant issued for the Defendant's arrest. The same course should be adopted whenever the magistrates consider the offence is in fact more serious than had been anticipated, eg if the offence is one of careless driving – this carries a fine and penalty points – the penalty points may 'tot-up' with previous ones to indicate the Defendant must be disqualified from driving. This will not be done in his absence, and the matter will be adjourned, the Defendant being summonsed to attend.

Sections 11 and 13 MCA 1980 set out the options open to the Magistrates if the Defendant fails to appear but has not indicated that he wishes to plead guilty under s12.

The Magistrates have a discretion to proceed in the Defendant's absence – s11(1) MCA 1980 – with a plea of not guilty being entered on his behalf. The Prosecution is unlikely to have difficulty in proving its case with its unchallenged evidence. For this reason, the Magistrates are unlikely to adopt this course if the offence seems at all serious. This course may not be adopted without initial proof that the Defendant has in fact been served with the summons.

Representation

Both Solicitors and Barristers have a right of audience in the Magistrates' courts. However, it is usual for a Defendant to be represented by a Solicitor or appear unrepresented (perhaps having been advised by the Duty Solicitor).

The information

The information performs two functions.

a It is the basis and justification for the issue of a summons ordering the Defendant to appear at the Magistrates' Court.

b It contains and constitutes the charge to which the Defendant must plead (see below).

It is function (b) that is of relevance at the start of the summary trial.

The first stage in a summary trial is the clerk 'putting the information' to the Defendant, and asking him if he pleads guilty or not guilty.

The Defendant must then 'plead' to the allegations. A number of the pleas available to a Defendant at a trial on indictment are not available in the Magistrates' Court. Put simply, the Defendant must plead guilty or not guilty.

If the Defendant pleads guilty, the procedure detailed below following conviction is followed. If the Defendant pleads not guilty, his trial begins.

Trial on indictment

Certain trials automatically proceed to the Crown Court.

If the magistrates have committed a defendant to the Crown Court for trial, a 'trial on indictment' will follow several months later.

In the summary trial, the magistrates themselves decide all questions in issue, whether they are questions of fact or law. However, a trial on indictment takes place before a judge and a jury; consequently there is a division in their respective functions.

The judge in a Crown Court is always a paid professional judge, usually a former barrister. The 'adversarial' method of trial is adopted in the English legal system: this means that each side presents its own case and the judge acts as a kind of 'umpire' during the course of the trial, ensuring 'fair play'. (This is to be contrasted with the 'inquisitorial' method adopted in other legal systems in which it is the role of the judge himself to question the witnesses.) At the end of the trial, it is also the function of the judge to be the sole arbiter of all question of law and to sentence a convicted defendant .

The role of the jury is to decide all questions of fact: the jury must decide whether they believe evidence presented to them or what weight to give to each piece of evidence. The final question they must decide is whether the defendant is guilty or not guilty, that is their 'verdict'.

Representation

Generally, the offences being tried in the Crown Court are more serious than those tried in the magistrates' courts. This fact is reflected in the increased formality and strictness of procedure and application of rules of evidence evident in the Crown Court. Therefore, although the defendant may represent himself, he is well-advised to be legally represented (legal aid is not difficult to obtain for this purpose).

Legal representation will almost invariably be by counsel (Barrister) as a Solicitor's right of audience in the Crown Court is very limited. Legal representation of the defendant is even more important in the light of the rule that the prosecution must be legally represented by counsel.

The Code of Conduct for the Bar sets out clear guidelines and rules as to how counsel should carry out their duties in a trial on indictment.

Prosecuting counsel must act as a minister of justice. Although he must present prosecution evidence as persuasively as possible he should not try to win at all costs. See Avory J in *R v Banks* [1916] 2 KB 621. In essence, the prosecution must act fairly towards the defence.

Defence counsel, however, need not act fairly to the prosecution, he is not in court as a 'minister of justice'. He owes a duty to the court not deliberately to mislead it, but apart from that he may use all proper means available to secure an acquittal.

The defence counsel's personal opinion is irrelevant and must not affect the way in which he presents the defence. If a defendant who insists on pleading not guilty tells his counsel he is guilty, his counsel may choose to withdraw from the case; if he continues representing the defendant he may not put forward a defence on behalf of the defendant he knows to be false but must confine himself to trying to establish that the prosecution has not proved guilt beyond reasonable doubt.

The plea and plea bargaining

The charge against the defendant is contained in a formal document called an 'indictment'. An indictment may contain one or more 'counts' each of which charges one offence.

At the start of a trial on indictment each count is 'put' to the defendant in turn so that he can plead to it. This procedure is called the 'arraignment'.

In the Crown Court the following pleas are available to the defendant

Guilty

The effect of this is that the defendant admits the truth of all allegations made by the prosecution against him in the indictment (or in relation to the particular count in the indictment to which he is pleading guilty).

A plea of guilty must be entered by the defendant himself; it may not be entered by his counsel on his behalf.

After a plea of guilty is entered, the sentencing procedure will follow (see below). If the defendant has pleaded guilty on one count, but not guilty on another, sentencing will be postponed until after the trial of the not guilty count.

Not guilty

The effect of this plea is to deny the offence charged and thus put the whole of the prosecution case into issue. If this plea is entered the trial procedure detailed below is followed. However, it is open to the prosecution to decide not to go ahead following a not guilty plea. This can be done in two ways:

a The prosecution may 'offer no evidence'. This is suitable when the prosecution considers that the defendant ought not to be convicted, perhaps in the light of new evidence. This then is the equivalent to an acquittal.

b The prosecution may ask the judge to allow the count to be left on the court file, to be marked as 'not to be proceeded with without the leave of either the court or the Court of Appeal'. This is appropriate when the prosecution considers that it still has evidence to prove the defendant's guilt, but that it would be a waste of money and time to do so, for example if the defendant had pleaded guilty to other related offences. With this course of action the defendant is not acquitted.

Guilty to a lesser offence

Under s6(1)(b) of the Criminal Law Act 1967 the defendant may offer a plea of not guilty as charged but guilty to a 'lesser' offence. An obvious example is in relation to a charge of murder where the defendant may offer a plea of not guilty to murder but guilty to manslaughter.

If the plea is accepted, then by s6(5) of CLA 1967, the defendant is acquitted of the offence charged but stands convicted of the lesser offence and sentencing will follow accordingly.

A plea of guilty to a lesser offence must be accepted by both the prosecution and the judge, if either is not willing to accept it it will be rejected and the defendant must choose between 'guilty' or 'not guilty' in relation to the offence charged. In the case of the 'Yorkshire Ripper', Peter Sutcliffe's offer of a plea of guilty to manslaughter was not accepted by the judge and his trial for murder went ahead.

Autrefois acquit and autrefois convict

These pleas are available to the defendant when he has been either acquitted or convicted of the offence charged in the indictment on a previous occasion. Obviously, it is rare that these pleas are suitable. The limits on the situations in which these pleas may be tendered were set down by Lord Morris of Borth-y-Gest in *Connelly* v *DPP* [1964] AC 1254.

In relation to the defendant's plea the following points should be noted:

Ambiguous pleas

A defendant may attempt to plead but use words in doing so which are ambiguous. In this event, the judge should explain to the defendant why his plea is ambiguous and a second arraignment should follow. Section 6(1) of the Criminal Law Act 1967 provides that if an ambiguous plea is then entered for a second time – a plea of not guilty must be entered on behalf of the defendant.

The plea must be voluntary

Unless the plea of guilty entered by the defendant is entered quite voluntarily, it is a nullity. The defendant could appeal and the Court of Appeal would quash the conviction and order a re-trial.

A plea will be involuntary if it is a result of pressure from either the defence counsel or from the judge himself. The degree of pressure from a judge which is relevant was considered by Lord Parker in *R* v *Turner* [1970] 2 QB 321. A judge may indicate to defence counsel that whatever the plea he intends to give a certain type of sentence; however, he may not indicate that if there is a plea of not guilty his sentence will be 'x' whilst if there is a plea of guilty his sentence will be 'y' (for example, x = custodial and y = non-custodial). As for pressure from defence counsel, it is clear that he may advise the defendant in the strongest of terms as long as the final decision remains with the defendant.

Inability to plead

If a defendant makes no reply to his arraignment, a jury is empanelled to decide whether he is 'mute of malice', that is by choice, or whether he is 'mute by visitation of God', that is for example because he is deaf or dumb. If he is found to be mute of malice a plea of not guilty is entered on his behalf and the trial proceeds: s6(1)(c) CLA 1967. If he is mute by visitation of God, the trial is adjourned until a method of communication is found.

Apart from muteness, it may be that the defendant is unfit to plead. Even if he is able to answer to his arraignment, it may be that the defendant is unfit to plead, the test being whether his intellect is so defective that he cannot understand the course of the trial so as to defend himself properly, for example, by instructing his legal representative. A jury should be empanelled in order to decide the question of whether or not the defendant is unfit to plead. If the jury decides that he is, he is not acquitted; rather, he must be admitted to a hospital specified by the Home Secretary. If his condition improves he will be tried for the offence charged: s5 of Criminal Procedure (Insanity) Act 1964.

Change of plea

A defendant may change his plea from not guilty to guilty at any stage of the trial: the indictment is put afresh to the defendant who then pleads guilty. It is more difficult to change a guilty plea to not guilty. An application to do so may be made at any stage of the trial before sentence is passed. However, the defendant may do so only with the judge's consent; this is a matter entirely within the judge's discretion: *R v McNally* [1954] 1 WLR 933.

Plea bargaining

Theoretically, there are several ways in which a defendant may 'bargain' with the prosecution and with the judge over his plea. Some of these methods are accepted in the English legal system and others are not. The whole topic was considered in the case of *R v Turner* [1970] 2 QB 321.

The following are methods which may be used by a defendant:

a   A bargain between the defence and the prosecution that if the defendant pleads guilty to a lesser offence the prosecution will accept the plea (see above). The judge's consent must also be forthcoming for this course of action to proceed.

b   A bargain between the defence and the prosecution that if the defendant pleads guilty to certain counts on the indictment, the prosecution will not proceed with one or more of the other counts. The two methods of doing this, that is by either offering no evidence or by leaving the charge on the count file, are discussed above.

Other methods of plea-bargaining are available in other jurisdictions, but not within the English legal system. Examples of these other methods include the following:

a   Agreements between the defence and the judge that if there is a guilty plea to one or more counts by the defendant, the sentence passed will take a certain form. This was expressly disapproved in *R v Turner* [1970] 2 QB 321. A guilty plea given in these circumstances is a nullity.

b   Bargaining between the defence and the prosecution to the effect that if the defendant pleads guilty to one offence, another will not be charged in the indictment. This does not take place in the English legal system as the decision to prosecute and what offences to charge is made without consulting the defence.

c   Bargaining between the defence and the prosecution to the effect that if the defendant pleads guilty, the prosecution will ask the judge for a light sentence. This is not possible because the prosecution takes no part in the question of what sentence the defendant should receive; it is entirely a question for the judge.

The trial procedure

If a plea of not guilty is entered by the defendant or on his behalf the trial must proceed. The trial procedure is as follows:

Empanelling a jury

At each Crown Court on each day a 'jury panel' is summoned, which consists of approximately 20–25 people. As soon as the defendant has pleaded not guilty the panel is brought into court. The clerk of the court has the name of each member of the panel written on a separate card; he shuffles the cards and picks out twelve at random, one at a time. Jury challenging may take place at this stage: this is discussed later in the chapter. If a juror is unchallenged, he takes his place in the jury box and takes the juror's oath:

> 'I swear by Almighty God that I will faithfully try the several issues joined between our Sovereign Lady the Queen and the prisoner at the bar and give a true verdict according to the evidence.'

Once twelve jurors are sworn in, the defendant is 'put in their charge'.

For further discussion of the role of the jury see below.

The prosecution case

The prosecution case begins with an opening speech by prosecution counsel. As the jury is likely to be unfamiliar with criminal procedure, the speech is likely to be explanatory of what they will see and hear and what their role is. The speech must also give the jury (and the judge) an 'overview' of the case against the defendant. The prosecution must then call its evidence. In general, witnesses must give their evidence orally in answer to questions split into examination-in-chief, cross-examination and re-examination.

The prosecution must call as witnesses all those who were called at any committal proceedings and all those who made written statements tendered under s102 of the Magistrates' Courts Act 1980. They may call further evidence provided the defence has been given notice of the same.

Submission of 'no case to answer'

A submission of no case to answer may be made on the same basis as in the magistrates' court. There is no case to answer if the prosecution has failed to adduce evidence on which a jury, properly directed by the judge in his summing up, could properly convict: *R v Galbraith* [1981] 1 WLR 1039.

In the Crown Court a submission of no case to answer is made in the absence of the jury and is a matter for the judge. If the judge decides there is no case to answer, the jury is called back in and directed to deliver a verdict of not guilty. If there is a case to answer – the trial continues.

The defence case

The defence evidence is presented in the same way as the prosecution evidence after the defence opening speech. Where the defendant himself is being called as a witness it is conventional for him to be called as the first witness for the defence. Indeed, this is provided for in s79 of the Police and Criminal Evidence Act 1984

Closing speeches

Both sides have a right to a closing speech. The prosecution closing speech is delivered first. He may review the evidence but may not comment on the fact that the defendant has not given evidence if that be the case.

Finally, the defence makes its closing speech giving the final word in the trial to the accused.

The summing up by the judge

At the end of the cases presented by the prosecution and defence the judge 'sums up' the trial to the jury. The following matters must be dealt with:

a The functions of the judge and jury. The judge decides all questions of law and the jury all questions of fact.

b The burden and standard of proof. The prosecution must prove that the defendant is guilty and the jury must be 'satisfied so that they are sure'.

c An explanation of the law concerning the offence charged. The jury must accept the judge's directions on the law.

d Any particular points concerning the evidence, for example, that the evidence of an 'accomplice' must be corroborated, otherwise it is unreliable.

e A review of the evidence actually given. The judge must give a fair summary and reminder to the jury of all material evidence given by witnesses for both sides. This will also include an appraisal of the defence put forward by the defendant.

f Finally, the judge must direct the jury to appoint one of their number as 'foreman' and to retire and reach a unanimous verdict.

Having looked very briefly at the role of the jury in criminal trials of indictable offences this may be an opportune moment to look at the function of juries generally in more detail.

The jury system in England

Introduction

The use of a body of sworn men to give a true answer on a given question or questions is not a device peculiar to the English legal system, nor was it even a development of the Norman administration. There are possible antecedents of the jury to be found in the Laws of Aethelred (997). This does not mean that the jury was the direct descendant of these institutions, but that the idea was a common one: it may be that the idea was introduced into Normandy before 1066 from the Holy Roman Empire, but this is mere conjecture. A body of sworn men appeared to the Norman kings of England as a useful means of gathering information and, indeed, was employed on a number of occasions. The most famous example of the use of 'inquisitions' was the great inquiry into the state of the realm ordered by William I, known as the Domesday Survey:

> '... Enquire by the oath of the sheriff and of the barons and of their frenchmen, and of all the hundred, of the priest, of the reeve, and of six villeins of every vill, what is the name of the manor, who held it in the time of King Edward, who now, how many hides, how many ploughs, how many men, how many villeins . . . how much it was worth, how much now; and all this at three times: the time of King Edward, the time when King William gave it and now ...'

The jury (jury = jurate = sworn) was at first only a method of royal administration and was not used to settle private disputes: however useful to the government it was a 'particularly drastic means of establishing its ... rights' and was resented by the people as royal interference and oppression.

However, on certain occasions favoured litigants were permitted by the Crown to have their rights ascertained by 'inquisition' (perhaps because of dissatisfaction with existing modes of proof): this was the next stage towards the development of a type of jury recognisable to modern lawyers.

History

From the late seventeenth century, London juries proved most awkward in that they proved reluctant to convict in certain types of cases – civil and intellectual liberties. The high point was the trial of the London Reform Societies' leaders in 1794.

Thus, by the start of the nineteenth century, the jury system was regarded as safeguarding the right of the individual against abuse of prerogative power; necessary at a time when criminal punishments were harsh and very few people had the vote. By the mid nineteenth century, this idea was disappearing and the jury began to decline as a result of the increase in civil litigation, the eclipse of Royal prerogative and the great increase in the proportion of criminal cases heard summarily before magistrates.

It is easy to see that there are historical reasons why the jury is considered to be the 'bulwark of our liberties' – Lord Denning MR in *Ward v James* [1966] 1 QB 273.

Today, trial by jury is not, however, the form of trial used in most courts. It has never been used in magistrates' courts, it is nowadays extremely rare in county courts; and it is used less and less in the High Court. Only in the more serious criminal cases has the principle of jury trial been continuously maintained.

Before 1854 most civil actions in common law courts had to be tried before a jury. The Common Law Procedure Act 1854 provided that a judge could hear a case alone with the consent of all parties and by 1933 about 50 per cent of all Queen's Bench Division actions were tried without a jury. Section 6 Administration of Justice (Miscellaneous Provisions) Act 1933 provided that the right to claim a jury in a civil case was limited to fraud, defamation, malicious prosecution and false imprisonment (and some other actions which have since been abolished). Even in these cases a jury may be refused if there are complex documents or accounts to be examined. NB: It is not the length and complexity but the prolonged examination of documents that is crucial (*Rothermere* v *Times Newspapers* [1973] 1 WLR 448). By 1965 the percentage of jury trials in the Queen's Bench Division had dropped to about 2 per cent.

In 1933 the Act left the grant of a jury in all other cases to the discretion of the court. Juries in personal injuries cases were unpredictable and, no doubt regarding for example, the defendant in motoring cases (an insurance company) as having unlimited resources, awarded disproportionate damages. In the leading case of *Ward* v *James* [1966] 1 QB 273 the Court of Appeal established that the discretion of the court to grant a jury is not completely untramelled, and that in actions for personal injuries trial should be by judges alone in the absence of very special circumstances. Lord Denning stated in that case that the Court of Appeal would not hesitate to upset an award of damages made by a jury where it was out of all proportion. The Court cannot substitute a figure unless both sides agreed, a new trial must be ordered. He also gave the following reasons for the decline of trial by jury in civil cases:

a Assessability – it is difficult for juries to assess fair compensation. It must be a conventional figure derived from experience.

b Uniformity – similar decisions in similar cases are necessary – juries vary widely.

c Predictability – is an advantage for the parties to predict and thereby settle out of court.

The jury in criminal trials

Trial by jury is now confined to trials on indictment before a Crown Court. As something like 95 per cent of all criminal trials take place in the Magistrates' Courts, it will be seen that in practice, few defendants today are tried by jury.

It is generally considered that the far greater expense involved in holding a jury trial (as opposed to a summary trial) is justifiable only for more serious offences.

Qualifications

The Juries Act 1974 lays down the rules for selecting a jury.

Persons eligible for jury service are:

Those aged 18–70, on the electoral roll, who have been ordinarily resident in the UK for at least five years since the age of thirteen. (Those between 65–70 have a right of excusal on grounds of health, etc.)

Those ineligible are:

a   members of the judiciary and others concerned with the administration of justice, eg barristers and solicitors;

b   the clergy;

c   the mentally ill.

Those disqualified from service are:

a   persons who have been sentenced to life or five years or more imprisonment;

b   anyone who has served a sentence of three months or more in prison during the previous ten years.

Those entitled as of right to be excused are:

a   MPs;

b   members of the armed forces;

c   members of the medical, legal, or similar professions.

Those entitled to be excused as a matter of administrative discretion are:

a   persons who have served on a jury in the last two years;

b   persons with some other good reason for being excused.

Composition of a jury

Jurors are summoned at random by Crown Court officials. Those summoned to attend on a particular day form a Jury Panel. Both the prosecution and defence are entitled to inspect the list of members of the Panel which will not include details of occupation. From the Panel, 12 jurors will be selected at random using ballot cards, to form the jury for a trial.

Empanelling the jury: challenge

It used to be the case that the defence could challenge up to three jurors per defendant without giving reasons. This was known as 'peremptory' challenge. This right was rarely exercised, but during the Angry Brigade Trial in 1972, thirty nine jurors were challenged. Peremptory challenge was abolished on 5 February

1989 by s118 Criminal Justice Act 1988. This appears to have been a very sweeping change in the law, especially when Parliament could simply have limited the number of challenges available to the defence in cases with multiple defendants.

The defendant may challenge *'for cause'*, either to the whole panel summoned or to an individual juror. The issue is then tried by the judge who has to rule for or against the objection. Challenging for cause is possible on three grounds – s12(4) of the 1974 Act:

a   the juror is not qualfied to serve;

b   the juror is biased;

c   the juror may reasonably be suspected of bias.

The prosecution has a right to make a provisional challenge in the form of 'standing by' a juror. Since the abolition of the peremptory challenge formerly available to the defence, the Attorney-General has issued guidelines which the prosecution should follow when exercising their right of standing by.

Practice Note [1988] 3 All ER 1086 provides 'The circumstances in which it would be proper for the Crown to exercise its right to stand by a member of a jury panel are:

a   where a jury check reveals information justifying exercise of the right to stand by and the Attorney-General personally authorises the exercise of the right to stand by; or

b   where a person is about to be sworn as a juror who is manifestly unsuitable and the defence agree that, accordingly, the exercise of the prosecution of the right to stand by would be appropriate.'

In *R v Mason* [1980] 3 WLR 617 (CA) Lawton LJ stated that it was generally accepted that the Police can investigate the background of jurors in three cases:

a   if it appears that a juror may be disqualified from serving;

b   if it is believed that a juror was involved in a previously aborted trial where there had been an attempt to interfere with the jurors;

c   if it is thought particularly important to ensure that no disqualified person serves – this varies according to what the Police consider 'necessary'.

The prosecution is, of course, also permitted to challenge 'for cause'.

In *R v Ford (Royston)* [1989] 3 WLR 762 it was held that the trial judge has no right to alter the racial compositon of a jury. Lord Lane, in the Court of Appeal, said the court had a discretion to excuse jurors on the grounds of personal hardship or conscientious objection to jury service, but did not have discretion to excuse jurors on more general grounds such as race, religion or political beliefs. To do so would be to assume bias where none was proved. Again the policy behind such a decision was to retain the principle of random selection.

Jury vetting

It has been said above that the panel is selected at random. Any party to the proceedings may inspect the panel from which the jurors are to be drawn, yet the only information which can be gleaned from this will be the names and addresses of the panel (NB selection from the electoral role). In theory it is open to a party to conduct his own inquiry into the background of such persons. This is likely to be costly and is rarely done – there may be up to 150 names on the panel.

This is not to say that it is never done. Jury 'vetting' – the investigation of jurors backgrounds to ensure that 'unsuitable' potential jurors are not selected – is the subject of much controversy and has divided judicial opinion. In a limited class of cases ('political' offences involving terrorism and breaches of the Official Secrets Acts, and (originally) serious 'gang' warfare crimes) the DPP may authorise the police to check the names on the panel to ascertain whether a potential juror is a known associate of the accused or is known to be sympathetic or antagonistic to the accused's cause.

Lord Denning in *R v Sheffield Crown Court, ex parte Brownlow* [1980] QB 530 disapproved (obiter) of the practice and considered it 'unconstitutional'. Parliament, in the 1974 Act, had not seen fit to disqualify all those with previous convictions and it is arguable that the courts should not sanction vetting since that would be to undermine what Parliament has decided should be the requirements. However, the prevailing judicial view is that of the Court of Appeal in *R v Mason* (1980). Moreover, in 1978 the Attorney-General published a set of guidelines for jury vetting in exceptional circumstances involving terrorism or national security: in them, the AG stated that in such circumstances, on his personal authority the records of the Police special branches could be checked and any resulting information passed on to the prosecuting counsel via the DPP.

Commentary on jury vetting

The constitutional position of this practice is much in doubt and the rules have been heavily criticised. Indeed, it has been pointed out (in *Justice Deserted* by *H Harman* and *J Griffiths* – NCCL) that these guidelines were formulated at the same time as the Juries Bill was being put through Parliament – and MPs were not informed of the guidelines which some have seen as unconstitutional.

Whether such a practice is desirable is also doubtful. The Juries Act contains no disqualification of persons who might be subject to improper pressure, nor of persons of 'extreme' political views. Clearly some will argue that this form of vetting constitutes a direct attack on the principle of random selection, which is meant to underpin the jury system.

Nonetheless, its legality, and that of the Crown's right to 'stand by' potential jurors, seems to have been firmly settled by the Court of Appeal in *R v Bettaney* [1985] Crim LR 142.

Following a Practice Note issued by the Attorney General [1988] 3 All ER 1086 it will only be right to check the backgrounds of potential jurors if:

a   national security is involved in which case the police may check security records of jurors, or

b   the case is concerned with terrorism in which case police may check the criminal records only of jurors to ensure no disqualified jurors sit on a jury.

The verdict

On completion of the case, the jury will retire to consider their verdict. They will be instructed to reach a unanimous verdict. The Criminal Justice Act 1967 s13 introduced the majority verdict. The law was altered to permit the judge to accept a majority verdict in certain cases.

If the jury cannot agree after a reasonable period of deliberation (now 2 hours) the judge may then direct them on a majority verdict. He may accept a verdict:

a   in a case where there are not less than 11 jurors, 10 agree, or;

b   in a case where there are 10 jurors, 9 agree.

This provision is now contained in the Juries Act 1974, s17.

The court will only accept a majority verdict of guilty if the foreman of the jury states in open court the number who agreed on, and dissented from the verdict. (Juries Act 1974 s17(3).)

It has recently been stressed by the Court of Appeal in *R v McIlkenny* (1991) The Times 1 April, that it is for the jury and the jury alone to decide whether a man was innocent or guilty. Where a court allowed an appeal, it was a direction to quash the conviction. There was no obligation to say whether the appellant was innocent or guilty.

The secrecy of the jury room

The jury does not give any reason for its decisions. It is contempt of court to question a juror. The court will not even make enquiries where after the verdict all the jurors are willing to swear that the decision was not unanimous (*Boston v WS Bagshaw* [1966] 1 WLR 1135) or where it is later contended that the majority wanted to acquit until a juror produced a list of previous convictions (*R v Thompson* [1962] 1 All ER 65.)

The secrecy of the jury's deliberations has recently been placed on a statutory basis:

Contempt of Court Act 1981

's8(1) Subject to subsection (2) below, it is a contempt of court to obtain, disclose or solicit any particulars of statements made, opinions expressed, arguments advanced or votes cast by members of a jury in the course of their deliberations in any legal proceedings.

(2) This section does not apply to any disclosure of particulars –

a) In the proceedings in question for the purpose of enabling the jury to arrive at their verdict, or in connection with the delivery of that verdict, or

b) In evidence in any subsequent proceedings for an offence to have been committed in relation to the jury in the first mentioned proceedings.

(3) ... proceedings (paraphrased) under this section only to be instituted by or with consent of AG or on the motion of a court having jurisdiction to deal with it.'

The above s8(1) confirms the existing well founded state of the law. This was enacted as a result of many criminal trials, especially at the Old Bailey in London being interfered with – known as 'jury tampering' or 'jury nobbling'.

Discharge of the jury

During the course of a trial the trial judge may discharge the jury or any individual juror. The former may occur if for example, it is accidentally disclosed that the accused has a criminal record, since this would be prejudicial to the defence case. In such a case trial will proceed again (in most cases) with a fresh jury.

The latter may occur if a juror falls ill. It should be noted that in these cases, a jury must not fall below nine.

Juries Act 1974 s16 – the judge may discharge a juror 'whether as being through illness incapable of continuing to act or for any other reason' (s16(1)). This will always be a question for the trial judge, although the Court of Appeal will interfere if injustice has resulted.

Once the jury has given its verdict, it will be discharged.

Arguments for and against the retention of the present system

For

a The jury, since it is randomly selected from a wide selection of the population, is best able to reflect the views of society and when a person's liberty is at stake it is a matter of principle that he should be tried by his peers.

b Fact finding is a matter of common sense and does not require specialised legal training and the twelve opinions of the jury are better than the single opinion of the judge since it is more likely to prevent individual biases governing the course of the fact finding.

c The jury is less 'prosecution-minded' than many judges and magistrates: *Keith Evans' 'Advocacy at the Bar'* notes the 'prosecution bias' of many circuit judges, though it gave rise to much controversy recently.

d The jury is particularly suited to judge questions of defamation (civil jury) since the test which is applied (*Sim* v *Stretch* [1936] 2 All ER 1237) is that of 'right-thinking people generally'.

e The jury is generally regarded by the public as the 'bulwark of individual liberties' who have great confidence in the present system of criminal trials as a result. Justice must be seen to be done.

f Juries are a barometer of public feeling on the state of the law. The case of Clive Ponting, charged with offences under the Official Secrets Acts with respect to his divulging information to a Member of Parliament about an alleged government cover-up, is an example. He was acquitted, perhaps largely because of the public outcry against a sentence of imprisonment passed on a secretary (Sarah Tisdall) in similar circumstances. In neither case was there a breach of security although there was undoubtedly a breach of confidence.

Against

a The jury is uneducated in the law and is often unable to weigh evidence correctly and appreciate the significance of certain matters. Complex fraud cases are particularly likely to cause problems for the lay juror.

b The present law of evidence in criminal cases is much distorted by the need to accommodate the biases and inexperience of the jury and to keep from them matters which would unduly prejudice them against the accused, but which are not actually relevant to the weighing of evidence in the case (eg informing them of the accused's criminal record which may be totally irrelevant to the present case).

c The jury may be too easily swayed by good oratory from counsel.

d *McCabe* and *Purves* in *The Shadow Jury at Work* suggest that the jury can be dominated by two or three strong-minded invididuals.

e It is perhaps not possible to guarantee that there has been absolutely no tampering with the jury.

f Juries often bring in perverse verdicts. Lord Hailsham LC said a few years ago in an interview with *Marcel Berlins* that the perverse verdict was the justification for the jury. It is by the bringing in of a perverse verdict that a jury can indicate its disapproval of a particular prosecution or of a particular law.

g Sir Robert Mark (former Commissioner of the Metropolitan Police) stated that confidence in the jury system is 'essentially a matter of faith' and 'is based on practically no evidence whatsoever'.

Liability in criminal law (1) | 22

The elements of crime

Most crimes are defined as containing two elements. These are referred to by the Latin labels mens rea and actus reus. The definition of the offence does not immediately label these respective elements – that is left to the courts to interpret.

As a working definition we can refer to actus reus as the 'doing' part of the definition of the offence or the proscribed conduct or in some cases as the state of affairs and the mens rea as the mental element. This working definition will however require further amendment as the actus reus often includes a mental element that is not part of the mens rea and the mens rea is a technical term with a more complex meaning than just a mental element.

Actus reus – state of affairs

The general rule is that there must be both mens rea and actus reus for criminal liability to attach. This is expressed in the maxim 'Actus non facit reum, nisi mens sit rea' (the act alone does not constitute guilt unless accompanied by a guilty mind). There are, however, certain important exceptions to this rule. So-called regulatory offences of crimes of strict and absolute liability are obvious examples. The reverse side of the coin is that there is no liability without an act. It is not sufficient to found criminal liability to have a guilty mind if there has been no actus reus. Mens rea is never sufficient. There must be some act. The criminal law is designed to control actions not thoughts. Whichever classification an offence falls into it has traditionally been accepted that there are three components to the actus reus. An early mastery of these will avoid complex difficulties later in the course when study of particular crimes is undertaken. These components are:

a *Conscious voluntary acts:* For example the conscious voluntary striking that is an element in assault. These require no proof of consequence.

b *Consequences:* This is when the prescribed result flows from the act. It has otherwise been described as 'result crimes'. An example of this type would be an assault occasioning actual bodily harm. The assault would be the conscious voluntary act but the actual bodily harm would be the consequence/result.

c *Surrounding circumstances:* This is when a state of affairs or a fact constitutes an element of the actus reus. The usually cited example is rape. The state of affairs is that at the time of the intercourse the woman had not consented. So her consent (or lack of it) is a surrounding circumstance.

Categorisation is important because the actus reus must coincide with the relevant mens rea. Usually, with regard to the third category – surrounding circumstances – the mens rea would be one of 'knowledge' while with regard to the others it would be either 'intention' or 'recklessness'.

It should be noted that in the case of a 'result crime' (where both circumstances and consequences must be proved as part of the actus reus) it is also necessary to prove that there is sufficient 'causal linkage' between the circumstances and the consequences. This problem is discussed in more detail under homicide where it is most commonly manifested.

Actus reus – omissions

As indicated above the criminal law usually prohibits acts of commission (positive acts); however, it may also punish omissions to act. This is the same as saying that the law imposes a duty to act. Such a principle is more usually found in tort, especially the law of negligence than one would expect to find in criminal law.

Whatever the moral position there is no general legal duty to go to the aid of someone who is drowning or is otherwise in danger, whether or not the 'bystanding spectator' would be in a position to act to save the victim. It is submitted however that there are four circumstances in which the law has imposed a duty to act and punished those who have failed to perform their legal duty. These are:

a Duties arising from family relationships – this category would include the duty of a parent towards their minor children. A case that involved the voluntary assumption of a duty was *R v Stone and Dobinson* [1977] Crim LR 166 in which the defendants took into their care an elderly relative and voluntarily offered to look after her. They did not do so but neglected her and failed to summon medical attention when it became obviously required. As a result the elderly relative died.

It was held that their neglect constituted the actus reus of manslaughter.

b Duties arising under contract – as in the case of *R v Instan* [1893] 1 QB 450 where there was a fatal omission by a niece to provide food and medical attention for her ailing aunt which resulted in a conviction for manslaughter.

c A general duty to act arising from a contract with a third party – as in the case of *R v Pittwood* (1902) 19 TLR 37 in which the accused was a level crossing gatekeeper who opened the gates to allow road traffic to pass over the tracks and went off for his lunch leaving the gates open. There was a crash between a train and a carriage which involved fatalities.

The accused was guilty of manslaughter because he was under a duty of care to the people whose safety he was employed to protect and his failure to live up to that duty was sufficient to constitute the actus reus of manslaughter as well as being a breach of his contract of employment.

d There are some statutory offences that impose liability for the omission to act. Section 25 Road Traffic Act 1972 makes it an offence if one is involved in a road accident either to fail to report it to the police within 24 hours or to give relevant insurance details to any person reasonably requesting them at the scene of the accident.

However, under *R v Miller* [1982] Crim LR 526 the Court of Appeal stated:

> 'Unless a statute specifically provides, or … the common law imposes a duty upon one person to act in a particular way towards another … a mere omission to act (cannot of itself lead to the imposition of criminal liability).'

Mens rea – general

The definitions of most crimes contain, whether expressly or impliedly, an element as to the requisite state of mind. What constitutes the mental element remains a matter for construction by the courts.

In spite of the Latin there is no need to establish evil in a moral sense. A preferred translation of the term would be 'proscribed state of mind'.

It is important to be aware that the mens rea differs depending on the definition of the offence. There is no single 'proscribed state of mind'. Thus whether it is malice aforethought (as in murder) or the dishonest intention permanently to deprive (as in theft) it is always referred to as the mens rea of the offence.

There is a rebuttable presumption that each ingredient of the actus reus will be accompanied by a corresponding ingredient of mens rea (*Sweet v Parsley* [1970] AC 132).

Note the recent case of *R v Le Brun* [1991] 3 WLR 653, in which the coincidence of mens rea and actus reus were considered. Where the act causing death is separated from the initial use of force in time, and mens rea and actus reus do not exactly coincide in time, this does not necessarily preclude a conviction for manslaughter.

In this case the appellant hit his wife, causing her to black out. He tried to carry her but dropped her head first on to the pavement, fatally injuring her. Lord Lane CJ remarked that 'The actual deed which causes death and the necessary mental state to constitute manslaughter need not coincide in point of time.'

Whatever the individual mens rea of the offence, the concept generally connotes two things:

a that the accused's act was voluntary – although there are important exceptions with regard to so called crimes of absolute liability eg *R v Larsonneur* (1933) 149 LT 542 (see below) where the accused was convicted of being an alien in the United Kingdom in violation of an exclusion order in spite of the fact that she was forcibly brought to the UK handcuffed to the Irish police; and

b that the accused foresaw the consequences of his conduct that in fact did occur. This proposition has recently been subjected to judicial scepticism.

However, if these were to be related to the corresponding actus reus then the mens rea that attaches to an actus reus of either acts or consequences would be one of intention or recklessness. In regard to an actus reus of surrounding circumstances the appropriate mens rea would be one of knowledge. This proposition applies to crimes of normal liability.

Mens rea – definitive

A major difficulty facing the student in this area is that there is no consistency in the use of terminology either among the leading academic texts nor even in the courts among the judiciary. It would therefore be useful to set out a short definitive section in which are offered brief explanations of the main terms. These are:

a *direct intent* – is a desire to bring about the consequences;

b *oblique intent* – even if the consequences are not desired where there is a certainty that they will flow from the act;

c *specific intent* – used variously to connote different states of mind, often used as an alternative to *direct intent*. *Smith and Hogan* preferred the expression 'ulterior' intent to denote an intention to bring about some consequence above and beyond the actus reus itself (see (e)).

d *Basic intent* – where the mens rea relates wholly to the actus reus and does not go beyond the actus reus, eg assault. Voluntary intoxication offers no defence to a crime of basic intent.

e *Ulterior intent* – where an intent additional to the actus reus is required. An example would be burglary under s9(1)(a) of the Theft Act 1968 where the actus reus of entering a building as a trespasser is accompanied by an additional mental element relating to the intention to steal, etc.

Some crimes are said to require proof of a specific or ulterior intent, which is often contrasted with basic intent. *Smith and Hogan* define basic mens rea as 'intention or recklessness with respect to all those circumstances and consequences of the accused's act (or state of affairs) which constitute the actus reus of the crime in question'.

Intention

By their very definition the courts have held that some crimes can only be committed intentionally. Intention in this respect does not bear its everyday usage meaning as it refers not only to a situation where the accused foresaw the consequences of his conduct and where it was his purpose to bring those consequences about (ie direct intention) but also where he knows that to achieve his aim he must bring about other forbidden consequences (ie oblique intention).

In their report on the Mental Element in Crime (No 89) The Law Commission do not fully define 'intention'. Nonetheless in their draft Bill (not yet adopted) it is provided that intention should be tested by posing the question 'Did the defendant either intend to produce the result or have no substantial doubt that his conduct would produce it.'

It is important to distinguish intention in the legal sense from motive. In this jurisdiction, motive in the stage of determination of guilt is almost entirely irrelevant (with some exceptions such as blackmail).

Motive remains, however, an important factor in mitigation of sentence.

Although, as stated, most crimes can be committed either intentionally or recklessly it is important to be aware that some crimes can only be committed intentionally. These are usually referred to as 'intentional consequence crimes' and include attempts where the intention to commit the substantive offence is of course relevant. (*R v Mohan* [1976] QB 1). Another example would be s18 Offences against the Person Act 1861 (wounding with intent) where the intention to cause grievous bodily harm is required (*R v Belfon* [1976] 1 WLR 741).

Recklessness

As stated above, recklessness is sufficient mental element for some types of crime. In this regard, recklessness could be defined as the unjustified taking of an unjustified risk.

There are of course activities where the taking of risks is justified, such as with regard to surgical operations carried out properly for a proper medical purpose. There is certainly a risk involved but as a matter of policy and good sense the law regards such a risk as prima facie justified.

The difficulty here concerns the meaning of the term 'reckless'. Until the decision of the House of Lords in *R v Caldwell* [1982] AC 341 (see below) it was generally accepted that recklessness was a subjective concept. This view was based on *R v Cunningham* [1957] 2 QB 396 in which the accused was charged under s23 Offences Against the Person Act 1861 with 'maliciously administering a noxious thing so as to endanger life'. The accused ripped a gas meter from a wall in order to steal from it and in so doing ruptured the gas pipe through which gas escaped. Gas seeped through the wall and a person in the next house was injured through inhalation of the gas. It was clear that Cunningham did not intend to injure the victim.

It was held that in order to be reckless the accused must actually know of the existence of the risk and go on deliberately to take it.

The test is thus subjective and involves a postulation of foresight of consequences. Recklessness thus amounted to the conscious taking of an unjustified risk.

It would appear that '*Cunningham* type' recklessness now applies in the following situations:

a   Where the word malicious is involved in the definition of the offence such as in the case of *W (A Minor) v Dolbey* [1983] Crim LR 681 where a person charged with malicious wounding under s20 OAPA 1861 had a conviction based on '*Caldwell* type' recklessness quashed on appeal. The Divisional Court held that the appropriate test in such an offence remained '*Cunningham* type'.

   W v Dolbey was followed by the Court of Appeal in *R v Rainbird* [1989] Crim LR 505. The appellant, a school caretaker, had fired an air-gun at some refuse bins where boys were trespassing; one of the boys was hit and injured. The appellant was convicted, following the trial judge's direction that the jury should consider whether a reasonable man would have realised the danger involved in firing the gun. The appeal was allowed as the judge had erred in applying an objective test to 'maliciousness'. The prosecution had to establish some foresight of consequences on the part of the accused.

b   *Rape*. Although soon after *Caldwell* it was thought that objective tests would be applied in rape cases it appears that it is now more appropriate to apply *Cunningham* type recklessness when required. (*R v Satnam and Kewal* (1983) 78 Cr App R 149 – a case involving reckless rape.) This would be entirely in line with the statutory effect given to the decision in *DPP v Morgan* [1976] AC 182 by the Sexual Offences Act 1976 that an honest but unreasonable mistake as to whether the woman was consenting would be a defence.

In the case of *R v Caldwell* [1982] AC 341 where the accused held a grudge against a hotel owner; he went out and got drunk, returned and tried to set fire to the hotel but only burned a hole in the curtain. Had *Cunningham* recklessness been applied he would have been acquitted because he was too drunk to appreciate the risk. But Lord Diplock, in the House of Lords, stated that *Cunningham* recklessness was restricted to common law offences and offences that involved the word 'malicious'. However, recklessness applies where the statutory definition involves 'recklessness' as opposed to 'malice': where the accused has not given any thought to the possibility of a risk existing, but had he stopped and thought about it a reasonable man would realise that there was a risk. So recklessness is now both subjective and objective, the change being the introduction of an objective test.

In *R v Farrell* [1989] Crim LR 376 the appellant had been convicted of malicious wounding. He appealed against conviction on the ground that the trial judge had directed the jury to find that the appellant had the requisite mens rea if he had been reckless in the '*Caldwell*' sense and the appeal was allowed. Malicious wounding required that the appellant should foresee the risk created by his actions. There was no scope for the concept of objective recklessness under s20 of the 1861 Act.

In *R v Caldwell* Lord Diplock, discussing 'reckless' when used in a criminal statute, in that case the Criminal Damage Act 1971, rejected the restricted meaning of the word emanating from *Professor Kenny*'s definition of 'malice' in his *Outline of Criminal Law*: '… in any statutory definition of crime "malice" must be taken … as requiring either:

a   an actual intention to do the particular kind of harm that in fact was done; or

b   recklessness as to whether such harm should occur or not (ie the accused has foreseen that the particular kind of harm might be done and yet has gone on to take the risk of it) …'

Instead he substituted the following in the context of the Criminal Damage Act 1971:

'In my opinion a person charged with an offence under s1 of the 1971 Act is reckless … if …

i) he does an act which in fact creates an obvious risk that property will be destroyed or damaged and

ii) when he does the act he has either not given any thought to the possibility of there being any such risk, or has recognised the risk ... and gone on to do it.'

The *Caldwell* definition was adopted by the House of Lords in *R v Lawrence* [1982] AC 510 (see: involuntary mansalughter below), a case involving the offence of causing death by reckless driving contrary to s1 Road Traffic Act 1972. In that case the House of Lords held that the actus reus of the offence is not merely driving without due care and attention but driving in a manner that creates an obvious and serious risk of causing physical injury to any other road user or substantial damage to property and the mens rea of the offence is driving in such a manner without giving any thought to the risk or, having recognised that it exists, nevertheless taking the risk. It is for the jury to determine whether the risk is obvious and serious adopting the standard of the ordinary prudent driver as represented by themselves.

One of the effects of the *Caldwell* decision is that it brings within the definition of recklessness those of limited intelligence or ability who would not have appreciated the risk even if they had thought about it (*Elliot v C* [1983] 1 WLR 939).

The extent of the *Caldwell* test was considered in the case of *Chief Constable of Avon and Somerset v Shimmen* [1986] Crim LR 800 in which the respondent had been charged with destroying a shop window, intending to destroy it and being reckless as to whether it was destroyed. The respondent was demonstrating his karate technique and while doing so broke the window. He had no intention to destroy the window. The magistrates had found that he had appreciated the risk but having considered it came to the conclusion that no damage would result from his demonstration. On a case stated the question was whether the respondent was reckless where he did an act that created an obvious risk that property would be destroyed or damaged and having considered the risk had subjectively concluded that no damage would result.

It was held that where it might not be recklessness where a person gave thought to but missed the obvious and substantial, it was recklessness where he was aware of the risk and took precautions that he believed to be adequate but which were in fact not adequate. That state of mind was not outside the *Caldwell* test as there was awareness of risk and that was sufficient. Case was remitted with direction to convict.

Remarks made obiter in *DPP v Khan* [1990] Crim LR 321 are indicative of judicial thinking on the question of *Caldwell* recklessness in the context of assault cases. K, a 15 year old schoolboy, was acquitted of assault at first instance on the basis that he had not meant to harm anyone. On appeal, however the Divisional Court directed conviction, on the basis that to place sulphuric acid into a hot air drier in some toilets so that it could be blown on to the next user could constitute assault, albeit indirect. There was no evidence that K had been aware of any risk that the next person to use the drier might be at risk.

The case of *R* v *Reid* [1991] Crim LR 269 confirmed that the tests as laid down in *Cunningham, Caldwell* and *Lawrence* must be taken into account in considering reckless conduct.

Coincidence of actus reus and mens rea

The general rule is that the mens rea must coincide in point of time with the actus reus, or in other words, at the time of performing the actus reus the accused had the proscribed state of mind.

There are however two situations in which the application of the above principle is difficult. These are:

a Where the actus reus is a continuing act. In the case of *Fagan* v *MPC* [1968] 3 WLR 1120 in which the accused accidentally drove his car over a policeman's foot yet when he became aware of the fact refused to remove the car immediately.

It was held that the actus reus of the assault was a continuing act which while started without mens rea was still in progress at the time the mens rea was formed and so there was a coincidence of actus reus and mens rea sufficient to found criminal liability.

b Where the actus reus is part of a larger transaction. The courts here will consider a continuing series of acts to be part of a single larger transaction. The application of this approach can be seen in the following two cases:

Thabo Meli v *R* [1954] 1 All ER 373 in which the appellants, in pursuance of a prearranged plan, brought their victim to a hut and struck him until he appeared dead. Believing him to be dead they threw him over a cliff. At the time they threw him over the cliff their victim was not dead. Evidence was presented to suggest that he died from exposure. The Privy Council upheld the murder conviction: as the actus reus and the mens rea were present throughout the transaction it was not necessary to separate them.

R v *Church* [1966] 1 QB 59 with similar facts to *Thabo Meli;* however there was no prearranged plan but the accused 'disposed of the body' in a panic which lead to the victim drowning. The court here stated that the manslaughter should be decided on the basis of the mens rea that existed at the start of the chain of events.

This reasoning is applied in order to avoid an unjust result that would exist if a literal interpretation were applied.

Conspiracy and incomplete crimes

Note that mens rea for conspiracy to commit an offence (or for attempts) is not necessarily to be equated with that required for the completed offence (see *R* v *Siracusa* [1989] Crim LR 712).

Strict and absolute liability

In criminal law the requirement to establish mens rea is usually the same as saying that criminal liability only occurs where there is blame. Strict liablity imposes liability in criminal law where there is no fault.

As a matter of statutory construction the courts have decided that if a statute omits any reference to words such as 'knowingly' it intends to impose strict liability. That means that there is no need to establish any mens rea. Note that this is not the same as saying there is no mens rea – merely that there is no requirement to establish it.

Strict liability

In these offences liability attaches without fault, so that they may be committed even though, as regards one or more important elements of the offence, the accused person had no mens rea.

Liability is strict, not absolute. Thus the need to prove mens rea is not ruled out completely by the fact that the offence is one of strict liability and it may be necessary to prove that the accused is aware of all the circumstances of the offence save that in respect of which strict liability is imposed.

In *R* v *Prince* (1875) LR 2 CCR 154, the accused was charged with and convicted of unlawfully taking an unmarried girl under 16 out of the possession and against the will of her father. Though Prince knew the girl was in her father's possession, he honestly and reasonably believed her to be over 16. On the other hand in *R* v *Hibbert* (1869) LR 1 CCR 184, H, who was charged with the same offence, was acquitted because, though he knew the girl was under 16, he did not know she was in her father's possession. These cases indicate that, though the girl's age involves strict liability so that a mistake as to the girl's age is irrelevant, the fact of parental possession involves mens rea, so that a mistake as to that element may preclude liability.

The majority of strict liability offences are created by statute. Whether the statute requires or dispenses with mens rea is a question of construction. Where the statute uses such words as 'knowingly', 'maliciously', 'dishonestly', 'with intent' etc it is necessary to establish mens rea. However, the absence of such words does not necessarily mean that the offence is one of strict liability. Thus in *Sherras* v *De Rutzen* [1895] 1 QB 918, the accused appealed against conviction for supplying liquor to a constable on duty. The accused reasonably believed the constable to be off duty as he had removed his armlet, which was the acknowledged method of signifying off duty. The accused's conviction was quashed because of his lack of knowledge that the constable was still on duty. Similarly, in *R* v *Russell* [1985] Crim LR 231, Russel was charged and convicted of having an offensive weapon in a public place contrary to the Prevention of Crime Act 1953. The accused claimed that he had put the cosh under the driving seat of his car and had forgotten it was there until the police found it. His conviction was quashed because the Court of

Appeal held that full mens rea was required, and 'has with him' meant 'knowingly has with him'.

The penalty, seriousness of the offence and the need to protect the public, are all relevant criteria in questions of statutory construction. This leaves a wide discretion in the hands of the judge.

The greater the need for public protection, so it is said, the greater the necessity for strict liability. Yet the harsher the penalty – and this presumably reflects the need for public protection – the greater justice requires the need for mens rea. This explanation is however wanting in that it does not cover the most serious offences where for example the public clearly needs protection from unlawful homicide yet there is no suggestion that murder be a crime of strict liability.

Another reason put forward in support of strict liability is founded on practicality. If mens rea had to be proved in every case, the prosecutor's task would often be made impossible, eg in a case involving dangerous machinery in a factory, it is the employer who has the means of supervision, knowledge and control of the equipment in question and it would be very hard to prove even negligence let alone intention or recklessness. However, it should be noted that in such cases where the prosecutor does not have to prove mens rea as to an element of the offence, the court may experience difficulty in imposing a fitting sentence, being unable, because the issue of mens rea has not been investigated in court, to distinguish between the deliberate and the inadvertent wrongdoer.

Such matters as statutory offences [sale of cars contrary to the then Hire Purchase legislation] (*R v St Margaret's Trust Ltd* [1958] 2 All ER 289 – also a case of corporate liability) dangerous drugs (*Warner v MPC* [1969] 2 AC 256) and pollution (*Alphacell Ltd v Woodward* [1972] 2 WLR 1320) have pushed the courts into applying strict liability, on the basis that the danger to the public is so great that it can best be countered by strict liability.

In *Alphacell Ltd v Woodward*, where the company was convicted for causing polluted water to enter the river, the appellants contended that they should not be convicted even if found to have 'caused' the pollution as required under the Act, unless it could be proved that they had done so intentionally, recklessly or negligently, the House of Lords rejected the argument and confirmed their conviction. Lord Salmon stated:

> 'If ... it were held to be the law that no conviction could be obtained under the (Act) unless the prosecution could discharge the often impossible onus of providing that the pollution was caused intentionally or negligently, a great deal of pollution would go unpunished and undeterred to the relief of many riparian factory owners.'

This reasoning was followed in *Atkinson v Sir Alfred McAlpine & Son Ltd* [1974] Crim LR 668 where it was held that the defendant company was guilty of failing to give written notice, as required by statute, of their intention to undertake work involving a particular chemical substance although they had no knowledge, nor reason to have such knowledge, that the work involved such use of the substance. The view taken was that the mischief aimed at by the legislature would not be met if 'know or ought to know' was read into the regulations.

In *Warner* v *MPC* (above) the offence related to possession of a prohibited drug. The accused contended that the drugs were in a box which he believed contained scent. The jury were directed that it was sufficient to show that the appellant was in control of the box and that it was immaterial that he was ignorant of the contents. The jury returned a verdict of guilty and expressed their view that the accused knew he had possession of drugs. The House of Lords upheld the conviction on the grounds that no substantial miscarriage of justice had occurred even though a majority of the House considered the jury had been wrongly directed and that a person cannot 'possess' the contents of a package without at least being aware of the general, if not the particular, nature of the contents.

Glanville Williams describes the result as 'An illogical compromise between liability with mens rea and strict liability.'

It has been argued that it would be better to replace strict liability offences with offences where liability would be dependent upon negligence. To some extent a move in this decision has been made by s29 Misuse of Drugs Act 1971 and s24 Trade Descriptions Act 1968, which places on the accused the onus of establishing his lack of fault.

The defence available under the Food and Drugs Act 1955 where a defendant can avoid liability if he can prove that the contravention was due to the act or default of a third party and that he used all due diligence to comply with the requirements does not abolish strict liability in respect of the offence. It merely exonerates the original defendant who may escape liability by proving both requirements referred to above. However, liability will still be deemed to be strict for the third party.

Since the House of Lords' decision in *Sweet* v *Parsley* [1969] 1 All ER 347 it seems that there is a judicial tendency to limit strict liability to regulatory or 'quasi-criminal' offences, ie offences which involve no moral stigma on conviction such as a failure to display an excise licence (*Strowger* v *John* [1974] Crim LR 123).

Absolute liability

Strict liability must be distinguished from absolute liability. A crime of absolute liability is one where mens rea is not required at all, not even to the extent of requiring a voluntary actus reus. In *R* v *Larsonneur* (1933) 24 Cr App R 74 it was held that an accused was still liable for the offence of 'being found' illegally in the UK even though she had been brought into the United Kingdom handcuffed to the Irish Police whilst an aliens exclusion order was in force against her.

The law of murder

Introduction

The syllabi covered in this book are primarily concerned with the law of homicide which concerns different offences at law the most important of which are murder, voluntary manslaughter and involuntary manslaughter. In all three there is only one actus reus – that is the killing of another. If the killing is unlawful it will be either murder or manslaughter. The distinction is found in the state of mind (mens rea) of the accused at the time of the offence.

Murder

Coke defined murder as '... when a man of sound memory, and of the age of discretion, unlawfully killeth within any country of the realm any reasonable creature in rerum natura under the king's peace, with malice aforethought, either expressed by the party or implied by law, so as the party wounded, or hurt, etc die of the wound or hurt, etc within a year and a day after the same.'

This definition forms a good basis on which to examine the law of murder.

Actus reus

Any person over ten years old who is neither insane nor suffering from diminished responsibility can murder. By virtue of s9 Offences Against the Person Act 1861 and s3 British Nationality Act 1948 if a United Kingdom citizen commits murder anywhere in the world the offence is indictable in Britain. Unlike the American law and some other jurisdictions, where the victim is British but the murder is committed by a non-British person outside the jurisdiction of the United Kingdom, then that offence is not triable in Britain; it remains a matter for the country in which the offence was committed.

Any living person capable of an independent existence can be the victim of murder. Thus a foetus or a person already dead could not be murdered. This is interesting since the law has offered no definition of death. The law is thus able to take account of changing medical technological achievements in the area of life support and preservation.

Murder involves the acceleration, albeit by a minute, of the time of death. Death must occur within a year and a day. This is to provide certainty. According to *Smith and Hogan* time runs not from the accused's act but from the time of the infliction of the injury. This is not normally different although it can be important with regard to say, for example, planting a bomb with a time delay mechanism.

Causation

An essential ingredient of the actus reus of the offences of homicide is the requirement to prove that the accused caused the death of the victim. This is both a question of fact and of law. As to the question of fact this can be left to the jury to determine. The question of law is of more interest here.

The accused's act need not be the sole cause. For liability to attach, the act of the accused must be the substantive and operative cause of death. The question becomes important when viewing an intervening act and considering whether it amounts to such as would break the chain of causation. This is a question of law.

In *R v Dyson* (1908) 1 Cr App R 13 it was held that even though the victim would have died from a disease, the blows accelerated the time of death. Those blows were also the substantive and operative cause of death.

Causation as a matter of fact and law involves looking at any intervening act and questioning whether in fact and in law that act is such as to break the chain of causation between the accused's act and the victim's death. If the accused mortally wounds the victim and one second later the victim is struck by lightning then the operative cause of death is the lightning and not the accused's blow.

However the courts have been reluctant to absolve the accused in circumstances where the 'intervening act' is consequential on the accused's own attack. The courts will trace causation back to the accused's attack. This principle is illustrated by reference to the following cases:

In *R v Smith* [1959] 2 All ER 193, S wounded the victim in a fight involving several other soldiers. The medical orderly was extremely pressed due to these 'near battle conditions' and the victim received what would in normal circumstances have been grossly negligent treatment. In the circumstances, however, the treatment was understandable and S was held to be guilty of the victim's murder.

In *Smith* the court distinguished *R v Jordan* (1956) 40 Cr App R 152. There it appeared that the victim died, not from wounds inflicted by the accused, J, but because of an injection given to him in hospital which was 'palpably wrong'. As evidence of this had not been before the jury, the Court of Appeal felt constrained to quash the conviction. However, their words are very guarded, and it is probably only where there is a distinct new cause of death that *Jordan* may be relied upon.

This is seen in *R v Blaue* [1975] 3 All ER 446. B appealed against his conviction for manslaughter. As a result of B's assault on a young girl, a blood transfusion became essential to save her life. The girl, who was a Jehovah's Witness, refused permission for this on religious grounds, and she died. B's conviction was upheld. The accused must take his victim as he finds him, including any religious beliefs he may have.

Note that no intervening cause is present here, merely a failure to prevent the death.

In *R v Malcherek; R v Steel* [1981] 2 All ER 422, the appellants had been convicted of murder following injuries to the victims who had later died in hospital after life support machines to which they had been connected were disconnected. The appellants contended that the trial judge had been incorrect in withdrawing from the jury the question of causation. Their appeals were dismissed on the ground that in both cases it was clear that the initial injuries were the reason for the medical treatment which in both cases was normal and conventional. The doctors had decided that the treatment had become futile and the court had to consider not whether the practice for determining brain death was satisfactory, but whether (applying *R v Smith* (1959)) the original wound was still the operating and substantial cause of death. Since there was no evidence that the original injury had ceased to be a continuing and operating cause of death at the time of the victim's death following the disconnection of the life support machines, it was held that the issue of causation was properly withdrawn from the jury in each case.

In *R v Cheshire* (1991) 93 Cr App R 251 the Court of Appeal confirmed the decision that problems involving negligent medical treatment would not break the chain of causation or amount to a novus actus unless the doctors had been reckless in their disregard for the patient's health. Even when, as in this case, some rare complication causes the death, it is still a direct consequence of the appellant's act.

If the accused puts his victim into a position where the victim risks his life in order to escape from apprehended harm from the accused then the accused will be liable for the consequences. Thus in *R v Halliday* (1889) 61 LT 701, Halliday was convicted of inflicting grievous bodily harm on his wife when she jumped from the window in escaping from him. See also the new case of *R v Williams, R v Davis* [1992] 1 WLR 380, in which the victim was killed trying to escape from a robbery. It was held that the chain of causation was not broken.

It seems that the accused will also be guilty where the fear he creates in another causes their death. In *R v Hayward* (1908) 21 Cox CC 692, the accused was found guilty of manslaughter when he chased his wife in a violent manner, and she fell dead because of the shock to her heart.

Similarly in *R v Pagett* (1983) The Times 4 February, the accused used a pregnant girl as a shield who was killed by shots fired instinctively by the police. It was held that the reasonable acts of the police in shooting in self-defence could not constitute a novus actus interveniens breaking the chain of causation between Pagett's conduct and the girl's death.

Mens rea

The mens rea of murder is malice aforethought.

Section 1 Homicide Act 1957 abolished the doctrine of 'constructive malice' whereby a person who caused death, albeit unintentionally, while committing a felony, was guilty of murder.

Thus the mens rea of murder is either:

a an intention to kill; or

b an intention to cause grievous bodily harm.

This is illustrated in the following cases:

In *R v Vickers* [1957] 2 All ER 741, the defence argued that the 1957 Act impliedly overruled the so-called doctrine of 'implied malice' ie that the accused was guilty of murder where he intended only to cause grievous bodily harm.

Here Vickers viciously assaulted an old lady, who died as a result. Lord Goddard CJ rejected the defence argument, though his judgment seems to be based on the assumption that a defendant intending grievous bodily harm is necessarily reckless as to the possibility of causing death.

The Court of Appeal in *R v Ellerton* [1978] Crim LR 162 held that *Vickers* was rightly decided and binding on it. It was however, in view of the doubts expressed in various decisions about the correctness of *Vickers*, still open to the House of Lords to hold that *Vickers*, was wrongly decided.

The House of Lords were given such an opportunity in *R v Cunningham* [1981] 2 All ER 863. There the appellant was charged with murder for striking a man round the head with a chair. The prosecution contended that while there was no intention to kill, there had been an intent to do really serious bodily harm. The appellant's plea of manslaughter was rejected and he was convicted of murder. He appealed to the Court of Appeal on the ground that intention to do seriously bodily harm was not sufficient for a murder conviction and that there had to be shown, in the absence of intention to kill, at least an intent to endanger life or cause such serious bodily harm as to be likely to endanger life. In dismissing the appeal, the Court of Appeal was bound by *Vickers*.

There has been some debate as to whether there exists a 'third head' to the mens rea of murder. The debate was fuelled by the House of Lords in *DPP v Smith* [1960] 3 All ER 161 in which S while carrying stolen goods in his car boot, was stopped by a policeman. To avoid capture, he accelerated away. The constable hung onto the car bonnet but was thrown off when S swerved. He fell into the path of an oncoming vehicle and was killed. Smith maintained that he had no intention of causing the constable any harm, but Donovan J directed the jury that if a reasonable man would have contemplated such harm, S was guilty. Though the Court of Appeal quashed the conviction the House of Lords restored it. There were two ways to interpret *Smith*; as an evidential rule or as a rule of law and thus a 'third head' of murder – that is where the accused performs an act which will, as a natural and probable consequence, result in death or serious injury.

As a result of the uproar caused by *Smith*, Parliament, in 1967, passed s8 of the Criminal Justice Act. Section 8 lays down the rule that when proving the defendant's intention, it is not sufficient to look at the natural and probable result of his actions. Instead, all the relevant circumstances must be examined by the jury, who must decide what this particular defendant actually did intend.

Thus if *Smith* was a rule of evidence, it was specifically overruled by statute. This was illustrated in the case of *R v Wallett* [1968] 2 QB 367 in which the Court of Appeal held that this in fact was the case. The accused shook a young girl until she died. Because, however, the trial judge inserted the words 'any ordinary person like himself' into his directions, which could be construed as an objective test, the conviction of murder was quashed and one of manslaughter substituted. The court is saying that, because of s8's overruling of *Smith* the crown must actually prove that the accused intended death or grievous bodily harm, this being a subjective test.

This approach was not followed in *Hyam v DPP* [1975] AC 55.

In order to 'frighten off' her lover's new mistress (B) the accused poured petrol through B's letter box, and set fire to it. The ensuing fire caused the death of two of B's children. The accused maintained that her only intention was to frighten B, and that she did not intend to cause death or serious bodily injury. On the way to B's house however, the accused stopped to make sure that her lover (J) was at his own flat, so that no harm would come to him.

By a three to two majority, the House of Lords upheld the conviction of murder. Lord Hailsham firstly rejected the argument that *Vickers* had been wrongly decided. Secondly, he held that s8 in fact did not overrule *DPP* v *Smith*. Thus *Smith* did not lay down an evidential rule, but a rule of law, ie a third head of murder. It is this third head that *Hyam* alters. His Lordship refused to overrule *Smith*, stating:

a that he could not be sure what he would be overruling;

b that he wished to keep the definition of grievous bodily harm, ie really serious bodily injury; and

c that he wished to keep the requirement for murder that the defendant's act must be 'aimed at someone'. The accused is guilty here because, having appreciated the risk, she nevertheless went ahead and put B in danger.

The approach of Lord Hailsham in *Hyam* does not now appear to be the correct approach. This became apparent in the following cases.

In *R* v *Moloney* [1985] 2 WLR 648, the accused had killed his stepfather with a shotgun after a party to celebrate the ruby wedding anniversary of his mother and stepfather. M and his stepfather had stayed up drinking and it seems that the victim challenged the appellant to a duel claiming that he could draw and fire a gun quicker than his stepson. The appellant gave evidence that he never intended to kill or injure his stepfather. However, he was convicted of murder after the judge had directed the jury that 'intention' included not just desiring something or knowing that it was certain to occur but also where he foresees that it will probably happen whether he desires it or not. The Court of Appeal dismissed his appeal. He appealed to the House of Lords, the Court of Appeal having certified a point of law of general public importance was involved, namely: 'is malice aforethought in the crime of murder established by proof that when doing the act which causes the death of another the accused either a) intends to kill or do serious harm or b) foresees that death or serious harm will probably occur, whether or not he desires either of these consequences.'

The House of Lords allowing the appeal unanimously held that there was no rule of substantive law that foresight of death or serious harm was an alternative to intention to kill or intention to do grievous bodily harm. Neither could it be viewed as equivalent to intention to kill or intention to do serious harm. Certainly foresight of consequences was relevant in deciding the question of intention in murder but only from the point of view of the law of evidence.

The House of Lords were shortly asked to reconsider this matter in *R* v *Hancock & Shankland* (1986) 82 Cr App R 264. The appellants who had caused the death of a taxi driver after they had pushed two concrete objects into the path of the taxi had been found guilty of murder after the trial judge had directed the jury in accordance with the House of Lords direction in *R* v *Moloney* (1985) on the issue of intention by reference to foresight of consequences in a murder trial. The jury had to consider: 'was death or grievous bodily harm a natural consequence of what was done, did the accused foresee that consequence as a natural consequence?' The

Court of Appeal had quashed their convictions for murder on the ground that the case of the *Moloney* guidelines might have misled the jury. The prosecution appealed to the House of Lords. The House of Lords held that the guidelines given in *R v Moloney* were unsatisfactory in the present case. In *R v Moloney* Lord Bridge had omitted any reference in the guidelines to probability or risk because he felt the word added nothing to the meaning he attributed to 'natural'. However, it was very doubtful that a jury should share that view.

The jury required an explanation that the greater the probability of a consequence the more likely it was that the consequence was foreseen and that if it was foreseen the greater the probability that it was also intended. The use of guidelines which are not rules of law could mislead the jury which was to decide the question of intention on the evidence before them.

These 'tests' are no substitute for the need to prove intention and are applicable only in the more extreme cases where intention is not immediately obvious from the evidence.

Thus under *R v Hancock & Shankland* the issue remains ultimately one of intention. Did the accused or either of them intend to kill or to cause anyone really serious harm? If the answer was negative then they lacked the mens rea necessary for the offence of murder.

The effect of this was seen in *R v Nedrick* [1986] Crim LR 742.

The appellant was convicted of murder after a child had burned to death in a house where the appellant had put a petrol bomb through the letter box. He admitted to starting the fire but stated he only wanted to frighten the owner of the home.

The Court of Appeal substituted a verdict of manslaughter. The judge had misdirected the jury relying on a passage in Archbold now disapproved of. In the light of *Moloney* and *Hancock* the direction was obviously wrong. Lane LCJ gave guidelines for directing a jury about intent in a murder case where the person charged did a manifestly dangerous act and someone died as a result:

'When determining whether the defendant had the necessary intent it might, therefore, be helpful for a jury to ask themselves:

1) How probable was the consequence which resulted from the defendant's voluntary act?
2) Did he foresee that consequence?

If he did not appreciate that death or really serious harm was likely to result from his act, he could not have intended to bring it about.

If he did, but thought that the risk to which he was exposing the person killed was only slight, then it might be easy for the jury to conclude that he did not intend to bring about that result.

On the other hand, if the jury were satisfied that at the material time the defendant recognized that death or serious harm would be virtually certain – barring some unforeseen intervention – to result from his voluntary act, then that was a fact from which they might find it easy to infer that he intended to kill or do serious bodily harm, even though he might not have had any desire to achieve that result.'

Note that when several people are involved in a murder the mens rea required is the same. In *R v Hyde*, *R v Sussex*, *R v Collins* [1990] 3 WLR 1115, the Court of Appeal ruled that when three persons were involved in a joint enterprise resulting in murder, and it was impossible to tell just who had struck the fatal blow, it was sufficient for conviction if any of the three had foreseen that their act might result in real harm, regardless of whether that person had actually struck the fatal blow.

The law of involuntary manslaughter

Involuntary manslaughter may be contrasted with voluntary manslaughter, where there is mens rea but also mitigating circumstances. An example might be *R v Cocker* [1989] Crim LR 740 and other cases of the 'mercy-killing' type (see also 22.5, following).

Involuntary manslaughter, of whatever category, has the same actus reus of murder but lacks any malice aforethought. We shall consider the following types of involuntary manslaughter, but it should be noted that this is not a closed list. There are other forms of involuntary manslaughter.

a Killing by gross negligence

b Causing death by reckless driving

c Causing death recklessly

d Unlawful act doctrine

e Goodfellow test

f Killing an unborn child

Killing by gross negligence

It appears to be gross negligence where the accused takes a risk in which the reasonable man would have foreseen the possibility of injury but the accused subjectively perceives of no such risk. It would not be necessary for the reasonable man to have foreseen a risk of death or really serious harm, foresight of any injury would suffice. The law in this area recently became uncertain when recklessness was defined in relation to some crimes to involve objective risk taking. This has blurred the distinction between recklessness and negligence. It seems that recklessness requires only a simple failure yet traditionally it was thought that this head of manslaughter could only be committed if the negligence was gross. This is illustrated in *R v Finney* (1874) 12 Cox CC 625. F was held not guilty of manslaughter when, after telling a lunatic to get out of the bath, his attention having been distracted, F put his hand on the wrong tap and poured scalding hot, instead of cold, water over him.

For the sake of clarity, and while acknowledging that *Bateman* is now doubted, it would be useful to refer to the speech of Lord Hewart CJ in *R v Bateman* (1925) 19 Cr App R 8 where he stated:

> 'In explaining to juries the test which they should apply to determine whether the negligence ... amounted or did not amount to a crime, judges have used many epithets, such as "culpable", "criminal", "gross", "wicked" ... but whatever epithet be used, and whether an epithet be used or not, in order to establish criminal liability the facts must be such that, in the opinion of the jury, the negligence of the accused went beyond a mere matter of compensation between subjects and showed such disregard for the life and safety of others as to amount to a crime against the state and conduct deserving of punishment.'

Lord Hewart in fact considers the word 'reckless' as the most appropriate; however, he does not mean to use the word in its subjective sense, but rather as 'objective' recklessness.

This head of manslaughter was applied in the following cases:

In *R v Stone and Dobinson* [1977] Crim LR 166, the accused's failure to obtain medical treatment for a person staying with them and suffering from anorexia nervosa caused her death. The court held that the accused were liable since they were indifferent to or had recklessly disregarded the danger to the health and welfare of the victim. It is not clear whether the case was decided on the basis of gross negligence or recklessness in its subjective sense. This case shows that a duty of care equivalent to the civil law duty may in extreme cases be enforced by the criminal law although it should be remembered that the woman was a relative of the accused and they had voluntarily assumed a duty of care towards her.

In *R v Dalby* [1982] 1 All ER 916 the prosecution contended there was a duty of care arising on the facts as between friends. It is not clear whether the jury convicted on this basis and the Court of Appeal made no comment on it.

In *R v Smith* [1979] 1 WLR 1445 a husband and wife concealed the body of their stillborn child and subsequently the husband, in accordance with his wife's wishes, failed to seek medical attention for her until a few days after she became unwell, and on calling for a doctor failed to give the full circumstances of the case so that the doctor did not attend at the home until after the wife's death. In his summing up, Griffiths J directed the jury that the accused must have shown a reckless disregard of his duty to care for the deceased's health. He gave an essentially subjective test of recklessness although there is an objective element to it in deciding whether the risk he took in not getting medical attention was in all the circumstances 'unjustified and unreasonable'.

The cases of *R v Prentice, R v Sulman; R v Adomako; R v Holloway* [1993] 3 WLR 927 are worth considering in the context of gross negligence. These three appeals against convictions for manslaughter were considered together because they raised similar legal issues. Prentice and Sulman were junior hospital doctors required to carry out a lumbar puncture and other procedures in relation to a patient suffering from leukaemia. The injections were not conducted properly and a drug which should have been administered by injection in the patient's arm was injected into his spine. The patient died despite the efforts of the doctors to rectify the error.

The appellants were convicted following a direction from the trial judge in terms of reckless manslaughter. Adomako was a locum tenens anaesthetist employed at a hospital. He was assisting during an operation on a patient for a detached retina. During the operation the tube from the patient's ventilator became detached. By the time the appellant became aware that something had gone wrong the damage caused to the patient had become irreversible and he died. The appellant was convicted of manslaughter following a direction from the trial judge, in terms of gross negligence as the basis for liability rather than recklessness. Holloway was a qualified electrician who was contracted to fit a central-heating programmer in a residential dwelling. The programmer was incorrectly wired by the appellant with the result that, during the operation of certain programmes, the metal parts of the heating system became live. Five months after the installation of the programmer, one of the occupants was killed as a result of electrocution, the death being caused by the incorrect wiring of the programmer. The appellant was convicted following a direction from the trial judge in terms of reckless manslaughter.

The Court of Appeal held that the appeals of Sulman, Prentice, and Holloway would be allowed and their convictions quashed. The appeal of Adomako would be dismissed. Where death was caused by a breach of duty on the part of the defendant, a prosecution on the basis of reckless manslaughter might be appropriate where the situation was one involving motor manslaughter as the risk of harm was created by the accused himself. Where the defendant had been under a duty to act in a situation where there was a pre-existing risk of harm to others not of his making, such as a doctor treating a sick patient, it was appropriate to apply a standard of fault that allowed the court to ask questions as to why the defendant might have made errors having fatal consequences. In this regard the Lord Chief Justice observed:

'It might well be unnecessary to ask such questions when the issue is simply as to whether the speed of a person's driving was reckless, but they are central questions when examining the degree of negligence of a skilled man exercising his trade. They are questions which obviously must be asked once the issue is defined as gross negligence, but might well not be asked under the *Lawrence* direction of recklessness.'

When *R* v *Adomako* went on appeal to the House of Lords ([1994] 3 WLR 288), the decision of the Court of Appeal was confirmed. The Lords stated, inter alia, that it was for the jury to decide whether, having regard to the risk of death involved, the defendant's conduct was so bad as to amount to a criminal act or omission. Such breach of duty would amount to involuntary manslaughter.

Causing death by reckless driving

Section 1 of the Road Traffic Act 1972 provides:

'A person who causes the death of another person by driving a motor vehicle on a road recklessly shall be guilty of an offence.'

The common law, by which a motorist who causes death by his driving may be convicted of manslaughter, remains unaffected by this section.

In *R v Lawrence* [1982] AC 510 the House of Lords has given an authoritative interpretation of reckless driving.

Note that in *R v Lamb* (1990) The Times 8 February, the Court of Appeal expressed the view that, in directing juries in cases of causing death by dangerous driving, trial judges should not deviate from Lord Diplock's formulation of 'recklessness' in *R v Lawrence*.

It is sufficient to show that the reckless driving was 'a cause' of death. It need not be the sole nor even substantive cause (*R v Hennigan* [1971] 3 All ER 133).

Causing death recklessly

The difficulty of ascertaining the correct head of manslaughter under which to charge an accused person has been somewhat relieved by the decision in *Attorney-General's Reference (No 4 of 1980)* [1981] Crim LR 493 where the Court of Appeal held that if an accused killed another by one or other of two or more different acts, each of which if it caused the death is a sufficient act to establish manslaughter, it is not necessary in order to found a conviction for manslaughter to prove which act caused the death.

It does seem that there might be a third head of manslaughter. Authority is slight, and the only important modern case is *R v Pike* [1961] Crim LR 114.

The accused administered a chemical to his mistress in order to increase sexual satisfaction. Though he had used the substance before, on this occasion it caused the victim's death.

The Court of Appeal upheld a direction that the accused was guilty if he knew that exposure to the substance would expose his mistress to the risk of some harm, and recklessly caused her to inhale it. It is uncertain whether or not this decision refers to recklessness as to death, or as to anything (and if so what) short of it.

It is submitted that a better approach in similar cases would be to leave the question to the jury on the broader ground of gross negligence.

In *Kong Cheuk Kwan v R* [1985] Crim LR 787, the accused was the master of a hydrofoil that had been in collision with another hydrofoil resulting in the death of one of the passengers. He was charged with manslaughter of the passenger. The accused was convicted of manslaughter after the judge had directed the jury that the relevant risk of causing some injury was not necessarily serious but not so slight that an ordinary prudent individual would feel justified in treating it as negligible. The accused appealed to the Court of Appeal of Hong Kong and thereafter to the Privy Council.

The Privy Council allowed the appeal and the conviction was quashed on the ground that the jury were misdirected. The *Bateman* test for gross negligence manslaughter was disapproved of. It was no longer necessary nor indeed helpful to make reference to compensation and negligence (ie the distinction between the civil standard of negligence and gross negligence sufficient to found criminal liability). A proper direction was one comparable to the model direction in *R v Lawrence* (above).

Unlawful act doctrine

According to this category of involuntary manslaughter the defendant must intend to commit an unlawful act which must be objectively dangerous and which must cause the victim's death.

It would be instructive to consider these elements in more detail.

The meaning of unlawful encompasses more than criminal. *R v Fenton* (1830) 1 Lew CC 179 is cited as a case where the act was not a crime but was a tort (in that case the tort was trespass when Fenton threw stones into a mine). However, this decision has been subject to much criticism and in *R v Franklin* (1883) 15 Cox CC 163 where the accused threw a box into the sea killing the victim, Field J held that this mere civil wrong was not part of a constructive head of manslaughter. In *R v Senior* [1899] 1 QB 823 where the accused neglected a child contrary to statute law (the predecessor of the Children and Young Persons Act 1933) he was held guilty of manslaughter as his conduct was unlawful and resulted in death.

It would seem that the act itself must be unlawful and not merely unlawful because of the negligent way in which it was performed. The leading case which lays down this proposition is *Andrews v DPP* [1937] AC 576. The facts were that the accused, driving too quickly and on the wrong side of the road, struck a pedestrian, who was carried forward on the bonnet and then run over. The accused was convicted of the manslaughter of the pedestrian.

Care must be taken in reading the judgment of Lord Atkin, as his lordship uses the words 'negligent and reckless' in an exact way. By 'reckless' it is submitted that his lordship referred to 'objective recklessness' or 'gross negligence'. Lord Atkin draws a distinction between acts which are unlawful in themselves, and acts which only become unlawful because of the negligent way they are carried out.

The accused must actually intend to commit the unlawful act. This can be seen by reference to *R v Lamb* [1967] 2 All ER 1282 in which there was held to be no unlawful act where Lamb pointed a loaded gun at the victim in jest which discharged and killed the victim. The accused did not appreciate that the gun might go off and had no intention of even frightening the victim. The accused also knew in fact that the victim would not be frightened. There could therefore be no assault.

It was thought following the decision in *R v Dalby* [1982] 1 All ER 916 that the act had to be aimed at some person, but that is now doubted. In *Dalby* the accused, a drug addict, unlawfully supplied a controlled drug to the victim, another addict. The victim injected himself and later took two further injections of an unspecified substance. The accused was unable to wake the victim at a later time but did not summon an ambulance until some time later when the victim was found to be dead. The accused was convicted of manslaughter either on the basis of an unlawful and dangerous act or alternatively that he was in breach of his duty of care to his friend and was grossly negligent by not calling an ambulance earlier.

The Court of Appeal held that if the conviction was based on the first of these grounds it was incorrect. To come within constructive manslaughter the act had to be directed at the victim and likely to cause immediate injury however slight.

In *R v Dalby* the conviction for manslaughter was quashed as an unlawful act of supplying dangerous drugs which the victim administered himself was too remote from the death that occurred.

However, it is now thought that *Dalby* was concerned merely with the question of causation and not with establishing an additional condition for constructive manslaughter.

This can be illustrated by reference to the following cases.

In *R v Pagett* (1983) The Times 4 February, having shot at police, the accused then used as a shield a pregnant girl who was killed by shots instinctively fired at the accused by the police. The Court of Appeal held that the accused had committed two unlawful acts, one by firing at police and the other by holding the girl as a shield in front of him when the police might well fire shots at him in self defence, either of which could constitute the actus reus of manslaughter. As a matter of law the reasonable acts of the police in shooting in self defence could not constitute a novus actus interveniens breaking the chain of causation between Paggett's conduct and the girl's death.

In *R v Mitchell* [1983] 2 WLR 938 the accused assaulted a third party who fell against the victim, an old woman who suffered a broken femur and later in hospital died from a pulmonary embolism caused by thrombosis of the leg veins directly resulting from the fracture. It was held that in these circumstances the accused was guilty of manslaughter and that it was unnecessary to show either that he had aimed an unlawful and dangerous act at the person who died or that the act had involved a direct contact or impact upon that person.

In *R v Goodfellow* [1986] Crim LR 468 the appellant was convicted of manslaughter after he set fire to a house in order to obtain rehousing from the local authority. Three people died in the fire. He appealed against conviction on the ground that the judge had misdirected the jury by referring to a passage in *Archbold* – later criticised in the case of *Kong Cheuk Kwan v R* [1985] Crim LR 787. The Court of Appeal dismissed the appeal.

The conduct of the appellant was capable of falling within either type of manslaughter. If a person inadvertently caused death by an unlawful act which was dangerous he was guilty of manslaughter. The case of *Dalby* was no more than a causation case – it should not be interpreted to require an intention to frighten or an intention to harm.

Furthermore had the judge directed on recklessness following the *Lawrence* test the jury might well have been satisfied that this was established.

The act must be likely, according to objective standards, to cause some harm, albeit not necessarily serious harm.

The following cases illustrate this proposition:

In *R v Larkin* [1943] 1 All ER 217, the accused threatened X a third party with a knife. The victim being groggy with drink fell against the knife and was killed.

Here Larkin was held guilty, as he was performing an unlawful act (an assault) which was likely to injure someone.

The objective test was confirmed in *DPP v Newbury* [1976] 2 All ER 365. The accused threw large stones from a bridge onto a train below. His conviction under this head of manslaughter was confirmed.

In *R v Dawson* (1985) 81 Cr App R 150 it was held to be a misdirection to the jury when a judge directed the jury that 'harm' in the context of constructive manslaughter included emotional or physical disturbance. Emotional disturbance on its own was not sufficient to constitute harm.

In *R v Watson* [1989] 2 All ER 865 the Court of Appeal recognised that, following *R v Dawson* (above) the unlawful act had to be dangerous in the sense that all sober and reasonable persons would foresee that it created a risk of some physical harm occurring to the victim, but added that, in applying this test, the reasonable person was to be imbued with all the knowledge that the defendant had gained throughout his burglarious trespass (ie his realisation of the occupant's frailty) and not just the appellant's limited or non-existent knowledge at the moment he first entered the property.

In *R v Ball* [1989] Crim LR 730 the appellant had been involved in a long running dispute with his neighbour, G, over her parking her vehicle on his land. An altercation developed culminating in the appellant grabbing a handful of cartridges, loading his shot-gun, and firing at G from approximately twelve yards. G was killed. The appellant was acquitted of murder, on the basis that he had honestly believed that he had loaded the gun with blank cartridges, and had only intended to frighten G, but was convicted of constructive manslaughter. Held on appeal that once it was established that the appellant had intentionally committed an unlawful act, the question of its dangerousness was to be decided by applying an objective test based on what the reasonable and sober person would have foreseen. There was no room, following *R v Dawson*, to impute to the reasonable man the mistake of fact made by the appellant.

Goodfellow test

In *R v Goodfellow* (1986) the Court of Appeal set out the three tests for manslaughter thus.

The *Lawrence* test is firstly, where the accused was acting in such a manner as to create an obvious and serious risk of causing physical injury to some person and secondly, that he, having recognised that some risk was involved, nevertheless had gone on to take it.

The *Church* test (an unlawful and dangerous act) is where the accused did an unlawful act such that all sober and reasonable people would inevitably recognise had to subject another person to, at least, the risk of some resulting harm, albeit not serious harm, and caused death.

The test as outlined in *Goodfellow* appears to be a mixture of the above two. The test here is:

a Was the act intentional?

b Was it unlawful?

c Was it an act which any reasonable person would realise was bound to subject some other human being to the risk of physical harm, albeit not necessarily serious harm?

d Was that act the cause of death?

'Killing' an unborn child

Two offences apply here, child destruction, under the Infant Life Preservation Act 1929, and attempting to procure a miscarriage, under the Offences Against the Person Act 1861. The former only applies to the killing of a foetus capable of being born alive. The latter applies from conception to birth, thus the two offences overlap. We do not deal with attempting to procure a miscarriage in these syllabi and deal only with the offence of child destruction which is defined by s1(1) of the Infant Life (Preservation) Act 1929 as:

> 'Subject as hereinafter, in this sub-section provided any person who with intent to destroy the life of a child capable of being born alive, by any wilful act causes a child to die before it has an existence independent of its mother, shall be guilty of felony, to wit, of child destruction, and shall be liable on conviction thereon to imprisonment for life; provided that no person shall be found guilty of an offence under this section unless it is proved that the act which caused the death of the child was not done in good faith for the purpose only of preserving the life of the mother.'

It can be noted that in *C v S* [1987] 1 All ER 1230 which involved the application of a man to prevent the woman carrying a baby he fathered from undergoing an abortion on the grounds that that would amount to the commission of the criminal offence of child destruction, the House of Lords held that the Infant Life (Preservation) Act 1929 applied to a foetus that was capable of being born alive and in a controversial decision held that that phrase related to capability of surviving at birth. Thus a foetus of less than 24 weeks gestation at current medical standards would not be capable of surviving at birth. Termination of a pregnancy at any stage up to the stage when the foetus is capable of surviving being born alive would not amount to child destruction.

This provision coexists with and indeed now must be taken to take priority over the provisions in the Abortion Act 1967 in that the Abortion Act speaks of allowing abortion up to 28 weeks gestation; that must now be taken to be modified.

The Abortion Act does not affect child destruction, therefore the only defence to this crime is within the Act, ie that the operation was performed in order to preserve the life of the mother – and the onus of proof here is on the Crown to show that this was not the case. The words 'preserving the life of the mother' were given a fairly liberal interpretation in *R v Bourne* [1939] 1 KB 687.

Though this case concerned the Offences Against the Person Act, no doubt the principle is relevant here also.

'It is not contended that those words mean merely for the purpose of saving the mother from instant death. I think those words ought to be construed in a reasonable sense, and, if the doctor is of opinion, on reasonable grounds and with adequate knowledge, that the probable consequences of the continuance of the pregnancy will be to make the woman a physical or mental wreck, the jury are quite entitled to take the view that the doctor who, under those circumstances and in that honest belief, operates, is operating for the purpose of preserving the life of the mother': per MacNaghten J.

Thus the common law does not confine the defence merely to a situation of immediate danger of death to the mother.

The courts place emphasis on the 'bona fide belief'. Thus much will depend on the position of the surgeon. In *Bourne*, the accused was a respected surgeon who performed the operation in a famous hospital, and took no fee. There the girl in question, who was only fourteen, was pregnant as a result of a rape. The accused was acquitted.

The result was different however, in *R v Newton* [1958] Crim LR 469, where the accused seemed to have performed the operation primarily for profit. There seems to have been no evidence that the accused had a bona fide belief that the operation was necessary.

Mitigations in the law of homicide

In the previous two sections we have discussed the law as it relates to murder, and to what is called involuntary manslaughter.

It should now be noted that certain mitigating factors may reduce a charge of murder to that of 'voluntary' manslaughter.

The applicable mitigating circumstances are as follows:

a provocation;

b diminished responsibility;

c suicide pact;

d infanticide.

These are the only four mitigating circumstances that are allowed. It is proposed to examine each in turn.

Provocation

If the accused is provoked into killing his victim, he is entitled to be convicted of manslaughter, but not murder. The common law definition of manslaughter, encapsulated in the judgment of Devlin J in *R v Duffy* [1949] 1 All ER 932 stated that provocation was 'some act or series of acts done by the dead man to the accused, which would cause a reasonable person and actually causes in the accused, a sudden and temporary loss of self-control, rendering the accused so subject to passion as to make him ... not master of his mind'.

Thus the test was both objective (would a reasonable man have been provoked to lose his self-control?) and subjective (was the accused provoked to lose his self-control?).

Note:

a That this test made the issue a question of law to be decided upon by the judge. The most curious consequence of this was that the courts constructed a model for the reasonable man and disallowed in evidence any quality of the accused which would not have been shared with the 'reasonable man'.

Thus in *R* v *Alexander* (1913) 9 Cr App R 139 evidence that the accused (unlike the 'reasonable man') was mentally deficient was disallowed.

b These 'qualities' were not confined to the mental aspect. In *R* v *Smith* (1915) 11 Cr App R 81 the court refused to admit evidence of the accused's pregnancy.

c In *Bedder* v *DPP* [1954] 2 All ER 801, the accused attempted to have intercourse with a prostitute. Due to his impotence, he failed and was taunted by the woman. The accused knifed her. The House of Lords held that evidence that the accused was impotent had been rightly excluded. The jury must consider the effect on a reasonable man of such provocation and he, of course, is not impotent.

The law was reformed in 1957, by s3 of the Homicide Act which provides:

> 'Where on a charge of murder there is evidence on which the jury can find that the person charged was provoked (whether by things done or by things said or by both together) to lose his self-control, the question whether the provocation was enough to make a reasonable man do as he did shall be left to be determined by the jury; and in determining that question the jury shall take into account everything both done and said.'

The position at common law under *Duffy* was that the provocation to be operative must relate to an act done by the victim to the accused. That was amended by s3 Homicide Act and there is now no such limitation. The difference is well illustrated in the case of *R* v *Davies* [1975] QB 691 where Davies shot his wife. The Court of Appeal held that the trial judge had been wrong in not allowing the jury to consider the conduct of a man with whom Davies' wife was committing adultery.

In *R* v *Johnson* [1989] 2 All ER 839 the appellant had made unpleasant comments to the deceased who retaliated by threatening the appellant with a beer glass. The appellant responded by fatally stabbing the deceased with a flick knife. The trial judge had refused to leave the defence of provocation to the jury on the ground that it had been self-induced, but the appeal was allowed. Section 3 provides that anything can amount to provocation, including actions provoked by the accused – the defendant had been deprived of the opportunity of having his defence considered properly by the jury.

It is also clear that the judge cannot now lay down a legal definition of the qualities of the 'reasonable man', neither can the judge remove the question of provocation from the jury where he considers that a reasonable man would not have been provoked on the evidence. However, note that s3 requires *some* evidence of provocation before the question need be considered by the jury and it is still for the jury to decide whether or not that evidence is there.

In *DPP* v *Camplin* [1978] 2 All ER 168 the House of Lords held that *Bedder* and similar cases were no longer good law and that a proper direction to the jury would be: 'a reasonable man is a person having the power of self-control to be expected of an ordinary person of the sex and age of the accused, but in other respects sharing such of the accused's characteristics as would affect the gravity of the provocation to him'.

In *R* v *Newell* (1980) 71 Cr App R 331 the Court of Appeal held that in order to be a characteristic within the terms of *Camplin* there had to be a sufficient degree of permanence to be seen as part of the individual's character. It could not be transitory and there had to be some real connection between the nature of the provocation and the particular characteristics of the offender.

In *R* v *Raven* [1982] Crim LR 51 the accused aged 22 had a mental age of nine. The jury were directed to consider the reasonable man test on the basis of a person aged 22 but with retarded development and a mental age of nine.

In *R* v *Ali* [1989] Crim LR 736 one of the grounds of appeal was that the trial judge, in directing the jury on the defence of provocation, had failed to focus their attention on the fact that the appellant was only 20, and might therefore not be expected to display the self control of a more mature man. The Court of Appeal dismissed the appeal, holding that where the accused was an adult, it would not normally be necessary for the trial judge to allude to the accused's age when directing on the defence of provocation. A 20 year old could be expected to display the self control of a 35 year old.

In *R* v *Marshall* [1993] Crim LR 957 it was stated by the Court of Appeal that glue sniffing could hardly be considered a characteristic of the reasonable man and hence the effects of such addiction on the accused's state of mind need not be taken into account in considering whether provocation existed.

R v *Cambridge* [1994] 1 WLR 971 illustrates clearly that a judge cannot remove the defence of provocation from the jury if there is any evidence at all from which the jury might have inferred provocation, no matter how slight. In this case the judge (wrongly) withheld from the jury the issue of provocation because it was not raised as an issue in the case, both sides having believed, incorrectly as it turns out, that no reasonable person could be provoked in the circumstances.

There must be evidence that there was a sudden and temporary loss of control on the part of the accused to establish the defence of provocation. No matter how grave the provocation by the deceased the defence cannot be left to the jury in circumstances where several days elapsed between the act of provocation and the fatal attack by the accused in accordance with a pre-arranged plan. This can be seen in the case of *R* v *Ibrams and Gregory* [1982] Crim LR 229.

In that case the conscious formulation of a desire for revenge was held to indicate that the accused had had time to think, to reflect, and that that would negative a 'sudden and temporary loss of self-control'. Thus the formulation of a desire for revenge would negate provocation although in some circumstances the provocation may last a long time and would be operative as a mitigation if it culminated in a sudden loss of self-control that may have been sparked off by a relatively trivial incident that would not of itself warrant the reasonable man losing his self control.

In *R v Thornton* (1993) 98 Cr App R 112 the question of provocation and a 'cooling-off' period came once more before the courts. The appellant had been subject to a long history of domestic violence and eventually stabbed her husband following an argument. The appeal against conviction was however dismissed, primarily because the appellant had admitted to having gone off to 'cool down'; and had become calm again and had then walked back into the room and stabbed her husband.

In this respect the existence of 'a cooling off period' is of the essence. The shorter the time between the provocation and the killing the more likely the mitigation was operative. The question of a cooling off period is not a matter of law but one of fact which if found to exist would negate provocation. In cases involving the accused fetching a weapon from a distance provocation would be available only in the absence of contrivance and design.

R v Ahluwalia (1993) 96 Cr App R 133 concerned the issue of whether a sudden loss of control is still a prerequisite to establish provocation. The appellant was an Asian woman who had entered into an arranged marriage. Her husband abused her verbally and physically over a number of years. He also conducted an adulterous affair about which he taunted her. On the night in question he had argued with her and promised to give her a beating the following morning. After he had fallen asleep, the appellant poured petrol over him and set him alight, causing burns from which he subsequently died. At her trial for murder the appellant contended that she had acted under provocation, in response to which the trial judge directed the jury to remember that the defence was only available to a defendant who suffered a sudden and temporary loss of self-control (the test laid down in *R v Duffy* [1949] 1 All ER 932). The appellant now sought to challenge her conviction for murder on the basis (inter alia) that the trial judge erred in directing the jury to look for evidence of a sudden loss of self control, and that they should have been directed to regard the fact that she was suffering from 'battered woman syndrome' as a characteristic in assessing how a reasonable married Asian woman would have reacted.

The appeal was allowed, the conviction quashed and a re-trial ordered. The evidence now available indicated to the Court of Appeal that she may have had an arguable defence on the basis of diminished responsibility, and as such she should be granted a retrial where the defence could be fully ventilated.

Similarly in *R v Richens* [1993] Crim LR 384 the Court of Appeal stressed the necessity for a sudden and temporary loss of control to be established.

In *R v Cocker* [1989] Crim LR 740 persistent pleading by the appellant's incurably ill wife for him to kill her was held not to be provocation. The evidence indicated that, far from losing self control, the appellant had been aware of his actions, and had killed in 'cold blood' – of particular significance was the fact that the appellant had paused while asphyxiating his wife only to continue following her entreaties that he should carry on.

It must not be thought that all cases of provocation prior to 1957 are now overruled.

In *Mancini* v *DPP* [1942] AC 1, the accused stabbed his victim with a knife. The accused claimed that the victim attacked him with a pen-knife, and thus his plea was self-defence. MacNaghten J did not direct the jury on the question of provocation, and the accused was convicted. His appeal was dismissed, the House of Lords holding that as the jury rejected the story of the pen-knife, there was effectively no real issue of provocation to be left. It would seem that were such a case to arise again, a similarly placed House of Lords would be entitled to say that, there being no evidence of provocation, the matter need not have been left to the jury.

It will no longer, though, be correct for the judge to tell the jury that the retaliation must 'bear a relationship to the provocation'. If one takes the view that there was evidence of provocation, but by an unarmed man in *Mancini*, then the judge, in a similar case, would not be entitled to withdraw the issue from the jury simply because the provocation was not sufficiently strong. It is for the jury to decide.

In *R* v *Brown* [1972] 2 QB 229 it was held that the rule in *Mancini* v *DPP* that there must be a reasonable relationship between the provocation and the retaliation is no longer a rule of law; it is now a question of fact for the jury.

In *R* v *Doughty* [1986] Crim LR 625 The appellant was convicted of murdering his 17 day old son. The appellant gave evidence that the child's crying had so annoyed him he had smothered the child to stop it crying. The judge ruled that the defence of provocation could not go to the jury as the episodes that the appellant referred to were natural and had to be endured.

The appeal was allowed. The defence should have been left to the jury. Section 3 of the Homicide Act 1957 was not restricted to cases where there was some element of 'wrongfulness' in the act of provocation.

The position can be represented in the following diagram which sets out in a flow chart the questions which the jury must consider:

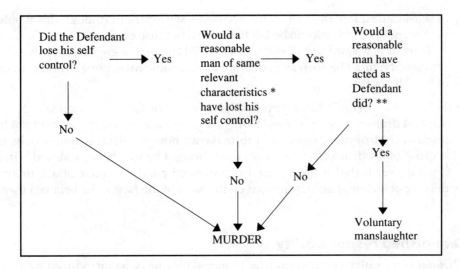

* 'Relevant characteristics' – in *DPP* v *Camplin* defined as 'those characteristics relevant to the provocation' (including age and sex and any others depending on the provocation offered)

** One must *not* apply any test of proportionality (the old case used to be *Mancini* – response had to be in proportion to the provocation – but this no longer applies) except as this is inherent in what a reasonable man would do.

If the accused makes a mistake as to facts which, had they been true, would have permitted him to plead provocation he should be judged on the basis of the facts as he believed them to be providing his belief was honest. In *Albert* v *Lavin* (1981) 72 Cr App R 178 it was considered that a mistake in relation to a defence had to be honest and reasonable but in *R* v *Williams* [1984] Crim LR 163 it was stated that a mistake in relation to a defence had simply to be honest. The reasonableness or otherwise of the belief was material only in deciding whether the belief was actually held.

Note the effect of mistake on the objective test.

The question will be:

a did the accused honestly believe a set of facts (his mistaken belief)?

b did he lose his self-control as a result?

c would a reasonable man, supposing these facts to be the case, have lost his self-control (and retaliated as the accused did) because of the situation created by those facts?

Drunkenness may affect provocation in two ways.

a It may result in the accused losing his self-control more easily. The law as shown in *R* v *McCarthy* [1954] 2 QB 105 disallowed the jury from considering the effect of self-induced intoxication on the accused's self-restraint (though this would now seem to be evidence to be left to the jury, because of s3).

Thus in *R v Wardrope* [1960] Crim LR 770 the jury were directed that the provocation must be such as to deprive a reasonable man, not a drunken man, of his self-control.

b In *R v Letenock* (1917) 12 Cr App R 221, however, the Court of Criminal Appeal allowed drunkenness to be raised where the intoxication led the accused not to lose his control more easily, but to make an honest mistake more easily, ie because of his drunken state the accused thought he was being attacked. Thus it would seem that if the accused is provoked partly because of a drunken mistake of fact he should be judged on the basis of the facts as he believed them to be.

Diminished responsibility

This defence, which reduces murder to manslaughter, was introduced by s2 of the Homicide Act 1957 which provides:

'Where a person kills or is party to the killing of another, he shall not be convicted of murder if he was suffering from such abnormality of mind (whether arising from a condition of arrested or retarded development of mind or any inherent causes or induced by disease or injury) as substantially impaired his mental responsibility for his acts and omissions in doing or being party to the killing.'

Smith & Hogan put the rationale for diminished responsibility thus:

'A man whose impulse is irresistible bears no moral responsibility for his act, for he has no choice: a man whose impulse is much more difficult to resist than that of an ordinary man bears a diminished degree of moral responsibility for his act.'

At a time when capital punishment was imposed on those convicted of murder this was an important development in the law that had failed to amend the M'Naghten Rules since 1843 in spite of considerable advances in psychiatry and understanding of mental illness. Thus diminished responsibility was intended originally to fill a gap left in the law to cover people commonly thought to be insane within the broad popular sense but who did not fit within the M'Naghten Rules.

The majority of cases where the defendant suffers from some mental aberration are now pleaded under s2. The burden of proof is on the defence here, on the balance of probabilities.

In *R v Campbell* (1986) The Times 4 November the Court of Appeal held that the wording of s2(2) Homicide Act providing that 'it shall be for the defence to prove' diminished responsibility not only dictated which party shouldered the burden of proof once the issue was raised but also left it to the defence to decide whether the issue should be raised at all. Thus although in cases where there is a prima facie evidence of self defence or of provocation that matter is to be left to the jury even if it was not raised by those appearing for the defence at trial there was no such rule with regard to diminished responsibility.

The trial judge must direct the jury as to the meaning to be attached to s2 of the Homicide Act 1957, but it is for the jury to decide whether, on the whole evidence, the accused was suffering from a substantial impairment of his mental responsibility for his acts. In *R v Spriggs* (1958) 42 Cr App R 69 the trial judge left the jury to decide whether or not the accused came within the section, with no explanation of its legal effect. Although this seems to be a case of allowing the jury to interpret the Statute, the Court of Appeal nevertheless held that this was correct. (This is now viewed as a wrong decision.)

In *R v Byrne* [1960] 3 All ER 1 the trial judge told the jury that the accused's inability to control his actions would not bring him within s2. The accused strangled a young woman because of inordinate sexual urges which he found impossible to control. The Court of Appeal held that the direction was wrong. It was for the jury to decide whether or not Byrne's conduct fell within the section and not the judge.

Note that this case does not lay down that such an irresistible impulse is within s2 as a rule of law, it merely leaves open the question of whether or not it is to be answered by the jury.

In *R v Seers* [1985] Crim LR 315 the Court of Appeal considered there was a misdirection to the jury to direct them that only partial or borderline insanity amounted to diminished responsibility. The accused had killed his estranged wife while suffering from a depressive illness. He was found guilty of murder after the judge had directed the jury as above. The Court of Appeal substituted a conviction of manslaughter after finding that the jury had been misdirected and however depressed the jury may have thought the accused to be it would have been highly unlikely they would have considered him to be partially insane.

In *R v Gittens* [1984] 3 All ER 252 the accused had killed his wife and raped and killed his 15 year old stepdaughter. The accused suffered from depression and on the day of the killings he had drunk in excess. The jury were directed to consider diminished responsibility and to ask themselves what was the substantial cause of his conduct. Only if it be shown that the abnormality of mind existed without regard to the drink was diminished responsibility established. The Court of Appeal, substituting a verdict of manslaughter on the ground of diminished responsibility for the verdict of murder, considered there had been a misdirection to the jury. The correct approach where alcohol or drugs were involved was that adopted in *R v Fenton* (1975) 61 Cr App R 261. The jury should have been directed to disregard the effect of drugs or alcohol since abnormality of mind from drink or drugs was not due to inherent causes and therefore not within the section. The jury then had to consider whether the combined effect of other factors that did fall within s2 were sufficient to amount to an abnormality of mind as substantially impaired the defendant's responsibility.

It will be appreciated that the circumstances where s2 will be relevant are very wide, and have included eg a person in a state of chronic depression and a mercy killer. This defence is often preferable to a plea of insanity, as manslaughter is a crime without a fixed penalty and therefore the court has a wide discretion in sentencing. Thus use will often be made of the power to make Hospital Orders under s60 of the Mental Health Act 1959.

Note also the effects of the Criminal Procedure (Insanity and Unfitness to Plead) Act 1991.

The purpose of the Act, which came into force on 1 January 1992, is to improve the position of the defendant whose fitness to plead is questioned at the outset of proceedings, and to increase the range of disposition options open to the court following the special verdict of 'not guilty by reason of insanity'. The Act makes no change to the 'M'Naghten Rules' (*M'Naghten's Case* (1843) 10 C & F 200) as regards the definition of insanity.

Fitness to plead

At present, a defendant can be found to be unfit to plead before the issue of liability is investigated. This can result in a defendant being detained in a secure hospital simply on the basis of his or her unfitness to plead. The 1991 Act is designed to improve the situation of such defendants by requiring a court, which has found a defendant unfit to plead, to continue with a trial of the facts to the extent of ascertaining whether or not the defendant committed the actus reus of the offence alleged. If the court concludes that he did not, the defendant should be acquitted. Whilst this development is to be welcomed, it should be remembered that the distinction between actus reus and mens rea is somewhat illusory in many cases, and it may be that in practice the court has no option but to investigate both elements.

Disposal

As indicated above, the defendant found unfit to plead could formerly have been detained in a secure hospital for an indefinite period. Under the 1991 Act, if such a defendant is found not to have committed the actus reus he must be acquitted.

If a defendant is found not guilty by reason of insanity, the 1991 Act increases the range of disposal options available to the court, provided the offence is not one that attracts a mandatory penalty. The court can now make a supervision and treatment order; a guardianship order; order the defendant's admission to hospital for a limited or unlimited period; or discharge the defendant completely.

Suicide pact

Under the Suicide Act 1961, suicide ceases to be a crime for the principal offender. Liability is possible, however, where at least two people are involved. This may be under either the Suicide Act itself, or the Homicide Act 1957.

By s2 of the Suicide Act:

'A person who aids, abets, counsels or procures the suicide of another or an attempt by another to commit suicide, shall be liable ...'

As usual, motive is irrelevant. Thus the procurement of a drug in order to cut short an agonising death is as much an offence as the counselling of an elderly relative to 'end it all' in order to inherit his money.

The consent of the DPP is required before this indictment can be laid.

In *Attorney-General v Able* (1984) 78 Cr App R 197 the accused were all members of 'EXIT' involved in the publication of a booklet giving practical advice to a person wishing to commit suicide. The booklet was only available to members of EXIT. The High Court were asked to consider whether the supply of the booklet contravened s2 Suicide Act 1961. The High Court held that supplying the booklet generally did not contravene s2 although the supplying of the booklet in a particular circumstance might amount to an offence contrary to s2 if it could be proved that the supplier intended it to be used by or to encourage a person to commit suicide where that person did read it and was encouraged to commit suicide or attempt to do so.

By s4 of the Homicide Act:

> 'It shall be manslaughter and shall not be murder for a person acting in pursuance of a suicide pact between him and another to kill the other or be party to the other being killed by a third person.'

and by s4(3):

> '(A suicide pact is) a common agreement between two or more persons having for its object the death of all of them, whether or not each is to take his own life, but nothing done by a person who enters into a suicide pact shall be treated as done by him in pursuance of the pact unless it is done while he has the settled intention of dying in pursuance of it.'

If the accused is charged with murder, the onus of proving a suicide pact is upon him, presumably on the balance of probabilities.

Note:

a A suicide pact is an offence under the Homicide Act and not under the Suicide Act; causing death in the course of carrying out a suicide pact is thus manslaughter.

b Complicity in another's suicide, under s2 of the Suicide Act, may only be charged where the victim kills himself. Thus if, on this charge, it is shown that the accused killed the victim, he is not guilty.

c Where the accused counsels the victim into allowing his life to be taken by X in the course of a suicide pact, this would seem to be the only situation where the accused may be guilty under both provisions.

d It should be noted that the reason for the mitigation is not that the deceased wished to die since euthanasia is no defence under English law but that the accused was prepared to take his own life and therefore will be assumed to be unbalanced.

Infanticide

The Infanticide Act 1938 1(1) states:

> 'Where a woman by any wilful act or omission causes the death of her child being a child under the age of twelve months, but at the time of the act or omission the balance of her mind was disturbed by reason of her not having fully recovered from the effect of giving birth to the child or by reason of the effect of lactation consequent upon the birth of the child, then notwithstanding that the circumstances were such that but for this Act the offence would have amounted to murder, she shall be guilty of ... infanticide, and may be dealt with as for manslaughter.'

Note:

a   The Act does not apply if the mother kills another child other than the one under twelve months old.

b   A conviction of infanticide may be returned on a charge of murder.

c   If on a charge of murder, the accused pleads guilty to infanticide, she must raise some evidence (the 'evidential burden') of this. The burden of providing murder still rests with the Crown.

d   The relationship with the defence of insanity and diminished responsibility.

Lawful homicides

There are certain circumstances in which the accused may be able to absolve himself completely from any criminal liability in connection with his causing death. He could do this by bringing himself within one of the recognised defences by which the homicide would cease to be unlawful.

These recognised defences are:

a   Killing while preventing crime or arresting offenders.

b   Self-defence.

c   In defence of property.

Killing while preventing crime or arresting offenders

This is covered by s3 of the Criminal Law Act 1967, which states:

> 'A person may use such force as is reasonable in the circumstances in the prevention of crime, or in effecting or assisting in the lawful arrest of offenders or suspected offenders or of persons unlawfully at large.'

The act overrules the previous complicated common law.

Reasonableness will depend on the circumstances. However, presumably the crime must be a serious one before a killing will be excusable, though the courts will no doubt give credit for what may be a decision taken in 'the heat of the moment'.

There is an overlap between this defence and the defence of self-defence.

Self-defence

As an attacker would obviously be about to commit a crime, there seems no doubt that a defendant could rely on s3 CLA. However there is still a common law right of self-defence.

Though there were previously doubts as to whether the defence applied to violence in relation to attacks on one's family, or friends, these seem resolved by *R v Duffy* [1967] 1 QB 63, where the Court of Appeal held that there was a liability, even among strangers, to prevent a felony.

Lord Morris in *Palmer v R* [1971] AC 814 stated:

> 'In their lordships' view the defence of self-defence is one which can and will be readily understood by any jury ... No formula need be employed by reference to it. Only common sense is needed for its understanding ... if there has been an attack so that defence is reasonably necessary it will be recognised that a person defending himself cannot weigh to a nicety the exact measure of his necessary defensive action. If a jury thought in a moment of unexpected anguish a person attacked had only done what he honestly and instinctively thought was necessary, that would be most patent evidence that only reasonable defensive action had been taken.'

It is worth quoting the remark of the American Supreme Court Justice *Oliver Wendell Holmes* that 'detached reflection cannot be expected in the face of an uplifted knife'. This is reflected in the following two cases:

In *R v Shannon* (1980) 71 Cr App R 192 the Court of Appeal held that it was necessary for the jury to consider the accused's state of mind in considering self-defence. If he was acting simply in angry retaliation or aggression, the defence was not available to him. However in deciding whether it was available to him, the jury should take into account the position of the accused at the time of the act, and in judging whether his actions were necessary apply ordinary commonsense principles.

In *R v Bird* [1985] Crim LR 388, the Court of Appeal held that a judge had misdirected the jury when he told them that self-defence was only available where an accused had evidenced in some way that he was unwilling to fight. Certainly an accused who was shown to be attacking could not claim self-defence. Proof that an accused tried to retreat was a method of rebutting the suggestion that the accused was an attacker, but was not the only method.

In *R v Scarlett* (1993) The Times 18 May where the appellant had forcibly used undue strength to eject the accused from his public house, in the mistaken belief that he was allowed to do so, the Court of Appeal held that if a genuine mistake were made, this would not affect the plea of manslaughter. Given that the appellant would have been allowed to rely on an honest but mistaken belief that the use of force was necessary, where for example he mistakenly believed himself to be being attacked, he should also be allowed to rely on an honest mistake as to the amount of force necessary in a given situation.

In defence of property

Though s3 applies here also, it would rarely apply when a death has resulted, as killing can seldom be justified. The most likely example would seem to be the burglar who is assaulted – therefore what would otherwise be manslaughter by unlawful act would become a lawful homicide providing reasonable force was used.

In *R v Barrett & Barrett* (1980) 72 Cr App R 212 the appellants were appealing against their convictions of assault occasioning actual bodily harm, after they had tried to repel bailiffs who were executing a proper warrant to take possession of a house which belonged to one of the appellants, on the grounds that the judge had directed the jury wrongly by saying that the use of force could not be justified even if they acted in the reasonable, albeit mistaken, belief that the bailiffs were trespassers. In dismissing the appeal the Court of Appeal held that the defence of honest mistake was not available in such circumstances where the rights in question had been the subject of litigation between the parties and where a competent court had stated what those rights were. Indeed on the facts here there would seem to be a mistake of law not fact. The Court of Appeal also stated that the subjective approach to the defence of mistake in rape adopted in *DPP v Morgan* [1976] AC 182 did not apply in civil matters and the House of Lords' observations in *Morgan* were not intended to invalidate the law of self-defence where excessive force was alleged to have been used – the test to be applied was objective still – namely was it reasonable?

Note:

a These defences are an 'extra' which go to nullify the effect of a completed crime. They do not negative mens rea.

b The accused may still intend the act that kills his would be assailant. Thus the accused must believe in the facts which give him the defence. If the accused's retaliation is only objectively reasonable (as where the victim is about to shoot him but the accused does not know this), then he cannot rely on self-defence. (See *R v Dadson* (1850) 2 Den 35.)

c The case of *R v Hussey* (1924) 18 Cr App R 160 would probably be decided differently today. Then the tenant had no recourse to law to save him from unlawful eviction and therefore then his use of force was considered reasonable.

The Criminal Law Revision Committee recommends that the justifiable force used in the defence of self, others, property, or in the prevention of crime should be regulated by a uniform test, that is:

a *a subjective test* – whether the defendant believed that the use of force was necessary; and

b *objective test* – whether on the facts as he believed them to be the force used was reasonable.

The Committee proposed two statutory provisions:

a a general provision that a person may use such force as is reasonable in the circumstances as he believes them to be in defence of himself or another, or property of his or another;

b amendment of s3 the Criminal Law Act 1967 to ensure that in criminal proceedings the uniform test is applied to force used in prevention of crime.

The Committee recommends a revision to the effect that self-defence as distinct from defence of property is justifiable only where the defendant fears an imminent attack and the question of whether or not he retreats before using force is simply a factor to be taken into account in deciding whether it was necessary to use force and whether the force was reasonable.

Note:

Duress has never been a defence to murder. Nor, it seems, will it be a defence to attempted murder, though it might succeed as a defence to a charge of conspiracy or incitement to murder.

In *R v Gotts* [1991] 2 WLR 878 the defendant, who had been convicted of the attempted murder of his mother, appealed on the basis of duress. He had been threatened by his father that, if he did not kill his mother, then he would himself be shot. It was held that the appeal must fail because duress was not available as a defence to murder or attempted murder.

Liability in criminal law (2) | 23

Theft and related offences: introduction

The offences against property, unlike those we have earlier examined, against the person, are largely in statutory form. Theft is the main offence against property, the major statutes being the Theft Acts of 1968 and 1978 and the Criminal Damage Act 1971. These three main Acts amend and consolidate a considerable amount of earlier legislation and common law; and were attempts to define in plain clear language, understandable to the ordinary person, various offences against property. It is clear, however, from the body of case law which has built up since the Theft Act 1968, that the concept of property is such a complex one, no amount of re-drafting or clarification will entirely solve the problem of definition.

When the Theft Act 1968 was drafted, it was decided to switch from the old basis of liability – interference with possession – to a new concept: interference with ownership. It was thought that ownership, being a wider concept, would prove more suitable for dealing with the different types of interest in property and especially intangible and intellectual property. One of the results of this switch-over was that the 1968 Act had to be largely re-drafted and replaced by the 1978 Act. The concept of ownership as defined in the 1968 Act was just too wide and too flexible.

The offence of theft; actus reus

The basic definition of theft is to be found in s1 of the Theft Act 1968 which provides:

'1) A person is guilty of theft if he dishonestly appropriates property belonging to another with the intention of permanently depriving the other of it; and 'thief' and 'steal' shall be construed accordingly.
2) It is immaterial whether the appropriation is made with a view to gain, or is made for the thief's own benefit.
3) The five following sections of the Act shall have the effect as regards the interpretation and operation of this section ...'

Many of the elements of the offence, such as property belonging to another and dishonesty, are found also in other offences under the Theft Acts. We shall consider first the *actus reus* of theft and the appropriation of property belonging to another.

Under s3 of the Act

'Any assumption by a person of the rights of an owner amounts to an appropriation ...'

The commonest form of appropriation is taking property away, but destroying property, treating property as one's own and selling or leasing it out will also be forms of assumption of rights of ownership. Some sort of positive conduct is needed and the appropriation must be unauthorised; see *R v Morris* [1983] 2 WLR 768 and *Eddy v Niman* [1981] Crim LR 501.

In *R v Gallasso* [1993] Crim LR 459 the definition of appropriation was considered further.

The appellant was a nurse caring for mentally disturbed adults. She was entrusted with looking after the financial affairs of her patients, in particular she was authorised to withdraw money from their accounts in order to pay for their day-to-day requirements. When J, one of her patients, received a cheque for £4,000, the appellant opened a second account in his name and paid the cheque into that account. The appellant subsequently transferred £3,000 from this second account to J's first account, and £1,000 from J's second account to her own account. Some time later the appellant used a cheque for £1,800, that had been sent to J, to open a cashcard account in his name. The appellant was convicted of theft in respect of the transfer of £1,000 to her own account, and in respect of the cheque for £1,800 that she used to open the cashcard account. The appellant appealed against conviction in respect of the cheque for £1,800 on the ground that she had not committed an appropriation. It was held that the appeal would be allowed, and the conviction for theft of the cheque for £1,800 quashed. In opening the cashcard account the appellant was acting in a proper manner in relation to the cheque, in the sense that she was confirming J's right to the money rather than usurping it. Whatever the appellant's secret dishonest intent, it could not convert her actions into an appropriation.

Property is defined in s4 of the Theft Act 1968 to include 'money and all other property, real or personal, including things in action and other intangible property'. Real property includes buildings and land, but there are special provisions relating to land in s4(2). Personal property includes moveables and may be tangible or intangible. A thing in action is intangible property which gives rise to a right of action: for example, a copyright, a trademark or a bank credit.

Money can, of course, take many forms; as a credit balance in a bank account it is actually a 'thing in action': the account-holder is a creditor and the bank is under an obligation to repay the balance to the creditor, or to honour valid cheques drawn on the account in favour of third parties. This means that if part or the whole of the credit balance of an account is dishonestly appropriated, what is stolen is not the tangible 'money', but an intangible 'thing in action' – the right of the creditor/account-holder to enforce payment for that amount from the bank.

If the bank is under *no* obligation to honour the cheque (for example, because the account is overdrawn and there is no agreed overdraft facility) then there is no 'thing in action' and thus no property to be stolen. It has also been held by the Court of Appeal that no theft is committed when a cheque is drawn by a dishonest account-holder on an account containing insufficient funds even when the cheque is backed by a cheque guarantee card so that the bank is obliged to honour the cheque on presentation. The Court held that there was no assumption of the bank's rights by the dishonest account-holder; there may well be an obtaining by deception, however (see 'Offences involving deception' below).

Not everything that is intangible is property within s4. It was held in *Oxford* v *Moss* (1978) 68 Cr App R 183 that information is not property capable of being stolen, so that borrowing an examination paper to look at the contents was found not to be theft of the information on the paper. It has also been held that electricity is not property (*Low* v *Blease* [1975] Crim LR 513), but a specific offence of unauthorised and dishonest abstraction of electricity is found in s13 of the Theft Act 1968.

The remainder of s4 contains rules for specific types of property. Land is covered by s4(2), which provides that land (or things forming part of land and severed from it, such as trees or minerals) can only be stolen in certain limited circumstances. First, where a trustee, personal representative or person authorised under a power of attorney or as liquidator, appropriates the land 'by dealing with it in breach of the confidence reposed in him' (s4(2)(a)). Thus a trustee, who is the legal owner of the trust property, will be guilty of theft if he dishonestly sells land which was subject to a trust. Secondly, where a person *in possession* of the land under a tenancy appropriates a fixture, this will be theft of the fixture.

Thirdly, the Act deals with things forming part of land and which may be severed from it, such as plants, trees or minerals. If a person who is *not in possession* of land cuts down trees or digs up plants or bushes, then this is theft (s4(2)(b)). However, merely picking flowers, fruit or foliage from plants growing wild on someone else's land is not theft unless it is done for a commercial purpose (s4(3)). It would not be theft to pick blackberries unless the fruit were to be sold in the local market. The same rule applies to mushrooms.

Lastly, s4 deals with 'wild creatures, tamed or untamed'. These are property, but cannot usually be stolen as they do not 'belong to' anyone (s4(4)). However, if the wild creature is ordinarily kept in captivity then it can be stolen. Likewise, if the creature has 'been reduced into possession' (caught) by another person, and possession has not since been lost, then the creature can be stolen from that person. A tame animal, such as a cat or a dog, is the property of its owner (as are domesticated animals such as horses, cows, sheep) and a dishonest appropriation will be theft.

Property must 'belong to another' before its appropriation can be defined as theft; and the term has an extended meaning depending on the type of property.

Under s5(1), property is regarded as belonging to anyone having possession or control of it or having a proprietary right or interest in it, certain kinds of equitable interest being excluded. The device of a constructive trust cannot be used to catch certain kinds of dishonest behaviour which would not otherwise come within s1.

In *Attorney-General's Reference (No 1 of 1985)* [1986] 2 WLR 733 a barman sold his own beer to customers. It was argued that the owners of the public house had a proprietary interest in the proceeds of the sale under a constructive trust. The Court rejected this argument saying that this sort of situation was not meant to be covered by s5(1) and a constructive trust could not be said to have arisen here. Potentially s5(1) can be interpreted widely; see for example *R* v *Turner* [1971] 1 WLR 901 in which it became apparent that given the necessary mens rea, a person can steal his own property from someone with a lesser interest. Turner had taken his car to a garage to be repaired. When it was repaired he took it from where it was parked, intending not to pay for the repair. The Court held that the car 'belonged to' the repairer at the time Turner took it, as the repairer had control over it. Turner was, therefore, guilty of theft.

Section 5(2) deals with trust property and provides, for the avoidance of doubt, that property belongs to any person who has a right to enforce the trust, such as a beneficiary. In the case of charitable trusts, this would be the Attorney-General.

There are some circumstances where legal ownership has passed to the defendant but for the purposes of the Theft Act the property is treated as still belonging to the original owner s5(3) states:

> 'Where a person receives property from or on account of another, and is under an obligation to the other to retain and deal with that property or its proceeds in a particular way, the property or proceeds shall be regarded (as against him) as belonging to the other.'

The obligation referred to must be a legal obligation (*R v Gilks* [1972] 1 WLR 1341); a purely moral obligation will not be enough. The courts have shown some uncertainty over the extent to which the existence of this legal obligation is a matter of law for the judge, or a question of fact for the jury. The current view is that it is mixed: the facts are for the jury, who must, therefore, decide the exact terms of any agreement; whether these terms give rise to the requisite legal obligation is then a question for the judge.

In *R v Brewster* (1979) 69 Cr App R 375 the Court of Appeal held that s5(3) would apply in the case of an insurance broker who acted as agent collecting premiums for insurance companies and then used the premiums to finance his own business. Under the terms of the contracts between the accused and the companies, he was under an obligation to retain the money collected and pass it to the insurance company. See, however, the case of *R v Hall* [1972] 2 All ER 1009 in which *Hall* was a travel agent who had taken money for holidays and not booked them. His business collapsed and the money was lost. Although *Hall* had a general obligation to fulfil his contract he did not have to deal with those specific notes and cheques in a particular way and the subsection did not, therefore, apply.

> 'Where a person gets property by another's mistake, and is under an obligation to make restoration (in whole or in part) of the property or its proceeds or of the value thereof, then to the extent of that obligation the property or proceeds shall be regarded (as against him) as belonging to the person entitled to restoration ...' (s5(3) Theft Act 1968).

As to the nature of 'obligations' under s5(3) see also, *R v Dubar* [1994] 1 WLR 1485.

Section 5(5) provides for a certain type of corporation, the corporation sole: certain offices (such as the Crown, or Bishop) possess a legal personality distinct from that of the person who happens to be the holder of the office at any particular time. This legal personality continues uninterrupted during periods when the office is not filled and the subsection provides that 'property of a corporation sole shall be regarded as belonging to the corporation notwithstanding a vacancy in the corporation.'

The remaining two subsections of s5 deal with cases where all legal rights in the property itself have been transferred to the thief, but because the thief is under some personal legal obligation with regard to the goods, the property is deemed to belong to another.

The mens rea of theft

The *mens rea* of theft, the state of mind that must accompany the appropriation, has two parts; dishonesty, and the intention of permanently depriving the owner of the property. Dishonesty is only partially defined in s2 of the Theft Act 1968 and the courts' response has been to leave the question of what is dishonest largely to the jury (or magistrates). The courts have, however, laid down certain general guidelines – see the cases that follow.

Dishonesty

Dishonesty is only partially defined in s2(1) of the 1968 Act, which sets out the situations where, as a matter of law, a person is *not* dishonest.

Those situations are:

a   Where he believes he has in law the right to deprive the other of the property permanently.

b   Where he believes that the other person would have consented to the appropriation if he had known the relevant circumstances: for example unauthorised 'borrowing' consumable goods from a neighbour or money from a friend's purse.

c   (Unless he is a trustee or personal representative), where he acts in the belief that the true owner cannot be found by taking reasonable steps.

Section 2(2) states that a person can be found to be dishonest notwithstanding his willingness to pay for the property. If an owner does not want to sell then it can be dishonest to take the property and leave payment against his will.

Section 2(1)(a) incorporates what is known as the 'claim of right'. The accused is not dishonest if he believes that he has a better legal right to the property than the other person; he may believe that he is the owner though this will not always give him a better legal right. A belief in a moral, as opposed to a legal, right to the property will not excuse, but there appears to be no requirement that the belief be a reasonable one, as long as it is honestly held. In *R v Robinson* [1977] Crim LR 173, for example, a belief that the accused was entitled to take from the victim a sum of money which the victim owed him was held to excuse, as a claim of right. In *R v Small* [1987] Crim LR 777 the Court of Appeal held that an honest belief that the property has been abandoned is a defence to theft, even if it is not reasonably held.

In situations not covered by s2 the meaning of the term 'dishonesty' is to be interpreted as an ordinary word in the English language and is a matter for the jury to decide. There has been considerable discussion among academics as to the amount of guidance to be given to the jury, and particularly as to the relevance of the views of the accused himself on his honesty or dishonesty. In the leading case *R v Feely* [1973] 2 WLR 201 the accused had, contrary to instructions, taken some money from his employer's till, intending to pay it back. The trial judge told the jury that the intention to pay the money back was irrelevant, and did not leave them to decide the issue of dishonesty. Lord Justice Lawton in the Court of Appeal held that dishonesty was a state of mind, and was, therefore, a question of fact, which must be left to the jury.

> 'We do not agree that judges should define what "dishonesty" means ... This word is in common use ... Jurors, when deciding whether an appropriation was dishonest can reasonably be expected to, and should, apply the current standards of ordinary decent people. In their own lives they have to decide what is, and what is not dishonest. We see no reason why, when in a jury box, they should require the help of a judge to tell them what amounts to dishonesty.'

Dishonesty is thus a question of fact, which is entirely for the jury to decide.

In the more recent case of *R v Ghosh* [1982] 3 WLR 110 the court set out a two-stage test for dishonesty:

a The jury must decide if the behaviour was dishonest by the standards of the ordinary decent person. If it was not, he is not guilty.

b If the defendant was dishonest by those ordinary decent standards he is only guilty if he *realised* that people would so regard his behaviour.

The test is, therefore, subjective but does not allow the defendant to claim he is honest when he knows that by the ordinary standards of society people would regard him as dishonest.

Intention permanently to deprive

It will usually be clear whether or not a person has an intention of permanently depriving. Taking money belonging to another, intending to repay, will involve an intention of permanently depriving the other of the particular notes and coins that were taken, although it is often referred to as 'borrowing'. Such a taking will be theft if it is dishonest, as s2(2) indicates. If the money is in a bank account, it will be theft of a thing in action and the intention of permanently depriving will normally be clear; there may also be theft of the cheque itself.

There will be cases where the intention of permanently depriving is not clear: cases, particularly attempts, where the accused has not yet found property to steal, and cases where the accused intends to return the property, but in circumstances which render the property of little or no value to its owner. The second of these difficulties is covered by s6 of the Theft Act 1968, and is examined below. The first is sometimes referred to as 'conditional intent' or, confusingly, 'conditional appropriation'. In some very limited cases this intention, though not actually present, will be presumed.

Section 6 of the Theft Act 1968 was designed specifically to clarify the meaning of the expression 'intention of permanently depriving'. It has two subsections:

'a) A person appropriating property belonging to another without meaning the other permanently to lose the thing itself is nevertheless to be regarded as having the intention of permanently depriving the other of it if his intention is to treat the thing as his own to dispose of regardless of the other's rights: and a borrowing or lending of it may amount to so treating it if, but only if, the borrowing or lending is for a period and in circumstances making it equivalent to an outright taking or disposal.

b) Without prejudice to the generality of subsection (a) above, where a person, having possession or control (lawfully or not) of property belonging to another, parts with the property under a condition as to its return which he may not be able to perform, this (if done for purposes of his own and without the other's authority) amounts to treating the property as his own to dispose of regardless of the other's rights.'

Thus, in effect, the second subsection gives more specific application and examples to be read in conjunction with the first, more general, subsection. This section has been heavily criticised, being called ambiguous, abstruse and 'sprouting obscurities at every phrase'. In fact it was made clear (in *R v Lloyd, Bhuee and Ali* [1985] 3 WLR 30) that s6 should be referred to only in exceptional cases.

Soon after the Theft Act 1968 came into force, Edmund-Davies LJ in *R v Warner* (1970) 55 Cr App R 93 warned that s6 must not be interpreted as in any way 'watering down' the definition of theft, which includes the intention of permanently depriving; it merely gives illustrations of such an intention, and clarifies its meaning. This approach has been broadly adopted by other judges.

Section 6(2) is not difficult to construe but it appears to apply in very limited circumstances: where the accused pawns another's property, for example, intending to redeem it and return it, but unable to guarantee that he will be able to do so. Gambling with another's property would be another example. The general provision in s6(1) is much more convoluted.

Lord Lane has given a useful analysis of s6(1) in *Lloyd* (above). As he points out, it is concerned with two types of activity. Firstly, the 'first part of s6(1) seems to us to be aimed at the sort of case where a defendant takes things and then offers them back to the owner for the owner to buy if he wishes. If the taker intends to return them to the owner only on such payment, then, on the wording of s6(1), that is deemed to amount to the necessary intention permanently to deprive'.

This is often referred to as the 'ransom' principle, and covers not only straightforward ransom cases but any case in which the taker makes his own terms and conditions for the return of the property, whether these are known to the owner or not. Where goods are taken as a joke, with no intention of keeping them in order to place them elsewhere, this will probably not come within s6 (see *R v Cahill* [1993] Crim LR 141).

Secondly, the section appears to draw a distinction between 'property' and 'the thing itself'. This distinction is not explained in the Act, but means that there will be occasions where 'the thing itself' is returned to the owner in such an altered form that the 'borrowing' is treated as 'equivalent to an outright taking' of the property. In debate in Parliament, the Government Minister gave the example of a person who 'borrows' a season ticket and uses it: he is guilty of theft (if dishonest) because he is acting as owner of the ticket; it will make no difference that he intends to return the ticket ('the thing itself') after it has expired. As far as the owner is concerned the property has been deprived of all its virtue. Lord Lane says:

> 'Borrowing is ex hypothesi not something which is done with an intention permanently to deprive. This half of the subsection, we believe, is intended to make it clear that a mere borrowing is never enough to constitute the necessary guilty mind unless the intention is to return the "thing" in such a changed state that it can truly be said that all its goodness or virtue has gone.'

Offences involving deception

The 'deception offences' are now an important group among property offences. The 1968 and 1978 Theft Acts between them contain a total of six main offences. The six have a number of common elements and may conveniently be discussed together. They are:

a Obtaining property by deception: s15 of the 1968 Act;

b Obtaining a pecuniary advantage by deception: s16(2)(b) and (c) of the 1968 Act;

c Obtaining services by deception: s1 of the 1978 Act;

d Securing the remission of a liability by deception: s2(1)(a) of the 1978 Act;

e Inducing a creditor, by deception, to wait for or forgo payment: s2(1)(b) of the 1978 Act;

f Obtaining exemption, by deception, from liability to make a payment: s2(1)(c) of the 1978 Act.

There is a certain amount of overlap between these offences and between the deception offences and theft. If the deception is such that it vitiates any consent the owner may have given to parting with his property, then the property will belong to another at the time of appropriation and both crimes (theft and obtaining by deception) will have taken place.

The borderline between theft and obtaining by deception has always been a grey area. In *R* v *Lawrence* [1982] AC 510, for example, the House of Lords affirmed that there was considerable overlap between the two.

To deal briefly with each of the first five of these in turn:

Obtaining property by deception

Section 15 of the Theft Act 1968 provides:

'a) A person who by any deception dishonestly obtains property belonging to another, with the intention of permanently depriving the other of it, shall on conviction on indictment be liable to imprisonment for a term not exceeding ten years.

b) For purposes of this section a person is to be treated as obtaining property if he obtains ownership, possession or control of it, and "obtain" includes obtaining for another or enabling another to obtain or retain.

c) …

d) For purposes of this section "deception" means any deception (whether deliberate or reckless) by words or conduct as to fact or as to law, including a deception as to the present intentions of the person using the deception or any other person.'

Deception includes words or conduct as to fact or law and includes deception as to the present intentions of any person. Either a deliberate or a reckless deception will suffice.

Words or conduct

A person's conduct may imply something which turns out to be untrue. This is a sufficient deception.

One of the commonest kinds of conduct deceptions occur where the defendant obtains goods by using a cheque or credit card, knowing that authorisation to use it has been withdrawn. There are particular problems in these cases in proving that the deception caused the obtaining. In *MPC v Charles* [1976] 3 WLR 431, the accused used a cheque and cheque card to obtain gaming chips at a gambling club, knowing he had exceeded his authorised limit. He was charged with obtaining a pecuniary advantage by deception (s16(2)(b)).

Referring to the deception involved, the House of Lords said that by writing a cheque backed by a cheque card the accused had impliedly represented that he was authorised to use the card, and his conduct was a sufficient deception.

Note that there is no general liability for omitting to 'undeceive' someone when the defendant has not caused the misapprehension. However, if the defendant by words or conduct has represented something which later becomes untrue, he is under an obligation to correct the misconception.

In *DPP v Ray* [1974] 3 WLR 359, Ray had ordered a meal intending to pay for it and later changed his mind. He left without paying. The House of Lords held that he had deceived the waiter by omitting to tell him that he no longer intended to pay. This situation is now also covered by s3 of the 1978 Act.

In *R v Lightfoot* (1993) 97 Cr App R 24 and *R v Mitchell* [1993] Crim LR 788 the Court of Appeal was concerned with the meaning of the words 'dishonestly' and 'intention permanently to deprive' in the context of s15. In *Lightfoot* the appellant obtained, signed and used a credit card addressed to a work colleague. In *Mitchell* the appellant, a theatre manager, attempted to redirect cheques paid by the theatre to creditors to an account of his own. In each case the appellant's argument was similar: that there was no attempt to permanently deprive the true owner of the cheque chard (*Lightfoot*) or cheques (*Mitchell*). The Court of Appeal held that such arguments must fail; 'dishonesty' had wider connotations. The real nature of the criminality lay in what the card or cheques represented, ie money, and there existed the necessary intention permanently to deprive the owner of this.

Obtaining a pecuniary advantage by deception

The importance of this offence (s16 of the Theft Act 1968) has been greatly reduced by its partial repeal and replacement by the Theft Act 1978. It is an offence to obtain, dishonestly and by deception, any pecuniary advantage. The scope of pecuniary advantage is exhaustively defined in s16(2):

> 'The cases in which a pecuniary advantage within the meaning of this section is to be regarded as obtained for a person are cases where –
>
> a) (repealed)
> b) he is allowed to borrow by way of overdraft, or to take out any policy of insurance or annuity contract, or obtains an improvement of the terms on which he is allowed to do so; or
> c) he is given the opportunity to earn remuneration or greater remuneration in an office or employment, or to win money by betting'

In the case of an insurance policy, the deception may mean that the insurer can declare the policy void. However, it has been held that the accused is still 'allowed to take out a policy of insurance' in these circumstances. More important, it has also been held that a person is 'allowed to borrow by way of overdraft' if he uses his cheque card to run up an overdraft without the bank's prior permission (see *R v Waites* [1982] Crim LR 369); in a case like this, the element of dishonesty may be crucial.

In the situations envisaged by s16(2)(c), although money is property, it may not be possible to bring a charge under s15 because the causal link is too weak. If the money is obtained as a direct result of the work done, or winning the bet, the deception will not be the operative cause. Hence the need for a separate offence. However, in *R v King and Stockwell* [1987] 2 WLR 746 the Court of Appeal upheld a conviction under s15 of attempting to obtain by deception payment for work that the victim agreed should be done. The Court said that it was for the jury to decide whether the deception had been the operative cause. Note that it is clear from *R v Miller* [1992] Crim LR 744 that the deception does not have to be permanent. Miller was an unlicensed taxi driver who enticed foreign tourists into using his 'taxi' by pretending he was licensed and the fare tariff was officially regulated. The Court of Appeal held that the various deceptions were the cause of the tourist using Miller's 'taxi' and it made no difference that at the final moment, faced with extortionate charges, the tourists must have known they had been deceived. The deception was operative at the relevant time.

Obtaining services by deception

Section 1 of the Theft Act 1978 provides:

'a) A person who by any deception dishonestly obtains services from another shall be guilty of an offence.

b) It is an obtaining of services where the other is induced to confer a benefit by doing some act, or causing or permitting some act to be done, on the understanding that the benefit has been or will be paid for.'

By referring to *any* deception, s1 makes it clear that although the services are a benefit which 'has been or will be paid for', and although the deception must be operative (it must *cause* the obtaining), there is no need for these two requirements to be linked.

Evasion of liability by deception

Section 2 of the Theft Act 1978 provides:

'a) Subject to subsection (b) below, where a person by any deception –

i) dishonestly secures the remission of the whole or part of any existing liability to make a payment, whether his own liability or another's; or

ii) with intent to make permanent default in whole or in part on any existing liability to make a payment, or with intent to let another do so, dishonestly induces the creditor or any person claiming payment on behalf of the creditor to wait for payment (whether or not the due date for payment is deferred) or to forgo payment;

iii) dishonestly obtains any exemption from or abatement of liability to make a payment;

he shall be guilty of an offence.

b) For purposes of this section "liability" means legally enforceable liability ...'

There is a close connection, and some overlap, between s2(1)(a), s2(1)(b) and s2(1)(c). In the first two cases, the liability is *existing* at the time of the deception; the deception is used as a way of avoiding a liability which is already in existence. What then is the difference between s2(1)(a) and s2(1)(b)? There are two differences.

Firstly, s2(1)(a) covers cases where the victim/creditor is persuaded to *remit*, or extinguish, the liability. Section 2(1)(b) covers cases where the creditor is induced to *wait for payment*. So s2(1)(a) is designed to deal with cases where, as a result of the deception, the debtor is 'let off' part or all of the debt for which he was liable at the time of the deception. It is not necessarily the case that the agreement to remit (as opposed to the pre-existing liability) is legally binding, and in the absence of consideration it generally would not be, especially in view of the deception. Under s2(1)(b), on the other hand, the debtor is ostensibly merely 'buying time'; the creditor does not agree to extinguish liability altogether.

Secondly, s2(1)(b) has an extra *mens rea* requirement, the intent to make permanent default.

Making off without payment
Section 3 of the Theft Act 1978 provides:

'a) ... a person who, knowing that payment on the spot for any goods supplied or service done is required or expected from him, dishonestly makes off without having paid as required or expected and with intent to avoid payment of the amount due shall be guilty of an offence.

b) For purposes of this section 'payment on the spot' includes payment at the time of collecting goods on which work has been done or in respect of which services has been provided.'

There is no definition of 'service' but presumably the definition of 'services' in s1(2) would be used. By s5(2), the definition of 'goods' given in s34 of the Theft Act 1968 is used:

'34(2)(b) "goods", except in so far as the context otherwise requires, includes money and every other description of property except land, and includes things severed from the land by stealing.'

Section 3(2) applies to circumstances such as garages, dry-cleaners, the repair of tools or machinery. It is implied in s3 that payment on the spot must not *only* be required or expected by the supplier, but actually legally *due from* the accused: a conviction under s3 was quashed on this ground in *Troughton* v *MPC* [1987] Crim LR 138: the accused after a dispute with a taxi-driver, apparently left without paying the fare; it was held that he was under no obligation to pay the driver, because he had not been taken to his destination and the driver was, therefore, in breach of contract. The expectation in the mind of the taxi-driver was not enough.

This interpretation of s3(1) is supported by s3(3) which provides:

'Subsection (a) above shall not apply where the supply of the goods or the doing of the service is contrary to law, or where the service done is such that payment is not legally enforceable.'

The mens rea for s3 includes dishonesty and knowledge that payment must be made and it must coincide in time with the making off.

R v Brooks and Brooks (1982) 76 Cr App R 66 makes it clear that making off actually means leaving the spot where payment is required. Furthermore, the mens rea must include an intention *never* to pay: *R v Allen* [1985] 3 WLR 107 in which the appellant was convicted of making off without payment. He had left a hotel without paying his bill of over £1,000. He claimed that he had genuinely hoped to be able to pay the bill. His conviction was quashed by the Court of Appeal and the House of Lords agreed with the the the decision of the Court of Appeal. It was held that the words 'with intent to avoid payment of the amount due' in s3 of the Theft Act 1978 should be interpreted to mean with intent never to pay.

R v Aziz [1993] Crim LR 708 makes it clear that the 'spot where payment is required' in s3 is clearly a reference to the defendant's state of mind and not to a specific location. It was sufficient that the requirement to pay had come into existence, and that the defendant was shown to have made off from the place where payment would normally be made. In the case of a taxi journey, the place for payment could be inside the cab, or standing outside the cab. The prosecution had to show that the intention to avoid payment existed at the time of the making off.

Robbery

All the offences in this chapter are concerned with property, and with the exception of criminal damage they all have links with theft and are found in the Theft Act 1968.

Robbery can be regarded as an aggravated form of theft. It combines an offence against the person with an offence against property, and is subject to a maximum punishment of life imprisonment, in contrast to a maximum of ten years for theft. Section 8 of the Theft Act 1968 provides:

'1) A person is guilty of robbery if he steals and immediately before or at the time of doing so, and in order to do so, he uses force on any person or puts or seeks to put any person in fear of being then and there subjected to force.
2) A person guilty of robbery, or of an assault with intent to rob, shall on conviction on indictment be liable to imprisonment for life.'

The essence of robbery is theft accompanied by force. The force must be used *in order to steal*, for the purpose of stealing, and this is part of the *mens rea* of the offence. It will normally be possible to infer this purpose from the fact that the use of force assisted the theft. Other ulterior motives, such as revenge or malice, will not by themselves displace the inference.

The timing of the force is important: it must occur at the time of the theft itself or just before it. So it will not be robbery to use force in order to escape after the theft is over (although the separate offences of theft and assault may be charged in such a case). It can be important, then, to know when the theft is complete, and this will depend on the appropriation. The attitude of the courts has been flexible; on the one hand, it has been held that the theft was complete, and robbery committed, on the basis of a momentary appropriation. In *Corcoran* v *Anderton* (1980) 71 Cr App R 104 the accused attacked a woman, pulling at her handbag so that she dropped it. They then ran away, leaving the handbag on the ground, but it was held that the appropriation, the 'assumption of the rights of an owner' (s3 of the Theft Act 1968) had been completed by the act of depriving the victim of physical control. On the other hand in *R* v *Hale* (1978) 68 Cr App R 415 Eveleigh LJ in the Court of Appeal said that although a theft had been committed when the accused seized a jewellery box, 'the act of appropriation does not suddenly cease. It is a continuous act and in this case the theft was still continuing when the accused tied up the victim'.

Burglary

Burglary appears to be a complicated offence because it can be committed in so many different ways. Its essence is trespass in a building (such as a private house or factory) for some criminal purpose. Section 9 of the Theft Act 1968 provides:

'1) A person is guilty of burglary if:

a) he enters any building or part of a building as a trespasser and with intent to commit any such offence as is mentioned in subsection (b) below; or
b) having entered any building or part of a building as a trespasser he steals or attempts to steal anything in the building or that part of it or inflicts or attempts to inflict on any person therein any grievous bodily harm.

2) The offences referred to in subsection (1)(a) above are offences of stealing anything in the building or part of a building in question, of inflicting on any person therein any grievous bodily harm or raping any woman therein, and of doing unlawful damage to the building or anything therein.'

The different types of burglary

The old law as contained in ss24–27 of the Larceny Act 1916 was extremely complex, with a number of different offences, including housebreaking (by day and by night) as well as burglary itself. The new offence of burglary comprises these offences (and others beside) in a more simplified form. The two main types of burglary are found in s9(1)(a) and s9(1)(b) of the Theft Act 1968.

Section 9(1)(a) provides that a person is guilty of burglary if:

'he enters any building or part of a building as a trespasser and with intent to commit any such offence as is mentioned in subsection (2) below.'

while in s9(1)(b) a person is guilty of burglary if:

'having entered any building or part of a building as a trespasser, he steals or attempts to steal anything in the building or inflicts or attempts to inflict on any person therein any grievous bodily harm'.

Thus the actus reus and mens rea in each case is different.

In s9(1)(a) the actus reus is essentially entry in to the building as a trespasser, the mens rea consisting of an intention formulated before or at the time of entry to commit one or more of the proscribed offences in s9(2). The offence is complete the moment the offender enters the building with the necessary intent, regardless of whether any subsequent offence is committed: *R v Walkington* [1979] 1 WLR 1169. The mens rea, the knowledge of being a trespasser and guilty intent must necessarily be present at time of entry; it cannot be presumed from later events: *R v Collins* [1972] 3 WLR 243.

Section 9(1)(b), however, requires a different actus reus and mens rea. Although the accused will of course be a trespasser on entry, it is enough if he recognises this fact after entry; he need not be aware of it at the time. The intention to commit some crime will not of course need to be present from the time of entry.

Finally, note that there is a third type of burglary – known as aggravated burglary. Created by s10 of the 1968 Theft Act, it applies equally to both s9(1)(a) and s9(1)(b) forms of burglary. To have a 'firearm, imitation firearm, weapon of offence or explosives' renders the accused liable to prosecution for aggravated burglary, an offence carrying the penalty of life-imprisonment. One of the most important aspects is the exact time at which the accused has with him such a weapon. The difference in actus reus is clear; in a s9(1)(a) burglary, the offender must have the weapon in his possession at the time of entry; for s9(1)(b) burglary at the time the further offence is committed. See for example *R v Francis* [1982] Crim LR 363 in which a conviction for aggravated burglary under s10 was quashed. Having prosecuted under s9(1)(b) the Crown failed to prove the offenders had weapons (in fact sticks) with them at the time when they stole from a house. They had in fact put their sticks down earlier as they explored the house.

Handling

Section 22 of the 1968 Act provides that a person is guilty of handling stolen goods if, knowing or believing them to be stolen, and acting other than in the course of stealing, he dishonestly does one of the following:

a Receives the goods.

b Arranges to receive them.

c Undertakes their detention, removal, disposal or realisation by or for the benefit of another.

d Arrange to undertake the above.

e Assists in their detention, removal, disposal or realisation, etc.

f Arranges to assist in the above.

A person receiving stolen goods may be liable even if he never personally sees or physically handles the goods. He does not have to receive them for the benefit of another, although he may do so. To receive goods which have been stolen will also constitute handling.

'Undertaking' implies an act by the defendant carrying out any of the above activities, rather than just tacit agreement or approval. The involvement will be more positive, eg by transporting goods or selling them. Any such acts must be by or for the benefit of another, normally the thief or another handler. The goods must actually be stolen by the time the arrangements are made for the offence of handling to be committed. The arranging must be by or for the benefit of another party.

'Assisting' implies co-operating with others in carrying out any of the above activities. Verbal assistance will suffice. In *R v Kanwar* [1982] 1 WLR 845 Kanwar tried to persuade the police that property which she knew to be stolen and retained by her husband, was in fact hers, and that her husband was retaining the property at her request. The Court of Appeal held this could constitute assisting in their retention by or for the benefit of another.

Blackmail

'Blackmail' was the name commonly given to a group of offences formerly contained in ss29–31 of the Larceny Act 1916. That term was officially adopted for the first time in s21(1) of the 1968 Act which provides:

'A person is guilty of blackmail if, with a view to gain for himself or another, or with intent to cause loss to another, he makes any unwarranted demand with menaces, and for this purpose a demand with menaces is unwarranted unless the person making it does so in the belief: a) that he has reasonable grounds for making the demand, and b) that the use of the menaces is a proper means of reinforcing the demand'.

The main elements of blackmail can be summarised as follows:

The actus reus consists of a demand with menaces. The demand can be any act or omission and can be made in any way, eg orally, in writing, expressly or impliedly. Whether an utterance amounts to a 'demand' seems to depend on whether an ordinary literate person would so describe it: see *Treacy v DPP* [1971] AC 537. There may be a 'demand' even when the wording is mocking, obsequious or couched as a begging letter or a polite request; provided the addition of menaces makes it clear that a threat is being made.

'Menaces' was used in s21(1), instead of threats, because the drafters claimed it was considered a stronger word than threats. 'Menaces' is said to be easily understood by any jury as an ordinary word in the English language; little judicial guidance has been forthcoming therefore to define exactly the meaning of the word in detail. The one limitation is that no threat will be sufficient to be a 'menace' within the meaning of s21 unless it is 'of such a nature and extent that the mind of an ordinary person of normal stability and courage might be influenced or made apprehensive so as to accede unwillingly to the demand': *R v Clear* [1968] 1 QB 68.

It should be noted (see *R v Garwood* [1987] 1 WLR 319) that the question of whether threats amount to 'menaces' is a subjective one, depending *not* on the state of mind of the victim, but on the facts known to the accused.

The mens rea of blackmail consists of a number of elements operating in combination:

a an intent to make a demand with menaces,

b a view to gain for himself or another *or* intent to cause loss, and c *either* no belief that he has reasonable grounds to make the demand *or* no belief that the use of the menaces is a proper means of reinforcing the demand.

To look at these elements a little more closely:

With a view to gain or intent to cause loss

Gain and loss are to be construed in terms of money or property only. Gain includes keeping what was already in the accused's possession and loss includes not getting something which the victim (or another) might otherwise gain.

Thus, the definition limits the offence to the protection of economic interests. Without this limitation the scope of s21 would be enormously wide.

Belief in a right to the gain

The test as to whether a demand is unwarranted is a subjective one. The defendant must believe both that he had reasonable grounds for making the demand and that also the methods he used to make the demands were proper. Section 21 does not use the word 'dishonestly' at any point. Thus the defence of a claim of right, discussed earlier (23.3) will not apply. The defendant might in fact have a claim of right to the money/property in question, but still commit the offence by virtue of knowing that the means by which he made his demand were improper.

In *R v Harvey* (1981) 72 Cr App R 139 'proper' was defined to exclude anything which a defendant knows to be unlawful. It is not open to the accused to argue that he felt, for example, morally justified in using improper means to obtain money from a third party who had behaved improperly towards him.

Criminal damage

The offences relating to the destruction of and damage to property are found in the Criminal Damage Act 1971. The most important offences are found in s1 of the Act which provides:

'1) A person who without lawful excuse destroys or damages any property belonging to another intending to destroy or damage, any such property, or being reckless as to whether any such property would be destroyed or damaged shall be guilty of an offence.

2) A person who, without lawful excuse destroys or damages any property, whether belonging to himself or another

a) intending to destroy or damage any property, or being reckless as to whether any property would be destroyed or damaged, and

b) intending by the destruction ... to endanger life of another, or being reckless ...

3) An offence committed under this section by destroying or damaging property by fire shall be charged as arson.'

Thus the actus reus consists of destroying or damaging property belonging to another, the necessary mens rea for criminal damage is intention or *Caldwell* type recklessness (see chapter 22).

'Property' is defined as tangible property, including land, and therefore differs from the concept of 'property' under the theft Acts. The destruction or damage need not be irreversible or irreparable, but it must be more than merely nominal. Although the offences created under s1 of the Act do not have the same connotation of dishonesty as offences under the Theft Acts, s5(2) of the Act creates a similar defence of honest belief.

Two recent cases on criminal damage illustrate the offence more clearly. In *R* v *Parker* [1993] Crim LR 856, the appellant deliberately started a fire in a council house where he was living as a lodger. He wanted to assist his landlady in her desire to be rehoused by the local authority. The house in question was semi-detached. The smoke from the fire spread to the adjoining house, but its occupants escaped any significant harm. The appellant was convicted of aggravated criminal damage contrary to s1(2) of the Criminal Damage Act 1971, and appealed on the ground that no life had actually been endangered. It was held that the appeal would be dismissed. Provided the actus reus of criminal damage was made out, the aggravated offence simply required proof of the relevant mens rea, in this case recklessness as to whether life would be endangered, regardless of whether this was actually the case.

In *R* v *Blake* [1993] Crim LR 586, the question of belief as a lawful excuse as a defence was raised. The appellant had participated in a demonstration, in the vicinity of the Houses of Parliament, against the involvement of Allied troops in the Gulf War. He was arrested after writing a biblical quotation on a pillar. The appellant contended that he had a lawful excuse for the criminal damage to the pillar, either because he had the consent of God as the owner of the property (s5(2)(a)), or because he had acted to protect other property (s5(2)(b)). The appellant was convicted of criminal damage and appealed. The appeal was dismissed. Belief that God was the person entitled to consent to the damage would not form the basis of a valid defence, no matter how genuine that belief was. Even if the appellant genuinely believed that property in the Gulf states could be protected by his protest, it was for the court, applying an objective test, to determine whether or not his action did, or could, protect property as he had contended. There was no sufficiently immediate threat to the appellant or others to found a more general defence of duress of circumstances.

Sanctions in criminal law | 24

Functions of the criminal law and the philosophy of sentencing

In order to understand the philosophy of sentencing it is important to appreciate what the criminal law seeks to achieve. We have examined this subject under the functions of law earlier, however, in this part it is proposed to refer specifically to the purposes of the criminal law.

Smith and Hogan – one of the leading academic student texts on criminal law – prefer the aims as laid out in The American Law Institute's *Model Penal Code* which provides that the criminal law be used:

a to forbid and prevent conduct that unjustifiably and inexcusably inflicts or threatens substantial harm to individual or public interests;

b to subject to public control persons whose conduct indicates that they are disposed to commit crimes;

c to safeguard conduct that is without fault from condemnation as criminal;

d to give fair warning of the nature of the conduct declared to be an offence;

e to differentiate on reasonable grounds between serious and minor offences.

The extent to which these aims are mirrored and achieved in English criminal law is a subject of much debate.

It would however be worth noting the views of the *Wolfenden Committee* that looked at the legality of homosexual relations and adopted an approach reminiscent of *John Stuart Mill*'s 'Harm Principle' when they found that the function of the criminal law was:

a to preserve public order, morals and decency;

b to protect citizens from what is offensive or injurious;

c to provide sufficient safeguard against exploitation of others, especially those who are vulnerable.

Wolfenden was adamant that it was not the criminal law's business to intervene in the private lives of citizens or to seek to enforce any pattern of behaviour further than is strictly necessary to effect the above mentioned functions.

Aims of sentencing

With regard to sentencing policy, views seem to diverge along largely political grounds. Sentencing is however important since most accused actually plead guilty and thus the court is turned into a sentencing tribunal rather than a forum for trial of either questions of fact or law. Sentencing remains the sole prerogative of the judge or magistrate. The factors that they take into account in arriving at their sentence have been and are the subject of much speculation, criticism and research.

It is possible to identify five principles of sentencing:

a retribution;

b rehabilitation;

c deterrence;

d justice;

e protection of society.

Retribution

The modern idea of retribution is that the sentence should fit the crime. Through the operation of a 'tariff system' the sentence as punishment would be proportionate to the moral blameworthiness and the seriousness of the offence. Courts have been very reluctant to accept the idea of a tariff system operating as to determination of sentence.

Nonetheless, the idea of retribution in sentencing is the one that has widest public acceptance. Closely linked with this idea is that sentencing performs a useful function in society in that it reinforces collective norms with society emphasising conduct considered impermissible.

Smith and Hogan take the view that retribution as a factor in sentencing is 'a relic of barbarism'. Indeed the Court of Appeal has indicated that it will intervene if there is a disproportion between the sentence and moral guilt.

Rehabilitation

This view suggests that crime is committed because the offender has somehow slipped from societal morals and that all that is required is to reinforce societal values internally to the offender and he will become a valuable contributing member of that society. Criminologists doubt this. It is the case however that offenders are members of society and that if sentenced to a custodial term they will have to return to society upon release.

However attractive the notion of rehabilitation is, the state of knowledge as to how best to achieve these goals is very limited. Where resources are finite and scarce, the rehabilitation of offenders inevitably assumes a low priority.

Rehabilitation may be wholly inappropriate for lesser crimes. A parking violation is a crime. What rehabilitative measures could one suggest?

Where an offender shows remorse, rehabilitation will have a secondary function to perform.

If prisons are indeed a university of crime it would seem to have the opposite effect on an offender to send him to prison where he can learn the more subtle aspects of crime.

Deterrence

There are two aspects to deterrence as a factor in sentencing:

Individual deterrence

There is considerable doubt as to the effectiveness of sentencing as a deterrent. The point made by Lord Parker LCJ that it is not the severity of sentence but the certainty of detection that acts as a deterrent to crime is a most incisive observation.

Within this area of individual deterrence there are some points to note:

The threat of punishment will not be effective with regard to crimes committed impulsively. This would include many crimes of violence.

Deterrence is likely to be more effective with certain people and less effective on others. To take this into account would be extremely difficult when considering sentencing.

The use of individual deterrence as the sole criterion for determining sentence is open to objection on moral grounds. It could be used as a justification for barbaric sentences unbecoming to a civilised society.

General deterrence

This acts as a warning to the rest of society not to engage in that activity (crime) otherwise a similar evil (sentence) will be visited upon them.

a It can be observed that for this to be effective there must be wide publicity of the sentence. It would be necessary for the general public to be aware of the measures that would be taken against those who violate a particular law.

b Secondly, there must be general public sympathy for the law and the way it is being administered. If this is absent no amount of severe sentencing would deter.

Having noted these important limitations to the use of a sentence as a general deterrent it can be further observed that a sentence designed for general deterrence would be unfair to the offender in that he was being made an example and that his sentence would not reflect his own moral blameworthiness but would mirror policy matters extraneous to his particular circumstances. This would conflict with the conception that sentencing conforms to a principle of justice, whereby the sentence fits the crime and like cases are treated in like manner.

Justice

An important consideration in determining appropriate sentence is that of justice. Supposedly at the heart of our legal system, the 'Lady of Justice' stands over our courts sword in hand but with balanced scales. Those balanced scales mean that all like cases be treated in a like manner. However, there seldom are any like cases, as the variety of circumstances is infinite.

Another manifestation would be the idea that wrongdoers should make reparation for their wrong to their victim. It is believed by some that this would lead to a reform of the offender. The scheme is however severely limited. It seems nonsensical to place a person who has assaulted his victim in that victim's home decorating their kitchen as a form of reparation. In other circumstances the offender may not be in a position to make material reparation and in some cases there may not be a clearly identifiable 'victim'.

Protection of society

Obviously this theory relates only to those sentenced for violent or anti social crimes. It would be important not to confuse protection of society with public revulsion at certain crimes and the exemplary sentences that are passed on those caught eg the Great Train Robbers.

Society has indeed a right to protect itself from persistent and dangerous offenders and this was reflected in the case of *DPP* v *Ottewell* [1968] 3 All ER 153 where the accused having been found guilty on two counts of assault occasioning actual bodily harm was sentenced to consecutive terms in circumstances where others were usually sentenced to concurrent terms. The House of Lords upheld the extended sentence as it was designed to protect the public from a persistent offender and not as a punishment for previous offences.

The courts will effect this aim by removing the offender from society for an extended period. One controversial area in which such sentences are used is with regard to espionage. This seems more to reflect retribution than protection of the public. If the person was a spy all the secrets he has passed on are already in the hands of a foreign power. Hilbery J in *R* v *Blake* [1962] 2 QB 377 said that the imposition of a forty two year prison sentence on the spy Blake was to be punitive, to deter others and as a safeguard to the country.

It is submitted that a better case could be made out for the imposition of such sentences on gangland crime bosses or other leaders of organised violent crime groups.

Range of available sentences

Criteria for sentencing

The Criminal Justice Act (CJA) 1991, s1(2) repeals s20 Powers of Criminal Courts Act 1973, and so now Magistrates and Crown Courts must only impose a custodial sentence where the court is of the opinion that either:

a the offence, or combination of the offence and one other offence associated with it, was so serious that only such a sentence can be justified; or

b where the offence is a violent or sexual offence, and that only such a sentence would be adequate to protect the public from serious harm from offender.

A 'sexual' offence means offences under the Sexual Offences Act 1956, Indecency with Children Act 1960, and the Protection of Children Act 1978.

Before the 1991 Act, 'so serious' was described in *R v Bradbourn* (1985) 7 Cr App R(S) 180 as the kind of offence which, when committed, would make right thinking members of the public, knowing all the facts of the case, feel that justice had not been done without a custodial sentence.

Section 2 of the CJA 1991:

'A custodial sentence shall be:

a) for such term as in the opinion of the court is commensurate with the seriousness of the offence, or the combination of the offence with other offences associated with it; or
b) where the offence is a violent or sexual offence, for such longer term as in the opinion of the court is necessary to protect the public from serious harm from the offender.'

'Associated offences' mean offences the defendant was convicted of in the same proceedings, where sentenced for two offences at the same time, or where one offence is taken into consideration at the time of sentencing of the other – s31(2).

Under s2, part (b) seems to allow for deterrence as a reason for a longer sentence, but not part (a). It is debatable whether part (a) allows the judge to consider reparation, and reform of the offender, as well as the need to give him his just deserts.

The major problem comes with s29 of the 1991 Act.

Section 29(1) states:

'An offence shall not be regarded as more serious for the purposes of any provision of the 1991 Act, by reason of any previous convictions of the offender, or any failure of his to respond to previous sentences.'

But this is subject to subs (2):

'Where any aggravating factors of an offence are disclosed by the circumstances of other offences committed by the offender, nothing in the Act shall prevent the court from taking those factors into account for the purpose of forming an opinion as to the seriousness of the offence.'

Subsection (2) seems to be an exception to (1), but there is no help from the White Paper. Perhaps it is meant to cover, as an example, a defendant who previously used a gun which he claimed went off accidentally during a rape, yet used a gun again this time; or a perpetrator of indecent assault, who appears to be pursuing one particular family. We need to wait for case law!

Pre-sentence reports – section 3

To consider if s1 applies to a particular defendant, the court must obtain and consider a pre-sentence report, unless the offence, or any offence associated with it, is triable only on indictment. Section 3(3)(a) provides that in addition to obtaining a pre-sentence report, the court shall 'take into account all such information about the circumstances of the offence (including any aggravating or mitigating factors) as is available to it'. The court must also obtain a pre-sentence report to decide on the *length* of custodial sentence, if one is given.

Sections 1, 2, 3, 4 and 5 apply with convictions before commencement of CJA 1991, as long as not sentenced yet.

Suspended sentences

Section 5 of the 1991 Act abolishes s47 Criminal Law Act 1977, ie partly served, partly suspended sentences. Section 5 also amends s22 Powers of Criminal Courts Act 1973 (PCCA 1973), and says the courts should not use a suspended sentence unless the case is one in which a sentence of imprisonment would have been appropriate, even without the power to suspend the sentence, *and* that the exercise of that power can be justified by the exceptional circumstances of the case.

Also now a fine or compensation order can be added to the suspended sentence – s22(2)(A) (as amended).

As for those over 21, a suspended sentence is a custodial sentence, and so ss1–3 of the Act apply.

Community sentences – ie non-custodial penalties

Section 6(1) – the court cannot pass a custodial sentence unless it is of the opinion that the offence, or combination of the offence and one other associated with it, is 'serious enough to warrant such a sentence'. The type of community sentence chosen must be the one 'most suitable for the offender'.

Probation orders

Section 8 of the 1991 Act repeals s2 of PCCA 1973, and adds a new s2 to it. The minimum age is reduced from 17 to 16. It can be combined with the new curfew orders and a compensation order. The court must be sure, before handing out a probation order, that supervision of the offender is desirable in the interests of:

a securing rehabilitation of the offender; or

b protecting the public from harm from him, or preventing the commission by him of further offences.

The minimum period is still six months, and the maximum is still three years.

c Section 9 – Conditions attached to probation orders. Section 9 amends s3 of the PCCA 1973. This allows the court to attach such conditions to the probation order it thinks 'desirable', but they must fall in with the two stated objectives of probation orders.

Section 10 – Community Service Orders

These can now be combined with other forms of sentence. Also, the maximum number of hours which may be imposed on a 16 year old is increased from 120 to 240 hours.

Section 11 – Combination orders

These are a new idea, and consist of a mixture of a probation order and a community service order. The probation part must be for not less than 12 months, and not more than three years, and the community service must be for not less than 40 hours and not more than 100 hours.

The offender must be 16 years of age or older, and have been convicted of an offence punishable with imprisonment, and the courts must be satisfied it is necessary in the same way as probation orders.

Section 12 – Curfew orders

These are a new idea, for those of 16 years or older. They can specify different places or periods of curfew, but it cannot last more than six months in total. They cannot involve curfew periods of less than two hours' duration, or more than 12 hours in any one day. The offender must consent to the order, and someone must be named to monitor the offender's whereabouts. Alternatively s13 allows for electronic monitoring, which at the moment is only being used on an experimental basis around the country.

Community orders relating to youths

Supervision Orders – s68 allowed now for those up to age 17, so the courts can decide between this order and a probation order with 16 and 17 year olds.

Attendance Centre Orders – s67 – Section 17(3) of the Criminal Justice Act 1982 is abolished (which prevented the passing of an attendance centre order on an offender with a previous custodial sentence.) The maximum number of hours for a 16 year old is raised to 36 to be in line with 17 year olds.

Compensation orders

For adults or youths – the maximum amount which can be ordered by the Magistrates Court in respect of each offence is increased from £2,000 to £5,000 – s17(3)(a) CJA 1991.

Procedural changes

Committals for sentence

Section 25 CJA 1991 amends s38 of the Magistrates' Courts Act 1980. The offender must now be not less than 18 years old, and the reasons for committal have been changed. The reasons now being that the court is of the opinion:

a that the offence or combination of the offences and other offences associated with it was so serious that greater punishment should be inflicted for the offence than the court has the power to impose; or

b in the case of a violent or sexual offence committed by a person not less than 21 years old, that a sentence of imprisonment for a term *longer* than the court has the power to impose is necessary to protect the public from serious harm from him.

It used to be the case that the court could commit in the light of the defendant's 'character and antecedents'.

Parole, remission and early release

Section 33 – there is abolition of the distinction between remission and parole, and in its place, a single concept of early release.

Early release is to be automatic after 50 per cent of the sentence for short-term prisoners (ie those sentenced to four years or less); but discretionary for long-term prisoners (four years or more).

When two-thirds of the sentence has gone, early release is automatic for all types of prisoners.

Early release is always given on licence (except with those serving less than 12 months originally) and this licence runs from the time of release up to the three-quarters point of the sentence.

What is the effect of being on licence? The prisoner is under a liability to serve the remaining part of the sentence in prison if convicted of a further imprisonable offence whilst on licence.

These rules are subject to s36(1) which says the Secretary of State may *at any time* release *any type* of prisoner on licence if he is satisfied that exceptional circumstances exist which justify that prisoner's release on compassionate grounds.

What of prisoners serving life? For discretionary lifers, s34 applies – he or she is given the right to have his or her case referred to the Parole Board (as it will still be called) once the part of his sentence specified by his sentencing court has expired.

As for mandatory lifers, s35(2) applies – the Secretary of State, the Parole Board and the Lord Chief Justice must all agree to his release on licence.

All these provisions are subject to a special rule for sexual offenders, under s44. Where the whole or part of his sentence was imposed for a 'sexual' offence, and the sentencing court so specifies, the offender will, after release on licence, be required to serve out the *full* term of his sentence, under supervision in the community, instead of the licence stopping at the three-quarters mark as with other prisoners.

Sentencing policy

Apart from offences which have a 'fixed sentence', such as life imprisonment for murder, the sentence passed is within the discretion of the judge or magistrates.

For some offences there are guidelines which set down a range of suitable sentences. If 'tariffs' are set down, a judge must exercise his discretion within the tariff. For example, if a defendant is convicted of rape, the maximum sentence he will face is life imprisonment. However, if the rape was committed by a man without violence against a woman with whom he was already familiar the tariff sentence would be about 2 years imprisonment. If the defendant raped a woman he did not know and violently, the tariff sentence will be up to 8 years.

The government, in its White Paper, *Crime, Justice and Protecting the Public*

(February 1990), signalled a shift in policy aimed at reducing the present prison population (around 50,000) and a movement towards community-based punishment.

Whilst the proposals comprised a greater element of rehabilitation, they were not designed to be a 'soft option'.

Greater availability has been made to magistrates and judges of community service and probation orders – aimed largely at non-violent offenders. Electronic 'tagging', at present in its experimental stage, will be increased in use – though it has encountered teething problems.

For those serving prison sentences, especially long terms of imprisonment, however, the changes signalled by the White Paper (and incorporated into the Criminal Justice Act 1991) will ring harsh. The old concept of parole after one third of the sentence has been served ('remission for good conduct') will not take effect. Instead there will be early release only after one half of the sentence has been served.

Fines will be more closely related to the offenders 'ability to pay' – many minor offenders are at present sent to jail for failing to pay fines.

Parents will be made more 'responsible', for their children's crimes – they may be forced to attend the youth courts and to pay fines in respect of their children's actions.

Note that many of the proposals outlined above in the White Paper *Crime, Justice and Protecting the Public* have been incorporated into the Criminal Justice Act 1991. The Act received the Royal Assent in July 1991. A small number of its provisions came into force during October 1991, but those dealing with sentencing and the early release of prisoners were not implemented until October 1992. The Act gives legislative force to the Government's view that just desserts should be the first aim of sentencing.

In September 1991 the Home Office published *Custody, Care and Justice: The Way Ahead for the Prison Service in England and Wales* (Cm 1647). The paper was a response to the *Woolf* report and to the report of Her Majesty's Inspector on suicides and self-mutilation in custody. It sets out a course for future developments in the prison service to the end of the century and beyond.

The paper identifies the Government's key priorities as being to: improve necessary security conditions; improve cooperation with other agencies; increase delegation of responsibility and accountability within the service; improve the quality of work for staff; recognise the status and particular requirements of unconvicted prisoners; provide a code of standards for activities and conditions in prisons; improve relationships with prisoners, including the provision of a statement of facilities and sentence planning for each prisoner; provide access to sanitation for all prisoners at all times; end overcrowding; divide larger wings into more manageable units wherever possible; and develop community prisons serving prisoners within given areas.

The remainder of the paper contains both firm proposals for action and suggestions for discussion. It is encouraging that the Home Office has recognised the need to develop a humane system of imprisonment, but it comes as no surprise that the implementation period extends into the next century.

Finally, groups such as Justice, the parliamentary law-reform group and the Labour Party have all called for a *'Sentencing Commission'* to be set up with the aim of standardising sentences meted out by the courts. This has been firmly opposed by the judges, under the auspices of Lord Lane, Lord Chief Justice, as an attack upon the independence of the judiciary. Sentencing 'guidelines' will thus remain, for the time being, the preserve of the Court of Appeal – of especial interest in the context of more serious crimes involving sex and violence.

Civil court proceedings | 25

Introduction

If one party sues another for some breach of civil law then proceedings will vary according to the particular area of civil law concerned. Obviously, in this book we are most concerned with breaches of contract, or a civil action following the commission of a tort: an accident at work or while driving. However, it should be remembered that there are many other forms of civil action which may be pursued through the courts, perhaps involving property law, matrimonial causes or company law and so on.

In a civil case the two parties are plaintiff and defendant (appellant and respondent) in appeals. The problems faced by litigants are similar regardless of the cause of action, and the remedy sought is (nearly always) monetary compensation. It should be remembered, though, that civil claims may be for widely varying amounts; some for millions of pounds (major industrial cases, shipping, aircraft and so on) and some for literally a few pounds only (small claims court cases).

The main form of action in The High Court and County Courts is what is known as adversarial. An adversarial mode of trial is based on the principle that each side is responsible for preparing its own case and collecting evidence and that having done so they will appear in court, not only to present *their* argument, but also to attack the arguments put forward by the opposition. The role of the judge is limited to that of referee, deciding in favour of whichever side presents the most convincing (but not necessarily the true) version of events. *Dugdale et al*, in *A-level Law* point out that under the adversarial method, the object of a hearing is not the discovery of the truth, but the promotion of a fair trial, in open court, before an independent judge. The judge's decision is made, on 'the balance of probabilities'.

The adversarial method is, however, time-consuming and consequently expensive. For this reason the adversarial mode of settling disputes has been modified in certain types of court, eg the small claims court. Most civil actions are brought in the county courts, though the more important may be heard in the High Court. As seen earlier (chapter 16) the 'importance' of a particular case is assessed primarily according to the amount of money involved.

Preliminary considerations

A prospective litigant considering whether or not to proceed needs to take a number of factors into consideration. In certain instances, although he may have an excellent cause of action and every chance of success in pursuing his claim, he may realise that for other reasons he would be well advised not to continue.

Such factors might include:

Financial status of the other party

There is little point in successfully obtaining redress from the court, if the defendant is unable to pay the award of damages made against him.

Costs

The financial status of the other party is obviously relevant here as well. Costs may very well be more than the amount of damages awarded.

However, it should also be borne in mind that a party who loses may have to pay not only his own costs but also those of his opponent; if a plaintiff has only a borderline chance of success in pursuing his claim, it may be worth thinking over, very carefully, what the cost might be if he does lose. Finally, note that a winning party may have any unreasonably high costs disallowed by the taxing-master (an official responsible for scrutinising legal costs) and may have to pay them himself. Thus even if a party wins, if the damages he obtains are minimal and some of his claims for costs disallowed, he may be severely out of pocket.

Time factor

A plaintiff may find that he has to wait a considerable time for a remedy, especially where a case goes to appeal. Unless the damages sought are substantial, it might not be worthwhile in time and effort expended, for the ordinary person claiming only a few thousand (or hundred) pounds.

Publicity

One of the reasons why arbitration has become so popular, is that it is possible to arrange an arbitration hearing in private. Similarly some parties may prefer to drop a case (or settle out of court in the case of a defendant) rather than pursue a cause of action which will result in unwelcome publicity.

Choice of defendants

A common situation, especially in personal injury cases, is that the plaintiff will have a choice: whether to sue the defendant who is an employee; or his employers who are vicariously liable for his actions. The logical thing is of course to sue the employers, who are presumably the richer party, and more likely to be able to pay up without difficulty. In other cases there may simply be more than one possible defendant – all of apparently equal status. There is no rule that says the plaintiff must sue them all, he can if he wishes; but he may single out one only. (In such cases the defendant may have a right to sue the others involved to recover damages/costs from them.) In singling out one defendant, a primary consideration will presumably be the financial status of the person(s) involved.

Legal aid

Legal aid is in theory available for most civil actions in an ordinary law court. However, because the criteria for eligibility are constantly being made more stringent the financial limits are now so low that the ordinary person will find that for routine personal injuries or a breach of contract case, the amount of aid forthcoming will be only minimal. It should be noted also, that as well as the financial criteria by which applicants are assessed; some local legal aid committees faced with too many applicants chasing too little money, operate a system whereby the applicant's chances of success are gauged. Thus sometimes an applicant with a 'cast-iron' case will obtain legal aid; while a 'borderline' case will not. (For further details on legal aid see chapter 20, above.)

Apart from legal aid to assist in the actual proceedings themselves, it may also be possible to get advice, either free or for a minimal sum, on preliminary matters.

Procedure before trial

Evidence

Each side is responsible for collecting its own evidence. Obviously the form evidence takes will vary according to the type of dispute involved. In a breach of contract action for example, the evidence might include a copy of the contract itself, paperwork showing previous dealings between the parties, photographs of, or the actual goods themselves, in the case of defects in the goods. In a personal accident case, say a motoring accident, the evidence might include police and insurance reports, photographs, medical reports, witnesses of the event and so on. Only very rarely is the plaintiff's word alone likely to be sufficient. Witnesses tend to present problems, because although a witness *may* be subpoena'd to attend a trial he cannot be forced to give a written statement beforehand. It should be noted as well that while there are statutory provisions to enable the plaintiff to obtain certain evidence, such evidence can only be obtained when the plaintiff has specifically alleged some cause of action. The plaintiff cannot demand evidence and trawl through it to find some cause of action. 'Fishing expeditions' as they are sometimes called are not permitted. Thus if a motorist is injured and specifically alleges that this is because his car was fitted with the wrong tyres at the last service at the garage, he could demand to see servicing records to establish this. However if he is not sure of the reason why his car swerved off the road he could not demand the servicing records simply to go through them looking for a likely cause of action.

Settling out of court

The majority of cases, especially in contract and tort, are settled before they ever go before the courts. Even those cases that do go to court, many are settled 'behind the scenes', while the case is still proceeding. Very few cases actually get to a point where the judgment is given.

It is the preliminary duty of any solicitor consulted, therefore, to attempt to settle the dispute before it goes further. Usually the first step is to write to to the opposing party (or, more usually, his solicitor). Often this initial communication is followed by further correspondence and, perhaps, meetings between the two sides. During these negotiations, one or both sides may make attempts to reconcile the dispute by offering concessions. The main problem is that if the preliminary efforts at settlement fail, then any such concessions might be seized on and used in court by the opposition. Thus, an admission by a workman that he may have been in part to blame for his accident, in return for an admission by his employers that they may be said to be partly to blame in not fencing machinery adequately, could be dangerous statements if the case does eventually go to court. For this reason concessional statements will usually be headed 'without prejudice' and as such, cannot be produced in evidence in court. They are said to be privileged documents.

Delay

In their efforts to reach a settlement, the parties involved in the dispute should not delay too long. Not only must a plaintiff take into account the limitation periods for the action which he is concerned to pursue, but also must take into consideration the fact that undue delay may result in the court dismissing the case. See the doctrine of laches and the equitable doctrine that 'delay defeats equity'. Thus although there is no formal time limit by which settlement out of court should be achieved, no negotiations should be so protracted that the chance of a successful court action is defeated.

Commencement of proceedings

Proceedings may vary in detail, depending on which court is chosen. Claims of up to £50,000 (which are the majority) will start in the County Court and amounts of over that in the High Court. Since s1 of Courts and Legal Services Act 1990 gave the Lord Chancellor the power to make orders varying these rules, it is anticipated that many more cases will be commenced in the County Court, even when the amounts involved are greater than the previous watershed of £50,000.

Although technically procedure is started in the County Court by taking out a summons, and in the High Court by taking out a writ, the two processes are very similar. The writ/summons notifies the defendant in general terms as to the nature of the claim and orders him to submit to the jurisdiction of the court.

On or with the writ/summons will appear a 'statement of claim' which should clearly and briefly explain what facts the plaintiff alleges and what remedy he seeks. Within 14 days of service of the writ/summons the defendant must acknowledge that he has been served with the document in question and if he does not do so judgment may be sometimes be awarded against him, there and then, in default. After acknowledgement he has a further 14 days during which to submit either a written defence and/or a counterclaim. If he fails to respond, the plaintiff can move to have judgment awarded against him.

Proceedings at this stage are known as interlocutory proceedings – they primarily consist of an exchange (assuming the defendant has decided to respond) of pleadings.

The main pleadings may be:

a   *statement of claim* (known as particulars of claim in County Courts) issued by plaintiff.

b   defence which is the defendants response to the statement of claim.

Note: in very simple cases these may be the only two pleadings. In more complex cases there may also be:

c   *counterclaim or reply* – defendants response to certain allegations of the plaintiff, making claims against the plaintiff in return.

d   requests for further and better particulars – may be served by either side. As the name would indicate these are requests for clarification of points arising in the pleadings.

These interlocutory proceedings may take a considerable time to complete. At close of proceedings one or both sides may ask for a:

e   *discovery of documents* to compel documents relevant to the case to be produced for scrutiny.

Either party may ask for:

f   *interrogatories* to be delivered; these are written questions on details arising from the earlier pleadings. They must be answered on oath.

Finally the plaintiff must, when all the foregoing is completed, take out a:

g   *summons for directions* in which any outstanding matters must be settled. For example a date and venue will be fixed and it may be decided which witnesses must attend in person and which may give evidence by sworn affidavits. The number of expert witnesses might be limited. If the case is unusual, eg a defamation case, it might be ordered to be heard by a jury. A summons for direction is a means of settling as many routine points as possible before the actual hearing.

The civil trial

Up to now, most of the work will have been done by the solicitors for each party. Most civil cases involve representation by barristers in the court itself, but more and more, since the Courts and Legal Services Act, solicitors have a right of audience in an increasing number of cases.

The burden of proof generally rests on the plaintiff, and in civil cases the burden of proof is lighter than in criminal cases; being to prove the plaintiff's case on a balance of probabilities.

The plaintiff's counsel will begin the civil trial, by outlining the main facts of the case and indicating what evidence he intends to produce to prove these facts. The evidence mentioned is then produced, including, possibly, witnesses. Such witnesses may be cross-examined by counsel for the defence as the giving of evidence proceeds. Then counsel for the defence proceeds in the same manner, with the plaintiff's representative having the right to cross-examine the defence's witnesses. At the end of the defence, each counsel will address the court, with counsel for the plaintiff making the last speech. In these final addresses each side sums up the strengths of their own argument and the weaknesses of their opponent's. Also any points of law may be argued.

In the odd case where a jury is being used, the judge will sum up the case to the jury, but this is, as stated, very unusual. In civil law juries are used primarily for defamation cases, but occasionally they have been used in such instances as false imprisonment, malicious prosecution or fraud. Usually, following the closing speeches, the judge will deliver his judgment. If the case is a particularly complex one the judge may opt to give a 'reserved judgment', a judgment given at a later date, so that the judge may have time to consider his decision.

Evidence

The rules of evidence (which are in fact much the same in criminal and civil cases) are primarily used to determine what evidence may be given, how it may be given and the level of proof required.

Certain facts: 'facts in issue', must be proved, otherwise the plaintiff's argument will fail. 'Res gestae' are facts, statements and other supportive evidence which show the alleged wrong was committed by the defendant. Such items are directly related to the case in hand and *must* be proved. Other information is generally deemed irrelevant and hence inadmissible.

Evidence can be categorised in a number of ways. For example a witness who actually saw what happened will give 'direct' evidence; other 'circumstantial' evidence may sometimes be deduced from several associated facts. Facts may be proved by 'oral' evidence – proof given by witnesses verbally, in court. Or it may be 'documentary' evidence; in which case the original documents normally need to be produced in court for inspection. 'Real' evidence will entail actually inspecting certain aspects of the case. The object in question might, if small enough be brought into court, or alternatively the judge might pay a site visit.

Certain forms of evidence are not permissible. Firstly, certain persons are not 'competent' to give evidence, for example children, or persons who are mentally unsound. Like all rules these are sometimes subject to exception: for instance the real objection to a child giving evidence is that he/she is too young to be aware of the implications of taking the oath. If a judge is satisfied that the child appreciates the seriousness of the situation, a child might quite validly be permitted to give evidence on oath. There are also witnesses who, though competent to give evidence, are not legally 'compellable'. Into this category would fall foreign diplomats and so on.

Secondly, their evidence might be inadmissible not because of who the party is, but because the 'proof' is merely opinion, or hearsay. Statements of opinion, however honestly held, are not admissible from the ordinary witness. However, it should be noted that expert witnesses who are, in effect, hired for their expert opinions are exceptions to this rule. They may give evidence relating to their opinions in their particular field of expertise. The rules relating to 'Hearsay' evidence mean that nothing which has been indirectly learned is acceptable by way of evidence. The witness may only tell the court what he *knows*, not what he has overheard, or learned in the course of conversation with another party.

There is one major exception to the hearsay rule, and it applies only in civil cases. By the provisions of the Civil Evidence Act 1968, so-called 'first-hand hearsay' is admissible. This will be an oral or written statement by someone not called as a witness, but who had actual knowledge of the event concerned. Obviously in the case of a first-hand witness it is desirable to call them before the court, but there are many reasons why this might not be possible. In such cases the 'first-hand hearsay' rule means that the statements of persons having direct knowledge may be used effectively.

Enforcement of civil judgments

In the chapters which follow we shall be discussing the various remedies available to an injured party whether injured by tort or breach of contract. But those remedies are in themselves useless unless the courts have the means to enforce a judgment. Those means vary according to the court involved and the type of remedy concerned. It is, for example, a very different proposition to attempt to enforce an injunction to securing payment of an award of damages. In the main, the High Court, as one would expect, has more potential means of enforcement than has the County Court. Those most commonly used are discussed below.

Where a defendant has been ordered to pay an award of damages and is unable or unwilling to do so the plaintiff may obtain from both the High Court or the County Court a writ of 'fieri facias' (fi fa) which is an order for the defendant's goods to be seized and, if necessary, sold to raise the money to pay the award. In the case of a defendant who is simply unwilling to perform the judgment, as opposed to unable, the very threat of seizure and sale is normally sufficient.

The plaintiff may apply to the High Court for:

a   a charging order; or

b   a garnishee order.

The main difference between these is that a charging order is placed directly on land (or possibly other goods like a boat, or shares in a company) belonging to the plaintiff. As and when the property charged is sold – and the plaintiff may force such a sale – the amount owing to the plaintiff will be deducted, on a priority basis, from the proceeds. A garnishee order, on the other hand, is an order placed on money owed to the defendant by a third party. Instead of paying the defendant, the third party must pay money directly to the plaintiff, until such time as the total amount owing under the judgment debt is paid. Similarly, he may apply to the County Court for an attachment of earnings order under the Attachment of Earnings Act 1971. Under such an order the employer of the defendant may be ordered to deduct money (often for months or years at a time) to pay the plaintiff's award.

There are various ways by which control may be taken of the defendant's property so that payment can be extracted for the plaintiff, but the defendant does not ultimately lose his property. For example a court may appoint a receiver to the defendant's property, or company who will intercept revenue and pay it to the plaintiff. Or a writ of sequestration will give the court control of the defendant's property and it may extract money from revenues until such time as the plaintiff is paid.

High Court judgments can be enforced through the County Courts. This sounds a rather roundabout way of enforcing judgment debt; but there are advantages: the main one being that the County Court has power to order payment to be made in instalments. If a defendant has little in the way of land or property, the High Court is often reluctant to use orders such as 'fi fa' (above). Payment by instalments is a practical way to recover at least some of the money owing.

All the above orders, writs and other methods concern the collection of monetary judgments. It should be remembered that some judgments involve other remedies, such as an injunction or specific performance. Probably the most common means of enforcement is by committal for contempt.

If a defendant ignores an order of the court, eg an injunction or an order of specific performance, he will be in contempt of court. The court has, in theory, unlimited powers of punishment for contempt. A defendant who will not comply may be committed (ie imprisoned) for an unlimited time until he has 'purged his contempt' (ie complied). In practice this power is rarely used, the mere threat of committal being sufficient to secure compliance with the judgment.

As an alternative to committal for contempt a writ of sequestration may be granted at the request of the plaintiff (see above). In cases of specific performance, for example an order to complete a contract to sell land, compliance may be effected by committal, as above, but writs of possession (to deliver land) and writs of delivery (to deliver goods) may sometimes be issued. The main problem here is that if a defendant has ignored an order of specific performance he is equally likely to resist a writ of possession/delivery. Ultimately the last threat may have to be that of committal for contempt.

Liability in tort (1) | 26

Introduction

There is often a large degree of overlap between crime and tort. If a criminal act harms the victim, it will usually be a tortious act as well. Thus the same act, for example dangerous driving which harms another driver or pedestrian, will be both a crime and a tort.

The law recognises certain rights, both personal and in respect of property, and will protect such rights against infringements, not by punishing the transgressor, as in criminal law, but by making the wrongdoer pay compensation to the injured person. However, not all conduct, no matter how undesirable, will be actionable. For example, there is in this country no right of privacy (though it has often been suggested there should be!). So, if a developer builds a housing estate on a field behind your home, he may rob you of a beautiful view, your hitherto secluded garden may now be overlooked and your house may sink in value; but none of this is actionable.

A tort is a civil wrong. Some students new to legal studies have difficulties defining the word 'tort'. *Professor Williams*, in attempting to define it, wrote:

> 'This word conveys little meaning to the average layman, and its exact definition is a matter of great difficulty even for the lawyer, but the general idea of it will become clear if one says that torts include such wrongs as assault, battery, false imprisonment, trespass, defamation of character, negligence and nuisance. It is a civil wrong, independent of contract, that is to say: it gives rise to an action for damages, irrespective of any agreement ...'

Liability in tort usually requires some element of fault or blame (for further discussion on this see chapter 35) though this is not always true. Broadly speaking the law of tort is not concerned with motive, in other words it is *what* has been done to injure another, not *why*.

There are cases where the defendant is liable even though the injury is clearly not his fault (for example, see vicarious liability in chapter 27). But on the whole tort is concerned with what happened to the plaintiff as a clearly foreseeable result of the defendant's action.

In the next section we shall look at negligence – perhaps the most important of all the torts, affecting many aspects of day-to-day life. There are other acts which may be tortious however, especially wrongs against property and goods and we shall be looking at some of these later.

The tort of negligence

Introduction

The tort of negligence contains specific legal principles. In some ways, it is misleading to call it 'negligence' in that the ordinary meaning of the word is 'carelessness'. Negligence in English law is more than mere carelessness, though. There are three things which must be proved by the plaintiff in a tort case. He must prove that the defendant owed him a duty of care, that that duty of care was breached and that he suffered damage as a result of the breach of duty. In order to breach a duty a wrongdoer must have been careless, but because not everyone who is hurt by someone's carelessness is owed a duty of care it takes more than mere carelessness to found an action in negligence.

Duty of care

A duty of care is owed to those people whom one can foresee as being so closely and directly affected by one's actions that they ought to be considered before one decides to act carelessly. For example, if you are driving a motor car, it is clear that other road users and people using the pavement alongside the road are likely to be hurt if you drive carelessly. Therefore, they are owed a duty of care. Many cases are not as simple as that of the driver of a motor car. For example, if someone is employed to lay new electricity cables under a pavement which runs close to factories who are those who ought to be considered by that person when he does his job? Should he be considering the possibility of harming pedestrians, road users driving close to the pavement, the companies which own the factories, visitors who go to the factories on business? Should he owe a duty of care to all of these classes of people or only to certain of them and if so to which classes? These questions are very difficult to answer. The courts have given general guidelines about to whom is owed a duty of care, but they realise that the circumstances of every case are different, so the rules must be put in general terms, so that the principles can be applied to a wide variety of cases with a high degree of consistency.

The general principle was laid down by the House of Lords in 1932 in the case of *Donoghue* v *Stevenson* [1932] AC 562.

The plaintiff drank a bottle of ginger beer which had been bought by a friend. She (the plaintiff) alleged that there was a decomposed snail in the bottle and that she suffered a serious illness. The House of Lords had to decide whether the law allowed a person with such a complaint to take an action against the manufacturer of the ginger beer in negligence. The House of Lords held, by a majority, that the law did recognise the tort of negligence in this sort of case, and laid down a general principle to be applied in all cases where one person alleged that he, or she, could recover for injury caused by the negligence of another. The following passage from the speech of Lord Atkin states the general principle to be applied when considering whether a duty of care is owed:

Lord Atkin:

'In English law there must be, and is, some general conception of relations giving rise to a duty of care, of which the particular cases found in the books are instances. The liability for negligence, whether you style it such or treat it as in other systems as a species of "culpa", is in no doubt based upon a general public sentiment of moral wrongdoing for which the offender must pay. But acts or omissions which any moral code would censure cannot in a practical world be treated so as to give a right to every person injured by them to demand relief. In this way rules of law arise which limit the range of complainants and the extent of their remedy. The rule that you are to love your neighbour becomes, in law, you must not injure your neighbour; and the lawyer's question, who is my neighbour? receives a restricted reply. You must take reasonable care to avoid acts or omissions which you can reasonably foresee would be likely to injure your neighbour. Who, then, in law is my neighbour? The answer seems to be – persons who are so closely and directly affected by my act that I ought reasonably to have them in contemplation as being so affected when I am directing my mind to the acts or omissions which are called in question.'

Several cases since 1932 have rephrased this principle in more modern language, but they all reflect this same general rule. It is recognised that there are some people to whom a duty of care is owed and some who may not recover if they are hurt by one's negligence. Those to whom a duty of care is owed are often called neighbours, and the principle stated by Lord Atkin is known as the neighbourhood principle. In recent cases such as *Anns v London Borough of Merton* [1977] 2 All ER 492 there have been attempts to restate the neighbour principle. In *Anns* Lord Wilberforce set down a two part test: part one can be regarded as a wide statement of the neighbour principle and part two contained a discretion to the court to limit, restrict or negate the application of a remedy even where the neighbour principle is satisfied for reasons of policy. An application of this can be seen in *Hill v Chief Constable of West Yorkshire* [1988] 2 WLR 1049 where the court thought that it would be undesirable if the victims of crime could bring actions against the police force where they could show the elements of negligence. The case of *Murphy v Brentwood DC* [1991] 1 AC 398, however, has now overruled *Anns*. The House of Lords decided that *Anns* was wrongly decided and that the law had been too widely drawn. See also *Department of the Environment v Thomas Bates and Sons* [1990] 3 WLR 457 which was decided on the same day by the House of Lords. The very wide definition of 'duty of care' as drawn up in *Anns* has now been redefined in these two cases.

The repercussions following the overruling by *Murphy* of *Anns v London Borough of Merton* continue. In *Targett v Torfaen BC* [1991] 141 NLJ 1698, the plaintiff was injured when he fell down the steps outside his council house. There was no lighting nor any handrail. The plaintiff was found to be 25 per cent to blame for his own injuries.

The defendants' argument that, following *Murphy v Brentwood DC* the council might not be considered personally liable for faulty design or structure of council houses was rejected by the Court of Appeal. *Murphy* concerned economic loss, it did not change the law where the plaintiff had suffered personal injury as a result of the negligence of the defendant. The council was liable for the plaintiff's injuries, less the amount of contributory negligence.

In *Caparo Industries plc v Dickman* [1990] 2 WLR 358, Lord Bridge distinguished between two approaches which could be adopted in identifying the existence of a duty of care: the 'traditional' approach where the existence of a duty of care was found in 'different specific situations each exhibiting its own particular characteristics'; and the 'modern' approach (such as that of Lord Wilberforce in *Anns*) where the courts had sought to identify a 'single general principle' which might be applied in all circumstances. He preferred the 'traditional' approach. This is an indication from the House of Lords that the courts now prefer to reason by analogy with precedent, rather than apply a wide, sweeping general principle as was the case in *Anns*.

Breach of duty of care: the concept of reasonableness

As mentioned above, it is not enough to show that the plaintiff was a neighbour of the defendant. The plaintiff must also prove that the duty of care was broken. In order to know whether the duty of care was broken it is necessary to discover the standard of the duty. In other words, how much care must everyone take towards his neighbours?

The general rule is that everyone owes a duty of care which requires him to act reasonably. The word 'reasonable' is very general; what is reasonable depends on all the circumstances of the case. For example, if A is driving along the road and suddenly swerves onto the pavement for no reason, knocking down B, he has not acted reasonably; but if he swerved in order to avoid being hit by a lorry which was coming in the other direction out of control, then he did act reasonably. In both cases the duty of care owed to B was the same, in both cases B was A's neighbour, in both cases the injury to B was the same. Nevertheless, the concept of reasonableness must be used in order to ensure that A is only liable to compensate B if he (A) was at fault. The legal standard is not that of the defendant himself but that of a reasonable person of ordinary prudence, care and skill (see *King* v *Phillips* [1953] 1 QB 429). It is no defence that a person acted, or thought, to the best of his abilities if this standard is below that of a reasonable man. The standard may not necessarily be reduced to take into account some special disability of the defendant, although as has been stated, all the surrounding circumstances of the case will be taken into account.

Thus, for example, a person who has poor eyesight, but drives nonetheless, will have the same duty of care as a person with ordinary vision. Similarly, a blind or deaf person who crosses a busy main road carelessly cannot complain if he is run over by a reasonably careful driver who does not know and cannot be expected to know of this disability (see *Bourhill* v *Young* [1943] AC 92 at p109). But compare cases where a person's disability is obvious at even a casual glance and cases where the disability, whatever it is, is not immediately apparent (on this, see the remarks of Stable J in *Daly* v *Liverpool Corporation* [1939] 2 All ER 142). The case of *Morrell* v *Owen* (1993) The Times 14 December concerning the duty of care towards disabled athletes on the part of the organisers of a sporting event, raises a number of queries. It is to be hoped that this case will go to further appeal to clarify the question of whether a concept of variable duty of care is now to be recognised by English law. Hitherto, such a concept has never been accepted, the rule being that the duty of care is the same for all (in this case the duty owed to able-bodied and disabled athletes would be the same).

With regard to children, however, it seems that the duty of care will be lowered according to age. In *Yachuk* v *Oliver Blais* [1949] 2 All ER 150, a Canadian case on appeal to the Privy Council, a boy of nine obtained, by deception, a container-full of petrol to make burning torches for a 'Red Indian' game. It was held, on appeal, that a boy of such an age was incapable of contributory negligence, he had no duty of care to himself or his playmates.

What is reasonable in every case, therefore, depends on all the circumstances of the case. It is, nonetheless, possible to lay down a general concept of reasonableness. The difficulty with doing so is that vague words must be used in the definition:

In the case of *Blyth* v *Birmingham Waterworks* (1856) 11 Exch 781 the defendants laid water pipes underground. They fitted safety valves in the pipes and one winter, because the weather was extraordinarily harsh, the safety valves were not effective and the plaintiff's house was flooded. The plaintiff sued in negligence arguing that his house would not have been damaged if the defendants had fitted valves which were strong enough to withstand such bad weather. The Court of Exchequer held that the defendants had not been negligent. It was held that the severity of the weather was so extraordinary that it was reasonable to fit the valves which were fitted because it was not foreseeable that the weather would be so bad. The general rule of the standard of care in negligence was set out by Alderson B:

> 'Negligence is the omission to do something which a reasonable man, guided upon those considerations which ordinarily regulate the conduct of human affairs, would do, or doing something which a prudent and reasonable man would not do.'

It can be seen that the principle of reasonableness is drawn in very general terms. This, again, is the result of the fact that the definition has to adapt to many different circumstances. Little guidance can be found in the cases as to what a reasonable man would or would not do. The point of the test is that it is objective and does not address the peculiarities of the particular individual defendant but considers what a reasonable man in the defendant's position at that time would do or would not have done. The court will then look at all the circumstances of the case.

It is a question of fact whether the defendant has failed to show reasonable care in the particular circumstances. The defendant is entitled to expect others to take reasonable care, but where experience has shown that others will take risks then the defendant will be failing in his duty of care if he does not take this into account.

The court may take into account the importance of the activity on which the defendant is engaged, though the fact that a person is driving an ambulance in an emergency, or some such situation, will not totally absolve the defendant from any duty of care (see *Watt* v *Hertfordshire County Council* [1954] 1 WLR 835.)

The defendant is entitled to balance the cost and practicality of any steps he might take as precautionary measures against harm resulting, against the likelihood of harm (*Latimer* v *AEC* [1953] AC 643). In making such an assessment, the defendant may take into account all his circumstances including financial (*Goldman* v *Hargrave* [1967] 1 AC 645).

Where a person holds himself as professing some particular skill, he will be expected to show the level of skill normally possessed by a reasonable person having that skill. Thus there may be different grades of skill according to the particular level of professional expertise. A consultant surgeon for example would have a higher duty of care than a young, recently qualified houseman. Similarly, a skill might be professed by several different persons in different professions. In *Philips* v *William Whitely* [1938] 1 All ER 566 for example it was held that a jeweller who pierced ears had to show only the standard of care of a reasonable jeweller, not a surgeon.

Causation

Even if there has been established a duty of care and that duty was breached, the linchpin in the law of negligence still has to be proved, namely causation. By causation is meant that the actual breach caused, both in law and fact, the actual loss complained of.

Two principles are involved. Firstly, it must be proved that as a matter of fact the damage was caused by the careless act. Secondly, it must be proved that the damage was reasonably foreseeable as a result of the carelessness. These two principles are known as the rules of causation and remoteness.

When considering remoteness the courts are concerned with a rule of law, not with a question of fact. The law says that only the damage which was of a reasonably foreseeable type can be recovered. The rule was laid down by the Privy Council in 1961 in *The Wagon Mound* [1961] AC 388.

The defendants were refuelling a ship and through the carelessness of one of their workmen, some of the oil spilled into the bay where the ship was moored. The plaintiffs had been using welding equipment at a nearby wharf. Some of the oil floated out of the bay and up to the wharf at which point it ignited because of sparks which had flown from the plaintiffs' welding equipment. The oil did not ignite directly, but only because some scraps of cloth which were floating on the surface had caught fire. The question for the Privy Council was whether the plaintiffs could recover in negligence. There was no doubt about the carelessness of the defendants in allowing the oil to leak onto the water in the first place, but they argued that they were not liable in damages because the setting fire to the wharf was not a direct consequence of their carelessness, or, to give it in legal terms, that the damage was too remote to be recoverable. The Privy Council held that the proper test of remoteness is one of reasonable foreseeability. In other words, it was held that as a matter of law the injured person can only recover damages to compensate him for the type of damage which was reasonably foreseeable; he may have suffered other damage, but he will not be able to recover damages for that. Viscount Simonds stated the rule as follows:

'It is a principle of civil liability, subject only to qualifications which have no present relevance, that a man must be considered to be responsible for the probable consequences of his act. To demand more of him is too harsh a rule, to demand less is to ignore that civilised order requires the observance of a minimum standard of behaviour.'

The point on causation can be illustrated by the case of *McWilliams* v *Sir William Arrol & Co Ltd* [1962] 1 WLR 295 where it was shown that the defendants were in breach of their duty towards their employee by failure to provide a harness for his safety when he was working at heights in a building site. Nonetheless the court found as a fact that the plaintiff's husband (who died as a result of a fall) would not have worn the harness even if one was provided. The cause of his death then was not the failure to provide a harness but the failure to wear one.

Remoteness of damage

If the type of damage is foreseeable the defendant will be liable for the full extent of the damage, even though the consequences are much more serious than could have been anticipated. The *Wagon Mound* (see previously) is, of course, the definitive case here.

Also, see *Smith* v *Leech Brain & Co Ltd* [1962] 2 QB 405, where a factory worker was splashed and burned by a spark of molten metal, which activated a pre-malignant growth he already suffered from. He died later from a cancerous tumour. It was held that this was not too remote, since the burn was foreseeable even though the gravity of its consequences was not.

The damage will be too remote if the chain of events is broken by some independent or new act intervening between the wrongful act and the new injury (*novus actus interveniens*) (see Defences, chapter 27).

However, compare the following cases:

In *Scott* v *Shepherd* (1773) 2 W Bl 892 a lighted firework was thrown by the defendant into a crowded covered market. Thrown by stallholders to protect their own stalls, it eventually exploded in the plaintiff's face, blinding him in one eye. It was held that the acts of the various stallholders in throwing the firework away from their stalls did not constitute a novus actus. The chain of causation was perfectly traceable and attributable to Shepherd.

In *McKew* v *Holland & Hannen & Cubitt Ltd* [1969] 3 All ER 1621 the chain of causation was broken and the damage pronounced 'too remote' by a court.

Here the plaintiff having been injured at work found that his left leg tended to give way without notice. On this particular occasion, while descending a steep flight of stairs with no handrail, he felt his leg going numb. In order not to fall head first he *jumped* and broke his right ankle. The court held that which consequences were the logical and reasonable result of an earlier act (in this case the injury at work) were sometimes difficult to trace with certainty.

Here they felt that the plaintiff's unreasonable act in jumping broken the chain of causation and rendered the injury to the right ankle. Had he simply fallen as a result of his leg going numb and giving way, any injury would not have been considered too remote.

Also, see *Bourhill* v *Young* [1943] AC 92, where a woman was dismounting from a tram in Edinburgh, and at the time at the rear of the tram, heard *but did not see* Young, the defendant, crash his motorbike while overtaking the tram on the inside. She was eight months pregnant and her baby was born dead.

The court held that the defendant did not owe her a duty of care. 'It was', said Lord Russell, 'material to consider what the defendant ought to have contemplated as a reasonable man … In these circumstances I am unable to see how he could reasonably anticipate that if he came into collision with a vehicle … the resultant noise would cause physical injury by shock to a person standing behind the tram car …'

She was beyond the area of foreseeable danger and Young was therefore not negligent towards her (though he may have had liability to other road users!).

See *Jones* v *Wright* [1991] 1 All ER 353 for a careful examination of the concept of remoteness and forseeability. The plaintiffs' case was a test case to determine liability of 150 or so other similar cases. All arose from a disaster at a football stadium, when 95 spectators were crushed to death and more than 400 injured. The question arose as to whether those who, for example, were present elsewhere in the ground, or witnessed the happening on television could claim for nervous shock. The court took the opportunity to examine closely the categories of persons entitled to sue.

The case of *Topp* v *London Country Bus (SW) Ltd* (1991) The Times 3 December involved a situation in which the defendants left their bus unattended with the keys in the ignition. The bus was stolen by 'joyriders' who knocked down and killed Mrs Topp. It was held that although it might be foreseeable that a vehicle thus left unattended would be stolen, the criminal acts of the 'joyriders' were not the liability of the defendants. Such results as the death of Mrs Topp were too remote to be considered the responsibility of the defendants and they had no duty of care.

Recently a new factor has emerged: proximity. It seems that the type of damage must not only be foreseeable, but the party to whom the duty of care is owed must be in a 'relationship of proximity'. Over the previous year or so, a number of cases have come before the courts involving claims for 'psychological' injuries sustained by those who witness some diaster, televised 'live', and who see or know that relatives or friends are present. One such case is *Alcock* v *Chief Constable of South Yorkshire* [1991] 3 WLR 1057 which was concerned with the Hillsborough football tragedy. Scenes of the disaster were televised and a number of friends and relations suffered nervous shock and related psychiatric disorders. The question arose as to whether such persons were eligible to claim.

The House of Lords held that mere foreseeability of psychiatric illness was not sufficient in itself to establish a duty of care. A relationship of proximity was needed. Such relationships extended to all ties of love and affection, and were not confined to spouses and parents. However the more distant the relationship the higher the burden of proof. The House of Lords stated however that the means by which shock was caused must be by *physical* proximity and scenes televised did not satisfy the requirements of this criterion.

Note also, that 'proximity' may not mean a relationship of love and affection as defined in *Alcock* (above) but may be financial, giving rise to a fiduciary relationship (see *Morgan Crucible Co* v *Hill Samuel Bank* [1991] 1 All ER 148).

See also *McFarlane* v *EE Caledonia Ltd* [1993] NLJ 1367 as to the duty owed to a bystander at a horrific event.

The case of *Page* v *Smith* [1994] 4 All ER 522 concerning personal injury, including nervous shock, and the question of remoteness of damage is important. The Court of Appeal, in considering liability for nervous shock, indicated that a person claiming for such injuries must prove himself to be a 'person or ordinary fortitude' which the plaintiff here was not. The plaintiff claimed that collision in a car accident with the defendant had, while causing only the most minor physical injuries, also triggered off a recurrence of myalgic encephalomyelitis from which he had suffered for many years. It was held that not only was causation impossible to establish, but the onset or recurrence of the illness was too remote for the defendant to contemplate.

Res ipsa loquitur

The literal translation 'the thing speaks for itself' or 'the facts speak for themselves', makes it fairly clear what is involved here. Under the doctrine of res ipsa loquitur, a plaintiff will be able to establish a prima facie cause of action when he can establish:

a on the evidence available it is reasonably likely that there was negligence by reason of some act or omission of the defendant; and

b that while it is not possible to prove exactly what act or omission set in motion the chain of events leading to injury; it is more likely than not that some act or omission of the defendant constituted failure to take proper care for the plaintiff's safety.

It must, in other words, be the sort of injury which just does not happen if those having the management of events use proper care. The maxim applies *only* when the causes of the accident are unknown but the likelihood of negligence is clear from the nature of the accident. Thus in *Turner* v *Mansfield Corporation* (1975) 119 Sol Jo 629, where the back of a refuse lorry raised up suddenly as it was driven under a bridge and also in *Gee* v *Metropolitan Railway Company* (1873) LR 8 QB 161, where a train door flew open; the question of negligence on the part of the defendant arose. While in the latter case it was held that there was some evidence of negligence on the part of the defendant; there was no such evidence in *Turner*. Res ipsa loquitur could be invoked in *Gee* but not in *Turner*.

The incident must be of a kind which could not happen without some degree of carelessness. Thus in *Byrne* v *Boadle* (1863) 2 H & C 722, a flour barrel fell from the upper storey of a warehouse onto a passer by in the street below. While there was no evidence as to exactly what happened, the court held that there must, of necessity, be negligence on the part of those responsible for the handling of the barrel of flour for it to fall at all.

Where the plaintiff successfully alleges res ipsa loquitur he raises a presumption of negligence against the defendant. But such a presumption may of course be rebutted. If the defendant can show how an accident happened and that there is no negligence on his part then he may not be liable. Obviously levels of proof vary. In certain cases the defendant may not prove sufficiently strongly that there was no negligence on his part, or that the cause of the action was inconsistent with any evidence of negligence on his part, then the court may have to decide on the balance of probabilities. This matter has never really been satisfactorily settled. In one of the more recent cases before the House of Lords: *Ward* v *Tesco Stores Ltd* [1976] 1 WLR 810, the plaintiff slipped on yoghurt spilled on the defendant's supermarket floor. It was held it was for the defendant to prove that the plaintiff would still have slipped even if the spilled yoghurt had been cleaned up instantly.

Trespass

Introduction

One of the oldest forms of liability in English law is the tort of trespass. An action lies in respect of a direct injury committed to property or to the person. Generally, the act or omission which constitutes the tort must be intentional on the part of the defendant, and it is actionable per se, that is, without proof of damage having been sustained by the plaintiff. The courts considered the protection of property rights, in particular, to be so important as to provide for an action to lie against anyone who 'trespassed' against property regardless of whether any actual damage has occurred.

There are four normal categories of trespass – trespass to land, trespass to goods, trespass to the person and the rule in *Wilkinson* v *Downton* [1897] 2 QB 57.

Trespass to land

This is the unlawful interference with possession of land. It may be committed by entering upon land in the possession of another person, or by placing objects upon it, or by remaining on land after permission to be there has been withdrawn, or by abusing a right of entry. The interest protected is possession, not ownership. The reason for this is a practical one. Disputes as to physical possession of land are the ones most likely to cause breaches of the peace, and so in the interests of security and 'the keeping of the peace' English law protected possession, not ownership, by means of the action for trespass to land.

Trespass to goods

Again, the interest protected is 'possession' of goods (personal property). The tort may be committed by an act which interferes with *possession*, without lawful justification. The action which lies in respect of interference with *ownership* of goods is the tort of conversion. Conversion is a tort of strict liability (ie intention or negligence is unnecessary) – the law regards the importance of certainty of title to goods as of paramount importance, so that a completely innocent purchaser of stolen goods may be 'liable' to the true owner from whom they were stolen, in conversion. This is quite different from trespass, where there is a normal requirement for both mens rea and actus reus.

Trespass to the person

General
This was, at one time, the only means by which a person physically attacked or injured in some way by another could obtain a remedy against that other. Trespass to the person may take one or more of three forms – assault, battery or false imprisonment.

Assault
This is committed where one person fears or anticipates a violent or humiliating physical contact from another, who has an apparent ability to carry out the threat of such contact. There does not have to be any actual physical contact, but mere words are not enough to be an assault, although they may negative a menacing gesture, preventing the gesture from amounting to an assault.

Battery
This is committed when one person intentionally causes physical contact with another person without the latter's consent, eg hitting him. A battery may be an assault as well, at least where the victim saw it coming. It has been described as 'the least touching in anger'.

False imprisonment
This action lies in respect of an unlawful interference with a person's physical freedom. The tort is committed where one person unlawfully restricts the physical freedom of another. Thus an unlawful arrest or imprisonment will amount to false imprisonment. Total restraint is necessary (ie there must be no practicable method of escape) but violence or actual physical restraint is not necessary. Since trespass is actionable per se, it is probably not necessary for the plaintiff to realise he is being detained, although on this point the authorities are inconsistent.

Wilkinson v Downton
In addition to these categories of trespass to the person, there is a further category sometimes referred to as 'residual forms of trespass to the person'. This is the rule

in *Wilkinson* v *Downton* [1897] 2 QB 57 in which Wright J said a defendant would be liable if:

a he wilfully did an act;

b which was calculated to do some physical harm to the plaintiff; and

c it actually did cause physical harm.

In *Wilkinson* a practical joker told a woman, untruthfully, that her husband had been badly injured. The defendant was held liable to pay compensation when the plaintiff suffered nervous shock and was seriously ill.

This form of tort has been accepted by the courts only comparatively recently. It falls within none of the other 'trespass categories'; it has few precedents and its extent is not yet fully determined.

Conclusion

Today, at least so far as injuries to the person are concerned, trespass has largely given way in practice to negligence as a means of securing compensation. It has been suggested in several cases that negligence, rather than intention, may be sufficient to give rise to liability in trespass. But in any personal injuries case where negligence is pleaded it seems that the appropriate action today is in the tort of negligence, not trespass. Indeed, Lord Denning has gone so far as to say that in such circumstances the only possible action open to the plaintiff was in negligence, not trespass, and other members of the Court of Appeal have agreed that negligence was to be preferred in such cases. Trespass, of course, is actionable without proof of damage, whereas negligence is not. The duty of care in negligence as developed since *Donoghue* v *Stevenson* [1932] AC 562 provides a far more flexible means of establishing liability for personal injury than trespass.

Nuisance

Introduction

As we have seen, the tort of trespass protects possessors of land from any direct interference with their possession of it. Trespass does not, however, extend to protect land owners or possessors from indirect interference with their use or enjoyment of their land, eg by noise emitted from neighbouring households, or smoke and other forms of pollution coming from neighbouring factories. Thus the tort of nuisance developed to protect persons having an interest in land from unreasonable interference with their use or enjoyment of it.

There are two aspects to the tort – private and public nuisance.

Private nuisance

Private nuisance may be defined as an 'unlawful interference with the plaintiff's use or enjoyment of land'. Any person who has an interest (not merely those who have possession) in land may sue, as the law was developed to ensure that legitimate expectations associated with interests in land should be protected. (See *Devon Lumber Co Ltd* v *McNeill* (1988) 45 DLR (4th) 300.) The emphasis is far less on the intention or negligence of the defendant than on the degree of interference suffered by the plaintiff. 'Unlawful' in this context simply means 'unreasonable' and it may be that the defendant's activity is to all other intents and purposes quite lawful, and that he intends no harm to the plaintiff.

In the case of *Sturges* v *Bridgman* (1879) 11 Ch D 852 the defendant operated a confectioner's business and the plaintiff alleged that the noise from the defendant's machinery interfered with his practice as a doctor. The court held that such interference was indeed unreasonable and amounted to nuisance. Here there was no intention or fault as such on the part of the defendant, who was nonetheless liable in nuisance and obliged, by means of injunction, to cease his noisy activity at that place.

The question of liability in private nuisance, then, is one of balancing the reasonableness of the defendant's activity against the reasonableness of the plaintiff's needs to use and enjoy his property in a particular way. For this purpose many considerations will be relevant; the character of the neighbourhood (for 'what would be a nuisance in Belgrave Square may not be a nuisance in Bermondsey'), the duration and frequency of the defendant's activities, and the question of whether the plaintiff has suffered any actual damage as a result of the defendant's activity (where there has been physical damage to the property itself, eg corrosion caused by smoke pollution, damp caused by leaky central heating systems, etc). The courts almost invariably find the defendant's conduct to amount to nuisance, regardless of the character of the neighbourhood.

In some circumstances, however, the defendant's motive may be relevant. Where the defendant does something purposely to annoy or injure the plaintiff then he may commit a nuisance where otherwise he would not be liable.

In the case of *Christie* v *Davey* [1893] 1 Ch 316 a music teacher complained that she was hampered in giving music lessons by loud noises, shouting and banging which came from her neighbours in the adjoining house. Her neighbours resented the fact that she gave music lessons, and purposely made a loud noise in order to hinder her in doing so. The court granted an injunction in favour of the teacher.

Private nuisance protects the use and enjoyment of land by those who have an interest in it. However, many people who do not have an interest in land may also be affected by activities which create noise, vibrations, or pollution in a particular area. They have no status to sue in private nuisance, but if a sufficient number of them are affected by the activities of the defendant, an action may lie in public nuisance. It is, however fair to say that the increasing number of remedies under legislation such as the Control of Pollution Act 1974 are slowly making this tort obsolete.

Public nuisance

Public nuisance is an unlawful act or omission which endangers the life, health, safety or comfort of some section of the public or obstructs the public in the exercise of some common right, eg obstruction of the highway or keeping dangerous premises near a highway, thus interfering with the common right to use the public highway. An action may not be brought by an individual unless he or she has suffered some special damage over and above that sustained by the rest of the section of the public affected. However, a 'relator' action may be brought by the Attorney-General to obtain an injunction to prevent the defendant from persisting with the activity complained of. That is, an action may be brought by the Attorney-General's department acting on behalf of (or at the relation of) the member(s) of the public affected. Public nuisance is also a crime which can be punished by means of fine or imprisonment.

'Unlawful' for the purposes of public nuisance, as for private nuisance, means 'unreasonable', ie unreasonably interfering with the health, comfort, safety, etc of a section of the public. Again, the intention or fault of the defendant is less relevant that the degree of harm being caused to the public, and an injunction may be granted without the defendant having been intentional or negligent as to the effects of his activities. However, so far as the individual action for damages (where 'special damage' has been sustained) is concerned, the courts tend not to find for the plaintiff unless some degree of fault on the part of the defendant can be shown. In some cases, there seems little difference between this form of liability and liability in the tort of negligence.

In the case of *Castle v St Augustine's Links Ltd* (1922) 38 TLR 615, C was driving his taxi when a ball driven from the thirteenth tee of a golf course struck his windscreen and caused loss of an eye. There was evidence that balls driven from this particular tee frequently landed on the highway. The court held that C could recover damages as the tee and hole were situated in a position so as to cause a public nuisance, and C had suffered special damage as a result.

The *Castle* case can be contrasted with the following case which was decided in negligence.

In the case of *Bolton v Stone* [1951] AC 850 the plaintiff claimed damages for a personal injury sustained when struck by a cricket ball from a cricket ground adjoining the street. The defendants (the cricket club) were not liable because the evidence showed that the event of a cricket ball travelling that far was extremely infrequent and in the circumstances the precautions taken had been adequate.

It is the frequency with which golf balls landed on the highway that made it possible to sue in *Castle*.

Rylands v Fletcher

Introduction

The rule in *Rylands* v *Fletcher* has its origins in the tort of private nuisance, and when that case was decided, by Blackburn J in 1865 and subsequently by the House of Lords in 1868, it is most likely that the judges thought they were not departing in any significant way from established principles. The rule has developed in such a way, however, that it is now considered as a separate head of liability, and one which, it is argued, imposes strict liability upon a defendant in certain circumstances. Whether or not it does impose strict liability today is subject to some doubt; the influence of the development of negligence and the 'no liability without fault' principle can be seen in the cases under this rule, as elsewhere in the law of tort.

Rylands v Fletcher (1866) LR 1 Ex 265 and (1868) LR 3 HL 330

B, a mill owner, employed independent contractors, who were apparently competent, to construct a reservoir on his land to provide water for his mill. In the course of the work the contractors came upon some old shafts and passages on B's land. These connected up with A's mines (A being B's neighbour). No one suspected this as the shafts appeared to be filled with earth, and the contractors did not block them further. When the reservoir was filled, water from it burst through the old shafts and flooded A's mines. Blackburn J held that there was no liability in negligence, trespass or nuisance, but that there was liability because of a special rule applicable in such cases. The House of Lords upheld the special rule, but it is the judgment of Blackburn J which is always cited.

'... the person who for his own purposes brings on his land and collects and keeps there anything likely to do mischief if it escapes, must keep it in at his peril, and, if he does not do so, is prima facie answerable for all the damage which is the natural consequence of its escape. D can excuse himself by showing that the escape was owing to the plaintiff's default; or perhaps that the escape was the consequence of vis major, or the Act of God; but nothing of this sort exists here, it is necessary to inquire what excuse would be sufficient. The general rule, as above stated, seems on principle just. The person whose grass or corn is eaten down by the escaping cattle of his neighbour, or whose mine is flooded by the water from his neighbour's reservoir, or whose cellar is invaded by the filth of his neighbour's privy, or whose habitation is made unhealthy by the fumes and noisome vapours of his neighbour's alkali works, is damnified without any fault of his own, and it seems but reasonable and just that the neighbour, who has brought something on his own property which was not naturally there, harmless to others so long as it is confined to his own property, but which he knows to be mischievous if it gets on his neighbour's, should be obliged to make good the damage which ensues if he does not succeed in confining it to his own property. But for his act in bringing it there no mischief could have accrued, and it seems but just that he should at his peril keep it there so that no mischief may accrue, or answer for the natural and anticipated consequences. And upon authority, this we think is established to be the law whether the things so brought be beasts, or water, or filth, or stenches.'

In the House of Lords an addition was made to the rule – the thing concerned must have been brought onto the land as part of a non-natural user of the land.

Thus, in order for the principle to apply, there must be:

a non-natural user of the land;

b an escape;

c damage to the plaintiff's property.

In deciding what constitutes a 'non-natural user of land' the courts have, in some cases, applied a standard of 'reasonableness' of the defendant's activity, or manner of keeping the relevant thing.

For example, in *Mason* v *Levy Auto Parts of England* [1967] 2 QB 530, D stored on their land large quantities of combustible materials which ignited under mysterious circumstances. It was held that in deciding whether this was a non-natural user of land under *Rylands* v *Fletcher* it was necessary to have regard to the quantities of combustible materials brought onto the land, the way in which they were stored and the character of the neighbourhood. In all the circumstances, this was a non-natural user. Thus the question of non-natural user appears to involve, in some circumstances, consideration of whether the defendant came up to the appropriate standard of care, ie a question of negligence. It is interesting to note that in this case McKenna J said:

'It may be that these considerations would also justify a finding of negligence. If that is so, the end would be the same as I have reached by a more laborious, and perhaps more questionable route.'

In *Cambridge Water Company* v *Eastern Counties Leather plc* [1994] 2 WLR 53 the defendants used a chlorinated solvent at their tannery which was situated some 1.3 miles from the plaintiff's borehole where water was abstracted for domestic purposes. This water became unfit for human consumption by solvent contamination when the solvent seeped into the ground below the defendants' premises and then percolated into the borehole. The plaintiffs brought an action in, inter alia, *Rylands*. In the High Court this action was dismissed on the grounds that the defendants had not made a non-natural user of their land, which was situated in an industrial village. On appeal, the Court of Appeal declined to determine the matter on the basis of Rylands but imposed liability on other grounds. The defendants appealed.

The House of Lords said that foreseeability of harm of the relevant type by the defendants was required to recover damages under the rule in *Rylands* v *Fletcher* (and also in nuisance). The House of Lords also held, contrary to the finding at first instance, that the defendants had made a non-natural user of their land. However, on the facts of the case the contamination was not foreseeable and the appeal was allowed.

In his judgment in *Rylands* v *Fletcher* Blackburn J indicated that there would be some defences available to the defendant under the rule. As developed in subsequent cases the defences are:

a volenti non fit injuria;

b common benefit to plaintiff and defendant (ie where the thing which causes the harm was brought onto the land for the common benefit of both parties, eg a shared water supply or sprinkler system for fire prevention);

c act of a stranger causing the escape;

d act of God causing the escape;

e statutory authority;

f default of the plaintiff.

In applying these defences, the courts have again allowed principles of 'fault' rather than strict liability to guide them. For example, the Court of Appeal has said that in pleading the defence of act of a stranger, the defendant had to show that he could not have controlled the stranger and that the escape was due to the latter's unforeseeable act without any negligence on the part of the defendant. If, on the other hand, the plaintiff could show that the act of the stranger could reasonably have been anticipated or its consequences prevented, the defendant would still be liable.

Similarly, in applying the defence of act of God, principles of fault liability appear in some judgments under *Rylands* v *Fletcher*. In one case the House of Lords held that, even where the escape was due to an act of God, the defendants were still under a duty to ensure that those potentially affected should be 'as secure against injury as they would have been had nature not been interfered with'.

The implication here is that the emphasis is on culpable failure to control a risk, rather than strict liability for the creation of the risk itself.

Thus, even under the so-called 'strict liability' rule in *Rylands* v *Fletcher* it seems that the courts have great difficulty in departing from the 'no liability without fault' principle. Actions under the rule are now extremely rare, partly because of the awkward technicalities of its application (eg the uncertainty of proving 'non-natural user'), but mainly because most such cases would be covered anyway by the tort of negligence, as was so clearly indicated by McKenna J in *Mason* v *Levy Auto Parts*.

Occupier's liability

Introduction

In this section we must consider three aspects of the tortious liability of an occupier of property towards those who use his premises. The law in this area is mainly statutory and it is not often necessary to apply the common law principles of negligence which have been discussed above. Nonetheless, the common law is of some importance. At common law there were three sorts of people who might visit one's property. An invitee was someone who entered the land for a purpose in which both he and the occupier had an interest. For example, a postman, who entered land to deliver mail; the postman's interest was in doing his job, the occupier's interest was to have his mail delivered. The second category of visitor was a licensee, who entered with the consent of the occupier, but for a purpose of his own. For example, a door-to-door salesman enters with the implied permission of the occupiers, but in doing so he is carrying on his own business and the occupier is not necessarily going to benefit from the visit. The third type of visitor was the trespasser, who entered without the permission of the occupier.

The common law recognised a different standard of care for each sort of visitor. Nowadays, the position of all three is covered by statute. The common law relating to invitees and licensees was replaced by the Occupiers' Liability Act 1957 and the duty of care owed to a trespasser is governed by the provisions of the Occupiers' Liability Act 1984. In this chapter we will follow the statutory pattern and deal with non-trespassers and trespassers in separate sections, but there is no longer any need to draw a distinction between invitees and licensees.

It is necessary, however, to mention the duties on an occupier under the Defective Premises Act 1972, because this sometimes gives a visitor extra protection on top of that given by the two Occupiers' Liabilities Acts.

Occupiers' Liability Act 1957

To whom is a duty owed?

It has already been stated that the 1957 Act does not draw a distinction between invitees and licensees, it treats them in the same way. One purpose of the 1957 Act was to do away with the distinction and to classify both common law invitees and common law licensees as 'visitors'. The matter is dealt with in s1 of the Act:

'1) The rules enacted in the two next following sections shall have effect, in place of the rules, of the common law, to regulate the duty which an occupier of premises owes to his visitors in respect of dangers due to the state of the premises or to things done or omitted to be done on them.

2) The rules so enacted shall regulate the nature of the duty imposed by law in consequence of a person's occupation or control of premises and of any invitation or permission he gives (or is treated as giving) to another to enter or use the premises, but they shall not alter the rules of the common law as to the persons on whom a duty is so imposed or to whom it is owed; and accordingly for the purposes of the rules so enacted the persons who are to be treated as an occupier and as his visitors are the same as the persons who would at common law be treated as the occupier and his invitees and or licensees.

3) The rules so enacted in relation to an occupier of premises and his visitors shall also apply, in like manner and to the like extent as the principles applicable at common law to an occupier of premises and his invitees or licensees would apply, to regulate –

a) the obligations of a person occupying or having control over any fixed or movable structure, including any vessel, vehicle or aircraft; and

b) the obligations of a person occupying or having control over any premises or structure in respect of damage to property, including the property of persons who are not themselves his visitors.'

These three sub-sections cover all the persons to whom an occupier of premises owes a duty of care under the Act. Sub-section 1) makes it clear that the Act takes the place of the common law in so far as it imposed liability where there were dangers on land or dangers in the use of land. The purpose of sub-section 2) is to define those people to whom a duty of care is owed. It states that all those persons whom the common law would regard as invitees or licensees are now classified as 'visitors' and that the same duty of care is owed to all of them. It also makes it clear that whether someone is to be treated as an occupier depends on whether he would be treated as an occupier at common law. It is important to note that in sub-section (2) the Act talks of persons who have the occupier's permission to enter his land including those who are treated as though they have permission to enter on to the land. This covers people like door-to-door salesmen who are rarely actually invited on to land, but are treated by the law as if they had been invited. The reason for the law implying an invitation is that in reality most people have no objection to door-to-door salesmen visiting them, and, if asked, would say that they would always allow such a person to visit their home. Sub-section 3) is important in that it recognises that there should be a duty of care owed to people who are visitors to boats and vehicles in the same way as there is a duty owed to visitors to land. Sub-section 3) also makes it clear that a duty of care is owed when property of a visitor is damaged as well as when he has suffered some personal injury.

McGeown v *Northern Ireland Housing Executive* [1994] 3 WLR 187 demonstrates the extent of the duty under the statute. The House of Lords declared that persons using a public right of way to gain access to premises could not be considered to be 'visitors' and the occupier would owe no duty of care under the 1957 Act. This decision may place limitations on the provisions of the 1957 Act, though it was stated that the existence of a public right of way was not necessarily completely inconsistent with the concept of occupier's liability.

Who owes the duty?

It has already been shown that the Act imposes a duty of care on occupiers. The Act (in s1(2)) states that whether someone is an occupier depends on whether the common law would treat him as an occupier. The leading case on the definition of an 'occupier' was, in fact, decided after the passing of the 1957 Act.

In the case of *Wheat* v *E Lacon & Co Ltd* [1966] AC 522 Mr Wheat was killed when he fell down a staircase at a public house. The staircase led from the downstairs part of the pub to the upstairs rooms which were run as a boarding house as well as being the private residence of the Manager of the pub and his wife. The owners of the premises, who were the defendants in the action, gave permission for upstairs rooms to be let to customers as boarding rooms. The question arose whether the owners of the public house, or the Manager, should be treated as the occupiers. The House of Lords held that whether someone is an occupier depends on whether he has control over the premises; and where a case revolves around part only of premises, whether someone is an occupier depends on whether he has control of that part of the property. On the facts of the case it was held that both the owners and the Manager were occupiers (as was his wife in that she ran the boarding house).

Lord Denning:

'In the Occupiers' Liability Act 1957, the word "occupier" is used in the same sense as it was used in the common law in cases on occupiers' liability for dangerous premises. It was simply a convenient word to denote a person who had a sufficient degree of control over premises to put him under a duty of care to those who came lawfully on to the premises.

Those persons were divided into two categories, invitees and licensees; but by the year 1956 the distinction between invitees and licensees had disappeared to vanishing point. The duty of the occupier had become simply a duty to take reasonable care to see that the premises were reasonably safe for people coming lawfully on to them; and it made no difference whether they were invitees or licensees. The Act of 1957 confirmed the process. It did away, once and for all, with invitees and licensees and classed them all as "visitors". This duty is simply a particular instance of the general duty of care, which every man owes to his "neighbour". When Lord Atkin eventually formulated the general rule in acceptable terms he, too, used occupiers' liability as an illustration. Translating this general principle into its particular application to dangerous premises, it becomes simply this: wherever a person has a sufficient degree of control over premises that he ought to realise that any failure on his part to use care may result in injury to a person coming lawfully there, then he is an "occupier" and the person coming lawfully there is his "visitor", and the "occupier" is under a duty to his "visitor" to use reasonable care. In order to be an "occupier", it is not necessary for a person to have entire control over the premises. He need not have exclusive occupation. Suffice it that he has some degree of control. He may share the control with others. Two or more may be "occupiers". And whenever this happens, each is under a duty to use care towards persons coming lawfully on to the premises, dependent on his degree of control. If each fails in his duty, each is liable to a visitor who is injured in consequence of his failure, but each may have a claim to contribution from the other.'

This case is important in two respects. Firstly, it shows that the normal rules on when a duty of care is owed must always be borne in mind. The second point of importance is that it makes it quite clear that more than one person may be under a duty of care to a visitor. On the facts of the case the owners of the premises were occupiers because they had certain duties of repairing the staircase under the terms of the lease. The manager and his wife were occupiers in that their lease of the premises gave them day-to-day control over the way in which the staircase was used and who used it.

What is the duty?

Lord Denning made it clear in the *Wheat* case that the 1957 Act derives from the common law in that the persons who owe a duty of care and the persons to whom that duty is owed are the same as at common law. Therefore, it is not surprising that the standard of care owed closely resembles the normal common law duty of reasonable care. In fact, however, the duty under the Act is not identical to the common law negligence duty. The duty owed by an occupier to a visitor is the 'common duty of care' and depends on the purpose for which the visitor is on the premises:

Section 2 of the Occupiers' Liability Act 1957 provides:

'1) An occupier of premises owes the same duty, the 'common duty of care', to all his visitors.

2) The common duty of care is a duty to take such care as in all the circumstances of the case is reasonable to see that the visitor will be reasonably safe in using the premises for the purposes for which he is invited or permitted by the occupier to be there.

3) The circumstances relevant for the present purpose include the degree of care, and of want of care, which would ordinarily be looked for in such a visitor, so that, for example, in proper cases -

a) an occupier must be prepared for children to be less careful than adults; and

b) an occupier may expect that a person, in the exercise of his calling, will appreciate and guard against any special risks ordinarily incident to it, so far as the occupier leaves him free to do so.'

Section 2 reflects the common law to a large degree, but is careful to relate the standard of care owed to the purpose for which the visitor is on the premises. The result of this is that the Act itself provides that it does not apply to trespassers. The examples given in s 2(3) are only examples – they are guides as to how the Courts should approach deciding the relevant standard of care in each particular case. It is implicit in s 2(3) that the occupier will not be held wholly responsible for injury to a visitor if the visitor was himself at fault; therefore, the Law Reform (Contributory Negligence) Act 1945 must be applied where appropriate.

The extent of the duty is demonstrated in *Cunningham v Reading Football Club* (1991) The Independent 20 March in which the club was held liable under the Occupiers' Liability Act 1957 s2 to five police officers injured while on crowd control duties at the club's ground. It was held that since the club knew the visiting fans contained an unruly element, and they knew how easily concrete could be broken from the stand and used as missiles, they should as reasonably prudent and careful occupiers have removed or minimised the risk. Although the police officers were actually injured by concrete thrown by visiting fans, it was the state ot the concrete in the stands which made the hooligans' acts possible. The club was liable both in negligence and under the Occupiers' Liability Act.

Trespassers

The common law

The law relating to liability for damage done to trespassers has recently been affected by the intervention of Parliament. It is, however, important to consider the common law prior to the statutory intervention which, in any event, must be looked at in order to understand the statute concerned. The House of Lords laid down the common law rules in 1972, but in doing so they overruled a case from 1929.

In *Addie* v *Dumbreck* [1929] AC 358 a child of four was killed when he trespassed on the defendants' land. He had been attracted to the land by a large wheel which formed part of a haulage system at a coal mine. Children often played on the site and the defendants knew this and had instructed their employees to warn children of the danger. On appeal from Scotland the House of Lords held that no duty of care was owed to a trespasser; the rule was formulated by the Lord Chancellor. Lord Hailsham LC:

'Towards the trespasser the occupier has no duty to take reasonable care for his protection or even to protect him from concealed danger. The trespasser comes on to the premises at his own risk. An occupier is in such a case liable only where the injury is due to some wilful act involving something more than the absence of reasonable care. There must be some act done with the deliberate intention of doing harm to the trespasser, or at least some act done with reckless disregard of the presence of the trespasser.'

The principle set out in *Addie*'s case that no duty of care was owed by an occupier towards trespassers was criticised on more than one occasion by the Court of Appeal for its harshness and in 1972 the House of Lords overruled the 1929 case.

In the case of *British Railways Board* v *Herrington* [1972] AC 877 the plaintiff was aged six when he was severely burned whilst playing on a railway track. He had been playing with his brother and some friends in a meadow, 'Bunces Meadow', which was owned by the National Trust. The railway track ran alongside Bunces Meadow and the railway operators, British Rail, knew for some time that children had been playing on the track since the fencing was in a bad state of repair. At first instance the boy was awarded damages and the Court of Appeal upheld the award. The House of Lords also held that he was entitled to damages.

All five Members of the House held that British Rail, the occupiers, had broken a duty of care towards the boy. Lord Wilberforce was a little reluctant to reach this conclusion, but did so nonetheless.

As regards the formulation of the rule applicable when asking whether a duty was owed in any particular case, the emphasis of all five speeches was the same. They all made it clear that we must use the neighbour test to see whether a duty of care is owed; but in the same way as that test is only in general terms, so only general statements were made about the times when a trespasser will be considered to be a neighbour. The first important point made was that the law must draw a distinction between lawful visitors and trespassers. The distinction must be drawn because a lawful visitor is owed the common duty of care, whereas the House of Lords held that a trespasser is owed a lower duty – the duty of common humanity. The duty of common humanity is a duty to take some steps to protect trespassers in certain cases only. A duty is owed where the occupier knows of the presence of the trespasser – on this matter all Members of the House agreed. If the occupier does not know of the presence of the trespasser, but knows that there is a chance that a person may trespass on his land, then he will owe a duty of care if the chance of a person trespassing is a 'substantial probability' (according to Lord Reid), or is 'likely' (according to Lord Morris and Lord Pearson) or is 'so likely that in all the circumstances it would be inhumane not to give him effective warning of the danger' (according to Lord Diplock).

Once it has been established that a duty of care is owed it is necessary to consider the standard of care. The speeches in *Herrington* were in agreement in saying that the standard of care owed is the standard of common humanity. But it was not said what this standard is, because that must inevitably be a question of fact from case to case. All that can be said about the duty of common humanity is that the occupier does not have to take as great steps to protect a trespasser as he would to protect a visitor. Also the amount of care which must be taken must depend on all the circumstances of the case, including the financial resources of the occupier.

The statutory position

In 1984 Parliament intervened in an attempt to lay down clear and uniform rules in the same way as had been done in 1957 in the context of lawful visitors:
Section 1 of the Occupiers' Liability Act 1984 provides:

'1) The rules in s 1(1)–(8) are to have effect instead of the common law rules to determine:

a) whether any duty is owed by a person as occupier of the premises to persons other than his visitors in respect of any risk of their suffering injury on the premises by reason of any danger due to the state of the premises or to things done or omitted to be done on them; and
b) if so, what the duty is.

2) "Occupier" and "visitor" bear the same meaning as under the Occupiers' Liability Act 1957.

3) An occupier owes a duty to a non-visitor in respect of any risk if:

a) he is aware of the danger or has reasonable grounds to believe that it exists;
b) he knows or has reasonable grounds to believe that the other is in the vicinity of the danger concerned or that he may come into the vicinity of the danger (in either case, whether the other has lawful authority for being in the vicinity or not); and
c) the risk is one against which, in all the circumstances of the case, he may reasonably be expected to offer the other some protection.

4) Where a duty is owed by an occupier, that duty is:

"to take such care as is reasonable in all the circumstances of the case to see that he does not suffer injury on the premises by reasons of the danger concerned."

5) The occupier may discharge his duty under the Act by "taking such steps as are reasonable in all the circumstances of the case to give warning of the danger concerned or to discourage persons from incurring the risk."

6) No duty is owed to a person in respect of risks which he willingly accepts as his; the question of acceptance of a risk is to be determined according to the principles which apply in cases where a duty of care is involved.

7) No duty is owed under the Act to persons on the highway.

8) No liability will be incurred for a breach of duty under the Act for loss or damage to property .

9) ... "injury" means "anything resulting in death or personal injury including any disease and any impairment of the physical or mental condition ...".'

The effect of this Act is, as s1(1) states, to replace the common law rules. The most difficult point as regards whether a duty is owed to a particular trespasser is in the interpretation of s1(3)(c). This states that the occupier owes a duty where there is a danger against which the trespasser may reasonably be expecting to receive some protection. Whether a particular risk is one from which an occcupier might reasonably be expected to protect a trespasser will, inevitably, depend on all the circumstances of the case. It may be that the courts will revert to the matters discussed in *Herrington* in order to decide where protection ought to be given. The standard of care is that the occupier should take such care as is reasonable to prevent the trespasser being injured by the danger concerned, according to sub-section 4; but this is explained in sub-section 5 as being a duty to warn the trespasser or to discourage trespassers. It is important to note that the duty is owed in relation to personal injury only, not in relation to the property of the trespasser.

Whether the Act will make much difference to the protection given to a trespasser can only be seen once the courts have interpreted the Act in different situations. It seems likely that the position of the trespasser is stronger now, in that the standard of care under the Act appears to be more stringent than the duty of common humanity recognised in *Herrington*.

Contractors

The third aspect of liability usually arises where the person who does the harm is not covered by the definition of 'occupier' mentioned above. Many people would call a builder who is working on a site the 'occupier' of the site whilst he is doing the work; but unless he has control over the site he is not treated as an occupier.

The law recognises a duty on someone like a builder to take care to people other than his employer. This duty is now laid down in the Defective Premises Act 1972. It is not necessary to set out the words of the Act, a brief summary will suffice.

Defective Premises Act 1972

Section 1 imposes a duty on a builder to see that the work is done in a proper manner with proper materials, so that on completion it will be habitable. This means that if the building is not fit for habitation when completed because of the poor standard of work, the builder will be liable not only to any landlord of the premises, but also to any tenant who may move in.

Section 3 imposes a duty of care on the builder which extends not only to any landlord and tenant at the time the work was done, but also to subsequent buyers and tenants. This section was needed because the common law did not recognise that a duty of care was owed to subsequent buyers or tenants.

Section 4 does not place a duty of care on the landlord himself. He may, in fact, be an occupier himself, under the test in *Wheat* v *E Lacon & Co Ltd* [1966] AC 522, so to this extent the Act can be seen to affect the position of occupiers. The section applies where a landlord has to repair defects and makes him liable in tort to anyone who suffers personal injuries because of the state of the premises.

In *Andrews* v *Schooling* [1991] 1 WLR 783, the plaintiffs took a long lease of a ground floor flat, but not the cellar. A considerable amount of building work was done to the flat, but not the cellar. The whole flat was later found to be suffering the effects of damp, originating in the cellar. The plaintiffs claimed breach of s1 Defective Premises Act 1972. The defendants argued that they had no liability because they had done no work at all to the cellar. The court rejected this argument. If a building was in some way unfit when works were complete, whether or not the problem arose from works negligently completed or because no work at all had been done, the defendants were liable.

Liability in tort (2) 27

Defences in tort

General defences

General defences are those which are available in more than one tort; these are to be contrasted with particular defences which may be raised in respect of a particular tort only. Both general and particular defences may be raised together in any action where this is appropriate. In this section of this chapter, seven general defences will be briefly examined.

Volenti non fit injuria (consent)

If a person consents either expressly or impliedly to suffer harm then he cannot afterwards sue in respect of it. The doctrine of volenti non fit injuria, or the 'assumption of risk' can be divided into two categories:

a where a person agrees to the infliction of an intentional harm which would otherwise be a tort, eg where a patient consents to a surgical operation by a doctor;

b where a person agrees to run the risk of accidental harm which would otherwise allow him to sue in tort.

See, for example, *Morris v Murray* [1991] 2 QB 6. Here the plaintiff had been drinking with a friend, a pilot, who later took him for a flight in his light aircraft. The friend was killed and the plaintiff was badly injured when the plane crashed. It was held that, by knowingly and willingly embarking on a flight with a drunken pilot, the defence of volenti would apply.

Consent to run the risk of accidental harm or to have intentional harm inflicted upon oneself may be implied or expressed. For example, a boxer cannot sue his opponent for damages for assault and battery because that is a risk he agrees to take when he enters the ring. Similarly, a footballer cannot complain about injuries which occur as part of the ordinary rough-and-tumble of a match.

See *Simms v Leigh Rugby Football Club* [1969] 2 All ER 923 where a player, whose leg was broken in a tackle, lost his action. Of course, had the tackle been a foul, he might not have been taken to have consented; see *Gilbert v Grundy* (1978) Sunday Telegraph 31 July.

Knowledge of a risk of accidental harm is not sufficient if the plaintiff did not in reality consent to run the risk. Thus where the plaintiff had no choice the defence cannot apply. For example, if the plaintiff was obliged to undertake a dangerous task as part of his job, his employer cannot claim that the plaintiff consented to the risk of injury. Clearly, consent to a danger is different to knowledge of the danger. In other words, the principle of volenti non fit injuria is based on free choice of taking a risk.

In *Smith v Baker* [1891] AC 325 a worker in a quarry continued to work, despite having several times pointed out to his employers that he was directly under the path of the crane which was loading rocks from the quarry, and that there was a serious risk of an accident. When, almost inevitably, he was injured by rocks falling from the crane, his employers pleaded volenti, saying that he was obviously aware of the risks and yet had continued to work.

In disallowing this defence, the court stated that *knowing* of the existence of a risk was not the same as *being willing* to face such a risk.

The doctrine of volenti non fit injuria cannot be pleaded by an employer in an action for damages based on breach of statutory duty, since the object of the statute should not be allowed to be defeated by a private agreement between employer and employee. However, where an employee is in breach of statutory duty and the party injured sues the employer (who is not himself in breach of statutory duty) as being vicariously liable for the tort of the employee, the employer can plead the defence if appropriate.

Volenti non fit injuria is often raised as a defence in cases where the plaintiff has been injured in an attempt to save persons or property from injury. The defence will only succeed in such cases if the action of the plaintiff was not reasonable.

Where a person who committed suicide was of unsound mind it could not be said that he was volens (ie that volenti non fit injuria applied) because his judgment was impaired and he could not be said to have 'waived or abandoned any claim arising out of his suicide': *Kirkham* v *Chief Constable of Greater Manchester Police* [1990] NLJ 209.

Inevitable accident

This may apply where the accident was one which was not avoidable by any precautions a reasonable man could be expected to take. It is rarely used, as it will generally be held that an 'accident' has a cause and is not unavoidable.

In *National Coal Board* v *JE Evans* [1951] 2 KB 861 the defendants damaged an electricity cable during excavations. Because they did not know and had no reason to know of the existence of the cable, this might be termed inevitable accident.

Act of God

This defence is available in 'circumstances which no human foresight can provide against, and of which human prudence is not bound to recognise the possibility'. It is most important in connection with the tort of *Rylands* v *Fletcher*. The distinction between the defence of Act of God and inevitable accident is that the former can be used only if the event is caused solely by natural forces, whereas the latter allows for a degree of human intervention.

In *Nichols* v *Marsland* (1876) 2 Ex D 1 a rainstorm 'greater and more violent' than any in living memory caused three ornamental lakes to overflow; the flood water destroyed four bridges and caused considerable other damage. The defence of Act of God was successfully pleaded.

Self defence

A person may use reasonable force to protect himself or other persons or his property against unlawful force. What is 'reasonable' is a question of fact to be decided according to all the circumstances. Therefore, if someone is attacked he may fight off his assailant without being liable in damages for assault and battery.

Necessity

This defence is available where the damage or loss was caused in order to prevent the occurrence of even greater damage or loss or was caused in defence of the realm. The action taken must be reasonable. It is to be distinguished from duress, which will not generally be a defence to an action in tort.

Statutory authority

Statutes may bestow upon public bodies authority to act in a way which would otherwise constitute tortious behaviour. Nothing authorised by statute will be unlawful.

Such authority may be absolute (where the authority is under a duty to act) or is permissive or conditional (where the authority has a power to act but is not bound to do so). In the latter case the public authority may only carry its power to act in a way which does not interfere with the rights of others, whereas in the former case, where the statutory authority is absolute, the body or authority concerned is not liable for damage resulting from the exercise of that authority so long as it has acted reasonably and there is no alternative way of performing the act.

Statutory authorisation is a particularly useful defence to local and other statutory authorities, especially when faced with actions for what would otherwise be a strict liability tort.

Note however that an act authorised by statute must be carried out with reasonable care and statutory authority is therefore not a defence if there is negligence.

Thus in *Metropolitan Asylum District v Hill* (1881) 6 App Cas 193 the authority had a duty to provide a smallpox isolation hospital. Though there was a choice of several potential sites they chose to build it in a residential area. When sued by neighbouring landowners for nuisance, it was held that the defence of statutory authorisation would not apply, because they could have exercised their statutory powers so as to cause fewer problems and danger.

Novus actus interveniens

This may be pleaded where the defendant has committed a wrongful act but it does not directly harm the plaintiff, but sets up a chain of events ending in damage suffered by the plaintiff. If the defendant can show that the 'chain of causation' was broken by a supervening event, he will not be liable, as he will have proved that it was not his original act but the subsequent act which caused the damage suffered.

Special defences

As has been already stated, there are special (as opposed to general) defences. These are defences which are usually available in relation to one specific tort only. For example, the defences available to a defendant sued in defamation cases are highly specific, though outside the content of these syllabuses.

Another example is contributory negligence which, as its name suggests, is largely a defence used in the context of negligence actions. (For further details on attribution of fault/blame see also chapter 35.)

This defence will arise where the damage suffered is partly because of the plaintiff's own neligent conduct. It should be distinguished from the general defence of volenti non fit injuria, where although the plaintiff may have consented to run the risk of injury his own behaviour is in no way negligent.

There are some who would argue that this is not a true defence, because even if established it will not nowadays absolve the defendant from all liability, but simply reduce the amount of compensation he may have to pay. At best it can perhaps be regarded as a damage limitation exercise to plead contributory negligence.

Where a plaintiff is partly to blame for his own injury, then the blame is shared (under the Law Reform (Contributory Negligence) Act 1945) on a percentage basis. A typical example of contributory negligence in operation is *Sayers* v *Harlow UDC* [1958] 2 All ER 342.

Mrs Sayers found herself locked in a public lavatory. Unable to summon help or to attract attention, she tried to climb out over the toilet door. Unfortunately, in so doing she rested her foot on the toilet roll which rotated. She fell and was injured.

The court found that 75 per cent of her injury was the responsibility of the Council in not maintaining the lavatories properly and providing a defective door lock; but 25 per cent of the blame was Mrs Sayers' own. Compensation, when assessed, was therefore awarded on that basis.

Vicarious liability

In certain circumstances a person may be held liable for torts committed by others. Examples are the vicarious liability of a parent for the torts of his child, of an employer for the torts of his employee or of a principal for the torts committed by his agent. This is not by any means a complete list of situations where vicarious liability will apply; but some forms of vicarious liability are more common than others. Probably *the* most commonly litigated form of vicarious liability is that of an employer for the wrongful acts of his employees.

It is that form of vicarious liability which we consider in this section.

It is essential to note that vicarious liability is concerned with the situation where one person is rendered liable for the tort of another, not with the situation where one person is rendered liable for his own tort. Although this distinction appears to be an obvious one, it can be difficult to draw the line in practice. For example, a National Health Service patient who suffers loss as a result of a negligently performed operation may decide to sue the Area Health Authority directly for its failure to provide adequate levels of staffing in the hospital or he may elect to sue the Area Health Authority as being vicariously liable for the negligence of one of its doctors.

Vicarious liability in employment law

Rationale for vicarious liability

One of the unusual features of the doctrine of vicarious liability is that, whilst there is general agreement as to the utility of the doctrine, the doctrine has no clear rationale. A number of possible rationales have been put forward, but none are wholly convincing. These rationales are as follows:

a the employer has control over his employee, therefore he is responsible for the acts of his employee. This, however, is a demonstrable fallacy because in many cases the employee is more skilled than the employer (for example doctors and pilots) and so it cannot be said in any meaningful sense that the employer has control over his employee;

b the employer was careless in selecting an employee who was negligent and he must accept responsibility because, by selecting a negligent employee, he set in motion the train of events which led to the negligent act of his employee. But no employee is immune from being negligent at some stage in his employment and to insist that an employer only employ non-negligent employees is to place an unreasonable and unjustified burden on the employer;

c the employer derives benefit from the service of his employee, so it is only right that he takes the burdens as well. This justification purports to give some economic and moral basis to the imposition of liability upon the employer. It may be thought, however, that, in a society which accepts the existence of the division of labour, we often benefit from the works of others without contributing to the cost of that work and the mere fact of receipt of a benefit is not, of itself, sufficient to justify the imposition of an obligation to pay for it.

d the employer is in a better position than the employee to compensate the victim of the tort. The employee will generally not have the funds available to meet the damages claim nor will he have an insurance policy to meet the claim, whereas an employer will normally have the latter if not the former. The employer is often in the best position to spread the loss because he can take account of the loss as a cost of the production process and thus pass the cost on as part of the cost of his product.

e by imposing liability on the employer, the employer is thereby given an incentive to ensure that the event does not occur again and that none of his other employees do the same thing.

It is probably true to say that there is no one justification for the imposition of vicarious liability. The best conclusion may be that of *Professor Williams* when he said in his article *Vicarious Liability and the Master's Indemnity* ((1957) 20 MLR 220, 232):

> ' ... that vicarious liability owes its explanation, if not its justification, to the search for a solvent defendant. It is commonly felt that when a person is injured ... he ought to be able to obtain recompense from someone; and if the immediate tortfeasor cannot afford to pay, then he is justified in looking around for the nearest person of substance who can plausibly be identified with the disaster. Where there is no immediate tortfeasor at all, the same sentiment works itself out through rules of strict liability.'

So the rationale of vicarious liability may be said to lie closest to category (iv). This lack of a coherent rationale for the doctrine does not appear to have troubled the judiciary. Lord Pearce in *Imperial Chemical Industries Ltd* v *Shatwell* [1965] AC 656, said:

> 'The doctrine of vicarious liability has not grown from any very clear, logical or legal principle but from social convenience and rough justice.'

Who is an employee?

As vicarious liability arises from the employment relationship and not from the relationship of employer and independent contractor it is important to distinguish between an employee and an independent contractor. This distinction may seem an obvious one, but it has caused the courts great difficulties. These difficulties are likely to increase today because of the growth of what is called 'a-typical' forms of employment, where it is difficult to tell whether the worker is an employee or not. These 'a-typical' forms of employment include homeworkers, casual workers (for example, those workers who have no fixed hours of work but are called in by their employer as and when required) and those who are told by their employers when they are hired that they are self-employed so that the employer can evade the employment protection legislation. All these categories of workers are likely to present the courts with considerable problems in determining their employment status.

The original test for distinguishing between an employee and an independent contractor was the 'control test'. This test had its origin in the judgment of Bramwell LJ in *Yewens* v *Noakes* (1880) 6 QBD 530 where he said that an employee was anyone 'who was subject to the command of the master as to the manner in which he shall do the work'. This test never meant that the employer in fact controlled the employee for every second of his working day, but that he had the *right* to do so. The control test was designed in Victorian times only to cope with manual and domestic workers and the like.

Difficulties with the 'control' test led to dissatisfaction with the test on the part of the judiciary and an attempt to find an alternative test for distinguishing between employees and independent contractors. So in *Stevenson, Jordan and Harrison Ltd* v *MacDonald* [1952] 1 TLR 101 Denning LJ formulated the 'business integration' test or the 'organisation' test. By this he meant that a worker who is an employee does his work as an 'integral part of the business' whereas an independent contractor is not 'integrated' into the business but is merely 'accessory' to it. While sounding neat in theory it was impossibly vague to apply in practice and was quickly abandoned.

The next attempt at formulating a test for distinguishing between an employee and an independent contractor occurred in *Market Investigations Ltd* v *Minister of Social Security* [1969] 2 QB 173. In this case an interviewer was hired by a research company. She was free to set her own hours of work, although the pattern of her work was set by the research company. She received no sick pay or holiday pay and she was free to work for others. It was held that she was an employee because she was not 'in business on her own account'. Although this test avoids the excesses of the 'business integration' test it is still unacceptably vague.

Another factor which has been given some weight by the courts is the parties' labelling of their own relationship. This approach reached its height in *Massey* v *Crown Life Insurance* [1978] 1 WLR 676 where a man who had agreed to be self-employed so that he could enjoy certain tax advantages sought to argue that he was an employee so that he could claim the benefits of the employment protection legislation. The Court of Appeal dismissed his claim, Lord Denning saying that 'having made his bed as being self-employed, he must lie on it'. But this approach has not been uniformly accepted. In *Young and Woods* v *West* [1980] IRLR 201 a skilled metal worker, who chose when he was hired to be treated as 'self-employed' so that he could obtain a tax saving of some £500 per year, was nevertheless held to be an employee when he presented a claim that he had been unfairly dismissed. The court held that the parties' labelling of their relationship was only one factor to be taken into account and that employees had to be protected from contracting out of their statutory employment rights.

The approach which the courts now adopt is to abandon the search for any one factor which will be conclusive in all cases and to examine all the facts of the particular case. An early example of this is the case of *Ready Mixed Concrete (South East) Ltd* v *Minister of Pensions* [1968] 2 QB 497. MacKenna J laid down three conditions for the existence of a contract of employment:

a the employee agrees to provide his work and skill to the employer in return for a wage or other remuneration;

b the employee agrees, expressly or impliedly, to be directed as to the mode of performance to such a degree as to make the other his employer; and

c the other terms of the contract are consistent with there being a contract of employment.

It should not be thought, however, that the courts confine themselves to these three factors. The courts will, in fact, consider a wide range of factors including the degree of control over the worker's work, his connection with the business, the parties' agreement, the regularity and nature of the work and methods of payment etc.

One final difficulty, which calls for comment at this stage, arises where an employer lends his employee to another employer. If that employee then commits a tort which employer is vicariously liable? The answer was provided by the House of Lords in *Mersey Docks and Harbour Board* v *Coggins and Griffith (Liverpool) Ltd* [1947] AC 1. They held that the proper test to apply was whether the hirer did or did not have the authority to control the manner in which the employee did his work and that the stipulations of the parties as to who was to be regarded as the employer were not conclusive. They held that the burden of proof was on the general employer (ie the one who hired out the employee) to show that he was not the employer and that the burden was a heavy one to discharge, and which according to Viscount Simon would only be discharged in quite exceptional cases. On the facts the general employers failed to discharge the burden on them because, although the hirers directed the employees as to what parcels they should lift with the crane, they had no authority to tell the employees how to use the crane. Other factors which may be of importance include who pays the wages, who can dismiss the employee, how long the employee is hired out for and whether machinery is also hired out. The latter factor may be important because where it is only labour which is hired out it is much easier to infer that the hirer is the employer, although even here the courts are reluctant to accept that the hirer has control (*Bhoomidas* v *Port of Singapore* [1978] 1 All ER 956).

The employee must commit a tort

This point may be said to be labouring the obvious, but it is inserted because in *Twine* v *Bean's Express Ltd* [1946] 1 All ER 202 Uthwatt J suggested that an employer could be vicariously liable even though the employee has not committed a tort (for the full facts of this case see below). This error was, however, corrected by the House of Lords in *Imperial Chemical Industries Ltd* v *Shatwell* (1965) (supra) where the crucial distinction between primary and vicarious liability was re-affirmed. Vicarious liability only arises where the employee commits a tort.

Course of employment

This is the most difficult issue in vicarious liability. There has been an enormous deluge of cases on this point and many of these cases are irreconcilable. All that can be said is that the courts have provided guidelines which they will use in considering whether the employee was acting within the course of his employment. The employee must, of course, have been acting within the course of his employment before the employer will be held vicariously liable for his employee's tort.

Perhaps the most famous definition of 'course of employment' is provided in the following terms by *Salmond and Heuston* in *The Law of Torts* (19th ed) at pp521–522:

'A master is not responsible for a wrongful act done by his servant unless it is done in the course of his employment. It is deemed to be so done if it is either (i) a wrongful act authorised by the master, or (ii) a wrongful and unauthorised mode of doing some act authorised by the master ... On the other hand, if the unauthorised and wrongful act of the servant is not so connected with the authorised act as to be a mode of doing it, but is an independent act, the master is not responsible: for in such a case the servant is not acting in the course of his employment, but has gone outside of it.'

This statement can be used as a basis for an analysis of the law, although it must be emphasised that it should not be taken as an exclusive statement of the law, but merely as being illustrative of the approach of the courts. It can be discussed under the following headings:

Negligent and careless acts

The fact that the mode of doing a job is wrongful and unauthorised will not prevent the employer being vicariously liable for it provided that at the time the employee was doing some act authorised by the employer. This has the effect of denying to employers the argument that the mere fact that the employee was going about his work in a negligent or mistaken manner takes the employee outside the course of his employment because the employer would not have sanctioned the commission of a negligent or mistaken act.

This can be demonstrated in its application to negligent acts by the case of *Century Insurance Co* v *Northern Ireland Road Transport Board* [1942] AC 509. The defendants employed S as a petrol tanker driver. While discharging petrol at a garage, S lit a cigarette. He threw away the lighted match, which caused a fire and an explosion in which the plaintiff's property was damaged. The House of Lords held that the defendants were vicariously liable for the tort of their employee. Although it was true that the driver had lit a cigarette for his own personal benefit and not for the benefit of his employers, this act of lighting a cigarette could not be viewed in isolation from the job he was doing at that time. At the time of the accident the driver was doing his job of discharging petrol from the tanker, albeit that he was doing his job in an unauthorised and negligent fashion. He was simply doing, in a mistaken manner, what he was employed to do.

Express prohibition

It follows from the definition provided by *Salmond and Heuston* that the mere fact that an employer has placed prohibitions upon the conduct of the employee will not, of itself, operate to restrict the course of employment (see to similar effect the judgment of Lord Dunedin in *Plumb* v *Cobden Flour Mills Co* [1914] AC 62). It may be objected that there is no good reason why an employer should be liable where he has expressly placed prohibitions upon the employee. But such an approach would make it too easy for employers to evade the impact of the vicarious liability doctrine by prohibiting their employees from committing torts. So the law has to strike a balance between denying to employers the ability to exempt themselves from the impact of this doctrine, while avoiding the imposition of liability for acts which are wholly unconnected with the work of the employee. The approach which the law has adopted is to permit employers to limit the acts which the employee may do within the course of his employment, but to deny them the ability to restrict the mode of doing the particular act in question. Thus stated, the crucial distinction is between the mode of doing the act and the act itself.

A comparison of the decisions in *Twine v Bean's Express Ltd* (1946) above and *Rose v Plenty* [1976] 1 WLR 141 illustrates the confusion that may occur between the doing of the act and the act itself test. In the former case the plaintiff's husband was given a lift in a van driven by an employee of the defendants. The plaintiff's husband was killed as a result of the negligence of the driver. The driver had been told that he could only give lifts to certain passengers and the plaintiff was not one of these passengers. Furthermore there was a notice restricting the class of authorised passengers inside the van. The Court of Appeal held that the defendants were not liable for the tort of their employee. There were two grounds to the decision of the court. The first was that the deceased was a trespasser and as such was not owed a duty of care by the defendants. The second point was that the driver was not acting within the course of his employment because at the time of the accident he was doing an unauthorised act, namely giving a lift to an unauthorised person.

This case was re-considered by the Court of Appeal in the controversial case of *Rose v Plenty* (above). The defendants expressly prohibited their milkmen from permitting boys to ride on their milk floats. Notices were also posted at the depot informing milkmen of this prohibition. In contravention of this order an employee allowed the plaintiff, a boy aged 13, to ride on his milk float while helping him with his deliveries and collections. As he was riding on the milk float the plaintiff was injured due to the negligence of the driver. The Court of Appeal held that the defendants were liable for the tort of their employee. Their prohibition had not affected the course of the employee's employment, it had simply affected the mode by which he could do his job. Lawton LJ dissented on the ground that he could not distinguish the present case from *Twine* and he was not prepared to say that the latter decision was wrong.

The majority, Lord Denning MR and Scarman LJ, distinguished *Twine* on two grounds. The first ground was that the deceased in *Twine* was a trespasser and was therefore owed no duty of care by the defendants. It was held that this ground of the decision could no longer stand because, since the decision of the House of Lords in *British Railways Board v Herrington* [1972] AC 877, it was clear that a limited duty of care is owed to trespassers.

The second ground on which the majority distinguished *Twine* related to the course of employment point. Lord Denning distinguished *Twine* on the ground that there the lift was not given for any purpose beneficial to the employer (presumably because the lift was given to an employee of another company), whereas in *Rose* the plaintiff's presence on the milk float was to further the employer's business. This latter point must be regarded as doubtful because, as was pointed out by Lawton LJ, the plaintiff was not furthering the employer's business but was doing the driver's job for him and making his life an easier one. Scarman LJ dealt more fully with the caselaw and vainly sought to show that the caselaw was reconcilable. He said that in *Twine* the employer's prohibition limited the scope of the employee's employment, whereas here the employer's prohibition did not alter the scope of the employee's employment but only affected the mode by which the job was to be done. However this reconciliation is only effective at the formal level because it does not explain how the courts define the act which the employee is employed to do, as against the mode in which he is to do the job. The more important aspect of the judgment may be that Scarman LJ argued that a broad approach should be taken to the question of the course of employment.

'Frolics and detours'

Considerable difficulty has arisen with vehicle drivers who depart from authorised routes. One could argue that as soon as an employee departs from his authorised route he goes outside the course of his employment. The generally accepted test was laid down by Parke B in *Joel* v *Morrison* (1834) 6 C & P 501 in the following terms:

> 'If [the driver] was going out of his way, against his master's implied commands, when driving on his master's business, he will make his master liable; but if he was going on a frolic of his own, without being at all on his master's business, the master will not be liable.'

In *Williams* v *A & W Hemphill Ltd* 1966 SLT 259, a Scottish case which went on appeal to the House of Lords, some interesting comments were made on this area of law. The case concerned a driver who had gone on a considerable detour when driving boys home, because the boys wanted to follow some girl guides who had been camping in a nearby field. While on this detour the bus was involved in an accident and some of the boys were injured. The driver was held to be within the course of his employment. Lord Pearce said that it was a question of fact in each case whether the employee had gone on a 'frolic of his own'. He considered *Storey* and said that had the driver been carrying, at the time of the accident, some important cargo belonging to the employer then the result might have been different. In *Williams* the continued presence of the boys on the bus made it impossible to say that this was a frolic of the driver's own. This latter case suggests that it is only a new and independent journey, which is solely undertaken for the selfish purposes of the employee, that will constitute a 'frolic of his own'.

Intentional wrongful acts

In cases involving intentional wrongful acts the courts have adopted a much more restrictive approach to the course of employment issue. This can be seen in the following two recent cases. The first is *Heasmans* v *Clarity Cleaning Co Ltd* [1987] IRLR 286. One of the defendant's employees, who was employed to clean the plaintiff's offices, used the plaintiff's telephone to make unauthorised international calls costing £1411. The Court of Appeal held that the defendants were not vicariously liable for the acts of their employee. Nourse LJ stated that the employee was employed to clean the telephones and not to use them. In using them he had not cleaned the telephones in an unauthorised manner, but had done an unauthorised act and so had gone outside the course of his employment. This extremely narrow approach to the course of employment issue is clearly at variance with the much broader approach found in *Rose* v *Plenty* (above). The second case is *Irving* v *The Post Office* [1987] IRLR 289. The plaintiffs claimed that the defendants had unlawfully discriminated against them on the grounds of their race. The plaintiffs lived next door to an employee of the defendants, called Mr Edwards, and they were not on speaking terms. Mr Edwards, during the course of his work sorting mail, saw an envelope addressed to the plaintiffs and wrote on the back of the envelope 'Go back to Jamaica Sambo' and drew a picture of a black smiling face. Mr Edwards was authorised to write on letters which he was sorting but only for the purpose of ensuring that the mail was properly dealt with. The plaintiffs argued that the defendants were vicariously liable for the racial abuse of Mr Edwards but it was held that, in writing racial abuse on the envelope, the employee was doing an unauthorised act and that therefore the defendants were not vicariously liable. The Court of Appeal placed strong reliance upon *Heasmans* v *Clarity Cleaning* (above) and held that the writing of the racial abuse was an act of personal malevolence by Mr Edwards, and they affirmed that it could not be assumed that, merely because the employment had provided the opportunity for the wrong, the employers were therefore liable. Fox LJ stated that 'out of fairness to employers' limits have to be set to the doctrine of vicarious liability, particularly where, as here, it was sought to make the defendants liable for the 'wilful wrongdoing' of their employee which they had in no way authorised.

Employer's indemnity
There is no doubt that employers and employees are joint tortfeasors, with the result that when the employer is held liable for the tort of his employee, the employer has the right to recover an indemnity under s1(1) of the Civil Liability (Contribution) Act 1978. In the typical vicarious liability case this would mean that the employer could recover a complete indemnity.

Employers' liability for independent contractors
In addition to being liable for the torts of their employees committed in the course of their employment, employers may also, in certain circumstances, be held liable for torts committed by independent contractors which they have employed. It must be stated that none of these cases of liability for the tort of an independent contractor are examples of vicarious liability. They are all examples of primary liability of the employer. The general rule, it should be noted, is that an employer is *not* liable for the tort of his independent contractor. The traditional justification for this is that the employer does not control the independent contractor and so there is no justification for imposing liability upon the employer for the tort of the independent contractor. One example of this general rule is the case of *Morgan* v *Incorporated Central Council of the Girls Friendly Society* [1936] 1 All ER 404. The plaintiff suffered injury when he fell down a lift-shaft on the defendants' premises. The reason for the accident was that the lift shaft had been negligently left

unguarded by a firm of independent contractors. It was held that the defendants were not liable for the negligence of the independent contractors.

An interesting challenge to this rule was launched in *D & F Estates Ltd v Church Commissioners for England* [1987] 7 Const LR 40. The defendants built a block of flats and the plaintiffs took a lease of one of the flats. After they had moved in the plaintiffs discovered that the plastering work, which had been done by a firm of independent contractors employed by the defendants, had been done defectively. So they sued the defendants for the cost of the repair plus other economic loss on the ground, inter alia, that the defendants were under a duty to the plaintiffs to supervise the work of the sub-contractors and that they had failed to discharge this duty properly. The plaintiffs' argument was based squarely on Lord Wilberforce's two-tier approach to the duty of care issue. This argument was, however, rejected by the Court of Appeal. Glidewell LJ stated that if the plaintiffs' argument was correct and 'a main contractor who properly sub-contracts part of the work owes to subsequent occupiers of the building a duty of care at common law to supervise the work of the sub-contractor, the normal rule that a principal is not responsible for the negligence of an independent contractor is much eroded.' The Court of Appeal was not prepared to sanction such an erosion and so dismissed the plaintiffs' claim.

An appeal to the House of Lords was dismissed and the decision is reported at [1988] 3 WLR 368.

Exceptions to the general rule

There are a number of exceptions to the general rule that an employer is not liable for the tort of an independent contractor. These exceptions may be classified as follows.

a The employer is liable where he has authorised the independent contractor to commit a tort (*Ellis* v *Sheffield Gas Consumers Co* (1853) 2 E & B 767). In such a case the employer is liable as a joint tortfeasor with the independent contractor.

b The employer is liable if he is negligent in choosing an independent contractor who is not competent to carry out the job or if the employer fails to instruct him properly or fails to check the work where he is competent to do so (*Pinn* v *Rew* (1916) 32 TLR 451).

c Statute law may impose upon the employer a duty of care which cannot be discharged by delegating performance to an independent contractor. Whether a statute does impose such an 'absolute' obligation upon the employer is, of course, a question of construction of the particular statute. One example of a statute which imposes such an absolute obligation upon employers is the Factories Act 1961.

d At common law certain non-delegable duties are imposed upon employers. 'Non-delegable' duty does not mean that the employer cannot, in fact, delegate performance to an independent contractor. What it means is that the employer cannot delegate responsibility for the performance of the task. There are a number of non-delegable duties which exist at common law, but there is no coherent policy behind the existence of these duties. There are six such common law duties which are worthy of consideration.

i   The first category consists of cases of strict liability at common law, such as the rule in *Rylands* v *Fletcher* and nuisance (chapter 26), where the employer is liable for the tort of the independent contractor.

ii The second, and to some extent analogous, category consists of cases where the employer has employed an independent contractor to do work which is classified as being 'extra hazardous'. The operation of this principle can be illustrated by reference to the case of *Honeywill and Stein Ltd* v *Larkin Brothers Ltd* [1934] 1 KB 191. The plaintiffs were engaged to do acoustics work and employed the defendants, as independent contractors, to take photographs of the cinema as part of their work. The defendants used flash photography which, at that time, required a tray of magnesium to be ignited above the camera lens. In doing this the defendants set fire to the cinema curtains. The plaintiffs paid the damages and then sought to recover from the defendants. It was held that the plaintiffs were liable to the owners of the theatre for the damage caused by the negligence of the defendants and that they were, in turn, entitled to recover damages from the defendants for breach of contract. The operation was a hazardous one and the plaintiffs had assumed an obligation to ensure that reasonable precautions were taken so that no damage would result and this obligation could not be delegated to an independent contractor. This rule does not apply where the activity is not extra hazardous (*Salsbury* v *Woodland* [1970] 1 QB 342). It is not easy to say what constitutes an extra hazardous activity, but it must be something which involves the risk of special danger to others, rather than being extra hazardous to the contractor himself.

iii The third category of non-delegable duties at common law relates to liability for the escape of fire (*Balfour* v *Barty-King* [1957] 1 QB 496).

iv The fourth category consists of cases where the work of the independent contractor is done on or over the highway, or some other place to which the public has access. Thus in *Tarry* v *Ashton* (1876) 1 QBD 314 an employer was held liable when a lamp which projected over the highway fell on the plaintiff. The employer was held liable even though he had contracted with an independent contractor for the repair of the lamp. He remained liable for the negligence of the contractor. Similarly in *Holliday* v *National Telephone Co* [1899] 2 QB 392 the contractor, a plumber, was soldering joints in telephone wires when he immersed a blowlamp in a pot of solder on the highway and it exploded injuring the plaintiff. It was held that the defendants, who had employed the plumber, were liable because they had a duty to see that the work was carried out with due care for the protection of those who passed along the highway (in this case the defendants' duty was derived from statute).

v   The fifth category consists of the employer's non-delegable duty in respect of the safety of his employees (*Wilsons and Clyde Coal Co* v *English* [1938] AC 57).

vi   The sixth category consists of the rule that a bailee for reward, who entrusts the goods he is supposed to be looking after to an independent contractor, remains liable for any loss or damage to the goods, in the absence of any contractual provision to the contrary (see *Morris* v *CW Martin & Sons Ltd* [1966] 1 QB 716 and *British Road Services* v *Arthur Crutchley* [1967] 1 WLR 835).

Remedies in tort

Introduction

Broadly speaking the law of tort is concerned with redress for the injured party rather than with the punishment of the person liable. In this respect it is quite unlike criminal law, where the primary aims are punishment and deterrence. The principal remedy in tort, an award of damages, is obtained with a view to putting the injured party back to his original position as far as money is able to do this. Obviously if the plaintiff has suffered serious physical injury, monetary compensation is never going to be the complete answer. Essentially, liability in tort is founded on fault and the student should see also chapter 35.

However, having said that tortious remedies are not concerned with punishment, it should be noted that there have been cases where the courts, regarding the defendant's conduct as especially blameworthy or outrageous, have awarded exemplary or punitive damages.

See *Sutcliffe* v *Pressdram* [1990] 2 WLR 271 in which the damages awarded were initially exemplary, although it is true that these were subsequently reduced to an amount representing the normal measure of compensation.

Damages

As a general rule, damages in tort may be recovered once and once only, as in principle only one action should be brought in respect of one cause of action. To this rule there are three exceptions:

a   where the defendant's wrongful act violates two distinct rights of the plaintiff; eg where as a result of the defendant's negligent driving the plaintiff's car is damaged and the plaintiff also suffers personal injuries, the plaintiff can bring two separate actions for damages;

b   where the wrongful act is a continuing one; eg wrongfully placing a thing on the plaintiff's land and leaving it there, or a continuing nuisance;

c   where the tort is actionable only on proof of damage; if, eg one negligent act causes the plaintiff on quite separate occasions to suffer quite distinct injuries.

Kinds of damages

Damages may be of different kinds, and they may fall into several categories simultaneously:

a *Nominal* – where a legal right of the plaintiff has been infringed by the defendant but the plaintiff has suffered no loss. Damages may total only a few pence.

b *Real* – where damages are awarded to compensate for the loss inflicted, the amount depending on the degree of injury.

c *Compensatory* – an amount actually reflecting the loss suffered in so far as this can be translated into pecuniary terms.

d *Aggravated* – where the defendant's conduct was such as to go beyond the bare tortious act and was calculated to injure or insult the plaintiff, the Court will award an additional sum in favour of the plaintiff.

e *Contemptuous* – where the infringement of the plaintiff's rights was a mere technicality or was morally justified, and the action should never have been brought.

f *Exemplary* – where the wrong act comprises oppressive, arbitrary or unconstitutional action by servants of the Government, or where the defendant's conduct was calculated to make a profit which might exceed the plaintiff's damages, or where such an award is expressly authorised by statute.

g *General or Unliquidated* – damages which do not have to be specifically proved.

h *Special or Liquidated* – specific items of loss or damage, eg 'one torn shirt'; 'cost of seven return taxi-rides to hospital for physiotherapy, at £3 per time' etc; pleaded in addition to general damages.

Measure of damages

The general principle is 'restitutio in integrum'; that the plaintiff should be put back in the position he would have been in had the tort not been committed. On the other hand the plaintiff should not make a profit – should not be *better* off than if the tortious act had not occurred. Obviously, in some circumstances, eg personal injury involving loss of a limb or other amenity, restitutio is not possible, so the Court makes a notional award of compensation in such cases.

a *Personal injury*. Damages may be recovered for pain and suffering, loss of amenity, loss of expectation of life, loss of earnings, medical and other incidental expenses, future loss of earnings, loss of earning capacity, future expenses – all as appropriate. Various deductions from the total may be made for State benefits (eg unemployment benefit) or other deductible benefits such as sick pay or wages paid by an employer, in order to ensure that the plaintiff is not over-compensated.

b *Loss of or damage to property*. Where the plaintiff's property has been totally destroyed, the loss is usually assessed at the market value at the time of destruction. Where the plaintiff's property has been damaged, the loss will usually be assessed at the cost of repair. Where the plaintiff has been wrongfully dispossessed of land, in addition to an order for recovery he may receive 'mesne profits' from the date of the issue of the writ to the date of repossession.

Self help

This may be something of a perilous remedy, as the person exercising it may not be the best judge of how much he is entitled to do without exceeding his rights and becoming a tortfeasor himself. Some examples of its use are:

Trespass

A trespasser may be expelled with reasonable force. Goods wrongfully taken may be peaceably recovered.

Nuisance

May be abated (ie removed). Notice must first be given to the offending party to remedy the nuisance, unless the conditions are so urgent that this is not practicable. The plaintiff must not cause unnecessary damage to the defendant, and the least troublesome method of abatement must be chosen if more than one way is possible

Injunction

This is the second most commonly sought remedy after damages, and in some cases, eg nuisance, may be the principal remedy. Injunctions are usually prohibitory, ie they prohibit the defendant from doing or continuing to do something which constitutes tortious conduct. In relatively rare circumstances a mandatory injunction may be granted which compels the defendant to do something to rectify the consequences of his wrongful act. The plaintiff may apply for an interlocutory injunction to prevent further commission of the act complained of until the full trial of the issue.

An injunction is an equitable and, therefore, discretionary, remedy; therefore, the equitable maxims discussed above (chapter 8) must be borne in mind by the Courts in deciding whether an injunction should be granted.

Under Lord Cairns' Act (Chancery Amendment Act 1852), damages may be awarded in lieu of an injunction. The following considerations should be applied:

a   Is the injury to the plaintiff's legal right a small one?

b   Is it capable of being estimated in money?

c   Can it be compensated by a small money payment?

d   Would it be oppressive to the defendant to grant the injunction?

An example of a case where it would be appropriate to award damages in lieu of an injunction would be where a part of a building trespasses on to the plaintiff's land as a result of a mutual mistake as to the true boundary between the plaintiff's and the defendant's land, and partial demolition to end the trespass would involve the defendant in considerable expense.

Specific restitution of property

This may be ordered for the recovery of land or goods which have been wrongfully interfered with.

Limitation of actions

This is really a defence to an action but is included here because of the way it restricts the availability of remedies.

By virtue of the Limitation Act 1980, all cases must be brought within a certain time from the tort being committed, or from the tort being discoverable. Under s2 the normal limitation period is six years, but under s11 the period is only three years if the claim is for damages for personal injuries.

The courts have spent a lot of time in recent years discussing when the limitation period starts to run. This problem arises frequently in cases where a building has been erected or designed negligently. In such cases the negligent act of design or erection occurs before the building shows any signs of being defective. The courts have had the choice of holding that the limitation period runs from the time the building is negligently built or from the first time that the defect could be discovered. The present law is that the limitation period runs from the time the damage to the building occurs. This is so even if the damage could not be discovered until some time later. For example, it may be that a building is erected which starts to crack the day after it is completed, but the cracks cannot be seen except by a very careful examination of the brickwork below ground level. It may be that the cracks do not extend above ground level for some time, but the limitation period would run from the time the cracks first appeared even though they could not then be found by the use of reasonable diligence. This present state of the law was laid down by the House of Lords in 1982 in the case of *Pirelli General Cable Works* v *Oscar Faber* [1983] 2 AC 1.

A chimney was built in 1969. It started to develop cracks early in 1970 but these were near the top of the 160 foot tall chimney and were not discovered until late in 1977, at which time a writ was issued. The House of Lords held that the six-year limitation period had started to run in early 1970 when the cracks first appeared and, therefore, that the writ was issued too late.

There are two important exceptions to the six-year and three-year periods. The first is that the fraud or concealment of the defendant postpones the limitation period. This is the result of s32 of the 1980 Act which provides that where the defendant has been fraudulent or has concealed his wrongdoing the limitation period only starts to run when the plaintiff could with reasonable diligence have discovered the fraud or concealment. The second important exception is that if the plaintiff was under 18 at the time of the alleged negligence, the limitation period only starts to run on the child's 18th birthday – the six-year or three-year period starts to run from then. This is the effect of s28.

The rule laid down in *Pirelli General Works* v *Faber* (above) that the cause of action accrues at the date on which the damage occurs, irrespective of whether the victim knew or could reasonably have known of the damage at the time, can be unjust where the plaintiff does not know of the damage for some years.

It should be noted that in *Nitrigin Eireann Teorantes* v *Inco Alloys Ltd* [1991] 141 NLJ 1518 that *Pirelli* was not followed. The defendants manufactured alloy tubing which was used by the plaintiffs in their chemical plant. The tubing was manufactured in 1981, cracking began to be discovered in 1983, repairs were made that year (though the cause of the cracking was not discovered) and in 1984 the alloy tubing ruptured completely, causing an explosion and extensive damage to the plaintiffs' premises. They brought their action in 1990. A preliminary issue was heard as to whether the plaintiffs had a cause of action at all and if so whether the action was time barred.

The court decided that the plaintiffs did have a cause of action in negligence and it was not time barred. The court found:

a   A cause of action had accrued to the plaintiffs, despite dicta in *D & F Estates* v *Church Commissioners for England* [1989] AC 177 and *Murphy* v *Brentwood DC* [1991] 1 AC 398, because the defect had not been discovered before the damage was done. Although the external sign of a fault (the cracking) was repaired, the cause was never diagnosed until after the explosion. The cause of action arose at the time of the explosion.

b   The case of *Pirelli General Cable Works* v *Oscar Faber* [1983] 2 AC 1, which was sought to be relied on by the defendants, could be distinguished because in the present case the cracking damage was not, in itself, the cause of action.

On the other hand, if the damage occurs many years after the negligent act, the defendant may find himself liable for the damage resulting from an act which took place many years ago; vital evidence may have been destroyed, witnesses dead and so on.

To deal with this situation, the Latent Damage Act 1986 was passed. This made two changes in the law:

Firstly, s14A gives to victims a three-year period in which to sue after the damage was discovered or was reasonably discoverable. Hence, even though the six-year period might have expired, the plaintiff still has three years from the date of discovery/reasonable discoverability of the damage in which to bring an action.

Secondly, since this could be potentially unfair to the defendant, s14B establishes a 'long stop', which provides that generally, no action may be brought after the expiration of 15 years from the date of the defendant's breach of duty, even if no damage is discoverable by the end of that period, and indeed, even if no damage has yet occurred, and therefore no cause of action has accrued.

Law of contract (1): 28
introduction

Definitions

It is notoriously difficult to define a very generalised concept like 'a contract', and it is perhaps oversimplifying matters to say that a contract is 'a legally enforceable agreement', but if we look at some standard definitions we see that this is a common theme.

Treitel: 'A contract is an agreement giving rise to obligations which are enforced or recognised by the law. The factor which distinguishes contractual from other legal obligations is that they are based on the agreement of the contracting parties.'

Anson: 'We may provisionally describe the law of contract as that branch of the law which determines the circumstances in which a promise shall be legally binding on the person making it.'

Pollock: described a contract as 'a promise or set of promises which the law will enforce'.

American Restatement (Second) of the Law of Contract, 1978: 'A contract is a promise or a set of promises for the breach of which the law gives a remedy or the performance of which the law in some way recognises as a duty.'

From these definitions it would appear that the law of contract is about promises and agreements; however the scope and operation of the subject – and the meaning of 'agreement' – cannot be adequately explained without a consideration of:

a The historical development of the law of obligations and the emergence of contractual remedies.

b The theories underlying the purpose of the law of contract which necessarily involve a consideration of prevailing economic and philosophical attitudes.

c The aims of the law of contract (and remedial goals).

d The concept of freedom of contract.

Historical development

In the fourteenth century the common law courts had established jurisdiction over certain civil wrongs, which were then called trespasses. Flexible forms of action came to be developed which allowed litigants to adapt these forms to the particular circumstances of the case. These were called 'trespasses on the case'. Amongst such actions were those in which the plaintiff alleged that the defendant had undertaken (in the Latin: 'assumpsit') a certain obligation and then by negligent misconduct had caused him damage. This was a significant development. The earlier form of action, known as debt, could only be brought for claims to a specific sum of money. More important, however, was the fact that the method of trial in debt was not by jury but by the ritual of swearing an oath. The writ of debt was eventually replaced by that of assumpsit (*Slade's Case* (1602)

4 Co Rep 92a). Assumpsit became the general remedy for informal contracts, and it was the concept of assumpsit that became the foundation of contract and quasi-contract. The old writ of debt has nevertheless left its mark on the modern law. The foundation of contract in assumpsit and debt is reflected, in broad terms, in two kinds of situations in which a contractual remedy might be sought.

a The first kind of situation is one where the plaintiff complains of an invasion of his rights by the defendant's breach of undertaking.

b The second kind of situation is one where the plaintiff seeks a contractual remedy to recover a sum of money owed to him by the defendant, often for goods sold or services supplied.

It could be said that the first situation reflects the assumpsit origin of contract and the second situation the origin in debt.

It will also be seen that contract, and tort have a common origin. There is also an increasing recognition by the judiciary that the traditional and long-accepted rigid division of the law of obligations into contract and tort is without historic foundation and unrealistic. See eg: *Brook's Wharf and Bull Wharf* v *Goodman Bros* [1937] 1 KB 534; [1936] 3 All ER 696; *Hedley Byrne & Co Ltd* v *Heller & Partners Ltd* [1964] AC 465; [1963] 2 All ER 575; and *The Albazero* [1977] AC 774; [1976] 3 All ER 129.

Theories of contract

The main question here is: Why should promises be enforced? Several answers to this question can be isolated: each of which has gained prominence according to the prevalent economic/social/political theory of the period:

a *Natural law: honour theory* – When the church had considerable influence on the mores of society it was thought that promises ought to be kept and the law should reflect this fact.

b *Laissez faire: bargain theory* – This idea, perhaps, represents the basis of 'classical' contract: the law should enforce bargains, supported by adequate quid pro quo moving from both sides, made by free men of full age and capacity. Such a theory was less acceptable when people realised that the market economy did not make all men free: accordingly contract became the means of social control by the state (eg Hire Purchase Act, Food and Drugs legislation etc). See also *Freedom of Contract* (below).

c *Welfare State: reliance theory* – This theory is based on the notion that where one person has altered his position to his detriment on the basis of another's promise, the other should make good the detriment, or give compensation if he goes back on his promise.

Contract and equity

Equity has contributed a wider view of the reasons for enforcing contracts than the narrow, consideration-based approach articulated at common law in cases such as *Eastwood* v *Kenyon* (1840) 11 Ad & El 438 and *Currie* v *Misa* (1875) LR 10 Exch 153. In particular, courts of equity have shown greater concern to enforce promises than to uphold bargains: the focus of attention is the promisor and the need for him to keep substantive faith.

This approach is easily confused with the common law approach and the confusion was compounded once equity ceased to be administered by a separate court. The reason for the confusion is that equity is only applied at the court's discretion. And this discretion – to enforce promises – will only be exercised, inter alia, where not to do so would cause more harm to the plaintiff than to the defendant. In other words, the plaintiff must satisfy the court that, in the circumstances which exist *at the time of the hearing* (not, as in common law, those which existed at the time of the alleged breach), he will lose more if the court does not act than the defendant will if the court does act:

See *Foster* v *Robinson* [1951] 1 KB 149 and *Binions* v *Evans* [1972] Ch 359.

The other major difference between law and equity relates to its remedies. Equity will enforce the promise directly through specific performance or injunction: where this is not appropriate, damages may be awarded, but computed not, as at common law, at the date of the breach of contract, but at the date when the court decides to act against the defendant for breaking his promise or undertaking: *Wroth* v *Tyler* [1974] Ch 30.

The aims of the law of contract

The main aims of contract are:

a   To realise expectations.

b   To guard against or allocate certain (commercial) risks.

c   To ensure smooth running of the commercial system: *Tsakiroglou & Co Ltd* v *Noblee Thorl GmbH* [1962] AC 93.

d   Not to rescue a party from a bad bargain (see *Tsakiroglou* case, above): however relief may be afforded to a party in cases of duress and undue influence.

e   To be an instrument of social control (see eg employment, sale of goods and consumer credit law).

Remedial goals

The remedial goals of a plaintiff in a contract action are traditionally said to be one of three possibilities:

a *Fulfilment of expectation interest.* This is often said to be the primary goal: the plaintiff seeks to be put into the position he would have been in had the defendant carried out the contract. Or:

b *Protection of plaintiff's restitution interest.* Here the plaintiff seeks just to be put into the position he was in before he entered into the contract – namely: return of any goods delivered or money paid. Or:

c *Protection of plaintiff's reliance interest.* Here the plaintiff is seeking compensation for work carried out, or expenses incurred, in reliance upon the contractual agreement. A good example is the case of *Anglia Television Ltd* v *Reed* [1972] 1 QB 60.

Note: Punishment of the defendant is not a contractual aim (see *Addis* v *Gramophone Co Ltd* [1909] AC 488).

Freedom of contract

The philosophy of laissez-faire which prevailed in the nineteenth century involved the belief that the law should interfere with people's activities as little as possible. In the area of the law of contract this belief found expression in the words of Sir George Jessel in *Printing and Numerical Registering Co* v *Sampson* (1875) LR 19 Eq 462:

> 'if there is one thing more than another which public policy requires, it is that men of full age and competent understanding shall have the utmost liberty in contracting, and that their contracts, when entered into freely and voluntarily, shall be held sacred and shall be enforced by Courts of Justice.'

This robust view was not shared by all nineteenth century judges and did not recognise that people are seldom free to choose whether or not to contract or to choose the other contracting party or to determine the terms of their contracts. In particular the one party often enjoys a monopoly or other economically dominant position.

In recognition of this, statutes – particularly in this century – have sought to impose terms and limit the power of economically dominant parties. We shall be examining the scope and effect of this legislative intervention later.

Formation of contract

General

A plaintiff will not be able to succeed against a defendant simply because he has suffered loss which has in some fashion been induced by the defendant. He must be able to show that the defendant's conduct has given the plaintiff a cause of action in law. He must show that a contract has been entered into, either with the defendant, or (where a misrepresentation is alleged) with a third party. If he cannot show that a contract has been entered into, he cannot succeed on an application of the law of contract. He may be able to obtain relief in equity or under the law of torts but that does not fall to be discussed in this section.

Elements of contract

Accordingly, it is said that the plaintiff must show several things to exist in order to establish that a contract has been entered into:

a that the parties had an intention to enter into legal relations;

b that one party made an offer to the other which was capable of acceptance;

c that the other accepted that offer unconditionally;

d that there was an exchange of consideration;

e that the terms were sufficiently certain that a court could ascertain what the parties have agreed on;

f that the contract was 'legal', for example not against public policy.

Note: In certain exceptional cases only, agreements are only valid if made in a certain form, for example in writing or under seal (see below).

If an agreement does not possess all these elements, it does not necessarily follow that the 'contract' is unworkable as between the parties, simply that should things go wrong it will not be enforceable in a court of law.

For example, the terms might be somewhat vague and woolly, enough for any court to say: 'this is not certain enough, it is too ambiguous, there is no definite proof the parties have reached an agreement'.

But the parties may know what they mean (even if outsiders do not) and the agreement may function perfectly well to the satisfaction of both. It is only if something were to go wrong and one of the parties to go before a court that the question of proof of the existence of an agreement might arise.

Thus there is a difference between contracts which are completely unworkable and invalid – an absolute nullity – and those contracts which are valid and in most cases workable but unenforceable in a court of law.

Certainty and form of a contract

Introduction

Even where an offer and acceptance have been established it may not be clear precisely on what terms the parties have reached agreement. Whilst it is not the function of the courts to make an agreement for the parties, they will not defeat the intention of the parties to contract merely because the agreement has been loosely-worded. Gaps in the contract may often be filled by reference to the custom of the trade or the course of dealings between the parties. If however, no such reference can be made, or it cannot be objectively determined what the parties intended then the courts may be forced to conclude that the lack of certainty militates against contractual validity.

Vagueness

If an agreement is too vague to permit a meaning to be given to it no enforceable contract can be construed. However, courts may be able to find a meaning to an apparently vague term by reference to custom or to what is reasonable (see the Scottish case of *Neilson* v *Stewart* 1990 SLT 346). Further, it may be possible to ignore certain meaningless words and still leave a valid contract. The approach of the courts is indicated by consideration of the following cases:

In *G Scammell & Nephew* v *Ouston* [1941] AC 251 the order stated that it was given 'on the understanding that the balance of the purchase price can be had on the usual hire-purchase terms ...'. The House of Lords held that the phrase was so vague that it could not be given a definite meaning. There were no usual terms in such a contract to which reference could be made.

In *Hillas & Co Ltd* v *Arcos* (1932) 147 LT 503 a seemingly vague phrase was able to be interpreted. The agreement of sale was for timber 'of fair specification'. The parties were persons fully acquainted with the particular trade and in the light of that, the House of Lords was able to affix a meaning to the phrase.

Nicolene v *Simmonds* [1953] 1 QB 543 illustrates that it may be possible to ignore certain words. A clause of the agreement stated that the sale was subject to 'the usual conditions of acceptance'. There were in fact no such usual conditions. The phrase was meaningless and the deletion of the phrase would not impair the validity of the contract.

Incompleteness

If there is an essential term yet to be agreed and there is no express or implied provision for its solution there is no binding contract.

Thus in *May and Butcher* v *R* [1934] 2 KB 17 the agreement provided that the price(s) to be paid and the date(s) of payment should 'be agreed upon from time to time' by the parties. The House of Lords held that there never was a concluded contract between the parties.

A contrast with the above case is provided by *Foley* v *Classique Coaches* [1934] 2 KB 1 in which there were two related agreements put into separate documents. The one agreement concerned the sale of petrol; the latter agreement stated that the petrol was to be supplied 'at a price to be agreed by the parties in writing and from time to time'. The Court of Appeal was able to distinguish this case from that of *May and Butcher*. Here the agreement for the sale of petrol was acted on for three years; it formed part of a bargain involving the sale of land which had been conveyed; and it contained an arbitration clause which was construed as applying to any failure to agree as to the price.

Statute

In the absence of express provision in an agreement, statute may be able to provide the missing terms.

Thus for example:

Section 8 Sale of Goods Act 1979

'1) The price in a contract of sale may be fixed by the contract, or may be left to be fixed in a manner agreed by the contract, or may be determined by the course of dealing between the parties.

2) Where the price is not determined as mentioned in sub-section (1) above the buyer must pay a reasonable price.

3) What is a reasonable price is a question of fact dependent on the circumstances of each particular case. '

Section 15(1) Supply of Goods and Services Act 1982

'Where, under a contract for the supply of a service, the consideration for the service is not determined by the contract, left to be determined in a manner agreed by the contract, or determined by the course of dealing between the parties, there is an implied term that the party contracting with the supplier will pay a reasonable charge.'

Form of the contract

We have already seen that the general rule is that contracts can be made informally, no special form is necessary.

The exceptions to the rule are all imposed by statute. The following contracts are required to be in writing:

a Bills of exchange and promissory notes – ss3(1), 17(2) Bills of Exchange Act 1882;

b Regulated consumer credit agreements (including hire purchase agreements) under the Consumer Credit Act 1974;

c Contracts of marine insurance are void unless made in writing in the form of a policy – Marine Insurance Act 1906;

d A bill of sale is void unless it is in writing in the statutory form – Bills of Sale (1878) Amendment Act 1882;

e Contracts for the sale or other disposition of land or interests in land may only be made in writing – s2 Law of Property (Miscellaneous Provisions) Act 1989;

f Contracts within the Statute of Frauds while not required to be in writing must be supported by written evidence of their existence.

Law of contract (2): agreement

29

Introduction

We have seen in the previous chapter that, while there are certain special forms of contract that *must* be made in a particular way (for instance, contracts for the sale of land must be in writing), most contracts may take any form. In fact most contracts are not in writing, despite a mistaken belief on the part of the layman that this must be so. Probably the majority of day-to-day contracts – buying a daily newspaper or a train ticket, paying the greengrocer – are verbal contracts. For larger purchases such as cars, refrigerators or televisions, many employers now produce standard forms and the use of these standard-form contracts has extended into many areas of everyday life; it seems particularly common where the industry in question is a monopolistic one. Obviously this 'take it or leave it' attitude leaves the unfortunate consumer with little choice when it comes to negotiation and one could not truthfully say that the parties were on equal terms or free to negotiate with any equality. We shall be returning to the subject of standard-form contracts later in chapter 30.

Generally contracts fall into two types:

a specialty contracts – those made under seal in the form of a deed;

b simple or parol contracts – any other form of contract, whether written, verbal, by conduct or some combination of these.

The law will not recognise all agreements. As we have seen, a party seeking to enforce an agreement in court must establish that certain factors are present before the existence of a contractually binding agreement can be proved. As to whether the courts *will* enforce it, this is entirely another matter; we shall look at defective contracts later. We shall be examining in the next few sections those elements which must be proved to exist in order to establish to the courts' satisfaction that there is a binding agreement between the parties.

Intention to create legal relations

Not every bargain gives rise to a contract. For example, if A says to B, his brother 'If you drive to the pub, I'll buy the first pint', and B agrees, a reasonable person would not expect that B would be able to sue A when he refuses to buy the first pint. The reason is that the nature of the agreement and the relationship of the parties would lead a reasonable person to believe that there was no contractual intention.

So when will a contractual intention be found? A distinction has to be drawn between agreements which are merely social and/or domestic and agreements which are commercial in nature.

Social and domestic agreements

The rule where agreements are social or domestic is that there is a *presumption* that the parties do not intend to create legal relations. The leading case is *Balfour* v *Balfour* [1919] 2 KB 571, where the defendant, a civil servant based in Sri Lanka, came to England with his wife (the plaintiff) and later returned to Sri Lanka alone, the wife remaining in England for health reasons. The defendant promised to pay plaintiff £30 per month as maintenance, but failed to keep up the payments. The wife sued.

It was held there was no intention to create legal relations and the wife could not succeed.

The burden in social and domestic agreements is on the plaintiff to rebut the presumption that in such arrangements there is not the necessary intention to contract.

Intention and consideration

In deciding whether there is a contractual intention it is often difficult to distinguish the intention from the question of whether consideration has been given. Natural love and affection is not consideration recognised at law. That is why no consideration was provided for the wife in *Balfour* v *Balfour*.

But in the case following there was consideration, at least to start with.

In *Jones* v *Padavatton* [1969] 1 WLR 328 Mrs Jones offered a monthly allowance to her daughter if she would go to England and read for the Bar. Her daughter reluctantly gave up her job in America and came to take Bar Finals. She was not very successful. Mrs Jones bought a house in London. She stopped paying the monthly allowance but she allowed the daughter to live in the house and receive rents from other tenants. Some three years later Mrs Jones brought an action for possession. The daughter counterclaimed for breach of the agreement to pay the monthly allowance and/or to provide the daughter with accommodation.

It was held that the first agreement may have been made with the intention of creating legal relations, but was only to be deemed to be for a reasonable time; that is, sufficient time to enable the daughter to pass her Bar Finals. It had lapsed after five years.

The second agreement was only a family arrangement and there was no intention to create legal relations.

Intention inferred from 'mutuality'

An illustrative case is *Simpkins* v *Pays* [1955] 1 WLR 975, where the defendant, her grand-daughter, and the plaintiff, a paying lodger, all entered weekly for a newspaper fashion competition in the defendant's name. There was no regular rule concerning the way in which payments were shared. One week a prize of £750 was won; on the defendant's refusal to share the prize, the plaintiff sued for a third.

It was held that, because it was a joint enterprise to which all contributed (although the court could not identify a formal offer or acceptance as such), this 'mutuality' made it clear that the necessary intention to be contractually bound was present.

Commercial agreements

Where the agreement is a commercial one there is a presumption that the parties intended to enter into legal relations. This means that the plaintiff does not have to prove intention in order to succeed; the court will presume its existence. The presumption can, however, be rebutted if a contrary intention is expressed. In *Rose & Frank Co v JR Crompton Bros* [1925] AC 445, a commercial agreement stated 'This agreement is not entered into ... as a formal or legal agreement, and shall not be subject to legal jurisdiction in the law courts.' It was held that no legally enforceable agreement existed.

Rebutting the burden of proof

The question of whether the burden of proof has been rebutted is, however, one of fact.

In *Edwards* v *Skyways Ltd* [1964] 1 WLR 349, an airline pilot was offered a 'golden handshake'; that is, a payment expressed to be ex gratia by his employers. They failed to pay. The pilot sued. The employers said that the offer of the ex gratia payment was not intended to be contractually binding.

The court declared that the burden of proof is on the person asserting that a commercial agreement is not intended to be legally binding. The onus was a heavy one and the employers had failed to prove their argument; they therefore had to pay the 'golden handshake'.

Also compare *J Evans & Son (Portsmouth) Ltd* v *Andrea Merzario Ltd* [1976] 1 WLR 1078 with *Kleinwort Benson* v *Malaysia Mining Corp Bhd* [1989] 1 All ER 785.

In the former case a representative of a firm of forwarding agents with whom the customer had dealt for a long time said that goods would henceforth be packed into containers and carried below deck. At the time that the statement was made, no specific contract of carriage was designated where it was held that the promise was intended to be legally binding. The Court of Appeal relied on the importance of the place of carriage to the customer and the fact that the customer would not have agreed to container carriage had that promise not been made.

In *Kleinwort Benson* the plaintiff bank agreed with the defendants to make a loan facility to the defendant's wholly-owned subsidiary. As part of the facility arrangement the defendants furnished to the plaintiffs two 'letters of comfort', each of which stated that 'it is our policy to ensure that the business of (the subsidiary) is at all times in a position to meet its liabilities to you under the (loan facility) arrangements'.

The Court of Appeal held that, on the facts, the letters of comfort were statements of present fact, and not contractual promises as to future conduct. They were not intended to create legal relations and gave rise to no more than a moral responsibility on the part of the defendants to meet the subsidiary's debt.

Note the case of *Walford* v *Miles* [1991] 28 EG 81, in which intention to create legal relationships (and other issues) was considered in the context of commercial contracts, by the House of Lords.

As to the intention to create legal relations, see also *G Percy Trentham Ltd* v *Archital Luxfer Ltd* [1993] 1 Lloyd's Rep 25, in which Trentham were engaged as main contractors on an industrial unit construction scheme in Hampshire. Archital carried on business as manufacturers of aluminium windows, screens and doors. Trentham engaged Archital as sub-contractors to complete windows and doors in the scheme in two phases. When the work was completed Trentham alleged that there were defects in both Phases 1 and 2 and claimed damages for breach of contract. Archital denied that the dealings ever resulted in binding contracts and denied that there were defects. The Court of Appeal held that the fact that there was no written, formal contract was irrelevant, a contract could be concluded by conduct. There was no stipulation that a contract would only come into existence if a written binding contract were concluded. Plainly the parties intended to enter into a contract, the exchanges between them and the carrying out of instructions in those exchanges, all supported Trentham's argument that there was a course of dealings between the parties which amounted to a valid, working contract. Similarly, the Court of Appeal dismissed the argument that since the contract in Phase 2 was negotiated on the basis of there being a valid contract in respect of Phase 1, then the Phase 2 negotiations were based on error. In the cases of both Phase 1 and Phase 2, the parties had the necessary intention to contract and, although there were never any integrated written contracts, both contracts were formed by conduct.

The offer

Definition

An offer is an expression of willingness to contract made with the intention (actual or apparent) that it shall become binding upon the offeror as soon as it is accepted by the person to whom it is addressed.

An offer can be made to one person or to a group of persons or to the world at large. The offeror is bound to fulfil the terms of his offer once it is accepted. The issue of whether there could be a valid offer to the world at large was considered in *Carlill* v *Carbolic Smoke Ball Co* [1893] 1 QB 256. The offer was contained in a newspaper advertisement. Bowen LJ said:

> 'It was also said that the contract was made with all the world – that is with everybody, and you cannot contract with everybody. It is not a contract made with all the world. It is an offer made to all the world; and why should not an offer be made to all the world which is to ripen into a contract with anybody who comes forward and performs the conditions?'

The offer may be made in writing, by words or by conduct. All that is necessary is that the terms of the offer are clear and that the offer was made with the intention that it should be binding if accepted.

Statements which look like offers

It is necessary to distinguish between true offers and statements which, though there may be a strong resemblance are not offers and not capable of being accepted so as to form a binding contract.

The following are examples of 'lookalikes' which are not true offers.

Invitation to treat

An invitation to treat made by one party to another is not an offer. An invitation to treat is made at a preliminary stage in the making of an agreement, where one party seeks to ascertain whether the other would be willing to enter into a contract, and if so, upon what terms. It is an invitation extended by one party to the other to enter into negotiations or to make an offer. An invitation to treat cannot be accepted so as to form a binding contract, since it is nearly always the invitee who is being asked to make the offer.

To distinguish between an offer and an invitation to treat it is necessary to look at the intention of the person making it, as revealed by his words or actions, and at the surrounding circumstances. It is not an offer unless it was made with the intention that it should be binding as soon as the person to whom it was addressed communicates his assent.

The words used by the parties are not themselves conclusive. An 'offer' may in fact be 'an invitation to treat' or vice versa. The court looks at both the words used and the surrounding circumstances to determine the real intention of the parties.

See *Gibson* v *Manchester City Council* [1979] 1 WLR 294, where Mr Gibson, a council tenant, received from MCC a letter saying (inter alia) that the Council '... may be prepared to sell the house to you at the purchase price of ... £2,180, freehold'. Mr Gibson applied to buy at this price, but in the meantime Council policy had changed and it refused to sell. It was held that the letter was only an invitation to treat and not capable of acceptance.

Catalogues or circulars are invitations to treat. So too is the display of goods in a shop window or on the shelves of a supermarket.

The leading case is *Pharmaceutical Society of Great Britain* v *Boots Cash Chemists (Southern) Ltd* [1953] 1 QB 401.

The defendants adapted their shop, or one of them, to a self-service system. A customer, on entering, was given a basket and, having selected from the shelves the articles he required, put them in the basket and took them to the cash desk. Near the desk was a registered pharmacist who was authorised, if necessary, to stop a customer removing any drug from the shop. The court had to decide whether the defendants had broken the provisions of s18 of the Pharmacy and Poisons Act 1933, which made it unlawful to sell any listed poison 'unless the sale is effected under the supervision of a registered pharmacist'. The vital and obvious question is where the 'sale' in fact took place, and at what time, and this depended upon whether the display of goods was an offer or an invitation to treat. The plaintiffs contended that it was an offer which was accepted when the customer put an article into his basket, and if this article was a 'poison' it was therefore 'sold' before the pharmacist could intervene. According to the defendants, the display was only an invitation to treat. An offer to buy was made when the customer put an article in the basket, and this offer the defendants were free to accept or reject. If they accepted, they did so only when the transaction was approved by the pharmacist near the cash desk. Lord Goodard at first instance, had no hesitation in deciding that the display was only an invitation to treat so that the law had not been broken, and the Court of Appeal upheld his reasoning and adopted his decision.

In *Fisher* v *Bell* [1961] 1 QB 394 a flick knife was displayed in a shop window with a price tag attached. The issue was whether the law prohibiting the display of such items for sale had been breached. It was held that the display of the flick knife was an invitation to treat. It was up to members of the public to make an offer which the shopkeeper might accept or reject as he pleased.

Advertisements will normally be considered to be invitations to treat. For example: *Partridge* v *Crittenden* [1968] 1 WLR 1204.

Here the appellants inserted in a periodical entitled *Cage and Aviary Birds* an advertisement, 'Bramblefinch cocks and hens, 25s'. The words 'offer for sale' were not used, but the advertisement was placed under the heading, 'classified advertisements'. The appellants were charged with unlawfully offering for sale a wild live bird.

It was held that the advertisement constituted an invitation to treat, rather than an offer. Similarly in *Grainger & Son* v *Gough* [1896] AC 325 the circulation of a catalogue by a wine merchant was held to be an attempt to induce offers from recipients, not an offer itself.

Again, a simple newspaper advertisement of an event is not an offer. For example: advertisement that a scholarship examination will be held. In *Rooke* v *Dawson* [1895] 1 Ch 480, this was held not to amount to an offer to a candidate that the examination would be held.

Requests for information, or the response to such requests

For example, in *Harvey* v *Facey* [1893] AC 552, the plaintiffs telegraphed the defendants in relation to a piece of land.

'Will you sell us Bumper Hall Pen? Telegraph lowest cash price.'

The defendants replied,

'Lowest cash price for Bumper Hall Pen, £900.'

The plaintiffs then telegraphed,

'We agree to buy Bumper Hall Pen for £900 asked by you.'

The Judicial Committee of the Privy Council held that the defendants' telegram was not an offer, but an invitation to treat, telling the plaintiffs the lowest price that they would accept for the land.

Declaration of intention

A declaration of intention is, similarly, not intended to form the basis of a contract and is not an offer. In *Harris* v *Nickerson* (1873) LR 8 QB 286, an auction sale was advertised, then later cancelled. The plaintiff who had travelled to the advertised place of sale, claimed travelling expenses and damages for inconvenience. He failed, since the advertisement was not an offer, merely an invitation to treat.

Auction sales

The question of whether an auctioneer's call for bids was an offer or an invitation to treat was considered in *Payne* v *Cave* (1789) 3 Term Rep 148.

It was there decided that the call for bids is an invitation to treat, a request for offers. The bids made by persons at the auction are offers which the auctioneer can accept or reject as he chooses.

This principle now has statutory form in s57(2) Sale of Goods Act 1979, which provides that a sale by auction is completed by the fall of the hammer and up until then a lot can be withdrawn. Likewise an auctioneer can generally withdraw lots before he accepts the bid.

Tenders

Where goods are advertised for sale by tender, the statement is not an offer, but an invitation to treat; that is, it is a request by the owner of the goods for offers to purchase them. It is not an offer to sell to the person making the highest tender: *Spencer* v *Harding* (1870) LR 5 CP 561

Likewise where a building contract is put out for tender, this is a request for offers by contractors which can then be accepted or rejected.

In *Harvela Investments Ltd* v *Royal Trust Co of Canada (CI) Ltd* [1986] AC 207 the Court of Appeal had to consider the proper construction of an invitation to submit tenders. The telex, inviting the tenders contained the term that:

> 'We bind ourselves to accept (the highest offer) provided such offer complies with the terms of this telex.'

In his judgment Waller LJ said, 'If it were not for the words "We bind ourselves to accept", this would have been a mere invitation to treat; but those words in my opinion make it an offer which the bidder being highest accepted' (at p 265).

(*Note*: the decision of the Court of Appeal was reversed by the House of Lords, but not on these grounds.)

In certain cases, although an invitation to submit tenders is no more than an invitation to treat, the wording of the invitation can imply certain legal obligations. See, for example, *Blackpool and Fylde Aero Club Ltd* v *Blackpool BC* [1990] 1 WLR 1195.

'Puffs' or boasts

Trade puffs which no one would expect to take seriously, for example: 'X sells cars the cheapest' or 'Y's insurance company offers the best rates', are not to be treated as offers. However there is a very narrow border line between trade 'puffery' and offers in the course of a trade promotion that the reasonable man would take seriously. (See the *Carlill* v *Carbolic Smoke Ball* case, below.)

Communication of offer

An offer must be communicated to the offeree, or he cannot accept it. This apparently common-sense rule can, however, on certain occasions be the cause of difficulties. For example, in 'reward' cases, a person who finds a lost article and tracks down the owner cannot, in theory, claim any reward offered because the offer of a reward was not known to him when he found the item in question. He cannot 'accept' an offer he did not know about.

Duration of an offer and its termination

An offer continues in existence capable of acceptance until brought to an end. There are a number of ways in which this can occur, the main ways are listed below:

Acceptance
Completing the contract will bring the offer to an end (see next section).

Rejection
Once the offeree has rejected the offer it ceases to exist and cannot be subsequently resurrected. There must however be a specific rejection not merely an enquiry or request for further details.

Counter-offer
A counter-offer will operate as a rejection.

In order to create a binding agreement the offer and acceptance must match. The offeree must accept all the terms of the offer. If in his reply to an offer, the offeree introduces a new term or terms, or varies the terms of the offer, then that reply cannot amount to an acceptance. Instead the reply is treated as an offer itself, a counter-offer, which the original offeror is free to accept or reject.

In *Tinn* v *Hoffman & Co* (1873) 29 LT 271, the offeree responded to an offer to sell 1,200 tons of steel with a request to purchase 800 tons. He was told that there had been no acceptance of the offer of sale. Instead there had been a counter-offer to purchase 800 tons, which the sellers were free to accept or reject.

A counter-offer not only fails as an acceptance. It also generally amounts to a rejection of the original offer, which cannot then be subsequently accepted. This is illustrated in *Hyde* v *Wrench* (1840) 3 Beav 334. The defendant offered to sell the plaintiff a farm for £1,000. The plaintiff offered £950, which the defendant refused. The plaintiff then purported to accept the offer of £1,000 and sought specific performance of a contract for the sale of land. It was held that no contract existed. The plaintiff had rejected the defendant's original offer with his counter-offer and that original offer no longer existed so as to be capable of later acceptance.

In order to amount to a counter-offer, the offeree's reply must itself be capable of acceptance. That is, it must contain either expressly or impliedly all the necessary terms.

Death
The death of either party before acceptance will normally terminate the offer. Insanity, insolvency or incapacity generally *may* terminate the offer depending on circumstances.

Lapse of time
Where an offer is stated to be open for a specific length of time, then the offer automatically terminates when that time limit expires. Where there is no express time limit, an offer is normally open only for a reasonable time.

In *Ramsgate Victoria Hotel Co* v *Montefiore* (1866) LR 1 Exch 109, the defendant offered to buy the plaintiffs' shares in June. He heard nothing more until the end of November when he was told that his offer had been accepted and he was required to pay the purchase price. On his refusal he was sued for that price. It was held that he was entitled to refuse as his offer had not been accepted within a reasonable time and had therefore lapsed.

Occurrence of a terminating condition
An offer may be made subject to a condition. If that condition is not satisfied, the offer is not capable of acceptance. Examples of such conditions are that the offer must be accepted within a stated time, or in an offer to sell goods, that the goods are in a saleable condition or that an applicant for life insurance is in the same state of health as he was when he made his application.

Revocation of offer
The offer may be revoked by the offeror at any time up until it is accepted: *Payne* v *Cave* (above).

The offeror is entitled to revoke, even if he has promised to keep the offer open for a specified time; unless the offeree had paid money or given some other consideration in return for such a promise (this is sometimes referred to as purchasing 'an option').

See *Routledge* v *Grant* (1828) 4 Bing 653, where the defendant offered to buy the plaintiff's house and said that he would keep the offer open for six weeks while Routledge made up his mind. Before the end of the six weeks, Grant withdrew (revoked) his offer. He was held entitled to do this at any time up to acceptance.

Revocation is only effective if it is communicated to the offeree, either directly or through the medium of a reliable third party (*Dickinson* v *Dodds* (1876) 2 Ch D 463). It may be express or by implication, provided the offeror's conduct shows a clear intention to revoke.

Acceptance

Definition

An acceptance is a final and unqualified acceptance of the terms of an offer. Unless it can be shown that there was such an acceptance, then there is no contract. In some cases it is obvious that there has been an unqualified acceptance of the exact terms of an offer. Where the offeror sets out his offer and requests an answer of 'yes or no' from the offeree, it is not difficult to determine whether or not there has been acceptance. Frequently however, progress towards agreement involves long and arduous bargaining by the parties. In those circumstances, the courts must look carefully at the dealings between the parties to decide whether there has in fact been an agreement and upon which terms.

Where an offer is made in the alternative, the acceptance must stipulate which alternative has been accepted. In *Peter Lind & Co Ltd* v *Mersey Docks and Harbour Board* [1972] 2 Lloyd's Rep 234 an offer to build a terminal was made by a tender quoting two alternative prices, fixed and 'cost-plus'. The offeree purported to accept 'your tender', without stating which price. It was held that there was no acceptance and hence no contract.

In addition to being a firm and unqualified acceptance of all the terms of the offer, the fact of acceptance must normally be communicated to the offeror before there is a concluded contract. The rules as to communication are dealt with below.

The manner of acceptance

Acceptance will usually correspond with the manner of the offer, for example if the offer was by letter so too will the acceptance be. There is, however, a convention that if the acceptance is some method speedier, more convenient and more reliable than that of the offer, this will be acceptable.

It is always open to the offeror to stipulate the mode of acceptance; in which case it will normally become a pre-condition of acceptance. There must be some positive words/act of acceptance and mere silence will never be sufficient.

An offeree who does nothing in respect to an offer is not bound by the terms of that offer. The offeror cannot, in other words, impose silence as acceptance by the offeree.

In *Felthouse* v *Bindley* (1862) 11 CBNS 869 the plaintiff and his nephew had been negotiating about the sale of the nephew's horse. Not having reached agreement the plaintiff wrote to his nephew saying, 'If I hear no more about him I consider the horse is mine at £3 15s'. The nephew did not reply, but had decided to accept the offer. He instructed the auctioneer who was selling his farming stock not to sell the horse as it had already been sold. The auctioneer mistakenly sold the horse and was sued by the plaintiff in conversion. The Common Pleas held that at the time of the auction no contract had been concluded for the sale of the horse between the plaintiff and his nephew.

In view of the fact that the nephew had decided to accept the offer and had informed the auctioneer accordingly, this decision is perhaps difficult to understand. The Exchequer Chamber, in affirming the decision on appeal, appears to have emphasised the alternative ground for the decision that the then requirements of the Statute of Frauds had not been complied with because there had been no delivery, part payment or memorandum in writing to vest the property in the plaintiff.

Though the decision at first instance in *Felthouse* v *Bindley* has been criticised on the facts the general principle laid down in that case, that an offeror cannot impose silence as acceptance, has not been challenged.

There is however a fine line between silence, which is never to be construed as acceptance and some activity which amounts to acceptance by conduct. Even some continuing inactivity may be considered acceptance.

Thus in *Rust* v *Abbey Life Insurance Co* [1979] 2 Lloyd's Rep 355, the plaintiff applied and paid for a 'property bond' which was allocated to her on the terms of the defendant's usual policy of insurance. After a period of some seven months the plaintiff sought recovery of the payment she had made on the basis that there had been no concluded contract. Her claim was rejected on the grounds that her application had been an offer and the issue of the policy an acceptance. It was further held, however, that, even if the issue of the policy had been a counter-offer, that counter-offer had been accepted by the plaintiff by her conduct in taking no action for the period in question.

In cases where two big businesses make a contract a 'battle of the forms' may arise.

The rule that offer and acceptance must correspond with each other gives rise to problems where each party wants to contract on the basis of standard terms and these terms differ. This would occur where neither of the contracting parties are private individuals. For instance, company A offers to sell goods to company B, stating that the sale will be subject to company A's standard terms, as printed on the back of the document containing the offer. Company B reply stating that they want to buy the goods, at the price offered, but that the sale should be subject to B's standard terms as printed on the back of B's order form, which differ materially from A's.

This problem, and the methods by which the courts should approach it was considered by the Court of Appeal in *Butler Machine Tool Co Ltd* v *Ex-cell-o Corporation (England) Ltd* [1979] 1 WLR 401.

Facts

23 May 1969: The sellers offered to sell a machine to the buyers for £75,535 to be delivered in 10 months. The offer included certain terms including a clause for variation of the price to the price ruling at the date of delivery. The offer was subject to an overriding clause that the seller's terms and conditions, as stated in the offer, 'shall prevail over any terms and conditions in the Buyer's order'.

27 May 1969: The buyers placed an order subject to their own, materially different, terms and conditions including, in particular, a term for a fixed price. At the foot of the order was a tear-off acknowledgement slip stating 'We accept your order on the Terms and Conditions stated thereon.'

5 June 1969: The sellers completed and returned the buyers' acknowledgement slip with a letter stating that the order was accepted on the basis of their quotation of 23 May.

At the date of delivery the sellers claimed an increase in price for the machine of c £3,000. The buyers refused liability to pay the extra price on the grounds that the contract was made under their terms and conditions at a fixed price. The sellers contended that it was their terms and conditions which prevailed and they were, therefore, entitled to the increased price.

It was held that the defendants' 'acceptance' was really a counter offer. The plaintiff had accepted this counter offer by sending back the tear-off slip and going on to perform the contract. The dispute which later arose, was decided on the basis that it was the defendants' terms which were the governing rules of the contract.

Motive for acceptance

The act that constitutes acceptance may be performed either with knowledge of the offer but for a motive other than that of completing the contract, or occasionally a person may 'accidentally' accept an offer without knowledge of its existence.

The question then arises as to whether such 'acceptance' can be valid.

In *Williams* v *Carwardine* (1833) 5 Car & P 566, the defendant offered a reward of £20 to anyone who gave information leading to the conviction of the murderers of Walter Carwardine. The plaintiff was aware of the offer, and thinking that she had not much longer to live, signed 'a voluntary statement to ease my conscience, and in the hopes of forgiveness hereafter'.

As a result of the statement, the murderer was convicted. The plaintiff was held entitled to enforce the agreement and obtain her reward. Patterson J said: 'We cannot go into the plaintiff's motives.'

In the Australian case of *R* v *Clarke* (1927) 40 CLR 227 a different conclusion was reached.

The Government of Western Australia offered a reward of £1,000 'for such information as shall lead to the arrest and conviction of' the murderers of two police officers, and added that, if the information should be given by an accomplice, not being himself the murderer, he should receive a free pardon. Clarke saw the offer, and he was an accomplice. Some time later he gave the necessary information. He claimed the reward from the Crown by Petition of Right. He admitted not only that he had acted solely to save his own skin, but that, at the time when he gave the information, the question of the reward had passed out of his mind.

The High Court of Australia held that his claim must fail. He was, in their opinion, in the same position as if he had never heard of the reward.

The position therefore seems to be that an acceptance which is wholly motivated by factors other than the existence of the offer has no effect. Where, however, the existence of the offer plays some part, however small, in inducing a person to do the required act, there is a valid acceptance of the offer.

Communication of acceptance

The general rule is that an acceptance must be communicated to the offeror. Until and unless the acceptance is so communicated, no contract comes into existence. Hence where, as in *Brogden* v *Metropolitan Railway Co* (1877) 2 App Cas 666 the offeree fails to inform the offeror whether or not the offer has been accepted, there is no acceptance. If the offeree decides to accept the offer and writes a letter of acceptance which he then forgets to post, again there is no effective acceptance of the offer. The same result would follow if the offeree communicated his acceptance only to his own agent.

In order for an acceptance to be accepted, it must be *brought to the attention of the offeror*. Hence, there is no contract if, as Lord Denning MR said in *Entores* v *Miles Far East Corporation* [1955] 2 QB 327 at p332:

> 'the words of acceptance are drowned by an aircraft flying overhead; or if they are spoken into a telephone after the line has gone dead or become so indistinct that the offeror does not hear them.'

Exceptions to the general rule

The general rule as to acceptance does not apply, or is modified in the following cases:

a Where the offeror expressly or impliedly waives the requirement that acceptance be communicated. However, see *Felthouse* v *Bindley* and the rules as to silence (above).

b Where the offeror is estopped from denying that the acceptance was communicated. This will be the case if it was in fact sent or spoken by the offeree, but was not received or heard by the offeror as a result of his own fault or omission. This would be the case in the example given by Lord Denning MR in *Entores* v *Miles Far East Corporation* (above):

> 'if the listener on the telephone does not catch the words of acceptance but nevertheless does not ask for them to be repeated.'

Probably the best known case on communication of acceptance is *Carlill* v *Carbolic Smoke Ball Co* [1893] 1 QB 256 the facts of which are too well known to bear repeating in full here. Note that in *Carlill* v *Carbolic Smoke Ball Co* the offer was contained in the advertisement by the company. Mrs Carlill accepted the offer by taking the smoke balls in accordance with the instructions. Acceptance was complete without the need to communicate the fact of acceptance to the company, an exception to the usual rule which requires communication before acceptance is complete. In practical terms there will normally be communication of the fact that the act has been performed in order to collect the reward that has been offered, but there is a complete contract in existence once the act of acceptance has been completely performed, whether or not the offeror is aware that this is the case.

Postal rules of offer and acceptance

Instantaneous communications

An acceptance is communicated when and where it is brought to the attention of the offeror, unless the postal rule applies, in which case the acceptance is communicated when the letter of acceptance is posted by the offeree.

Methods of communication are divided into those where communication is virtually instantaneous:

> face to face conversation,
> telephone,
> telex,
> fax,

and into those where there is a time lag between the dispatch and receipt:

> letters,
> telegrams.

The postal rule applies only to letters and telegrams, though there are 'grey' areas: for example whether a telephone answering machine is an instantaneous communication or governed by postal rules.

Where the method of communication is instantaneous, then the offer is accepted when the offeror actually hears the acceptance. If the offeree speaks his acceptance but it is not heard by the offeror, then it has not been effectively communicated.

In *Entores* v *Miles Far East Corporation* (above), the issue was where a contract had been made. The plaintiffs were a London company and the defendants an American corporation with agents in Amsterdam. Both the plaintiffs and the Amsterdam agents used telex machines. The plaintiffs made an offer to the Amsterdam agents by telex, to buy goods from them. This offer was accepted, also by telex. The defendants were alleged to have broken this contract and the plaintiffs wished to show that the agreement had been made in England, so that legal proceedings could be commenced in England for breach of contract. The defendants contended that the postal rule applied, so that the offer was accepted when the telex was dispatched, in Holland.

Parker LJ said:

'Where ... the parties are in each other's presence, or, though separated by space, communication between them is instantaneous, there is no need for such a rule of convenience (the postal rule). To hold otherwise would leave no room for the operation of the general rule that notification of the acceptance must be received. An acceptor could say: "I spoke the words in your presence, albeit softly, and it matters not that you did not hear me"; or "I telephoned you and accepted, and it matters not that the telephone went dead and you did not get my message" ... So far as telex messages are concerned, although the despatch and receipt of a message is not completely instantaneous, the parties are to all intents and purposes in each other's presence just as if they were in telephonic communication, and I can see no reason for departing from the general rule that there is no binding contract until notice of the acceptance is received by the offeror. That being so, and since the offer was made by the plaintiffs in London and notification of the acceptance was received by them in London, the contract resulting therefrom was made in London.'

The Court of Appeal decision was approved by the House of Lords in the case of *Brinkibon Ltd* v *Stahag Stahl und Stahlwarenhandelsgesellschaft mbH* [1983] AC 34.

The plaintiffs were an English company and the defendants an Austrian company, based in Vienna. After negotiations, the defendants offered to sell steel bars to the plaintiffs. The plaintiffs accepted this offer by a telex sent to the defendants in Vienna. The contract was not performed and the plaintiffs commenced proceedings for breach of contract, in England. The defendants claimed that the contract was made in Austria, so that the English courts did not have jurisdiction.

The House of Lords held that where there was instantaneous communication between the offeror and the offeree the formation of a contract was governed by the general rule that a contract was concluded where and when acceptance of the offer was received by the offeror. Since the telex communication from the buyers in London to the sellers in Austria was instantaneous the contract was made in Austria.

The House of Lords considered the possibility that there might be circumstances in which, although telex was used, communication was not in fact instantaneous. This could occur where a telex was sent at night or when the offeror's office was closed.

Lord Wilberforce said, in relation to such circumstances:

'No universal rule can cover all such cases; they must be resolved by references to the intentions of the parties, by sound business practice and in some cases by a judgment where the risk should lie.'

The postal rule

The postal rule applies where there is a lag between despatch of an acceptance and receipt of that acceptance by the offeror. That is, where acceptance is by letter or telegram. In such a case, acceptance is communicated when the offeree posts the letter or telegram. This is an exception to the general rule, under which acceptance is complete once it is brought to the attention of the offeror.

It is best explained as a rule of convenience. Where acceptance is by post, there are three possible moments when that acceptance could be complete:

a when the letter is posted by the offeree;

b when the letter is delivered to the offeror;

c when the letter is actually brought to the attention of the offeror.

It is easier to keep accurate records of the date and time at which a letter was posted, than the moment when it was delivered or the time when the offeror actually became aware of its existence. Hence it can be argued that in the interests of certainty as to the time when the contract was formed, the time of acceptance should be the time of posting.

A second ground upon which this departure from the general rule can be supported is that of the allocation of risk. Where postal acceptance has been expressly or impliedly stipulated by the offeror (see below) then the offeree may reply by that method. Postal communication bears the risk of letters being lost or delayed in the post. If acceptance was only complete when a letter was received by the offeror, then the offeree would not know whether or not he was a party to a binding agreement until the letter was received and if in fact the letter never does arrive, the offeree could find himself acting on the assumption that he was a party to a contract when this does not turn out to be the case.

The risk borne by the offeror where acceptance is complete upon the posting of the letter of acceptance is that he is then bound by the agreement before he actually is aware of the acceptance. If the letter of acceptance is delayed or lost, then the offeror may assume that his offer was not accepted and enter into a contract for the disposal of the same goods. This would be a breach of the original contract. However, it was the offeror who stipulated acceptance by post, and hence it can be argued that he should bear the risk.

The postal rule in its present form was first laid down in *Adams* v *Lindsell* (1818) B & Ald 681. A letter is 'posted' when it is put into the control of the post office (for example handing the letter over the counter at a post office or posting it into a letter box).

Re London & Northern Bank [1900] 1 Ch 220 showed that it is *not* sufficient to hand the letter to a postman on his way to the sorting office, or an off-duty postman outside the post office.

Note: The postal rule will not always apply, simply because acceptance was posted.

In *Holwell Securities* v *Hughes* [1974] 1 WLR 155, an offer to sell required acceptance to be made 'by notice in writing to the intending vendor'. Notice was posted but never received. It was held that there was no contract because the wording of the offer made it clear that the vendor was not prepared to consider a contract to be in existence until he received the written notice. The postal rules did not apply here because the terms of the offer indicated to the contrary.

Finally, note that the postal rule only applies to acceptance, an offer or a letter of revocation will be effective only on arrival.

In *Byrne* v *Leon van Tienhoven* (1880) 5 CPD 344 a firm in Cardiff offered by letter to sell tin to a firm in New York. Later, the firm sent another letter revoking this offer, but while this was in transit and before its delivery, the New York firm posted their letter of acceptance. It was held that the letter of acceptance came first, creating a contract; the letter of revocation could not take affect until it had arrived and been communicated.

One question which has been frequently discussed is whether an offeree can withdraw his acceptance after it has been posted, by a later communication which somehow reaches the offeror before the acceptance.

There is no clear authority in English law. A strict application of the postal rule would not permit such withdrawal. This view is supported by decisions in New Zealand in *Wenckheim* v *Arndt* (NZ) 1 JR (1873) and South Africa in *A–Z Bazaars* v *Minister of Agriculture* [1974] (4) SA 392 (c). The contrary view is argued by *Professor Hudson* in (1966) 82 LQR 169. He holds that the postal rule is merely one of convenience and ought not to be inflexibly applied.

Telegrams and telexes

The 'postal rule' also applies to acceptance by telegram. See *Bruner* v *Moore* [1904] 1 Ch 305. It does not apply to acceptance by telex. The problem in relation to acceptance by telex is not *when* the offer has been accepted because communication is nearly instantaneous, but *where* it has been accepted. This is significant for determining whether English law governs the contract or whether the English court has jurisdiction to hear a case or to order service of notice of a writ outside the jurisdiction. (Students interested in this aspect should refer to a textbook on Conflicts of Law.) It is axiomatic that the contract is complete on acceptance. If A in Belgium accepts an offer by telex made by B in England, the contract could be capable of being made in Belgium or England. It will, however, be very rare that the contract will be deemed to have been made in Belgium. This question was first discussed in *Entores* v *Miles Far East Corporation* (1955) (above) and has been upheld in the *Brinkibon* case (see above).

Consideration

Introduction

For all practical purposes consideration is what the parties exchange; it is the whole point of making the bargain. It therefore seems appropriate to include the subject in this chapter on agreement. As we have seen, the law is not concerned with the fairness or otherwise of the parties' bargaining, simply that there should be *some* contribution from each party; whether money, goods, or promises.

Although subjected to criticism by theorists, the courts have traditionally defined consideration in terms of a dichotomy of benefit to the promisor (the person making the promise) or detriment to the promisee (the person to whom the promise is made). These requirements are alternative. For instance where A guarantees B's bank overdraft the promisee bank suffers detriment by advancing money to B but no benefit to A, the promisor, need be shown.

The benefit/detriment dichotomy can bear two separate meanings. Firstly it may be used in the sense of any act, forbearance or promise that has economic value ('factual' benefit/detriment). Secondly it is used in the sense of an act, forbearance or promise the performance of which is not already legally due ('legal benefit/detriment). The Courts have never consistently drawn the above distinction but, as will be seen, there are a number of cases where there was undoubted actual benefit/detriment but there has been held to be no legal consideration.

Consideration can be 'executory', or 'executed'. Executory consideration is a promise yet to be fulfilled and executed.

Consideration is the completed performance of one side of the bargain.

Most contracts have a mixture of the two types of consideration.

Rules governing consideration

Generally, it can be said that there are four principles governing the sufficiency and nature of consideration. These principles are hedged about with exceptions. The principles are:

a   consideration must move from the promisee;

b   consideration need not move to the promisor;

c   past consideration is not good consideration;

d   consideration must be sufficient but need not be adequate;

The effect of the last principle is ameliorated by the operation of equity by what is now known as 'promissory estoppel'. The position at common law will be examined first. Each principle and the exceptions to it will be dealt with in turn.

Consideration must move from the promisee

As has been indicated above, a person may provide consideration either by conferring a benefit upon another or by undertaking to suffer a detriment to himself. It is, however, a personal obligation. A cannot generally promise C that B will confer a benefit or suffer a detriment in consideration for a promise by C to A, unless, of course, A assumes liability to C for the non-performance of that activity by B. The justification for this is that the consideration has not moved from the promisee.

In *Thomas* v *Thomas* (1842) 11 LJ QB 104, a testator wanted to give a house to his widow. The executors of his will promised the house to the widow 'in consideration of such desire' provided that she promised to keep the house in repair and to pay ground rent of £1 per annum. It was alleged that no binding agreement had been reached because the consideration was expressed to be moving from the testator and not from the widow. It was held that the promise to keep the house in repair (and the token payment of £1) constituted consideration moving from the widow and she was entitled to remain in the house.

In *Dickinson v Abel* [1969] 1 WLR 295, the occupier and beneficiary under a trust of a farm asked a prospective purchaser of the farm 'What's in it for me?' The prospective purchaser said that he could have £10,000 if he (the purchaser) bought the farm for £100,000 or less.

No services were offered by the occupier or expressed by the purchaser. The occupier could not know what was in the mind of the purchaser so that there could not be any contractual consensus as to the consideration to be provided by the occupier. No term could be implied which amounted to consideration.

Consideration need not move to the promisor

Where the consideration provided is the suffering of a detriment to the promisee the consideration cannot move to the promisor.

So in *Carlill v Carbolic Smoke Ball* (above) the consideration for the promise by the Smoke Ball Company was using the smoke ball which the plaintiff had bought. That conferred no direct benefit on the Smoke Ball Company and so did not move to the promisor. It was, however, a detriment to herself.

Past consideration is not good consideration

The rule is well established. It can be seen in operation in *Roscorla v Thomas* (1842) 3 QB 234, where the defendant promised the plaintiff that a horse which had been bought by him was sound and free from vice. In fact it was not.

It was held that the express promise that the horse was sound and free from vice had been made after the sale and therefore no consideration for the promise was given.

Similarly in *Eastwood v Kenyon* (1840) 11 Ad & El 438, the guardian of a young girl had raised a loan to pay for her education and maintenance. On her marriage her husband agreed to repay the amount of the loan. He failed to do so. The guardian sued him.

It was held that there was no liability on the part of the husband because the consideration was past consideration. With reference to the argument that the husband had a moral obligation to repay the loan the court said that no such argument could exist in English law. It would annihilate any need for consideration at all.

In *Re McArdle* [1951] Ch 669 a promise made 'in consideration of your carrying out certain alterations and improvements to the property' was held by the Court of Appeal to be unenforceable as all the work had been done before the promise was made.

These cases contrast with that of *Lampleigh v Braithwait* (1615) Hob 105, where Braithwait had murdered someone (M) and asked Lampleigh to do his best to obtain a pardon for him. Lampleigh journeyed to and from Newmarket for him. Braithwait afterwards promised to pay Lampleigh £100. It was held that the promise to pay £100 coupled with the prior request as part of the same activity amounted to good consideration.

The principle extrapolated from this case crystalised into its modern form in *Re Casey's Patents* [1892] 1 Ch 104.

A and B who were joint owners of certain patent rights wrote to C stating: 'In consideration of your services as the practical manager in working our patents we hereby agree to give you one third share of the patents.' It was held that C could rely on this agreement, as he was deemed to have given consideration for it.

See also the more recent case of *Pao On* v *Lau Yiu Long* [1980] AC 614 in which a promise made by one party not to sell shares before a certain date (in one agreement) was held to provide consideration for a second agreement to indemnify, even though the agreement not to sell was made separately, and before the indemnity agreement.

The Privy Council, in *Pao On*, laid down the necessary preconditions for an act done before the giving of a promise to constitute consideration for the promise:

a The act must be done at the promisor's request;

b The parties must have understood that the act was to be remunerated either by a payment or the conferment of some other benefit; and

c The payment, or the conferment of a benefit, must have been legally enforceable had it been promised in advance.

Thus, provided these conditions are met, 'past' consideration may in certain circumstances be good consideration.

Consideration must be sufficient but need not be adequate

The word 'sufficient' in this context is incapable of precise definition. In reality it is used as little more than shorthand for the body of rules which prevent certain acts or promises from constituting valid consideration although the rules discussed above may have been satisfied.

A promise or act must have some financial value no matter how small. In *White* v *Bluett* (1853) 23 LJ Ex 36 it was held that a son's promise not to bore his father with complaints (for the father's promise not to sue him on a promissory note) was not good consideration.

Certain types of case have given rise to difficulty. In three situations in particular the question has arisen, whether such acts are capable of being good consideration. They are:

a duties owed by law;

b duties owed under an existing contract;

c duties owed to third parties.

Duties owed by law. If the duty relied upon to constitute consideration is already owed at law, it may not constitute good consideration. If, however, the promisor agrees to do more than is required at law the consideration will be sufficient. This contrast can be illustrated by *Collins v Godefroy* (1831) 1 B & Ad 950, and *Glasbrook Brothers v Glamorgan County Council* [1925] AC 270. In *Collins v Godefroy* a plaintiff was subpoenaed to give evidence for the defendant. The plaintiff alleged that the defendant had promised to pay her expenses.

It was held that, since the defendant was obliged by law to answer the subpoena, giving evidence could not be consideration sufficient to support the promise to pay her expenses.

Contrast this case with *Glasbrook Bros v Glamorgan County Council*, where the police were under a duty to protect a coal mine during a strike. They were asked by the manager of a coal mine to provide a stronger guard than the police would otherwise have done. A rate was agreed for the provision of this service. It was held that the *extra* protection afforded was good consideration, and sufficient to require the payment promised to be made.

Duties owed under an existing contract. The rule is that if A is bound to do something by virtue of a contract with B, performance of the duty or the promise to perform cannot be consideration for a further promise by B.

The same principle is said to be derived also from *Stilk v Myrick* (1809) 2 Camp 317. Some sailors had deserted a ship. The captain of the ship promised to divide their wages among the remaining sailors if they would work the ship home short-handed. It was held that there was no consideration, because the sailors were already bound to work the ship home. This decision has long been considered suspect.

In the case of *Williams v Roffey Bros & Nicholls (Contractors) Ltd* [1989] NLJ 1713 it was held (by the Court of Appeal) that when a party to an existing contract later agrees to pay an extra 'bonus' in order to ensure that the other party performs his obligations under the original contract, that the agreement is binding if the party agreeing to pay the bonus has thereby obtained some new practical advantage or avoided a disadvantage. Although this case limits the application of *Stilk v Myrick*, the rule still continues in a restricted form.

It was recently made clear by the Court of Appeal in *Re Selectmove* (1994) The Times 13 January that despite *Williams v Roffy Bros & Nicholls* (above), the courts will continue to follow the principle laid down in *Foakes v Beer* (1884) 9 App Cas 605 that an agreement to pay in instalments is unenforceable. This is the case even if a creditor might derive practical benefit from such an agreement. Such benefit and promise to pay in instalments are not adequate consideration to make such an arrangement legally enforceable.

Duties owed to third parties. When a person is already contractually bound to perform a particular act, to promise to another that the contract will be performed can be good consideration.

The principle that a promise to perform, or the performance of, a pre-existing contractual obligation to a third party can be valid consideration was affirmed by the Privy Council in *New Zealand Shipping Co Ltd* v *AM Satterthwaite & Co Ltd, The Eurymedon* [1975] AC 154, and was reconfirmed in *Pao On* v *Lau Yiu Long* (above).

Promissory estoppel

'Promissory estoppel' is the name that has been given to the equitable doctrine which has as its principal source the obiter dicta of Denning J (as he then was) in *Central London Property Trust Ltd* v *High Trees House Ltd* [1947] 1 KB 130.

Reference has already been made to the fact that, of the four rules governing consideration (above), the fourth – 'that consideration' must be sufficient but need not be adequate' – operates particularly harshly.

We have seen that because performance of an existing duty cannot be consideration for a new promise that, a fortiori, partial performance of a duty cannot be consideration for a new promise. On the other hand the introduction of a new element into the existing duty will support a new promise. The cases which are authority for this view are mainly cases which concern debts. In *Pinnel's Case* (1602) 5 Co Rep 117a Pinnel sued Cole for £8 10s due on a bond in November 1600. Cole's defence was that at Pinnel's request he had paid him £5 2s 6d on 1 October and that Pinnel had accepted this payment in full satisfaction of the original debt.

Pinnel's Case is therefore cited as the authority for the proposition that: 'Payment of a lesser sum on the day in satisfaction of a greater sum cannot be any satisfaction for the whole.' The rule was approved by the House of Lords – *Foakes* v *Beer* (1884) 9 App Cas 605 although Lord Blackburn in the latter case, dissenting in all but name, said the true ratio of the former case was:

> ' ... that where a matter paid and accepted in satisfaction of a debt certain might by any possibility be more beneficial to the creditor than his debt, the Court will not inquire into the adequacy of the consideration ...',

and that the further statement that a lesser sum on the day could never be satisfaction was unnecessary and erroneous.

The facts of *Foakes* v *Beer* were that B obtained judgment against F who subsequently asked for time to pay. B agreed to take no proceedings whatever on the judgment in consideration of an immediate payment with the balance paid by instalments. F complied with the terms of the agreement and paid the whole of the judgment debt but B thereafter sued for interest on the principal sum and the House of Lords held that she was entitled to succeed on that claim.

The harshness of the rule in *Pinnel's Case* has to a great extent been ameliorated by the doctrine of promissory estoppel.

It has been defined thus:

> 'Where by his words or conduct one party to a transaction makes to the other an unambiguous promise or assurance which is intended to affect the legal relations between them (whether contractual or otherwise), and the other party acts upon it, altering his position to his detriment, the party making the promise or assurance will not be permitted to act inconsistently with it.' (Snell's Principles of Equity, 27th Ed).

The modern starting point of the doctrine is generally accepted to be the *High Trees* case (*Central London Property Trust* v *High Trees House Ltd* [1947] 1 KB 130), but the authority and legitimacy of the doctrine appears to come from cases from the last century.

In the *High Trees* case, in 1937, the defendants leased a block of flats from the plaintiff for 99 years at a rent of £2,500 per annum. By 1940, because of the war, the defendants were unable fully to let the block and the plaintiffs agreed to reduce the rent to £1,250. In 1945, when conditions had returned to normal and the block was fully let again, the plaintiffs sought to return to the full rent.

Denning J held that the plaintiffs could thereafter recover the full rent because their promise to accept half only was intended to apply during the war whilst the block was not fully let. Such is the ratio decidendi of the case. Promissory estoppel only raises its head in obiter dicta, because his Lordship said that had the plaintiffs sued for the balance in respect of the period 1940–45, they would not have recovered.

In avoiding the rule in *Pinnel's Case* Denning relied particularly on *Hughes* v *Metropolitan Railway Co* (1877) 2 App Cas 439, where the appellant landlord served on the respondent tenants a notice to repair within six months; the effect of the respondents' failure to comply being that the appellant could forfeit the lease. Following service of the notice the parties commenced negotiations for the respondents to buy the lease, which proceeded for almost six months when the appellant terminated them and sought to forfeit the lease for the respondents' failure to repair. The House of Lords held that by the negotiations the appellant impliedly promised that he would not bring proceedings upon the respondents' failure to repair within six months and that he could not subsequently take advantage of the respondents relying on this.

The doctrine is limited and applies only where it would be inequitable to allow the plaintiff to succeed in spite of his promise.

In *D & C Builder Ltds* v *Rees* [1966] 2 QB 617 the defendant owed £482 to the plaintiffs and refused to pay. Eventually, because they themselves were in financial trouble, the plaintiffs agreed to take £300 which they said would be in 'full satisfaction'. Rees put considerable pressure on the builder to accept less – there was an element of duress. It was held that promissory estoppel should not apply here, because it would be grossly unfair and inequitable. Instead the normal *Pinnel's Case* rules applied and the builder was held able to recover the remaining £182.

Promissory estoppel is ripe for examination in the House of Lords. The cases in the Lords in which the doctrine has been discussed have all ultimately turned on other issues and their Lordships' remarks in that House had indicated that their Lordships feel that the time is ready for a pronouncement by the highest court in the land.

'I desire to add that the time may soon come when the whole sequence of cases based on promissory estoppel since the war, beginning with *Central London Property Trust Ltd* v *High Trees Houses Ltd* may need to be reviewed and reduced to a coherent body of doctrine by the courts. I do not mean to say that any are to be regarded with suspicion. But, as is common with an expanding doctrine, they do raise problems of coherent exposition which have never been systematically explored. However, this may be, we are not in a position to carry out this exploration here and in the present proceedings.' Per Lord Hailsham LC in *Woodhouse AC Israel Cocoa Ltd SA* v *Nigerian Produce Marketing Co Ltd* [1972] AC 741.

Law of contract (3): 30
contents of a contract

Introduction

Having established that a contract satisfies the requirements for validity, that is that there has been an agreement supported by consideration and that it is in the necessary form (where that is required), the next stage is to determine the scope of the obligations incurred by the parties. One of the first matters to consider is how far the parties themselves can agree between them on the terms of the bargain and how far they may be governed by common law or statute. A great deal will obviously depend on the nature of the contract. A 'one-off' individual contract between two private individuals is, clearly, more likely to be specifically negotiated to the requirements of the two people concerned than say, a purchase of a car from a network dealer, where the contract will most likely be a standard-form contract, leaving few if any opportunities for negotiation to the individual consumer. Similarly a contract concerning an area which is 'statute regulated' for example, a sale of goods contract, will leave the parties very little room to manoeuvre as to negotiating terms – the relevant legislation lays down a fixed series of implied terms.

During the course of the preliminary negotiations the parties will make a whole series of statements to each other. Not all of these will necessarily form part of the contract. Early statements which may induce the contract, but do not form a part of it are called representations. Should they prove incorrect, the injured party may have a cause of action for misrepresentation (see chapter 31, following). Some early statements *will* become terms of the contract, and the contract will probably incorporate some additional terms. These terms will not all be equally important in the eyes of the law. The most important, the core of the contract are called conditions, the lesser statements are warranties.

The main problem is to sort out which is which. Even where the contract is in writing, there is no guarantee that *every* term is included, sometimes oral additions or alterations may have been made. When a contract is totally verbal it is particularly difficult to establish whether a statement has been incorporated or not as a term, and what importance the parties attached to the statement (whether it is a condition or a warranty). Remember, the parties are in dispute, so any agreement they may seem to have reached may have long since disappeared in the course of 'hostilities'.

The difficulties are further compounded that parties do not always expressly agree all terms; many are implied. We shall look, in the next sections, first at express terms and subsequently at implied terms.

Express terms

Express terms are those specifically mentioned and agreed upon by the parties. They do *not* have to be in writing. If a contract is in writing and the document is signed the signatory is usually assumed to have agreed to everything in the document. (See also, however, exclusion clauses below.)

If the contract is verbal, although the parties may have apparently agreed, it may subsequently transpire that they each have a different idea of what the other is saying. This is not confined to verbal contracts, as it can happen with written terms; but it is more likely to happen where there is no permanent record to refer to.

Where there are express terms, but the parties are at cross-purposes over the meaning of words used the courts have evolved rules to ascertain the true meaning of the terms causing difficulty. These rules can be split into:

a rules of law;

b rules of evidence.

Rules of law

These rules can be shortly stated:

a the aim is to discover the intention of the parties;

b their intention must be found in the document itself (although see the observations of Lord Wilberforce in *Reardon Smith Line* v *Yngvar Hansen-Tangen* [1976] 1 WLR 989. This is known as 'the parol evidence rule';

c the popular meaning of words is to be applied unless the context indicates that some other meaning is intended;

d technical words should be given their technical meaning;

e the contract should be construed so as to avoid absurdity or inconsistency;

f Mercantile contracts should be construed according to mercantile usage;

g the courts may look at customs of particular places to interpret the contract;

h the contract should be read as a whole;

i where clauses are inconsistent or repugnant to each other effect should be given to that part which is intended to carry the real intention of the parties on a consideration of the contract as a whole;

j where there are printed and written words greater significance should be placed on the written words as more likely to exhibit a true intention;

k where a general word is preceded by several words illustrating a class of behaviour or meaning or intention, the general word shall be limited 'ejusdem generis', that is, it only applies to matters which are in a similar category to the preceding words. For example, the words, 'be destroyed by fire, flood, storm, tempest or other inevitable accident' could not cover losses caused by acts or default of the parties to the contract.

Rules of evidence

The 'parol evidence rule' is frequently said to derive from the rule in *Goss* v *Lord Nugent* (1833) 5 B & Ad 58:

'verbal evidence is not allowed to be given ... so as to add to or substract from, or in any manner to vary or qualify the written contract.'

There are, however, innumerable exceptions to the parol evidence rule: These 'exceptions' include:

a to show that an implied term is inapplicable;

b to show when the contract is due to commence;

c to show that one party is acting in a particular capacity, eg as agent;

d to show a collateral promise;

e to help construe an ambiguous document.

In all the above cases (and others) verbal evidence may be given on extrinsic matters.

Implied terms

Terms may be implied by the courts, implied by custom or usage or implied by statute. We shall look at each, briefly in turn.

Terms implied by the courts

It is a moot point whether the implication of terms into a contract is a question of law or whether it can in some circumstances be a question of fact. *Treitel* takes the view that the implication may be either of fact or law, whereas *Chitty* considers that the implication is one of law for the court. There are, in any event, generally said to be two circumstances in which terms are implied at common law:

a Where the contract does not deal with a matter expressly but a term is said to be intended by the parties. That intention is discovered by looking at the words of the agreement and their surrounding circumstances.

b Where the contract does not expressly deal with the matter but it creates a relationship in which such a term is usually implied.

In the first case, intention of the parties, the circumstances in which a term will be implied are where its inclusion can be inferred from the agreement. It is sometimes referred to as the 'officious bystander' test for an implied term, because of the test laid down in *Shirlaw* v *Southern Foundries (1926) Ltd* [1940] AC 701 HL:

'Prima facie that which in any contract is left to be implied and need not be expressed is something so obvious that it goes without saying; so that, if while one of the parties were making their bargain, an officious bystander were to suggest some express provision for it in the agreement, they would testily suppress him with a common, "oh, of course".'

The dividing line between those cases where a term may be implied is narrow and difficult to draw. Two examples illustrate the problem. The first is *Luxor (Eastbourne) Ltd* v *Cooper* [1941] AC 108, where it was held a term would not be implied that an estate agent was entitled to commission where he introduced a purchaser but no sale followed. The court was not satisfied that both parties, as reasonable men, would have agreed to it if it were suggested to both of them.

The second example is *Shell* v *Lostock* [1976] 1 WLR 1187. Here it was held that no term could be implied forbidding abnormal discrimination between competing purchasers of Shell petrol because the parties would not have agreed to such a term. The court indicated that it would always be reluctant to find an implied term where the parties had agreed in the form of a carefully drafted written contract.

In the second case, where term(s) may be implied from the relationship of the parties the classic example of this is *Liverpool City Council* v *Irwin* [1977] AC 236 HL. It was held that it was an implied term of a lease of a maisonette in a Council block that the landlord should take reasonable care to keep the common parts of the block in a reasonable state of repair. The House of Lords held that the subject matter of the lease and the relationships created by the tenancy demanded, of its nature, the contractual obligation on the landlord.

It seems that the courts are reluctant to extend implications from the relationships between the parties beyond the recognised categories of such relationships.

Terms implied by custom or usage

Terms may be implied by custom or usage of a particular trade or business, market or locality. The custom must be invariable and certain. A contract may be construed as incorporating a relevant custom unless it is inconsistent with the terms of that contract. Examples of terms implied by custom or usage are:

Hutton v *Warren* (1836) 1 M & W 466
A tenant established a right to a reasonable allowance for labour expended on the land even though the lease did not contain a term to this effect.

Lord Eldon v *Hedley Brothers* [1935] 2 KB 1
The usage of a particular trade, the hay trade, was implied into a contract, to vary what would otherwise have been the time property in the goods passed. The Sale of Goods Act 1979 s18 provides that when goods are subject to being weighed or measured to determine the price, property does not pass until that act is done. The usage in the trade, however, was that when hay was bought in the particular manner relevant in this case, property passed at the time the contract was made, and a term to this effect should be implied into the contract.

British Crane Hire Corporation v *Ipswich Plant Hire* [1975] QB 303

The owner of a crane hired it out to a contractor who was engaged in the same business. It was held that the owner's terms, which were usual in the business, were binding on the hirer although they had not actually been communicated at the time of hiring. There was, in the view of the Court of Appeal a 'common understanding' that these terms applied.

Note: A custom or usage cannot be incorporated into a contract if it is expressly or impliedly excluded by the terms of the contract. Nor can it be incorporated if it is inconsistent with the tenor of the contract as a whole.

Terms implied by statute

Examples of this are numerous. For example, the Sale of Goods Act 1979 implies numerous terms. Sections 12–15 of this Act imply terms about the title of the seller to the goods, the quality of the goods, fitness for purposes, correspondence with description and so on.

Sections 12–15 are imposed on both parties *in consumer sales* and govern the parties whether they wish it or not. They cannot be excluded. Other implied terms in other parts of the Act can be freely altered (or excluded altogether) by the parties if they so wish.

(For further details of this and other aspects of sale of goods see chapter 34.)

Conditions, warranties and innominate terms

Introduction

The ways in which the obligations under a contract are construed are various. The most important distinction is between those contractual obligations which entitle an innocent party to repudiate a contract in the event of a breach and those which merely enable a person to claim damages. The classic division is between 'conditions', a breach of which gives the innocent party an option to repudiate, and 'warranties', a breach of which does not. The expression 'warranty' is also used to mean a contractual promise, or term, so it is important to have in mind the use to which the word is being put. The word 'condition' also has another meaning. It may mean a stipulation that a contract should be brought to an end, or should not be enforceable except on the happening of a given event. The condition is then properly called a 'condition subsequent' or a 'condition precedent' respectively.

In addition to the classic division between conditions and warranties, there is a third class of term called an intermediate term or innominate term. This is usually thought to be different from a condition because it is not necessarily certain at the outset whether the term will enable a person to repudiate in the event of its breach.

When is a term a condition?

Frequently, the terms of a contract are not conveniently labelled by the parties as 'condition' and 'warranty'. Even if the parties do employ such labels, it does not follow that their use may be conclusive as to what may constitute a condition or warranty. For example, if the words 'it is warranted that ...' are used it will not follow that breach of the term will not be a breach of condition. If the parties have not expressed themselves on the issue of what is to be a condition enabling repudiation for breach and what is not, the courts have to decide. This may be a formidable task.

In *Poussard* v *Spiers & Pond* (1876) 1 QBD 410 an actress was employed to play the leading part in a French operetta as from the beginning of its run. She was unable to take up her role until a week after the season had started. The producers, who had had to engage a substitute, refused her services. It was held that her promise to perform as from the first night amounted to a condition and that its breach entitled the producers to treat the contract as discharged.

On the other hand, in *Bettini* v *Gye* (1876) 1 QBD 183, a singer was engaged to sing for the whole of the season in theatres and at concerts. He undertook to appear six days in advance for rehearsals. He only arrived three days in advance. The defendant sought to terminate the contract. It was held that he could not. The rehearsal clause was subsidiary to the main part of the agreement. Accordingly, it was only a warranty that the singer would arrive six days in advance.

The courts, therefore, seek to distinguish a condition from a warranty by deciding upon the importance of the term to the contract as a whole, and from that decision inferring the intention of the parties.

In *Behn* v *Burness* (1863) 3 B & S 751, the court had to evaluate a statement in a charter party that a ship was now in the port of Amsterdam. The statement was inaccurate. The question was whether that promise was a condition or a warranty. It was held that the term was a condition.

The intention of the parties is to be ascertained at the time of entry into the agreement.

In *The Mihalis Angelos* [1971] 1 QB 164, the owners of a vessel let it to charterers for a voyage from Haiphong to Hamburg. The owners said that the vessel was 'expected ready to load about 1st July'. It was found as a fact that there was no reasonable ground for expecting that the vessel would be ready to load on 1 July.

It was held that the expected readiness clause was a condition.

Warranties

This term is notoriously difficult to classify.

It is already suggested that the word 'warranty' is used in a multiplicity of senses. *Chitty* suggests that 'the emergence of the new category of "intermediate" or "innominate" terms (see below) seems likely to have reduced the number of occasions when a term will be classified as a warranty in this sense (the breach of which by one party does not entitle the other to treat his obligations as discharged), almost to vanishing point, save in the very exceptional circumstances where a term has been specifically so classified by statute.' He is referring principally to the Sale of Goods Act 1979.

Innominate or intermediate terms

Hong Kong Fir Shipping v Kawasaki Kisen Kaisha [1962] 2 QB 26

The defendants chartered the vessel 'Hong Kong Fir' from the plaintiffs for 24 months; the charter party provided 'she being fitted in every way for ordinary cargo service'. It transpired that the engine room staff were incompetent, and the vessel spent less than nine weeks of the first seven months of the charter at sea because of breakdowns and consequent repairs required to make her seaworthy. The defendants repudiated the charter party and claimed that the term as to seaworthiness was a condition of the contract, any breach of which entitled them to do so. It was held that the term was neither a condition nor a warranty, and in determining whether the defendants could terminate the contract it was necessary to look at the consequences of the breach to see if they deprived the innocent party of substantially the whole benefit he should have received under the contract. On the facts this was not the case, because the charter party still had a substantial time to run.

Diplock LJ said:

'There are, however, many contractual undertakings of a more complex character which cannot be categorised as being "conditions" or "warranties" ... Of such undertakings all that can be said is that some breaches will and others will not give rise to an event which will deprive the party not in default of substantially the whole benefit which it was intended he should obtain from the contract; and the legal consequences of a breach of such undertaking, unless provided for expressly in the contract, depend upon the nature of the event to which the breach gives rise and do not follow automatically from a prior classification of the undertaking as a condition or warranty.'

A term is most likely to be an innominate term when it is capable of being broken in both a very trivial or a very serious manner, so that a duty to provide a seaworthy ship would fall within this category (*Hong Kong Fir* (above)) as could a duty to proceed with 'all convenient speed' to a port of loading (*Freeman v Taylor* (1831) 8 Bing 124) and as would an obligation on a shipmaster to obey the charterer's orders (*Federal Commerce and Navigation Co v Molena Alpha Inc* [1979] AC 757).

Exclusion clauses

Introduction

An exclusion (or exemption) clause is one which purports to exempt wholly or in part liability for certain breaches of contract or for the happening of certain events.

If the exemption is only partial then the clause may be called a 'limitation of liability clause'. The courts have always been wary of such clauses. As with any other clause, it must, of course, be incorporated into the contract; at common law such a clause is also construed 'contra proferentem', that is, against the interests of the person seeking to rely on the clause. The Unfair Contract Terms Act 1977 has gone further, so that some exclusion clauses may be wholly void and some may be relied upon only so far as they satisfy the 'requirement of reasonableness' specified in the Act. In some cases also, provisions of the common law must be considered.

In order for an exclusion clause to be relied upon three factors must be established:

a that the clause was incorporated into the contract;

b that it covered the damage complained of;

c that it is not affected by common law or statutory rules which might render it invalid.

We shall look at each requirement in turn.

Incorporation

Incorporation may be achieved either by signature or notice.

Signature

The usual rule is that a person is bound by whatever he signs, whether he has read the document or not.

In *L'Estrange* v *Graucob* [1934] 2 KB 394 a woman signed a contract to buy machinery. The contract contained a clause that: '… any express or implied condition, statement or warranty … is hereby excluded.' It was, as the court remarked, 'in regrettably small print'! Although she had not read the document in full, it was held that her signature bound her, and when the machine proved defective Miss L'Estrange had no remedy.

Notice

This may be further broken down according to the form of notice involved.

Notice by display

Notices exhibited in premises which purport to exempt liability for loss or damage are common. For example: 'Car parked at owner's risk' in a car park, or 'The Management undertake no liability for loss or damage occasioned to customer's apparel' in a cloakroom, are instances of notices which are intended to have contractual force. Whether such clauses do have contractual force is dependent upon whether the notice is in a position where it can be seen before or at the time of entry into the contract. A leading case is *Olley* v *Marlborough Court Ltd* [1949] 1 KB 532, where a husband and wife arrived at a hotel. They paid for their board and residence in advance. They went to the hotel room. A notice was displayed in the room exempting the hotel from liability for loss or damage to items left in the room. During their stay, the wife's fur coat was stolen. It was held that the contract was made before the notice was seen, so that the contractual liability could not be excluded.

Notice in a document

There are five questions which should be asked.

a Is the document contractual?

b Has reasonably sufficient notice been given?

c Is the clause unusual?

d Could acceptance have been avoided?

e When is the contractual dealing concluded?

The following cases give some idea of the sort of problems that may arise. Most of the cases concern documents such as tickets, order forms or receipts.

In *Chapelton* v *Barry Urban District Council* [1940] 1 KB 532, deck chairs were stacked by a notice asking the public who wished to use the deck chairs to get tickets and retain them for inspection. The plaintiff paid for two tickets for chairs but did not read them. The reverse of the ticket contained exclusion clauses from liability for personal injury. The plaintiff was injured when a deck chair collapsed. It was held that the local authority defendant could not rely on the exclusion clause, because it was on a document no one would ever assume to be a contractual document.

(Also, even if it *had* been a contractual document, it was handed to the plaintiff after he had hired the deck chair.)

In *Sugar* v *London, Midland and Scottish Railway* [1941] 1 All ER 172 the words 'for conditions see back' which appeared on the face of the document was obliterated by the date stamp. It was held that reasonably sufficient notice had not been given.

In *Richardson, Spence & Co* v *Rowntree* [1894] AC 217 the plaintiff contracted with the defendant to be taken as a passenger on a steamer from Philadelphia to Liverpool. The fare was paid and the plaintiff received the ticket which was folded up and in part obliterated by red ink. She knew that the ticket contained writing but not that it contained terms. It was held that no reasonably sufficient notice had been given.

See also the Australian case of *Dillon* v *Baltic Shipping Co* [1991] 2 Lloyd's Rep 155 which, while not of course binding in this country, illustrates perfectly the problems likely to be encountered in 'ticket' cases.

Note that the requirement is only that *reasonably* sufficient notice be given. It is an objective and not a subjective test. If the plaintiff has a peculiarity not common to the rest of the population such that he does not know of the terms he will not be protected by his ignorance if a reasonable man would have known of them.

In *Thompson* v *London, Midlands and Scottish Railway Co* [1930] 1 KB 40, the plaintiff was injured when she stepped off a train which had stopped before reaching the platform. Her ticket contained terms which referred to timetables which limited liability. She could not read the words on the ticket because she was illiterate.

It was held that she was bound by the clauses limiting liability. A reasonable man would have been able to read the ticket and to know that exclusion clauses referred to might be consulted in the timetable.

Note, also, that if a clause is particularly unusual it seems special rules of notice may apply.

It seems that the more unusual or unreasonable the clause the more difficult it may be to incorporate into the contract at common law. This is principally an argument promoted by Lord Denning MR. He first made this observation in *J Spurling* v *Bradshaw* [1956] 1 WLR 461, where he suggested that 'the more unreasonable the clause is the greater the notice which must be given of it ...' He expressed like views in *Thornton* v *Shoe Lane Parking* [1971] 2 QB 163. In that case a ticket was issued from an automatic machine in a car park. The car park premises contained a notice which was visible on approach that all cars were parked at owner's risk. The ticket, which was issued as the driver approached, emerged from the machine. He would take the ticket and drive on. The ticket contained printed wording that it was issued subject to conditions displayed inside the premises. The conditions inside the premises were in small print and very wide and excluded liability for damage to cars and customers.

Lord Denning said that the clause was so wide and destructive of rights that in order to be effective it would have to have a red hand pointing to it and be printed in red ink and so the rule became known as the 'Red-Hand Rule'.

Megaw LJ said that when a restriction was not usual the defendant must show that he had fairly brought to the notice of the other party his intention to attach an unusual condition.

Because of these considerations the plaintiff was not bound by the clauses inside the premises, because they could not be seen until after entry and, with an automatic barrier system, it was impossible to change one's mind after entry.

In *Interfoto Picture Library Ltd* v *Stiletto Visual Programmes Ltd* [1988] 1 All ER 348 the Court of Appeal re-affirmed the principle that where a condition in a contract was particularly onerous or unusual and would not generally be known to the other party the party seeking to enforce that condition had to show that it had been fairly and reasonably brought to the other party's attention.

Notice by a course of dealing

If notice has not been given by display as in a contractual document, it may have been given by 'a course of dealing'. This situation will arise where the parties have dealt together in the past on a number of occasions such that one party can be presumed to know the terms and conditions upon which the other operates. It does not seem to matter that the party against whom the clause is used does not know in fact what those terms are, provided that he has had every opportunity to find out what they are.

In *Henry Kendall & Sons* v *William Lillico & Sons* [1969] 2 AC 31 the parties had contracted on more than 100 occasions in the years preceding the contract which was broken. On each occasion there was a verbal contract which was followed by a 'sold note'. The 'sold note' contained conditions. They would not have been incorporated into the first few contracts.

On the other hand, the recipients knew that the notes contained conditions, but they had not read them.

It was held that their conduct in continuing to trade showed a desire to be bound by the conditions.

In contrast with the above is *McCutcheon* v *David MacBrayne Ltd* [1964] 1 WLR 125, where the plaintiffs' agent had dealt with the defendants on many occasions. Sometimes he had signed a 'risk note' and sometimes he had not. The risk note contained conditions. On this occasion no risk note was signed. It was held that the plaintiffs were not bound by the conditions. There was no course of conduct because there was no consistency of dealing.

In *Hollier* v *Rambler Motors (AMC)* [1972] 2 QB 71 Salmon LJ held that three or four transactions over a period of five years could not be described as 'a course of dealing'.

Does the clause cover the damage complained of?

Introduction
Once it has been established that the clause is a term of the contract and has not been successfully excluded it must be shown to cover the damage complained of.

In *Andrews* v *Singer* [1934] 1 KB 17 a clause which read 'all conditions, warranties and liabilities implied by statute common law or otherwise' was held not to exclude liability for an *express* term.

The 'contra proferentem' rule
In construing exemption clauses the courts will interpret them 'contra proferentem', that is against the interests of the person seeking to rely on it.

In *John Lee & Son (Grantham) Ltd* v *Railway Executive* [1949] 2 All ER 581 the plaintiffs leased a warehouse from the defendants. In the lease was a clause which purported to exempt liability for loss and damage which would not have arisen but for the tenancy. The goods were damaged by a spark which gave rise to a fire. On the basis of the 'contra proferentem' rule, the loss did not arise from the relationship of landlord and tenant and so the clause was not applicable, and could not be used to exclude liability for loss.

Similarly, in *Wallis, Son & Wells* v *Pratt & Haynes* [1911] AC 394, a provision that a seller gave no 'warranty, express or implied' did not exclude him from liability for breach of a *condition*. And in *Houghton* v *Trafalgar Insurance Co* [1954] 1 QB 247 the insurance policy excluded the insurer from liability 'whilst the car was carrying any *load* in excess of that for which it is construed'. It was held that the clause did not exclude liability where the car was carrying an excess number of *passengers*.

Fundamental breach

Where there has been a breach of a fundamental term or any other fundamental breach of contract it is a question of construction whether the exclusion clause is drafted sufficiently widely to apply to the breach. In *Suisse Atlantique Société D'Armament Maritime* v *NV Rotterdamsche Kolen Centrale* [1967] 1 AC 361, a charterparty contained a clause limiting damages to $1000 per day for each 'lay day' beyond the permitted number (that is, days spent waiting in port). The number of excess days was 150. The owners claimed a greater loss.

It was held that the clause was an agreed damages clause and not an exclusion clause so that the question of fundamental breach did not arise, and even if it had, the clause would have been effective.

However, the House of Lords went on to say that as a rule of *construction* (not of law) an exemption clause should not, in the absence of clear words, be applied to breaches which tended to defeat the main purpose of the contract.

Thus a clause should not be assumed to be intended by the parties to cover fundamental breach where one party does something totally different from what he undertook to do (eg supplies a central heating system instead of double glazing).

This was re-affirmed in *Photo Production* v *Securicor Transport* [1980] AC 827

The defendants agreed to provide a visiting patrol service to the plaintiffs' factory at £8 15s per week. The contract contained an exemption clause to the effect that the defendants 'should not be responsible for any injurious act or default by any employee of the company unless such act or default could have been foreseen and avoided by the exercise of due diligence on the part of the company as his employer.' In fact a patrolman deliberately lit a fire and the factory was substantially burnt down.

It was held that the defendants were protected by the exemption clause. The view expressed in *Harbutt's 'Plasticene'* [1970] 1 QB 447 that a breach of contract by one party, accepted by the other as discharging him from his further obligations under the contract, brought the contract to an end, and, together with it, any exemption clause, was disapproved. The proper question was whether, as a matter of construction, the exemption clause relieved the defendants from liability. Here, there was an apportionment of the risk as between plaintiff and defendant and the risk of arson was not accepted by the defendant.

Negligence

The Unfair Contract Terms Act now renders clauses purporting to exclude liability for negligence largely ineffective (see below). But even where the statute does not apply the courts have required clear words to satisfy the exclusion of liability for negligence.

Where a party can be made liable on some ground other than negligence the clause will be construed as applying to that other ground, and not to negligence.

The principle was stated by Lord Greene MR in *Alderslade* v *Hendon Laundry Ltd* [1945] KB 189 as follows:

'... where the head of damage in respect of which limitation of liability is sought to be imposed by such a clause is one which rests on negligence and nothing else, the clause must be construed as extending to that head of damage, because if it were not so construed it would lack subject-matter. Where, on the other hand, the head of damage may be based on some ground other than that of negligence, the general principle is that the clause must be confined to loss occurring through that other cause to the exclusion of loss arising through negligence. The reason for that is that if a contracting party wishes in such a case to limit his liability in respect of negligence, he must do so in clear terms, and in the absence of such clear terms the clause is to be construed as relating to a different kind of liability and not to liability based on negligence.'

The reasoning behind this approach was made clear in *Gillespie Brothers* v *Roy Bowles Transport* [1973] QB 400 where Buckley LJ said:

'... it is inherently improbable that one party to the contract should intend to absolve the other party from the consequences of the latter's own negligence. The intention to do so must therefore be made perfectly clear for otherwise the court will conclude that the exempted party was only to be free from liability in respect of damage occasioned by causes other than negligence for which he is answerable.'

In *Smith* v *South Wales Switchgear Ltd* [1978] 1 All ER 18 the House of Lords held that a clause did not contain an *express* provision excluding liability for negligence unless it contained the word 'negligence' or some synonym for 'negligence'.

The courts have distinguished between cases where the defendant could be held liable only if he were negligent and cases where liability could arise from some other cause.

Thus in *Hollier* v *Rambler Motors* (above) the clause purported to exclude liability 'for damage caused by fire to customers' cars on the premises'. The Court of Appeal held that the clause did not apply to negligence. Fire could occur from a large variety of causes, only one of which is negligence on the part of the occupier of the premises.

Limitation clauses

In *Ailsa Craig Fishing Co* v *Malvern Fishing Co* [1983] 1 WLR 964 the appellants owned a boat which sank in Aberdeen Harbour. The vessel was a complete loss. The respondents were required by contract with inter alia the appellants to provide continuous security cover for the boat. The contract contained two contentious clauses and the issues were:

a whether they were available to the respondents even though the respondents had completely failed to comply with the contract; and

b how the clause was to be interpreted.

The court said that the clause was one which limited liability and that the contract had to be construed as a whole to see whether the limitation of liability clause should apply to a fundamental breach. Although a limitation of liability clause had to be clearly and unambiguously expressed and construed 'contra proferentem', it should be given its ordinary and natural meaning. This should be construed less rigidly than an exemption clause because it would be more likely to accord with the true intention of the parties.

The clause must not be invalidated by statute or common law

The Unfair Contract Terms Act 1977 (UCTA) is the most important piece of legislation affecting exemption clauses; but there are other Acts which have similar effects (for example, the Carriage by Railway Act 1972 and the Public Passenger Vehicles Act 1981 provide that public transport companies cannot exclude or limit liability for death or personal injury of passengers).

Ambit of the Act

The Act applies to contract terms and to notices which are non-contractual and which purport to exclude or restrict liability in tort. It seeks to limit the circumstances in which terms and notices restricting or limiting liability may apply, but it does not affect the basis of liability nor does it apply to any other 'unfair' terms. The Act, furthermore, does not affect the issues of incorporation and interpretation which must be left to the common law.

Most of the Act applies only to 'business liability', that is liability for things done by a person in the course of a business. The person intended primarily to benefit from the Act is the person who deals as a 'consumer' with a person acting in the course of business.

Section 12 of the Act provides:

'1) A party to a contract "deals as consumer" in relation to another party if:

a) he neither makes the contract in the course of a business nor holds himself out as doing so; and

b) the other party does make the contract in the course of a business; and

c) in the case of a contract governed by the law of sale of goods or hire purchase, or by section 7 of this Act, the goods passing under or in pursuance of the contract are of a type ordinarily supplied for private use or consumption.

2) But on a sale by auction or by competitive tender the buyer is not in any circumstances to be regarded as dealing as consumer.

3) Subject to this, it is for those claiming that a party does not deal as consumer to show that he does not.'

('Business' includes a profession and government, local government, local authority or public authority activities – s14.)

Generally, the Act can be said to cover three areas:

a the exclusion or restriction of liability for negligence (defined in section 1(1)) to apply to:

i a contractual duty of care

ii a tortious duty of care

iii a common duty of care under the Occupiers Liability Act 1957.

b the exclusion or restriction of liability for certain terms implied by statute into sale of goods contracts, hire purchase agreements and some other supply contracts.

c some contract terms which exclude or limit liability for breaches of contract or which purport to entitle the other party to render a contractual performance substantially different from that which was reasonably expected of him.

Negligence liability

This is covered by s2 of the Act. No one who acts in the course of a business can, by either incorporating terms in a contract or displaying a notice, exclude liability either in contract or tort for death or bodily injury arising from negligence. He can exclude/limit liability for loss of property or financial loss, but only if the exemption is reasonable.

To prove reasonableness is difficult, though where two large businesses are concerned the courts are more inclined to take a lenient approach.

See, for example, the following cases.

In *Waldron-Kelly* v *British Railways Board* [1981] 3 Cur L 33 a suitcase was lost. The Board relied on their limitation clause restricting liability to £27, whereas the total value of suitcase and contents was £320. The County Court held the limitation clause to be unreasonable and the Board could not rely on it. And, in *Woodman* v *Photo-Trade Processing* (1981) The Times 20 June, wedding photographs were ruined when being processed. The firm relied on their limitation clause, restricting liability to the cost of a new film. The courts held this to be unreasonable.

Finally in *George Mitchell (Chesterfield) Ltd* v *Finney Lock Seeds Ltd* [1983] 2 AC 803 the purchasers of cabbage seeds were supplied with commercially useless seed of the wrong description so that their crops were lost. The contract contained an exclusion clause which purported to limit the liability of the seller to the cost of the seeds, some £200. The purchasers' claim was for damages of £61,513 for breach of contract.

The House of Lords held the limitation clause to be unreasonable.

More recently the House of Lords considered the question of exclusion of liability for negligence in the two cases of *Smith* v *Eric S Bush* and *Harris* v *Wyre Forest District Council* [1989] 2 WLR 790. In affirming the decision of the Court of Appeal in *Smith* and reversing the Court of Appeal's decision in *Harris* the House of Lords held that a valuer who valued a house for a building society or a local authority owed a duty of care to the purchaser of the house. However, the valuer could disclaim liability to exercise reasonable skill and care by an express exclusion clause but such a disclaimer had to satisfy the requirement of reasonableness in s2(2) of the Act. In both these cases it would not be fair and reasonable to impose on the purchasers the risk of loss arising from the incompetence or carelessness on the part of the valuers. The disclaimers were, therefore, not effective to exclude liability for the negligence of the valuers.

In his speech Lord Griffiths said that it was impossible to draw up an exhaustive list of factors to be taken into account in deciding whether an exclusion clause met the requirement of reasonableness, but certain matters should always be considered. These were:

a Were the parties of equal bargaining power?

b In the case of advice, would it have been reasonably practicable to obtain the advice from an alternative source taking into account considerations of costs and time?

c How difficult is the task of being undertaken for which liability is being excluded?

d What are the practical consequences of the decision on the question of reasonableness? This involves the sums of money at stake and the ability of the parties to bear the loss, which raises the question of insurance.

Finally, although the majority of decisions appear to go against exclusion clauses, this is not always the case; especially where the parties are of roughly equal bargaining power.

See *Photo Production* v *Securicor Transport* [1980] AC 827 where S contracted to guard the plaintiff's factory. The security patrolman deliberately started a fire, which ultimately burned the factory down. Both parties were established businesses on a roughly equal footing and freely negotiated the terms of the contract. Both parties were insured (the plaintiff, in particular, for the loss of the building). The court declared itself satisfied that both the parties had intended the exclusion clause as it stood, and declared it reasonable. This protected Securicor for a liability for damage to property caused by negligence or for any other reason and operated to exclude all liability. The plaintiff was unable to claim.

Sale of goods, hire purchase and other supply contracts
Sections 6–7 deals with both business and non-business liability and makes some exclusion clauses totally ineffective and others subject to the test of reasonableness. (For further details on sale of goods contracts see chapter 34.)

The 1977 Act Schedule 2 includes a code of guidance to help determine what is 'reasonable'.

Matters to be taken into account include:

'a) the strength of the bargaining positions of the parties relative to each other, taking into account (among other things) alternative means by which the customer's requirements could have been met.
b) whether the customer received an inducement to agree to the term, or in accepting

it had an opportunity of entering into a similar contract with other persons, but without having to accept a similar term;

c) whether the customer knew or ought reasonably to have known of the existence and extent of the term (having regard, among other things, to any custom of the trade and any previous course of dealing between the parties);

d) where the term excludes or restricts any relevant liability if some condition is not complied with, whether it was reasonable at the time of the contract to expect that compliance with that condition would be practicable;

e) whether the goods were manufactured, processed or adapted to the special order of the customer.'

For the operation of these guidelines see cases like: *Photo Production* v *Securicor Transport* (1980) and *George Mitchell* v *Finney Lock Seeds* (1983) (both above), and also *R W Green* v *Cade Bros Farm* [1978] 1 Lloyd's Rep 602. Here the contract was for the sale of seed potatoes by potato merchants. The contract limited the liability of the sellers to returning the price. The potatoes proved to be infected with a virus. As the potatoes were uncertified, and hence cheaper, Griffiths J upheld the limitation clause as reasonable. However he struck down as unreasonable a clause requiring the buyers to give notice of a claim within three days of delivery.

Separate 'guarantees' of goods
Manufacturers and suppliers sometimes provide what they call 'guarantees' or 'indemnities' or 'warranties'. (The terms are all equally meaningless!) Such guarantees will sometimes purport to contain exclusion clauses. Section 5 of UCTA provides that if goods are of a type normally supplied for private use or consumption then no term in the guarantee can purport to exclude/limit the manufacturer's or supplier's liability for defective goods, if the defect is caused by negligence.

Also s10 UCTA provides:

'A person is not bound by any contract term prejudicing or taking away rights of his which arise under or in connection with, the performance of another contract, so far as those rights extend to the enforcement of another's liability which this part of the Act prevents that other from excluding or restricting.'

This means that evasion of the provisions of UCTA by means of a secondary contract is prevented.

Exceptions to the Act
The Act does not apply to the following:

a   the liability of people not acting within the course of business (except s6);

b   insurance contracts;

c   certain parts of contracts relating to land;

d   apart from s2(1) which does apply: contracts of marine salvage as towage, charterparties of ships or hovercraft, contracts for the carriage of goods by ship or hovercraft;

e section 2(1) and (2) do not apply to contracts of employment except in favour of the employee;

f contracts for the international supply of goods.

Save as set out above, a contract properly governed by English law may not include provisions excluding the Act.

A person cannot exclude liability by choosing a foreign law wholly or mainly to avoid the Act.

Law of contract (4): 31
defective contracts

Some contracts which appear perfectly valid may nevertheless be wholly or partly vitiated because of some defect when they were formed.

We have already looked at lack of certainty and informality, where a contract needs to be made in a particular form. In the sections that follow we shall discuss other vitiating factors, especially mistake, misrepresentation, duress and undue influence, illegality and lack of capacity of the parties (or one of them).

Mistake

The general rule is that mistake does *not* affect the validity of a contract.
Having said that, there are so many exceptions to the rule that an operative mistake of fact may affect the contract to a point where, if sufficiently serious, it will render the contract void.

A great deal will therefore depend on how one defines an 'operative' mistake.

Certainly a mistake of law will never affect the validity of a contract – witness the saying that 'ignorance of the law is no defence'!

Terminology differs – mistakes will be found to be defined differently by different authorities; also many of the definitions overlap.

Some of the most common mistakes and their effect on contracts are studied below.

Mistake as to documents

Where a person, by signing a document, enters into contractual relations with another party, it may be possible for him to avoid liability under the contract if he signed the document under a mistaken belief as to the essential nature of the document by raising the plea 'non est factum', namely that 'it is not my deed'. This is an exception to the general rule that a person who signs a document is bound by it, whether or not he reads it or understands it, and was originally applicable where the mistaken party was unable to read the document owing to illiteracy or blindness; further it could also only be pleaded where the document was in fact a deed. The plea has evolved through judicial decisions so that now it applies to any written contract, and though some special circumstance must now attach to the mistaken party, it no longer need be inability to read.

In *Foster* v *Mackinnon* (1869) LR 4 CP 704 the defendant, an elderly gentleman, was induced to indorse a bill of exchange, having been told that it was merely a guarantee and not having seen the face of the bill. The bill was later indorsed to the plaintiff who sued on it. Byles J held it invalid 'not merely on the ground of fraud … but on the ground that the mind of the signer did not accompany the signature; in other words, that he never intended to sign and therefore in contemplation of law never did sign the contract to which his name is appended.'

Likewise, in *Lewis* v *Clay* (1898) 67 LJ QB 224, at the request of a third party, one N, the defendant signed in a number of cut-open spaces on otherwise concealed documents, believing he was witnessing N's signature. In reality he had signed promissory notes in favour of the plaintiff worth approximately £11,000. The plea succeeded on the grounds that promissory notes were altogether different to merely attesting a formal signature.

However, contrast this with *Gallie* v *Lee* [1971] AC 1004, where Mrs Gallie intended to assign the lease of her house so as to enable her nephew to borrow money. The assignment she actually signed was prepared fraudulently by Lee who had promised to arrange the loan and was an assignment to Lee himself who mortgaged the house to the Anglia Building Society and absconded with the proceeds.

Mrs Gallie claimed (unsuccessfully) 'non est factum' – she was old, could not, at that time, read (she had lost her spectacles) and would never have signed the document had she realised its true nature.

Because she had been negligent in not seeking independent advice and because the nature of the document (an assignment of a lease) was not so very different from what she believed it to be, the House of Lords held that non est factum could not apply.

Mistakes as to identity

A mistake by one party may sometimes invalidate a contract. It will be a unilateral mistake. Normally the law assumes the identity of the person with whom one contracts to be immaterial; it is therefore for the person claiming that the contract has been affected by the mistake to prove that the identity of the other party was crucial. This is easier in cases where the parties are not '*inter praesentes*' (face to face).

Some examples may help to establish the difficulties involved in proving that identity is all important.

In *Phillips* v *Brooks* [1919] 2 KB 243 a man called North entered the plaintiff's shop and asked to see some jewellery, and selected some pearls and a ring, of total value £3,000. He wrote a cheque, saying as he did so, 'You see who I am. I am Sir George Bullough', a person known by reputation to the plaintiff, and gave an address which the plaintiff checked in a directory. The plaintiff allowed North to take the ring away, valued £450, and North pledged it with the defendants for £350 who took it bona fide and without notice of the fraud. When North's cheque was dishonoured the plaintiff sought the return of the ring, claiming the contract was void. The issue was whether the plaintiff intended to sell the ring to the person present in the shop, or whether the offer was directed at Sir George Bullough only. It was held that the plaintiff's intention was the former; he may have thought his customer was Bullough, but the evidence did not bear out the argument that the offer was made to him alone.

The inference that the judge drew was that the parties intended to thus contract.

In *Ingram* v *Little* [1961] 1 QB 31 the plaintiffs were three elderly ladies who advertised their car for sale. A rogue calling himself Hutchinson visited their home and agreed to purchase the car for £717. When he tried to make payment by cheque they refused to accept it, and to persuade them otherwise he told them what he claimed to be his full name and address and details of his local business interests. One of the plaintiffs checked his details in a telephone directory at the local post office and found them apparently correct. As a result he was permitted to take the car away in return for his cheque, which was dishonoured.

The Court of Appeal held that the contract was void, the identity of the purchaser being of the utmost importance. They intended only to sell after checking the name and address of 'Hutchinson'.

The most recent case of *Lewis v Averay* [1972] 1 QB 198 disagrees with *Ingram v Little*. Here the plaintiff advertised his car for sale and a rogue called round to see it and offered to buy it, claiming to be the actor 'Richard Greene'. He signed a cheque for £450 'R A Green' and asked to take the car away with him. The plaintiff asked for proof of his identity and the rogue showed him an admission pass to Pinewood Studios in the name of 'Richard A Green'. The plaintiff in consequence allowed him to take the car. The cheque was dishonoured and the defendant purchased it bona fide for £200. The Court of Appeal held that the contract with the rogue was voidable only, that the plaintiff had failed to show that he did not intend to contract with the person actually present.

In *Cundy v Lindsay* (1878) 3 App Cas 459 a rogue called Blenkarn ordered bed-linen by post from the firm of Lindsay and Co. He signed his letter as from the firm of Blenkiron and Co, a reputable dealer, with whom Lindsay had previously contracted. He intercepted the parcel of goods and resold the linen to Cundy. The crucial factor in this case was the question of identity. Lindsay's never intended to deal with Blenkarn, but only Blenkiron and Co. Not surprisingly there was held to be no contract.

In *King's Norton Metal Co v Edridge, Merrett & Co* (1897) 14 TLR 98 the plaintiffs sold goods to a firm called 'Hallam and Co' which did not exist, the real buyer was a rogue called Wallis. It was held that the contract was not void for mistake, because if the plaintiffs were willing to deal with an unknown firm, without checking on them, obviously identity could not be said to be crucial.

Finally, look at the case of *Lake v Simmonds* [1927] AC 487, where the appellant was a jeweller, and he had in the past made a number of small sales to a woman, Esme Ellison, who described herself as the wife of a wealthy customer, Van der Borgh. He permitted her to take away two extremely valuable necklaces 'on approval' to show to her 'husband'. She was in fact Van der Borgh's mistress and she absconded with the jewellery. The appellant sought to claim for the loss on his insurance policy which excluded liability for jewellery 'entrusted to a customer', but covered theft. The question turned on whether there was a contract between the jeweller and Ellison, and the House of Lords held there was no contract; the jeweller intended to deal with the wife of Van der Borgh, and that was the reason he parted with the goods. This was held to be a mistake as to identity and not merely attributes. *Phillips v Brooks* was distinguished on the ground that the sale had been concluded before North made his claim to be Bullough, the effect of which had been to affect the mode of payment the jeweller was prepared to accept and to induce him to let North take the ring away. It should be stated that although this is an arguable interpretation of the facts, it was in no way at the heart of the decision of the case and Horridge J did not rely on it. Further in *Lake* v *Simmonds* this line of reasoning was adopted by Viscount Haldane alone and is not supported by the other speeches. The logical conclusion of the chain of thought is that if North had at the outset announced himself as Sir George Bullough, the contract would have been void because the jeweller intended to contract with Bullough only, as the jeweller in *Lake* was held to have intended to contract with the wife of Van der Borgh only.

Mistake as to the existence of the subject matter

This type of mistake encompasses instances where the subject matter never existed, has ceased to exist before the contract was completed, or involves some defect (for example of title) that makes the subject matter of the contract meaningless.

Thus, see the following cases.

Strickland v *Turner* (1852) 7 Ex 208
The plaintiff purchased an annuity and, unknown to the parties, the annuitant was already dead. He was able to recover the price paid, the consideration having totally failed.

Raffles v *Wichelhaus* (1864) 2 H & C 906
A cargo of cotton was described as being on the *SS Peerless* from Bombay. Unknown to either party there were two ships of that name sailing from Bombay within a few weeks of each other. The contract was held void.

Cooper v *Phibbs* (1867) LR 2 HL 149
A agreed to take the lease of a fishery from B, though contrary to the belief of the parties at the time A was tenant for life of the fishery and B had no title. The House of Lords granted rescission in equity, though Lord Atkin was of the opinion that the contract was void at common law and regarded the case as analogous to a situation where a contract is void for mistake owing to non-existent subject matter (above).

McRae v *Commonwealth Disposals Commission* (1951) 84 CLR 377
The defendants accepted the plaintiff's tender of £285 for the purchase of a wrecked oil tanker, described as laying on Jourmaund Reef, off Papua New Guinea. There was no such reef, nor any wrecked tanker in the indicated area, and in consequence of this, and of having incurred considerable expense in preparing the salvage operation, the plaintiff sued for damages for breach of contract.

On appeal the court held that, far from considering this a case of non-existent subject matter, the defendants had in fact warranted that the tanker existed and were liable accordingly.

As an Australian case, *McRae* is of only persuasive authority in the English courts. The decision has in fact led to a wide reappraisal of the law relating to non-existing goods.

Mutual mistake

It has already been said that there is a great deal of overlap between the different classifications of mistake. Clearly, for example, *Raffles* v *Wichelhaus* (above) would fit equally well into this category.

The main question at issue is whether the mutual mistake the parties make is sufficiently serious and fundamental to render the contract void (or at least voidable).

See, for instance *Bell* v *Lever Bros* [1932] AC 161, where agreements to make severance payments to senior employees were made on the assumption (by all parties) that the employees were entitled to such payment. In fact they could, unknown to the company and not realised by the employees, have been sacked at any time for misconduct.

It was held, however, that the 'golden handshake' agreements were valid, the mistake made by *all* the parties was simply not serious or fundamental enough to order the contract void (or voidable).

In *Galloway* v *Galloway* (1914) 30 TLR 531 the plaintiff contracted to hire a room from the defendant to watch the King's coronation procession. Shortly before the contract was made the procession was cancelled. The plaintiff recovered moneys paid to the defendant on the grounds that the agreement was made on a missupposition of facts which went to the whole root of the contract.

While in *Norwich Union Fire Insurance Society* v *Price* [1934] AC 455 the respondents shipped a cargo of lemons, issued under a policy of marine insurance, with the appellants. In the belief that the lemons had been damaged by an insured-against peril, and sold in consequence, the appellants paid over the insurance moneys. In fact the lemons had not been damaged and had been sold because they were ripening. The Judicial Committee of Privy Council held that the appellants could recover the moneys as having been paid under a mistake of fact. The mistake was 'vital' and the contract was therefore void. The Judicial Committee said there was nothing in *Bell* v *Lever Bros* to suggest otherwise.

More recently in *Associated Japanese Bank International Ltd* v *Credit du Nord SA* [1983] 3 All ER 902 a Mr X purported to sell machinery (which did not exist to the Associated Japanese Bank (AJB) and then leased it back. Credit du Nord (CDN) contracted with AJB to act as Mr X's guarantor that he would pay the rent.

The contract of guarantee was held void for mistake – the whole subject matter on which the guarantee was based did not exist.

As has already been stated there is much overlap between different categories. Obviously a number of the cases listed as examples of mutual mistake would fit equally neatly into that category of mistake in which the subject matter does not exist – res extincta – and vice versa.

William Sindall plc v *Cambridgeshire County Council* [1994] 1 WLR 1016 is a classic case of mutual mistake in a sale of land. It is of particular interest because of the Court of Appeal's careful and systematic examination of remedies.

The courts' attitude to most mistakes is best summed up in *Leaf* v *International Galleries* [1950] 2 KB 86. Here the plaintiff purchased from the defendants a painting which both mistakenly believed to be by Constable. The plaintiff sought rescission for misrepresentation, but the Court of Appeal said, obiter, that although the mistake may have been in one sense essential or fundamental, it did not avoid the contract.

It is clear therefore that although a particular quality may be of great importance to the contracting parties themselves, the courts look at the matter in a slightly different way by considering the essential nature of the subject matter, and not necessarily giving any weight at all to the hopes, desires and disappointments of the parties.

Consequences of mistake

Depending on whether the mistake is 'operative' or not, a mistake may (see *Leaf* v *International Galleries*, above) have no effect on the contract at all.

It seems however that most mistakes if sufficiently serious will render a contract either void, that is a complete nullity, or voidable, that is it may be avoided at the option of the injured party.

It is to be noted that the attitude of common law towards mistake is a good deal harsher than that of equity, which provides a number of remedies for the mistaken party.

For further details see chapter 33 on Remedies.

Misrepresentation

We noted in the previous chapter that all the statements made in the course of the pre-contractual negotiations become terms of the contract. There is a difference between representations (often called 'mere' representations) and true terms, and this difference is most important with regard to the remedies available, should either terms or representations prove to be incorrect or be broken.

Defining misrepresentation

A misrepresentation is a false statement of fact made by one party to the other prior to the making of the contract, with a view to inducing the other party to act on it. The statement must have been intended to be acted on, it must actually have induced the other party to make the contract.

We shall look at certain aspects of this definition more closely.

The misrepresentation must be one of fact

Therefore statements as to the law, or of opinion, will not be included.

In *Bisset* v *Wilkinson* [1927] AC 177 the vendor, whilst in the process of selling his farm which had not previously been used as a sheep farm, was asked by the plaintiff as to the number of sheep the farm could sustain. An opinion, which turned out to be incorrect, was given.

It was held that this statement was merely the honest expression of an opinion, and not a statement of fact as to the actual capacity of the farm.

But notice that a statement of opinion that is not genuinely held, or a statement as to future intention that the maker knows he will not be able to carry out, *are* misrepresentations, but are notoriously difficult to prove.

In *Edgington* v *Fitzmaurice* (1885) 29 Ch D 459 the directors of a company issued a prospectus inviting subscriptions for debentures stating that the issue was for investment purposes. The plaintiff advanced the money in reliance on that statement and in the erroneous belief that the debenture holders would have a charge upon the property.

It transpired that the real object of the loan was to enable the directors to pay off pressing debts.

The Court of Appeal held that the plaintiff was entitled to rescind the contract on the basis of misrepresentation.

Although the statement was a promise of intent the court held that the defendants had no intention of keeping to such intent at the time they made the statement.

The defendants knew that they would not be able to keep their promise.

In recent years this view has become more prevalent. In *Esso Petroleum Co Ltd* v *Mardon* [1976] QB 801, a petrol company which offered an inaccurate forecast of the probable sales of a filling station was liable in damages to a tenant who contracted with the petrol company on the basis of the forecast.

In *McNally* v *Welltrade International Ltd* [1978] IRLR 497 an employment agency was liable for misrepresentation about a prospective employee's suitability for a job he had applied for.

The statement must have been made with a view to inducing the other party to enter the contract and must have been an inducement

There can be no liability in respect of a falsehood which does not induce the party to enter into the contract.

The best illustration of this in operation is where A makes a false statement as an inducement for B to contract but B contracts regardless either knowing the statement to be false or not even being aware of the statement in the sense that it did not influence his mind.

There will be no reliance, and hence no inducement in the following circumstances:

a The misrepresentation did not come to the plaintiff's notice. Thus where false reports of a company's financial affairs had been published but the plaintiff had not read them: *ex parte Biggs* (1850) 28 LJ Ch 50.

b The plaintiff relied not on the misrepresentation but on his own judgment. In *Attwood* v *Small* (1838) 6 Cl & F 232 the plaintiffs negotiated with the defendant for the sale of certain mines. The plaintiffs asked questions as to the capabilities of the property. The defendant's answer was verified by persons appointed by the plaintiffs.

Six months after the sale was complete the plaintiffs found that the defendant's statement had been inaccurate and they sought to rescind on the ground of misrepresentation.

The court held that the plaintiffs could not rescind the contract since they had not been induced to contract by the defendant's statement but rather by their engineer's own report.

And in *Redgrave* v *Hurd* (1881) 20 Ch D 1 a party was induced to purchase a solicitor's house and practice by innocent misrepresentations as to the value of the practice. He was allowed rescission even though the books and papers which he had been invited to examine, and did not, would have revealed the falsity of the representations.

It must be a statement

The basic rule is that silence is not in itself misrepresentation. Thus if one party is labouring under a misapprehension there is no need to correct it.

There are three fundamental exceptions to this rule:

a The representor must not misleadingly tell only part of the truth: *Dimmock* v *Hallett* (1866) 2 Ch App 21.

b Later events falsifying a representation must be disclosed.

This includes the situation where an individual makes a false statement believing it to be true. If he subsequently discovers that he was in error he is under a positive duty to disclose the truth. Similarly, this applies where later events falsify an initially correct assertion. For example, *With* v *O'Flanagan* [1936] Ch 575, where a medical practice became valueless between the time of making the statement and the date of sale. It was held that the vendor should have communicated this.

c *Contracts uberrimae fidei*

Certain contracts impose a duty of disclosure. These are known as contracts uberrimae fidei. (Contracts of the utmost good faith).

The main contracts that fall within this category are contracts of insurance, family settlements and contracts where there is a fiduciary relationship.

Examples of a fiduciary relationship are – solicitor and client, trustee and beneficiary, bank manager and client, inter-family agreements, but not apparently master and servant.

Note also, that conduct (eg displaying a sign or behaving in a certain way) can amount to a statement even though nothing is actually said.

Types of misrepresentations

At one time misrepresentation divided neatly into two categories, it was either innocent, or fraudulent. By and large, there were few remedies for innocent misrepresentation, and the burden of proof on the misled person, to establish fraudulent misrepresentation was a heavy one.

However, there have been in recent times two major developments:

a the decision by the House of Lords in *Hedley Byrne* v *Heller* in 1964 (see below) which provided a remedy in damages for negligent misstatements at common law;

b the reforms provided by Misrepresentation Act 1967.

As a consequence of these developments misrepresentations can now be categorised as:

a fraudulent misrepresentations;

b negligent misstatements at common law;

c misrepresentations under s2(1) Misrepresentation Act 1967;

d innocent misrepresentations.

These categories will be examined in more detail below.

Consequences of misrepresentation

A misrepresentation is fraudulent in the three instances set out by Lord Herschell in *Derry* v *Peek* (1889) 14 App Cas 337, where it is made with knowledge of its falsity, or without belief in its truth, or recklessly not caring whether it is true or false.

The victim of a fraudulent misrepresentation has the following courses of action open to him;

a he may affirm the contract and claim damages for the tort of deceit;

b he may rescind the contract and claim damages as aforesaid;

c he may plead fraud as a defence to an action against him for breach of contract.

For fraudulent misrepresentation the measure of damages is tortious; in tort the purpose of an award of damages is to put the injured party in the position he would have been in if the wrong had not been committed. The contractual measure is designed to put such party in the position he would have been in if the contract had been performed, that is if the promise were true.

Normally, in tort actions, an award of damages is limited by the test of remoteness, that is the defendant will be liable only for damages that were reasonably foreseeable.

An important development in the law relating to misrepresentation was initiated in *Hedley Byrne & Co Ltd* v *Heller & Partners Ltd* [1964] AC 465, where the plaintiffs in this action had suffered loss by extending credit to a certain firm. They had been induced to do so by a reference, carelessly given by that firm's bank, which, in effect, vouched for the firm's creditworthiness. The bank escaped liability because of a disclaimer clause – the reference was stated to have been given 'without responsibility'. But the House of Lords made it clear that without this clause the bank would have owed a duty to the plaintiffs.

The importance of this case lies in its recognition that the duty arises not only in situations of fiduciary and contractual relationships, but in situations where there is a 'special relationship' between the parties.

This special relationship will arise where the representor has (or purports to have) some special skill or knowledge and knows (or should know) that the representatee will rely on the representation.

The main impact of the case for the law of contract was the clear emergence of the category of negligent misrepresentation for which a remedy lay in damages. But this has been somewhat overtaken by the enactment of Misrepresentation Act 1967.

Also note the case of *Caparo Industries plc* v *Dickman* [1990] 2 WLR 358 in which the House of Lords reversed the decision of the Court of Appeal holding that the auditors did not owe a duty of care either to individual shareholders or to potential investors. Lord Bridge stated that the crucial facts in cases such as *Hedley Byrne* (above) and *Smith* v *Eric S Bush* [1989] 2 WLR 790 were that the defendants were 'fully aware of the nature of the transaction which the plaintiff had in contemplation, knew that the advice or information would be communicated to him and knew that it was likely that the plaintiff would rely on that advice or information indeciding whether or not to engage in the transaction in contemplation.' But he said the situation was 'entirely different' in a case such as *Caparo* where the 'statement was put into more or less general circulation and might foreseeably be relied on by strangers to the maker of the statement for any one of a variety of different purposes which the maker of the statement had no specific reason to anticipate.' In the latter case the essential requirement of 'proximity' was missing.

Section 2(1) of the Misrepresentation Act provides:

'Where a person has entered into a contract after a misrepresentation has been made to him by another party thereto and as a result thereof he has suffered loss, then, if the person making the misrepresentation would be liable to damages in respect thereof had the misrepresentation been made fraudulently, that person shall be so liable notwithstanding that the misrepresentation was not made fraudulently unless he proves that he had reasonable ground to believe and did believe up to the time the contract was made that the facts represented were true.'

Royscot Trust Ltd v *Rogerson* [1991] 2 QB 297 makes it clear that the innocent party is entitled to claim for any loss flowing from the innocent misrepresentation, even if the loss could not have been foreseen.

Section 2(1) requires analysis.

a It is clear that where the representation had induced the contract there is no need to prove a 'special relationship': *Howard Marine and Dredging Co Ltd* v *A Ogden & Sons (Excavations) Ltd* [1978] QB 574.

b It reverses the burden of proof. Once the representee has proved that there has been a misrepresentation which induced him to enter into the contract the onus is on the representor to prove both his belief in the truth of the representation and reasonable ground for his belief.

c Section 2(1) also applies where the representation is made by an agent on behalf of the contracting party *(Gosling* v *Anderson* (1972) 223 EG 1743) but the agent is not personally liable.

The effect of s2(1) was considered by the Court of Appeal in *Howard Marine* v *Ogden* (above).

The defendants wished to hire two barges from the plaintiffs. The plaintiffs quoted a price for the hire in a letter which made no mention of the carrying capacity in weight of the barges. During subsequent negotiations, in response to a query, the plaintiffs' representative gave a figure for the carrying capacity, which though an honest answer was incorrect. The figure was given on the basis of the representative's recollection of the figure given in Lloyd's Register. The correct figure appeared in shipping documents which the representative had seen, but had forgotten. Because of their limited carrying capacity the defendant's work was held up. They refused to pay the hire charges. The plaintiffs sued for the hire charges and the defendants counter-claimed damages. By a majority the Court of Appeal found the plaintiffs liable under s2(1).

The Act has only to a limited extent altered the position with regard to innocent misrepresentation, that is where the representor has discharged the burden of proof imposed by s2(1).

Prior to the Act the only remedy available for innocent misrepresentation was rescission. Damages were not obtainable but Equity devised a measure of compensation, known as indemnity compensation, for loss directly attributable to innocent misrepresentation.

The difference between indemnities and damages is illustrated by the case of *Whittington* v *Seale-Hayne* (1900) 82 LT 49, where the plaintiffs, poultry breeders, were induced to enter into a lease of property belonging to the defendants by an oral representation that the premises were in a sanitary condition. The lease that was later executed did not contain this representation, which was not, therefore, a term of the contract. The premises were in fact insanitary. The terms of the lease required the plaintiffs to pay rent to the defendants and rates to the local authority and they were also obliged to effect certain repairs to the premises. The plaintiffs could recover these expenses as they were bound under the lease to make these payments. They could not recover removal expenses and consequential loss as these did not arise from obligations imposed by the lease.

The Misrepresentation Act 1967 now allows, subject to certain limitations, damages in lieu of rescission.

(For further details as to remedies see chapter 33.)

Duress and undue influence

Duress

The original common law of duress confined the doctrine within very narrow limits. Only duress to the person was recognised during the nineteenth century, and this required actual or threatened violence to the victim. Instances of duress to the person, in these terms, are rare in the present day. A modern example of such duress is *Barton v Armstrong* [1976] AC 104. Here a decision of the Privy Council, in which A threatened B with death if B's company did not pay a substantial sum of money to A. This is an important decision on the question of whether or not the victim would have entered into the contract but for the threat. This question provoked a difference of opinion both in the Court of Appeal of New South Wales and in the Privy Council. It will be considered further, below.

The nineteenth century limitation on duress meant that it could not be applied to 'duress of goods'. If a person, unlawfully detained, or threatened to detain, another's goods, this was not considered to be sufficient duress to enable a contract to be avoided.

Today economic pressure can amount to duress.

In *Universe Tankships Inc of Monrovia v International Transport Workers' Federation* [1983] 1 AC 366 trade union pressure stopped a ship leaving port. Eventually it was allowed to do so, but only on condition that the owners paid money into a union welfare fund. This agreement was held void for duress and the owners were allowed to recover the money paid into the fund.

Also see *D & C Builders v Rees* (1966) (above) in which the builders had 'virtually been held to ransom'.

Similarly in *Atlas Express Ltd v Kafco Ltd* [1989] 3 WLR 389 Kafco, a small firm, received a huge order from Woolworths the retail chain. Kafco contracted with Atlas, the haulage firm, to carry the goods at an agreed fee. Later Atlas realised it had badly undercalculated costs and told Kafco that they would make no further deliveries unless Kafco paid almost twice the fee. Desperate to keep the Woolworths contract Kafco agreed, but later refused to pay the extra. It was held that the imposition of the extra charge amounted to duress.

The case of *Dimskal Shipping Co SA v International Transport Workers' Federation, The Evia Luck* [1991] 4 All ER 871, illustrates the fact that, to constitute economic duress, the pressure imposed by one party on the other must be improper.

The Evia Luck was a ship owned by the plaintiffs, a Panamanian registered company whose vessels sailed under the Panamanian flag of convenience. The International Transport Workers Federation (ITF) had been conducting a long campaign against flags of convenience. While the ship was in harbour in Sweden, it was boarded by agents of ITF, who informed the master, and the owners, that the ship would be blacked and loading would not be continued until the company entered into certain agreements with ITF. These included payment of back-pay to the Greek and Filipino crew, new contracts of employment at higher wages and guarantees for future payments. At first the owners would not agree and the ship was in fact blacked. Yielding to pressure, the company agreed to sign the various agreements, which were expressly declared to be governed by English law. The company incurred losses of some £100,000 or more, due to delays in loading and sailing, and having to pay back-pay to the crew. In discussing whether the actions of the ITF constituted duress, the House of Lords decided that the fact that Swedish law considered such acts legitimate was irrelevant; the contract was governed by English law, under which such pressure was improper.

In *CTN Cash & Carry Ltd* v *Gallaher Ltd* [1994] 4 All ER 714, the Court of Appeal refused to consider a threat to perform a lawful act as economic duress. It would, they said, open up categories of duress to include 'lawful act duress' which would have far-reaching implications in commercial circles and lead to undesirable uncertainty.

Undue influence

Undue influence is an equitable doctrine. Equity has long recognised less direct pressures, particularly where confidential or personal relationships are involved.

Generally improper pressure has to be *proved* specifically.

In *Williams* v *Bayley* (1866) LR 1 HL 200 a promise to pay money was set aside because it was obtained by a threat to prosecute the promisor's son.

Sometimes the law will *presume* that undue influence exists, because of some special relationship between the parties.

A transaction can be set aside in equity where undue influence is presumed from the relationship between the parties. The presumption can be rebutted (see below); the onus is on the party receiving the benefit to show that it was not obtained by undue influence: *Powell* v *Powell* [1900] 1 Ch 243.

The relationships where undue influence is presumed have been held to be:

a Parent and child: *Wright* v *Vanderplank* (1855) 2 K & J 1.

b Solicitor and client: *Wright* v *Carter* [1903] 1 Ch 27.

c Doctor and patient: *Mitchell* v *Homfray* (1881) 8 QBD 587.

d Trustee and beneficiary: *Ellis* v *Barker* (1871) LR 7 Ch App 104.

e Religious adviser and disciple: *Roche* v *Sherrington* [1982] 1 WLR 599.

The presumption does not apply between husband and wife: *Bank of Montreal* v *Stuart* [1911] AC 120.

As to undue influence and constructive knowledge see the recent cases of *Barclays Bank plc* v *O'Brien* [1993] 3 WLR 786 and *CIBC Mortgages plc* v *Pitt* [1993] 3 WLR 802.

Illegality

Different methods of classification of illegal contracts have been adopted by writers, some of whom prefer to classify illegal contracts according to the effects of the illegality. The effects, however, vary, depending on the nature of the contract and the behaviour of the parties. For example one or both parties may be prevented from suing on the contract at all, or one or both parties may be prevented from suing on a particular undertaking, or, if the doctrine of severance applies (see below), one or both parties may be prevented from suing on part of a particular undertaking. The classification that is adopted here is into:

a contracts contrary to some principle of law;

b contracts contrary to public policy.

Contracts in restraint of trade fall into category (b), but are dealt with separately because of their importance.

We shall examine, first, the types of illegal contracts and then the effect of the illegality.

Contracts contrary to some law

Not only may the intention of the contract itself be unlawful, but sometimes also the manner of performing the contract is unlawful. Similarly a contract which is lawful in Britain, but unlawful in a friendly country, is considered, illegal. Certain contracts are contrary to the provisions of legislation.

See the following examples.

Contracts to commit a crime

If a contract has as its object the deliberate commission of a crime then it is illegal and the courts will not enforce it.

In *Bigos* v *Bousted* [1951] 1 All ER 92 the defendant wished to send his daughter to Italy for health reasons but because of Exchange Control Regulations could not get sufficient funds out of the country to make her an adequate allowance while abroad. He contracted with the plaintiff that if she made £150 of Italian money available to his daughter in Italy he would give her £150 in England and gave the plaintiff some share certificates as security. The whole transaction failed and the defendant sought recovery of his share certificates.

It was held that the courts would not aid the defendant to recover his share certificates as the whole transaction was illegal.

Contract to commit a civil wrong

If the contract is to deliberately commit a civil wrong such as to assault a third party (*Allen* v *Rescous* (1676) 2 Lev 174) or give fraudulent preference to a creditor (*Cockshott* v *Bennett* (1788) 2 TR 763) it is illegal and unenforceable.

If the parties are ignorant of the fact that by the contract they are committing a civil wrong then it is not illegal. Therefore, if X agrees to sell Y goods which, in fact, belong to a third party both are liable in conversion. However, no case seems to have held such contracts illegal and s12 Sale of Goods Act 1979 would appear to lend support to the theory that they are not.

If one of the parties to the contract knows that the contract is illegal, for example, where the seller of goods knows they belong to a third party, then it appears that only the innocent party is entitled to rely on the contract.

In *Clay* v *Yates* (1856) 1 H & N 73 the plaintiff agreed to print a book for the defendant which had a libellous dedication. The plaintiff discovered afterwards that the dedication was libellous and printed the book without it. He then claimed the cost of printing the book. The defendant argued it was an entire contract and that the plaintiff could not recover anything as he had only given part performance.

Contracts which though lawful in Britain would be unlawful in some friendly foreign state

This group is often also found categorised under contracts which are against public policy (see below).

See *Foster* v *Driscoll* [1929] 1 KB 470 in which an English contract negotiated by an English partnership to smuggle whisky into the USA at the time of the 'Prohibition Era' was held illegal, even though the contract was quite legitimate here. See also *Howard* v *Shirlstar Container Transport Ltd* [1990] 1 WLR 1292 as an example of the sort of contract which might interfere with foreign relations.

Contracts declared illegal by statute

Some contracts expressly declare the whole contract illegal.

Thus, for example, the Life Assurance Act 1774 forbids the insurance of a life in which the person has 'no insurable interest'.

In *Harse* v *Pearl Life Assurance Co* [1904] 1 KB 588 it was held that the plaintiff had no insurable interest in the life of his mother, whom he had insured. The policy was held illegal and he could not recover premiums paid.

Some statutes do not specifically declare contracts illegal, but provide that the contract in question shall only be carried out with the necessary licence.

Thus sales of alcohol and road haulage require the relevant licence. Other contractual requirements may be to keep records, or provide a rent book, and so on.

One question that often arises is whether the whole contract is to be considered void if the statutory requirements are not complied with. A great deal depends on the purpose of the legislation in question.

Thus in *Archbold's (Freightage)* v *S Spanglett* [1961] 1 QB 374 a contract by an unlicensed road haulier was held valid, because the purpose of the legislation was designed to assist in the administration of road transport only.

But in *Cope* v *Rowlands* (1836) 2 M & W 149 an unlicensed broker in the City of London was held not to be entitled to sue under a contract negotiated by him. The whole purpose of the legislation was to ensure the probity of the individual brokers and therefore *any* unlicensed contracts were illegal.

Contracts contrary to public policy

There are perhaps eight or nine such categories of contract, depending on which authority you read.

They include:

a   contracts to pervert the course of justice;

b   contracts purporting to oust the jurisdiction of the court (note however that it is perfectly legal to have a clause in an agreement to refer a matter to a private tribunal for a decision before going to court. But, if such a clause deprives the parties of their right to go to court, it is contrary to public policy and void);

c   maintenance and champerty contracts (unusually, two cases concerning champerty have recently come before the courts. *Advanced Technology Structures* v *Cray Valley Products* (1992) The Times 29 December concerned an agreement which was held to be champertous because it involved trafficking in litigation, whereas in *Giles* v *Thompson; Devlin* v *Baslington* (1993) The Times 1 June the contracts in question were held not to promote or initiate litigation and were therefore not champertous);

d   contracts which promote sexual immorality;

e   contracts which concern family and matrimonial affairs – thus a contract in restraint of marriage, or to sell a child;

f   procurement of public offices and honours;

g   contracts which interfere with friendly foreign states or to trade with enemy states or those against whom sanctions are imposed;

h   contracts to deceive public authorities/government bodies.

Contracts in restraint of trade

The most likely possibilities are that such a contract will be agreed on either when a person takes up employment (that he will not go to work for a competitor or set up in business on his own) or on the sale of a business (that the seller will not set up as a rival to the purchaser of his business).

These are not the only two forms of restraints, but they are the most common.

The courts regard *all* contracts or covenants in restraint of trade as prima facie illegal. Only if they can be proved reasonable can they be enforced.

The origin of modern law is in the speech of Lord Macnaghten in *Nordenfelt* v *Maxim Nordenfelt Guns and Ammunition Co* [1894] AC 535 from which the proposition emerged that:

Although a covenant in restraint of trade is prima facie unenforceable, it will become enforceable if it is reasonable. The matters which are pertinent are:

a the legitimate interests of the parties;

b the public interest.

The criteria for determining reasonableness will depend on the nature of the transaction in which the restraint is imposed.

Watson v *Prager* [1991] 1 WLR 726 illustrates the fact that the whole contract must be unreasonable at base. It is irrelevant whether one party or other performed the contract as well, or as fairly or reasonably as he could. The nature of the terms determined whether the contract was in restraint of trade or not.

Covenants which restrain an employee's activities after the termination of the employment have always been construed more jealously than covenants which restrict the trading activities of the vendor of a business. The reason is that there is a greater parity of bargaining power between the vendor and purchaser of a business than between an employee and employer. That does not mean, however, that the court will go to extravagant lengths to find a covenant restricting the employee's activities void. In *Home Counties Dairies Ltd* v *Skilton* [1970] 1 WLR 526 the defendant (a milkman) covenanted that he would not serve or sell 'milk or dairy produce' to any customer or former customer of his employer for a period of one year. It was argued that this was too wide because it would prevent him from working in a grocer's shop. The restriction was held valid and necessary to protect his employer against potential loss of customers.

The legitimate interests which can be protected by an employer are less than those which can be protected by the purchaser of a business. Whereas the purchaser of a business can be deemed to be entitled to the goodwill of the business free of competition, the same is not true of an employer. He cannot protect himself against competition but only against the use of something in which he has a proprietary interest, such as a list of customers. See *Fitch* v *Dewes* [1921] 2 AC 158.

Although an employer's principal concern is likely to be about soliciting customers, it does not follow that this is the only interest which he can protect. In *Eastham* v *Newcastle United Football Club* [1964] Ch 413, Wilberforce J thought that other covenants in restraint might protect legitimate interests and be enforceable. In that case he was considering the 'retain and transfer' system (where an employee could not transfer sides without the consent of both the sides from which and to which, he wished to change). In fact he did not find that this was an interest to be protected.

The area to which an employee or vendor can be limited in plying his trade is a matter which goes to the reasonableness of the clause. Again, it may follow that a purchaser of a business has a greater interest to protect than an employer and can impose wider restraints.

In *Nordenfelt* v *Maxim Nordenfelt Guns and Ammunition Co* (1894) (above) a worldwide restraint was held valid. N entered into a contract for the the sale of his worldwide business. He undertook not to compete with it (inter alia) in the trade or business of guns, gun making, explosives etc, for 25 years or anywhere in the world. The clause was held valid in so far as it is set out above.

On the other hand, in *Mason* v *Provident Clothing and Supply Co Ltd* [1913] AC 724, a covenant by a canvasser, employed to sell clothes in Islington, not to enter into a similar business within 25 miles of London was held void. The area was too large.

It is frequently said that a covenant will be void if it is contrary to the public interest. There is little direct authority. In *Wyatt* v *Kreglinger & Fernau* [1933] 1 KB 793 the employers of a wool broker promised him a pension on his retirement provided that he did not re-enter the wool trade and did nothing to their detriment. He claimed for arrears of his pension. It was held that he could not recover. One of the reasons given in the judgments was that the stipulation against competition was contrary to the public interest.

In *Deacons* v *Bridge* [1984] 2 All ER 19 the Privy Council upheld a restraint on a former partner in a firm of solicitors the effect of which was that he would not act as a solicitor in Hong Kong for a period of five years for any client of the firm or any person who had been a client during the three years preceding his departure from the firm. Their Lordships did not consider that a five year restriction was unreasonable and also thought that such a restriction was reasonable in the public interest.

In *Kerr* v *Morris* [1986] 3 All ER 217 the Court of Appeal held that a restraint on a doctor, a member of a partnership practising within the National Health Service, which precluded him from practising within a certain area, or treating patients of the partnership, was not contrary to the public interest.

Interpretation of restraint clauses

As already stated *all* restraints are considered prima facie illegal.

The burden of proof in establishing reasonableness lies on the party seeking to rely on the restraint.

The question of 'severability' may arise if the contract has several different restrictions. The court may strike out those parts of the contract it considers unreasonable and enforce the rest.

It will never 'reword' or alter restraint contracts, though if the existing meaning is ambiguous the court may give the most logical common-sense meaning to the words.

Thus in *Littlewoods Organisation* v *Harris* [1972] 1 WLR 1472, Harris was employed by Littlewoods. A restraint covenant in his contract of employment forbade him to work for GUS (L's main rival) for 12 months after leaving.

Harris claimed that the restraint was too wide. The court heard that while Littlewoods had only a mail order business in England, GUS had numerous types of business throughout the world. The court held that the restraint had clearly been intended to apply only to protect Littlewoods' mail order business in England and only that part of it should be enforced.

Effects of illegality

The attitude of the courts to illegal contracts may best be summed up in the maxim 'the loss lies where it falls'.

The general rule is that the court will not assist either party to an illegal contract to recover money paid or property transferred under the contract. Since the parties have embarked on an illegal transaction, they can expect no assistance from the court in respect of it and if money is paid or property passes, this will not be interfered with even if it appears unjust.

Several exceptions exist where the court will aid a party to recover property or money. These are:

Where the parties are not in 'pari delicto'

This is especially true where the parties are in such a position that one has a decided advantage over the other. The 'innocent' party must establish that he was unaware that at the time of making the contract it was illegal.

Repentance

If a party enters into an illegal contract, knowingly or otherwise, he may be able to change his mind.

The repudiation must be voluntary and it must be in time.

In this sort of case the usual test is whether the 'repentant' party would be claiming the right to repudiate had the contract worked.

For example in *Bigos* v *Bousted* (1951) (above) the courts said that, had things gone well with the contract, Bousted would quite happily have completed it. It was only because the transaction had failed that he was claiming repudiation.

Collateral contracts

Any agreement which is made to help with the performance of an illegal contract is itself illegal and unenforceable. Thus, an insurance policy on an illegal agreement is illegal (*Toulmin* v *Anderson* (1808) 1 Taunt 227) and any loans or payments of money to aid the performance of an illegal contract are also illegal (*M'Kinnell* v *Robinson* (1838) 3 M & W 434).

If an agreement is in itself legal, it will not, however, be rendered illegal merely because a collateral transaction to aid or further its performance happens to be illegal. Therefore, if a charterparty is itself legal, it will not be invalidated merely because a policy of insurance relating to it is illegally drawn up.

Incapacity

The general rule is that everyone is fully capable of entering into contracts and enforcing contracts and that everyone may have a contract enforced against him. However there are certain categories of persons (both human and artificial persons) whose contractual capacity is limited.

Obviously, if a contract is made by such a person this may have repercussions as to its validity.

Prima facie the law presumes that everyone has capacity to contract. A few classes of person are under a disability:

a minors;

b mentally disordered persons;

c drunken persons;

d corporations.

Minors

A minor (or infant) is anyone under the age of 18. As a general rule minors are given special protection by law. A minor can sue an adult with whom he has made a contract, but in similar circumstances he himself may not be sued. Minors may make all sorts of contracts, but in the eyes of the law these can be divided into just two categories:

a contracts for necessaries (which are valid);

b voidable contracts, which may be of two types:

   i those binding on the minor unless he repudiated them during minority or within a reasonable time thereafter; and

   ii those which were not binding upon him unless and until he ratified them after attaining his majority.

What are necessary goods?
There are goods 'suitable to the condition of life of the ... (minor) and to his actual requirements at the time of the sale and delivery': Sale of Goods Act 1979 s3(3). It must be shown, first that the class into which the goods fall is capable of being described as necessary, and second, that the goods supplied, even if within such a class, were actually necessary at the time of the contract.

Thus, given the style of dressing at the time, a waistcoat would fall into a class of objects capable of being called 'necessary', but the eleven fancy waistcoats supplied to an undergraduate in *Nash* v *Inman* [1908] 2 KB 1 were not deemed to be necessary to him. Clothes, food, drink, medicine, etc will fall within the definition of necessaries. The onus of showing that the goods are necessaries lies on the supplier.

At common law it has been held that a minor cannot be made liable on a loan to him to purchase necessaries: *Darby* v *Boucher* (1694) 1 Salk 279. By statute the former position was that contracts of loan were declared to be 'absolutely void'. This provision was contained in the Infants Relief Act 1874, but this Act has now been repealed by the Minors' Contracts Act 1987.

If the loan is actually spent on necessaries it can be recovered (or such part of it as may have been so spent) in equity. See *Marlow* v *Pitfield* (1718) 1 P Wms 558.

Contracts of service are valid if the service is, taken as a whole, beneficial to the minor – eg an apprenticeship, or articles of clerkship, which may on occasions appear exploitive, but which have beneficial consequences long term. See *Clements* v *London and North Western Railway* [1894] 2 QB 482. However an apprenticeship was said to be oppressive, and not beneficial, in *De Francesco* v *Barnum* (1890) 45 Ch D 430, where the dancing master stipulated in the contract that his pupil should not accept remunerative engagements without his consent during the apprenticeship, nor marry until it was over.

On the other hand there was an interesting clash of values in *Chaplin* v *Leslie Frewin (Publishers) Ltd* [1966] Ch 71. A minor made a contract to sell the story of his disreputable life: Lord Denning MR concluded that:

'... it is not for his good that he should exploit his discreditable conduct for money, no matter how much he is paid',

but Dankwerts and Winn LLJ considered the contract beneficial in so far as Chaplin was well paid at a time when he would otherwise have had to rely on National Assistance. The scandal, the majority felt, would not be harmful, for there was 'clear proof that he had no taste nor decency' and 'no right to claim to any reputation'.

In *Doyle* v *White City Stadium* [1935] 1 KB 110 a minor, who was a professional boxer, contracted with the British Boxing Board of Control and agreed to adhere to the rules of the Board. It was held that the contract was binding on him because he could not have earned his living otherwise.

Voidable contracts

Other than contracts for necessaries, most contracts made by minors exist unless or until avoided.

Once a minor avoids a contract, he has no liabilities which accrue thereafter, but he remains bound to meet obligations which have already arisen.

A minor may, on reaching his majority, ratify contracts made by him in his infancy. Once ratified they become enforceable and cannot be avoided (Minors Contracts Act 1987 s1(a)).

Drunken persons and those mentally disordered

These two may be treated together, because although their physical/mental state may be very different; the law treats them in a very similar way. Indeed their whole status is very much that of infants.

A person certified mentally unsound by virtue of the Mental Health Act 1983 Pt VII has no right to enter into contracts anyway.

For those temporarily insane or drunk, the contract is voidable at the option of the affected person if they can prove that they were so insane or so drunk that they did not know what they were doing and that the other party was aware of this.

The only exception to this rule is in regard to necessaries. Contracts for necessaries (defined as with infants) are binding and cannot be avoided on regaining sobriety or sanity. A drunken or insane person must pay a reasonable price for necessaries.

Corporations

What is a corporation?

Where two or more persons associate in order to enter transactions, their association may be incorporated or unincorporated. If it is unincorporated – by a partnership – then it cannot incur liability apart from its members. No-one can sue the partnership as such, but only its members, who are personally liable for any debts, to the full extent of their assets.

An incorporated association can incur liability apart from that of its members. It can hold assets in its own name and is liable for its own debts. The liability of members and controllers is limited in some pre-arranged way – eg as in a company limited by guarantee, or, the most common form of corporation, the 'limited liability' company. An incorporated association has contractual capacity.

What limitations are placed on a corporation's contractual capacity?

This depends upon whether the corporation is:

a chartered, or

b statutory.

A chartered corporation is created by Royal charter. It has full contractual capacity so far as the other contracting party is concerned, but if it exceeds what it is authorised to do by its charter, the Attorney-General may bring proceedings to revoke the charter, or a member may seek a declaration that the contract is invalid.

A statutory corporation is one which has been set up in the manner prescribed by statute. The most common type is the limited company, which can be created by individuals following the procedure laid down in the Companies Act 1985.

A limited company must register a Memorandum of Association with the Registrar of companies and this must contain an 'objects clause' specifying the purposes for which the company has been set up. If the company enters into a contract outside the scope of this clause, it is void.

A body which acts outside its authority is said to act ultra vires: *Ashbury Railway Carriage & Iron Co v Riche* (1875) LR 7 HL 653.

Reason for disability?

It is felt that shareholders and other persons doing business with the corporation on the faith of its publicly declared enterprise should not suffer as a result of its going beyond those bounds.

Reservations

Objects clauses were drafted very widely, in the case of companies, so as to render them useless as a guide to what the company intended to do.

Moreover, a company may not raise ultra vires against a party who contracts with it in good faith, though such a person may use ultra vires as a defence to an action under the contract by the company against him.

This provision was introduced into English legislation as a result of an EEC Directive in 1972 and now appears in the Companies Act 1985 s35.

Law of contract (5): 32
discharge of contracts

Introduction

A contract may come to an end in four main ways, performance, agreement, frustration and breach of contract. We shall be looking in more detail at breach in the next chapter, but the other three methods of discharge will be examined in more detail below. It is important to realise from the outset that while some methods of discharging the contract arise directly out of the terms of the original contract (performance, breach) others are brought about by new extraneous events intervening. Some may be within the control of the parties (agreement) some may not (frustration). We shall also look at two other matters which, though not directly concerned with discharge of the contract, affect the right to sue. They are the rules relating to limitation, and the doctrine of privity of contract.

Note *Harrods Ltd* v *Schwarz-Sackin & Co Ltd* [1991] FSR 209 in which the question arose as to whether, when the contract ended, any terms could continue to be applied. The Court of Appeal held that unless a term was specifically declared to be binding after termination, it would cease to have any effect when the contract ended.

Discharge by performance

Generally, parties must perform *precisely* all the terms of the contract in order to discharge their obligations.

In contracts for the sale of goods the Sale of Goods Act 1979 contains strict rules. Section 30 affords the buyer the right to reject goods if the seller delivers less or even more goods than he contracted to sell. Section 13 imposes the condition that the goods must correspond with the description. An illustration of the precise requirement of this section appears from *Re Moore & Co and Landauer & Co* [1921] 2 KB 519, where tins of fruit delivered in cases of 24 and not the stipulated cases of 30 constituted a breach of s13.

The decision in this case is now, perhaps, doubtful. It was critised as being excessively technical by Lord Wilberforce in *Reardon Smith Line* v *Yngvar Hansen-Tangen* [1976] 3 All ER 570 at p 576.

A classic example of hardship caused by this rule is *Cutter* v *Powell* (1795) 6 Term Rep 320.

A seaman who was to be paid his wages after the end of a voyage died just a few days away from port. His widow was able to recover none of his wages because he had not completed performance of his contractual obligation.

The strict rule as to performance is mitigated in a number of instances.

Divisible contracts

It is a question of construction whether a contract is entire or divisible. An *entire* contract is one where the agreement provides that complete performance by one party is a condition precedent to contractual liability on the part of the other party. With a *divisible* contract part of the consideration of one party is set off against part of the performance of the other. Divisible contracts are frequently to be found in the building trade eg where a builder agrees to build a house for £2,500, with £1,000 to be paid on completion of the foundations, £1,000 on erection of the superstructure, and £500 six months after completion of the house in accordance with the specifications.

Then, if after the foundations are laid the builder fails to do any further work, he can, nevertheless recover £1,000.

But, see *Sumpter* v *Hedges* [1898] 1 QB 673 where the plaintiff had agreed to erect upon the defendant's land two houses and stables for £565. He did part of the work to the value of about £333 and then abandoned the contract. The defendant completed the buildings.

It was held that the plaintiff could not recover the value of the work done as he had abandoned it.

Substantial performance

When a man fully performs his contract in the hope that he has done all that he agreed to do, or has supplied all he agreed to supply, but subject to defects of so minor a character that he can be said to have *substantially* performed his promise, it is regarded as far more just to allow him to recover the contract price diminished by the extent to which his breach of contract lessened the value of what was done, than to leave him with no right of recovery at all.

The doctrine of substantial performance dates back to the judgment of Lord Mansfield in *Boone* v *Eyre* (1779) 1 Hy Bl 273n.

In *Dakin & Co* v *Lee* [1916] 1 KB 566 builders promised to build a house according to specification and failed to carry out exactly all the specifications, eg concrete not four feet deep as specified, wrong joining of certain rolled steel joists, concrete not properly mixed. It was held (by the Court of Appeal) that the builders were entitled to recover the contract price, less so much as ought to be allowed in respect of the items found to be defective.

Also see *Hoenig* v *Isaacs* [1952] 2 All ER 176 in which a carpenter/decorator nearly finished a job, but did some of it badly. The agreed contract price for the completed work was £750. Since he had very nearly finished he was awarded the whole sum of £750, less £56 – the cost of putting right what he had done wrong.

Completion of performance prevented by promisee

Where a party to an entire contract *is prevented by the promisee* from performing all his obligations, then he can recover a reasonable price for what he has in fact done on a quantum meruit basis in an action in quasi-contract.

In *Planché* v *Colburn* (1831) 8 Bing 14 the plaintiff was to write a book on 'Costume and Ancient Armour' for a series and was to receive £100 on completion of the book.

After he had done the necessary research but before the book had been written the publishers abandoned the series.

He claimed alternatively on the original contract and on a quantum meruit.

The claim on the original contract seems to have disappeared in the course of the argument, but, on the alternative submission

It was held:

a that the original contract had been discharged by the defendants' breach, (or more properly that the plaintiff had accepted the defendants' breach as discharging the contract?);

b that no new contract has been substituted;

c that the plaintiff could obtain 50 guineas as reasonable remuneration on a quantum meruit. This claim was independent of the original contract and was based on quasi-contract.

Acceptance of partial performance

Where the plaintiff to whom the promise of performance was made receives the benefit of partial performance of the promise under such circumstances that he is able to accept or reject the work and he accepts the work, then the promisee is obliged to pay a reasonable price for the benefit received. But it must be possible to infer from the circumstances a fresh agreement by the parties that payment shall be made for the goods or services in fact supplied.

In *Christy* v *Row* (1808) 1 Taunt 300 a ship freighted to Hamburg was prevented 'by restraint of prices' from arriving.

Consignees accepted the cargo at another port *to which they had directed it to be delivered*. It was held that the consignees were liable upon an implied contract to pay freight pro rata itineris (contract implied from their directions re alternative port of delivery).

In *Sumpter* v *Hedges* (above) Collins LJ said:

'Where, as in the case of work done on land, the circumstances are such as to give the defendant no option whether he will take the benefit of the work or not, then one must look to other facts than the mere taking of the benefit in order to ground the inference of a new contract. In this case I see no other facts on which such an inference can be founded. The mere fact that a defendant is in possession of what he cannot help keeping, or even has done work upon it, affords no ground for such an inference. He is not bound to keep unfinished a building which in an incomplete state would be a nuisance on his land'.

Tender of performance

Tender of performance is equivalent to performance in the situation where one party cannot complete performance without the assistance of the other and the one party makes an offer to perform which the other refuses.

In *Startup v M'Donald* (1843) 6 M & G 593 the plaintiffs agreed to sell 10 tons of oil to the defendant and to deliver it to him 'within the last 14 days of March', payment to be in cash at the end of that period. Delivery was tendered at 8.30 pm on 31 March. The defendant refused to accept or pay for the goods because of the late hour.

It was held that tender was equivalent to performance and the plaintiffs were entitled to recover damages for non-acceptance.

Rolfe B said:

'In every contract by which a party binds himself to deliver goods or pay money to another, he in fact engages to do an act which he cannot completely perform without the concurrence of the party to whom the delivery or the payment is to be made. Without acceptance on the part of whom who is to receive, the act of him who is to deliver or to pay can amount only to a tender. But the law considers (the latter) as having substantially performed it if he has tendered the goods or the money … provided only that the tender has been made under such circumstances that the party to whom it has been made has had a reasonable opportunity of examining the goods or the money tendered, in order to ascertain that the thing tendered really was what it purported to be. Indeed, without such an opportunity an offer to deliver or pay does not amount to a tender.'

Where goods are tendered they must be correct in quantity and quality.

Where *money* is tendered as payment it must be in the form of 'legal tender' or such other form as is agreed eg a cheque.

To amount to a valid tender of money, the party seeking to perform must produce the correct sum of money (change cannot be required) in the form of 'legal tender', ie Bank of England notes for any amount; gold coins for any amount; coins of cupro-nickel or silver exceeding ten new pence in value for any amount up to £10; coins of cupro-nickel or silver of not more than ten new pence in value up to £5; coins of bronze for any amount up to twenty new pence (Coinage Act 1971 s2).

If the party making the tender of payment is sued for breach of contract he must make payment of the sum tendered into court whereupon the costs of the action will be borne by the plaintiff. See *Griffiths v School Board of Ystradyfodwg* (1890) 24 QBD 307.

It is the duty of the party obliged to pay to seek out his creditor and if he sends the money in any way and it is lost in the course of transit the risk is on the debtor and he will have to pay again, unless the creditor requests a particular manner of delivery, eg by post, in which case the debtor will be discharged as long *as he exercises reasonable care* even where the money is lost in transit, thus the risk is on the creditor.

Where there is a valid tender of *goods* the party tendering is discharged, but where there is a tender of *money* although the debtor is absolved from further obligation to tender, the obligation to pay the debt, when called upon, remains.

Note that to constitute accord and satisfaction agreement must be established between the debtor and creditor. See *Stour Valley Builders v Stuart* (1993) The Times 9 February.

Discharge by agreement

Eodem modo quo oritur, eodem modo dissoluitur – what has been created by agreement may be extinguished by agreement.

An agreement by the parties to an existing contract to extinguish the rights and obligations that have been created is itself a binding contract, provided that it is either made under seal or supported by consideration. Accordingly, a distinction needs to be drawn between agreements which are executed on one side where the party seeking to be released must show that he has been giving consideration for the release or that the release is under seal, and agreements which are wholly executory where consideration may be found in the mutual release by each party of his rights under the contract.

Discharge by deed is equally effective as regards unilateral or bilateral discharge but where the agreement for discharge is not under seal the legal position varies according to whether the discharge is bilateral or unilateral.

There are three main ways in which discharge by agreement can be achieved:

a   The parties may have made provision in their original agreement for such an eventuality. For example they may have agreed that the contract will end if a certain event happens. Or they may say that the contract will only continue to exist while a particular state of affairs exists.

b   Unilateral discharge. This takes place where only one party has rights to surrender. Where one party has entirely performed his part of the agreement he is no longer under obligations but has rights to compel the performance of the agreement by the other party.

For example, A agrees to sell 1 cwt of coal to B for £X and A delivers the coal only to find out that B has suddenly incurred a tremendous expense. A, out of sympathy, agrees that B shall not pay for the coal. But where is the consideration moving from B in support of A's promise to forgo his right to the £X? There is none. There is merely a bare promise from A.

For unilateral discharge, unless the agreement is under seal, consideration must be furnished in order to make the agreement enforceable.

In this context, the agreement is termed the *accord* and the consideration which makes it binding is known as the *satisfaction*. See above under bilateral discharge.

Bills of Exchange Act 1882 provides an exception to the general rule that a unilateral discharge requires consideration: where the holder of a bill of exchange or promissory note unconditionally renounces his rights against the acceptor the bill is discharged. The renunciation must be in writing or the bill must be delivered up to the acceptor.

c   The contracting parties may agree to vary the existing contract, or create a new contract by novation.

Frustration

Introduction

The doctrine of frustration operates in situations where it is established that due to subsequent change in circumstances the contract is rendered impossible to perform, or it has become deprived of its commercial purpose by an event not due to the act or default of either party.

This is not to be confused with initial impossibility which may render the contract void ab initio. See 'Mistake' above and s6 Sale of Goods Act 1979 (see chapter 34, following).

Originally, the law declared that if a man bound himself by contract then that man was absolutely bound notwithstanding anything which may subsequently have transpired making it difficult or impossible to perform the contract.

> 'It amounts to this: when the law casts a duty upon a man which, through no fault of his, he is unable to perform he is excused from non-performance; but if he binds himself by contract to do a thing, he cannot escape liability for damage by proof that as events turned out performance is futile or even impossible.'

The classic statement of the concept appears in *Paradine* v *Jane* (1647) Aleyn 26, a Civil War case involving dispossession of tenants by one Prince Rupert of the Rhine. The tenant pleaded that he should be relieved under the contract with the landlord for he had been evicted and thus had obtained no material benefit from the lease. He was held liable under the lease.

The turning point away from absolutist construction of contractual obligation came with the decision in *Taylor* v *Caldwell* (1863) 3 B & S 826.

Caldwell agreed to let a music hall to Taylor so that four concerts could be held there. Before the date of the first concert the hall was destroyed by fire. Taylor claimed damages for Caldwell's failure to make the premises available. It was held that the claim for breach of contract must fail since it had become impossible to fulfil. The contractual obligation was dependent upon the continued existence of a particular object.

The interesting point to note was that until this time the law refused to acknowledge that a party could be relieved from a contract unless there was some express condition entitling him to be so relieved in the event of subsequent impossibility.

Examples of frustrating events include:

Destruction of the specific object essential for performance of the contract
See *Taylor* v *Caldwell* (above).

Personal incapacity where the personality of one of the parties is significant

In *Condor* v *The Barron Knights* [1966] 1 WLR 87 a drummer engaged to play in a pop group was contractually bound to work on seven nights a week when work was available. After an illness Condor's doctor advised that it was only safe to employ him on four nights a week, although Condour himself was willing to work every night. It was necessary to engage another drummer who could safely work on seven nights each week. It was held that Condor's contract of employment had been frustrated in a commercial sense. It was impracticable to engage a stand-in for the three nights a week when Condor could not work, since this involved double rehearsals of the group's music and comedy routines.

The non-occurrence of a specified event

Compare *Krell* v *Henry* [1903] 2 KB 740 with *Herne Bay Steamboat Company* v *Hutton* [1903] 2 KB 683.

In *Krell*, Henry hired a room from Krell for two days, to be used as a position from which to view the coronation procession of Edward VII, but the contract itself made no reference to that intended use. The King's illness caused a postponement of the procession. It was held that Henry was excused from paying the rent for the room. Holding of the procession on the dates planned was regarded by both parties as basic to enforcement of the contract.

In the latter case Herne Bay Steam Boat Company agreed to hire a steamboat to Hutton for a fee of £250 for a period of two days for the purpose of taking passengers to Spithead to cruise round the fleet and see the naval review on the occasion of Edward VII's coronation. The review was cancelled, but the boat could have been used to cruise round the assembled fleet. It was held that the contract was not frustrated. The holding of the naval review was not the only event upon which the intended use of the boat was dependent. The other object of the contract was to cruise round the fleet and this remained capable of fulfilment.

Supervening illegality

In *Denny, Mott & Dickson* v *James Fraser & Co* [1944] AC 265 a contract for the sale and purchase of timber contained an option to purchase a timber yard. By a wartime control order trading under the agreement became illegal. The appellants wanted to exercise the option. It was held that the order had frustrated the contract so the option could not be exercised.

Similarly in *Re Shipton, Anderson & Co Ltd and Harrison Brothers & Co Ltd* [1915] 3 KB 676 a contract was concluded for the sale of a quantity of wheat lying in a warehouse. The Government requisitioned the wheat, in pursuance of wartime emergency regulations for the control of food supplies, before it had been delivered, and also before ownership in the goods had passed to the buyer under the terms of contract of sale. It was held that the seller was excused from further performance of the contract since it was now impossible to deliver the goods because of the Government's lawful requisition.

Delay

Inordinate and unexpected delay may frustrate a contract. The problem is to know how long a party must wait before the delay can be said to be frustrating. In *Pioneer Shipping Ltd* v *BTP Tioxide Ltd, The Nema* [1982] AC 724 Lord Roskill said:

> '... it is often necessary to wait upon events in order to see whether the delay already suffered and the prospects of further delay from that cause, will make any ultimate performance of the relevant contractual obligations "radically different" from that which was undertaken by the contract. But, as has often been said, businessmen must not be required to await events too long. They are entitled to know where they stand. Whether or not the delay is such as to bring about frustration must be a question to be determined by an informed judgment based on all the evidence of what has occurred and what is likely thereafter to occur. Often it will be a question of degree whether the effect of delay suffered and likely to be suffered, will be such as to bring about frustration of the particular event in question.'

Also see *Jackson* v *Union Marine Insurance Co* (1873) LR 10 CP 125 where a ship was chartered in November 1871 to proceed with all possible despatch, danger and accidents of navigation excepted, from Liverpool to Newport where it was to load a cargo of iron rails for carriage to San Francisco. She sailed on 2 January, but next day ran aground in Caernarvon Bay. She was refloated by 18 February and taken to Liverpool where she underwent extensive repairs which lasted till August. On 15 February the charterers repudiated the contract. It was held that such time was so long as to put an end in a commercial sense to the commercial speculation entered upon by the shipowner and the charterers. The express exceptions were not intended to cover an accident causing such extensive damage.

The scope of the doctrine

> 'The doctrine of frustration must be applied within very narrow limits'

per Viscount Simonds in *Tsakiroglou & Co Ltd* v *Noblee Thorl GmbH* [1962] AC 93.

More recently Lord Roskill said that the doctrine of frustration was 'not lightly to be invoked to relieve contracting parties of the normal consequences of imprudent commercial bargains': *Pioneer Shipping Ltd* v *BTP Tioxide Ltd, The Nema* [1982] AC 724, 752.

The doctrine is subject to the following limitations.

a The doctrine cannot override express contractual provision for the frustrating event. However, this does not apply if the supervening event is illegality: *Ertel Bieber & Co* v *Rio Tinto Co Ltd* [1918] AC 260.

b The mere increase in expense or loss of profit is not a ground for frustration. In *Davis Contractors Ltd* v *Fareham UDC* [1956] AC 696 the plaintiff agreed to build 78 houses in eight months at a fixed price. Due to bad weather, and labour shortages, the work took twenty-two months and cost £17,000 more than anticipated. The builders said that the weather and labour shortages, which were unforeseen, had frustrated the contract, and that they were entitled to recover £17,000 by way of quantum meruit. It was held that the fact that unforeseen events made a contract more onerous than was anticipated did not frustrate it.

c Frustration must not be self induced: *Maritime National Fish Ltd* v *Ocean Trawlers Ltd* [1935] AC 524. Here Maritime chartered from Ocean a vessel which could only operate with an otter trawl. Both parties realised that it was an offence to use such a trawl without a government licence. Maritime was granted three such licences, but chose to use them in respect of three other vessels, with the result that Ocean's vessel could not be used. It was held that the charterparty had not been frustrated, consequently Maritime was liable to pay the charter fee. Maritime freely elected not to license Ocean's vessel, consequently their inability to use it was a direct result of their own deliberate act.

The burden of proving events which prima facie frustrate the contract lies on the party relying on frustration. If there is an allegation that the frustration is self-induced, the burden then shifts to the person alleging self-inducement.

The effects of frustration

Frustration automatically brings a contract to an end and renders it void.

In the case of *Fibrosa Spolka Akcyjna* v *Fairbairn Lawson Combe Barbour Ltd* [1943] AC 32 the House of Lords held that money paid over on a total failure of consideration was recoverable. This case, however, was equally inflexible: recovery was dependent upon a total failure of consideration and there was no provision for restitution of pre-frustration expenditure by one of the parties. As a result Parliament intervened with the Law Reform (Frustrated Contracts) Act 1943.

The Reform (Frustrated Contracts) Act 1943

This statute remedies the defects of the common law. It is very flexible and this is probably why there are no reported English decisions in the Act.

Section 1:

'... (2) All sums paid or payable to any party in pursuance of the contract before the time when the parties were so discharged (in this Act referred to as "the time of discharge") shall, in the case of sums so paid, be recoverable from him as money received by him for the use of the party by whom the sums were paid, and, in the case of sums so payable, cease to be payable:

Provided that, if the party to whom the sums were so paid or payable incurred expenses before the time of discharge in, or for the purpose of, the performance of the contract, the court may, if it considers it just to do so having regard to all the circumstances of the case, allow him to retain or, as the case may be, recover the whole or any part of the sums so paid or payable, not being an amount in excess of the expenses so incurred.

(3) Where any party to the contract has, by reason of anything done by any other party thereto in, or for the purpose of, the performance of the contract, obtained a valuable

> benefit (other than a payment of money to which the last foregoing section applies) before the time of discharge, there shall be recoverable from him by the said other party such sum (if any) not exceeding the value of the said benefit to the party obtaining it, as the court considers just, having regard to all the circumstances of the case.'

Section 1(6) allows an action given by subsection 1(3) to be brought against one party even though the benefit was bestowed on a third party.

Section 2(3) permits contracting out.

Section 2(4) enables severance of a part of a contract which has been performed from a part which has been frustrated, but only where a part of a contract 'can properly be severed from the remainder of the contract'.

Certain types of contract are excluded from the Act, including insurance contracts, contracts for sale of specific goods which perish (see chapter 34: Sale of Goods) and contracts for carriage of goods by sea.

Limitation of actions

It has already been remarked that after a certain time the law bars any action taken to enforce a contract.

The limitation rules concern not so much discharge of contracts as the period during which an action must be brought.

The Limitation Act 1980 lays down certain simple rules as follows:

a Actions based on a simple or parol contract will be barred after six years have elapsed from the date when the cause of action accrued.

b Actions based on contracts made under seal, by deed, can be brought up to twelve years from the date of the cause of action.

c Actions to recover land can be brought for up to twelve years from the date when the cause of action accrued.

These rules are simple and specific. The only problem is to discover what is meant by the term 'cause of action'. It is not at all the same thing as the date of making the contract though sometimes these will coincide. A right of action normally accrues, when the breach occurs. Thus if a loan is made over a 25-year period with payments every quarter and the debtor defaults in the tenth year, the right of action accrues on the debtor's default; not the date of the contract which was ten years ago.

Sometimes the cause of action cannot be discovered for some time, because of its nature. In that case the time period begins to run from the point when the defect or breach of contract is discovered or should reasonably have been discovered.

In *Lynn v Bamber* [1930] 2 KB 72 some fruit trees were sold in 1921 as being of a particular variety. It was not until they had grown to maturity in 1928 and fruited, thereby revealing themselves as being of inferior quality, that it was possible to see that there had been a breach of contract. The limitation period began to run from this date.

Two additional factors are worth noting.

a   If the plaintiff is under some disability, such as infancy, or mental illness, the limitation period will not start to run until the disability has ended.

b   Unless the limitation period has actually ended it can be extended almost ad infinitum by the party in breach acknowledging his liability in a signed document. The limitation period begins to run afresh and can, of course, be renewed over and over again.

Privity of contract

The general rule when considering discharge of contract, and particularly breach is that rights of enforcement can vest only in a party to the contract.

This is because the law only seeks to enforce contracts supported by consideration (see chapter 29, above).

Thus an agreement between A and B cannot confer any legally enforceable benefit on a stranger, nor can a stranger be adversely affected by obligations under their contract. Only A and B are concerned and only A can sue B, or vice versa.

The leading case on this aspect is *Tweddle v Atkinson* (1861) 1 B & S 393 where the plaintiff married Mr Guy's daughter. The plaintiff's father and Mr Guy effected an agreement whereby each would pay a sum of money to the plaintiff. Both the fathers reneged on this agreement and subsequently died. The plaintiff sued the executor of Mr Guy for the sum promised. Crompton J:

'It is admitted that the plaintiff cannot succeed unless this case is an exception to the modern and well established doctrine of the action of assumpsit. At the time when the cases which have been cited were decided the action of assumpsit was treated as an action of trespass upon the case, and therefore in the nature of a tort; and the law was not settled, as it now is, that natural love and affection is not a sufficient consideration for a promise upon which an action may be maintained; nor was it settled that the promisee cannot bring an action unless the consideration for the promise moved from him. The modern cases have, in effect, overruled the old decisions; they shew that the consideration must move from the party entitled to sue upon the contract. It would be a monstrous proposition to say that a person was a party to the contract for the purpose of suing upon it for his own advantage and not a party to it for the purpose of being sued. It is said that the father in the present case was agent for the son in making the contract but the argument ought also to make the son liable upon it. I am prepared to overrule the old decisions, and to hold that, by reason of the principles which now govern the action of assumpsit, the present action is not maintainable.'

Wrightman J:

'Some of the old decisions appear to support the proposition that a stranger to the consideration of a contract may maintain an action upon it, if he stand in such a near relationship to the party from whom the consideration proceeds, that he may be considered a party to the consideration. But there is no modern case in which the proposition has been supported. On the contrary, it is now established that no stranger to the consideration can take advantage of a contract, although made for his benefit.'

The rule in effect laid down by *Tweddle* v *Atkinson* has become accepted as one of the tenets of the Common Law.

In *Adler* v *Dickson* [1955] 1 QB 158 a passenger on board a ship was injured by the combined negligent conduct of the captain and the bosun. Her ticket (issued by the shipping company) provided that 'passengers are carried at passengers' entire risk'. Nevertheless she successfully sued both captain and bosun. Her contract was between herself and the shipping company and the exclusion clause was a part of that contract. Any exclusions therefore did not cover the employees – because of the doctrine of privity of contract they had no obligations, but *also no rights* under the contract.

The doctrine of privity of contract is subject to exceptions. Thus for example:

a agency contracts;

b collateral contracts;

c trusts.

may be taken as exceptions to the general rule, and there are others. We shall look at the three main exceptions in turn.

Agency

A person may contract as agent for a third party (his principal). The principal is then bound and the agent is not privy to the contract and cannot (generally) sue or be sued upon it. Sometimes problems arise regarding sub-agencies. An agent can create privity of contract between himself and a sub-agent, and thus there is no direct contractual relationship between the principal and the sub-agent.

Collateral contracts

In *Shanklin Piers* v *Detel Products* [1951] 2 KB 854, the plaintiffs had employed contractors to paint a pier. They told them to buy paint made by the defendants. The defendants had told them that the paint would last for seven years. It only lasted for three months. It was held that the plaintiffs could sue the defendants on a collateral contract. They had provided consideration for the defendants' promise by entering into an agreement with the contractors which entailed the purchase of the defendants' paint.

The court was able to find consideration moving from the plaintiffs – *Shanklin Piers* – without substantial difficulty. The case of *Charnock* v *Liverpool Corporation* [1968] 1 WLR 1498 gives rise to some doubts about the presence of consideration. The plaintiff's car was damaged. A contract existed between his insurance company and a garage (the defendant) for repairing the plaintiff's car. It was held that there was also a collateral contract between the plaintiff and the defendant to do the repairs within a reasonable time. The court found that the consideration was the leaving of the car at the garage. This was not, of course, a detriment to the plaintiff but it was a benefit to the garage.

Trusts

Although contractual rights cannot be established for a stranger, a trust can occur, conferring benefits on such a person, giving rights that can be legally enforced. Any form of property can form a trust. If A and B contract, B promising to pay C £100, then C cannot sue for the £100, because he is a stranger to the contract. But, if it can be proved that A and B had not created a contract but a *trust*, then A the trustee or C the beneficiary under the trust can sue for the £100 – in equity.

In *Re Flavell* (1883) 25 Ch D 89 a contract between two parties provided that in the event of one of the parties' death, the widow would be entitled to certain payments. The action was brought by one such widow. Her claim in contract failed, but she succeeded in equity as she managed to show to the court that she was the beneficiary under a trust made by the above parties in her favour.

Compare this decision, however, with *Re Schebsman* [1944] Ch 83. Schebsman was employed by a Swiss company, who agreed that his appointment should be ended by means of a golden handshake to the value of £5,500 to be paid in instalments and in the event of death to his widow. The widow sued for the failed payment, but it was held that she would fail as she could show no evidence of a trust. (In contract she failed because she was not privy to the contract.)

It appears from these two cases that two conditions must be fulfilled in order for the court to be convinced of the existence of a trust.

First, there must be a clear intention to create a trust; the words 'trust' and 'beneficiary' need not be used although it would clarify matters if they were.

Second, it must be clear that the parties did not intend to *alter* in any way whatever, the rights they had created, eg if A and B make a contract to pay C £100, they have created a non enforceable benefit to C (non enforceable by C) and C cannot sue. But if A and B create a trust their freedom to modify the trust is curtailed.

Law of contract (6): 33
remedies for breach

Breach of contract

The nature of a breach

A failure to perform the terms of a contract constitutes a breach. As we have seen in chapter 30: Contents of a Contract, not all breaches entitle the innocent party to treat the contract as repudiated.

A breach does not automatically discharge a contract. It is simply that a sufficiently serious breach (breach of a condition or a breach with serious consequences) will give the innocent party the option of treating the contract as repudiated (that is: treat the contract as 'at an end'). It is not rescinded ab initio and the word rescission is, accordingly, a misleading term to use. The word repudiation is more satisfactory. When a contract is said to be 'at an end' it means that the innocent party, or in some cases, both parties are discharged from further performance of their primary obligations under the contract, but in place of the primary obligation a secondary obligation may arise. This secondary obligation is (usually) to pay a monetary compensation for the non-performance. See *Photo Production* v *Securicor Transport* [1980] AC 827.

Note: The innocent party may choose to continue with the contract and simply sue for damages.

A breach which is sufficiently serious to give the innocent party this option of treating the contract can occur in one of two ways. Either:

a one party may show by express words or by implications from conduct at some time before performance is due that he does not intend to observe his obligations under the contract – called anticipatory breach; or

b he may in fact break a condition or otherwise break the contract in such a way that it amounts to a substantial failure of consideration.

Anticipatory breach

Where the breach occurs before the time fixed for performance, this is known as anticipatory breach. The innocent party is not under any obligation to wait until the date fixed for performance before commencing his action but may immediately treat the contract as at an end and sue for damages. Alternatively, he may affirm the contract by treating it as still in force. The innocent party has this right of election and is bound by his choice. If within a reasonable time he does not indicate that he accepts the other party's repudiation so that the contract is discharged, then the contract remains open for the benefit of and the risk of both parties.

The breach was accepted in *Hochster* v *De La Tour* (1853) 2 E & B 678. An employer told his employee (a travelling courier) before the time for performance arrived, that he would not require his services. The courier sued for damages at once.

It appears that the right to keep the contract alive subsists even where the innocent party is increasing the amount, and not mitigating, the damages which he may receive from the party in breach. In *White & Carter (Councils) Ltd v McGregor* [1962] AC 413 the appellants (advertising contractors) agreed with the respondent (a garage proprietor) to display advertisements for his garage for three years. The respondent repudiated the agreement and cancelled on the same day. The appellants refused to cancel and performed their obligations. They sued for the contract price.

It was held that they were entitled to the full contract price. Where a party elects to treat the contract as continuing, it can be seen as a form of waiver. The innocent party effectively waives his right to treat the contract as rescinded.

Substantial failure of consideration

The consequences of breach can be so serious that the injured party may have no choice but to consider the contract at an end. One example might be if the subject matter of the contract no longer existed. But subject to this reservation an injured party does not *have* to end the contract unless he wants to. He can avoid the contract, or can affirm it. If he affirms he may chose to accept the defective or varied performance from the other side (and possibly claim damages for the difference in price) or he may possibly have to opt for some other remedy, eg specific performance (see post) to enforce the performance of the contract.

If the injured party does wish to end the contract he must do so reasonably quickly; the right to rescind may be lost due to delay, especially if innocent third parties acquire rights under the contract. Not every breach will be sufficiently serious as to allow an injured party such a choice, however. Where the breach in question is only a breach of warranty, the sole remedy is damages; the right to opt for repudiation does not exist.

Damages

General

Damages are meant to compensate the injured party for any consequences of the breach of contract which the law recognises. The underlying principle is to put the injured party financially as near as possible, into the position he would have been in had the promise been fulfilled.

Damages are assessed on the actual loss to the plaintiff, and not on the gain to the defendant. They are compensation, not punishment.

Loss can be financial, damage to property, personal injuries or even distress to the plaintiff, though the latter is rare in contract cases. (See *Hayes v James and Charles Dodd* (1988) The Times 14 July.)

There are several ways in which the plaintiff can be compensated for his loss; the plaintiff is entitled to choose whichever form of compensation he feels is most appropriate to his case.

Loss of bargain

Damages for loss of bargain are assessable to put the plaintiff

'so far as money can do it ... in the same situation as if the contract had been performed'.

In a contract for the sale of goods which are defective, the plaintiff will under this heading be entitled to damages reflecting the differences between the price paid under the contract and the actual value of the defective goods.

Reliance loss

Damages to put the plaintiff in the position he would have been, if the contract had never been made, by compensating him for expenses he has incurred in his abortive performance. Under this heading, expenses which the plaintiff was never obliged to incur may be recovered.

In *McRae v Commonwealth Disposals* (1951) 84 CLR 377 the plaintiff recovered £3,000 spent on sending out a salvage expedition to salvage a wrecked tanker, in a specified position, which they had purchased from the defendant. The tanker had never, in fact, existed.

Reliance loss incurred before the contract was entered into may be recovered in certain instances.

In *Anglia Television v Reed* [1972] 1 QB 60 the plaintiffs incurred expenses in preparation for filming a television play. They subsequently entered into a contract with the defendant to play the leading role. The defendant repudiated the contract. The plaintiffs tried hard to find a substitute but failed and had to abandon the play. The plaintiffs sued the defendant for expenses of production amounting to £2,750 incurred by the plaintiffs on production before the contract. It was held that they were entitled to recover the whole of the wasted expenditure.

'Mr Reed must have known perfectly well that much expenditure had already been incurred on director's fees and the like. He must have contemplated – or at any rate, it is reasonably to be imputed to him – that if he broke his contract, all the expenditure would be wasted, whether or not it was incurred before or after the contract.' per Lord Denning MR.

Restitution

Where a bargain is made, and the price paid, but the defendant fails to deliver the goods then the plaintiff is entitled to recover the price paid plus interest thereon. Note that tort principles of assessment apply to assessment of damages for loss of profit. See *Beoco Ltd v Alfa Laval Co Ltd* [1994] 4 All ER 464.

Incidental and consequential losses

Incidental losses are those which the plaintiff incurs after the breach has come to his notice. They include the administrative costs of buying a substitute or sending back defective goods or hiring a replacement in the meantime.

Consequential losses may be loss of profits, eg reliance loss, or further harm such as personal injury or damage to property. Thus if the defendant sells the plaintiff a cow which is diseased and infects the plaintiff's other cows, then the plaintiff can claim for not only damages in selling a defective cow, but the losses caused to the other cows.

Remoteness of damage

Not every type of damage caused to the plaintiff as a result of the breach of contract will be recoverable. If the loss flowing from the breach of contract is too remote then it cannot be recovered. Losses, to be recoverable, must have been within the reasonable contemplation of the parties.

In *Hadley* v *Baxendale* (1854) 9 Exch 341 a shaft in the plaintiff's mill broke and had to be sent to the makers at Greenwich to serve as a pattern for the production of a new one. The defendant agreed to carry the shaft to the makers, but in breach of contract, delayed it so that a stoppage of several days occurred at the plaintiff's mill. The plaintiff claimed damages for £300 for loss of profits during this period, and was awarded £50. The defendant appealed. It was held that there were two principles upon which the jury should have been directed.

> 'Where the parties have made a contract which one of them has broken, the damages which the other party ought to receive in respect of such breach of contract should be such as may fairly and reasonably be considered as either arising naturally, ie according to the usual course of things, from such breach of contract itself, or such as may be reasonably supposed to have been in the contemplation of both parties at the time they made the contract as the probable result of the breach.' per Alderson B.

Damages are recoverable under two limbs under *Hadley* v *Baxendale*.

a Damages which may fairly and reasonably be considered as arising naturally.

b Damages which may reasonably be supposed to have been in the contemplation of the parties at the time of the contract.

If the loss resulting from the damage falls within either category under *Hadley* v *Baxendale*, then it is recoverable. Therefore, in *Hadley* v *Baxendale*, as the stoppage was not the natural consequence of the delay the defendant was not liable under the first limb. He was not liable under the second limb either, as this required that the damage ie the stoppage would be contemplated by both parties at the time of the contract, as a probable result of the breach. The plaintiff had only told the defendant that the shaft was the broken shaft from a mill; if he had told the defendant that the mill would be idle if there was any delay, then the defendant might have tried to limit his liability as he would then, in the circumstances, have been clearly in breach.

The first limb covers loss which would usually be expected to result from the breach. The second limb will only operate where special circumstances under which the contract was actually made are communicated to the defendant by the plaintiff.

Since *Hadley* v *Baxendale* a number of cases have arisen and these rules have been further refined and built upon.

Thus in *Victoria Laundry (Windsor) Ltd* v *Newman Industries Ltd* [1949] 2 KB 528 Victoria Laundry wished to expand business and needed a new boiler. Newman Industries wished to supply one, but delivered six months late after a road accident. During this time Victoria Laundry were losing profits the new boiler would have earned, and this included certain lucrative contracts for the Ministry of Supply. Victoria Laundry claimed these profits as damages.

The firm was held able to recover *normal* loss of profits, because the supplier should have anticipated this; but it was not entitled to recover for further loss of profits from losing their government contracts. The supplier could not be expected to know about these, and had not been specifically told.

The principles relating to remoteness of damage were further considered in the House of Lords in 1969 and given greater refinement.

In *The Heron II* [1969] 1 AC 350 the owner of 'Heron II' agreed to carry a cargo of sugar from Constanza (Rumania) to Basrah (Iraq). The voyage normally took 20 days but in breach of contract this voyage took 29 days. In those nine days the Basrah sugar market fell and the plaintiff suffered loss of profit.

It was held that the loss of profits could be recovered because the possibility of dealings on the sugar market must have been in the contemplation of both parties.

However compare *Horne* v *Midland Railway* (1873) LR 8 CP 131 with *Simpson* v *London and North Western Railway* (1876) 1 QBD 274. In *Horne* the defendant contracted to carry a consignment of shoes to London by 3 February but delivered a day late. As a result of the delay the plaintiff lost an opportunity of selling the shoes at an exceptionally high price. It was held that the defendant was not liable for this loss, although he knew the plaintiff would have to take the shoes back if they were not delivered by 3 February, he did not know the plaintiff would lose an exceptionally high profit.

In *Simpson* the defendant contracted to carry the plaintiff's samples of cattle food from an agricultural show at Bedford to another at Newcastle. He delivered certain goods to an agent of the defendant's at Bedford showground. The goods were marked 'must be at Newcastle by Monday certain'. No express reference was made in the contract of carriage to the Newcastle show. The samples arrived at Newcastle after the show was over. It was held that the defendant was liable for loss of profits which the plaintiff would have made had the samples reached Newcastle on time. The plaintiff's purpose and intention could readily be inferred from the circumstances which clearly indicated that the contract was one to carry samples to the Newcastle show and not simply to Newcastle.

Note that is not the *amount* of loss suffered that determines whether the plaintiff is entitled to damages, but whether the harm that results should be within the bounds of foreseeability.

In *Wroth* v *Tyler* [1974] Ch 30 the defendant contracted to sell his house to the plaintiff but later refused to complete the transaction in breach of contract. In the meantime house prices rose sharply and the plaintiff claimed the difference between the contract price and the market value at the date of the trial. The defendant argued that he should not be liable for the full difference between the contract price and the market price, because he could not have contemplated the exceptionally large rise in house prices between 1971 and 1973. However, he admitted he could have contemplated some rise in house prices.

It was held that the defendant might escape liability for a type or kind of loss which he could not have contemplated, but there was no authority to show that the quantum should be contemplated.

However the test does not mean that the defendant is liable for all losses once liability has been founded. In the *Victoria Laundry* case the defendant was only held liable for a reasonable amount of the profits, not for the actual amount of profits the plaintiff lost on not having the contracts for the Ministry of Supply.

Accordingly, whether or not a plaintiff may recover damages depends substantially upon the type of loss that the court is prepared to identify. So, in *H Parsons (Livestock) Ltd* v *Uttley, Ingham & Co Ltd* [1978] QB 791, the court thought that it was within the contemplation of the parties that a hopper which was unfit for its purpose of storing food in a suitable condition for feeding pigs might lead to 'illness' of or 'physical injury' to the pigs, even though the pigs had died of a rare intestinal disease, which could not have been foreseen. See the judgment of Scarman LJ, in particular, on remoteness of damage in contract and in tort.

Mitigation of damages

There are three rules:

a   The plaintiff cannot recover for loss which is consequent upon the defendant's breach of contract where the plaintiff could have avoided the loss by taking reasonable steps;

b   The plaintiff cannot recover for any loss he has actually avoided, even though he took more steps than were necessary in compliance with the rule above;

c   The plaintiff may recover loss incurred in taking reasonable steps to mitigate his loss even though he did not succeed.

In *Payzu* v *Saunders* [1919] 2 KB 581 the plaintiff agreed to buy certain goods from the defendant over a period of nine months with payment within one month of delivery, and deliveries monthly. The plaintiff failed to make prompt payment for the first instalment and the defendant in breach of contract, refused to deliver any more instalments under the contract, but offered to deliver the goods at the contract price if the plaintiff paid cash on delivery of the order. The plaintiff refused this and claimed damages being the difference between the contract price and the market price. It was held that the plaintiff had permitted himself to sustain a large measure of the loss which as a prudent and reasonable person he ought to have avoided. He had the cash available to meet the defendant's demands and could have mitigated by purchasing off the defendant at the contract price as the defendant offered instead of going into the market to purchase at a higher price. He was therefore not entitled to damages.

Note, however, that only *reasonable* steps need be taken to mitigate loss.

Liquidated damages and penalty clauses

In some cases the parties, forseeing the possibility of breach make some provision for it.

The parties to the contract may make a genuine assessment of the losses which are likely to result in the event of a breach and stipulate that such sum shall be payable in the event of a breach of contract.

Such clauses enable a party to know his liability in advance. If, however, the clause is not an assessment of losses but intended as punishment on the contract-breaker, then the clause is a penalty clause and is void.

A liquidated damages clause will be effective in the event of a breach and the plaintiff will not recover more than that sum. No action for unliquidated damages will be allowed. Where the clause is a penalty clause, then in an action for breach of contract it is disregarded.

Penalty or liquidated damages?

The parties may often be in dispute over whether the clause was a penalty or liquidated damages clause. Various rules have been formulated to deal with such contingencies.

The mere fact that a payment is described in a contract as a 'penalty' is not of itself decisive. The court will look at the construction of the clause itself and the surrounding circumstances and may, on these, conclude that what is described as a penalty clause is, in fact, a liquidated damages clause.

In *Dunlop Pneumatic Tyre Co Ltd* v *New Garage and Motor Co Ltd* [1915] AC 79 Lord Dunedin laid down three rules concerning penalty clauses:

a The use of the words 'penalty' or 'liquidated damages' may prima facie be supposed to mean what they say, yet the expression used is not conclusive.

b The essence of a penalty is a payment of money as in terrorem of the offending party; the essence of liquidated damages is a genuine covenanted pre-estimate of damages.

c Whether a sum stipulated is penalty or liquidated damages is a question of construction to be decided upon the terms and inherent circumstances of each particular contract, judged as of the time of making the contract, not as at the time of breach.

In *Jobson* v *Johnson* [1989] 1 WLR 1026 an agreement for the sale of shares in a football club to the defendant's nominee was made. Para 6 of a side letter to the agreement provided for default including that the defendant would, on default, transfer to the vendors shares totalling not less than 44.9 per cent of the issued share capital in the football club, together with variable monetary payments depending on which instalment(s) was/were defaulted. The defendant having defaulted, the vendors assigned their rights to the plaintiff who sought to enforce the contract.

It was held:

a that whether a clause was a penalty clause was a question of construction, to be decided in the light of the circumstances at the time of making the contract and that in the present case since para 6 provided for repurchase of the shares at a fixed price regardless of the extent of the defendant's default it amounted to a penalty clause.

b that the penalty clause was unenforceable to the extent that it provided for compensation to the innocent party in excess of his actual loss.

c There is a presumption (but no more) that it is a penalty when 'a single lump sum is made payable by way of compensation on the occurrence of one or more or all of several events, some of which may occasion serious and others but trifling damage'. (Lord Watson in *Lord Elphinstone* v *Monkland Iron Co* (1886) 11 App Cas 332).

d It is no obstacle to the sum stipulated being a genuine pre-estimate of damage, that the consequences of the breach are such as to make precise pre-estimation almost an impossibility.

In *Bridge* v *Campbell Discount Co Ltd* [1962] AC 600 the plaintiff bought a car on hire purchase and paid a deposit plus one monthly instalment. He could not keep up the payments and returned the car to the finance company. Clause 9 of the agreement required the plaintiff to pay, by way of depreciation, such sum as would make his total payments up to two thirds of the purchase price (£206 in this case). Although this clause was to compensate for depreciation, it in fact decreased the amount payable, the longer the plaintiff kept the goods and continued the payments. It was held that the clause was penal because if the plaintiff was liable to pay the 'penal sum of £206 without relief of any kind' ... 'It means that equity has committed itself to this absurd paradox: it will grant relief to a man who breaks his contract but will penalize the man who keeps it' per Lord Denning.

If the clause is in fact a penalty clause then it is void and the plaintiff can ignore it and sue for his actual loss.

In *Philips Hong Kong Ltd* v *Attorney-General of Hong Kong* (1993) The Times 15 February makes it clear that unless the parties are on very unequal terms, the desirability of achieving certainty in commercial contracts is paramount. Wherever possible terms previously agreed by the parties are to be considered valid liquidated damages clauses rather than penalties.

Specific performance

Introduction

There are cases where damages, although obtainable for the breach, are an inadequate remedy because they will not give the plaintiff adequate compensation for his loss. For example, the plaintiff may have contracted to purchase a particular plot of land from the defendant for which compensation can provide no satisfactory equivalent in the event of the defendant's breach.

Specific performance is an equitable remedy for breach of contract. The court has a discretion to order specific performance where it is just and equitable to do so. The plaintiff is not entitled to it as of right.

If the plaintiff can show that damages are inadequate, then the court may entertain his claim for specific performance. Damages will be inadequate in the following cases:

Where the plaintiff cannot get a satisfactory substitute

Where land or other premises are involved their specific performance is readily granted since the law takes the view that a buyer is not readily compensated by damages.

Antiques, valuable painting and other irreplaceable items may be the subject of an action for specific performance.

In *Nutbrown* v *Thornton* (1804) 10 Ves 159 specific performance was ordered of a contract to supply machinery or plant which could not be readily obtained elsewhere.

In cases where the plaintiff has contracted to obtain services of a personal quality from the defendant. For example, to sing or take part in a film, then he will *not* get specific performance but may obtain an injunction.

Where damages are difficult to assess

For example, specific performance will be ordered of a contract to sell or pay annuities.

Where the amount allowable as damages is not a secure financial equivalent

In *Beswick* v *Beswick* [1968] AC 58 A promised B to pay an annuity to C in consideration of B's transferring the goodwill of the business to A. It was held that although the promise did not give C any right of action, because she was not a party to the contract, it could be specifically enforced by B's personal representative against A. This was because damages would have been purely nominal since the promisee or his estate had suffered no loss. A would have been unjustly enriched by being allowed to retain the entire benefit of the other contracting party's performance without performing his own promise.

Factors to be considered in awarding specific performance

Mutuality

There must be mutuality before specific performance is available. Therefore the plaintiff can only have this remedy if the contract can also be enforced by the defendant.

There will be no mutuality if there exist some unperformed obligations of the plaintiff which cannot by their nature be enforced, for example, personal service contracts or contracts requiring constant supervision.

'The court does not grant specific performance unless it can give full relief to both parties.'

Hardship

This is a ground for not ordering specific performance where it would cause the defendant hardship.

In *Denne* v *Light* (1857) 8 De GM & G 774 the court refused to order specific performance against the buyer of farmland which was wholly surrounded by land belonging to others, and over which there was no right of way.

Unfairness

The court will refuse the remedy to the plaintiff if he has acted unfairly or dishonestly. The equitable principle is that the plaintiff must come to equity with clean hands. See *Coatsworth* v *Johnson* (1886) 54 LT 520 and *Walters* v *Morgan* (1861) 3 De GF & J 718 where the defendant agreed to grant the plaintiff a mining lease over land he had just bought. Specific performance was refused as the plaintiff had produced a draft lease and induced the defendant to sign the agreement in ignorance of the value of the property. The plaintiff had hurried the defendant into signing the lease before he knew the value of the property.

Mere inadequacy of consideration is not a ground for refusing specific performance, *Collier* v *Brown* (1788) 1 Cox CC 428, unless it is coupled with factors such as mistake or fraud.

Conduct of the plaintiff

Specific performance will be refused if the plaintiff fails to perform a promise which induced the defendant to contract.

In *Lamare* v *Dixon* (1873) LR 6 HL 414 the plaintiff induced the defendant to agree to take a lease of cellars by orally promising they would be made dry. The promise had no effect as a misrepresentation as it related to the future. The court refused the plaintiff specific performance since he had made no attempt to perform his promise.

Impossibility

Equity will do nothing in vain, thus specific performance will not be ordered, for example, against the defendant who has contracted to sell land which he either does not own or has already conveyed elsewhere. See *Castle* v *Wilkinson* (1870) LR 5 Ch App 534.

Supervision
The court is reluctant to grant specific performance where this would require constant supervision.

In *Ryan* v *Mutual Tontine Westminster Chambers Association* [1893] 1 Ch 116 a lease of a service flat provided that the lessors should provide a porter who was to be 'constantly in attendance'. It was held that this undertaking could not be specifically enforced. It would require 'that constant superintendence by the court which the court has always in such cases declined to give.'

In *Posner* v *Scott-Lewis* (1987) The Times 12 December, however, the court granted an application for specific performance of a lessor's covenant to employ a resident porter for certain duties. Mervyn Davies J distinguished the facts before him from those in *Ryan*, where supervision of the execution of the undertaking had been required. Here neither personal services, nor a continuous series of acts were required, but merely the execution of an agreement containing provision for such services.

Uncertainty
The agreement must be definite enough to be enforced both legally and specifically (ie the court must be able to formulate its decree).

In *Joseph* v *National Magazine Co* [1959] Ch 14 the defendant undertook to publish an article to be written by the plaintiff but could not agree with him as to the precise wording. It was held that specific performance must be refused as there was no definite manuscript, publication of which could be ordered.

Delay
There is no limitation period for obtaining specific performance, however the plaintiff should pursue his remedy within a reasonable time, otherwise the equitable doctrine of laches may operate to bar his claim ie 'equity assists the vigilant not the indolent'.

If both sides regard the contract as a leisurely transaction then the plaintiff may obtain specific performance after two years.

Particular contracts

Contracts involving personal service
The court will not order specific performance of these contracts. Section 16 Trade Union and Labour Relations Act 1974 states that no court shall compel an employee to do any work by ordering specific performance of a contract of employment or by restraining the breach of such contract by injunction.

An employer cannot be forced to employ somebody against his wishes and the general rule is that the court will not order re-engagement of an employee but will instead award compensation. In one case, however, an employer was forced to retain an employee he dismissed.

In *Hill* v *CA Parsons & Co Ltd* [1972] Ch 305 the plaintiff was employed by the defendant for 35 years. Within two years of retirement which would mean certain pensions etc, the defendant ordered the plaintiff to join a certain trade union which he refused to do and got a month's notice.

It was held that an interim injunction should be granted to ensure the employment continued to give at least six months' notice. However specific performance was not granted.

Building contracts

The general rule is that a contract to erect a building cannot be specifically enforced. Several reasons exist for this, including:

a Damages may be an adequate remedy as the owner can engage another builder.

b The contract may be too vague and not describe the building with sufficient certainty.

c Specific performance may cause difficulties relating to supervision.

Where the first two reasons are not applicable the court will in effect ignore the third and order specific performance.

In *Wolverhampton Corporation* v *Emmons* [1901] 1 KB 515 the plaintiff acquired land for an improvement scheme and sold part of it to the defendant who covenanted to demolish houses on it and build new ones. The demolition was carried out and plans for new houses approved.

It was held that specific performance would be ordered since the defendant's obligations were precisely defined by the plans, and damages would be inadequate because the defendant had possession of the site and the plaintiff could not get the work done by employing another contractor.

Entire and severable contracts

Where the court cannot grant specific performance of a contract as a whole it will not interfere to compel specific performance of part of that contract.

Where parts of a contract are severable specific performance of each part can be separately granted.

Injunctions

Introduction

A court may be able to restrain a party from committing a breach of contract by injunction. The remedy is most appropriate where the contract contains a negative stipulation by which the defendant precludes himself from acting in a manner inconsistent with his positive contractual obligations.

There are three main types of injunction available:

a an *interlocutory injunction*, which is designed to regulate the position of the parties pending trial;

b a *prohibitory injunction* which orders the defendant not to do something, for example, X contracts with Y to obtain all the beer for his pub from Y. A prohibitory injunction could be issued to prevent him buying from Z;

c a *mandatory injunction* which orders the defendant to undo something he has agreed not to do.

Unlike specific performance the defendant cannot resist a prohibitory injunction on the ground that it is burdensome to him.

Interlocutory injunctions

These could possibly be used to prevent a breach of contract by the defendant before it actually occurs. The circumstances in which this is likely to occur are hard to envisage, but the rules governing the grant of such an injunction were laid down by the House of Lords in *American Cyanamid Co v Ethicon Ltd* [1975] AC 396. The basis of this case is that the plaintiff must show there is a serious issue to be tried at the trial and that the balance of convenience is in his favour in grating the injunction. See also *Fellowes & Son v Fisher* [1976] QB 122, where the subject matter of a contract is in danger of being moved out of the jurisdiction in a case where a claim for damages or for an agreed sum is being heard and the sale of that subject matter is likely to be used to pay the damages, then it would appear that the plaintiff can apply for an interlocutory injunction to restrain the defendant from removing the subject matter from the jurisdiction. Such injunctions are known as 'Mareva' injunctions. See *Mareva Compania Naviera SA v International Bulk Carriers SA, The Mareva* [1980] 1 All ER 213.

Prohibitory and mandatory injunctions

These will not be granted if the effect is to directly or indirectly compel the defendant to do acts for which the plaintiff could not have specific performance. Thus an employee cannot be restrained from committing a breach of his positive obligation to work (s16 TULRA 1974: above).

A service contract may, however, contain certain express negative obligations which can be enforced by injunction without compelling the defendant to work or infringing the rule that the plaintiff could not have obtained specific performance.

In *Lumley v Wagner* (1852) 1 De GM & G 604 the defendant contracted to sing for the plaintiff in his theatre for three months, and at the same time, not to sing elsewhere during this time without the plaintiff's consent. A third party, one Gye, offered the defendant a larger sum to sing for him. It was held that there was no power to make the defendant sing or encourage her to sing at plaintiff's theatre.

However, the court could persuade her to do so by preventing her singing elsewhere by imposing an injunction to that effect.

Lumley v *Wagner* has been criticised particularly as regard the perilous position in which it puts those who have agreed, and later refuse to perform, personal contracts. In *Warner Bros Pictures Inc* v *Nelson* [1937] 1 KB 209 the defendant, an actress, agreed to act for the plaintiff and at the same time not to act or sing for anybody else for two years without the plaintiff's written consent, and no other employment could be taken up during this period without the plaintiff's consent. It was held that the defendant could be restrained by injunction from breaking this undertaking. She would not be forced to act for the plaintiff because she could earn a living by doing other work.

The law seems to be moving away from this rule in the *Warner Bros* case and it appears that an injunction will not now be granted unless it leaves the defendant with some reasonable alternative means of earning a living.

In *Page One Records Ltd* v *Britton* [1968] 1 WLR 157 'The Troggs', a pop group, contracted to appoint the plaintiff their sole agent and manager for five years and agreed not to act themselves in such capacity and not to appoint any other person for that time. They fell out with the manager and wanted to replace him. The plaintiff sought an injunction. It was held that an injunction must be refused because to grant it would in effect, compel 'The Troggs' to continue to employ the plaintiff and thus would amount to enforcing the performance by the plaintiff of a contract for personal services.

Damages in lieu of specific performance or injunction

Damages were originally only available at common law. However, s2 Chancery Amendment Act 1858 gave the Court of Chancery the power to award damages in lieu of specific performance (now s50 Supreme Court Act 1981) commonly referred to as Lord Cairns' Act.

Section 50 Supreme Court Act 1981

Where the Court of Appeal or High Court has jurisdiction to entertain an application for an injunction or specific performance, it may award damages in addition to, or in substitution for, an injunction or specific performance.

In contractual cases other than those concerning land there is little point invoking s50 of the SCA 1981 where there is a valid contract and a breach of this is proved. However the plaintiff may invoke the Act on two occasions.

a Damages may be awarded under the Act even though there is no completed cause of action. See *Leeds Industrial Co-operative Society* v *Slack* [1924] AC 851. In such cases it would not be possible to get damages at common law, for example, damages in lieu of a quia timet injunction and damages for breach of a restrictive covenant to which the defendant was not a party;

b Damages awarded to the plaintiff may be greater under the Act than at common law. Damages under the Act are assessed in the same manner as at common law. But, where damages are awarded at common law the principle is that such damages are normally assessed as at the date of the breach, a principle which is recognised and embodied in s51 Sale of Goods Act 1979.

This is not an absolute rule and if 'it would give rise to injustice, the court has power to fix such other date as may be appropriate in the circumstances' per Lord Wilberforce in *Johnson* v *Agnew* [1980] AC 367. Here the plaintiff obtained a decree of specific performance on a contract for the sale of a house to the defendant. The plaintiff had bought a new house in the meantime and he could not keep up the mortgage instalments on the house he had sold to the defendant. The mortgagee took possession and sold the house making specific performance impossible. The plaintiff then claimed to have the specific performance decree cancelled and damages in lieu of specific performance requested. The date of breach of the contract was about 21 January 1974, the decree of specific performance was drawn up and entered on 26 November 1974 and specific performance became impossible on 3 April 1975, when the mortgagee took possession and sold. The Court of Appeal fixed the date of assessment of damages at 26 November 1974, but in the House of Lords. It was held the damages should be assessed as at 3 April 1975.

> 'As the vendors acted reasonably in pursuing the remedy of specific performance the date on which that remedy became aborted (not being the vendor's fault) should logically be fixed as the date on which damages should be assessed' per Lord Wilberforce.

Damages may often be awarded in addition to specific performance, but again, the only clear examples of use of this are in contracts for the sale of land.

In *Grant* v *Dawkins* [1973] 1 WLR 1406 the vendor's title to land was subject to an encumbrance which amounted to a breach of contract. The plaintiff, it was held, could get specific performance of what title the defendant had plus damages based on the cost of discharging the encumbrance.

Claims on a quantum meruit

In some situations a claim for damages may not be appropriate. For example, the plaintiff may be prevented, by the conduct of the defendant, from completing his part of the contract. The plaintiff may have invested time and money in the contract, but not be able to say that he has actually completed the contract.

This remedy (which, literally translated, means 'as much as he has earned') is particularly appropriate in two types of contract:

a fixed fee contracts, where the *whole* contract must be performed in order to be paid;

b work done under a contract which is void. The plaintiff will not be able to recover damages for breach of contract, because of course no contract exists but he may be entitled to a quantum meruit.

Thus in *Planché* v *Colburn* (1831) (above) where the plaintiff was commissioned to write a book for £100 and, having completed the research and part-written the book, found his publisher repudiating the contract; it was held the plaintiff was entitled to £50 for work already done.

In *British Steel Corporation* v *Cleveland Bridge Engineering Co Ltd* [1984] 1 All ER 504 BSC supplied steel to the defendants while still negotiating terms. When the contract fell through, BSC was held entitled to a quantum meruit payment for steel supplied prior to the collapse of negotiations.

And in *Craven-Ellis* v *Canons Ltd* [1936] 2 KB 403 the plaintiff received payment on a quantum meruit basis for work done in the capacity of managing director when it turned out that his appointment was in fact void.

Rescission

The right to rescind has already been discussed in earlier chapters, especially in connection with defective contracts.

The right to rescind is an equitable remedy and, as such, is easily lost.

As soon as it becomes impossible to restore the parties to their pre-contractual position it becomes impossible to effect 'restitio in integrum'. This may happen when:

a the subject matter of the contract is used or consumed, or destroyed;

b innocent third parties acquire rights; for example if the subject matter is delayed.

Note, also that because rescission is an equitable remedy it is only available to those who act equitably. The right may be lost after excessive time has lapsed, for example ('delay defeats equity').

Finally, the right to rescind will be lost if the injured party affirms the contract. Rescission is only available if the contract is voidable; there is no such option open to a party to a void contract. Once the choice has been exercised, it is final. Affirmation can be express or implied from conduct (eg retaining and using, or selling the subject matter of the contract).

Sale of goods 34

Definitions

'Contract of sale' – a contract whereby the seller transfers, or agrees to transfer, the property in goods to the buyer, for a money consideration called the price, Sale of Goods Act 1979 s2(1). All section references to this part of the manual are to sections of this Act unless otherwise stated.

'Sale' – a contract of sale whereby the property in the goods is transferred at once.

'Agreement to sell' – a contract of sale under which the transfer of the property is to take place at a future time or subject to a condition, s2(5).

'Property' – the right of ownership (also referred to as 'title').

'Goods' – all chattels personal other than things in action and money, s61(1).

'Specific goods' – goods identified and agreed upon at the time a contract of sale is made, s61(1). For example, 'that 1976 Rover 3500'.

'Unascertained goods' – existing goods not specifically identified but referred to by description, eg 'one of the Rover 3500 cars in your showroom' or '500 tons of wheat out of the cargo of 1,000 tons on board the SS Mars'.

'Ascertained goods' – goods which are identified in accordance with the agreement after the contract is made.

'Existing goods' – goods actually in existence when the contract is made.

'Future goods' – goods to be manufactured or acquired by the seller after the making of the contract of sale, s5(1).

Formation of the contract

The general rules of contract apply (see, eg s3 as to capacity). No particular form is required, s4.

Perishing of the goods

In the case of a contract for the sale of *specific* goods:

a If, without the knowledge of the seller, the goods have perished *at the time the contract is made*, the contract is void, s6.

b If, without the fault of either party, the goods *subsequently* perish, the contract is void if the risk has not yet passed to the buyer, s7; if the risk has passed, the buyer bears the loss.

The risk passes with the property, except:

a where otherwise agreed; or

b where delivery has been delayed through the fault of either party in which case the goods are at the risk of the party at fault in respect of any loss that might not have occurred but for such fault, s20, eg *Sterns* v *Vickers* [1923] 1 KB 78.

120,000 gallons of spirit out of 200,000 in a tank was sold. A delivery warrant for the 120,000 gallons was given to the buyer who failed to act upon it, consequently the spirit deteriorated. It was held that the risk lay with the buyer as the deterioration was his fault in that he had not collected the spirit as he should have done.

The price

The price must be paid wholly or partly in money; it may be fixed in the contract or in an agreed manner, eg by a third party, s9, or by the course of dealing between the parties; otherwise the buyer must pay a reasonable price, s8.

Time of payment

Stipulations as to time of payment are not of the essence, unless otherwise agreed, s10(1). Failure to pay by the agreed date, if any, does not therefore release the seller from his own obligations under the contract.

Implied terms

Conditions and warranties

In addition to the *express* terms of the contract, certain terms relating to the goods are *implied* in the contract of sale by SGA 1979. These terms may be either conditions or warranties. A *condition* is a term which goes to the root of the contract, breach of which entitles the buyer to reject the goods and treat the contract as repudiated, in addition to claiming damages.

A *warranty* is a collateral term, the breach of which gives rise to an action for damages, but does not release the buyer from his own obligations.

Whether a term is a condition or a warranty depends upon the construction of the contract. The buyer may elect to treat a breach of condition as a breach of warranty only, and he must do so, if the contract is not severable and he has accepted any part of the goods, s1(4).

The implied terms are as follows:

As to title: s12

A *condition* that the seller has a right to sell, eg *Rowland* v *Divall* and *warranties* of quiet possession and freedom from encumbrances.

In *Rowland* v *Divall* [1923] 2 KB 500 the plaintiff 'bought' a car from the defendant who, it transpired, was not the owner. The true owner recovered the car. It was held that the plaintiff could recover the price he had paid from the defendant.

As to sales by description: s13

A *condition* that the goods supplied shall correspond with the description; this section is applied very strictly in favour of the buyer – see *Re Moore & Co* and *Landauer & Co*; where the buyer has not seen the goods but relies on the description, it will be a sale by description (even if the goods are specific goods, eg *Varley* v *Whipp*); but it may be a sale by description even where the buyer has seen the goods, eg *Beale* v *Taylor*; and if the sale is by sample as well as by description there is a further implied condition that the bulk corresponds both with the sample and with the description.

In *Re Moore & Co and Landauer & Co* [1921] 2 KB 519 a consignment of canned fruit was ordered to be delivered in boxes of 30 tins. Some of the boxes supplied contained only 24 tins. It was held that the consignment did not conform to the description.

In *Varley* v *Whipp* [1900] 1 QB 513 a reaping machine was ordered by a buyer, the machine having been described by the seller as new the previous year. In fact it was much older.

It was held that the machine did not comply with the description.

And in *Beale* v *Taylor* [1967] 1 WLR 1193 the subject matter of this contract was described as a 1961 Triumph Herald convertible. The plaintiff saw the car and bought it. In fact it turned out to be two different cars joined together. It was held that the car did not comply with the description.

As to quality: s14

A *condition* that the goods are of merchantable quality if the seller sells the goods in the course of a business.

This implied term will not apply to defects specifically drawn to the buyer's attention before the contract is made, nor will it apply if the buyer has examined the goods before the contract is made as regards defects which that examination ought to have revealed, eg *Thornett & Fehr* v *Beers & Sons* [1919] 1 KB 486.

A buyer of barrels of glue inspected the outside of the barrels. Had he looked inside the barrels he would have seen there was a defect in the glue. It was held that because of the examination, the seller was under no responsibility for the defect.

Goods are merchantable if they are as fit for a purpose for which goods of that kind are commonly bought as it is reasonable to expect having regard to any description applied to them, the price, and all other relevant circumstances; compare *BS Brown & Sons Ltd* v *Craiks Ltd* [1970] 1 WLR 752.

A buyer ordered cloth at 36p per yard. The cloth supplied was not suitable for dressmaking which was the buyer's particular purpose, though it was perfectly suitable for industrial purposes. The price of industrial cloth was only 30p per yard. It was held that the difference of 6p per yard did not make the goods unmerchantable.

Note that the Sale and Supply of Goods Act 1994 came into operation as from

January 1995. This, primarily, introduced a *new* s14 into the Sale of Goods Act 1979. 'Reasonable fitness for purpose' under s14(3) (see below) remains unchanged. But the concept of merchantable quality is to be replaced by a condition as to 'satisfactory quality'. It may be that this will lead to a lowering of the requisite standards under the previous section, but only when cases begin to present themselves before the courts will the trend of judicial interpretation be ascertained.

As to fitness for purpose

A *condition* that goods sold in the course of a business are reasonably fit for the purpose expressly or by implication made known to the seller by the buyer. Thus the buyer need not expressly state the purpose for which the goods are required if it is obvious, eg *Frost* v *Aylesbury Dairy Co Ltd* [1905] 1 KB 608.

Milk contained typhoid germs. It was held that the milk was not fit for its purposes eg drinking – even though it had not been stated by the buyer that the milk would be drunk.

But this condition will not be implied if the circumstances show that the buyer did not rely, or that it would have been unreasonable for him to rely on the seller's skill or judgment.

As to sales by samples: s15

A *condition* that the bulk will correspond with the ample in quality; a *condition* that the buyer will have a reasonable opportunity of comparing bulk with sample, and a *condition* that the goods shall be free from any latent defect rendering them unmerchantable.

Exemption clauses

Normally, the implied terms may be varied or negatived by express agreement or by trade usage.
But:

a   an express term does not negative an implied term unless it is inconsistent therewith;

b   any express term exempting the seller from all or any of the implied obligations as to title in s12 (see (b) above) shall be void (s6(1) UCTA);

c   in a consumer sale any term of the contract which purposes to exclude or restrict the operation of Sale of Goods Act ss13 to 15, is void. A consumer sale is defined as 'a sale of goods (other than a sale by auction or by competitive tender) by a seller in the course of a business where the goods are of a type ordinarily bought for private use or consumption and are sold to a person who does not buy or hold himself out as buying them in the course of business'. The onus is on the seller to prove that a particular sale is not a consumer sale (s6(2); s12 UCTA);

d in the case of 'non-consumer sales' (eg where the buyer is in business to re-sell) an exemption clause is not enforceable to the extent that the buyer satisfies the court that it would not be fair and reasonable for the seller to rely on that term (s6(3); s11(2); s11(5) UCTA).

Passing of property

The property passes at the time the parties intend it to pass, s17; but the property in *unascertained* goods cannot pass until they have been ascertained, s16.

In the absence of evidence to the contrary, the property is deemed to pass in accordance with the following rules, s18:

a *Unconditional* contract for sale of *specific* goods in a *deliverable* state – property passes when contract is made, even though time of payment or of delivery is postponed. In *Tarling* v *Baxter* (1827) 6 B & C 360 the buyer bought a haystack. Before he took it away it was destroyed by fire. It was held that property had passed and so the loss fell on the buyer. Goods are in a 'deliverable state' when they are in such a state that the buyer would be bound to take delivery of them under the contract, s61.

b Contract for sale of *specific* goods, still to be put in a deliverable state – property does not pass until this has been done and buyer has notice thereof.

c Contract for sale of *specific* goods in a deliverable state, price to be ascertained by the seller weighing, measuring, etc – property does not pass until this is done and buyer has notice thereof.

d Goods delivered on *approval* or *sale or return* or similar terms – property passes when the buyer:

i signifies his approval or acceptance to seller; or

ii does any other act adopting the transaction; or

iii retains the goods without giving notice of rejection within a fixed or reasonable time.

e Contract for sale of *unascertained* or *future* goods sold by description – property passes when goods of that description and in a deliverable state are *unconditionally appropriated* to the contract by one party with the consent of the other, eg by seller delivering to buyer or to a carrier on his behalf, without reserving the right of disposal. The buyer's assent to the appropriation may be given either before or after the appropriation and may be implied. In *Pignatoro* v *Gilroy* [1919] 1 KB 459 a buyer ordered some bags of rice which he was to collect when they were ready from the seller. The seller informed him the bags were ready. The buyer, however, did nothing for three weeks. The bags were stolen during this time. It was held that the buyer had by his inaction assented to the appropriation and thus the property in the goods, and the risk of loss had passed to him.

Transfer of title

The general rule is 'nemo dat quod non habet:' no one can transfer title to goods except the true owner or his authorised agent. Exceptions:

Estoppel

Where the owner is *estopped* by his conduct from denying the seller's authority to sell, eg by 'holding out' a person as his agent, s21(1).

Sale by factor

Where goods are sold by a factor to a person taking in good faith without notice of any lack of authority, s21(2)(a).

Sale under common law or statutory power

Where goods are sold under a common law or statutory power of sale or under a court order, s21(2)(b), eg by a pawnbroker or sheriff.

Sale in market overt

The sale of goods in market overt was always recognised as an important exception to the 'nemo dat' rule. It was however open to abuse. Probably the main area open to criticism has been the steady growth of 'car boot sales'. Whatever the reason the concept of market overt has now been abolished by the Sale of Goods (Amendment) Act 1994, s1.

Sale under voidable title

Where goods held under a voidable contract are sold to a person taking in good faith without notice of the defect before the seller's title has been avoided, s23; this section applies, for instance, where the contract is voidable for fraud, eg *Lewis* v *Averay* but not where it is void, eg *Cundy* v *Lindsay*. For these cases see mistake in contract – chapter 31).

Sale by buyer or seller in possession

Where the buyer or seller is, with the consent of the other party, in possession of the goods, or of the documents of title to the goods, and he sells the goods to a third person who takes them in good faith without notice of the claims of the other party, the third person will obtain a good title, s25; a change in the nature of the seller's possession (for instance, from possession as owner to possession as a bailee or even as a trespasser) does not affect the operation of the rule.

Sale by hirer of motor vehicles

Where the hirer or buyer of a motor vehicle under a hire-purchase or condition sale agreement sells the vehicle to a *private* purchaser who takes it in good faith without notice of the agreement; similar protection is afforded to the first private purchaser from a trade or finance purchaser (Hire Purchase Act 1965 ss27–29).

Performance

The basic duties imposed by a contract of sale are *delivery* of possession of the goods by the seller, and *acceptance* and payment by the buyer, s27; unless otherwise agreed, delivery and payment are concurrent conditions, s28. Whether the buyer is to collect the goods or the seller is to send them to the buyer is to be determined by the terms, express or implied, of the contract between them, s29(1).

Delivery

Unless otherwise agreed, the place of delivery is the seller's place of business or residence. If the seller has agreed to send the goods to the buyer, he must do so within a reasonable time, at a reasonable hour, and at his own expense, s29; moreover a seller who is required to deliver at the buyer's premises will be discharged if the goods are delivered to a person having apparent authority to receive them, eg *Galbraith & Grant Ltd* v *Block* [1922] 2 KB 155.

Sellers were contractually bound to deliver a crate of champagne to the buyer's house. There it was received by a respectable looking and apparently authorised person. The champagne was never seen again. It was held that the sellers were entitled to the price from the buyers.

If the seller delivers more or less than the quantity contracted for, or delivers goods of the contract description mixed with other goods, the buyer may reject the whole of the goods or that part which does not conform with the terms of the contract, s30. The buyer cannot accept those goods that do not conform, unless the parties agree.

The buyer need not accept delivery by instalments, unless he has agreed to do so. In the latter event, if the goods are to be paid for separately, and there is a failure to make or take delivery of one or more instalments, the breach may constitute the repudiation of the whole contract or a severable breach giving rise to a claim for damages only, depending upon the circumstances, s31. The test is the quantity of goods involved in relation to the contract as a whole and the likelihood of repetition of the breach: *Maple Flock Co Ltd* v *Universal Furniture Products (Wembley) Ltd* [1943] 1 KB 148.

The case involved a contract for the delivery of 100 tons of rag flock at a rate of three loads per week. The first 15 deliveries were satisfactory, the 16th was not, but the buyer nevertheless accepted a further four loads all of which were satisfactory. The buyers then refused to take any further deliveries. It was held that they were not entitled to do this. There was little likelihood of the breach being repeated.

Delivery of the goods to a carrier is prima facie a delivery of the goods to the buyer, but the buyer may decline to treat is as such if the seller has failed to make a reasonable contract of carriage and the goods are lost or damaged in the course of transit, s32.

Acceptance

The buyer is deemed to have accepted the goods when (s35):

a he intimates his acceptance to the seller; or

b the goods have been delivered to him and he does any act in relation to them inconsistent with the seller's ownership; or

c he retains the goods longer than is reasonable without intimating to the seller that he has rejected them.

But he is not deemed to have accepted them, where he has not previously examined them, until he has had a reasonable opportunity of examining them, and the seller must afford him this opportunity on tendering delivery if so requested, s34.

If the buyer properly refuses to accept the goods he is not bound to return them to the seller, s36; an unjustified refusal renders him liable to the seller for any loss thereby caused, s37.

Remedies of the unpaid seller

In the event of non-payment, the seller has remedies against the goods and against the buyer.

Remedies against goods

An unpaid seller has the following rights over the goods:

a A lien on the goods, if the property has passed and the seller is still in possession. If credit has been given no lien can exist until the period of credit has expired, or the buyer is insolvent, s41.

The right may be lost by waiver, eg by assenting to a sub-sale, or loss of possession, s43.

b *Right to stop the goods in transit* (stoppage in transit) and retake delivery while they are in the possession of a carrier if the buyer becomes insolvent, s44. The goods are still in transit if the buyer rejects them and the carrier continues in possession of them; but the goods cease to be in transit if the buyer takes delivery before they reach their destination, or where the carrier either acknowledges to the buyer that he holds the goods on his behalf or where he wrongfully refuses to deliver the goods to the buyer, s45.

c Right to *withhold delivery*, co-existent with the above rights, if the property has not passed to the buyer, s39(2). (Note, that this is not a lien – no one can have a lien over his own goods.)

d An unpaid seller who has exercised his right of lien or stoppage in transit has a right of *resale* only if:

i   the goods are of a perishable nature; or

ii   the seller gives notice of his intention to resell, and the buyer does not tender the price within a reasonable time thereof; or

iii the right of resale is expressly reserved in the contract s48.

The effect of resale is to rescind the original contract and the whole of the proceeds belong to the unpaid seller.

The unpaid seller's rights of lien or stoppage in transit against the goods are not affected by any sale or other disposition thereof by the buyer unless:

iv   the seller has assented to it; or

v   a document of title to the goods has been transferred to the buyer, and the buyer has further transferred it to a person taking it in good faith and for value, s47.

Remedies against buyer

a *Action for the price*: the seller can sue the buyer for the price if:

i   the property has passed to the buyer; or

ii   a date for payment, irrespective of delivery, has been agreed, even though the property has not passed, s49.

b *Action for damages for non-acceptance*: if an action for the price is not available, the seller may claim damages if the buyer wrongfully refuses to accept and pay for the goods. The measure of damages is the estimate loss directly and naturally resulting in the ordinary course of events from the buyer's breach of contract. Where there is an available market for the goods in question the measure of damages is prima facie to be ascertained by the difference between the contract price and the market price at the date of the breach, s50. However, if there is no available market, then the seller is entitled to damages for the loss of his bargain and this depends on the state of demand for the goods. See the recent case of *Shearson Lehman Hutton Inc* v *I MacLaine Watson and Co Ltd (No 2)* [1990] 3 All ER 723 as to assessment of what constitutes an 'available market'.

Remedies of the buyer

The buyer may have one or more of the following remedies in the event of a breach of contract by the seller:

Remedies for damages for non-delivery

This is available if the seller wrongfully neglects or refuses to deliver the goods, s51. The damages are calculated in the same manner as in paragraph 32.10(b)(ii).

Specific performance

Such an order may be made if the contract is for specific or ascertained goods, and the court thinks that this is an appropriate remedy, s52.

Action for breach of warranty

On a breach of warranty, or of a condition which the buyer chooses or is required to treat as a breach of warranty, the buyer may set off his claim for damages against the purchase price, or bring an action against the seller for damages for the breach, or both, s53.

A breach of condition, which can be treated as such, enables the buyer to reject the goods and to claim damages for the breach.

Liability and the fault principle | 35

The basis of liability

To determine the circumstances in which a person may be legally liable, ie answerable to the law, for his acts or omissions, is one of the most fundamental functions of law in any society. The basis on which liability has traditionally been attached is on the basis of fault.

Perhaps the most obvious application of the fault principle is in the criminal law which is concerned with the punishment, deterrence and rehabilitation of individuals whose misdeeds are considered by the law to be not only wrongs against other individuals, but also against society as a whole. Thus, as discussed elsewhere in this book, criminal proceedings are generally brought under public authority ('The Crown') against the wrongdoer, and criminal law is classified as part of 'public law', that is, the law which regulates the relationship between the individual and the state.

Tort and contract law, on the other hand, are classified as part of 'private law', regulating relationships between individuals and other individuals. The main concern of the law here is to provide compensation to the innocent party for breach of an obligation committed (whether by act or omission) by another. The main difference between contract and tort is that in contract the obligations are the creation of the parties themselves whereas in tort the obligations are imposed by law, regardless of any agreement between the parties concerned.

Laissez-faire individualism

As stated a common thread running through these three divisions of English law is the fundamental principle of 'no liability without fault'. Perhaps the most obvious way of determining individual liability under the law is to use the concept of 'blameworthiness' or 'fault'. This is a clear example of abstract conceptions of 'morality' and 'justice' being incorporated into the law, ie the person who is to blame for injury incurred by another should be the one to bear the loss, or to be punished for his fault, as the case may be.

The high-water mark of the principle 'no liability without fault' in English law was the nineteenth century. This was the period of economic individualism and 'laissez-faire', in which there was minimal interference by the state in the business and commercial life of the community. The law of contract as developed by the judges during this period was based on the assumption that private individuals should be left alone to regulate their own affairs and interests, to make their own terms and conditions and the law would only intervene where there was a breach of an undertaking which had been voluntarily accepted through a freely-negotiated contract.

The nineteenth century emphasis on laissez-faire individualism has given way, under economic and political pressures, to a much more interventionist role for Government and state. The Welfare State, through state agencies such as local authorities and legal institutions, now plays a large and increasing part in the regulation of individual activities and relationships. In contract law, for example, a whole range of consumer protection legislation regulates considerably the terms on which certain contracts may be made, recognising that in some circumstances 'equality of bargaining power', an assumption on which the laissez-faire philosophy was based, is a mere fiction. In tort, legislation providing for compulsory insurance and state benefits has had some influence on the development of the law, and in the criminal law, growth in regulatory legislation in many spheres of activity has been accompanied by the creation of many 'strict liability' offences, in which the principle of 'no liability without fault' plays little or no part. In addition the concept of vicarious liability has assumed great importance, particularly in the employment field and in the tort of negligence. In vicarious liability as with 'strict' liability, there need be no fault on the part of the defendant for him to be liable in law.

Exceptions to the fault principle

Whilst it is recognised that much liability in English law is based on the fault principle that seeks to hold the person at fault responsible for his blameworthy acts or omissions there are now some important exceptions that are sufficient to cast doubt on the assertion that there is no liability without fault.

The now famous dicta of Lord Radcliffe in *Bolton v Stone* [1951] AC 850 to the effect that the law of negligence is concerned less with what is fair than with what is culpable demonstrates the harshness of the fault principle in application. If there is no culpability then there is no liability. However today with other considerations such as welfarism in mind the law has developed the concept of strict liability and even in some extreme cases the concept of absolute liability.

Criminal law

In criminal law the requirement that 'mens rea' or a guilty state of mind be established really amounts to saying that criminal liability is imposed only on blameworthy activity.

The concept of strict liability in the context of criminal law means that this is not entirely true. As a matter of statutory construction, the courts have decided that where the legislature has omitted any reference to words such as 'knowingly' or some equivalent in the definition of the offence, then it is intended to impose strict liability. Strict liability means that with regard to at least a part of the 'actus reus' there is no requirement to establish any mens rea – that is to say that there is no requirement to establish intentional recklessness or even negligence as to one or more of the elements of the actus reus. This is not the same as saying that there is no mens rea. For example, with regard to the offence of selling meat which is unfit for human consumption whether the meat is fit or unfit carries no mental element so even the most careful and clean butcher would be liable. However, there is a mental element with regard to the selling.

Where there is no requirement to establish any mens rea then the offence is said to be one of absolute liability or in the preferred term a 'state of affairs offence'. An example of this can be found in the case of *R v Larsonneur* (1933) 149 LT 542 in which the accused was an alien the subject of an exclusion order under which it would be an offence for her to enter the United Kingdom. She was brought to the United Kingdom handcuffed to the police very much against her will and was convicted of violating the exclusion order! There was no mental element involved in the offence and that as soon as the state of affairs (being in the United Kingdom during the currency of an exclusion order against her) came into existence the accused had committed a crime.

It is clear that in these examples from the criminal law there is some liability being imposed in the absence of fault.

Tort

In tort there are also some examples of liability being imposed without fault. There is some strict liability in tort although it is limited. A case involving private nuisance, was *Sturges v Bridgman* (1879) 11 Ch D 852 where a confectionary manufacturer was obliged by means of an injunction to cease his noisy activity in his own premises because the court felt that it was an unreasonable interference with the neighbouring doctor's surgery. There was no intentional harm and indeed what the defendant was doing was otherwise perfectly legal but for the interference in fact. I would take the view that this was more a case of balancing conflicting interests in the use of land than as an exception to the fault principle.

Perhaps the major instance of liability without fault in tort can be found in the area of vicarious liability. This is when one person is held liable for the tort of another person. Essentially this concept was developed as a mechanism to find a defendant who could pay the damages to the plaintiff especially in respect of the liability of the employer for the torts of the employee. The employer will be liable for the torts of the employee committed in the course of the employee's employment providing that the employee is not 'on a frolic of his own'. It is said that the employers ought to exercise control over the way in which their employees work and that in any event they profit from the employment relationship. In the case of *Twine v Bean's Express Ltd* [1946] 1 All ER 202 the driver disobeyed instructions and gave a lift to a person who did not help with his job. For the death of that person the employers were held not to be liable. However, in the case of *Rose v Plenty* [1976] 1 WLR 141, where the facts were rather similar with one material exception, the court found that the employers were vicariously liable. That exception was that the persons given lifts assisted with the deliveries that were the job of the employee. The essence of the distinction between these cases lies in the purpose for which the act was done. Even in circumstances such as those prevailing in *Rose v Plenty* liability is imposed even when the employer gave express and explicit instructions to the employee not do that very thing which he then did so incurring liability vicariously on the employer. Even though in certain circumstances the employer may have a right to sue the employee as in *Lister* v *Romford Ice and Cold Storage Co* [1957] AC 555 this will often be an exercise in futility as the employee is unlikely to be adequately insured or to otherwise have the resources available to pay. Indeed if he did have the necessary resources there would be no need for the plaintiff to seek to establish vicarious liability as he could have sued the employee directly. It is thus clear that the very nature of vicarious liability is such that it involves liability for someone else's fault.

Whilst these are examples of some of the exceptions to the general rule they are sufficient to show that the statement that there can be no liability without fault is too general to be true.

The need for reform

The case of *Bolton* v *Stone* [1951] AC 850 has been referred to above. In that case Lord Radcliffe was acknowledging that there could be situations when the law of negligence insisting on culpability would lead to an unfair result. Perhaps the very case in which he was sitting would be a clear example of this. The injured plaintiff suffered loss as a result of the injury sustained when hit by a cricket ball whilst she was standing outside the cricket ground. However, there was no one at fault in that the club had done all that a reasonable person would do in the circumstances, having regard to all the relevant factors, such as social utility of the action in question (cricket), expense of avoiding harm and likelihood of harm coupled with seriousness of harm. Thus had the plaintiff suffered the same injuries as a result of someone dropping a cricket ball or throwing a cricket ball outside the game of cricket then she may have been able to recover damages. As the law stands as stated by Lord Radcliffe only those who suffer loss as a result of someone else's fault will be able to recover damages. The rationale is clear. If the loss is no one's fault who should be made to pay? In essence this rationale dates back to the era of laissez faire individualism.

As stated, in England, where a person is injured, in order to recover damages he has to establish that someone else was at fault. That is taken to mean that someone else owed him a duty of care and it was the unreasonable breach of that duty that in fact and in law caused the loss he has suffered and for which he is claiming damages. Whether fairness is served by the requirement to establish culpability (fault) will form the essence of this answer. For damages are regarded as a private matter between the defendant and the plaintiff in each individual case. In theory, the state takes no active role in this regard.

To say that the state takes no active role is not entirely true. Ever since the advent of the welfare state in this country the state has paid benefit to those who fall sick or who otherwise are unable to work. There are disability allowances and payments are made. These are of course funded out of central government sources

– primarily through taxation. These payments do not however take account of the individual responsibility that may be borne for the injury and to a certain extent the fault based principle can be seen as serving the purpose of compensating those injured while at the same time penalising those who caused the injury by requiring them to pay damages. The problem is that this method takes no account of those who do suffer loss through accident but who either are unable to establish fault or the party against whom they can establish fault is not in a position financially speaking to pay the full amount of damages to which they would otherwise be entitled. To use a metaphor, the law cannot extract blood from a stone.

Professor Atiyah in *Accidents, Compensation and the Law* criticised English tort law on the grounds that it is expensive to operate, that the necessity of proving fault means that the process of compensation is arbitrary and that only a small proportion of accident victims are compensated. A suggestion frequently made is to adopt a system similar to that which exists in New Zealand. In that country, a no fault compensation scheme was introduced in 1972 whereby accidental injury (including occupational diseases) are compensated by recourse to a central fund regardless of fault. The common law action in tort in respect of such injuries is abolished. Naturally benefits are less than awarded in common law actions yet it covers loss of earnings (to 80 per cent) and some lump sums are made available to compensate permanent disability. The success of this scheme is indicated by the fact that none of the major interest groups expressed in their submissions to a Parliamentary Committee considering a return to the old tort system any desire so to return.

The most recent inquiry into the law of tort in England was the Royal Commission on Civil Liability and Compensation for Personal Injury, appointed in 1973 under the Chairmanship of Lord Pearson. That Report did not support the institution of a no fault compensation scheme such as in New Zealand. In an apparent attempt to disguise a split of opinion in the Commission the Report stated that consideration of such a scheme was precluded by the terms of reference given to it.

If introduced, such a scheme would firstly provide that there would no longer be any need to prove fault. This would mean that all the rules of negligence would not apply. It would also result in all persons who have suffered injury through accidental causes being able to recover compensation. Since more would recover they would not all receive such large amounts as are currently being awarded. The cake would have to be more evenly divided. Such a scheme would be administered by central government and would operate as a sort of taxation system with everyone paying a small sum in each year similar to the current National Insurance Contributions that fund unemployment benefits.

As noted above, in New Zealand the state has abolished the fault based principle and in its place instituted a state scheme whereby any person who is injured in an accident will receive as of right, compensation from the state. There is no requirement to establish that anyone was at fault. It was initially thought that lawyers in New Zealand would be in opposition to this, however, experience has shown that they actually prefer this method. The New Zealand scheme concentrates on the needs of the injured individual and as a form of insurance all taxpayers in the country contribute towards the fund from which these payments are made. It could be argued that this method does not penalise those at fault but it does have what I would subjectively regard as the advantage of compensating all who suffer accidents without the lottery of the necessity of proving fault.

The New Zealand scheme is in essence a state organised insurance scheme of loss distribution by which is meant that all contribute a little and draw on the fund if the need arises. One drawback with the New Zealand scheme is that those who could prove fault do not receive as much in the way of damages as they would in a fault based system. The cake is of a limited size – there is only so much to go around. Either large sums are awarded to those who can prove fault or smaller amounts (although by no means negligible) are paid as of right to all who are injured in an accident.

In Britain in the area of medical negligence, the British Medical Association (BMA) is advocating a no fault compensation system. This is largely in response to two factors. Firstly, the frequency of cases involving medical negligence is rising sharply and secondly, the size of damages being awarded is increasing dramatically.

In the case of *Samir Aboul Hosn* damages were awarded in excess of one million pounds for loss sustained through medical negligence. This award generated a lot of debate about the way in which damages are assessed and awarded. The result of claims such as this is that the National Health Service loses money that would otherwise be used to expand medical services. Health Authorities paid out £7,400,000 in 1985 to meet claims for medical negligence. Since then the quantum of awards has increased substantially and it is likely to increase further. This also puts a heavy strain on insurance schemes and doctors fear that premiums will reach the proportions currently experienced in the United States.

One side effect of this is that doctors have admitted that they are now over cautious and carry out more tests and consult more often with senior colleagues in order to safeguard against a negligence claim. This may be a good thing if resources were unlimited. That is not the case.

In the light of this, it might appear that a no fault compensation system would be recommended. However, the Centre for Socio-Legal Studies of the University of Oxford, in a recent report published in the British Medical Journal, suggests that to introduce a no fault compensation scheme which would benefit those who go without compensation because they cannot prove fault would have an important detrimental effect in that one of the major deterrents of medical negligence practice would disappear. It is suggested that one of the major advantages of the present fault based system is that it encourages doctors to be careful and to maintain, if not actually improve, standards. It is submitted that such a view confuses recklessness with negligence.

It is by no means certain that the choice is really between the old nineteenth century maxim 'no liability without fault' and the system whereby all who suffer loss through accidents are compensated.

The current system of tort/fault based liability has important deterrent factors. However these are minimalised since in most cases the defendant has already taken steps to minimise his loss though insurance. Thus the private insurance sector are performing the task that the state compensation scheme in New Zealand perform. The difference that certainly exists between the two schemes relates to the type of admissible claim.

From a Marxist perspective *Abel* argues that the fault based system is a tool of the capitalist class in that through the doctrine of the maximisation of profits business tends to sacrifice health and safety. A capitalist, argues *Abel*, will calculate the likely profit and loss from running the risk and may conclude that it would be cheaper to allow negligence. In the light of incidents such as the Bhopal disaster it is to be doubted whether this rather simplistic analysis is valid.

A further difficulty experienced with any compensation scheme is of course the equation of non pecuniary loss such as pain and suffering with monetary damages. We lack the know-how to replace lost limbs and therefore it seems as if the only way in which we can compensate for non-pecuniary loss is through money. It is not argued that this is a replacement, merely compensation.

There are, in our own fault based system, circumstances under which liability attaches and damages become payable on parties that lack any first degree fault. The doctrine of vicarious liability is of relevance here, as it provides that a person may be liable in law for the negligence of someone else. The doctrine usually applies to employers with regard to the negligence of their employees during the course of their employment. It is said that there is no fault on the part of those held vicariously liable, however, one doubts this. The employer is liable for failure to control his employee, for failure to exercise care in the hiring of a person who was negligent or in any event from profiting from the relationship with an employee who happened on occasion to be negligent.

With regard to road traffic accidents there is a requirement that all drivers have compulsory insurance. There even exists a Motorists Insurance Bureau funded by all the insurance companies (and therefore indirectly by all those who possess compulsory insurance) for the victims of accidents caused by a person who, in violation of the legal duty on him, does not have driving insurance yet who has caused loss. This is a half way house between the two ideas and is perhaps more satisfactory. However the requirement to establish fault is still present.

In the interests of those who suffer loss the case for the abolition of the fault based system and its replacement with a centrally funded insurance scheme, along the lines of that adopted and working well in New Zealand, is convincing. Also it would appear to be more just.

Thus the principle of no liability without fault in tort, contract and crime is subject to important exceptions and in certain circumstances may be argued to be inadequate to meet the needs and expectations of a modern society.

Jurisprudence: a brief reading list

It should be stressed that this list is not meant to be a comprehensive list of all works referred to in the book. It is, as stated in Chapter 7, a guideline only to the main jurisprudential authorities, as mentioned in the first stages of the book.

AUSTIN, J: *Lectures in Jurisprudence*, 5th edition, ed. Campbell, 1885.
BENTHAM, J: *Introduction to Principles of Morals and Legislation*, ed. JH Burns and HLA Hart, 1970.
BUCKLAND, WH: *Some Reflections on Jurisprudence*, 1945.
DEVLIN, PA: *The Enforcement of Morals*, Oxford University Press, 1965.
DIAS, RWM: *Jurisprudence*, 5th edition, Butterworths.
DIAS, RWM: *A Bibliography of Jurisprudence*, Butterworths.
DWORKIN, R: *Law's Empire*, Fontana, 1986.
DWORKIN, R: *Taking Rights Seriously*, Duckworth, 1977.
GRIFFITH, JAG: *The Politics of the Judiciary*, 2nd edition, 1981.
HART, HLA: *Law, Liberty and Morality*, Oxford University Press, 1968.
HART, HLA: *The Concept of Law*, 1961 (reprinted 1976).
HOBBES, T: *Leviathan*, ed. CB McPherson, Penguin, 1968.
HOHFELD, WN: *Fundamental Legal Conceptions as Applied in Judicial Reasoning*, Yale University Press, 1934.
HOLMES, OW: *The Common Law*, 1881.
POUND, R: *Jurisprudence*, 1943–44.
RAWLS, J: *A Theory of Justice*, 1972.
SALMOND, JW: *Jurisprudence*, 12th edition, 1966.

Index